MUSICAL EMOTIONS EXPLAINED

Musical Emotions Explained is a magnificent publication that has been painstakingly researched to illuminate the many, varied ways music can express and arouse emotions. It provides the most authoritative single authored text on the topic so far. As a highly readable and informative publication, it superbly unlocks the secrets of musical affect for experienced researchers through to lay readers alike.

—Gary E. McPherson, Ormond Chair of Music and Director, Melbourne Conservatorium of Music, Australia

Anyone who wants to understand more about the most essential quality of music—its ability to move us—needs to read this book. Juslin's writing is gripping and thoughtful as he takes us on a journey through the latest research on this most interesting intersection between science and art.

—Daniel J. Levitin, Author of *This Is Your Brain on Music* and *The World in Six Songs*

Music Emotions Explained is a tour de force. In this extraordinary book, written with passion and humor, Patrik Juslin shares insights gleaned from decades of ground-breaking research. Breadth and depth are nicely balanced as grand, over-arching themes are richly supported by systematic and detailed research findings. This book will serve as an inviting introduction to students or interested laypersons but also as a touchstone to which professionals will return frequently for guidance and inspiration.

—Donald A. Hodges, Professor Emeritus, University of North Carolina at Greensboro, USA

Patrik Juslin here deftly synthesizes several decades of psychological research, much of it his own, on how music both expresses emotion and moves us emotionally, in the course of developing an empirically grounded, evolutionarily based, philosophically informed theory of the phenomenon in question, doing so with style and wit. *Musical Emotion Explained* is wide ranging, engagingly written, full of arresting claims, and studded with telling anecdotes. It is a book that everyone who has ever marveled at the affective power of music should read.

—Jerrold Levinson, Distinguished University Professor, Department of Philosophy, University of Maryland, USA

Musical Emotions Explained is essential reading that sets the new gold standard resource for understanding the *delicious pleasures* of music experience. Using lucid, witty and compelling arguments, Patrik Juslin illustrates a set of core mechanisms that collectively account for music-evoked emotions. Scholars, general readers and musicians will be inspired by this landmark work, which will stimulate research for decades to come.

—Bill Thompson, Distinguished Professor, Macquarie University, Sydney, Australia

It goes without saying that Patrik Juslin is one of the world's top experts on the science of musical emotion. What this book reveals is that he is a hugely persuasive and accessible interlocutor. It really feels as though one is in conversation with a friend who is thinking issues and arguments through with the reader, step by step. Of course all the important literature is covered, but this is far from a dry literature review. Juslin's book should excite and stimulate layreaders and professional colleagues alike to deepen their understanding of what makes music emotional.

—John Sloboda, Research Professor, Guildhall School of Music & Drama, London, UK

The best comprehensive and critically explanatory tome to-date on one of the most fascinating and still poorly understood topics in music research, written by the foremost international expert on music and emotion. A treasure for decades to come.

—Michael Thaut, Professor of Music, Neuroscience and Rehabilitation Science, University of Toronto, Canada

In *Musical Emotions Explained*, Patrik Juslin probes and proffers many psychological and philosophical concepts of musical emotions toward unpacking numerous mysteries surrounding the arousal and expression of musical affect. The results of his meticulous research have profound implications for experiencing, creating, valuing, and teaching music. Written with great care and passion, this brilliant book is a must-read for anyone who takes a serious interest in the nature and values of music in people's lives.

—David Elliott, Professor of Music and Music Education, New York University, USA

Patrik Juslin has been at the forefront of research into music and emotion for more than 20 years. Adding to what is already an astonishing body of work, this hugely impressive monograph is the culmination of that remarkable programme of research. Witten in an accessible and engaging style, and covering a huge range of perspectives, this is a book that will undoubtedly become a classic in the psychology of music, an indispensable resource for researchers in the field, and a fascinating read for those who may be new to the topic.

—Eric Clarke FBA, Heather Professor of Music, University of Oxford, UK

PATRIK N. JUSLIN

MUSICAL EMOTIONS EXPLAINED

Unlocking the secrets of musical affect

OXFORD
UNIVERSITY PRESS

OXFORD
UNIVERSITY PRESS

Great Clarendon Street, Oxford, OX2 6DP,
United Kingdom

Oxford University Press is a department of the University of Oxford.
It furthers the University's objective of excellence in research, scholarship,
and education by publishing worldwide. Oxford is a registered trade mark of
Oxford University Press in the UK and in certain other countries

First Edition published in 2019

Impression: 1

Published in the United States of America by Oxford University Press
198 Madison Avenue, New York, NY 10016, United States of America

British Library Cataloguing in Publication Data
Data available

Library of Congress Control Number: 2018965945

ISBN 978–0–19–875342–1

Printed and bound by
CPI Group (UK) Ltd, Croydon, CR0 4YY

PREFACE

For as long as I can remember, I have been fascinated by the emotional power of music.

I was deeply moved by music from an early age. When I grew older and started playing music myself, I discovered that I was not alone in this wonder.

As a young musician, I made my own attempt to be expressive and move listeners. Whether I succeeded or not is for others to judge, but the unspoken intimacy of creating music on stage with fellow musicians include some of the best moments of my life. At that particular moment, I was not particularly concerned about how music works; it made me feel good and that was all I needed. But my curiosity never really left me. Eventually, as an adult, I discovered that there was a whole field of research devoted to understanding how we come to experience music: music psychology. As a result, I have devoted over 20 years of my professional life to exploring the relationship between music and emotion. This book is about what I have learnt so far.

For a long time, I resisted the idea of a book of this kind. It seemed to me that the field of music and emotion was in such a mess that an attempt to write a book on this topic would amount to intellectual suicide. The theory and findings needed to tell a coherent story just weren't there. What has changed?

Over the last 15 years, we have seen amazing developments in the field, with large masses of data collected and, increasingly, the development of theories that can help to account for these data. Several of the issues most fiercely debated in the humble beginnings have been, or are slowly becoming, resolved. You could say that the study of music and emotion is coming of age.

Readers who are familiar with this domain and have seen the steady flow of publications in recent years may wonder whether we really need another publication on this topic. I think we do. One reason is that most research is either scattered across various publications or presented in a way that is not accessible to most readers. (*Handbook of Music and Emotion*, edited by myself and John Sloboda and published in 2010, may seem daunting to even the most seasoned reader.) Thus, it has been difficult for anyone who is not actually an expert in the field to get some sense of the progress made.

More importantly, no-one has yet attempted to pull together the fragmented research into a more complete picture. We have by now discovered many principles for how music can both express and arouse emotions—principles that fit together. Hence, for the first time it seems feasible to present an integrated perspective on the topic. Also—although I could, of course, be mistaken—it appears that the research on the topic has reached something of a peak, so this could be a good time to take stock of the findings.

I am not saying that there is nothing more to discover. Far from it, this book will make it clear that there are still many gaps in our knowledge. Even so, I think there is now a core of scientific knowledge about music and emotion that will stand the test of time.

It has been a joy and privilege to be involved in this process of discovery. Through this book, I hope to share some of the insights that my colleagues and I have gained along the way. In a sense, I consider this book recompense for the taxpayers who have supported my research over the years.

As anyone vaguely familiar with science knows, it is a never-ending story. All knowledge is preliminary—it *will* be refined, extended, and even revised. What I hope, however, is that this book will at least make its readers "confused on a higher level"—to borrow a phrase that my mentor, Alf Gabrielsson, liked to quote during his music psychology lectures. Indeed, if I am successful in my endeavor, you may even become *less* confused about your responses to music after reading this book.

The book cites literature from ancient Greece to the year of 2018, but it does not attempt to offer an exhaustive review of all the scientific publications in this vibrant field; that would be virtually impossible given the pace of developments in recent years (at least, if the aim is to produce a book that is pleasurable to read). I have thus cited only those publications that I feel are integral to the story I want to tell. (If I happened to leave out a publication that you think is important, I apologize in advance.)

The great philosopher Bertrand Russell said that the writing of his *Principia Mathematica* was such a huge mental effort that it destroyed his brain. (Luckily, I only read that quotation *after* beginning work on this book.) I am, of course, no Bertrand Russell; and this book is surely no *Principia Mathematica*, but I can relate to some of the hardship attested to by Russell. Writing a book *is* hard work (for me at least).

The best time I had in writing this book was quite early on when I wandered around like an idiot fantasizing about how fantastic the book would be, and much later on, when I noted that my manuscript began to have *some* semblance of a book. Between these two phases, there were periods of hard work and anxiety, interspersed with brief moments of flow and euphoria. It helped to remind myself, of course, that I didn't write the book for myself, I wrote it for you. Fortunately, there were love and music to console me in moments of despair.

My own musical journey over the years has taken me from the Beatles and James Brown to Miles Davis and Igor Stravinsky, but the one "musical companion" who has stayed with me since I was young and first laid my hands on a guitar is Eric Clapton. I followed his musical endeavors through all the ups and downs, and to be fair there were quite a few of the latter. But his musical peaks were riveting. I can honestly say that no other musician has given me so many musical emotions as Eric Clapton. For that reason alone, it seems fitting to dedicate this book to him. (Thank you for the music - it's been a blast.)

Patrik N. Juslin
November 23, 2018

ACKNOWLEDGMENTS

All egos in academia notwithstanding, science is a truly social enterprise. A large number of researchers from all over the world have contributed to the body of research summarized in this book.

First, I would like to thank my colleagues—past and present—in the music psychology group in Uppsala: Gonçalo Barradas, Marie Djerf, Gertrud Ericson, László Harmat, Jessika Karlsson, Ingrid Lagerlöf, Petri Laukka, Simon Liljeström, Erik Lindström, Siv Lindström, Guy Madison, Melissa Ovsiannikow, Laura Sakka, and Maria Sandgren. I owe a special debt of gratitude to my mentor, Alf Gabrielsson, who introduced me to this topic. I thank him for kind permission to quote several examples from his unique study of strong experiences with music.

I would also like to offer my heartfelt thanks to the scholars with whom I have collaborated over the years, briefly or for longer periods. These include Tanja Bänziger†, Roberto Bresin, Tuomas Eerola, Anders Friberg, Terry Hartig, Marie Helsing, Sara Isaksson, Daniel Javitt, John Limmo, Lars-Olov Lundqvist, Gary McPherson, Roland Persson, Klaus Scherer, Erwin Schoonderwaldt, Bill Thompson, Renee Timmers, Daniel Västfjäll, and Aaron Williamon. I am especially grateful to John Sloboda, with whom I had the pleasure of editing two previous volumes on music and emotion.

I also wish to acknowledge a number of colleagues who supported the Uppsala group in various ways over the years: Eric Clarke, Ian Cross, Lola Cuddy, Stephen Davies, Irène Deliège, Sue Hallam, Ingrid Hammarlund, David Hargreaves, Donald Hodges, David Huron, Stefan Koelsch, Reinhard Kopiez, Carol Krumhansl, Andreas Lehmann, Jerrold Levinson, Åke Pålshammar, Richard Parncutt, Aniruddh Patel, Ann-Sofie Paulander, Isabelle Peretz, Suvi Saarikallio, Emery Schubert, Michael Spitzer, Johan Sundberg, Michael Thaut, Fredrik Ullén, and Marcel Zentner.

I am further indebted to funding agencies that made my research possible, most notably the Swedish Research Council and the Bank of Sweden Tercentenary Foundation. Funding was easy until I turned to the subject of aesthetics! I am also grateful to the Royal Academies of Music in London and Stockholm, the Conservatory of Music B. Marcello in Venice, and the College of Music in Piteå for their collaboration in some of the research projects described in the book. Thanks also to the students I have taught during my music psychology courses for keeping me on my toes.

I owe a big thank-you to Martin Baum and Charlotte Holloway at Oxford University Press for their steadfast yet unobtrusive support throughout the whole project. Special thanks to Costis Chatzidakis for illustrations, Michael Durnin for music engravings, and Janet Walker for copy editing. Thanks also to Châteauneuf du Pape for pleasures along the way, and to all the musicians (you know who you are) with whom I have had the privilege of creating music. I am also grateful to my friends for the good times we have shared and to my parents for their unconditional love and support. My deepest, most heartfelt thanks goes to the singularly most important person in my life, the one who constantly inspires me to become a better human being and who is my most reliable source of emotion outside the musical domain: my partner Susanne (*tu est mon tout*). Last but not least, thank *you* for reading this book!

SUMMARY CONTENTS

Part I: Introduction 1

Part II: Expression and Perception of Emotion 59

Part III: Arousal of Emotion 203

Part IV: Aesthetic Judgment 399

Appendix: The Lens Model Equation and Its Use in Modeling Musical Communication 515

References 517

Name Index 563

Subject Index 571

CONTENTS

Part I: Introduction

1. Setting the Stage: Overture in C Major 3
2. The Book's Composition: Aim and Structure 11
3. The Value of a Psychological Approach 28
4. Music, Experience, and Affect 39

Part II: Expression and Perception of Emotion

5. What Is Meant by Emotional Expression? 61
6. Empirical Studies: What Have We Learned? 79
7. Music as Expression: Objections and Obstacles 99
   Box 7.1: Interlude—Perspectives from Musicians 115
8. Breaking the Code: The Musical Features 122
9. How Are Music and Emotion Links Studied? 139
10. Viewing Music Through a Brunswikian Lens 147
11. The Voice of Angels? Iconic Expression 156
12. Further Layers: Intrinsic and Associative Expression 169
13. Deviation from the Exact: The Role of the Performer 188

Part III: Arousal of Emotion

14. Beyond Perception: When Music Moves Us 205
15. Does Music Arouse Emotions? How Do We Know? 210

16. The Prevalence of Emotional Reactions 231

17. How Does Music Arouse Emotions? 247

18. Jumping at Shadows: Brainstem Reflex 265

19. Get into the Groove: Rhythmic Entrainment 275

20. Mirroring the Expression: Contagion 287

21. Ring My Bell: Evaluative Conditioning 303

22. Blast from the Past: Episodic Memory 316

23. Seeing in the Mind's Eye: Visual Imagery 330

24. What Comes Next? Musical Expectancy 343

25. Predictions, Implications, Complications 364

Part IV: Aesthetic Judgment

26. Aesthetics: The Hard Problem? 401

27. Traditional Approaches to Aesthetics 410

28. What's Special? Adopting the Aesthetic Attitude 422

29. Aesthetic Criteria: Meet the Usual Suspects 433

30. A Novel Approach Towards Aesthetic Judgment 452

31. Aesthetics and Affect in Broader Perspective 469

32. The Last Chorus: Putting It All Together 488

33. Coda: Final Outlook 509

Appendix: The Lens Model Equation and Its Use in Modeling Musical Communication 515

References 517

Name Index 563

Subject Index 571

PART I

INTRODUCTION

CHAPTER 1

SETTING THE STAGE

Overture in C Major

> When I hear certain pieces of music, my vital forces seem at first to be doubled. I feel a delicious pleasure, in which reason has no part; the habit of analysis comes afterwards to give birth to the admiration; the emotion, increasing in proportion to the energy or the grandeur of the ideas of the composer, soon produces a strange agitation in the circulation of the blood; tears, which generally indicate the end of paroxysm, often indicate only a progressive state of it, leading to something still more intense. In this case I have spasmic contractions of the muscles, a trembling in all my limbs, a complete torpor of the feet and the hands, a partial paralysis of the nerves of sight and hearing; I can no longer see, I scarcely hear; vertigo.
> Hector Berlioz (Goulding, 1995, p. 319)

Spoken like a true romantic. This quote from the French composer, Hector Berlioz, may seem over the top. (But given that he wrote a composition called "Symphonie Fantastique," what did you expect?) Yet, this colorful description may serve to introduce the topic of this book.

It is a topic that that may be summarized by two simple observations: wherever there are human beings, there is *music*; and wherever there is music, there is *emotion*. How are music and emotion related? This book aims to give you the best possible answers to this question that the psychology of music can provide.

In Part I, I will introduce the field of music and emotion. Why is it important? Why did I choose to write this book? How might the field of psychology help you to understand your responses to music? What is an emotion? Why do we have emotions? Should we distinguish between perceived and felt emotions? By addressing these issues, I will set the stage for an exploration of the manifold ways in which music may engage our emotions.

1.1 Why Do Musical Emotions Matter?

Music occurs in every known human culture. It accompanies people's activities from the cradle to the grave, and it has done so for a *very* long time. The oldest surviving song is approximately 3,400 years old (Beyer, 2011)—adding new meaning to the term "golden oldies." But music is even older; the oldest musical instruments found are approximately 40,000 years old (Turk, 1997). This means that music is older than agriculture, writing, and money.

We still do not know for sure whether human beings have an evolved ability to create music, or whether musical activities merely exploit abilities that have a different origin and purpose (Patel, 2008). But evidence that music is ancient, universal, and involves specialized brain structures suggests that music is part of our biological makeup (Levitin, 2006).

What we do know is that in both "primitive" cultures and modern society, a considerable amount of time is spent on singing, music, and dance (Werner, 1984). Not just time, either. According to musicologist David Huron (2001), people in North America spend more money on music than on prescription drugs.

What is it that drives us to engage with music? There is, of course, no simple answer to this question because the reasons are many and may also be different, depending on the historical and cultural context.

There are a number of theories about the possible origins and functions of music: it may originally have served a purpose in parent–infant bonding, language acquisition, work coordination, transmission of cultural knowledge, sexual courtship, or social coherence (for discussions see Cross, 2016; Hodges & Sebald, 2011).

There are also theories which claim that music served no purpose at all (Pinker, 1997), even though evolution seems to have provided us with an innate potential for musical activity. All theories about the origins of music are, of course, speculative. Thus, Eckart Altenmüller, Reinhard Kopiez, and Oliver Grewe suggest that, "from a scientific viewpoint the question of the origin of music is difficult, if not impossible, to answer" (Altenmüller, Kopiez, & Grewe, 2013, p. 314).

Fortunately, we do not have to go back in time to obtain a sense of the rich benefits that musical activities bring us in the flow of everyday life. The notions are all (too) familiar, but they ring true. Both musicians and listeners will tell you that music brings people and cultures together; that it is a source of aesthetic pleasure; that it may contribute to health and well-being; that it is a powerful form of communication; or that music is a creative form of self-expression. Music can be all these things and more.

Note that running like a thread through all these notions about music is *emotion*; it is the common currency, regardless of whether you seek out music for entertainment, healing, self-expression, or aesthetic experience. Hence, questions about music and emotion are at the heart of why we listen to it. They are central to how music affects us, and how music is affected by us—the way we write and perform it.

Presumably, you picked up this book because you already think that the emotions play a paramount role in musical activity. If not, the remaining parts of the book can hopefully convince you.

1.2 Putting the Emotions into Perspective

But wait a minute; there is something I need to confess and I know that it may seem bizarre for *me* to say this, particularly in the context of this book and after my previous comments. *Emotion is not everything*. The fact that I devote a whole book to this aspect of music should not be taken to mean that I think other aspects of music are unimportant. Sometimes, however, it may be necessary to explore a specific topic in depth to truly understand it.

Still, I want to acknowledge from the outset that for some people, emotions are not essential to their engagement with music. I have no problem with that. People engage with music in many different ways, and there is no "right" way to approach music. One could, for instance, listen to music primarily to contemplate the cleverly wrought musical structures of a gifted composer. Who is to say that this way of hearing music is more or less sensible than one focusing on emotions? Moreover, this book adopts a scientific perspective, which means that my aim is descriptive, not prescriptive.

Clearly, for a lot of people music is nothing more than a "pleasant pastime," or even a nuisance to be endured in shops during the Christmas holidays. "Is music the most important thing we ever did" asked Ian Cross in an article published in 1999. That seems like a stretch.

Some people claim that music (or a specific piece of music) literally saved their life during moments of deep despair (Clapton, 2007, p. 264; Gabrielsson, 2011, p. 151). There is no doubt that many people regard music as very important in their lives. As you are reading this book, I assume that you are one of those people. Could you imagine a world without music?

What seems beyond doubt is that music has never been more prevalent than in our modern society (North & Hargreaves, 2008). Most people in the developed world hear music every day. In a significant proportion of these everyday episodes, the music arouses an emotional state in the listener (Juslin, Liljeström, Västfjäll, Barradas, & Silva, 2008; Juslin, Liljeström, Laukka, Västfjäll, & Lundqvist, 2011; Juslin, Barradas, Ovsiannikow, Limmo, & Thompson, 2016).

The emotions run the gamut from mild appreciation to extreme euphoria. Indeed, listeners actively employ music to change their emotions, to release emotion, to match their current emotion, to enjoy or comfort themselves, and to relieve stress (Juslin & Laukka, 2004). A listener in a survey study explained: "I don't think any other art form can give me the same joy and strong experiences as music" (Gabrielsson, 2011, p. 447).

Such sentiments are echoed by musicians: "Emotion is the most important thing in music for me," explained the singer Björk in a TV documentary. "What is the point of music if it does not have an emotional impact," asked Emmylou Harris during a Polar prize TV interview. "Our business is emotion and sensitivity," declared Janet Baker (Watson, 1991, p. 238). Scientific findings indicate that artists often create music to "move" others or themselves—or simply to express themselves (Boyd & George-Warren, 2013). All these aspects will be carefully reviewed later in this book.

It is *not* a stretch, then, to claim that one of the more common motives for listening to music is to influence one's emotions. Even those listeners who insist that they are interested in the *music* rather than in their own emotions are presumably indirectly motivated by the pleasure that their "interest in the music" brings them. If you find that music is a purely "intellectual adventure," then consider how even the term "adventure" implies some level of excitement. Without some minimum of affective involvement, it would seem almost irrational to engage with music.

There is no need to claim that musical emotions are important for every musician or listener, but as a researcher, I conclude—based on scientific findings—that for a significant proportion of the listeners in the world, emotions are regarded as a key aspect of their experience, even the main motive for listening to music. Emotions are, as we shall see, deeply intertwined with most of the ways in which we use and relate to music in daily life.

The finding that emotion is felt to be crucial for many music listeners makes it a "legitimate" subject for scientific investigation. The possibility that music may affect subjective well-being and physical health (MacDonald, Kreutz, & Mitchell, 2012) through emotional experiences renders the study of music and emotion more than just "legitimate": it is outright important.

There are several applications of music and emotion research such as music therapy, film music, marketing, healthcare, and the gaming industry. Professionals that could benefit from knowing something about music and emotion research include musicians, music critics, teachers, producers, nurses, sound engineers, and psychotherapists. For me, it is ultimately about curiosity—an urge to explore how "mere sound," as it were, affects us so deeply.

1.3 Why did Freud Not Enjoy Music? The Mystery of Musical Emotions

The truth is that researchers have struggled to understand emotional responses to music. It is often described as one of the great mysteries in life, which has puzzled serious thinkers from Plato to Darwin and William James, and all the way to modern-day affective scientists. "How does music communicate emotions, and why do we enjoy having our emotions stirred in this way? No one knows" (Johnson-Laird, 1992, p. 13).

Included amongst the scholars puzzled by music is psychoanalyst Sigmund Freud (Figure 1.1), who reportedly did not enjoy music—albeit for a very specific reason:

Figure 1.1 Sigmund Freud, frustrated by his inability to understand his responses to music.
Illustration by Costis Chatzidakis.

> [W]orks of art do exercise a powerful effect on me ... [I] spend a long time before them trying to apprehend them in my own way, i.e. to explain to myself what their effect is due to. Wherever I cannot do this, as for instance with music, I am almost incapable of obtaining any pleasure. Some rationalistic, or perhaps analytic, turn of mind in me rebels against being moved by a thing without knowing why I am thus affected and what it is that affects me. Freud, 1914/1955, p. 211

This apparent lack of a rational explanation for our emotional responses to music could also perhaps explain why most scholars shied away from studying musical emotions for so long. Neuroscientist Isabelle Peretz notes that emotional reactions have often been regarded as "too personal, elusive, and variable to be studied scientifically" (Peretz, 2001, p. 106), and philosopher Peter Kivy similarly argues that emotions tend to be "very personal and idiosyncratic" (Kivy, 2001, p. 71).

Indeed, although there are certain pieces of music that many listeners find moving—examples will be offered later—a more common tendency is that different listeners respond *differently* to the same piece of music. For example, a piece of "heavy metal" music may be annoying to some listeners, whereas others find it highly enjoyable (Gowensmith & Bloom, 1997).

French composer Jean-Claude Risset recounted an event where he played one of his musical compositions, *Mutations*, to an audience in 1970. The piece features an endlessly ascending *glissando*,[1] beginning roughly two minutes and 40 seconds into the music, and Risset was intrigued to find how different listeners' responses were: One felt "exhilarated" by the "liberation from gravity," whereas another experienced "anxiety," because the sound was reminiscent of the sirens during the Second World War (Cochrane, 2013a, p. 28).

Such individual patterns can be quite frustrating for scientists who wish to discover general principles. Hence, Emil Gutheil expressed doubts whether research on music and emotion "can ever reach the goal of science, namely to *discover laws of cause and effect* in order to *predict the results*" (Gutheil, 1952, p. 11).

[1] A *glissando* is a continuous glide from one pitch to another, for instance from low to high pitch. A related term is continuous *portamento*.

But do not be alarmed: in this book, I will show you that despite their elusiveness, emotional responses to music are far more predictable than is commonly believed. Behind the apparent mess there are systematic principles at work.

Not only that: our emotional experiences with music tell a story about who we are—both as individuals and as a species. At the individual level, musical emotions reflect our memories, experiences, preferences, motivations, interests, and personality traits. At the biological level, the emotions reflect our human ability to interpret and use sound as sources of information in order to guide future behaviors by way of our emotions. In subsequent parts of the book, we will explore what this means for our music experiences in everyday life.

CHAPTER 2

THE BOOK'S COMPOSITION

Aim and Structure

2.1 Why Did I Write This Book?

A lot has been written about the relationship between music and emotion throughout the ages by music philosophers, music theorists, and musicians. I do not aim to provide a comprehensive history of the topic here. Such an account is still to be written. (For a brief overview, I refer the reader to Cook and Dibben, 2010).

Historical writings range from the classic theories of art in ancient Greece, which construe art as "mimesis" (the imitation of nature) or "catharsis" (the purification of the soul through affective experience); and the so-called doctrine of the affections (*Affektenlehre*) of the seventeenth and early eighteenth century, holding that music should convey particular "affects" (i.e., idealized emotional states) and have listeners feel these same states, in accordance with quite detailed prescriptions; to the aesthetics of feeling and sensation (*Empfindungsästhetik*) of the late eighteenth century, which involved greater freedom to use fantasy and intuition to express more subjective feelings; and the following nineteenth century conflict between those scholars who argue for the value of music as "pure and contentless form," and those who argue that music's value lies in its ability to refer to extra-musical phenomena in the world (including the emotions).

Historical surveys can be interesting, and many popular notions about what music is or should be can clearly be traced back to age-old notions. However, a historical view will arguably not give us the kind of evidence-based input needed to *explain* emotional responses to music. The old theories simply will not do. Philosopher Malcolm Budd reviews the most influential of these theories and finds them all wanting (Budd, 1985). In fact, by the early 1990s, philosophers could still not—by their own admission—explain how music arouses emotions (e.g., Kivy, 1993, p. 6).[1]

Had I wished to be provocative, I would have said that philosophers had their chance to explain how music arouses emotions in listeners for over 2,000 years, and that they blew it.

Fortunately, I have too much respect for their work to say that, and it is beyond doubt that philosophers have contributed considerably to our understanding of musical expression of emotions (Davies, 1994). I will not attempt to review all the philosophical work undertaken because it is impossible to do this rich source of discussions justice here.[2] However, we will return to what philosophers might have to offer when we consider aesthetic judgments of music (Part IV).

In this book, I will adopt a different approach. The focus is on how *modern psychology* may explain emotional responses to music. As we will see, psychology was a relative latecomer to the intellectual party. Even so, it may hold the key when it comes to making sense of this complex field.

Can music arouse emotions in listeners? If so, which emotions? How, exactly, does it do so? Why do listeners often respond with different emotions to the same piece of music? Are emotional reactions to music different from other emotions? What is it that makes a musical performance expressive? Are composers and performers able to communicate specific emotions to listeners? How do emotions and preferences relate to aesthetic judgments of music?

This is the first monograph in psychology to tackle these questions and more in a comprehensive synthesis of the literature. Although drawing heavily on my own 20-year research program, I aim to cover the field in a

[1] Later, when philosophers *were* able to discuss possible explanations, they did so mainly by referring to work by music psychologists (e.g., Robinson, 2005).

[2] For a very courageous attempt to summarize prominent philosophical theories of music, see Hodges (2017).

representative manner, highlighting the significant contributions made by researchers around the globe.

Given the flow of publications in recent years, I believe we need an integrative framework more than ever. My goal is to provide a unified perspective on music and emotion, so that various aspects fit together, but make no mistake: this book represents *my* take on the subject—not everyone may agree with the perspective offered.

My views will be based on the best theory and evidence available at the time of writing. Although I will occasionally rely on my experience as a musician and active music listener, the emphasis will be on scientific research. The field has long been marked by controversy (see, e.g., Juslin & Västfjäll, 2008), but the last two decades have seen an emerging consensus regarding many issues. This book will highlight such areas of agreement among researchers. Where there is still disagreement, I will discuss different opinions, and point out what I consider to be the most promising direction at the current stage of research.

Fortunately, many of the problems that have been debated over the years can be resolved empirically, by collecting evidence. Hence, empirical findings play a key role in the story. I want to communicate these findings to a broader audience who may still be largely unaware of the recent breakthroughs in the field. In doing so I hope to dispel some myths that surround expression and emotions in music—myths that have prevented the full application of knowledge about music and emotion in various practical settings, such as music education (Hallam, 2010).

2.2 What Took Us So Long?

I hinted earlier that psychologists were late to the party. This brings us to the first of a series of paradoxes that characterize the study of music and emotion:

> PARADOX 1: "Emotion" is often considered a key aspect of music experience. Yet, this topic was largely neglected by psychologists until the 1990s.

If you were to pick up a handbook on music psychology (or emotion psychology, for that matter) in the late 1980s or 1990s, chances are that you would discover a book without a single chapter on emotional responses.[3] For a newcomer to the field, this may seem utterly bizarre. What were researchers thinking? Why didn't the field develop sooner, considering how essential emotions are for musical activities?

Rather than concluding that earlier scholars were nutjobs, we should perhaps blame it on the prevailing zeitgeist of the 1980s. To understand this, and help to resolve Paradox 1, we should briefly consider the history of music psychology.

Some readers may be surprised to learn that music psychology was a subdomain of psychology right from the start in the late nineteenth century (e.g., Downey, 1897). At this time, psychology looked to physics as the model for "the new behavioral science." The focus was on "controlled experiments" that aimed to reveal general "laws" about how humans come to perceive the world (Goodwin, 2008).

Likewise, early music psychology mainly involved experiments focusing on basic psycho-physical and perceptual processes, rather than on how we experience music. The subsequent developments in psychology did little to change this. First came the era of "behaviorism" (Skinner, 1953), which claimed that only external behavior could be the focus of a proper science—emotions were "subjective inner states" that could play no role in such a science. Then came the so-called cognitive revolution (Gardner, 1985), which regarded the human mind as a computer—a metaphor that also seemed incompatible with a focus on emotions (though the computer HAL in the movie *2001: A Space Odyssey* certainly seemed to behave emotionally toward the end).

After a slow and tentative start, psychological research on music and emotion took off in the 1990s, when emotion was finally recognized as a legitimate topic in music psychology. (I was fortunate enough to begin my

[3] There were exceptions, however, most notably *Music Cognition* by Jay Dowling and Dane Harwood (1986).

research at just the right time.) Even then, however, there were several problems that made life miserable for music and emotion researchers.

First, it is difficult to capture emotions in a controlled laboratory environment—the favorite workspace of the music psychologist. Emotions may be fleeting and elusive, sensitive to the artificial context of the research laboratory. Only when music psychologists moved away from (only) laboratory-based experiments on perceptual and cognitive processes to a broader exploration of the ways in which music is used and experienced in everyday life did scholars gain a better understanding of the phenomena under investigation (Juslin & Sloboda, 2010).

Second, researchers lacked a theoretical framework that could guide their work. There was a general sense that traditional theories of emotion were not capable of explaining responses to music (Ellsworth, 1994). Yet, it was not clear what should come in their place. It is fair to say that much of the early work was "a-theoretical," which is never a good thing in science. We need theories to make sense of the data collected.

Third, studies of music and emotion initially met with some resistance. Music educator Robert Woody sensed "a general aversion among musicians to scientific study of music, especially when related to topics such as emotion, expression and aesthetics" (Woody, 2002, p. 214).

In addition, the academic study of music has often adopted a view about the appreciation of music that musicologist Nicholas Cook succinctly sums up: "You should listen attentively, respectfully, in a detached manner (avoiding being too caught up in the sensory or emotional ebb and flow of the music), and informed by appropriate knowledge" (Cook, 1998, p. 25). This attitude is partly linked to an emphasis on classical music in much academic work, a type of music that is not typical of most music in the world, and that represents a minority interest even among Western listeners, as pointed out by David Hargreaves (1986).

This illustrates the fact that the study of music and emotion tends to bring a politics of sorts: discussions about music and emotion often revolve around questions about value. Here, I am not just thinking about issues concerning the value of *pieces* of music (which is treated in Part IV) but rather of the value of our *responses* to the music. Not all responses, it seems, are regarded as equally "valuable," "appropriate," "sophisticated," or "aesthetically warranted." Such views are sometimes expressed explicitly by scholars, other times they are implicit in their reasoning. It is a matter of which emotions music *ought* to express or arouse, and who decides whether these responses are appropriate.

In my opinion, these are not issues that a science of music and emotion should be concerned with—science is descriptive, not normative. Still, these lines of thought occur in the literature and color the views of some scholars. Therefore, we should be aware of them if we wish to understand the domain. I believe that normative views sometimes cloud the (scientific) judgment of scholars, and for that reason I will highlight them throughout the book.

Some people resist studies of music and emotion because they want to "preserve the magic." As the composer Leonard Bernstein commented, "Why do so many of us try to explain the beauty of music, thus apparently depriving it of its mystery?" (Watson, 1991, p. 9). Despite having spent the past 20 years investigating music and emotion and the links between them, my fascination and sense of wonder about music has not decreased at all—in fact, it has increased. For reasons that will become clear, most of the underlying psychological processes are not affected by one's having knowledge about them; they live their own lives. But considering all the difficulties listed earlier, how can we make progress in this complex field?

2.3 Keys to Progress: Six Premises

Based on insights from my own 20-year quest to unravel the mysteries of music and emotion, I have come to believe that real progress can only be achieved if we accept a number of basic premises about music and emotion. These premises constitute six themes, which will recur throughout the book.

- Theme 1: Emotions depend on evolved mechanisms

The first premise is that in order to understand emotional responses to music, we must adopt an evolutionary perspective. Consider the timeline shown in Figure 2.1. Life on Earth began approximately 4.5 billion years ago; mammals began to develop about 200 million years ago. The Neanderthals began to roam the earth around 500,000 years ago. Modern humans, or *homo sapiens,* appeared around 200,000 years ago (Harari, 2014).

As already explained, music-making has been part of the human behavioral repertoire for roughly 40,000 years. However, many emotional mechanisms evolved well before music appeared on the earth. Emotions involve old parts of the brain partly shared with many other species (Panksepp, 1998), in particular mammals, which began to develop 200 million years ago. Therefore, chances are slim that our ancient emotional mechanisms evolved to handle the intricacies of driving in New York City, surfing the dark web, or fiddling with the knobs of the Moog synthesizer.

What this means is that *human music-making most likely evolved on the foundation of existing emotional mechanisms with a longer evolutionary history*. Although uses of music are influenced by social conventions that developed over many centuries (Clarke, Dibben, & Pitts, 2010), they are also constrained by psychological mechanisms. The only known causal process capable of

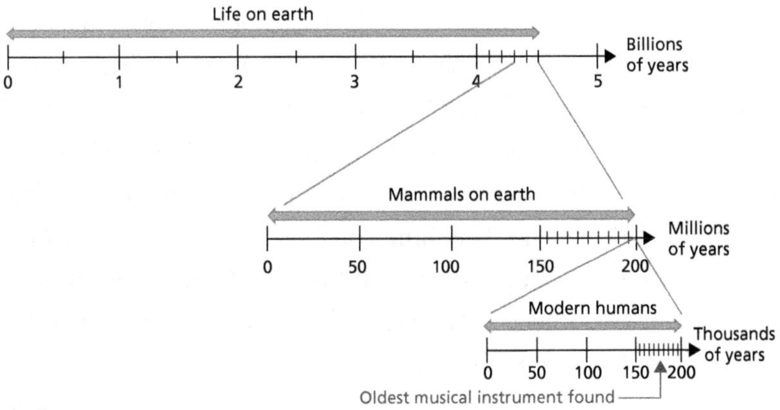

Figure 2.1 Evolutionary timeline and the advent of music.

producing such mechanisms is biological evolution (Tooby & Cosmides, 1990). Still, despite a general acceptance of the theory of evolution, few music researchers incorporate an evolutionary perspective into their studies of emotional responses.

In this book, I will attempt to show that an evolutionary approach can help to explain many of the peculiarities of musical emotions. Responses that at first glance do not seem to make sense may, indeed, make perfect sense—once we understand the "architecture" of our ancient emotions. Although our music experiences appear *uniquely rewarding*, they are, ultimately, based on the same evolved brain mechanisms as our other experiences of emotions in daily life (Juslin, 2013a).

- Theme 2: Music engages multiple emotion mechanisms

A second premise is that *there is no single psychological mechanism that can explain all our emotional reactions to music.* This premise follows, in a sense, naturally from the first: an evolutionary perspective suggests that the human brain and body involves several instances of *functional redundancy*; that is, that different structures can serve a similar behavioral function (cf. Brunswik, 1956). In nature, there are often multiple means to an end. Our emotions are no exception. There are multiple pathways from events to emotions.

I sense that researchers often struggle to accept and come to terms with this aspect, the multiple causes of emotions. For too long, music and emotion researchers have tended to focus on a single mechanism in the hope that it could carry the whole burden of explanation. Invariably, it failed—not necessarily because the theory was wrong but because it provided only part of the overall puzzle. The same conclusion was reached by Malcolm Budd when he reviewed philosophical theories: "A new theory of music is needed … It will, I believe, have to be less monolithic than the theories I have rejected" (Budd, 1985, p. 176).

In this book, I present a different kind of theory of music and emotion consisting of multiple mechanisms at various levels of the brain. In Part III,

I describe no less than nine distinct mechanisms that can explain how music may arouse felt emotions in listeners, either alone or in combination.

Thus, a consistent theme of the book is the manifold ways in which music may engage our emotions, with much of the subtlety, richness, and complexity of our experiences resulting from the combined effects of multiple sources, which come and go across various contexts (Chapter 32). Many debates in the field reflect failure to see that musical emotions are not unitary.

- Theme 3: There are definitive limits to human introspection

The experiences that music creates belong at center stage in a book on musical emotions. Yet, the reflective, conscious experience of the world that we tend to take more or less for granted is a novel development, seen from an evolutionary perspective. It coincided with the vast expansion of the part of the human brain most recently developed, the neocortex (Striedter, 2005). Note, however, that this top layer of the brain is partly independent of many older and more "primitive" brain circuits associated with emotion and largely shared with other species (Panksepp, 1998).

The discovery that many emotion mechanisms can function independently of our conscious thoughts and intentions may help to explain why musical expression is often described as "a channel of the unconscious" (Boyd & George-Warren, 2013), dependent on "intuition" and "instinct" (Casals, 1970).[4] Recall that Sigmund Freud—virtually the inventor of our modern notion of the subconscious—was frustrated with music precisely because he had no conscious access to the causes of his emotional responses.

A third premise, therefore, is that *because several of the psychological processes involved in music and emotion are subconscious, researchers cannot rely merely on phenomenological report to explain emotion.* Most of what goes on in the causal process may not be consciously available, and we may attribute causality

[4] "Ultimately, the paramount role is that of intuition. For me the determining factor in creativity, in bringing a work to life, is that of musical instinct" (Casals, 1970, p. 97).

to salient stimuli, even when salience is unrelated to the causal effect (Fox, 2008).

For example, if you—like Freud—do not understand the causes of your emotional response, it appears natural to search the contents of your current attention for some plausible "candidate cause." But the focus of your immediate attention may not be the actual cause of your response to the music.

Hence, although phenomenological description may give us clues about *possible* causes of our emotions, we must remember that the music experience is the very thing that needs explaining rather than being that explanation (Juslin, 2013a). I believe that psychological experiments are key in order to "tease out" the implicit processes involved in our emotional reactions to music. Being able to *manipulate* features of a musical event directly to evaluate its influence on the listener helps to resolve the problem of limited conscious access to psychological processes.

- Theme 4: Emotional responses to music are intrinsically social

The human species is fundamentally a social one (Berry, Poortinga, Breugelmans, Chasiotis, & Sam, 2011). It has been argued that the real secret behind the human dominance of the world is our ability to cooperate in large groups (Harari, 2014).

Some researchers have speculated that the absolute brain size increased in *homo sapiens* mainly because larger brains allowed for more sophisticated social interactions (Striedter, 2005). We continually interact with other people, and our behavior is greatly influenced by the presence of others. Even when alone, we rely on social knowledge to make sense of our lives.

Music is no different in this respect. Music is made *by* humans *for* humans. Most theories about the origins of music have "a social element" (e.g., work coordination, communication, courtship, and bonding). Music often serves "social functions"—for example, to enhance a listener's sense of cultural identity and social belonging, or to create an appropriate atmosphere during social ceremonies (Hodges & Sebald, 2011; Saarikallio, 2012).

A fifth premise, then, is *the inherently social nature of musical activities.* Not only is music often created together with other people, as well as enjoyed together with other people (e.g., during a concert); the social context will also strongly influence the nature and intensity of our responses to music. Indeed, even when you listen to music alone, you respond to musical sounds in a social way. Your brain treats the sounds as "intentional" and "communicative" (as will be shown in Chapters 5, 13, and 20)—and with good reason.

This social way of responding may occur with instrumental music and it is even more obvious when it comes to music featuring lyrics. Don Henley of The Eagles explains: "Songs just keep you company, that's all. They make you feel less lonely; they make you feel like there's somebody else out there that feels the way you do" (Boyd & George-Warren, 2013, p. 296). In fact, researchers have discovered that music listening might lead to the discharge of the hormone oxytocin in the brain, which is closely linked with physical intimacy (Nilsson, 2009). You are, it appears, quite literally "touched" by music.

- Theme 5: Musical emotions depend on music–listener–situation interactions

It is widely accepted by researchers that events that cause emotions are psychological rather than physical (e.g., Oatley, 1992). There is no physical situation that will invariably arouse a specific emotion. Emotions depend on psychological evaluations, which take individual and contextual factors into account. Think back on the example of how emotional reactions to the composition by Jean-Claude Risset varied drastically depending on personal experience, such as memories of sirens during the Second World War (Chapter 1).

A fourth premise, then, is that all responses to music occur in a complex interaction between the *music*, the *listener*, and the *situation* (Figure 2.2), as argued by the Norwegian researcher Harald Jørgensen (1988). Each of these factors can influence your response. As soon as there is a change in one of

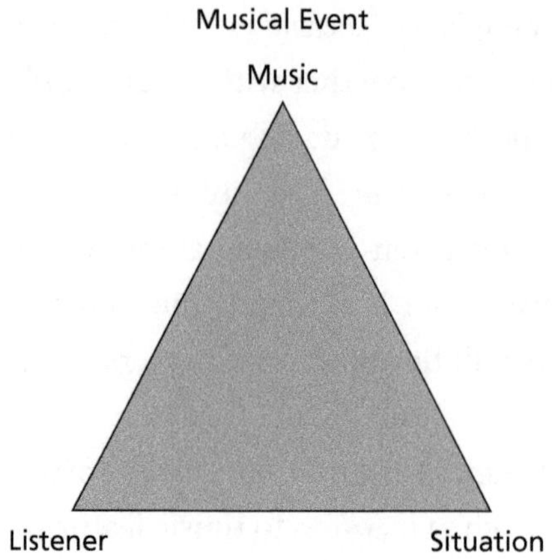

Figure 2.2 Interaction between music, listener, and situation.

them, the nature of your musical experience is likely to change, in more or less subtle ways.

Consider some examples. Your experience may be affected by *musical* features, such as tempo, rhythm, timing, melody, articulation, timbre, harmony, phrasing, instrumentation, texture, and genre. It may further be affected by *individual* features, such as age, gender, personality, education, music experience, cultural background, psychological status (e.g., mood, attention, whether you are tired), and personality traits. Finally, it may be affected by *situational* factors, such as location (e.g., at home, at a concert, outdoors), social context (e.g., listening alone or with friends), other activities occurring at the same time (e.g., jogging, dancing), acoustic conditions (listening in headphones or through loudspeakers, sound quality), or visual impressions (e.g., performer gestures).

One could argue—only half-jokingly—that musicologists tend to focus only on the music, psychologists only on the listener, and sociologists only on the context. In reality, all three factors influence our music experiences immensely (for some examples, see Chapter 25).

As a result, I suggest that *you can never have exactly the same music experience twice*. Even if you manage to play exactly the same music, under precisely the same circumstances (a tall order in itself), the fact remains that *you* are not exactly the same person as you were the last time you heard the music. With every hearing of the piece, you will have gone through additional experiences in life, and your familiarity with the piece has increased.

This is as much part of the attraction and joy of music listening as it is a headache for the psychology researcher, who wishes to draw general conclusions about music experiences. The implication is that reactions to music can never be fully explained by reference to the music alone. (This should be borne in mind when, later in this book, I summarize musical features linked to the expression of specific emotions.)

2.4 Terminology and Organization of the Book

Many researchers argue that the field of musical emotion has lacked conceptual specificity and precision. Previous disagreements have not only reflected a lack of relevant empirical data but also conceptual confusion. When researchers speak of *feelings, moods, emotions, passions, affects,* or *sentiments,* what do they mean by these terms? Do they refer to similar phenomena or not?

To make matters worse, the meaning of these terms has changed over time. For instance, the word *affect* is used in a different way today from how it was used in the seventeenth century. (For a review of the history of the emotions, see Plamper, 2015.) The term "emotion" was—like many good things—introduced by the French. The philosopher René Descartes launched the term *émotion* in 1649, before which both French and English writings mostly referred to the "passions."

For a music psychologist such as myself, it certainly helps that our discipline is not focused on history. Yet, even in the present time, terminological issues abound. It is not just a matter of words: the problem goes straight to the heart of how we *define* and *conceptualize* the phenomena under investigation. Having implied earlier that philosophers failed to explain how music can arouse emotions, I should be graceful enough to acknowledge that philosophers would have a field day picking apart the work of psychologists, due to their sloppy treatment of conceptual distinctions in previous studies.

In any case, it seems clear that the subject needs to be broken down into smaller constituents, based on a set of key distinctions, in order to make sense of the field. Accordingly, Table 2.1 presents a set of simple working definitions of terms used throughout the book. These will be further elaborated in the following parts.

My definitions are in the majority of cases consistent with the use advocated in the *Handbook of Affective Sciences* (Davidson, Scherer, & Goldsmith, 2003) and *Handbook of Music and Emotion* (Juslin & Sloboda, 2010). They reflect the increasing consensus among scholars today. However, we need to be conscious of the fact that these terms are not always used in the same way in other—and, in particular, older—writings in music psychology. Note that the term "musical emotions" occurring in the title of this book is used as mere shorthand for "emotions related to music."

This book is largely organized in accordance with the conceptual distinctions in Table 2.1. Part I outlines basic principles of psychology and emotions, followed by Parts II and III, which focus on the expression, perception, and arousal of emotions, and Part IV, which considers how emotions may relate to aesthetic judgments and preferences for music. Each part presents a theoretical model that can help to organize the findings.

There is a kind of logical progression to the specific order of the four parts, as will hopefully be even more apparent later. Suffice to say, a musical communication process often begins with an *expression* of emotion that can be *perceived* by the listener, and that hopefully also *arouses* some emotion in the listener, which in turn may lead the listener to regard the music as *aesthetically valuable* and thus to *like* it (Figure 2.3). This way of conceptualizing music is not without its critics, but I save that discussion for Part II. There are, of course, exceptions to the sequence shown in Figure 2.3, but such exceptions do not, in my view, detract from this being the most plausible and pedagogical way in which to describe the different processes.

Academic books can be challenging, and there are some "shortcuts" in the book which may suit some readers. Thus, the Parts on expression of

Table 2.1 List of working definitions.

Affect	This term is used as an umbrella term that covers all evaluative—or "valenced" (positive/negative)—states (e.g., emotion, mood, preference). The term denotes such phenomena in general. If that is not intended, a more precise term (e.g., mood, emotion, preference) is used instead.
Emotion (e.g., happiness, sadness)	This term is used to refer to a quite brief but intense affective reaction that usually involves a number of sub-components—subjective feeling, physiological arousal, expression, action tendency, and regulation—that are more or less "synchronized." Emotions focus on specific "objects" and last from a few minutes to a several hours.
Musical emotions	This term is used only as shorthand for "emotions that were somehow induced by music," without any further implications about the precise nature of these emotions.
Mood	This term is used to denote such affective states that are lower in intensity than emotions, that do not have a clear "object," and that are much longer lasting than emotions (i.e., several hours to days). Moods do not involve a synchronized response in components like expression and physiology (e.g., gloomy).
Feeling	This term is used to refer to the subjective experience of emotions or moods. One component of an emotion that is typically measured via verbal self-report.
Arousal	This term is used to refer to physical activation of the autonomic nervous system. Physiological arousal is one of the components of an emotional response, but could also occur in the absence of emotion (e.g., due to exercise). Arousal is often reflected in the "feeling" component (i.e., the subjective experience).
Preference	This term is used to refer to more long-term affective evaluations of objects or persons with a low intensity (e.g., liking of a particular type of music).
Personality trait	This term is used to refer to relatively stable affective dispositions, which are characterized by low intensity and a behavioral impact which is usually the result of an interaction with situational factors (e.g., a neurotic personality).

(*continued*)

Table 2.1 Continued

Emotion induction	This term will be used to refer to all instances where music arouses an emotion in a listener—regardless of the nature of the process that evoked the emotion.
Emotion perception	This term will be used to refer to all instances where a listener perceives or recognizes emotions in music (e.g., "a sad expression"), without necessarily feeling an emotion him- or herself.
Communication	This term will be used to refer to a process where a sender conveys an emotion to a receiver who is able to decode the emotion concerned. Note that the term "communication" will be used regardless of whether the transmitted emotion is "genuinely felt" or simply "portrayed" by the performer in a symbolic manner. (Music's potential to convey referential information is separate from the issue of whether the music is the result of felt emotion or a sending intention or both.)

Adapted from Juslin, P. N., & Sloboda, J. A. (Eds.). (2010). *Handbook of music and emotion: Theory, research, applications*. By permission of Oxford University Press.

emotions and arousal of emotions, respectively, can be read separately; for instance, if you are eager to learn how music arouses strong emotions, you can skip directly to Part III. However, reading Part II first might offer a deeper understanding of the topic because expression may contribute to aroused emotions. Similarly, if you are mainly interested in expression, you can read only Part II. Yet, a fuller appreciation of expression may require some sense of how it may figure in the arousal of emotions (Part III).

Part IV focuses on a mechanism hitherto neglected by most music psychologists that is closely linked to the value of music: aesthetic judgments. It can be read on its own, but it also explains how judgments of aesthetic value can be related to both preferences and emotions. Part IV also ties together all previous sections by showing how various aspects (e.g., perceived versus aroused emotions) and mechanisms (e.g., episodic memory versus aesthetic

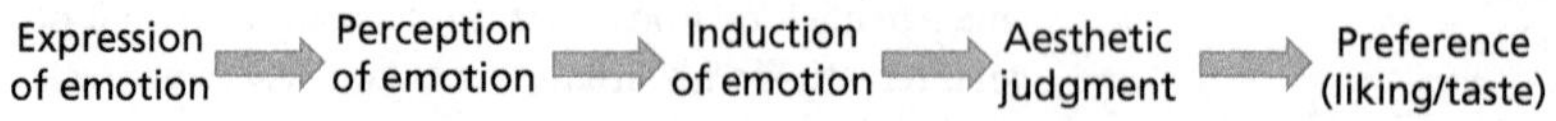

Figure 2.3 Default relationships between primary concepts.

judgment) *combine* to create the kind of complex emotional experiences that we have come to expect from music listening.

I have tried to provide plenty of accessible music examples to illustrate the ideas in the book. However, I have done so with some hesitation—primarily because one of the themes is that emotional responses to music can never be explained by the music alone. They always reflect a complex interplay between the music, the listener, and the context. Hence, at least *some* of these musical examples may work for me or for the participants who visited my laboratory, but not for you. You may have to find your own personal examples that embody the principles I discuss in the various parts of the book.

Before looking closer at how music may be involved in the expression, perception, and arousal of emotions, as well as how such emotions can relate to aesthetic judgment and preferences for music, we must first review basic concepts of psychology and emotions. These will provide the foundation—the "rhythm section," if you will—of the book.

CHAPTER 3

THE VALUE OF A PSYCHOLOGICAL APPROACH

3.1 The Mind's Science

Psychology is commonly defined as the study of mental processes and behavior. It is both an academic discipline and an applied science. The main focus is on describing and explaining how we sense the world (perception), how we think (cognition), feel (emotion), and behave (action).

The roots of the discipline can be found in philosophical problems, though unlike philosophy, psychology is an *empirical* science; that is, psychologists think that we can rely on evidence to resolve theoretical disputes (Eysenck, 1994). Consistent with this view, my belief is that most, if not all, issues regarding music and emotion can be resolved empirically.

The focus on empirical data reflects the predominately *scientific* orientation of psychology. Briefly, science refers to the acquiring of more or less objective knowledge, by means of observations under controlled conditions, and the interpretation of data with the help of theories. As explained in the *Handbook of Music and Emotion*, psychologists aim to discover antecedents to the behavior requiring explanation, and to uncover the mechanisms whereby the antecedents bring about the observed behavior (Sloboda & Juslin, 2010).

Music psychology, then, focuses on mental processes and behaviors that occur in connection with music (Gabrielsson, 2016). It aims to observe and develop theories about the processes involved in composing, performing, and listening to music (for a complete review of the field of music psychology, see Hallam, Cross, & Thaut, 2016).

3.2 Whose Topic? Levels of Scientific Analysis

To complicate matters, human behavior is influenced by a large number of factors, such as the current stimulus (at this very moment, the text you are reading), our genes, our body and its needs (e.g., hunger, thirst, sleep), our thoughts and emotions, the social situation, the culture we were brought up in, previous life experiences, and personality traits. This suggests that behavior can only be fully understood by taking into account the work in neighboring disciplines, such as biology and sociology.

This largely multidisciplinary character is evident also in the study of music and emotion, which may be fruitfully approached from many different perspectives. Although emotion is clearly a psychological concept—considering its focus on mental processes and behavior (see Chapter 4)—studies of music and emotion often transcend traditional lines of inquiry.

Thus, for example, when we attempt to explain our emotional responses to a piece of music, we can hardly avoid analyzing musical structures (musicology), measuring bodily and brain responses (neurophysiology), or looking at how the social context influences our responses (sociology). I will therefore adopt an eclectic approach to the subject of this book, gathering relevant ideas and findings from a variety of sources and disciplines.

Still, although I will take on board important contributions from neighboring fields, I will also argue that psychology is uniquely situated to explain emotional responses to music. In my view, it is no coincidence that the most successful attempt to analyze emotional reactions to music by a musicologist drew heavily on contemporary psychological theories such as gestalt psychology (see Meyer, 1956; and Chapter 24 in this book). Why, then, is psychology key to understand musical emotions?

3.3 Explaining Music and Emotion: It's All About Meaning

Malcolm Budd has defined music as "the art of uninterpreted sounds" (Budd, 1985, p. ix). This seems to be a common view—that music is "pure sound" or "abstract patterns of notes" without any meaning. But this line of thought will not get us very far, in my opinion, if we wish to explain emotional responses to music.

I will instead argue that music is *constantly interpreted*. Even if we are not aware of it, our brain is constantly scanning the sound environment for "clues" about the world (Juslin, 2013a). Sometimes, such interpretations may lead to the arousal of *felt* emotion. More frequently, perhaps, we merely detect information *about* emotions in sounds. (I will soon return to these distinct aspects.)

At its core, the study of music and emotion is concerned with relationships between "musical events" and "emotional responses." (I define the "musical event" broadly here as the joint information in the *music*, the *listener*, and the *situation*.) The interface between them consists of psychological processes in the human mind. Most researchers have been content to look to the music itself for an explanation, and there is no doubt that a detailed grasp of the musical structure is important. But it is *not enough*.

When we ask ourselves why certain note patterns, but not others, evoke an emotion in us we can easily overlook the fact that our responses to those note patterns depend only in part on the notes themselves. To understand our responses, we need to look *beyond* the musical structure and consider the *meaning* extracted from the musical event. What kind of meaning, then, may we find in music?

In a study by the British musicologist, Nicola Dibben (2001), listeners were asked to describe what they actually *heard* when played extracts of music (as well as other everyday sounds)—surprisingly, a very rare task in music studies. Although the listeners reported perceiving musical structure, they were more likely to describe what the sounds *meant* to them; that is, the listeners typically heard beyond the acoustic characteristics, and picked up information concerning such aspects as the source of the sound, musical genre, emotions, social context, physical proximity to the sound source, and performer skill (see also Clarke, 2005). "Sound really means something, it suggests something to you," notes singer Jackson Browne (Boyd & George-Warren, 2013, p. 275).

Psychology is key to understanding *how* and *why* a listener goes from "sound" to "significance." We need to consider the underlying mechanism that turns information about a musical event into perceived or aroused emotions—a functional description of what the mind is doing when the music is being perceived (e.g., retrieving a memory) in order to extract or create meaning.

3.4 Why Don't We Just Ask the Listeners or Musicians?

How, then, may we access the psychological processes that "mediate" between the musical event and our response? Could we not simply ask listeners? Or better yet, could we not just interview musicians to find out how emotional responses to music work? After all, they are the ones who write and perform the music that moves us.

As it turns out, musicians are often reluctant to talk about the processes that underlie musical creation. "I believe so strongly that it is dangerous for artists to talk," explained the composer Benjamin Britten (Watson, 1991, p. 27). Artists may prefer to "let the music do the talking," to use a familiar cliché. They certainly like to quote the humorist, Martin Mull, who quipped that "writing about music is like dancing about architecture." (To be fair, they have a point: talk or writing about music can never fully capture what it is like to create or experience music.)

Even when musicians *do* talk about the topic, their accounts may not be terribly helpful. As Kate Hevner observed: "if the great artist could speak to the audience verbally as effectively as he does musically, our efforts would be unnecessary, but seldom he expresses himself except through the medium of his art, and when he does, it is usually not in the terms calculated to be most useful and helpful" (Hevner, 1935, p. 204).

To illustrate this point in a humorous way, let me just quote the singer and songwriter in the band The Jam—Paul Weller—who once "explained" that, "The Jam is The Jam and they play Jam music" (Dimery, 2005, p. 402). Composer Jean-Claude Risset says he has an "unclear" view on emotion in music, and that he has "hardly tried to unravel it" (Cochrane, 2013a, p. 24). His colleague, Samuel Barber, confessed that he is puzzled about the creative process: "As to what happens when I compose, I really haven't the faintest idea" (Watson, 1991, p. 89).

To be sure, there *are* examples of musicians being able to explain some emotional features of their writing or performance. Throughout this book, I will continuously insert quotations from musicians to illustrate key points. However, there are also examples of musicians providing accounts of how they create music, which on closer examination turn out to be surprisingly inaccurate (Behne & Wetekam, 1993). How can this be so?

The short answer is that most of what goes on in the human mind is not available to *introspection*; that is, the examination of one's own conscious thoughts and feelings. Being able to create great music is one thing. Being able to explain exactly how this happens is something else. Consider a tennis player who is able to control the tennis ball perfectly and yet is unable to explain the physical laws that govern the ball's trajectory.

3.5 Consciousness: The Tip of the Iceberg

During the last 50 years, psychologists in various subdomains have reported evidence that shows that a large amount of information processing in the brain occurs below the level of consciousness (e.g., Eysenck, 1994). Indeed, it has been found that "introspective evidence" may be remarkably uninformative, even misleading. This is because consciousness contains information about the results or products of psychological processes rather

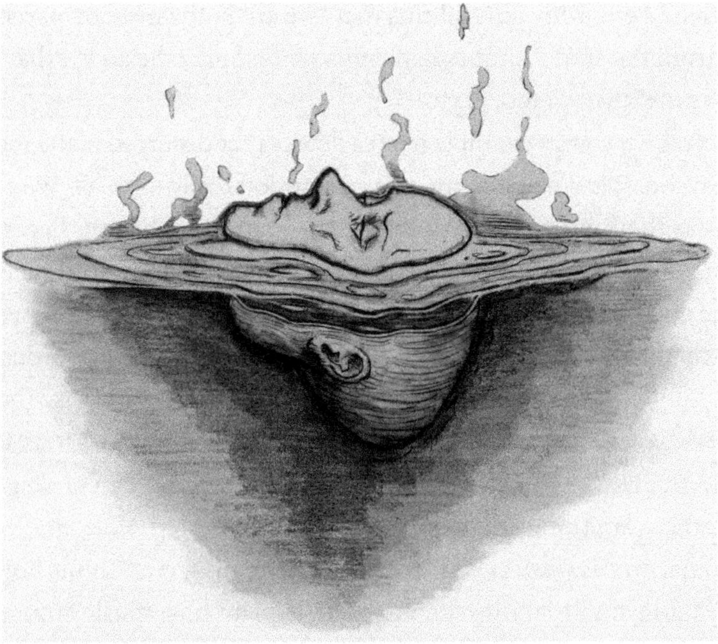

Figure 3.1 Consciousness—the tip of the iceberg.
Illustration by Costis Chatzidakis

than the processes themselves, and some products may never enter into conscious awareness (Kihlstrom, 2013).

Thus, most psychologists subscribe to an "iceberg" theory of mind (Figure 3.1), where the conscious mind corresponds to the visible tip of a large iceberg. We tend to exaggerate the importance of the conscious mind just because we do not have access to the (much larger) non-conscious mind.

If most of the processes involved in our responses to music occur subconsciously, it is not so strange after all that we find it difficult to talk about how music works. It further opens up the possibility for "misattributions" of the causes of our musical emotions (as discussed in section 30.5).

All of this can explain why music philosophers, however clever they may be, have made only limited progress with respect to what I consider the primary issue in the field: to explain how music causes emotions. In my view, philosophers are to some extent prisoners of their own introspection. They cannot conduct experiments to "tease out" implicit effects on the brain.[1] Peter Kivy duly admits that "we are in the need of 'psychology', right from the start," although, being a philosopher, he adds, "that is what bothers me" (Kivy, 1990, p. 150).

Let me give you an example from a debate that occurred in the 1990s, before psychological work on music and emotion really took off. We can refer to this as the Kivy–Radford debate. Kivy denied that he ever becomes sad when he listens to music that expresses sadness, but Radford maintained that he does "catch" the sadness of the music. In his closing argument, after admitting that neither he nor Radford knows how music can arouse emotions, Kivy ponders "where do we go from here? If it is the case that some listeners experience music as I do ... and some experience it as Radford does ... then the argument about whether or not music can or does arouse the garden-variety emotions is at an end" (Kivy, 1993, p. 9).

In other words, they were forced to agree to disagree ("this is how *I* hear music"); to admit that they are unable to explain how music arouses emotions; and to conclude, disconcertingly, that there is nothing further to be added. Why? Because they could not rely on data concerning the underlying psychological processes to resolve the dispute empirically.[2] Whether music is able to arouse sadness in listeners and how this "works" are both questions that may be addressed in psychological studies.

3.6 The Unique Role of a Psychological Inquiry

As explained earlier, music psychologists were among the last to address emotion. Yet, I will go out on a limb here and suggest that psychology has made more progress in explaining how music arouses emotions in the last 20 years, than what philosophy has in the past 2000 years.

[1] However, they may point out logical inconsistencies in the work of psychologists (e.g., Davies, 2001).

[2] In hindsight, I think it is clear that the two philosophers were talking about different processes. Radford seems to be talking about what I refer to as *emotional contagion* (Chapter 20), whereas Kivy is talking about what I refer to as *aesthetic judgment* (Chapter 30). I regard these as different mechanisms which arouse different kinds of emotions. When viewed in this light, Kivy and Radford's debate makes more sense.

What psychology may offer the study of music and emotion, among other things, is a method that can help us to "tease out" the underlying processes, and test specific hypotheses about the causes. The "flagship" in the psychological "toolkit" is the *experiment*, in which one or more variables are actively manipulated in order to explore their causal effects on another variable such as emotion. This methodology offers ways to explore music experiences without relying exclusively on language and introspection (Clarke, Dibben, & Pitts, 2010).

"The proof of the pudding lies in the eating," the old saying goes. A music psychologist may be able to manipulate features of the music and the social context directly so as to produce predicted emotions (perceived or aroused) in the listener. If we are able to create the actual emotion in a controlled way based on theoretical predictions, this represents the best evidence that we have understood the underlying process. Later in this book, we will see examples of such psychological experiments.

3.7 Some Caveats: Limitations of a Psychological Approach

I believe that psychology is uniquely situated to explain the links between music and emotions. However, there are also some limitations of the psychological approach that should be borne in mind. One limitation involves the fact that psychological experiments require that all relevant concepts are operationalized. *Operationalization* is the process of strictly defining variables into measurable factors. This requirement limits the level of complexity that can be handled in any single experiment. For that reason, psychological experiments are sometimes criticized for their "simplicity" by scholars in neighboring fields.

Such criticisms are, occasionally, well founded: There *are* examples of ridiculously simple studies which turn music and emotion research into parody, but I will not cite any of them. Obviously, psychologists should study music at a sufficient level of complexity.

At the same time, we should appreciate the conditions under which empirical research is carried out. It is not easy to cover all angles of a subject once we leave the safe haven of armchair speculation. Seemingly crude experimental designs may reflect practical limitations rather than insensitivity with regard to musical matters. As noted by Eric Clarke and colleagues, the effects of contextual factors that cannot all be manipulated in the same study are acknowledged in the interpretation of the results rather than in the design of the experiment (Clarke et al., 2010).

Such practical limitations of the psychological approach are redeemed, perhaps, by the power with which experiments enables us to draw valid conclusions about cause and effect. Whereas, for instance, musicologists interpret the expressive content of pieces of music by analyzing the score—suggesting *possible* ways of hearing the music—psychologists, by contrast, adopt a scientific approach where the expressive effects of specific musical features are tested in experiments, asking what *is* the actual impact of a specific musical feature on listeners' experiences?

Even so, psychologists cannot tackle all issues of interest in the study of music and emotion equally well—and some questions they cannot really answer at all. For instance, how did people experience music 300 years ago? This is clearly not something psychology can comment on; because psychology is an empirical science, it can only explore the music experiences that occur in our modern-day context. Then again, to "reconstruct" emotional experiences from the past is a tricky business for any discipline. As musicologist Daniel Leech-Wilkinson notes: "our Schubert is not the Schubert of 100 years ago. How he compares with Schubert's Schubert we cannot know" (Leech-Wilkinson, 2013, p. 46). (How, then, do we know that it is different?)

Further, psychologists are not really concerned with unique works of art such as Beethoven's Ninth Symphony, but rather with principles involved in the perception of artworks *in general*. Specific artworks are of interest in as far as they provide examples of more general principles that psychologists can incorporate into *models* of the underlying processes. Since any attempt to create a model will tend to involve simplification, psychology has been criticized for being "too reductionist."

However, reductionism is merely the explanation of a complex phenomenon in terms of more basic principles—a fundamental feature of all science. Indeed, the whole point of creating a model is to obtain a *simplified* representation of a phenomenon in terms of its *essential* points and their relationships. A model facilitates understanding and communication concerning the phenomenon, and renders experimental manipulation more feasible (Edwards, 1992). If we really wish to preserve every irrelevant aspect, and be left with a complex and intractable mess that is utterly incomprehensible, we already have that—it is called *the real world*. This, then, is why psychology—just like any other discipline—leaves certain things out.

Accordingly, Clarke and colleagues have argued that music psychology differs from musicology which focuses on the history and analysis of musical texts, and from sociology which focuses on the social and political contexts of musical activities (Clarke et al., 2010). The focus of psychological studies is not on how music *could* be heard ("suggestive" analyses in musicology), on how music *ought* to be heard ("normative" analyses in philosophy), or on how music perhaps once *was* heard ("reconstructive" analysis in history), but rather on how music *is* heard by listeners in the here and now. In fact, you can probably volunteer to take part in a music experiment somewhere *today*.

Psychological research may certainly take socio-cultural and historical variables into account. ("Good reductionism" seeks lower levels of explanation, but does not ignore the contributions of higher levels; Workman & Reader, 2008.) However, at some point, such an endeavor goes well beyond what might reasonably be regarded as falling within the purview of psychology. Psychological models do not aim to capture broader socio-cultural forces in society fully, just as sociological models do not aim to outline brain mechanisms underlying behavior. After all, that is why we have multiple disciplines.

In a sense, then, it is rather pointless to criticize psychology—as some scholars do—for not being sociology or musicology, or vice versa; it only makes sense to criticize psychology for being poor psychology. This is, in fact, what I will do in Chapter 17: I shall criticize previous psychological studies of music and emotion for not being "psychological enough" or, more precisely, for ignoring the underlying psychological mechanisms. A primary message of this book is that, for too long, scholars have tried to understand musical emotions simply in terms of *direct* relationships between musical features and emotions, as if nothing had to happen in between them for an emotion to occur.

Before looking closer at these processes, we must first take stock of how psychologists have approached the general domain of affect—including the emotions.

CHAPTER 4

MUSIC, EXPERIENCE, AND AFFECT

4.1 What is Music?

In this chapter, I will begin the process of defining emotions. First, however, I should perhaps define the other component of the equation: music.

This remains a controversial issue, and we must accept that there is no generally accepted definition; all definitions depend on cultural and historical context. As soon we propose a certain definition, an artist will jump at the opportunity to create a piece that defies this definition (think of John Cage's piece, 4'33"). As pointed out by Nicholas Cook, "'music' is a very small word to encompass something that takes as many forms as there are cultural or subcultural identities" (Cook, 1998, p. 5).

There are familiar dictionary definitions in the developed world, for instance that music is "the art of combining vocal or instrumental sounds (or both) to produce beauty of form, harmony, and expression of emotion" (Allen, 1992). This cannot be the whole story because clearly not all types of music aim for "beauty" or "harmony." Simply listen to "Anarchy in the UK" by the Sex Pistols, or the second movement of Anton Webern's String Trio, Opus 20.

Anthropologist Alan Merriam argues that music involves three main aspects: sound, behavior, and concept (Merriam, 1964). Most definitions focus perhaps too much on the sounds, which have changed dramatically across the long history of music-making. Might it be the case that music is better conceived of as behavior? Musicologist Christopher Small coined the term "musicking" to highlight the active nature of music, as reflected in composing, performing, and listening (Small, 1999). In other words, music is something we *do*.

Other scholars have offered conceptual definitions that cannot be denied, but that fail to offer much information about the phenomenon itself—for example, that music is "everything that one listens to with the intention of listening to music" (Berio, Dalmonte, & Varga, 1985, p. 19), or that music is simply "whatever people choose to recognize as such" (Nattiez, 1990, p. 47). Providing a satisfactory definition of music would probably require a book in itself.

What we may conclude without hesitation, however, is that the concept of music (much like the emotions it arouses; see Part III) is not unitary (Turino, 2008). There are so many distinct types of music, and perhaps an even larger number of different ways of approaching and using music, that the one thing we *really* want to avoid is to narrow down our notions of what music is (or can be). As long as we recognize the "plurality" of types of music, we are hopefully on the right track. Having said that, I should acknowledge that the research discussed in this book primarily focuses on Western music, a limitation that should be kept in mind.

4.2 What's in a Music Experience?

Another way of "defining" music is to consider the *contents* of our actual experiences. What does a music experience comprise? Some clues come from a pioneering survey study by the Swedish music psychologist, Alf Gabrielsson.

In the late 1980s, Gabrielsson started a project that aimed to explore the contents of "strong experiences with music" (sometimes also referred to as "peak experiences"), a topic hitherto not addressed satisfactorily by music psychologists. The task given to the participants was to describe in their own words "the strongest experience of music they had ever had."

The survey resulted in more than 1000 reports, which were summarized in a subsequent book (Gabrielsson, 2011). Gabrielsson found that simply *reading* these reports could be very moving. I will cite examples from this study later because they highlight many of the phenomena that music and emotion researchers need to explain.

Gabrielsson and his co-worker, Siv Lindström Wik, carefully analyzed the verbal reports by using content analysis methods. The result was a descriptive scheme (Table 4.1), consisting of the following aspects: general, physical and behavioral, perceptual, cognitive, emotional, existential and transcendental, and personal and social. As can be seen, each category also features further subdivisions of the experiential content.

The point is not that every music experience will include *all* of these aspects; that would be exhausting. Rather, the scheme may serve to illustrate the outer boundaries for what any music experience might potentially include. Each instance will most likely feature just a subset of the aspects (see Table 4.1 for explanation of these). To illustrate, this morning you may have heard (3.1) a piece of music on the radio while driving to work; the perception of a melody (3.8) evoked a memory (4.5), which in turn aroused a positive feeling of nostalgia (5.2) and a sense of confirmed personal identity (7.3). Your next music experience may involve a different selection of aspects.

In this book, I will focus on the emotional component of music experience. But to understand emotional responses, we will have to relate them to other components. The analytic categories shown in Table 4.1 are, in a sense, only an abstraction. It may seem odd, then, to single out one component of music experience (emotion). However, this is the only way we can cover the subject in sufficient depth. Even this book-length treatment will leave out several aspects of musical emotions.

Table 4.1 Different aspects of music experience: the SEM descriptive system.

1. *General characteristics*
1.1 Unique, fantastic, incredible, unforgettable experience
1.2 Hard-to-describe experience, words insufficient
2. *Physical reactions, behaviors*
2.1 Physiological reactions
2.2 Behaviors, actions
2.3 Quasi-physical reactions
3. *Perception*
3.1 Auditory
3.2 Visual
3.3 Tactile
3.4 Kinaesthetic
3.5 Other senses
3.6 Synaesthetic
3.7 Intensified perception, multimodal perception
3.8 Musical perception-cognition
4. *Cognition*
4.1 Changed attitude
4.2 Changed experience of situation, body and mind, time and space, part and whole
4.3 Loss of control
4.4 Changed relation/attitude to the music
4.5 Associations, memories, thoughts
4.6 Imagery
4.7 Musical cognition-emotion
5. *Feelings/Emotions*
5.1 Intense/Powerful feelings
5.2 Positive feelings
5.3 Negative feelings
5.4 Different feelings (mixed, conflicting, changed)
6. *Existential and transcendental aspects*
6.1 Existence
6.2 Transcendence
6.3 Religious experience
7. *Personal and social aspects*
7.1 New insights, possibilities, needs
7.2 Music: New insights, possibilities, needs
7.3 Confirmation of identity, self-actualization
7.4 Community/Communication

Based on Gabrielsson, A. (2011). *Strong experiences with music: Music is much more than just music.* By permission of Oxford University Press.

It is crucial to distinguish the components because features that apply to one component of music experience may not apply to other components. For instance, our *perception* of music and its dynamic changes over time may be "ineffable" (i.e., difficult to describe in words), but this may not be true of our *emotions* (see Chapter 7). Moreover, we should not treat "emotion" as equivalent to "music experience"; not all instances of music experience involve emotion. As will be apparent in Parts II and III, we may often hear music without perceiving or feeling any emotion at all.

This book, then, focuses on that subset of instances where the music experience *does* feature an emotion—whether perceived or felt by the listener. I propose that when emotions do occur, they contribute by adding a more deeply *personal* significance to our music experience—for instance, by connecting it to our life history. This brings us to another problem, however: what exactly is an emotion anyway?

4.3 (Musical) Affect Comes in Many Shapes and Forms

For laypersons, what we refer to as "feelings" may seem to exist on a broad single spectrum of experiences. You might feel "sad," "tired," "strange," or "like eating a pizza." Researchers, however, tend to distinguish between different sub-categories of affect (e.g., Oatley, Keltner, & Jenkins, 2006, pp. 29–31). The aim is to achieve greater precision when dealing with these phenomena scientifically.

The term "affect" itself is often used by researchers as an umbrella term which covers various affective phenomena such as emotions, moods, and preferences. The defining feature is *valence*; that is, the evaluation of an object, person, or event as being positive or negative. Most scholars also require a certain degree of *physiological arousal* in order to distinguish affect from a purely intellectual judgment (Frijda & Scherer, 2009). However, the level of arousal may vary from very low to extremely high, depending on the type of affect.

Conceived in this way, affect in relation to musical activities might comprise anything from *preference* (e.g., liking of a particular piece of music) and *mood* (e.g., a mild, object-less, and long-lasting state produced by, say, subtle background music) to *aesthetic judgment* (e.g., an assessment of the aesthetic value of a piece based on criteria such as beauty and novelty), and *emotion* (e.g., a more intense but short-lasting reaction to music, such as joy).

It is essential to distinguish the various kinds of affect because they differ in characteristics such as duration, intensity, and degree of behavioral impact (Scherer, 2000). Although I will touch upon each of these kinds of affect in the subsequent sections, the main focus will be on emotions.

4.4 In a Nutshell: The Psychology of Emotions

"What is an emotion?" asked the psychologist William James in a famous article in the journal *Mind* over 100 years ago (James, 1884; see also Fox, Lapate, Shackman, & Davidson, 2018, Question 1). The question appears simple enough, but to define emotions is difficult (Plutchik, 1994). Kleinginna and Kleinginna identify 92 definitions from textbooks, articles, and dictionaries (Kleinginna & Kleinginna, 1981). Since then, the number has increased.

Paula Niedenthal and Markus Brauer conclude pessimistically that an integrative theory of emotions seems impossible—because a definition of emotion can only be useful within the context of a specific research program (Niedenthal and Brauer, 2012). Maybe they are right.

Sometimes, though, we do not actually need a perfect definition to make progress in a field. In fact, it can be argued that such a definition is the end result—rather than the starting point—in exploring a field, and "what we seek is not, in the end, to define emotions, but to understand them" (Oatley & Jenkins, 1996, p. 97). But where do we begin?

We could start by noting that "emotion" is what scholars like to call a psychological construct. We cannot actually see emotions, we cannot touch them. Instead, it seems, we have to "infer" them from different types of "evidence"—a smile, tears, or blushing; a thrown chair; the verbal declaration of sorrow; an unselfish act. One way to begin to define emotions, then, is to specify a set of features that characterize the concept.

Whereas lay people may think of emotions mainly in terms of the phenomenological *feelings* they produce, researchers prefer to define emotions in terms of a wider range of aspects. To capture these, I have previously offered the following working definition:

> Emotions are relatively brief, intense and rapidly changing responses to potentially important events (subjective challenges or opportunities) in the external or internal environment, usually of a social nature, which involve a number of subcomponents (cognitive changes, feelings, physiology, expressive behavior, and action tendency) which are more or less 'synchronized' during an emotion episode. (Juslin, 2011, p. 114)

Notice that I say *potentially* important events. Our emotions are not a direct reflection of the objective importance of an event; rather, they occur when some part of the brain "concludes" that something is potentially at stake in the event. In addition, separate individuals may evaluate the same event quite differently depending on personal aspects such as memories or motivations.

The physiological reaction may be the aspect that gives emotions their distinct phenomenological feeling (James, 1884). It confers a sense of embodiment—the "heat" of the emotion. "What kind of an emotion of fear would be left, if the feelings neither of quickened heartbeats nor of shallow breathing ... were present, it is quite impossible to think" (James, 1884, pp. 193–194). Thus, emotion researchers often rely on physiological measurements to confirm that an emotional response is occurring (Chapter 15).

Emotions—just like pieces of music—are dynamic processes. They unfold, linger, and then dissipate over time. Thus, most psychologists like to think of an emotion as a sequence of events. However, they may well disagree about the precise sequence and about where the emotion episode begins. Is it when an antecedent event occurs (e.g., when you hear a piece of music)? Or when the event is evaluated (e.g., you think the music is beautiful)? Or when the subjective feeling occurs (e.g., you experience pleasure)?

Part of the difficulty in determining the beginning or end of an emotion episode could reflect that affective processing is really a *continuous* process. Some scholars argue that people are always in *some* affective state, even if they are not aware of it (Barrett, Mesquita, Ochsner, & Gross, 2007). When the state is intense and involves a salient stimulus, we tend to call it an "emotion." When the state is less intense, and its causes are not immediately apparent, we tend to call it a "mood."

Neuroscientist Richard Davidson suggests that emotions may be conceptualized as *phasic* perturbations, superimposed on the *tonic* affective background provided by the mood (Davidson, 1994). To illustrate: you may be in a slightly irritated mood in the afternoon due to, say, hunger and fatigue, but when someone accidently drops a can of jam on your foot, that is when you really lose control and begin to "emote."

4.5 Responses to Music: Emotions or Moods?

Evidence suggests that, in principle, music listening can influence both emotions and moods. The term "mood" appears commonly in writings about music. Philosophers, in particular, are inclined to argue that music arouses mere moods (i.e., objectless affective states), rather than emotions, perhaps because listeners—including philosophers—are commonly unaware of the "object" of their emotions when music is involved. (Recall Freud's frustration cited in Chapter 1)

However, this view ultimately rests on a mistaken assumption: that the "intentional objects" of emotions are always conscious. This is not really the case. More likely, we are commonly unaware of the cause of our emotions. In a classic experiment by Arne Öhman and Joaquim Soares, subjects with spider phobia showed physiological fear reactions to masked pictures[1] of spiders that they were unable to detect at a conscious level (Öhman & Soares, 1994). Although subjects were clearly unaware of the "intentional object" of their reaction, it would be incorrect to label it "mood." Similarly, I suggest that we tend to talk about moods in relation to music, although we are actually dealing with emotions.

To see why the concept of emotion is more relevant than that of mood, we must examine the nature of mood in more detail. One of the leading scholars in mood research, Robert Thayer, has described mood as a kind of "clinical thermometer" (Thayer, 1996, p. 4), which reflects a number of external and internal factors such as sleep, health, daily cycles, exercise, nutrition, and overall level of stress. Moods do not typically reflect single events but rather the overall status of the person—how we are doing in general. Moreover, as explained earlier, moods are usually lower in intensity and more long-lasting than emotions. If we take a close look at the findings reported to date in relation to the definitions of mood and emotion, they suggest that by and large music arouses emotions rather than moods.

Empirical evidence shows that musical arousal of emotions involves a specific "object" (the music, or more specifically information in the music processed in relation to individual and situational factors; e.g., Juslin, Harmat, & Eerola, 2014; see Part III). Furthermore, evidence indicates that the affective states aroused by music last for a relatively brief duration (Scherer, Zentner, & Schacht, 2002); that they usually have a rather

[1] *Backward masking* is a technique that involves presenting one visual stimulus (a "mask") immediately after another brief (circa 30 milliseconds) "target" visual stimulus, resulting in a failure consciously to perceive the first stimulus.

strong intensity (Gabrielsson, 2011; Juslin, Liljeström, Västfjäll, Barradas, & Silva, 2008; Juslin, Liljeström, Laukka, Västfjäll, & Lundqvist, 2011, Juslin, Barradas, Ovsiannikow, Limmo, & Thompson, 2016a); and that they induce physiological responses (Krumhansl, 1997). All these features are associated with emotions rather than moods (Beedie, Terry, & Lane, 2005; see also Table 2.1).

There is no doubt that music is one factor that can influence mood. In fact, studies suggest that music is one of the most frequent and effective ways of regulating mood (e.g., Thayer, 1996). However, I propose that when music influences our moods, it does so *indirectly* by affecting our emotions (the *phasic* aspect of affect). And moods are also affected by many other factors like sleep, health, daily cycles, exercise, nutrition, and overall levels of stress (Thayer, 1996). Hence, the long-term effect of music on mood is likely to be rather limited in the greater scheme of things—unless you are one of those people who listen to music all day long, every day of the week.

4.6 It Moves Me: Why Emotions are Most Important

I want to argue that of all the various affective states that music can arouse, none is more *important* than the emotions. To the degree that music affects moods, these are less likely than emotions to be remembered (since intense affective reactions are remembered better; Reisberg & Hertel, 2004), and will have a weaker impact on subsequent behavior (Scherer, 2000).

Emotions are what "drive" people to seek out novel experiences of music or to decide to pursue a career in music (see Chapter 14). Remember also that music is a dynamic event, constantly changing. This timescale is clearly more consistent with emotional reactions than with the longer lasting moods. Our experiences involve attention focused on musical events in the here and now. Sure, music may subtly influence moods, but this is not the key issue. Consider the magic, the wonder, the fascination, the heartbreak of a peak experience with music—emotion is what it is all about.

When the cards are on the table, there is still no definitive evidence of a clear-cut distinction between moods and emotions. (The distinction is originally based on "folk psychology" and "intuition," rather than scientific evidence). It may turn out that mood and emotion share more similarities than differences.

I will, nonetheless, adopt a prudent approach here, allowing for the possibility that emotions and moods really are different. Whether they are different sides of the same coin or not does not have any strong bearing on the psychological principles reviewed later in this book. I will focus on the more temporary and high-intensity variety that we call emotions, and that seems to be the driving force behind most people's engagement with music.

4.7 Are Emotions Categorical or Dimensional?

What are emotions like, then? We could start with some simple observations from everyday life. First, emotions seem to vary in their intensity (compare slight irritation to rage). Second, many emotions appear to involve qualitatively distinct feelings (certainly, it *feels* different to be afraid as opposed to be nostalgic). Third, some pairs of emotions seem to be more similar than other pairs (joy and contentment are more alike than are joy and disgust). Finally, some emotions seem to be each other's opposites (happiness–sadness, love–hate, calm–worry). How can we describe emotions in order to capture these characteristics?

The two dominant views in emotion psychology are *categorical* and *dimensional* approaches, respectively.[2] According to the categorical approach, we experience emotional episodes as categories, which are distinct from each

[2] These are sometimes referred to as "theories." I prefer to refer to them as "approaches' because they represent broad perspectives on similarities and differences between emotions, which can involve very different emotion theories of a more particular kind. For instance, component process theories (Scherer, 2001) and basic emotion theories (Ekman, 1992) are both categorical, but they differ in other respects.

other—such as happiness, sadness, anger, surprise, fear, and interest (Izard, 1977; see also Hutto, Robertson, & Kirchhoff, 2018).

To understand what is meant by emotion categories, we may compare them with colors. There are different shades of *sadness*, just as there are different shades of *blue*, but at a certain point we cross a categorical boundary where there is a qualitatively abrupt shift from one category (sad, blue) to another category (angry, red) in our experience. Many researchers also believe that emotions, just like colors, can be "mixed" (Plutchik, 1994). Categorical theories come in different forms, which we will become acquainted with in Chapters 11 and 16.

The dimensional approach tries instead to conceptualize emotions based on their approximate placement along a few broad and continuous affective dimensions. The most popular version is the *circumplex model* proposed by James Russell (1980), perhaps because it is easy to understand. It consists of a two-dimensional and circular structure, featuring the two dimensions *pleasure* and *arousal*. It may illustrate the fact that emotions vary in their degree of similarity, and that certain emotions are usually thought of as opposites (see Figure 4.1). However, just like categorical approaches, dimensional approaches come in different forms (see Part II).[3] Both approaches have struggled with the issue of the number of categories/dimensions required and the precise nature of these.

In my view, it is doubtful whether the issue of which approach—categorical or dimensional—provides the best description of emotions will ever be fully resolved. It seems that the debate between proponents of each approach has run out of steam. Part of the reason might be that emotions irrevocably involve both dimensional and categorical tendencies (Damasio, 1994).

To illustrate, it is beyond doubt that emotions vary in terms of arousal level and that even discrete categories of emotion may vary in intensity (a

[3] For instance, models may be one-dimensional (e.g., arousal; Duffy, 1941); two-dimensional (e.g., positive affect–negative affect; Watson & Tellegen, 1985); or three-dimensional (e.g., energy arousal–tense arousal–valence; Schimmack & Grob, 2000).

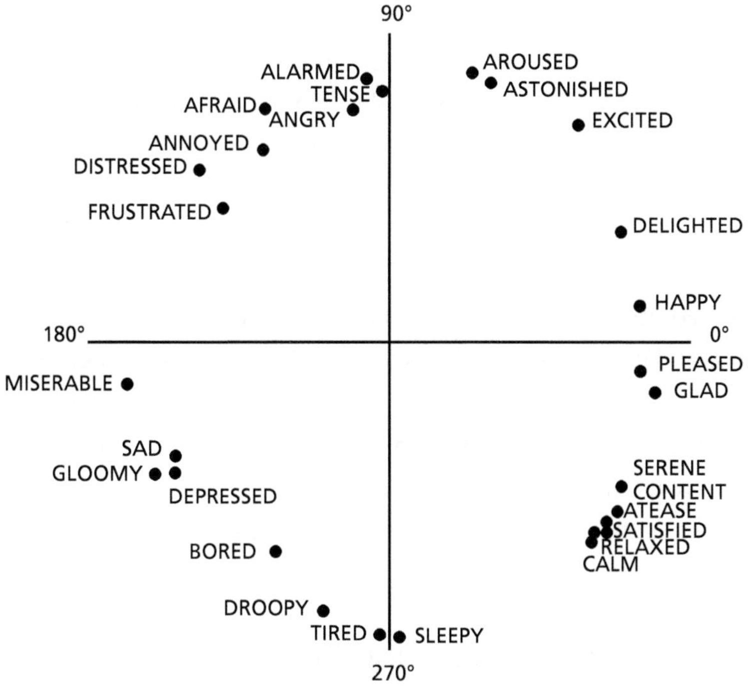

Figure 4.1 Circumplex model of emotions.
Reproduced from Russell, J. A. (1980). *A circumplex model of affect*. Journal of Personality and Social Psychology, 39, 1161–1178. © 1980 American Psychological Association.

continuous dimension). Still, it is equally true that there are emotions that are *qualitatively* different such that they are best viewed as categories. In fact, even an affective dimension like *valence* appears to imply a category: We talk about "positive" and "negative" valence, and although this dimension is supposedly continuous, there must be a "cross-over" at some point where a feeling turns from more negative into more positive—and *voilà*, there we have a categorical boundary (Qiu, Wang, & Fu, 2018).

In music, changes in the intensity, quality, and complexity of an emotion can often occur from moment to moment, and such changes may be captured in terms of shifts along such emotion dimensions as *arousal* and *valence*. However, the same emotions shifts may also be analyzed in terms of qualitatively distinct categories (e.g., joy). Both these views can capture important aspects of how we experience music, and complement each other nicely in research.

Still, if push comes to shove, I would choose a categorical over a dimensional approach, for two reasons, one practical and one theoretical. The practical is that categories are needed to capture and do justice to the complex emotions experienced by listeners (as reviewed in Chapter 16). Subtle emotions such as nostalgia, awe, and interest cannot be reduced to coordinates in a two-dimensional emotion space without losing valuable information concerning the listener's experience.

The theoretical reason is that, ultimately, the most basic assumption of the dimensional model seems to be incorrect. When actually tested, emotions show discreteness, in terms of category boundaries, rather than continuity in the emotion space (e.g., Haslam, 1995; Laukka, 2005). It makes perfect sense to treat emotion as categories. This will be clearer if we consider why we have something like emotions in the first place.

4.8 Who Needs Emotions? A Functionalist Analysis

To understand *why* we have emotions, we must look closer at their evolutionary origin. Most researchers today believe that the forerunners of our modern-day emotions are to be found in adaptive responses that increased the chances of individual (and hence also genetic) survival throughout evolution (e.g., Oatley, 1992; Panksepp, 1998; Plutchik, 1994). How so?

Biologists assume that there is a set of survival problems that most living organisms have in common, and that these problems in turn require adaptive responses (read *emotions*) to deal efficiently with them. An organism needs to avoid danger (*fear*), search for food (*curiosity*), cooperate with others (*happiness*), compete for resources (*anger*), procreate (*desire*), avoid toxic substances (*disgust*), and care for offspring (*tender love*).

Such responses are considered the "prototypes" of human emotions. The categories are often referred to as "basic" or "primary" emotions (Ekman, 1992). Note that because many of these emotion categories arose during the process of mammalian evolution, we can expect to find *homologies* between human and non-human emotions.[4] Indeed, some of the mechanisms involved in emotional reactions to music do not seem to be unique to humans (Juslin, 2013a; see Part III).

The emotions of modern humans involve additional "conceptual layers" (Barrett, 2006), which add considerably to the complexity of human emotions; thus, in addition to the basic emotions noted above, we also have more *complex emotions* such as nostalgia and remorse. Further, we have what we may call the *moral emotions* which deal with social norms (Buck, 2014) and *aesthetic emotions* which concern various aspects of art (Juslin, 2013a). We can also share *collective emotions* during social events (Scheve & Salmela, 2014).

Different types of emotions will assume different degrees of importance in the various parts of this book. I will argue that the basic emotions have a privileged position in the *expression* and *perception* of emotions in music (see Part II), but that the complex emotions—especially positive ones—gain in importance as we move on to the *arousal* of felt emotions (see Part III), and that the moral and aesthetic emotions will be involved mainly in the context of *aesthetic judgment* of music (see Part IV). The various subtypes of emotions are shown in Table 4.2.

Because of their larger "cognitive machinery," humans show greater flexibility than other animals in choosing their actions when "emoting." Human emotions involve wide cultural differences in emotional practices (Mesquita, Vissers, & De Leersnyder, 2015) which are reflected also in how music relates to emotions (Becker, 2004). Given our greater intellect, reason, and culture we may be tempted to think that emotions are somehow less important in human life, but make no mistake: emotions are still the prime motivators of behavior in everyday life. As pointed out by Donald Hebb, our intellect is the humble servant of our emotions and instincts (Hebb, 1949).

Emotions are clearly involved in everything we consider important in life. The problem is to explain how music fits into this perspective. How and why does a piece of music engage the ancient emotion circuits which

[4] In evolutionary biology, *homology* typically refers to a state of similarity in structure and anatomical position (but not necessarily in function) between different organisms that may arise from a common evolutionary origin (*Biology Online*: <https://www.biology-online.org/>).

Table 4.2 Subtypes of emotions and their discussion in different parts of the book.

	Part 2	Part 3	Part 4
	Expression	*Arousal*	*Aesthetics*
Basic emotions	•	•	•
Complex emotions	•	•	•
Collective emotions	-	•	-
Mixed emotions	•	-	•
Moral emotions	-	-	•
Aesthetic emotions	-	-	•

contributed to our survival throughout evolution? A first clue comes from recognizing the "dual functionality" of emotions.

In this book, I will adopt a view on emotion advocated by psychologist Keith Oatley, who argues that emotions are really "communications": they convey information—to ourselves (internally) and to others (externally) (Oatley, 1992; cf. Darwin, 1998/1872):

1. *Internally*, emotions function as signals in the brain that some change of priority is needed. Such signals are required in any system that consists of "modules" which specialize in specific types of activity and are somewhat autonomous. (For example, you can presumably walk and check your cellphone at the same time because the motor control of your body can be handled independently of the visual analysis of your latest text message.)

However, modular systems require coordination. Because they work with multiple goals simultaneously, there is a need for interruption when one goal suddenly becomes more urgent than the one that is controlling the current psychological process. (For example, when you suddenly realize that you are about to walk over a cliff, the text message on your phone does not appear so important anymore. An interruption signal is needed to shift your priorities.)

Given that we often have multiple (and sometimes conflicting) goals, the idea is that emotions arose initially to help organisms prioritize between distinct behavior options under conditions of limited time, knowledge, or cognitive resources; that is, "when no fully rational solution is available for a problem of action, a basic emotion functions to prompt us in a direction that is better than a random choice" (Johnson-Laird & Oatley, 1992, p. 201). Specifically, emotions prompt us in a direction which has proved successful in our evolutionary past (e.g., fleeing in the face of apparent danger).

Although emotions do not specify either exactly what has happened or exactly what should be done about what has happened, they make us *inclined* to behave in certain manner (e.g., approach, avoid). It is easy to see now why categories are needed. Emotions function to guide decisions about future behaviors. A continuous dimension of, say, valence is all very nice, but how are you going to use it? Exactly *how much is enough* to motivate a change in our behavior? We need some "cut-off" or "stop rule" to make a decision . Once we have that, we have a *category boundary* (Juslin, 2013b). In short, categories aid inferences and decision-making (Markman & Rein, 2013).

2. *Externally*, expressions of emotions convey crucial information to other individuals and affect social interactions. For example, if you can infer another speaker's emotion, you may also be able to understand or predict his or her behavior; your own emotional expression can in turn influence that person's behavior (Juslin, Laukka, & Bänziger, 2018). Communication of emotions is thus believed by some scholars to lie at the very core of social organization in humans (Buck, 2014). Communication of emotions is of crucial importance in music as well (see Part II).

This dual functionality of the emotions (internal versus external) is linked to a distinction already hinted at several times in previous sections.

4.9 Perception versus Arousal of Emotion

Thus far, my discussion has largely focused on emotional reactions (e.g., that you feel joyful), but there is another way in which emotions can be related to music. This leads us to a distinction of key importance for the field (e.g., Meyer, 1956), which may be traced to ancient Greece (Cook & Dibben, 2010) and is encountered in both Western and non-Western cultures (Becker, 2001).

On the one hand, you may simply *perceive* (or recognize) a certain emotion "expressed" or "represented" in the music (e.g., you may recognize sadness expressed in a funeral march I play for you on the piano). On the other hand, you may feel an emotion in yourself (e.g., you can become truly *moved* to sadness when you hear the ballad "Someone Like You" by Adele). Indeed, Aristotle argued, in the *Poetics,* that works of art both represent emotions and induce them in the spectator.[5]

How can we conceive of these two processes in the case of music? It is all about information occurring in musical events. As noted by Eric Clarke (2005), listeners can "pick up" a number of different kinds of information (cf. Gibson, 1979) from a musical event. They might hear concrete things, such as which instrument is playing. They may be able to deduce something about the skill level of the performer. In some cases, they may recognize the performer of the music, or in the case of "live" music, even the very concert at which it was recorded. Further, the sounds may specify a certain cultural context (e.g., Western music), style (e.g., free jazz), and perhaps a period (e.g., the late 1950s), as gleaned from sound quality and recording technology.

Some of the information in a musical event might relate to emotion, but it can do so in two different ways. *Perception* of emotion involves (merely "cognitive") detection of emotional meaning ("expression") in a musical event (see Part II). Thus, for instance, you might detect sadness in the slow movement of Beethoven's "Eroica" symphony. The induction or *arousal* of

[5] Various conceptions of art are further discussed in Chapter 28.

emotion, by contrast, involves detection of information that has what I will call emotional implications—information that for one reason or another warrants an emotional reaction (Part III). This second type of information sometimes overlaps with that of perceived emotions (see the *contagion* mechanism in Part III which involves a response to the expression in the music).

Arousal of emotions more frequently involves a distinct type of information not related to the perceived emotions (if any) in the music. (To illustrate, a piece of music might *arouse* an emotional memory, which does not in any way reflect the emotions *perceived* in the music.)

I have previously referred to this distinction as the "locus" of the emotion (Juslin & Zentner, 2002, p. 11): "Is the emotion in the music or in the listener?" However, this way of putting it is ultimately misleading because *both* perception and arousal of emotions are psychological processes that occur "in the listener"; *both* depend on various structural features of the music; and *both* may occur together sometimes while listening to music.

Yet, it is important to distinguish them for at least three reasons. First, their underlying mechanisms could be different. Second, measuring aroused emotion is more difficult than measuring perceived emotion, and requires a different set of methods (Chapter 15). Third, the types of emotions usually expressed and perceived in music may be different from the set of emotions usually aroused by music. Even during a given listening episode, the emotion you perceive in the music (e.g., sadness) might be different from the emotion you *feel* as a result of perceiving the same music (e.g., nostalgia) (e.g., Taruffi & Koelsch, 2014).

The distinction between perceived emotion and aroused emotion is, of course, not unique to music. Consider facial expressions: you may simply recognize a facial expression of joy in a stranger's face or you may experience joy yourself—for instance, if the smile occurs in the face of your own child. There is evidence of a differential responding in the brain, too:

Tor Wager and co-workers analyzed a large number of brain-imaging studies of emotion, and were able to conclude that perception and arousal of emotions involve "peak activations" of different areas of the brain (Wager, Barrett, Bliss-Moreau, Lindquist, ... Mize, 2008; see also Juslin & Sakka, in press). This supports the notion that these are distinct psychological processes (Davidson, 1995).

Some of the confusion in the field of music and emotion has been due to a failure to clearly distinguish these two processes, both theoretically and empirically. (For further discussion, see Gabrielsson, 2002.) Music listeners are not always aware of—or concerned about—this distinction in everyday life. Still, studies show that they can make the distinction, if properly instructed.

In a study by Marcel Zentner, Didier Grandjean, and Klaus Scherer (2008), several hundred people were required to rate a large set of emotion terms for the frequency with which they perceived and felt each to music. By asking for both types of response simultaneously, they reduced the risk that listeners would be misconstruing the *arousal* question as a *perception* question. Music was rated as particularly effective in arousing certain emotions (e.g., calm). Other emotions were more likely to be perceived than felt (e.g., angry). Consider your own responses: you can perhaps *feel* admiration when you hear a great piece of music, but rarely do instrumental pieces of music *express* admiration.

The distinction between perception and arousal of emotion is used to organize this book. Part II explores how listeners perceive emotions expressed in the music, whereas Part III focuses on how music arouses felt emotions in listeners. I should add that though perception and arousal of emotion are different processes, they often co-occur—and may indeed influence each other in a number of different ways (see Chapter 32).

With these conceptual foundations in place, we are now ready to explore the relationship between music and emotion in more depth.

PART II

EXPRESSION AND PERCEPTION OF EMOTION

CHAPTER 5

WHAT IS MEANT BY EMOTIONAL EXPRESSION?

> In the end, the essence of music performance is being able to convey emotion. (Levitin, 2006, p. 204)

5.1 Prelude from Vienna

Imagine you had a time machine and could travel back to Vienna in the nineteenth century. In the evening, you attend a concert at the Wiener Musikverein. When, finally seated, the chatter of audience expectation is silenced, out of the darkness appears a pale and slender figure, carrying a violin. Just a few moments later, you realize that it is the great Niccolo Paganini (Figure 5.1).

Of course, we do not know how you would experience the ensuing music, but some sense of the impact is given by a critic who was there—witnessing Paganini in full flight:

> He put the bow to his instrument … and then, the first notes, bold and fiery, sang through the hall. At once the spell began to work. Was this really the music of a violin?
>
> What grandeur in these slurred notes, what absolute purity!
>
> There came roulades of double-stop harmonic notes, and a long run across four octaves, played staccato in a single stroke of the bow …
>
> Then came a noble, moving theme, which sounded as though a human voice was singing …
>
> After the seemingly endless applause had subsided, Paganini began to play the second movement. It was an adagio, and showed the virtuoso from quite a different angle. There were none of the devilish tricks that had stunned the

audience during the first movement. A sublime, angelic song of great noblesse and simplicity touched the hearts of the listeners ...

The notes followed one another as though growing out of the instrument, and it seemed incredible ... that this wooden object was not an integral part of the man who played it, a part of his very soul ...

An infinitely tender pizzicato accompanied the melody, and it finally soared away into a happy dance tune. (Farga, 1969, pp. 171–172)

Like blues singer Robert Johnson many years later, Paganini was accused of having made a pact with the devil to obtain his extraordinary skill. Paganini

Figure 5.1 Legendary Italian violin virtuoso Niccolo Paganini in concert.
Illustration by Costis Chatzidakis.

was an impressive technician and a "showman." For instance, he secretly cut the strings on his violin so they would break during the show, "forcing" him to finish the piece on one string.

Far more importantly, however, he had an emotionally expressive playing style which captivated his audience. (Technical skill alone is rarely sufficient for a performer to gain a strong following.) Opera composer Gioachino Rossini claimed to have wept only three times in his life: "the third time was when I first heard Paganini play" (Watson, 1991, p. 241). What is the secret behind such expressivity?

5.2 Aims and Questions

In this section, we will look closer at a phenomenon that is almost universally acknowledged across the disciplines—namely, that music is heard as expressive of emotions by listeners (Budd, 1985; Davies, 1994; Elliott, 2005; Gabrielsson & Juslin, 2003; Turino, 2008). Musicologist Deryck Cooke went as far as proclaiming that music is a language of the emotions (Cooke, 1959).

This view finds support amongst many (but not all) musicians: "Music is a language that doesn't speak in particular words. It speaks in emotions," claims guitarist and songwriter Keith Richards (Loewenstein & Dodd, 2004, p. 4). Composer Richard Wagner argues that "the language of tones belongs equally to all mankind ... melody is the absolute language in which the musician speaks to every heart" (Watson, 1991, p. 99).

Music may not be a language in the *technical* sense of the word. Kate Hevner observed that musical elements have no fixed semantic meaning of their own (Hevner, 1935). Still, there is clearly some merit to the notion that music is expressive of emotions. "Emotional expression is often regarded as central to the purpose and meaning of art," writes philosopher Tom Cochrane (Cochrane, 2013b, p. 75; see also Chapters 28–29).

Expressivity is not only important in itself; perception of emotional expression may also be "contagious" such that it *arouses* emotions in the listener (see Chapter 20), as highlighted in the review of Paganini's performance. In Gabrielsson's 2011 study of strong experiences with music, "the emotional expression" was one of the most commonly reported causes by the participants (although we should keep in mind the limitations of self-reports when it comes to establishing causes of aroused emotions; see Chapter 3).

Why is music perceived as expressive of emotions? Can musicians actually convey emotions to listeners? Which emotions does music express? How are the different emotions expressed? What is the role of the performer? Are there cross-cultural similarities in how the emotions are expressed? How is emotional expression related to the human voice? Can a computer express emotions? How is music able to convey complex emotions? Why are some authors critical of regarding music as an expression of emotions?

In addressing these questions, I will illustrate how the themes from Chapter 1 are relevant to an understanding of expression and perception of emotion in music: It is, ultimately, a social and largely tacit process involving multiple sources of emotion of ancient origins, which are influenced by various factors in the music, the listener, and the context. Opera singer Luciano Pavarotti called music "the most perfect expression of any emotion," and this part of the book will explore the reasons why this may indeed be the case.

When scholars and laypeople use the term "expression," it is not always perfectly clear what they mean, and they do not always mean exactly the same thing. The notions of expression and perception of emotion seem simple enough. Still, discussions of expression can rather be confusing because different scholars may well have different things in mind when they use these concepts. Hence, it may be helpful to look closely at what these concepts might entail in earlier research.[1]

[1] Readers should be aware that a lot has been written about musical expression over the years by philosophers and music theorists. I will not provide a full review of these works, but will cover those notions that are relevant for a psychological approach to the subject. For a book-length overview of previous work, see Davies (1994); for chapter-length reviews, see Cook & Dibben (2010) and Gabrielsson & Juslin (2003).

5.3 Different Types of Meaning

As noted in section 3.3, I believe that music (or sound more generally) is constantly interpreted by the listener—whether implicitly or explicitly. Music and emotion is thus linked to the concept of *meaning*. A full discussion of different attempts to define this concept is beyond the scope of this section (but see Cross & Tolbert, 2016). Suffice to say that in the present context, the concept of meaning implies that music can *refer* to something, either to itself or to something beyond (Cross, 2012).

Whether music has meaning, and, if so, what kind, have been matters of much debate. Most commentators appear to conclude that music has *some* kind of meaning (e.g., Berlyne, 1971; Cook, 1998; Davies, 1994; Langer, 1957; Meyer, 1956).

One of the genuine pioneers in studies of emotional expression in music is Kate Hevner (Figure 5.2). Her carefully chosen words on the issue of meaning are instructive:

> There is probably no one who would maintain either that music invariably has a meaning, that all listeners give it meaning, that any one listener always give music meaning, or that there is always agreement on the meaning of any one composition. Likewise, there is probably no one who would maintain that the opposite of these statements are true - that no music has meaning or that there is never any agreement on the meaning of any composition. (Hevner, 1935, p. 187)

To the extent that at least some music has some meaning for some listeners some of the time, what is the nature of this meaning? Music theorist Leonard Meyer made an important distinction between "absolutists" and "referentialists" (Meyer, 1956). Absolutists claim that musical meaning is "intra-musical"; that is, music refers only to itself (so-called *embodied meaning*) and should be conceived as "pure" and "autonomous" patterns of notes. Referentialists, however, believe that music obtains its meaning by referring to extra-musical phenomena (so-called *designative meaning*)—including emotions.[2]

[2] The opposition between these views came to the fore during the nineteenth century clash between the proponents of *program music* (a type of classical music that attempts to depict an extra-musical narrative or event in the music; e.g., Richard Wagner, Richard Strauss) and those of *absolute music* (e.g., Eduard Hanslick, Igor Stravinsky).

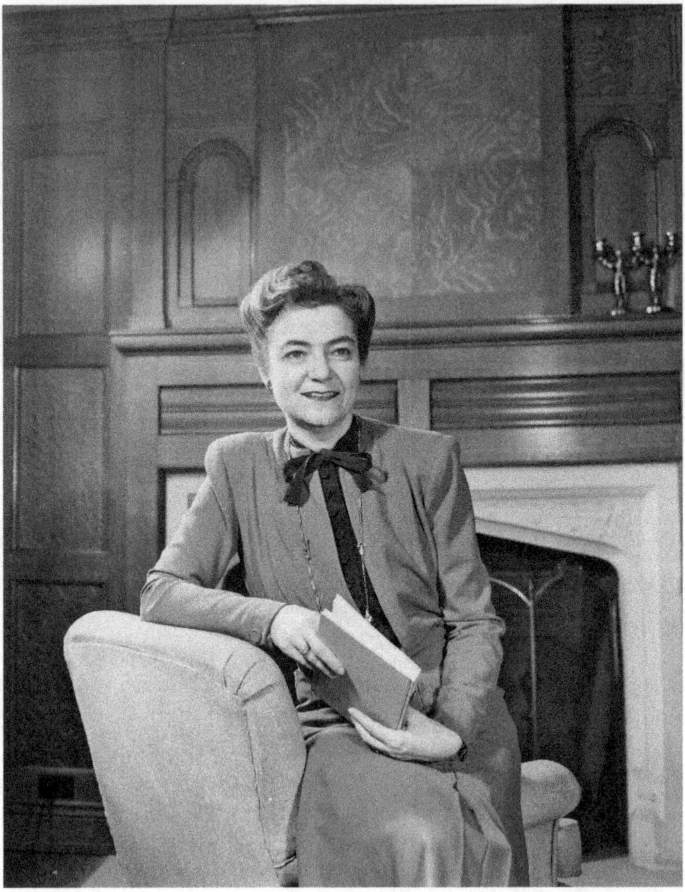

Figure 5.2 Kate Hevner—pioneer in research on emotional expression in music. *Reprinted with permission from Indiana University Archives. Copyright © 2018 The Trustees of Indiana University.*

The two aspects of musical meaning are not exclusive. They may co-occur, even in the same piece of music (Hodges & Sebald, 2011; Meyer, 1956). However, certain types of music may appear to invite an absolutist view; for instance, think of Johann Sebastian Bach's "The Art of the Fugue", Arnold Schoenberg's "serial" compositions, or certain kinds of "free jazz." Other types of music seem to have been conceived with a referentialist view from the start, such as Antonio Vivaldi's "The Spring" or Arthur Honegger's "Pacific 231." In types of music that feature lyrics, referential content is obviously present. This includes, most likely, most of music heard in the world on any given day.

Importantly, "absolutists" do not necessarily deny that music can arouse felt emotions, they merely deny that the meaning of the music lies in its *referring* to emotions (and other extra-musical phenomena). This will become clearer, perhaps, if we consider another, yet related, distinction between *formalists*, who argue that the value of music is mainly intellectual, and *expressionists*, who argue that the value of music is mainly emotional. For example, Meyer may be labeled an "absolute expressionist," because he considers the value of music largely in emotional terms (expressionist), but the emotions he considers derive from "intra-musical" meaning (absolutist) (Meyer, 1956).

In contrast to some of his followers, Meyer did not make the mistake of overstating the importance of absolutism: "The prominence given to this aspect of musical meaning does not imply that other kinds of meaning do not exist or are not important" (Meyer, 1956, p. 2). (Are you listening, music theorists out there?)

It seems to me that certain classical composers, in particular, are fond of regarding music as autonomous note patterns. Yet there is something *irresistible* about the extra-musical side of musical meaning. Another pioneer in research on emotional expression, Melvin Rigg, notes that the human tendency to find music expressive is so strong that "if the composer leaves no interpretation of his production, it is usually not long before one is invented" (Rigg, 1942, p. 279). We cannot help but make a connection between the music and the "external" world.

While it is certainly possible, and perhaps even interesting, to consider music in terms of purely embodied meaning, it is, ultimately, doubtful whether we can ever really perceive music in that way. Doing so would require that we could "turn off" a large chunk of brain machinery that is constantly and involuntarily involved in making sense of all sounds that surround us. In fact, this processing of meaning in sounds continues to some degree, even when we are sleeping (Coenen, 2010).

Furthermore, if you listen to, say, "The Art of the Fugue", and you decide to listen to the piece as "absolute music," how could you avoid hearing

"Bach" in the notes? This is referential meaning. Hearing music in absolute terms—as pure note patterns—would require you to have no previous experience at all or that you can abolish all personal associations and memories. Such music listening is possible, but only if you are a robot.

Hence, a more plausible view is that music listening is *always* referential, more or less, even if you try to focus your conscious attention on the musical patterns; referential meaning is still being processed by the brain pre-attentively. The composer Béla Bartók confesses, "I cannot conceive of music that expresses absolutely nothing" (Watson, 1991, p. 41). But what is it that the music is expressing?

5.4 Does Music Refer to Emotions?

Referential views are discussed in the vast literature on "expression in music." (For reviews, see Davies, 1994; Gabrielsson, 2016; Jørgensen, 1988; Scruton, 1997.) The various theories proposed suggest that music contains many different kinds of meaning. Throughout history, music has been viewed as expressive of human character (Halliwell, 1987), motion (Shove & Repp, 1995), tension (Nielsen, 1987), gender (Dibben, 2002), social organization (Adorno, 1976), cultural and social identities (Folkestad, 2002), religious faith (Lippman, 1986), and social conditions (Lomax, 1968). But the one hypothesis that recurs, through the ages, is that music is expressive of emotions (Budd, 1985).

So, how *do* listeners hear music? Some preliminary clues come from a survey study that we conducted in Uppsala several years ago (Juslin & Laukka, 2004). I noted in Chapter 3 that self-reports may not fully reliable when it comes to determining the causes of musical emotions, whether perceived or aroused. However, when it comes to exploring what listeners perceive, self-reports may be more helpful, because perception tends to involve conscious experience and attention. Surprisingly, very few studies have consulted ordinary listeners when it comes to characterizing musical expression.

In our survey study, 141 listeners were asked what—if anything—music expresses. They were required to tick any item that seemed reasonable from a long list of alternatives. They could also add their own alternatives. Most listeners checked many options, but "emotions" was most frequently selected (100%), followed by "psychological tension" (89%), "physical aspects (e.g., motion, force, energy)" (88%), "beauty" (82%), "sound patterns" (80%), "events and objects" (e.g., birds, cannons, or the sea) (77%), "experiences that cannot be described in words" (72%), "religiosity" (60%), "social conditions" (57%), "personality characteristics" (50%), "musical conventions" (38%), and "other" (6%).

What can we conclude from the results? First, they clearly suggest that referential meaning in music is multi-dimensional. Music may be perceived to be expressive of a number of things—apart from emotions. It is important to remember this later, when we single out the emotional aspect. Second, note that although there were individual differences concerning several of the alternatives, there was *complete* agreement that music expresses emotions.

Similar data were obtained in a study of expert musicians—from both classical and popular music—but "only" 99% of them believed that music expresses emotions (Lindström, Juslin, Bresin, & Williamon, 2003). Performers were also much more inclined to think that music can be expressive of personality characteristics (89%) than were listeners (50%). Indeed, it is frequently argued that works of classical music, and their emotional expressions, may be reflective of their composers' temperaments. Just compare the playful ease and harmony of Mozart's music with the dark and passionate intensity of Beethoven's music.

It appears, then, that although listeners can potentially perceive different types of meaning in music, "emotion" may be the most salient one. Later we will see why this may be the case. It could be argued that such findings are more reflective of the "beliefs" and "folk theories" that performers and listeners have about music, than they are of any real circumstances. (We may like to *think* that music is expressive of emotions, even though it really is not.)

However, evidence that there is some substance to the intuitions of philosophers, musicians, and listeners comes from a large number of studies where participants are asked to judge the emotional expression of different pieces of music. (For a detailed review, see Gabrielsson & Juslin, 2003.)

Imagine the following scenario. You are invited to take part in an experiment. The researcher explains that you will listen to a series of excerpts from various pieces of music. Your task is to report which emotion is expressed in each piece. To illustrate: you may be asked to choose one emotion word from a list ("forced choice"), or to check any number of adjectives on a list ("adjective checklist") to describe the expression. Or you may be asked to rate each piece on a scale from 1 to 5 with regard how expressive it is of each emotion ("adjective ratings"). Or you may be asked to simply report which emotion you perceive, using your own words ("free phenomenological description"). Or you may be instructed to rate the perceived expression in real time, while you are listening, using a dedicated computer interface ("continuous response method"). Or you might use some combination of the above procedures. As you can probably imagine, the results will differ somewhat depending on what response format you are using.

Researchers have mostly used short excerpts of music in their investigations (Eerola & Vouskoski, 2013). This is partly because if longer excerpts are used, the expression might *change* across the excerpts, leading to inconsistent responses (Hevner, 1935). Consider the dramatic expressive changes that occur over time in an excerpt such as Gustav Mahler's Symphony No. 1 in D Major, IV: "Stürmich bewegt." Jumping to various parts, it is hard to believe that they all belong to the same movement.

Using short excerpts also offers an additional advantage—that the researcher may include a larger number of pieces to rate without taxing the listener, enhancing the *representativity* of the sample. The number of excerpts used in previous studies varies from 2 to 384. The latter number is from one of my own studies (Juslin & Lindström, 2010). Simply imagine having to listen to so many pieces in a single session! Most pieces used belong to Western tonal music—in particular, classical music. This limitation should be kept in mind when we look at the major findings shortly.

The task of matching emotion labels to pieces of music is the most common approach in the music-psychology domain, traditionally. To describe music in emotional terms is a task that comes naturally for most listeners. "Students asked to find meaning in musical compositions exhibit the greatest docility and ease in complying with the experimenter's request," remarks Hevner (1935, p. 194). In fact, most listeners find it considerably easier to describe the music in emotional terms, than in purely musical structural terms. As already mentioned in section 3.3, we tend to hear *meanings*, rather than structural features, in the music (Dibben, 2001).

I review results from studies of emotional expression in music in the next chapter, but I can reveal one major finding: *listeners are generally consistent in their ratings of the emotional expression in music*. In other words, the ratings are systematic and reliable, and may even be predicted with reasonable accuracy based on various features of the music (see Juslin, 1997b; Yang & Chen, 2011; examples will be provided in Chapters 9 and 10). Not only that, but it would appear that listeners can judge the emotional expression very quickly. A presentation lasting half a second might suffice for listeners to perceive whether a musical expression is, say, *happy* or *sad* (Bigand, Vieillard, Madurell, Marozeau, & Dacquet, 2005; Peretz, Gagnon, & Bouchard, 1998).

Listeners are able to perceive and rate emotions in music when asked to do so in experiments, but does this occur *spontaneously*, when listeners are not prompted by an investigator? Some clues come from the fact that pieces of music are commonly "tagged" with emotion labels on the Internet, and that CD and vinyl record sleeves often include emotion terms. (See also the review of the Paganini concert at the beginning of this chapter.)

More formal evidence comes from Gabrielsson's study of strong experiences with music, indicating that the emotional expression of the music was one of the primary causes of listeners' responses (Gabrielsson, 2011, p. 422). In the survey study by Juslin and Laukka, 76% of the participants reported that they perceive music as expressive of emotion "often" (Juslin & Laukka 2004). All of this suggests that emotions are salient in most listeners' perception of music.

Quite clearly, there is *some* kind of link between music and emotion perception, which seems broadly consistent with the notion that "music can refer to emotions." The question is how we should characterize this link.

5.5 Is the Term "Emotional Expression" Really Appropriate?

I have argued that listeners are strongly inclined to hear music as expressive of emotions, and that they can easily match verbal emotion labels to pieces of music consistently. A number of different terms have been used by scholars to refer to these phenomena. (All are linked to the concept of meaning.)

For example, music has been said to "express," "signify," "represent," "portray," or "convey" emotions. Although any of these terms could probably be used, I will use the term "express," partly because it is the most frequently used term in the literature, but also because the term does capture something important about the *origin* of musical expression .

In *one* sense, perhaps, the term "emotional expression' is misleading. It is only on occasion that musicians are truly expressing their *own* emotions at the moment of composing or performing (see Interlude in Box 7.1). Yet the fact that people tend to use the term "emotional expression" suggests that music, somehow, *reminds* them of the ways human beings express their states of mind in daily life—why would they otherwise use this term? "The very concept of expression strongly suggests the model of someone's expressing some feeling to someone else" (Goldman, 1995, p. 59). We should ask, is the model an apt one?

Philosophers like to point out that music is "non-sentient": it does not inherently possess any innate emotion that can be expressed. So, why do listeners perceive it as expressive of emotions (Davies, 2001)?

This has always appeared to me a very odd way of approaching the phenomenon. First, it is not that unusual that we perceive non-sentient things (e.g., a tree) as expressive. We have an "anthropomorphic" tendency to perceive expressive form even in inanimate objects (Juslin, 2003), as has been long recognized by anthropologists (Eibl-Eibesfeldt, 1989). To illustrate: the sound of a slowly closing door may sound "weary" or "complaining" to our ears.

With regard to music, however, it is not clear that we even need to evoke anthropomorphism. In Chapter 11, I will show you that part of the emotional content in music is due to expressive form which derives from other forms of non-verbal, spontaneous communication, such as gesture and tone of voice, so that there is, in fact, a strong link to "emotional expression," in the original sense of the term.

Second, if we find it puzzling that music is heard as being expressive of emotion, because "musical sounds do not have emotions," then we should be *equally* puzzled when we ascribe emotion to sounds such as crying or laughing. These sounds do not have emotions either. In both cases there is an "agent" producing the "noises," and in both cases the "noises" themselves do not "have" any emotions. The "noises" are produced by "agents" who *are* capable of having emotions.

In sum, then, there is no real mystery here once we realize that musical sounds are created by human beings—usually with an expressive intention of some kind (Box 7.1).

5.6 Expression: Are there Different Uses of the Term?

It is not strange that we often hear music as "expressive"—it would be stranger if we did not. However, in both musical and non-musical contexts, the term "emotional expression" can refer to a number of different scenarios, which may create confusion in discussions of the topic.

Look at Figure 5.3: on the left, there is the potential "expression" of an emotion by a musician (a composer or performer); on the right, there is the potential "perception" of an emotion by a music listener. Between them, we find the actual "sounds" involved. Surrounding them is the "context."

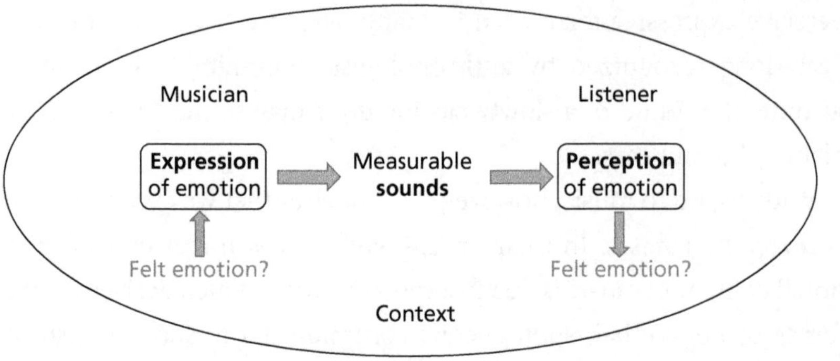

Figure 5.3 Expression of emotions in music.

This simple illustration can serve as the basis for further characterization of various possibilities when it comes to conceptualizing expression.

First, consider the musician's perspective. *If* he or she does "express" an emotion, this process may reflect a *felt* emotion or it may just reflect an *expressive intention* to convey an emotion in a symbolic manner. Both certainly occur (for evidence, see Box 7.1). The empirical question of whether the acoustic patterns will be different depending on whether an emotion was truly felt or "only" the result of an expressive intention has been long debated and is yet to be resolved. (This issue is often discussed regarding stage acting too; Roach, 1993.) Either way, the end result will be the generation of some sounds that can be recorded and analyzed, and that listeners may perceive.

It is important to note here that the music's potential to convey referential information to a listener is separate from the question of whether the sounds were the result of felt emotion, a sending intention, or both. In addition, not all intentions need to be conscious (for further discussion, see the collected works of Freud and his neo-Freudian disciples). This is why works of art—including music compositions and performances—are sometimes revealing even to those who created them.

Now consider the listener's perspective: *if* he or she *does* perceive an emotion, this may involve a *felt* emotion, or it may not. The listener may well perceive or "recognize" an emotion in the music without necessarily feeling any emotion. Alternatively, the listener might feel an emotion which is totally different from the one perceived in the music (cf. Part III); for instance, *perceiving* the music as expressive of sadness while *feeling* pleasure (see Chapter 32).

Most researchers assume that the listener's perception of emotion is relatively independent of any felt emotion (although this is debatable). The implicit understanding is that we can judge perceived emotions in a "cool," "rational" manner, independently of our own feeling (e.g., you can *recognize* the joy expressed in "Walking on Sunshine" by Katrina and the Waves, even if you happen to *feel* annoyed when hearing it).

If this assumption is true—that rating expression is mainly a cognitive process—then it implies that emotion perception is quite easy to measure: you can simply *ask* listeners about what they perceive in the music. This may explain why studies of emotion perception have relied almost exclusively on verbal self-report, in contrast to studies of arousal of *felt* emotions, which often involve a broader range of measures (Chapter 15).

Note that "expression" and "perception" of emotion are, in principle, independent entities. For example, the composer or performer might express an emotion (true or symbolic) which goes undetected by the listener. Similarly, the listener might perceive an emotion in the music that the composer or performer did not intend to express. "I can only suggest an interpretation of my music, but I cannot impose it," observes composer Jean Claude Risset (Cochrane, 2013a, p. 29).

Alan Goldman recounts the classical argument that the artist's intended meaning should be irrelevant to what the work means because "if she successfully conveys what she intends, the intention will be evident in the work itself; and if the intention is unfulfilled or unsuccessfully conveyed, then it is once more irrelevant to what the work itself means" (Goldman, 1995, p. 59).

Whatever the merits of this philosophical argument, it is certainly true that a composer does not know how a listener will react to the music at the moment of composing, and the listener does (in most cases) not know the

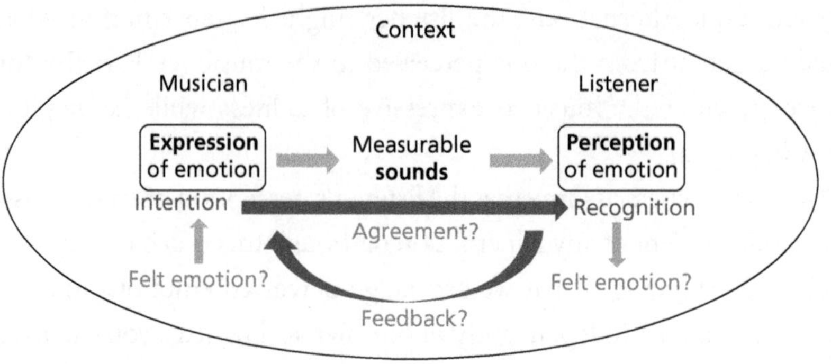

Figure 5.4 Communication of emotions in music.

exact circumstances surrounding the creation of the music, including the composer's or performer's intention.[3]

Conceived this way, the notion of "expression" does not require there to be a correspondence between what the listener perceives in a piece of music and what the composer (or performer) may have intended to express (if anything). Each side can be studied independently.

However, as we shall see (Interlude in Box 7.1), many musicians and listeners seem to have something more in mind when they talk about "emotional expression" in music. They like to think of this process in terms of "communication." The notion of communication requires that there is both an *intention* to express a specific emotion and *recognition* of this same emotion by the listener (Figure 5.4).

The "sender" constructs an "internal representation" of some feature of the world such as an emotional state, and then intentionally carries out some symbolic behavior that conveys the content of that representation. The "receiver" must perceive the behavior, as well as recover from it an "internal representation" of the content it signifies (Johnson-Laird, 1992).

[3] This is one of the problems for the so-called authenticity project, where musicians seek to play the music as the composer intended it. As noted by Nicholas Cook, this is "not so much hard, as impossible" because when consulting period treatises, "the result is usually a series of tantalizingly disconnected clues which you have to link together through the exercise of judgment, imagination, guesswork, and musical intuition" (Cook, 1998, p. 2). And still, "you cannot escape your own time" (ibid).

The listener may, additionally, come to experience (or feel) the emotion in question, but this is *not required* for it to qualify as a case of "communication" (think of how we communicate other contents in everyday life without arousing any emotions). This way of conceptualizing "expression" is often referred to as "the transmission model" (Serafine, 1980).

Finally, note the feedback arrow at the bottom of Figure 5.4. This is meant to illustrate those situations (e.g., a "live" concert) where the performer can receive feedback from the listeners (e.g., the audience), such that there exists a genuine, continuous interaction during a musical performance. Guitarist Peter Frampton explains:

> Knowing how I feel on stage and when I communicate that feeling to the whole audience, it starts to become a sort of emotional feedback... People in the audience are reacting to my actions and my mood as well as the music. I know that I can control the feeling in the audience. (Boyd & George-Warren, 2013, p. 146)

This is part of the attraction of attending a concert. However, most musical experiences in the Western world involve listening to recorded music (Juslin, Barradas, Ovsiannikow, Limmo, & Thompson, 2016; Juslin, Liljeström, Västfjäll, Barradas, & Silva, 2008)—musical events where the feedback loop does not apply. How could the listener provide "online" feedback to the performer, if the music was recorded at an earlier date?

If we extend the time-frame, however, it seems feasible to conceive of artists and audiences influencing each other over time, through a kind of reciprocal relationship (e.g., Hargreaves, MacDonald, & Miell, 2005). Whether such influences should be labeled "communication" is perhaps debatable, considering that most of the effects will not involve any sending intention.

In any case, the feedback loop may perhaps be applicable in another sense. The composer or performer is also a listener and may gauge the music created partly based on his or her own emotional reactions (Sloboda, 1999). As Mozart acknowledges in a letter, "I pay no attention to anybody's praise or blame... I simply follow my own feelings" (Watson, 1991, p. 381). I have heard many musicians say that they primarily aim to please themselves, but that if they succeed in this endeavor, they are bound to please others else as well.

The present discussion has, hopefully, illustrated why discussions of expression might be confusing. Different scholars may have different scenarios in mind when they use the term "emotional expression" (e.g., focus on the musician versus the listener, "true" expression versus "symbolic" expression, independent expression/perception processes versus communication, feedback cycle versus no feedback).

Psychological research on emotional expression summarized in Chapter 6 has mostly focused on the listener side—*how listeners perceive emotions in music*—rather than on whether and how musicians may have intended to express any emotional contents (but see Interlude in Box 7.1 for a few studies of composers and performers). Hence, although musical expression must originate in performers' and composers' behaviors, it is more common in the literature to define musical expression from the listener's point of view: "expression's domain is the mind of the listener" (Kendall & Carterette, 1990, p. 131).

This quotation also serves to highlight another point: that the perceived expression is the result of *psychological processes* in the listener, rather than being only "in the music." If it were otherwise, we would have a hard time explaining why there are individual differences in perception of emotions. As Leonard Meyer observes, "ultimately, it is the listener who must make connotation concrete" (Meyer, 1956, p. 266).

Because neither expression nor perception *requires* a felt emotion, most studies measure how musicians express emotions or how listeners perceive emotions, without investigating if the processes are accompanied by felt emotion or not. Emotion perception in music is treated as a "cool" and "detached" process. Let us now take a closer look at the empirical findings.

CHAPTER 6

EMPIRICAL STUDIES

What Have We Learned?

6.1 How Precise is Musical Expression? Conflicting Views

As noted in Chapter 5, psychological studies of emotional expression indicate that there is a great deal of agreement in listeners' judgments of perceived emotion in music. Yet if we broaden our perspective for a moment and look at neighboring disciplines, we find that the literature presents a more confusing picture.

Some scholars regard "expression" as something vague and flexible—almost idiosyncratic. Musicologist Ian Cross comments that music is "a strangely malleable and flexible phenomenon" (Cross, 2012, p. 265), because "one and the same piece can bear quite different meanings for performer and listener, or for two different listeners" (p. 266); and philosopher Susanne Langer submits that "it is a peculiar fact that some musical forms seem to bear a sad and a happy interpretation equally well" (Langer, 1957, p. 238). (She does not offer any musical example.)

Other authors seem to view expression as something far more precise, something for which terms like agreement and accuracy seem appropriate (Juslin, 2000a). Manfred Clynes argues that emotional expressions "can be shown to be subject to the highest degree of order and precision" (Clynes, 1977, p. xxxi). They operate "like keys in the locks of our nervous system" (p. xx). Hence, "a good composer who intends a particular portion of music to communicate joy can do just that" (p. 77).

Are these authors really writing about the same phenomenon? Could both views really be correct? We have just encountered the second paradox in the study of music and emotion.

PARADOX 2: Some scholars consider musical expression of emotions precise and reliable, while others insist that musical expression is vague and idiosyncratic.

To resolve this paradox, we need to look closer at what different scholars could possibly mean when they say that music is expressive of a specific emotion—or, more importantly, how they measure it. Even if we limit ourselves, for the time being, to the listener's side of the equation, and focus purely on perceived (as opposed to felt) emotion, there are still many different ways of approaching this phenomenon empirically.

6.2 Three Ways to Measure Perceived Expression

Note that there are different ways in which music may be said to express an emotion. First, a listener could perceive *any* emotion in a piece of music, and in a non-trivial sense, it would be odd to argue that the listener is "wrong."

To illustrate this, if I have the impression that the second movement of Beethoven's Piano Sonata No. 8 in C minor, Opus 13 ("Pathétique") is expressive of "tenderness," who is to argue with me? You may respond that *you* perceive it as "melancholic" rather than "tender," or even that most people hear it that way (backing it up with empirical evidence from a listening test, including numerous participants); but you cannot reject my claim that *I* perceive tenderness. The subjective impression of an individual listener cannot be disputed on "objective" grounds.[1]

[1] This is, of course, what lead to an impasse in the Kivy–Radford debate I mentioned in section 3.5. The debate was reduced to acknowledging that Kivy experiences music his way, and that Radford experiences it his way.

One way to measure emotional expression is thus to simply accept the *unique impressions* of individual listeners: whatever a listener perceives in a piece of music *is* what this music is expressing—for him or her at least. (This appears to be the view adopted by MacDonald, Kreutz, and Mitchell when they argue that "we are ... free to interpret what we hear in an infinite number of ways"; MacDonald, Kreutz, & Mitchell, 2012, p. 5).

With the possible risk of upsetting some scholars, I would also count *hermeneutic analyses* by musicologists in this category.[2] Their analyses may be informed, sophisticated, and interesting, and may potentially enrich our hearing of a piece of music. However, because their interpretations have not been subject to empirical testing with other listeners, I suspect many of the meanings are "idiosyncratic" in the sense that most listeners would fail to perceive them unless carefully instructed how to do so. Music analysts show us how music *might* be heard, or how they think it *ought* to be heard (Cook & Dibben, 2010), based on their special knowledge. It is a different matter how most listeners actually hear it.

To illustrate, in Robert Hatten's analysis of a section of the *Cavatina* in Beethoven's string quartet (Opus 130), he suggests that "the 'willed' (basically stepwise) ascent takes on a hopeful character supported by the stepwise bass" (Hatten, 1994, p. 213). I doubt that most listeners would spontaneously perceive "hope" in this section (or its "support" from the bass line).

If we accept such interpretations by single listeners, musical expression of emotion seems boundless. There is no end to what a piece of music can signify to a specific listener on a specific occasion in a specific social or cultural context.

This is *not* the kind of view that most psychologists have adopted in their studies, presumably because they wish to establish less "idiosyncratic" and more "general" tendencies. Thus, most psychologists adopt a more restrictive view which holds that music is expressive of a specific emotion only to the extent that there is a certain level of *agreement* among

[2] A *hermeneutic* approach refers here to the processes of appropriation, interpretation, and understanding of meaning in music by a music theorist.

different listeners about the emotion expressed, presumably because there is *something* in the actual music that tends to cause a similar impression in different listeners. (Many listeners might agree that the final movement of Tchaikovsky's Symphony No. 6 in B minor, Opus 74, is expressing various shades of *sadness*.)

If we measure emotional expression in terms of agreement, it alters our focus to the general *psychophysical relationships* between musical features and perceptual impressions. Although such a view still allows for individual differences (cf. Campbell, 1942), it shifts the balance towards the causal features in the music that listeners' impressions are founded on—a high degree of consensus among listeners implies that there *is* something to agree about in the music. (However, the observed agreement may well be limited to a specific type of emotional content, style of music, or cultural setting.)

There is a third sense in which the present phenomena may be conceived and measured. If we define musical expression in terms of communication, we can also measure emotional expression in terms of *communication accuracy*—the extent to which listeners are able correctly to infer or recognize the emotion that the composer or performer intends to express (Gabrielsson & Juslin, 1996; Rigg, 1942; Senju & Ohgushi, 1987; Thompson & Robitaille, 1992).

Some readers might perhaps find it a bit odd to use a term such as "communication accuracy" in the context of music, yet I think it is reasonable to assume that many artists *are* concerned about whether their interpretation is received by the audience the way that they had intended. "Unless you think of what the music carries, you will not convey it to the audience," notes the classical violinist Yehudi Menuhin (1996, p. 406); and the music theorist Leonard Meyer seems to concur: "Certainly the listener must respond to the work of art as the artist intended" (Meyer, 1856, p. 41). Most listeners are clearly curious about the intentions of artists.

A performer may, for instance, wish to highlight an emotional character latent in a piece. The degree to which performer and listeners agree about the resulting emotional expression might pragmatically be seen as a measure of whether the communication was successful or not. Note that measuring perception of emotional expression in terms of accuracy is quite different from measuring it in terms of listener agreement. To offer an example, listeners may agree *with each other* about which emotion is conveyed in a piece of music, yet their joint impression may disagree with what the composer or performer *intended*. This, then, would be a case of a high degree of agreement albeit low accuracy in judging what the artist meant to convey (Juslin, 2013b).

I raise these different senses in which music may be regarded as expressive of emotions because different ways of measuring emotional expression will provide different answers to questions such as "which emotions can music express?" There are probably fewer emotions for which there is *agreement* amongst listeners than there are emotions that a *single* listener could potentially perceive in a piece. Even fewer emotions might be relevant if we consider only those emotions that may be reliably *communicated* from a performer to a listener (i.e., where the intention to express an emotional character is correctly recognized by a perceiver).

As a reader, you may personally prefer one of these views on emotional expression in music, but there is undeniably some truth to all of them. In Chapter 12, I will propose a conceptual model which covers all the ways in which music could be said to "express emotions"—from the most personal to the most communal aspects of perceived expression. We will thus be able to resolve the second paradox of music and emotion.

6.3 Which Emotions Does Music Express?

Just as there are many different ways to conceptualize expression in music, there are different approaches that may be adopted to investigate empirically which emotions music can express. One simple approach is to *ask music listeners* directly—using the agreement criterion to index perceived emotions.

Table 6.1 shows data from three separate studies in which listeners were asked what emotions music can express. In each study, participants could

Table 6.1 Ratings of the extent to which specific emotions can be expressed in music. Data from three studies.

	Kreutz (2000)	Lindström et al. (2003)	Juslin & Laukka (2004)
Subjects	50 students	135 expert musicians	141 volunteers
No. of emotions	32	38	38
Rank ordering:			
1.	**Happiness**	**Joy**	**Joy**
2.	**Sadness**	**Sadness**	**Sadness**
3.	Desire	**Anxiety**	**Love**
4.	Pain	**Love**	Calm
5.	Unrest	Calm	**Anger**
6.	**Anger**	Tension	**Tenderness**
7.	**Love**	Humor	Longing
8.	Loneliness	Pain	Solemnity
9.	**Fear**	**Tenderness**	**Anxiety**
10.	Despair	**Anger**	Hate

Note. Only the 10 most highly rated emotions in each study have been included in the table. Those emotion categories that correspond to the basic emotions are set in bold text. (Anxiety belongs to the "fear family," and tenderness to the "love" family, see, e.g., Shaver, Schwartz, Kirson, & O'Connor, 1987.) The original lists of emotion terms contained both "basic" and "complex" emotions, as well as some terms commonly emphasized in musical contexts (e.g., solemnity).

choose from a long list of emotion labels. Shown are the rank orders with which each of the top 10 emotion terms was selected.

As can be seen, *happiness, sadness, anger, fear,* and *love/tenderness* were all among the top 10 emotions. This tendency is quite similar across the three datasets, despite the fact that the studies featured different samples (musicians versus students, different countries) and selections of emotion terms (ranging from 32 to 38 terms). Note that the five emotion categories largely correspond to the so-called basic emotions mentioned in section 4.8. I shall argue later that these categories form a *core layer* of musical expression upon which more complex emotions might be added. The last column on the right-hand side of Table 6.1 includes two complex emotions: *longing* and *solemnity*. The term *calm* is also highly rated in two of the lists. It may be regarded as the opposite of *arousal* (a broader emotion dimension; cf. section 4.7) and is highly correlated with *tenderness* in musical expression.

The ratings by the musicians (middle column in Table 6.1) are notable because they include the two terms, *tension* and *humor*. *Tension* is not a discrete emotion, but rather a dimension of emotion (just like *arousal*) which occurs to different degrees in different emotions (high *tension* is particularly typical of negative emotions, such as *anxiety*). It is not surprising that musicians rate *tension* highly. Music-theoretical discourse often speaks of "musical tension" as a result of the intricate interplay between various structural aspects of the music (Lerdahl & Krumhansl, 2007; see Chapter 12 for further discussion).

Humor is a frequently occurring expression in certain genres, perhaps most typically jazz music, where musical quotations, such as fragments or motifs from another song or a famous solo, are inserted for humorous effect. Being a musician myself and having been around musicians a lot over the years, I find that there is a certain brand of "musician's humor."

Many performers find it endlessly amusing to "play around" with music, imitating famous musicians or beginners, over-emphasizing typical features of a genre, playing a piece with what is obviously an inappropriate interpretation, perfecting a wholly ridiculous timbre, or revisiting musical licks from an era which has not "aged well."

Apart from these (usually) "off-duty" activities, humor does seem to "sneak into" otherwise serious compositions also; thus, for instance, in the *Scherzo* of Beethoven's Fifth Symphony, there is a moment where "clumsy double-basses are made to scamper like elephants, and are then abruptly pulled up and started again." (Scholes, 1923, p. 170; score given on p. 143).

The results from the survey data discussed earlier indicate that there is *some* agreement about which emotions are easiest to express in music, but it could be argued that the results reflect mere beliefs; that they do not prove that these emotions really *are* the easiest to express. A second approach, then, is to look at which emotions tend to produce the highest levels of listener agreement in perceptual ratings.

Alf Gabrielsson and I carried out an extensive review for the *Handbook of Affective Sciences* which featured all empirical studies published up until that point (Gabrielsson & Juslin, 2003). We concluded that the highest agreement amongst listeners occurred for emotion categories such as *happy/triumphant, sad/melancholic, angry/violent,* and *gentle/relaxing,* and emotion dimensions such as *arousal* and *valence.* Again, the results suggested that certain basic emotion categories may be easier to express in music than others; a lower degree of agreement was observed for complex emotions (e.g., *jealousy, pity, cruelty, eroticism, devotion*) as well as various types of non-emotional content (e.g., narratives).[3]

We should, however, be careful not to make *too* sweeping claims about what music can or cannot express. As I will explain further in Chapter 11, the perceived expression is in part determined by how the content is "coded" in the music. Hence, the contents perceived will depend to a considerable extent on the particular circumstances: the context, the style, and the individual listener. There is no doubt that some emotions (e.g., *happiness, sadness*) are expressed more commonly and easily in music than others, but the expressive qualities are partly dependent on musical genre, with some emotions being more salient in certain styles or genres than in others, as discussed by philosopher Jerrold Levinson (2015).

It should also be noted that the studies discussed earlier have focused on instrumental music. Most music heard in the world features lyrics. Because lyrics and their accompanying music tend to express similar emotional meanings, analyses of lyrics may offer another measure of which emotions are expressed most frequently in music.

Using a large database, musicologist Gunter Kreutz analyzed the contents of 1785 (English) lyrics from songs across several centuries (Kreutz, 2000).

[3] Although evidence is lacking, we can hypothesize that expressions will produce higher levels of listener agreement when a composer or performer *set out* to convey a particular emotion in the piece (which is not always the case), than when he or she did not.

The top 10 most common emotion categories represented in the lyrics were *love, pain, joy, sadness, longing, tiredness, hope, loneliness, fear,* and *anger.* (Note that there is considerable overlap with the emotions that participants believed music is able to express in Table 6.1.)

The number one spot was occupied by *love.* This is consistent with Daniel Levitin's claim that the most frequent form of musical expression, "from the Psalms of David to Tin Pan Alley to contemporary music" (Levitin, 2006, p. 246), is the love song, "the best courtship display of all" (p. 267; see also chapter 20 in Gabrielsson, 2011).

Cynthia Whissel (1996) also offered a number of examples of how analyses of lyrics in pop music can aid our understanding of the emotional expression in music. Relying on computer-driven *stylometric analysis,* she examined the emotional meaning of all Beatles songs written by Lennon and McCartney between 1962 and 1970, 155 songs in total. Although the songs were jointly copyrighted as "Lennon–McCartney," Todd Compton has shown that most of the songs were written by only one or the other composer after 1964 (Compton, 1988).

Whissel discovered differences in emotion between both composers and years (Whissel, 1996). Based on an analysis in terms of emotion dimensions such as pleasantness and activation, the Lennon–McCartney songs as a whole became less pleasant, less arousing, and less cheerful over time, reflecting a move away from love songs. Lennon generally wrote songs that were less pleasant and sadder than those of McCartney. A follow-up study showed that Lennon wrote more songs in a minor key than McCartney (Whissel & Whissel, 2000).

The question of which emotions are most frequently expressed in music is far from resolved, and the answer may differ across time, to some extent, if it is true that artists tend to express the emotions of their generation (Boyd & George-Warren, 2013), or that compositional style may partly reflect significant world events, such as world wars (Simonton, 2010; Interlude in Box 7.1). However, in Chapter 12 I will return to this issue and postulate a set of prototypical emotions in musical expression, partly based on the psychological processes through which music may carry emotional meaning.

6.4 Can Musicians Communicate Emotions to Listeners?

Howard Gardner suggests that "music can serve as a way of capturing feelings, knowledge of feelings, or knowledge about the forms of feelings, communicating them from the performer or creator to the listener" (Gardner, 1993, p. 124). Can a composer communicate emotions to listeners?

Because it is often difficult to determine post hoc which intentions the composer possessed with a piece of music (e.g., because the composer might be dead, or simply unwilling to discuss the creative process), few studies thus far have investigated the extent to which a composer is able to convey specific emotion categories to listeners.

A rare exception is a study by Bill Thompson and Brent Robitaille (1992), who asked five highly experienced musicians to compose short melodies that should express six emotions: *joy, sorrow, excitement, dullness, anger* and *peace*. The musicians were required to rely on information that is contained in musical scores (e.g., pitch, tempo, and volume information). Figure 6.1 offers an example of a score intended to express *sorrow* by one of the composers.

"Dead-pan" performances of the resulting compositions on a computer sequencer were played to 14 listeners moderately trained in music who successfully recognized the intended emotion. The results indicate that music composers can communicate at least *some* emotions reliably to listeners. These findings are all the more impressive if we consider that the use of

Figure 6.1 Part of musical score intended to communicate sorrow to listeners.
Reproduced from Empirical Studies of the Arts, 10, *Thompson, W. F., & Robitaille, B., "Can composers express emotions through music?", pp.79–89. Copyright © 1992, © SAGE Publications.*

"dead-pan" performances meant that several aspects of performance (e.g., timing patterns) were excluded from the communicative process.[4]

What about the performance? The same piece can be performed in several different ways, all of which will strongly affect the listener's impression of the emotional expression (Juslin, 2001). However, if we wish to explore the role of the performance, we soon encounter a problem: how can we tease out the expressive effects of the performance from those of the composition or song?

One solution is to ask performers to play the *same* piece of music in a number of different expressive ways. This is exactly what we did in a series of studies in Uppsala (e.g., Gabrielsson & Juslin, 1996; Gabrielsson & Lindström, 1995; Juslin, 1995, 1997a,b, 2000a; Juslin & Madison, 1999): professional musicians were required to perform a short piece of music so as to convey specific emotions such as *sadness, happiness, tenderness,* and *anger.* This is similar to studies of emotion in speech where actors are required to pronounce the same sentence with different "tones of voice"—the so-called *standard content paradigm* (Juslin & Scherer, 2005).

How did the performers respond? As it turns out, most of them enjoyed the task. They found it interesting and challenging. More importantly, results showed that professional performers were generally able to communicate basic emotion categories to listeners simply via the manner in which they performed the piece (though there were individual differences between performers in communication accuracy even at a professional level). How accurately can performers communicate a specific emotion to listeners?

In the most extensive review of emotional expression in music performance to date, featuring 41 studies, a meta-analysis of communication accuracy showed that professional performers were generally able to communicate five "basic emotion" categories—*happiness, anger, sadness, fear,* and *tenderness*—to listeners with an accuracy about as high as in facial and vocal

[4] A "dead-pan" performance is one in which all notes are played exactly as notated (in a "mechanical" manner), lacking all the subtle variations that human performers typically add to make the music sound "expressive" and "musical" (Chapter 13).

expression of emotions, a finding that surprised quite a few researchers (Juslin & Laukka, 2003).

The overall decoding accuracy, across emotion categories, is equivalent to a "raw" accuracy score of 70% correct in a forced-choice task using five response options (20% correct is the accuracy we could expect merely by chance), though the communication may be successful even when using a free-labeling task (e.g., Juslin, 1997c). Amateur musicians communicate emotions less accurately, mainly because they tend to apply musical features inconsistently (Juslin & Laukka, 2000; Rohwer, 2001; see also Chapter 10).

The high degree of accuracy applies only to the "basic emotions" mentioned. When studies have tried using more complex emotions, the accuracy has usually fallen (Gabrielsson & Juslin, 1996). When researchers have explored whether performers may communicate non-emotional ideas, the data have also been disappointing; this point is brought home by the low degree of accuracy reported in a study which used more abstract labels such as *deep* and *sophisticated* (Senju & Ohgushi, 1987). Such concepts could not be conveyed nearly as accurately as emotions (e.g., *sad*) could.

In summary, previous studies indicate that some emotions are easier to convey in music than others. In terms of the nomenclature of emotions outlined in Table 4.2 we can conclude that the top 10 emotions expressed in music are "basic" emotions rather than "complex," "cognitive," or "moral" emotions. Although there is a core of truth to this observation, the picture is more complex. Music *can* express more "complex" emotions under certain conditions (Juslin, 2013b), as will be further described in Chapter 12.

6.5 Does Music Convey Mainly Broad Emotion Categories?

We saw earlier that listener agreement may be impressive with regard to basic emotion categories, such as happiness and sadness, and that composers and performers can accurately communicate these emotions to listeners. However, this conclusion needs to be qualified.

As a rule, although there is typically a high level of agreement among listeners about the *broad* emotion category expressed in the music, there is less agreement about the nuances *within* the category (Brown, 1981; Campbell, 1942; Downey, 1897; Juslin, 1997c)—at least without additional context provided by lyrics, visual impressions of the performers, program notes, or (historical) knowledge of genre conventions.

Ivy Campbell notes that although "over 90% of the [participants] agreed that certain selections expressed 'gayety,' as to whether this 'gayety' was 'carefree,' 'lively,' 'merry', there was no such agreement" (Campbell, 1942, p. 7). It is not that music pieces intended to express, say, *anger* and *jealousy* sound exactly the same to listeners, it is simply that listeners are not able to tell which piece is which.

A study by Melvin Rigg further illustrates this tendency, within a communication paradigm: 24 college students judged the expression of each of 18 music excerpts, presented across three tasks (Rigg, 1942). The pieces of music featured, for instance, Siegfried's Funeral March from "Götterdämmerung" by Wagner, Turridu's Farewell from "Cavalleria Rusticana" by Mascagni, and Butterfly's Death Scene from "Madame Butterfly" by Puccini.) Due to his careful selection of pieces, Rigg knew what the music was supposed to express and could use this criterion to evaluate the listener's accuracy in the rating tasks.

First, the listener had to decide whether the piece in question was predominately "sad–serious" or "joyful"—a broad characterization. Seventy-three % of listeners could tell whether the music was sad or joyful. Following this initial identification, the listener had to make a more accurate judgment and say whether the piece portrayed, for instance, "death," "sorrow," or "religion"; at this stage the classification accuracy dropped to 41%. Finally, the listener had to make an even finer discrimination, deciding whether, say, the "death" sub-category of the "sad–serious" main category referred to "a death scene," "a funeral march," or "an elegy." The accuracy dropped to a meager 25%. Rigg thus concluded that "it may be that only the main categories and not the nuances are expressed" (Rigg, 1942, p. 12; see also Downey, 1897).

Some scholars have paradoxically argued that musical expression of emotions is *more* precise than language could ever be. Susanne Langer claims that "music can reveal the nature of feelings with a detail and truth that language cannot approach" (Langer, 1957, p. 235). How can this view be reconciled with the findings just cited, suggesting that musical expression of emotions is *broad* and somewhat imprecise?

First, in some of the cases concerned, I suspect that the "precision" considered has more to do with the experience of *musical* nuance than with *emotional* nuance. (This is discussed further in section 7.2.) Clearly, language is incapable of capturing every nuance of the music, which may shift by every tenth of a second.

Second, and more importantly, I will argue later that one can distinguish different "layers" of emotional expression, some of which are broad and others which are precise. I will show that musical expression of emotion is *broad* and *robust* at the inter-individual level, albeit *precise* and *unreliable* at the individual level. These tendencies can be explained in terms of different types of coding (see Chapter 11).

Thus, although you may have the *subjective impression* of a precise expression as an individual listener ("This music *really* expresses a such-and-such an emotion *perfectly*"), comparison with other listeners will show that as far as *inter-individual agreement* is concerned, the reliability applies only to the broad emotion category.

Although the inter-individual "fuzziness" of musical expression of emotions may be regarded as a serious limitation by some, others have argued that it may be a strength. Because musical expression is slightly "flexible" or "imprecise," it enables the listener to project his or her own interpretation onto the music in a way that would be impossible with, say, ordinary language.

Kate Hevner suggests that "it is due to this flexibility that each individual listener may find in the music just that particular shading of its general mood which is most desired ... the mood of the music, stated in these more general terms, is ideally adapted for the expression of the specific personal experience with which he is led to associate it" (Hevner, 1935, p. 188).

In a similar vein, John Sloboda argues that, "our own subconscious desires, memories, and preoccupations rise to the flesh of the emotional contours that the music suggests. The so-called 'power' of music may very well be in its emotional cue-impoverishment. It is a kind of emotional Rorschach blot" (Sloboda, 2005, p. 227).[5]

Is the imprecision of musical expression a weakness or a strength? You decide. In section 12.3, I will describe a model that may explain both the shared and idiosyncratic aspects of musical expression in terms of the underlying psychological processes.

6.6 Not Quite Emotions: Meet the Vitality Affects

Many expressive qualities in music involve subtle changes over time, which make possible the expression of shifting, blending, or conflicting emotions. Such changes may be captured by Daniel Stern's concept of "vitality affects" (Stern, 1985). Stern suggested this term to capture a set of elusive qualities related to shape, intensity, contour, and movement. These qualities are best described in dynamic terms, such as growth and decay, tension and release, crescendo and diminuendo, and accelerando and ritardando—terms indispensable to characterize Beethoven's music.

The vitality affects are not emotional states themselves, but rather abstract *forms* of feeling that may occur both together with, and in the absence of, "proper emotions." (Indeed, Stern has later referred to them as "forms of vitality"; Stern, 2010.) Vitality affects occur at the *intermediate* level, between low-level features of the music and high-level concepts such as emotions.

[5] The Rorschach test is a psychological test in which a subject's perceptions of inkblots are recorded and then analyzed psychologically in order to reveal a person's personality characteristics or emotional functioning.

Stern suggested that the vitality affects are particularly important in the early communicative acts between mother and infant, where they react to one another through a constant matching of gestural events, a process referred to as *attunement* (see also Malloch & Trevarthen, 2010). Attunement is also key in certain types of active music therapy (Bunt & Pavlicevic, 2001)—in those cases between a therapist and his or her client.

Vitality affects are quite reminiscent of philosopher Susanne Langer's famous theory of how music symbolizes our feelings: music, suggests Langer, represents the *dynamic form* of emotional life, not specific emotions. Thus, when Langer notes that "some musical forms seem to bear a sad and happy interpretation equally well" (Langer, 1957, p. 202), this may be because vitality affects are not emotions themselves, and because some vitality affects can be common to many different emotions. To illustrate, a sudden accelerando may appear in cases of joy expressions as well as in anger expressions. Considering its temporal nature, music is arguably the art form best equipped to express vitality affects.

Now we can perhaps resolve the previous apparent inconsistency. Music can express vitality affects in a precise manner, but this does not imply that music can express discrete emotions in an equally precise manner. We may agree that an expressive change, at a specific moment in a piece generally expressive of sadness, is a "crescendo" with a certain shape, but we may *not* agree on how to label the exact resulting emotion. Is it a tragic outburst? Intense despair? Sadness tinged with anger? (This is where more idiosyncratic aspects enter the picture.)

Quite often when music theorists discuss "musical affect" (Lerdahl, 1991), they appear to be thinking about something akin to vitality affects rather than emotions proper. I believe this is because vitality affects are closely linked with the "intra-musical" aspects of expression that music theorists are so fond of analyzing (see Chapter 12).

For conceptual clarity, it may be helpful to distinguish such expressive qualia from emotions. (The term "qualia" is used by philosophers to refer to qualitative characteristics of experiences.) Musical expression involves a number of feeling-like qualia such as "groove" (Ashley, 2014), "swing" (Vuust

& Kringelback, 2010), and "topics" (Ratner, 1980). These are interesting aspects of music experiences, but they are not emotions. Hence, I will not discuss them further here.[6]

6.7 It All Depends: Moderating Variables

Listeners' agreement about expression varies depending on several *moderators*. These are variables that can influence the strength of a statistical relationship or experimental effect. Examples may include the piece of music, the style, the social context, and the methods used in the listening test (e.g., procedure, response format).

Thus, for example, we have found in our laboratory that some songs or pieces are expressive of a clear and distinct emotional quality, whereas others are far more ambiguous in character. (Note that composers and musicians, like other artists, may sometimes *strive* for ambiguity in expression.). Similarly, some genres of music (e.g., pop songs) may have more "recognizable" emotional expressions than others (e.g., serial music).

Amongst the moderators, we may also include a range of contextual and individual variables. Table 6.2 offers a simple list of variables that might potentially moderate the effects found in expression studies. Which of these are relevant depends on the musical setting (e.g., listening at home versus attending a "live" concert).

Many artists are visually quite expressive, and we know that visual impressions can aid the decoding of expressive intentions in performers. For example, watch the video of blues singer and guitarist B. B. King's performance of "How Blue Can You Get?" at the Sing Sing prison in 1972. Several studies suggest that visual impressions alone can convey much expressive information about performances (for a review, see Davidson & Broughton, 2016).

[6] For further examples of non-emotional expressive aspects, see the volume edited by Fabian, Timmers, and Schubert (2014).

Table 6.2 Examples of moderator variables in expression research.

Type	**Examples of factors**
Piece-related	The musical composition itself Notational variants of the piece Consultations with composer or composer's written comments Musical style/genre
Instrument-related	Acoustic parameters available Instrument-specific aspects of timbre, pitch etc. Technical difficulties of the instrument
Performer-related	The performer's structural interpretation The performer's expressive intention with regard to the mood of the piece The performer's emotion-expressive style The performer's technical skill The performer's motor precision The performer's mood while playing The performer's interaction with co-performers The performer's perception of/interaction with audience
Listener-related	The listener's music preference The listener's music expertise The listener's personality The listener's current mood The listener's state of attention The listener's learning history
Context-related	Acoustics Sound technology Listening context (e.g., recording, concert) Other individuals present Visual impressions Larger cultural and historic setting The overall purpose of the musical event Whether the music is formally evaluated

Based on Juslin, 2003.

In contrast, when listening to recorded music, recording technology will play a larger role. Variables such as microphones, sound effects, and spatial localization can all influence the listener's perception of the emotional expression (Dibben, 2014; Garofalo, 2010; Tajadura-Jimenez, Larsson, Väljamäe, Västfjäll, & Kleiner, 2010). Few psychological studies thus far have tested such contextual variables by means of experimental methods.

There are also numerous methodological moderators of importance. First, as you may expect, one observes a higher level of agreement when listeners choose a word from a short list than when listeners report their impressions using their own words. Moreover, there are strong order effects in judgments of emotional expressions, which is why most experiments impose a random order of pieces for each listener and compute the average across listeners. A musical excerpt that potentially sounds happy may sound even more happy if it is preceded by a sad excerpt.

Contrast effects can also work to an advantage in expression. Some scholars have argued that music may express more "complex" emotions (e.g., relief, hope) via the ways in which different expressive sections follow one another (e.g., Davies, 1994), although this notion has not yet been tested. If you are a regular music listener, it has perhaps occurred to you that the expressive impact of a song or piece might be strikingly different depending on its position in a "playlist." Sequencing of songs on albums is an art in itself, which some producers (e.g., Glyn Johns) take a great deal of pride in perfecting. It is also a crucial factor during "live" concerts, when the set list is often unknown to the audience (see section 25.7).

All things considered, it is difficult to estimate in a more general sense how much agreement there really is about musical expression. With knowledge about the moderators, I may easily run an experiment that "proves" *either* that agreement is high *or* that it is low simply through how I design the study (e.g., stimulus choice, stimulus order, response format, instructions).

This may seem alarming, but it is simply a fact of life. In science, as soon as you ask a question, the precise way in which you formulate it will affect the kind of answer you will get. How we operationalize the variables of interest also affects the outcome, as shown earlier with the concept of emotional expression (section 5.6).

Nonetheless, I think we can safely conclude that at least some emotions are quite accurately and consistently decoded by listeners across a variety of contexts within the same culture—and sometimes even across cultures. Indeed, studies show that perception of emotion in music is robust in that listeners' judgments seem only marginally influenced by musical training, age, and gender of the listener (Gabrielsson & Juslin, 2003). This suggests that our perception of emotions in music relies to some extent on psychological mechanisms that are not unique to music, a notion I will return to in Chapters 11 and 12.

CHAPTER 7

MUSIC AS EXPRESSION

Objections and Obstacles

7.1 The Case Against Musical Expression of Emotions

The previous chapter demonstrated that there is some agreement among listeners about what emotion pieces of music express, and that music performers may communicate at least some emotions to listeners in a reliable manner. Yet such findings do not by themselves prove that this is how musicians or listeners conceive of music.

In this chapter I will address problems and objections surrounding the notion of music as the expression of emotions. There are scholars who are strongly critical of this view of music. Issues concerning expression, communication, and emotion tend to invite controversy, and some authors go to extreme lengths to reject any link between music and emotion.

One example can be found in an essay by philosopher Nick Zangwill. He argues that "it is not essential to music to *possess* emotion, *arouse* emotion, *express* emotion, or *represent* emotion. Music ... has nothing to do with emotion" (Zangwill, 2004, p. 29). Zangwill is, of course, entitled to his opinion, but in the light of empirical findings concerning how most people in the Western world conceive of music, his view appears oddly out of touch with reality (see Box 7.1).

Yet such an opinion is hardly new. Enid Robertson notes that "the emotional response is not an essential part of musical appreciation ... This view, that music is the expression of the emotions, is held by most unmusical people" (Robertson, 1934, p. 199). Ouch! She goes on to suggest that "a true appreciation of music always involves an intellectual approach" (p. 203).

Usually, however, the resistance against emotions is subtler. For example, in a recent anthology devoted to investigating "what it means to be expressive" in music performance, the editors tried their best to define emotions *out* of the concept of "expression" (Fabian, Timmers, & Schubert, 2014, pp. xxi–xxii), but apparently unsuccessfully (p. 349). Emotion reasserted itself in many of the chapters, nonetheless! As Nicholas Cook duly notes, "turned away at the front door, expression simply re-entered at the back" (Cook, 2014, p. 331).

The most hilarious moment in the book—for me—is when the editors conclude in their final commentary that there is an "emergent theme" in the book to not consider specific emotions (Fabian, Timmers, & Schubert, 2014, p. 353)—as if this was an "empirical finding" of some sort—after having directly instructed the authors that "any such meaning should be minimized" (p. xxii). (The editors provide no clear reason why emotions should be avoided.) How can such resistance be explained?

As is commonly the case, the controversy boils down to values. Part of the resistance against emotions can be explained by concerns that an argument that the value of music resides in its emotional or communicative functions could render music merely a "tool" for communication of emotions (Budd, 1989).

It *is*, in fact, a plausible idea that music initially developed from a means of emotion sharing and communication to "an art form in its own right" (Juslin & Laukka, 2003). Still, as Philip Johnson-Laird notes, it is a peculiar aspect of human communication that, sometimes, the symbols themselves rather than their interpretation may come to be the crucial part of the "message" (Johnson-Laird, 1992). Hence, music can to a limited extent be appreciated as autonomous tone patterns—and *ought* to be, according to some scholars.

Arguments against emotional expression or referential meaning in general can be construed as attempts to defend the "unique" value of music as an "autonomous" art form. The issue of how to do music justice as an art form is a legitimate concern, but the solution is not to deny that music is linked in crucial ways to the emotions. Yet this seems to be the price that some scholars are willing to pay to avoid emotions hogging the spotlight, as they have a strong tendency to do, whenever allowed to enter the picture.

This could be the reason that some famous composers have rejected emotional expression in music. Impressions can be misleading, however, and some of the sternest critics might reveal a more nuanced view on closer examination. My favorite composer of classical music (along with Beethoven), Igor Stravinsky (Figure 7.1), has often been credited as rejecting expression and emotion (which is paradoxical to me, since his music is among the most expressive I have ever heard).

There is a famous quotation by him, often interpreted as the ultimate defense of absolutism: "Music is, by its very nature, essentially powerless to

Figure 7.1 Composer extraordinaire Igor Stravinsky—not an enemy of emotional expression.
Illustration by Costis Chatzidakis.

express anything at all, whether a feeling, an attitude of mind, a psychological mood, a phenomenon of nature" (Stravinsky, 1975, pp. 53–54).

He later claimed that the quotation had been over-publicized, saying that "even the stupider critics could have seen that it did not deny musical expressivity" (Stravinsky & Craft, 1981, p. 101). A little harsh, perhaps, but other remarks seem to confirm that Stravinsky was not resistant to the notion of music as expression of emotions:

> Many people seem obsessed with the idea that I do not desire to express emotion in my music. They are completely mistaken. The emotion is there all right—I myself feel it and express it, and for those who cannot or will not share it, I can only suggest that they consult a psychiatrist! (Stravinsky, 1934)

Again, a bit harsh, Igor, but point taken. (I should confess that, as a rule, I find Stravinsky's music more enjoyable than his writing.) Stravinsky added, however, that "listeners are too ready to condemn the 'new' music because it is not overflowing with the type of melody and emotion to which they are accustomed and which they can recognise at a first hearing" (Stravinsky, 1934).

In other words, the real issue discussed here is not so much whether or not there is musical expression of emotions but rather *what kinds* of emotions are, or ought to be, expressed. For the first but certainly not the last time, we encounter the politics of music and emotion; that is, normative views on the subject. Stravinsky's words imply that his music expresses emotions that are different in kind from those that listeners might hear in the popular music of the day.[1] This seems fair enough. Still, the fact remains: when the cards are laid down, Stravinsky does not deny that (his) music is expressive of emotions.

[1] Think of the music by the composer Alban Berg. Although loosely based on Arnold Schoenberg's twelve-tone technique and mostly "atonal," Berg's compositions still manage to achieve a strange beauty and expressiveness. Listen, for instance, to his violin concerto ("To the memory of an angel"): it strikes me that this is what expressive music from another planet might sound like.

One possibility is that the young Stravinsky had become influenced by the theoretical views of Eduard Hanslick (1854), influential music critic, musicologist, and composer in nineteenth-century Vienna. Clearly, Zangwill bases his views partly on the writings by Hanslick, as reflected in the title of his essay, "Hanslick was right" (Zangwill, 2004). Hanslick was the most outspoken, self-declared "absolutist" of the day, forcefully defending the "autonomy" of music.

Still, as Kivy observes, Hanslick strays from his own music-philosophical standpoint in his work as a critic: "He cannot but describe music in emotive terms, because the emotive properties will not be denied: they will be heard, and Hanslick has ears to hear them" (Kivy, 2001, p. 43). The lofty ideal of pure, absolute music does not survive its first contact with reality, it seems.

In the Foreword to the eighth edition of his book *On the Musically Beautiful*, Hanslick admits to "share completely the view that the ultimate worth of the beautiful is always based on the immediate manifestness of feeling" (Hanslick, 1854, p. xxii). The problem, he notes, is rather the notion of music as "representation." Hence, on close examination it is not absolutely clear that even Hanslick denies the importance of emotion in music. The formalists in musicology took what they could from his writings and ran with it.[2]

So far, we have mainly focused on the critique of the notion of music as expression of emotions. The notion of music as communication has also been criticized. The "transmission model" of music has been described as "old-fashioned" (Serafine, 1980) or "naive" (Swanwick, 1985), as a "romantic notion" of music (Budd, 1989). Yet, as we shall soon see, there is much evidence to support this notion. So why, then, is the communicative aspect

[2] There is another, arguably less subtle, way of addressing Hanslick's resistance against emotions, which might be cheered by *some* readers, at least. Most listeners in the Western world hear music as expressive of emotions, and consider this a crucial aspect of music so, really, who cares what a music critic wrote on the topic 160 years ago?

of music dismissed by some scholars? Again, there is "politics" involved. Philosopher Lydia Goehr argues that:

> As soon as we talk about music as communication, we imply a topography and arising from it a politics ... The politics is played out between the sometimes complementary and sometimes conflicting concerns of composers, performers, and listeners ... Should the entire process be regarded as the recreation of the composer's original *intention?* ... Or then again is music really a performing art? ... Or again, should not everything be evaluated from the point of view of the recipient? After all it is he who pays! (Goehr, 1992, p. 125)

In classical music, at least, it is usually the composer who has the upper hand, as observed by Melvin Rigg (1942):

> The composer is usually accorded the privileged position in the interpretation of his own works. If he announces that his symphony represents the restless striving of the human spirit against the decree of Fate, then for another musician to fail to find this meaning becomes a confession of musical insensitivity. It may be suspected that we have here a case analogous to that of the Emperor's clothes, no one daring to reveal that he does not see a non-existent significance. (Rigg, 1942, p. 281)[3]

A communication perspective, it seems, may accord too much power to the listeners. It comes as no surprise, then, to learn what priorities many composers have: "It is better to make a piece of music than to perform it, better to perform one than to listen to one," proclaims composer John Cage, to take just one example. (And, of course, it is better to write a book about music than to merely compose it!)

Another form of resistance against both the notions of music as expression of emotions and of music as communication is based on the fact that not *all* composers or performers seek to convey emotions, or that those who do it don't do it *all the time*.[4] However, this is a weak argument: it is like

[3] Rigg, a psychologist, points to "the value of an experimental approach" (Rigg, 1942, p. 281) in empirically resolving the question of what meaning is present or not in a piece of music, using agreement or accuracy as an index.

[4] Not every culture values music as a means to emotional expression. Here I focus primarily on Western cultures.

claiming that emotion theories are invalid simply because we do not experience an emotion all the time.

The theories of expression and communication of emotions presented in this book concern those cases—and they seem to be quite a few—where musicians *do* try to convey an emotion or when listeners *do* perceive an emotion in the music. In those cases where the music is *not* conceived this way, the theories simply do not apply. A musical communication model is just that, it does not purport to cover everything (else) that music is or can be.

7.2 *Wovon Man Nicht Sprechen Kann, Darüber Muss Man Schweigen*

As discussed earlier, some of the controversy surrounding emotions in music concerns which emotions music is expressing, and how they should be labeled. Hence, this section focuses on the problems of language. You might have guessed that from the heading, even if you did not understand the German. It is a quotation by philosopher Ludwig Wittgenstein, which translates as "whereof one cannot speak, thereof one must be silent" (Wittgenstein, 1922).

As you have probably noticed by now, psychologists are rather keen on having listeners report their experiences of perceived emotions in words. This can seem deceptively simple, but when interpreting the results, the difficulty involved in translating emotional experiences into verbal labels should be kept in mind. The interpretation of such labels can also be difficult.

People have different vocabularies. They may use or interpret words differently. Some people are better at describing emotions verbally than are others. Individuals with the personality trait *alexithymia* suffer, among other things, from difficulties in identifying their own emotions and describing the emotions of other people. The term *emotional granularity* refers to an ability to differentiate between emotions: some people describe emotions in very specific terms, others tend to describe emotions more vaguely (e.g.,

Lindqvist & Barrett, 2008). In addition, different cultures use different terms for the same emotion (Russell, 1991).

We must also remember that words and emotions are distinct entities. As noted by Jean Starobinski, "emotions come before the words that name them" (Starobinski, 2013, p. 329); that is, we must not confuse the emotions themselves with the imperfect words we use to refer to them.

When two listeners use different terms (e.g., *melancholy* versus *gloominess*) to characterize a piece, this does not *necessarily* mean that they have perceived different emotions. Hevner argues that apparent disagreement amongst listeners over the emotional expression may be due to the slightly different connotations that different listeners place on particular words, rather than differences in the perceived expression—though the two can be difficult to tease apart empirically (Hevner, 1935).[5]

Hevner's solution was to develop a unique self-report scale for expression in music, which aimed at capturing broad categories (Hevner, 1936). As seen in Figure 7.2, Hevner's "adjective circle" consists of a large number of terms, arranged into eight clusters in a circular configuration. Terms within each cluster are supposed to be close in meaning; adjacent clusters deviate by cumulative steps until reaching a contrast in the opposite position of the circle. To illustrate, *happy* is the opposite of *sad*, and *vigorous* is the opposite of *serene*.[6]

The advantage of this scale is that even if two listeners may prefer to use somewhat distinct verbal terms to describe a piece—say, *sad* versus *depressing*—their responses can still be treated as belonging to the same overall category. What strikes me from a modern perspective, however, is that some of the words in Hevner's adjective circle appear to refer to music-perceptual "qualia" (e.g., *vigorous, sparkling*), rather than emotion categories, reducing the conceptual precision of the scale.

[5] One way to tease apart these two aspects may be to ask listeners to make similarity judgments instead of verbal labeling. If two listeners sort pieces of music into specific emotion categories in the same way, it does not matter whether they label the categories somewhat differently; they appear to perceive the nuances in the pieces in the same way (Brown, 1981).

[6] Hevner's "adjective circle" is actually a forerunner to Russell's (1980) "circumplex model" (Figure 4.1), with its implicit dimensionality (e.g., cluster 2 versus cluster 6 = *pleasure*; clusters 7/8 versus clusters 4/5 = *arousal*).

7
exhilarated
soaring
triumphant
dramatic
passionate
sensational
agitated
exciting
impetuous
restless
tumultuous

6
merry
joyous
gay
happy
cheerful
bright
sunny
gleeful
vivacious
entrancing
fun

5
humorous
playful
whimsical
fanciful
quaint
sprightly
delicate
light
graceful
jovial
sparkling

8
vigorous
robust
emphatic
martial
ponderous
majestic
exalting
energetic
mighty
potent
imposing

4
lyrical
leisurely
satisfying
serene
tranquil
quiet
soothing
peaceful
comforting
easygoing
gentle

1
spiritual
lofty
awe-inspiring
dignified
sacred
solemn
sober
serious
noble
pious
sublime

2
pathetic
doleful
sad
mournful
tragic
melancholy
frustrated
depressing
gloomy
heavy
dark

3
dreamy
yielding
tender
sentimental
longing
yearning
pleading
plaintive
nostalgic
wistful
touching

Figure 7.2 Kate Hevner's adjective circle.
Reproduced from Hevner, K. (1936). *Experimental studies of the elements of expression in music.* American Journal of Psychology, 48, 246–268. *Copyright 1936 by the Board of Trustees of the University of Illinois. Used with permission of the University of Illinois Press.*

This problem was addressed in an alternative version of Hevner's adjective circle outlined by Emery Schubert (Schubert, 2003, presented in Table 7.1). Note that the emotion clusters in the updated version are quite similar to the most highly ranked emotions in Table 6.1, suggesting that this version can be a useful "tool" to capture relevant aspects of musical expression of emotion, at least for broad emotion categories. (It has not been used in any study to date, as far as I know.)

Dedicated self-report scales might address *some* of the verbal problems, but there is another potential problem: some music listeners—as well as some scholars—claim that the emotions perceived in music cannot be described in words *at all*; they are "ineffable" (Raffman, 1993). I agree that *some* aspects of music experience are very difficult to describe in words (though there is an abundance of poetry concerned with describing music). I doubt, however, that this difficulty applies to the emotions.

I believe the problem involved in describing music experience verbally really has more to do with the difficulty of capturing what it is like to perceive *the music* per se; "it's very hard for people to write about music. How do you describe music," asks singer and songwriter Tom Petty (Smith, 1988,

Table 7.1 Emery Schubert's updated version of Hevner's adjective circle.

	M	***SD***	**Source**		**M**	***SD***	**Source**
Cluster A				**Cluster F**			
Bright	6.04	1.63	HF,6,a	Dark	5.84	1.95	HF,2.f
Cheerful	5.35	1.82	HF,6,a	Depressing	4.64	2.31	HF,,2,f
Happy	5.29	1.97	HF,6,a	Gloomy	4.64	2.18	HF,2,f
Joyous	5.22	2.01	HF,6,a	Melancholy	5.36	2.17	H,2,f
Cluster B				Mournful	4.64	1.76	HF,2,f
Humorous	4.67	2.25	H.5,	Sad	5.53	2,02	HF,2,f
Light	6.02	1.73	HF,5,b	Solemn	5.09	2.11	HF,1,f
Lyrical	6.23	1 74	HF,4,c	**Cluster G**			
Merry	4.30	1 88	HF,6,a	Heavy	5.61	1.72	H,2,
Playful	5.17	2 01	HF,5,a	Majestic	5.81	1.87	HF,8,g
Cluster C				Sacred	4.92	2.35	HF,1,g
Calm	6.06	1.76	HRW,4,4,	Serious	5.08	2.15	HP,1,
Delicate	5.13	2.15	HF,5,c	Spiritual	5.30	2,06	HF,1,g
Graceful	6.02	1.71	HF,5,c	Vigorous	5.06	1.84	HF,8,g
Quiet	5.69	1.97	HF,4,c	**Cluster E**			
Relaxed	5.04	2.05	RW,	Tragic	4.71	1.99	HF,2,f
Serene	4.66	2.15	HF,4,	Yearning	4.10	2.39	HF,3,e
Soothing	5.69	1.92	HF,4,c	**Cluster I**			
Tender	4.26	2.18	HF,3,c	Agitated	4.86	2.06	HF,7,I
Tranquil	5.29	1.97	HF,4,c	Angry	4.07	2.53	RW.,
Cluster D				Restless	4,63	2.23	H,7,
Dreamy	4.79	1.89	HF,3,d	Tense	1.71	1_77	RW,,
Sentimental	4.48	2_18	HF,3,d	**Cluster H**			
				Dramatic	6,54	152	HF,7,h
				Exciting	5.58	1.96	HF,7,h
				Exhilarated	4.27	2-08	HF,7,h

Table 7.1 Continued

	M	*SD*	Source		*M*	*SD*	Source
				Passionate	5.92	2.00	H,7,
				Sensational	4.83	2.31	H$_1$7,
				Soaring	4.25	227	H,7,
				Triumphant	5.27	2.03	HF,7,g

Note. The columns show: mean score on a scale of 0 to 7 ± one standard deviation, the source of the word (H = original Hevner adjective list, F = Farnsworth, R = Russell, W = Whissell), the original cluster *number* in Hevner's list, and the original cluster *letter* in Farnsworth's list. The latter two items will be of interest for readers who are familiar or wish to become familiar with the Hevner and Farnsworth papers. For example, "bright" in the new Cluster A is reported as (6.04 ± 1.63, HF,6,a), indicating that the mean suitability rating for this word in describing music was 6.04, with a standard deviation of 1.63. The word occurs in Hevner's and Farnsworth's lists (hence, HF) and appears in Cluster 6 of Hevner's list and Cluster a in Farnsworth's list (hence, 6,a). "Relaxed" in the new Cluster C is reported as (5.04 ± 2.05, RW), indicating a mean suitability score of 5.04 with a standard deviation of 2.05. The word appears only in the Russell and Whissell lists (RW). As it does not appear in either Hevner's or Farnsworth's lists, the last two comma positions remain empty. Farnsworth's clustering labels are retained in the headings but have been rearranged to restore the (approximate) circular configuration suggested by Hevner, with Cluster H joining to Cluster A. That is, clusters move in the sequence A, B, C, D, F, G, E, I, H, then back to A.
Schubert, E. (2003). Update of the Hevner adjective checklist. Perceptual and Motor Skills, 96, 1117–1122.

p. 402). Composer Camille Saint-Saëns concurs: "There is nothing more difficult than talking about music" (Watson, 1991, p. 48).

Our perception of *musical nuance* is clearly hard to describe in words, but we should not confuse musical nuance with emotional nuance. It is simply not the case that every note in music expresses its own emotional category, just as not every letter in a novel conveys its own emotional category.

The musical shape may be indicative of gradual shifts in emotion intensity or valence over time, but those changes have a somewhat longer time frame, and *can* be captured in words (e.g., the vitality affects; see section 6.6). In addition, most languages in the world contain several hundreds of words that refer to emotions (e.g., Johnson-Laird & Oatley, 1989). For something that cannot be described in words, there are an awful lot of words to describe it.

If we *do* perceive specific emotions, those states will be amenable to description in common language, but describing them well may require practice. A professional wine taster may not simply *perceive* more nuances in wines, but may also be better at *finding the right words* to capture these nuances. Similarly, describing emotions in music or elsewhere is presumably a skill that can be developed, just like any other. In fact, it is often only in poetry and literature that we find descriptions of feelings that truly resonate with our own experience (Nielsen & Kaszniak, 2007).

Sometimes when there is low listener agreement regarding what emotions a particular piece of music expresses or when listeners struggle to characterize the expression of a piece, it is due to the specific piece itself; certain pieces *are* more emotionally ambiguous in expression. Claude Debussy's "Beau Soir" (e.g., as performed by Yo-Yo Ma) has a quite elusive, vague, and quickly shifting expressive character, which is not easily labeled in terms of a single category. (Listener agreement and communication accuracy depend *equally* on the "sender"/"stimulus" and the "receiver"; see Chapter 10.)

Yet, even when we have difficulties in the moment of finding the right emotion word to describe a piece, we can probably still characterize it in *relative* terms, by comparing it to other pieces. ("This piece sounds less tender than the previous piece.") Thus, then, we have already come *some* way towards characterizing its emotional expression. For instance, listen to the beginnings of the various movements of Beethoven's String Quartet No. 14 in C-sharp Minor, Opus 131, and notice the changes in expressive character from one movement to the next.

Some scholars (e.g., Fabian, Schubert, & Timmers, 2014) argue that music can be expressive in general, without being so in a particular way. I think this is absolute nonsense. A piece of music may have a more or less clearly discernible and discrete emotional expression, yet every piece of music has certain musical features which will make it different in "expressive character" from another piece with other musical features. Hence, *music is always expressive in a particular way.*[7] The trick is how to describe the expression in a manner that people will find acceptable.

[7] I do not deny that musicians may have the *intention* to "play expressively" in a general (transitive) sense; what I deny is that a performance can ever be *heard* as expressive "in general" without being more expressive in one way rather than another.

7.3 Not Lost in Translation: Emotion Terms versus Expression Marks

Researchers have repeatedly asked listeners to match pieces of music to emotion labels. The selection of emotion labels has mostly been done in a post hoc manner, after the fact, based on statements by philosophers or music theorists, suggestions in previous studies of expression, as well as intuition, folk psychology, or personal experience. Taken all together, the emotion labels that have been used are counted in hundreds, though much of this variety is due to the use of (more or less) synonymous affect terms (e.g., happiness, joy, gaiety, elation; cf. Gabrielsson & Juslin, 2003).

Nevertheless, certain emotions (e.g., *sadness, happiness*) occur more often than others across studies. Modern studies often refer to these as the basic emotions (section 4.8). As already noted, these emotions might be easier to express or communicate than other emotions. A focus on these emotions is natural if we consider that people regard them as typical emotions (Shaver, Schwartz, Kirson, & O'Connor, 1987) and that they figure prominently in performance treatises (e.g., Hudson, 1994), sleeve notes to music CDs and vinyl records, and reviews of albums and concerts (e.g., the Paganini review at the start of Chapter 5). Eric Clapton at one point expressed the explicit ambition "to make the saddest album ever" (Clapton, 2007, p. 269).

It may be true that not all musicians conceive of musical expression in terms of precisely these terms, but they *do* seem inclined to communicate the *expressive characters* that the terms refer to, judging from the actual acoustic characteristics of the music. For example, musicologist Daniel Leech-Wilkinson provides numerous examples of expressive gestures used by singers to express emotional categories such as *fear, sadness, anger,* and *love* in lieder composed by Franz Schubert (Leech-Wilkinson, 2006).

The basic emotions do not exhaust the expressive possibilities (more complex emotions are considered in Chapter 12), but they are, in a sense, unavoidable aspects of musical expression, simply because they represent "anchor points" in the different quadrants of the emotion space in terms of *valence* and *arousal*; see Figure 7.3. A piece of music which expresses, say, negative valence and evokes a low arousal response *will* be perceived as "sad" to some extent, regardless of how we may wish to label its expressive character.

Yet, some musicians (and scholars) become uncomfortable when expression in discussed in terms of "garden-variety" or "everyday" emotions, especially when researchers refer to them as basic emotions (Juslin, 2013b); this, they point out, is *not* how they approach their music. I suspect that the concept of basic emotions somehow seems to imply a low level of musical sophistication. After all, who would like to have any aspect of his or her music compositions or performances described as "basic"?

However, as we explain elsewhere, the phrase "basic emotion" does not imply that the music itself is "basic": "basic emotions may be expressed in the most sublime manner" (Juslin & Lindström, 2010, p. 356). The term simply highlights the fact that the basic emotions are at the core of human emotions and have a long evolutionary past (Plutchik, 1994). In addition, for most theorists, the concept of basic emotions implies that there are more complex emotions which "build upon" more basic ones (e.g., Johnson-Laird & Oatley, 1989).

One way to reduce resistance against the idea of basic emotions amongst musicians is to demonstrate their natural relationships to the everyday praxis of performers, even in classical music. Might it be the case that these terms, used merely as shorthand for broad categories of emotion in musical expression in previous studies (Juslin, 2001), may be "translated" to some "language" more familiar to the working musician?

In classical music, scores often feature *expression marks*, which serve to indicate not only the tempo of the piece but also the intended expressive character. Such expression marks—often given in Italian (*furioso*) or German (*sehr Langsam*)—are more frequent during some musical eras than others. (They hardly occur before 1500 AD.) Yet most performers of classical music are accustomed to seeing them in scores. Perhaps it would be worth investigating how expression marks relate to basic emotions.

In a rare study conducted in Uppsala, professional musicians and psychology students were asked to rate a highly varied set of pieces of classical music with regard to 20 expression marks rated as common by music

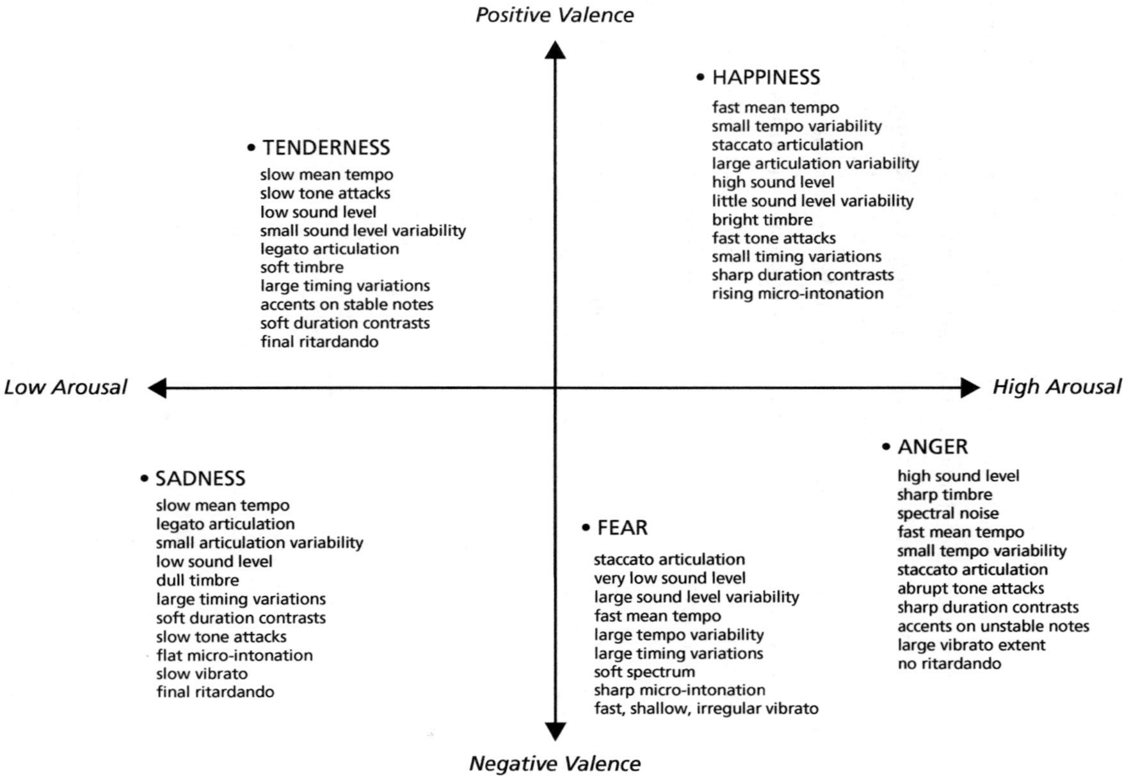

Figure 7.3 Two-dimensional emotion space in music.
Reproduced from Juslin, P. N. (2010). *Expression And Communication of Emotion in Music Performance*. In P. N. Juslin & J. A. Sloboda (Eds.), Handbook of music and emotion: Theory and research. By permission of Oxford University Press.

experts and 20 emotion terms rated as feasible in a musical context (Wiik, 2012). Ratings on expression marks and ratings on emotion terms were done independently by musicians and psychology students, respectively.

When these ratings were combined, statistical analysis yielded strong correlations between expression marks and emotion terms, in particular for the basic emotions (Table 7.2). Note, for example, the large correlations for *furioso–angry* and *dolce–tender*. Yet, there were also correlations for more complex emotions, such as *cantabile–nostalgia* and *maestoso–pride*.

These results may not be particularly surprising, considering that expression marks frequently feature reference to motional and emotion characters, but the point is that when psychologists talk about basic emotions, they may well be referring to exactly the same expressive qualities as classical musicians consider in expression marks through their daily work.[8] This confirms the relevance of psychological research on the matter.

Table 7.2 Examples of correlations between commonly used expression marks in musical scores and basic emotion labels used by psychologists.

Expression mark	**Emotion label**	**Correlation** (r)
Dolce	Tenderness	98*
Espressivo	Desire	.85*
Furioso	Anger	.92*
	Disgust	.79*
Grave	Sadness	.88*
Scherzando	Happiness	.76*
Spiritoso	Surprise	.94*
Temoroso	Anxiety	.97*
	Fear	.82*

* $p < .01$

Reproduced from Frontiers in Psychology, *Hypothesis and Theory*, Patrik N. Juslin, 'What does music express? Basic emotions and beyond'. Copyright © 2013 Juslin. Published under the terms of the Creative Commons Attribution 3.0 Unported license (https://creativecommons.org/licenses/by/3.0/).

[8] In this study, the expression marks seemed to have a less precise meaning than the emotion terms, suggesting that it may be advantageous to use the latter—at least for research purposes.

The greater lesson from this section is that we should not get too hung up on the superficial verbal labels used to refer to the underlying emotion categories. Whether we like to think of music in terms of expression marks or emotion labels, or prefer to avoid labeling of emotion altogether, there is little doubt that many musicians conceive of music in terms of expression of emotions (see Box 7.1). Hence, it appears highly apt to examine this process further.

Box 7.1 Interlude—Perspectives from Musicians

Musicians are conspicuously absent from academic discussions about expression. Why is that? Perhaps, researchers feel that musicians lack the required training to understand science. Or perhaps musicians feel reluctant to dwell on this subject, preferring to "let the music do the talking." Thus, for instance, Menuhin argues that "the interpretation should speak for itself" (Menuhin, 1996, p. 329). As explained in section 3.5, much of the brain processing underlying music and emotion is tacit and so it is difficult to talk about anyway.

However, what does occur, time and time again, is evidence that musicians regard emotional expression as important. Much of this evidence is anecdotal and informal, although there are a few studies that report relevant data and I will summarize them here.

The goal is not to prove that composers and performers always strive to express emotions, it is merely to show that there is a *tendency* to do so, in particular amongst popular musicians. While we can certainly find exceptions, there is a common theme that music is an expression of emotions, even a language of sorts. John Coltrane: "A musical language transcends words. I want to speak to their souls" (Irvin & McLear, 2000, p. 48).[a]

It should be noted from the outset that emotions may play various roles in musical creativity: they can provide the motivation to start writing the music; they may shape the actual process of composition; the can be used to evaluate the results of the process; they can be involved in the act of performing the music, sometimes even hindering a performance (e.g., stage fright). Many of these subjects have yet to be properly investigated (but see Persson, 2001; Woody & McPherson, 2010).

[a] Several quotes from composers, performers, and others suggesting that music is a "language" can be found in Watson (1991).

Emotion and expression in composing

Do composers create music while under the influence of emotion? This question cannot be answered satisfactorily at this time: we simply do not have the empirical data. Clearly, it is not *necessary* to experience an emotion to create great music, nor is it necessary to have an intention to express an emotion in order to write a wonderful piece of music, including one that is *heard* as expressive by listeners.

I agree with Vladimir Konečni that the process of music composition is likely to be dominated by *reason*, rather than emotion: "contemplation, analytical and technical skills, problem solving, and planning" (Konečni, 2012, p. 141). For some composers, emotion might *inspire* the process of creation. More commonly, perhaps, composers express emotions in a symbolic manner (see section 5.6), relying not on "current, acute emotions, but their memories and knowledge of them" (Konečni, 2012, p. 148; for similar views, see Langer, 1957).

Is it important to know whether a composer wrote a piece in order to express an emotion? It may not be important from the listener's perspective. A piece of music may well be heard as expressive of a particular emotion, regardless of whether the composer wrote this piece with this emotion, another emotion, or no emotion at all in mind. As explained in section 5.6, the question of whether a piece of music was intended to express a specific emotion is logically independent of whether a listener will perceive a certain emotion.

Yet, it is an interesting question what role emotions or expressive intentions may play on the "sender" side of the process. What appears beyond doubt is that *some* composers write music having been inspired by emotions and/or intending to express emotions *some* of the time. This may be more common in popular music than in classical music.

A unique investigation by Jenny Boyd and Holly George-Warren (2013) provides insight into the creative process of popular musicians, using a rich material based in part on Boyd's Ph.D. thesis from 1989. The study features 75 interviews with eminent musicians, conducted between 1987 and 1991.

The musicians represent the whole spectrum of "popular music": rock, jazz, blues, soul, funk, hip-hop, pop, folk, and country. Keith Richards, Eric Clapton, John Lee Hooker, George Harrison, Ravi Shankar, Joni Mitchell, Hank Marvin, Stevie Nicks, B.B. King, Roger Waters, Don Henley, Steve Winwood, Branford Marsalis, Patti Smith, Randy Newman, Tony Williams, Graham Nash, Ice-T, Peter Gabriel, Rosanne Cash, Jackson Browne, and others share their innermost thoughts on musical expression and creativity.

Boyd and George-Warren conclude that "one of the strongest motivations to create, according to several artists, is the need to express deeply felt emotions" (Boyd & George-Warren, 2013, p. 274). To assist in the process, some artists (e.g., Don Henley of the Eagles) have learnt to "trigger" certain feelings to inspire their writing (p. 275). Anthony Kiedis explains that "when something happens in your life that really stimulates a specific emotion, I think you are inclined to write about it" (p. 276).

Other sources such as biographies and interviews usually offer similar views. "Emotions guide us, it is very instinctive," comments Jean-Benoit Dunckel of the electronic duo Air (Irvin & McLean, 2000, p. 641). Singer and songwriter Joni Mitchell refers to her highly rated album *Blue* as "probably the purest emotional record I will ever make."[b] Songwriter Roger Waters of Pink Floyd continues:

> My writing was such that I could never make anything up. *Dark side of the moon*, for example, in terms of its construction and lyrical content, as well as the music, is simply how I was feeling in 1972. I found that the more direct I've been with my feelings, the better I felt about work at the end of the day. (Smith, 1988, p. 360)

Classical composers may be relatively less inclined to create to music in the grip of emotion. Many composers and theorists like to conceive of music as "an abstract narrative." They take pleasure in the cleverly wrought structures, free from everyday concerns (Clarke, Dibben, & Pitts, 2010, pp. 67–68). This suggests a more intellectual pursuit—a consideration of note patterns from a more decidedly "aesthetic" perspective (Part IV), even if we suspect that composers cannot avoid *evaluating* their work partly based on their own emotional response.[c]

Rather than expressing acute emotions in the composition, as posited by the expression theory in the philosophy of art, "a more plausible view is that composers try to use various structural factors in order to achieve certain intended expressions ... with no or little direct connection to their present feelings" (Gabrielsson & Lindström, 2001, p. 223).

Yet, even composers of classical music might create while "emoting". When a servant found G. F. Handel weeping after having completed Part II of "The Messiah" (featuring the famous Hallelujah chorus), the composer explained: "I did see all heaven before me, and the great god himself" (Watson, 1991, p. 148).

In 1893, the Russian composer Pyotr Tchaikovsky premiered what is often regarded as his best and incidentally most moving composition—namely his

[b] An article in *Mojo* magazine stated that "loneliness, grief and infatuation were just three themes of an album which has become a sacred text of nostalgic introspection and a source of almost healing power ... it's the honesty and unmediated emotion of *Blue* that still resonate with anyone who has ever lost sleep over love" (quoted in Irvin & McLean, 2000, p. 250).

[c] Igor Stravinsky may not have sought to compose pieces that pleased his audience, but I presume he made compositional decisions that pleased *himself* at least, which means "affect" was still involved in the process.

Symphony No. 6 in B minor, Opus 74 ("Pathétique"). Writing to his nephew prior to the premiere, Tchaikovsky disclosed that "the programme is subjective through and through, and during my journey, while composing it in my mind, I often wept bitterly" (Porter, 1966). The piece was novel in form because instead of closing with an *Allegro*, the final movement was an extensive *Adagio* (marked *lamentoso*) which is often regarded as a prototypical expression of *sadness* in music.

Dean Keith Simonton provides some evidence of a more indirect link between emotions and musical composition. He has been able to compute a reliable, quantitative index of "melodic originality" (described further in Part IV), based on melodic themes of ten of the most eminent composers of classical music, according to a previous survey by Farnsworth (1969). Melodic themes scoring high in melodic originality tend to be perceived as unpredictable, interesting, complex, and arousing (Simonton, 2010).

Simonton correlated this measure with the amount of "biographical stress" in the composer's life at the time of the composition of each music theme, an index based on the occurrence of stressful and traumatic events such as legal difficulties, interpersonal conflicts, and economic problems, everything from lawsuits and unrequited love to divorce and duels. (A composer's life is apparently not as boring as you might think!)

Data showed that the two indices were positively but moderately related. In times of higher stress, the composer wrote themes that tended to have a higher melodic originality; melodic originality also tended to increase during more general traumatic world events, such as war. Note, however, that Simonton's results do not show that acute emotions are involved in the very act of *composing* the music; they only suggest that emotional life events may indirectly influence the style of composition.

The actual process of composing may require a more tempered state, as confirmed even by the "emotional" composer, Pyotr Tchaikovsky: "those who imagine that a creative artist can … express his feelings at the moment when he is *moved*, make the greatest mistake. Emotions, sad or joyful, can be expressed only *retrospectively*" (Fisk, 1997, p. 157).

Much the same could probably be said about music performers, many of whom report that they cannot allow themselves to be in too strong a grip of an emotion, in order to maintain "control" and perform well (Scherer, 2013; Van Zijl & Sloboda, 2011; see also Chapter 13).

Emotion and expression in performing

It would seem that only some composers intend to express emotions in their songs or pieces. The link to emotional expression may be more consistent in the daily work of the performer. Boyd and George-Warren suggest that the audience prefers those artists that are most expressive to those that are mere "technical wizards" (Boyd & George-Warren, 2013). Only a few studies have looked at how performers approach this matter.

We carried out a questionnaire study featuring 135 musicians at an expert level (69 males and 66 females) from music conservatoires in three countries: Italy, England, and Sweden. (These featured the Royal Colleges of Music in London and Stockholm as well as the Conservatory of Music B Marcello in Venice.) The musicians were asked to respond to 48 items with regard to how they think of expression in music—starting with broad questions and gradually narrowing in on emotions (Lindström, Juslin, Bresin, & Williamon, 2003).

Early in the survey, the musicians were asked to rate different characteristics in terms of how much they appreciate these in other musicians. The results clearly suggested that expressivity was regarded as the most important characteristic, much more important than aspects such as technical skill, stage presence, personal style, and theoretical knowledge. (The importance of expressivity was also highlighted in a study of music students by Robert Woody, 2000.)

Open-ended responses to the question "In your view, what does it mean to play expressively?" were analyzed by content and divided into categories. The results suggested that the performers define playing expressively mainly in terms of "communicating emotions" (44%) or "playing with feeling" (16%). These categories were not always easy to distinguish in the performers' responses, but the first involves more focus on conveying something to an audience, whereas the second involves more focus on the performer's own feelings while playing. A third group (34%) provided answers in terms of "focus on the music itself" (e.g., conveying the structure). This can perhaps be construed as a more "absolutist" view on musical expression (Chapter 5).

Of particular interest is that 83% of the performers reported that they deliberately try to express specific emotions in their performance "always" or "often." Further, nearly all (92%) believed that they express emotions without consciously thinking about it—highlighting the often tacit aspect of emotional expression. Several performers reported that they also "feel" the intended emotion while they are playing (Always 23%; Often 65%; Seldom 12%; Never 0%).

Singers, however, occasionally avoid felt emotions. Experiencing (too) much emotion can affect the singer's control over the voice, as discussed in an interview study by Klaus Scherer (2013). Tenor Thomas Moser explains that: "A singer must remain in complete control of his body at all times otherwise he can't sing. So I can't let myself go with the emotion when I'm singing" (Scherer, 2013, p. 56). Similarly, soprano Gillian Keith observes that "there are situations in which feeling genuine emotion will be beneficial to the performance," but also adds that "my throat would get very tight if I let myself get carried away by these extreme emotions" (p. 59).

How can we resolve these different views on the role of a performer's experienced emotions in the construction of an expressive performance? It may depend on the stage of preparation. Unique insights come from a small study conducted by Anemone Van Zijl and John Sloboda (2011). Eight students from British conservatoires or universities took part in the study, which followed them throughout the entire process of developing an interpretation. Both interviews and playing diaries were used to capture the process.

In analyzing the results, Van Zijl and Sloboda distinguished between "emotions in the music" (e.g., "great sadness; loneliness; desire") and "emotions felt by the performer" (e.g., "I have to remain calm throughout"). In the latter category, they further distinguished between "practice-based emotions" (e.g., "frustration") and "music-based emotions" (e.g., "feeling the sadness to be expressed in the music"). So how did the role of the performer's emotions change across the stages of preparation?

"Practice-based emotions" dominated initially while trying to solve technical problems. Then, "music-related emotions" came to the fore, guiding the student's interpretational choices. As the process developed, "feeling the musical emotions" transformed into "knowing the musical emotions"—finding the appropriate musical features to put the desired expression across. At the point of the performance, some students felt emotions were added again. But as one of the students observed, "I can't imagine any way I could get carried away too much with emotion" (Van Zijl & Sloboda, 2011, p. 212).

The expert musicians in the survey study (Lindström et al., 2003) were asked which factors determine what emotion they try to express in their performance: 36% referred to "external" factors, such as the music itself, the historical context, the composer's intentions, the mood of the piece, or audience reactions; 29% referred to "internal factors" such as the performer's own moods and emotions—often the specific state in the moment; and finally, 34% referred to a mixture of "internal" and "external" factors. Most musicians reported feeling free to interpret pieces of music according to their own preferences (Always 22%; Often 64%; Seldom 14%).

All musicians in the study by Van Zijl and Sloboda (2011) said that their interpretation of a piece was based mainly on their own feelings (Van Zijl & Sloboda, 2011, p. 207); when their feelings did not "fit" with performance directions (e.g., the composer's intention or expression marks), or conventions, they found that they had to compromise their feelings to some extent (cf. Persson, 2001).

Emotion and communication

Is "the transmission model" appropriate for music? Indeed, several biographies, surveys, and interviews with performers (both classical and popular) suggest that they conceive of music in terms of "communication" (Boyd & George-Warren, 2013; Carreras, 1991; Denski, 1992; Menuhin, 1996; King, 1996; Persson, 2001). As Beethoven scribbled on the original score of his "Missa Solemnis": "From the heart, may it go to the heart" (Scherman & Biancolli, 1972, p. 951). Again, there are only few relevant studies on the topic.

Caroline Minassian, Christopher Gayford, and John Sloboda (2003) conducted a survey study featuring 53 classical performers exploring which factors are statistically associated with an "optimal" musical performance. Performances judged as "optimal" tended to be those where the performer (i) had a clear intention to communicate (usually an emotional message); (ii) was emotionally engaged with the music, and (iii) believed the message had been received by the audience. These results are perfectly consistent with the transmission model of musical communication (see section 5.6).

Interviews with pop musicians by Boyd and George-Warren provide further evidence that music is usually seen as a form of communication. Singer Sinéad O'Connor: "Music is the most powerful form of emotional communication" (Boyd & George-Warren, 2013, p. 295). Blues guitarist Buddy Guy: "The feeling I get when I'm playing to an audience is 'Am I reaching you?' Am I getting to these people through communication with my music?" (p. 147).

In their study of jazz musicians, Karen Burland and Luke Windsor observe that "communicating with the audience was of primary concern and all musicians spoke of their awareness of the audience—its experience of the performance" (Burland & Windsor, 2014, p. 110). Paul Berliner confirms that listeners feel that they are part of a "communication loop" at intimate jazz venues (Berliner, 1994). This reminds us that "musicking" is an inherently *social* activity—one of the recurring themes throughout the book.

CHAPTER 8

BREAKING THE CODE

The Musical Features

Having established that expression and perception of emotions are important phenomena in music, we are ready to have a closer look at how the psychological processes actually work. A first step is to have look at the musical features. Which are the relevant ones? How do they co-vary with specific emotion categories and dimensions? How are they modulated by musical style, culture, and historical context?

It is a recurring notion from ancient Greece that there are *systematic relationships* between musical structure and expression of emotions. Plato argues that the Lydian mode is intimate, tender, and complaining whereas the Phrygian mode is ecstatic, passionate, and wild.[1] Plato is so concerned about the emotional effects of certain modes that he thinks they should be censored in order to not influence an impressionable youth negatively. (This seems oddly reminiscent of modern debates about "dangerous music".)

Numerous treatises featuring descriptions or prescriptions concerning which compositional and performance practices can be used to convey specific emotions have been published hence, especially during the baroque era (e.g., Bach, 1778/1985; Mattheson, 1739/1954).

Note, however, that these writings were based on personal experience, intuition, folk theory, or speculation. When it came to specifying the features

[1] Both Plato and Aristotle endorse the Dorian mode. For a good explanation of the Dorian mode, please see <http://www.simplifyingtheory.com/modes-ionian-dorian-phrygian-lydian-mixolydian-aeolian-locrian/>.

needed to express specific emotions, different scholars varied considerably in their prescriptions, and many of the proposals were quite vague. The prescriptions were, for obvious reasons, not tested and confirmed by means of scientific methods. Modern studies differ from previous treatises by using psychological experiments to uncover "causal relationships" between musical features and perceived emotions (Juslin & Lindström, 2010; see Chapter 9).

8.1 Which Features are Linked to Which Emotion Categories?

My review of links will initially focus on the five emotions most frequently studied thus far (*sadness, happiness, anger, tenderness*, and *fear*). I will also consider how musical features correlate with broader emotion dimensions, such as *tension, arousal*, and *valence*. I believe that these emotion categories and dimensions form the "core" of musical expression, though more complex emotions can also be conveyed depending on the circumstances (see Chapter 12).

The musical features investigated include variation in tempo, mode, harmony, tonality, pitch, melodic contour, melodic intervals, rhythm, sound level, timbre, timing, articulation, accents on specific notes, tone attacks and decays, and rate and speed of vibrato (in frequency and/or amplitude). A distinction is frequently made between more *composer*-related features, such as mode and pitch (usually indicated in the score of notated music), and more *performer*-related features, such as sound level and micro-timing (usually *not* specified in detail in the score).

Studies confirm that composition and performance tend to manipulate different features, and have different emotional capabilities (Quinto, Thompson, & Taylor, 2013)—but there is no sharp boundary between them. To illustrate, a composer might suggest a certain tempo by inserting an expression mark in the score, but the ultimate decision about tempo is made by a performer or conductor. Also, it is not clear that the distinction makes sense in certain genres of music where the difference between piece and performance is "blurred" (Dibben, 2014).

For that reason, I will summarize all features jointly, regardless of whether they occur in the score or not. Most music in the world is not score-based, anyway. I will describe the features using designations such as "high" or "low," "fast" or "slow," rather than in terms of precise values ("60 beats per minute"). This is because feature levels need to be interpreted in a *relative* sense; levels are strongly context-dependent. A "baseline" or "reference level" against which to assess the level of a feature (e.g., tempo) is usually provided by the genre. (A "slow" speed-metal song can be faster than a "fast" piece of Romantic piano music, for example.)

Baselines cannot only be ascribed to genre, though. As Leonard Meyer notes, "every piece of music establishes norms ... which are peculiar to that particular work" (Meyer, 1956, p. 246). Thus, a section of a piece that is considerably faster than a previous section of the same piece will tend to be perceived as "fast," regardless of any stylistic norm. For the very same reason, there are fairly strong "order effects" (see section 6.7) in listening tests: A researcher needs to counterbalance or randomize the presentation order of music pieces in order to obtain an unbiased estimate of the perceived expression.

In addition to norms provided by the genre or the piece (which are highly culturally variable), there are also more "absolute" norms. These are provided by the *embodiment* of emotion, and its expression (discussed further in Chapter 11). These absolute norms can explain why many studies of perception of emotional expression find relatively small effects of musical training and also why cross-cultural communication appears to be possible for at least *some* emotions (section 8.3).

Before beginning my review of the links between feature and emotion, let me repeat one key point: that perception of emotional expression in music depends not *merely* on features in the music but also on factors in the listener and the situation (and combinations of all these). I argue that, in a relative sense, the expression and perception of emotion is *more* strongly dependent on "just" musical features, than is arousal of felt emotion (cf. Part III), but there are still several moderators of the effects.

Let us now look closer at the feature–emotion links. (If you play a musical instrument, it can be helpful to have that instrument in your hands when you browse the results so that you can try out some of the emotions cited) Table 8.1 presents a wide range of musical features associated with the expression of five emotion categories. It might be helpful to consider a few music examples of each emotion category.

- For an example of *sadness*, listen to the fourth and final movement (Finale, marked *Adagio lamentoso*) of Symphony No. 6 in B Minor, Opus. 74, "Pathétique", by Pyotr Ilyich Tchaikovsky.
- For an example of *happiness*, listen to the third movement (*Scherzo*) of the the Piano Quintet in A Major, D. 667, by Franz Schubert (often referred to as "The Trout Quintet").
- For an example of *anger*, consider the second movement (*Allegro*) of Symphony No. 10 in E minor, Opus 93, by Dmitri Shostakovich.
- For an example of *tenderness*, consider the fourth movement (*Larghetto*) of Serenade for Strings in E Major, Opus 22, by Antonín Dvořák.
- For an example of *fear*, consider the opening of "II. Sérénade: Modérément animé," from Claude Debussy's Sonata for Cello and Piano in D Minor, L. 135. (For something more like a nervous breakdown, consider the start of Shostakovich's String Quartet No. 8 in C Minor, Opus 110, II. *Allegro Molto*.)

So far, most studies have analyzed only a few features, and the amount of study carried out on a specific feature is inversely related to the difficulty of quantifying it. Thus, most features in Table 8.1 are rather simple. More complex features, such as harmonic progression and musical form, remain yet to be thoroughly investigated in psychological experiments.

It should be acknowledged, however, that when more complex aspects *have* been studied, the results have sometimes been disappointing. For instance, attempts to test Deryck Cooke's (1959) theory about the meaning of specific melodic intervals (e.g., Gabriel, 1978; Hampson, 2000; Kaminska

Table 8.1 Summary of musical features used to express five different emotion categories.

Emotion	Feature
Happiness	*fast tempo, small tempo variability*, major mode, simple and consonant harmony, *medium-high sound level, small sound level variability*, high pitch, much pitch variability, wide pitch range, ascending pitch, perfect 4th and 5th intervals, *rising micro intonation, raised singer's formant, staccato articulation, large articulation variability*, smooth and fluent rhythm, *bright timbre, fast tone attacks, small timing variability, sharp contrasts between "long" and "short" notes, medium-fast vibrato rate, medium vibrato extent, micro-structural regularity*
Sadness	*slow tempo*, minor mode, dissonance, *low sound level, moderate sound level variability*, low pitch, narrow pitch range, descending pitch, *"flat" (or falling) intonation*, small intervals (e.g., minor 2nd), *lowered singer's formant, legato articulation, small articulation variability, dull timbre, slow tone attacks, large timing variability* (e.g., rubato), *soft contrasts between "long" and "short" notes, pauses, slow vibrato, small vibrato extent, ritardando, micro-structural irregularity*
Anger	*fast tempo, small tempo variability*, minor mode, atonality, dissonance, *high sound level, small loudness variability*, high pitch, moderate pitch variability, ascending pitch, major 7th and augmented 4th intervals, *raised singer's formant, staccato articulation, moderate articulation variability*, complex rhythm, sudden rhythmic changes (e.g., syncopations), *sharp timbre, spectral noise, fast tone attacks/decays, small timing variability, accents on tonally unstable notes, sharp contrasts between "long" and "short" notes, accelerando, medium-fast vibrato rate, large vibrato extent, micro-structural irregularity*
Fear	*fast tempo, large tempo variability*, minor mode, dissonance, *low sound level, large sound level variability, rapid changes in sound level*, high pitch, ascending pitch, very wide pitch range, large pitch contrasts, *staccato articulation, large articulation variability*, jerky rhythms, *soft timbre, very large timing variability, pauses, soft tone attacks, fast vibrato rate, small vibrato extent, micro-structural irregularity*
Tenderness	*slow tempo*, major mode, consonance, *medium-low sound level, small sound level variability*, low pitch, fairly narrow pitch range, *lowered singer's formant, legato articulation, small articulation variability, slow tone attacks, soft timbre, moderate timing variability, soft contrasts between long and short notes, accents on tonally stable notes, medium-fast vibrato, small vibrato extent, micro-structural regularity*

Note: Shown are the most common findings. Features set in *italics* can usually be modulated by the performer.
Adopted from Juslin & Lindström, 2010.

& Woolf, 2000) or to explore the effects of large-scale musical form (e.g., Konečni, 1984) have generally failed to establish predictable tendencies. Similarly, the common view that certain musical keys, such as E major, are linked to specific emotions has been disproved by experiments (e.g., Rigg, 1942; Powell & Dibben, 2005).

It may well be that most of the weight of the expression process is actually carried by gross features, such as overall tempo, pitch, and loudness, rather than more "subtle" aspects of the music. The latter aspects contribute to other aspects of the aesthetic value of the music (e.g., enhancing beauty; Part IV). The reason why some musical features may have a more decisive or consistent role than others is discussed in Chapter 11.

The results in Table 8.1 represent at least part of the code used to express emotions in music, but needless to say, the mere application of these patterns of features will not by itself result in "great" music. It *will* result in music with a clearly perceptible emotional expression, but as noted from the outset, there is much more to music than just emotion. There is, arguably, a well-founded concern that a too "formulaic" application of the feature patterns can result in "stereotypical" expression; the trick is to apply the features in a creative manner that avoids too many expressive clichés.[2]

8.2 Which Features are Linked to Which Emotion Dimensions?

Most studies have not taken into consideration the dynamic changes in emotional expression that may take place during a piece. Consider the dramatic expressive contrasts that occur, for instance, in Gustav Mahler's symphonies. Music researchers have devised new techniques to investigate such moment-to-moment changes in expression (for a review, see Schubert,

[2] Composer Jean-Claude Risset notes that "much popular music abuses of a few effects are akin to manipulation" (Cochrane, 2013a, p. 26).

2010), and these techniques may be used to capture various emotion dimensions (section 4.7).

Researchers have tried to reduce listeners' judgments of emotional expression to a set of more fundamental factors. The resulting dimensions have frequently corresponded to those obtained in other studies of emotions: *high arousal* versus *low arousal; positive valence* versus *negative valence; tension* versus *relaxation* (e.g., Kleinen, 1968; Nielzén & Cesarec, 1981; Wedin, 1972). However, Lage Wedin obtained a novel dimension that may be related to musical style (e.g., *solemnity* versus *triviality*), and that might reflect a distinction between "serious" and "popular" music in the music examples rated (Wedin, 1972).

Dimensional models (e.g., tension versus relaxation) may be ideal to capture the "vitality affects" discussed in section 6.6, but as far as specific emotions are concerned, dimensional models are generally too coarse to capture relevant differences in perceived emotions. Thus, for instance, the "circumplex" model (Russell, 1980), in terms of *arousal* and *valence*, does not adequately differentiate emotions such as *anger* and *fear*, which occupy the same position in the emotion space (Figure 4.1), yet they are expressed quite differently in music (Table 8.1). Furthermore, recall from Chapter 4 that dimensional models are inconsistent with the category boundaries seen in emotion perception (Laukka, 2005) and people's emotion representations (Haslam, 1995).

Nonetheless, I submit that dimensional approaches may be useful to explore what I will call *intrinsic* sources of emotional expression, which are strongly linked to the gradual unfolding of the local musical structure (see Chapter 12). We tend to perceive an increase in *tension* in musical segments that include an increase in dissonance, sound level, pitch, and harmonic or rhythmic complexity (e.g., syncopations); we tend to perceive *positive valence* in music with major mode, consonance, rhythmic regularity, and low complexity; and we tend to perceive increases in *arousal* when there are increases in tempo and sound level, combined with high pitch, staccato articulation, intervallic leaps, and large vibrato extent.

The dimensions are not wholly independent: an increase in *tension* will typically involve a decrease in *positive valence,* and many of the features associated with *arousal* are similarly associated with *tension*. Quite often, music features subtle and gradual changes along these dimensions (e.g., vitality affects) within a broader emotion category that remains the same throughout the musical segment (cf. Meyer, 1956).

Sometimes, listeners do not perceive any discrete emotion in the music. They merely perceive a certain level of "arousal" or, say, "positive valence." When this happens, it is usually because the musical features are too few (e.g., due to the limitations of a specific instrument) to enable more precise signification—some features are common to many emotions. Alternatively, it is because the features are varied in a manner that is inconsistent with a single emotion category. Composers and performers do not always aim for a clear and consistent emotional expression. Sometimes emotional ambiguity is more interesting to explore.

8.3 Are Musically Expressed Emotions Universal?

I have now considered a number of links between musical features and emotion categories or dimensions. Are these musical emotions invariant across different cultures? This (apparently) simple question is perhaps the one I encounter most frequently when I present my work to lay audiences. Still, the question is difficult to answer in a simple manner because there are both similarities and differences across cultures, depending on the focus and level of analysis.

There is a common notion that music is a "universal language" that can be understood across every culture (Watson, 1991). While it is true that we can *hear* all types of music and that we can potentially even enjoy most of the music, it is debatable whether we *understand* all music in quite the same way. That may, of course, be true even *within* cultures. We could probably argue all day about what it means to understand music, but there are definitely some occasions when an understanding is clearly in doubt.

Just to give you some idea of how difficult it may be to assess music from a different culture, I will recount an amusing incident from George

Harrison's benefit concert for Bangladesh in 1971 (a forerunner to Live Aid and similar star-studded concerts). Harrison was very fond of Indian music and invited his friend (and teacher), the sitar virtuoso Ravi Shankar, to open the concert. At the opening of Shankar's section (which may be heard on a "live" album from the concert), he and his fellow musicians play selected notes for a minute or two, after which the (predominately) Western audience hesitantly starts to applaud, to which Shankar says, "thank you, if you enjoy the tuning so much, I hope you will enjoy the music even more."

As philosopher Stephen Davies explains, there is a certain condition that needs to be fulfilled in order for a listener to grasp the emotional expression of a piece of music, namely that the person is "a qualified listener" (Davies, 2001). This may sound elitist, but Davies has something far more fundamental in mind:

> Qualified listeners are at home with the type of music in question, with its genre, style, and idiom. They know when the melody begins and ends, when the piece is over. They can recognise mistakes and can distinguish predictable from unusual continuations. They may not be able to articulate this knowledge, most of which is acquired through unreflective exposure to pieces of the relevant kind. (Davies, 2001, p. 29)

I noted earlier that when we rate the expression of a piece of music, we rely on a "baseline," "reference level," or "norm" against which to assess a certain feature level (e.g., tempo). The norm is often provided by the musical style or by the other sections of the same piece.

Thus, as Davies notes, one of the reasons that it could be difficult to interpret the emotional expression of a piece of music from a different culture is that we lack the required "reference levels" to hear, say, a tempo as "fast" or "slow." To understand the "norms" of the style is part of what it means to be a "qualified listener."

At the same time, I submit that *some* degree of universal or cross-cultural communication of emotions is possible, because we tend to rely also on more general and natural baselines of sorts, in terms of characteristics of

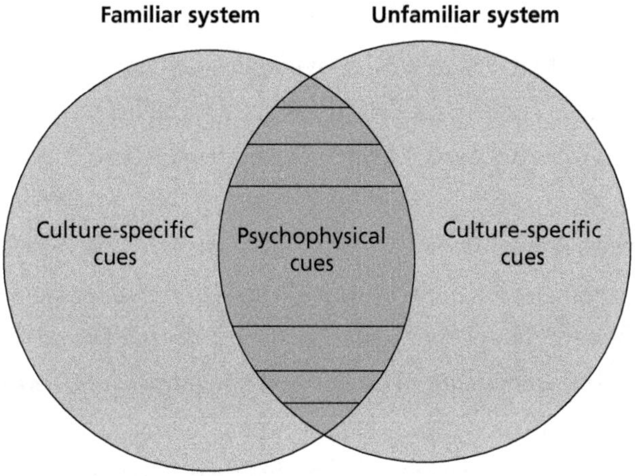

Figure 8.1 The cue-redundancy model (CRM).
Reproduced from Balkwill, L.-L, & Thompson, W. F. (1999). *A cross-cultural investigation of the perception of emotion in music: Psychophysical and cultural cues*. Music Perception, 17, 43-64. Copyright © 1999, University of California Press Journals.

emotional speech and pendular movements of our body.[3] Think of the typical speed of walking, your heartbeat, or the pitch of your speech. Based on such "embodied criteria," we may be able to hear *any* piece as generally fast or low in pitch.

The extent of cross-cultural specificity further depends on the precise features considered: "Some aspects of music (e.g., tonality, melody, and harmony) are relatively more culture-specific, whereas other aspects ... are more culture-independent (because they are based on nonverbal communication of emotion)" (Juslin, 1997b, p. 248). This is nicely illustrated in the so-called cue-redundancy model proposed by Laura-Lee Balkwill and Bill Thompson (1999) (see Figure 8.1).

In short, the model shows that when we are confronted with an unfamiliar culture, there are both "psychophysical cues" that are universal and overlap between the two musical systems and "culture-specific cues" that are not shared by the two cultures. Emotion recognition will be possible to the extent that the culture-overlapping part of the cues is not too small.

[3] The common expression mark, *Andante*, in a musical score roughly corresponds to a moderate walking speed.

With this model in place, let us now consider some evidence.[4] Early studies did not offer any definitive evidence—except perhaps of the difficulties in conducting cross-cultural research. A telling example is a study by Morey (1940), who used a gramophone to play five pieces of classical music, chosen to express *fear, reverence, rage, love,* and *no particular emotion* to Loma villagers in Zealua, native West Africans. He asked them about the expression suggested to them by the pieces. Nine participants left without answering. We might speculate that they found either the task or the music strange or incomprehensible. The answers provided by the remaining participants showed little correspondence to the intended emotions.

Subsequent studies have provided mixed results, partly dependent on the type of music used. By selecting pieces that are perceived as expressive of emotion via simple features such as tempo, loudness, and timbre—what Thompson and Balkwill referred to as psychophysical cues—you may find a fair level of cross-cultural agreement, as in the meta-analysis of music performance studies conducted by Juslin and Laukka (2003). On the other hand, by selecting pieces whose expression derives mainly from more complex—and arguably culture-specific—features of the composition, such as harmony, you will observe a larger "in-group advantage" (Gregory & Varney, 1996).

What I am trying to convey here is that without a representative sample of pieces (a tall order indeed) you could quite easily support either position—cross-cultural invariance or diversity—simply depending on how you select the music. This shows why it is so difficult to provide a straight answer to the question of whether emotions expressed in music are universal or not. It depends.

One view, however, can most definitely be ruled out by now, namely the notion that musical expression of emotions is determined *only* by cultural influences (enculturation). If expression and perception of emotion were determined only by culture, then we would expect to find that listeners are completely unable to recognize emotions in music from a foreign culture.

[4] For a more extensive review, see Thompson and Balkwill (2010).

This is not the case. Instead, current evidence indicates that there *is* cross-cultural recognition of basic emotions in music (e.g., Balkwill & Thompson, 1999; Fritz et al., 2009; Laukka, Eerola, Thingujam, Yamasaki, & Beller, 2013).

It appears safe to conclude that emotional expression in music involves *both* "universal" and "culture-specific" aspects. This is what we would expect from the different types of "coding" involved (Chapter 11). One can speculate about the reasons for cross-cultural differences in the types of music people play and listen to. These include a complex set of factors, such as climate, social organization, technological development, and history (Gabrielsson, 2016).

Regardless of their origin, one may conceptualize the cross-cultural differences in perceived emotional expression as a special case of a more general principle, which applies also *within* cultures, namely the dependence on musical style.

8.4 Is Emotional Expression Dependent on Style?

The short answer is, of course, yes. How could it not be? Emotional expression is dependent on musical features (see Table 8.1), and certain features are characteristic of particular styles (Rentfrow & Gosling, 2003). Speed metal? Fast tempo. Romantic piano music? Rubato. Blues? Pentatonic scales. Opera? Wide vocal vibrato. Baroque? Terrace dynamics. To some extent, then, different styles *must* have different expressive characteristics.

It would be a grave mistake, however, to think that this observation necessarily invalidates the code description shown in Table 8.1. I cannot think of any example of a style where, for example, *sadness* is expressed by the use of major mode, staccato articulation, rising pitch contours, and fast tempo. As will be made clear in Chapter 11, this code is far from arbitrary; it has deep evolutionary origins.

More plausibly, style will influence the finer details and nuances of the emotional expression. We can perhaps talk of "expressive dialects" of specific styles, such that models of emotional expression in a particular genre will not "map" perfectly onto the models of a different genre (Eerola, 2011)[5]. In addition, there may be certain *conventions* for expressing emotion which are associated with a particular style (e.g., baroque music) and are "laid on top" of the overall code presented earlier (further discussed in section 12.2).

Still, there is little evidence to suggest that the *major* portion of the expressive code used to express specific emotions in today's music world derives from style-specific aspects. When some musicologists claim to have found evidence of strong stylistic differences, it is usually when they have analyzed expressive aspects *other* than the emotions (Fabian, Timmers, & Schubert, 2014).

Few studies in music psychology have investigated stylistic aspects of *emotional* expression (but for some recent excellent musicological examples, see Leech-Wilkinson, 2006, 2013; Spitzer, 2010, 2013). There are several ways in which musical style may influence emotional expression.

First, style is important simply because expressions are often evaluated by reference to a norm constituted by the typical characteristics of a style or genre (e.g., Meyer, 1956; Robinson & Hatten, 2012). I hypothesize that listeners tend to "adjust" their judgments of emotional expression based on their implicit or explicit knowledge about the typical characteristics of the style in question. If we are unfamiliar with the style, it will be difficult to make such adjustments.

However, analyses by musicologists often underestimate the problem that there are many different norms that can be used by listeners, and that it is not easy to know which one is relevant in a specific case. We may call this "the reference class problem." In listening to, say, Beethoven's String Quartet No. 14 in C-sharp minor, Opus 131, which reference class is the listener using as the norm for his or her judgments? Is it the stylistic features of "classical music," or "Viennese classicism," or "Beethoven's music," or "Beethoven's late quartets?" (Fortunately, judgments of expression in music do not rely *only* on stylistic norms.)

[5] In the case of Eerola's study (2011), however, it should be noted that it focused on emotion dimensions rather than emotion categories; that it used stepwise regression (where the specific order in which features are entered influences the results) instead of simultaneous regression; and that its models were probably "over-fitted" to the specific styles. Unit-weight models (Dawes & Corrigan, 1974) will probably work much better across styles and could bear more similarities to how humans make judgments.

Second, style may influence which emotions are usually expressed in the music (Levinson, 2015). Some readers might find it odd to conceive of music expressing an emotion such as anger. However, consider, for instance, B.B. King's angry vocal delivery of the lines "I gave you seven children/And now you want give them back" on the song "How Blue Can You Get" from the classic album *Live at the Regal*. In fact, an angry expression is common in some genres such as heavy metal: "it's a very aggressive music, and that's a big part of it" (Steve Harris, guitarist in Iron Maiden; Driver, 2001, p. 304).

Genres are linked to many other emotions. Punk music often expresses *contempt* for society (e.g., "I'm a Lazy Sod" by the Sex Pistols). Prokofiev's inclusion of "wrong notes" in an otherwise traditional musical context gives his works an expression of *sarcasm* (Pogue & Speck, 1997). In contrast, the classic pop album *Pet Sounds* by the Beach Boys has been described as expressive of *spiritual tenderness* (Irvin & McLear, 2000, p. 64). Consider the expression of *triumph* at the end of Gustav Mahler's Symphony No. 2, which would hardly be possible to achieve in quite the same way by, say, a folk singer with an acoustic guitar.

Hence, when drawing conclusions about which emotions are expressed in music, we need to remember that the prevalence of emotions depends on style and context; to some extent, expressive styles reflect what the music is "for" (the *functions* of the music; see Part III). To take an obvious example, the music used at funerals will tend to have a different emotional expression than the music used in nightclubs.

8.5 Is Emotional Expression Dependent on Historical Context?

My earlier comments suggest a third way in which musical style may influence emotional expression: the historical context. Are there stylistic changes in emotional expression over time?

Views on expression and emotion have clearly changed considerably over time (Benestad, 1978; Gabrielsson & Juslin, 2003; Hudson, 1994; Ratner,

1980), as have the features of the music themselves. Again, I do not believe that the "foundation," the musical features summarized in Table 8.1, have changed. (To illustrate, *sadness* was not generally expressed with *fast* tempo and *major* mode 200 years ago.) The changes over time are more plausibly a matter of degree and manner of implementation.

Thus, for instance, Daniel Leech-Wilkinson has observed that preferences for specific means of *emphasis* have changed: "A prominent note in a score that in 1910 was emphasized by sliding up to it from the note below, in 1950 might have been emphasized by vibrating on it, and in 1990 by increasing and decreasing its amplitude" (Leech-Wilkinson, 2006, p. 60). In other words, although the inclination to emphasize certain notes is constant over time, the specific means to achieve this may differ. In that sense, "almost every aspect of performance style has changed over the past century" (p. 42). Why is this the case?

For one thing, views on musical expression and emotion do not occur in a vacuum: they are influenced by the concurrent views on affect in science and society, more generally. (Compare the hydraulic theory of emotions of Freud during the nineteenth century with current brain theories of emotion.) The history of emotions (Plamper, 2015) has influenced discourse on music and emotion to a considerable extent.

Music theorists are keenly aware of broad changes in expressive style over time: the music of the Baroque was perceived by audiences as highly emotional (allegedly—since we cannot run experiments!), with composers/performers using plenty of tricks such as rich ornamentation to enhance the expressive intensity of the music.

Expression of emotions during "classicism" was more restrained, reserved, and controlled. A fair assessment is that Beethoven's intense music brought "classicism" into the era of "romanticism," shifting the focus again towards emotional expression.[6] In addition, the Romantic composers

[6] The composer Camille Saint-Saëns suggested that what gives J. S. Bach and Mozart a place apart is that these composers "never sacrificed form to expression" (Watson, 1991, p. 68). Personally, I prefer Beethoven because he never sacrificed expression to form.

brought a stronger focus on "subjective" and "personal" expression, often getting inspiration from mother nature (e.g., thunderstorms).

So-called contemporary music which followed at the beginning of the twentieth century tended to abandon tonality altogether, and was described by several music critics as expressive of "ugly" emotions, bordering on "mental unhealth" (Slonimsky, 1969; see also Huron, 2006).

Glenn Schellenberg and Christian von Scheve examined whether two emotional features (mode, tempo) in American popular music have changed over time, using a sample featuring more than 1,000 Top 40 recordings, spanning five decades (Schellenberg & von Scheve, 2012). The authors concluded that there was an increase in the use of the minor mode and a decrease in mean tempo, which suggests that popular music became generally more sad-sounding over time.

To some degree, historical changes in expressive style reflect technical developments. One clear example relates to loudness (or, more precisely, sound pressure level). When the *piano forte* was introduced, it enabled a far greater amount of dynamic contrast in the music. Beethoven exploited this effect in his piano sonatas to enhance the emotion intensity.

Consider how the introduction of electric portable microphones enabled singers such as Frank Sinatra to develop a much softer and more intimate "crooning" singing style. Think of how the Marshall stacks (i.e., piles of guitar amplifiers) of the late 1960s and early 1970s enabled the development of an aggressive style of "hard rock", which would have been unthinkable with the thin-sounding amplifiers of the early 1960s. The band Cream has been credited with starting this development, giving birth to hard rock. (The trio's drummer, Ginger Baker, was not flattered, suggesting that they should have had an abortion.)

Timing aspects have also changed as a result of the technical development. A peculiar form of expression began to occur on the scene when artists combined samples from different musical performances—sometimes from completely different genres—into new pieces of music. These tracks would have odd "grooves" and expressive patterns that would arguably never occur in a "real" ensemble performance, simply because the different parts did not quite fit together. For better or worse, new types of expression resulted.

In summary, then, styles of emotional expression clearly change over time, but historical changes in expression are mostly beyond the scope of a psychological analysis because we cannot collect empirical data from events that occurred in the distant past. This will become clear if we consider how psychologists investigate musical features.

CHAPTER 9

HOW ARE MUSIC AND EMOTION LINKS STUDIED?

When trying to establish links between musical features and specific emotions, the first step is usually to conduct an experiment in which listeners rate the emotional expression of different excerpts of music—either music from commercial recordings or pieces created specifically for the study. The next step is to extract musical features associated with emotion categories.

9.1 In What Ways Can Relevant Features Be Extracted?

One approach is to analyze the *musical score* of the pieces (e.g., Gundlach, 1935; Imberty, 1979; Thompson & Robitaille, 1992). This may offer rather substantial information about potentially relevant features. Yet, not all important expressive features are indicated in the score. In addition, of course, not all music is notated.

A second approach is to rely on *experts*, such as music theorists and musicians, asking them to rate various aspects of the musical structure (e.g., Watson, 1942; Wedin, 1972). This may help to obtain additional musical features of importance.

A third approach is to measure *acoustic parameters* of the music (e.g., sound level, timing, frequency spectrum of the timbre), using dedicated computer software[1] (e.g., Juslin, 1997a; Schubert, 2004). This strategy is especially useful to capture more subtle features of a music performance (e.g., timing patterns; see Chapter 13). Acoustic measurements of musical features may produce results that differ from those of human participants, since there is no one-to-one correspondence between physical measures and subjective impressions.

The fourth and final approach is the most reliable if we wish to draw clear conclusions about cause and effect: One can manipulate specific musical features in *synthesized* (computerized) performances to evaluate how they influence a listener's judgments of emotional expression. This is, in fact, the only way to evaluate objectively the causal effect of individual features.

To see why this is so, consider the following: the musical features of a piece of music rarely vary one at the time. More commonly, various features change in tandem (e.g., the volume may increase when the tempo increases). I will refer to this as an *intercorrelation* between features. (For explicit reports of such intercorrelations, see Table 2 in Juslin, 2000a; see also Juslin, 1997a; Kratus, 1993). Intercorrelations make it difficult for researchers to disentangle or isolate the possible causal effects of individual features.

9.2 How Can Causal Effects Be Tested? Music Synthesis

Analyses of pieces of music have suggested several features that musicians—composers or performers—can use to express a specific emotion (Table 8.1). However, such analyses do not by themselves prove that listeners actually *use* all of these features in their judgments of emotional expression (Juslin, 1997b).

Thus, for instance, it is possible that certain features that have been reported to be expressive of specific emotions simply happen to *co-occur* with other features that "do the job," without themselves contributing to the

[1] A useful software package that may be accessed for free for research is PRAAT (<http://www.fon.hum.uva.nl/praat/>). It is intended for the analysis of emotions in speech but covers many features of importance for music. Another tool that is uniquely adapted to music but is more difficult to use is the MIR toolbox (Lartillot, Toiviainen, & Eerola, 2008).

listener's judgment. To test the validity of hypotheses regarding the causal role of features derived from analysis, it is necessary to conduct listening tests that use synthesized stimuli. (For this reason, a music psychologist must regard music-theoretical analyses of emotional meaning in music as "speculative" or "preliminary": It has not (yet) been shown that the features analyzed have a causal effect on listeners' judgments.)

Music synthesis is a technique of systematically manipulating and/or editing pieces of music on computers and synthesizers, and is an important "tool" in studies of emotional expression. It allows a researcher to "control" every feature of the music, which is necessary in order to evaluate the effect of a musical feature

There are two different approaches to synthesis of expression in music, which may answer distinct types of questions. Based on the distinction introduced by Brunswik (1956), I have called them *representative design* and *systematic design* (Juslin, 1997b). It is the systematic design that truly enables a proper evaluation of cause and effect. First, however, let us have a look at the representative design.

Representative design means that one tries to "recreate" the emotional expression of a music performance by programming a computer to play in exact accordance with emotion-specific patterns of musical features obtained in previous studies (cf. Chapter 8). Ideally, the musical patterns used to synthesize the expression should be representative of real pieces in the sense that they display similar statistical characteristics (e.g., range) with regard to their musical features.

The first attempt to deliberately recreate emotional expressions in a representative manner was a study I conducted in the mid-1990s (Juslin, 1997b), for which I had to go through the arduous task of programming an old, analog synthesizer, the *Synklavier*. (Benny Andersson used this instrument to compose songs for ABBA in the 1980s.)

I manipulated the tempo, sound level, frequency spectrum (timbre), articulation, tone attacks, timing (durational contrasts, ritardando), vibrato extent and speed, and pauses of the music performances in accordance with previous findings (see Table 8.1). I could show for the first time that it is

		Tempo		
		slow	medium	fast
Pitch	high	high pitch slow tempo	high pitch medium tempo	high pitch fast tempo
	low	low pitch slow tempo	low pitch medium tempo	low pitch fast tempo

Figure 9.1 Example of factorial experimental design.

possible to program a computer to communicate specific emotions so that these are recognized by naïve listeners with an accuracy similar to—or even higher—than the accuracy achieved by a human performer (Juslin, 1997b, Exp. 1; see also Bresin & Friberg, 2000).

Such synthesized pieces may be regarded as "computational models," which confirm the "overall" validity of the code description by showing that it really "works" with regard to listeners. However, such models do not prove that listeners really are *using* all features in their judgments because just as in a human performance, the musical features are entangled.[2]

In order to unambiguously attribute the variance in a listener's judgments of emotions to *individual* features, one must use a *systematic* design, or, more specifically, a *factorial design*. This is where a synthesis approach shows its true potential.

An experiment using a factorial design presents all possible combinations of the levels of the musical features manipulated (see Figure 9.1). This removes all intercorrelations between features, making it possible to assess the causal effect of every feature. Notice that features are manipulated systematically, changing only one at a time while keeping other features constant. (Not all musical features described earlier in Table 8.1 have been tested in this manner yet.)

[2] Moreover, such synthesized performances do not sound as musically satisfying as human performances do, because they lack other aspects of musical expression that are also important (see Chapter 13).

An early attempt to manipulate features independently was made by Klaus Scherer and James Oshinsky (1977). They synthesized eight-tone sequences using a Moog synthesizer, and manipulated them in two levels regarding amplitude variation, pitch level, pitch contour, pitch variation, tempo, envelope, and filtration cut-off level. Listeners then rated the stimuli on three scales corresponding to emotion dimensions (*pleasantness, activity, potency*). They also indicated whether each version expressed any of the following seven basic emotions: *anger, boredom, disgust, fear, happiness, sadness*, and *surprise*.

Similarly, I (Juslin, 1997b, Exp. 2) manipulated synthesized performances of "Nobody Knows" with regard to tempo (slow, medium, fast), sound level (low, medium, high), timbre (soft, bright, sharp), articulation (legato, staccato), and tone attacks (slow, fast), using a factorial design. Listeners rated the performances on six adjective scales: *happy, sad, angry, fearful, tender*, and *expressive*.

Both studies showed that listeners' judgments of each emotion can be accurately predicted, based on a linear and additive combination of the features. (These results were replicated by Juslin & Lindström, 2010; and Eerola, Friberg, & Bresin, 2013). By demonstrating that expression of emotions in music can be modeled statistically, these seminal studies stimulated efforts in computer science to model musical emotions using machine-learning techniques (e.g., Yang & Chen, 2011).

9.3 Interactions Between Features: Fewer and Smaller Than Believed?

We have seen that a number of musical features are relevant to our understanding of music's expression of emotion; a single feature is hardly ever sufficient to suggest a specific emotion. It seems to be *the combined effect* of several features that does the trick. But do these features interact with each other? And, if so, are the interactions important?

We often use the word "interaction" in everyday life, but *interaction* bears a precise meaning in statistics. It means not only that the effects of the features operate simultaneously, but also that their results are "non-additive": their combined effect is not just a sum of their individual effects. Put differently, an interaction means that the effect of one feature (e.g., tempo) partly depends on the value of another feature (e.g., articulation).

Some researchers believe that the interactions are the most important aspect of the emotional expression process (e.g., Gabrielsson, 2016). Alf Gabrielsson and Erik Lindström argue that "music abounds with interactions" (Gabrielsson & Lindström, 2001, p. 243). Still, this issue has not been the subject of much research to date. A few studies have obtained evidence of interactions between pitch and rhythm (e.g., Schellenberg, Krysciak, & Campbell, 2000) and between tonal progression and rhythm (e.g., Lindström, 2003, 2006). However, the range of features explored in these studies was limited, which meant that they were unable to estimate the *relative* contribution of the interactions (as compared to the individual effects of the features) to the overall expression process.

An extensive attempt to explore the role of feature interactions was made in a study conducted in Uppsala (Juslin & Lindström, 2010). Eight features (pitch, mode, melodic progression, rhythm, tempo, sound level, articulation, and timbre) were systematically varied in a factorial design by means of synthesis. Musically trained participants were asked to judge the resulting 384 versions of music on emotion scales. Relationships between musical features and listener judgments were modeled using multiple regression analysis. What we found was that only a small fraction of the total number of possible interactions made any significant contribution to the listeners' judgments.

There are several types of interaction that *could* have occurred in the results, yet there were no "catalytic" interactions (where two features are effective only when they occur together), "terminative" interactions (where the combined effect of two features is not greater than that of either feature by itself), or "antagonistic" interactions (where combining two features leads to their effects counteracting each other; Neale & Liebert, 1986).

Instead, the typical scenario was that the effect of one musical feature was moderated by that of another. Some interactions recurred across many models: tempo × articulation interactions contributed to four of the five regression models and was particularly strongly correlated with judgments of *fear* and *happiness.* (For example, the effect of tempo on *happiness* ratings was particularly strong when it was combined with staccato—as opposed to legato—articulation.)

Still, the major conclusion was that the lion's share of the variance was accounted for by the simple main effects. In the regression models for *happiness* and *sadness,* which may be the two most commonly expressed emotions in music, the main effects could explain 83–88% of the variance in listeners' judgments; adding the interaction effects to the models enabled us to explain only an additional 4–7% of the variance. We concluded that although there *are* interactions between features, we should not overstate their importance: they may be fewer and smaller than previously believed.

Testing interactions between musical features requires use of factorial designs (Figure 9.1). Lack of independent manipulation of cues could explain why several of the early studies of emotional expression in music have concluded, somewhat unjustifiably, that there are strong interactions between musical features. Note that the occurrence of a fast tempo in a piece of music rated by listeners as *sad* is not evidence of an interaction, say that the effect of tempo has been modified by the musical context. The *happy* effect of the fast tempo could simply have been "overridden" by a large number of *other* additive features, which indicated a *sad* piece. The piece might have been rated as even more *sad,* had the tempo been slow too.[3]

We have seen that music synthesis is a valuable tool to study expression. The downside of computer manipulations—"the dark side of the Moog," if you like—is that they may sound "artificial." They lack "ecological validity," as researchers like to put it. (This is abundantly clear for anyone who has heard the original music examples on the Moog synthesizer used by

[3] Some of the inconsistencies in the literature concerning links between musical features and emotions (Gabrielsson & Lindström, 2001) could well be due to this problem.

Scherer and Oshinsky (1977); "musically sophisticated" are not the words that spring to mind!) The best strategy may be to *combine* analysis of real pieces of music with synthesis of systematically manipulated pieces, so as to benefit from the advantages of each one: the ecological validity of the former, the statistical conclusion validity of the latter.

CHAPTER 10

VIEWING MUSIC THROUGH A BRUNSWIKIAN LENS

Studies of emotional expression in music present some puzzling findings, which may only be explained if the nature of the process is examined in greater detail. Consider again the results summarized in Table 8.1. At first sight, these findings might appear to suggest that musicians and listeners simply rely on *emotion-specific patterns of musical features*. However, the truth is more complicated.

First, consider the fact that different musical instruments will offer different opportunities for varying musical features. *If* the process depends on specific patterns of features, what happens if not all features can be varied? Does the whole communication process break down?

Second, a musical feature may be used in a similar manner in more than just one emotional expression. For instance, a fast tempo could occur in both expressions of *happiness* and expressions of *anger*. This implies that a single feature is not an 100% reliable indicator of any given emotion.

Furthermore, what Table 8.1 presents is the most *common* result for each feature. In reality, there is a lot of inconsistency in the findings, some of which are due to stylistic differences, individual differences between composers or performers, and the fact that musicians need to strike a balance between many aesthetic goals (e.g., beauty, novelty; see Chapter 28), of which emotional expression is only one.

The consequence is that the musical features in actual music rarely correspond precisely to the "ideal" patterns presented in Table 8.1. In other words, there is considerable *variability* in the features that occur across various pieces with the *same* perceived emotional expression. From this perspective, it is beginning to look more and more like a mystery that the communication of emotion in music can work at all. This, then, is another paradox of musical emotions:

PARADOX 3: Emotions can generally be communicated accurately from a musician to a listener based on musical features, despite the fact that different circumstances offer very different features to the performer's and listener's disposal.

As a PhD student in the early 1990s, I struggled to come to terms with this paradoxical nature of emotional expression (which at the time I studied mainly in the context of the performance of music). What I needed was a "tool" to help explain the peculiar characteristics of emotional expression in music. (Some were so peculiar that researchers did not even seem to notice that they were so.)

10.1 What is Brunswik's Lens Model?

Help came from quite unexpected quarters during a course on visual perception as part of my undergraduate training in Uppsala. Amongst the usual "heavyweights" in perception research, such as David Marr and James J. Gibson, there was another, more obscure researcher, whose chapter was not even included in the required reading.

His name was Egon Brunswik, and his theory of visual perception appeared to be regarded as old-fashioned and as something of a failure. (It later found a new home in studies of cognitive judgment, thanks to the pioneering work of Professor Kenneth Hammond at the University of Colorado at Boulder) However, when I read about this theory—out of curiosity—I noticed that his way of approaching visual perception was a perfect fit with the problem I was studying as a PhD student: how various musical features contribute to the expression of emotions.

As a result, I suggested that we should apply his so-called lens model to the issue of musical communication (Juslin, 1995, 1997a, 2000a). The original version of the lens model (Brunswik, 1956) aimed to depict the relationship between an "organism" and its "environment," and, in particular, how visual impressions are "mediated" by a number of imperfect "cues" in the environment that the organism is utilizing to make "inferences" about perceptual objects.

The (modified) lens model in Figure 10.1 shows how the performer *encodes* (i.e., expresses) emotions by means of a set of acoustic *cues* (e.g., variation of tempo, sound level, or timbre) that are *probabilistic* (i.e., uncertain), albeit partly redundant. The emotions are *decoded* (i.e., recognized) by the listener, who utilizes these same cues to infer or recognize the expression.

Why are the cues described as probabilistic? It is because, as I explained earlier, they are not perfectly reliable indicators of the intended expression. For instance, a high sound level (volume) is not a perfectly reliable indicator of *happiness* expressions, because a high sound level occurs also in *anger* expressions. The relationships between cues and emotions are merely correlational—they have a *tendency* to co-occur—but there is no one-to-one mapping. If you hear, for instance, a fast tempo in a musical performance, this increases the probability that its expression was intended to express *happiness,* but it does not guarantee it.

What are the practical consequences if cues are probabilistic? It means that performers and listeners have to *combine* many cues for reliable communication to occur. This is not a just matter of "pattern matching," however. If it were, musicians would be in trouble, because in many circumstances, they cannot achieve the exact patterns presented in Table 8.1.

Fortunately, as explained in Chapter 9, the cues contribute in a largely *additive* fashion to listeners' judgments: Each expressive cue is neither necessary, nor sufficient, but the larger the number of cues used by a musician, the more reliable the communication (Juslin, 1995).

Further help comes from the *redundancy* of the cues. Redundancy means that more than one cue can convey somewhat similar or overlapping information (they are intercorrelated, to use the more technical term from Chapter 9). The redundancy among the cues partly reflects how sounds are produced on musical instruments. A harder string attack on the electric guitar will produce a tone that is both louder and sharper in timbre. But the redundancy also reflects how humans like to perform music.

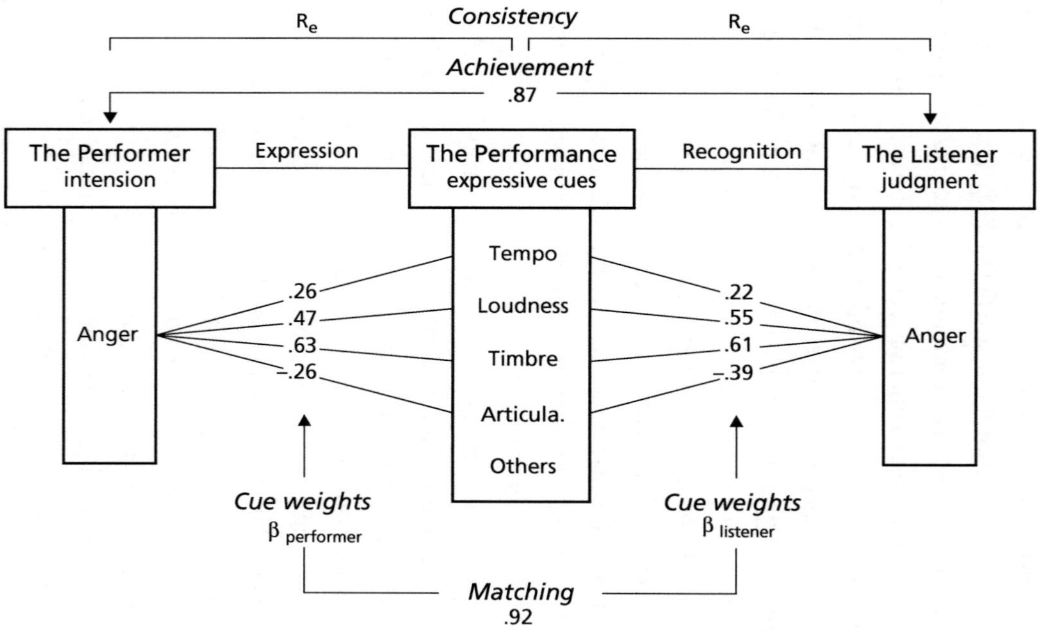

Figure 10.1 The lens model of musical communication.

For instance, musicians have a clear tendency to link tempo and sound level. If you listen to a slow piece of Romantic piano music, such as Robert Schumann's "Träumerei," you may notice that when the tempo slows down, the sound level follows suit. This is merely one of many intercorrelations between musical features. This redundancy has both pros and cons, but for now suffice to say that when many cues convey similar information, the communicative process becomes more "robust"; that is, it becomes less sensitive to deviations from an "ideal" use of features.

10.2 How Can the Communicative Process Be Quantified?

The correlational and partly redundant nature of the cues may be nicely captured by applying a statistical analysis technique termed multiple regression analysis to either side of the lens model, performer and listener (see Juslin, 2000a, for examples). Thus, one can obtain a precise description of how musicians and listeners, respectively, use the cues. The following concepts in the lens model are key to understand the nature of the process (see Figure 10.1):

- *Achievement* (r_a) refers to the relationship between the performer's expressive intention (e.g., intending to express *sadness*) and the listener's judgment (e.g., perceiving *sadness*). It is a measure of how well the performer succeeds in communicating a given emotion to listeners.
- *Cue weight* (β_1, β_2, β_3, ...) refers to the strength of the relationship between an individual cue (e.g., articulation), on the one hand, and a performer's intentions or a listener's judgments, on the other. Cue weights illustrate how the individual cues are used by performers and listeners respectively (e.g., that the performer is using a slow tempo to express *sadness*).
- *Matching* (G) refers to the degree of similarity between the performer's and the listener's use of cues, respectively. For effective

communication to occur, the performer's use of cues (i.e., his or her cue weights) must be reasonably "matched" to the listener's use of cues: they must "speak the same language." (Failure to do so can be due to cultural differences in use of cues; see section 8.3)

- *Consistency* (R_e, R_s) refers to the degree of consistency with which the performer and listeners, respectively, are able to use cues (that they are systematic and rely on the same strategy throughout). All things equal, the communication will be more effective if the cues are used consistently. Professional performers can be highly consistent (Juslin, 2000a), but amateur performers vary considerably in their consistency (Juslin & Laukka, 2000), partly due to their imperfect control over individual musical features.

It is possible to obtain a precise statistical measure of each of these concepts. I have further shown that the lens model equation (LME) developed by Hursch, Hammond, and Hursch (1964) in the context of studies of cognitive judgment can be used to relate mathematically models of performers and listeners (Juslin, 2000a; the lens model equation is shown in the Appendix).

Such an analysis enables us to explain why the communication of an emotion was successful or not. Was it because the performer uses the cues in a different way from that of the listener? For example, did the performer perhaps use *staccato* articulation to express *tenderness*, when *legato* articulation would have been more effective? Or was it because the performer used the cues in an inconsistent manner? As you may have guessed, this type of analysis could benefit the training of tomorrow's musicians (Juslin et al., 2006).

My "original" version of the lens model was limited to performance cues (Juslin, 1995), but listeners' perception of emotion may also be affected by an interplay between composer and performer cues. Thus, we have outlined an *expanded lens model* (Juslin & Lindström, 2010; see Figure 10.2), in which both composer cues and performance cues are featured in order to make it possible to study their relative contribution. Interactions between performer cues and composer cues may also be included as separate predictors in the regression models.

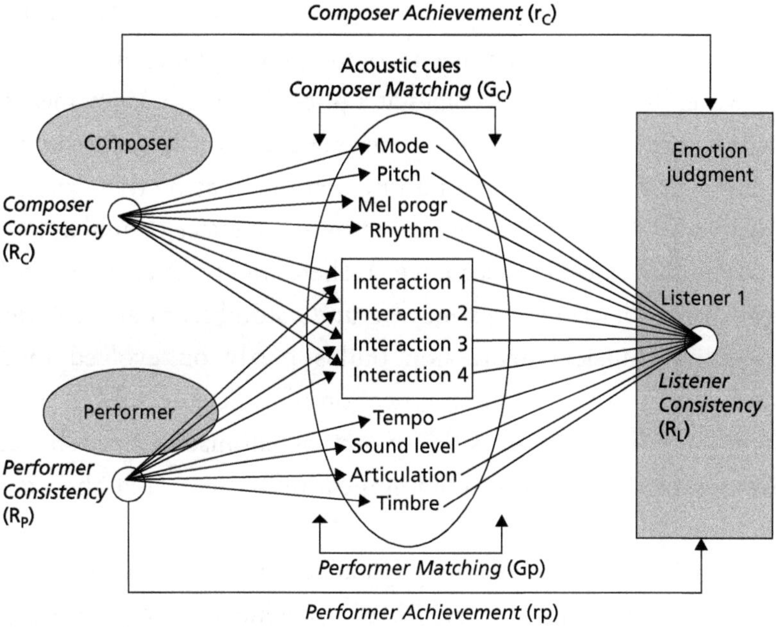

Figure 10.2 The expanded lens model (ELM).
Reproduced from Juslin, P. N., & Lindström, E. (2010). *Musical expression of emotions: Modeling listeners' judgments of composed and performed features.* Music Analysis, 29, 334–364. (Special Issue on Music and Emotion)© 2011 The Authors. Music Analysis © 2011 Blackwell Publishing Ltd.

10.3 What Can We Learn from the Lens Model?

The lens model might appear simple. Even so, it has some important implications for studies of communication. If the cues are redundant to some degree, more than one way of using the cues could lead to a similarly high level of decoding accuracy. This is because different cues may "substitute" for one another, so-called *vicarious functioning* (Juslin, 2000a; cf. Brunswik, 1956). To illustrate, if a performer is unable to vary one feature in the way needed to convey a particular emotion, then he or she can manipulate another (redundant) feature even more to "compensate" for the missing effect of the first feature.

The lens model can explain why there is accurate communication of emotions, even when the cues are used inconsistently across different performers or pieces of music. Multiple cues that are partly redundant yield a robust emotion-communicative system that is "forgiving" towards deviations from (nominally) optimal use of the cues (Juslin, 2001).

However, the robustness comes at a price. The redundancy means that similar information is conveyed by several cues, which limits the amount of unique or non-overlapping information that may be transmitted. This explains why emotional expression in music operates mainly in terms of broad emotion categories (section 6.5). There is a "limited bandwidth."[1]

The above characteristics may be understood from an evolutionary perspective. Musical expression builds partly on evolved mechanisms for the non-verbal communication of basic emotions in the voice (Chapter 11). Selection pressures in our ancient history have shaped the priorities of this emotion communication system, and they favored redundancy.

Brunswik's words—concerning visual perception but clearly apt here—were that this type of system prioritizes "smallness of error at the expense of the highest frequency of precision," which leads to "compromise and falling short of precision, but also the relative infrequency of drastic error" (Brunswik, 1956, pp. 145–146).

Can you see how a communication system with this characteristic may have survival value? Ultimately, it is more important to avoid making serious mistakes (e.g., mistaking *anger* for *happiness*) than to have an ability to make subtle discriminations among states (e.g., reliably detecting all different kinds of *happiness*). The concerns of a musician in our modern world are, of course, rather different, but musical expression of emotions is still partly constrained by ancient psychological mechanisms, for better or worse.

In sum, the redundancy amongst musical features (cues) might help to explain why musical expression tends to involve broad emotion categories (as opposed to very specific and fine-grained categories) and can also resolve the "paradox" that musical communication of basic emotions is accurate,

[1] This is true mainly for the "core" layer of emotional expression (iconic coding) discussed later in Chapter 11.

despite variability in patterns of musical features that composers and performers use to express emotions. Vicarious functioning of musical features opens the door for personal creativity, while also preserving the ability to communicate emotions in a widely recognized manner. Musical expression is simultaneously individual and universal.

CHAPTER 11

THE VOICE OF ANGELS?

Iconic Expression

I have outlined a number of musical features that may be used to express emotions, such as *happiness* and *tenderness*. I have also shown that these features have certain characteristics that constrain their use, but I must still explain *why* and *how* the features come to denote emotions in the first place. (Saying that music expressive of *sadness* has low pitch does not explain *why* low pitch is associated with *sadness*.)

Such an account can help us to resolve the second paradox of music and emotion. Recall that some authors regard musical expression as something "subjective" and "ambiguous," whereas others as something that involves a great degree of inter-individual agreement. If we explore more closely how musical expression actually "works," we will see that there is some truth to each of these perspectives. Music contains distinct "layers" of expression, some of which have a "universal" character and others which build more on conventions and personal associations.

11.1 Different Types of Coding

The first step is to look at how the emotional meaning is coded in music. *Coding* refers to the specific manner in which the music "carries" the emotional meaning. I intend to show that the emotional contents of musical expression are *constrained* by the type of coding available and that distinct types of content are conveyed through different types of coding (Juslin, 2013b).

About 30 years ago, Jay Dowling and Dane Harwood published a classic textbook in music psychology, *Music Cognition*, one of the first written (Dowling & Harwood, 1986). In the book, the authors outlined an influential categorization of music and emotion links, largely based on the ideas of Charles Peirce.

Peirce focused on the role of signs. A *sign* is something that stands for something in some respect or capacity. A sign "represents" something else in order to suggest it to a perceiver. Peirce divided signs into three categories, each of which Dowling and Harwood apply to a musical setting:

- *Icon* refers to how music carries emotional meaning based on *formal resemblance* between the music and some other event or object that has an emotional tone.
- *Symbol* refers to how music carries emotional meaning based on *syntactical relationships* within the music itself; one part of the music may refer to another part of the music.
- *Index* refers to how the music carries emotional meaning based on an *arbitrary association* (e.g., temporal or spatial contiguity) between the music and some other event or object that has an emotional tone.

Using the term "symbol" to refer to a specific category of sign is perhaps unfortunate because the term *symbol* is often used as a synonym to *sign*. All three types of sign may be involved in symbolic communication, referring to something else, such as an emotional state.

Hence, my colleague John Sloboda and I have referred to these categories as *iconic*, *intrinsic*, and *associative* sources of musical expression in an attempt to make the meaning of the terms easier to grasp (Sloboda & Juslin, 2001). In this and the following chapter, I will consider each type of coding and its implications for the types of emotions that can be expressed. Then I will consider how the different codings may combine to convey more complex emotions.

11.2 Iconic Sources: Formal Resemblance

Philosopher Susanne Langer has proposed that there is an *isomorphism* between the structure of feelings and the structure of music (Langer, 1957). Formal characteristics that might be similar include "patterns of motion and rest, of tension and release, of agreement and disagreement" (Langer, 1957, p. 228). "Music sounds the way moods feel," as famously declared by Carol Pratt (1931).

Langer's ideas seem intuitively appealing for anyone who has listened to classical music in particular. Yet, one problem with the theory is that it must provide a *specification* of the structure of feelings and how this can be measured, without which her hypothesis has little explanatory force (Cook & Dibben, 2010).

Another issue is Langer's claim that music represents only the *dynamic form* of emotional life, not specific emotions. My personal opinion is that Langer's theory applies mainly to the vitality affects (discussed in section 6.6); it cannot explain how music may express discrete emotions, because different emotions may well involve the same vitality affects (e.g., tension release).

Perhaps there is a more promising approach when it comes to explaining how music may express specific emotions through an iconic resemblance. Has it ever occurred to you that playing on a musical instrument sometimes sounds a lot like *the human voice*? Or that musical expression is reminiscent of human gesture? You are not alone.

Several theorists have suggested that it may be useful to map formal similarities between musical structure and non-verbal expression of emotions, such as human gestures (Clynes, 1977; Davies, 1994) and tone of voice (Juslin, 1997a; Kivy, 1980). Singer Nancy Wilson expressed admiration at how the pioneer guitarist Jimi Hendrix "spoke through his guitar" (Boyd & George-Warren, 2013, p. 118).

There is evidence that spontaneous non-verbal expressions of emotions convey discrete emotions (Juslin, Laukka, & Bänziger, 2018), so if music is somehow able to "mimic" their features, this might explain why listeners hear specific emotions in music.

Although this approach appears promising, some authors have noted a potential problem with it. Resemblance alone is not sufficient to explain the impact of the link, as pointed out by Bill Thompson: "Music could be said to represent any number of events that it clearly does not: the rise and fall of local housing market, changes in the speed and direction of a football in flight, the acceleration and deceleration of cars in a traffic jam, and so on" (Thompson, 2015, p. 180).

If we can potentially hear so many different kinds of formal similarities between musical structures and extra-musical phenomena, why do we perceive primarily *emotions* and not all the other phenomena that also have a similar form?

First, we tend to give priority to the emotions *in general.* Consider TV programs. From "low-brow" soap operas and sit-coms, to "high-brow" theater and film, all are all ultimately about human emotion. Because emotions concern issues of the highest priority (section 4.8), we have an inbuilt bias to view "emotional stuff" as more interesting than "non-emotional stuff." Simply think about how difficult it is to ignore a highly emotional person or event.

Second, and more importantly, I argue that there is a more direct and natural link between musical sounds and emotional expressions, than between musical sounds and other "extra-musical" phenomena. The reason may be found in the human voice.

I have repeatedly (Juslin, 1995, 1997a, 1998, 2001) theorized that the iconic code used in emotional expression in music is based on innate and universal *affect programs* for vocal expression of emotions. My *functionalist* framework, inspired by Herbert Spencer (1857), assumes that the origin of iconically coded expressions is to be sought in involuntary and emotion-specific physiological changes that occur during emotional reactions (Chapter 4) and that have a strong influence on various aspects of vocal production (Juslin & Scherer, 2005).

Put simply, when in the grip of a strong emotion, physiological arousal will influence the phonation, articulation, and resonance of the voice in ways that reflect the felt emotion. If you are *angry*, this leads to increased tension in the laryngeal musculature coupled with increased sub-glottal air pressure. This changes the sound production at the glottis, and hence alters the timbre of the voice. Gradually during evolution, organisms evolved the ability to trigger these expressive patterns intentionally (Buck, 2014). By imitating the above-mentioned timbre acoustically, a musician may express *anger* in a manner that can be easily recognized by any listener, regardless of musical training.

I refer to this principle as "Spencer's law" (Juslin & Laukka, 2003). Note that such a direct relationship is lacking for other extra-musical phenomena that we could potentially hear in music, such as sea waves. It is due to this natural link between felt, embodied emotion and emotion-specific acoustic patterns that I consider the term "emotional expression" apt in a musical context, even if performers may not necessarily experience the emotion at the moment of performance; the code they are using *does* derive from emotional expression proper. It represents the closest we come to an "absolute" norm for hearing musical features.

Because iconic coding is linked to emotions in the voice, this type of coding will tend to prioritize expression of emotions that have a distinct pattern in the voice, primarily basic emotions (cf. Chapter 4) and whose pattern can be feasibly imitated in a musical setting. (Some vocal inflections could be difficult to imitate on a musical instrument.[1]) Selection pressures throughout evolution have favored efficient and robust communication of basic emotion categories, because they concern our most fundamental life issues (Juslin, 1998).

The idea that music is linked to the voice is not new. Several authors throughout history have called attention to this special relationship. Marcel

[1] For example, the "guttural" sound of disgust in the voice may be difficult to achieve on a musical instrument. In singing, it is obviously easier: consider the singing of Johnny Rotten on the Sex Pistols album *Never Mind the Bollocks*.

Proust notes that "there are in the music of the violin ... accents so closely akin to those of certain contralto voices that one has the illusion that a singer has taken her place amid the orchestra" (Watson, 1991, p. 236).

Think further of how we often refer to the "musical" aspects of speech (Fónagy & Magdics, 1963). This is particularly obvious in infant-directed speech, where mothers use changes in duration, pitch, loudness, and timbre to regulate their infant's level of emotional arousal by means of "musical contours" (Papoušek, 1996). During infancy, there is no sharp division between non-verbal expression of emotions in speech and in singing.

Perhaps the line between the two was similarly blurred in the evolutionary origins of music. The German physician and physicist Hermann Von Helmholtz—one of the pioneers in music psychology—notes that "an endeavor to imitate the involuntary modulations of the voice, and make its recitation richer and more expressive, may therefore possibly have led our ancestors to the discovery of the first means of musical expression" (Helmholtz, 1863, p. 371).

Even Leonard Meyer, who devotes the lion's share of his classic book to how musical expectancies may arouse felt emotion (Part III), acknowledges the role of voice parallels in the expression of emotions: "Because moods and sentiments attain their most precise articulation through vocal inflection ... it is possible for music to imitate the sounds of emotional behavior with some precision" (Meyer, 1956, p. 268). These are speculations, however, and do not prove that there is a link to the voice.

Is there empirical evidence to support the proposed link between musical expression and the voice? Let us start with the most crucial type of evidence. The hypothesis assumes that there are similarities between the two communication channels in terms of the acoustic features used to express specific emotions. Without such similarities, the whole idea seems doomed from the start.

In 2003, my former student, Petri Laukka, and I published an extensive review article in *Psychological Bulletin* which arguably provided the first (strong) evidence of cross-modal parallels. In the review, we analyzed data from 104 studies of vocal expression (emotional speech) and 41 studies of emotional expression in music performance. Both types of study used the so-called standard paradigm (cf. Chapter 6), where the focus is on *how* something is conveyed rather than on *what* is conveyed.

We looked at the accuracy of communication, and the patterns of acoustic features used to communicate five basic emotions. Our conclusion was that music performers use the same emotion-specific patterns of acoustic features that are involved in emotions in speech. Table 11.1 offers a summary of the results. Note the striking parallels between the two channels.

There is further support for the hypothesis that emotional expression in music is partly based on a code borrowed from vocal expression

Table 11.1 Summary of cross-modal patterns of acoustic cues for speech and music.

Emotion	**Acoustic cues**
Anger	fast speech rate/tempo, high voice intensity/sound level, much voice intensity/ sound level variability, much high-frequency energy, high Fo/ pitch level, much Fo/pitch variability, rising Fo/pitch contour, fast voice onsets/tone attacks, and micro-structural irregularity
Fear	fast speech rate/tempo, low voice intensity/sound level (except in panic fear), much voice intensity/sound level variability, little high-frequency energy, high Fo/pitch level, little Fo/pitch variability, rising Fo/pitch contour, and a lot of micro-structural irregularity
Happiness	fast speech rate/tempo, medium-high voice intensity/sound level, medium high-frequency energy, high Fo/pitch level, much Fo/pitch variability, rising Fo/pitch contour, fast voice onsets/tone attacks, and very little micro-structural regularity
Sadness	slow speech rate/tempo, low voice intensity/sound level, little voice intensity/ sound level variability, little high-frequency energy, low Fo/ pitch level, little Fo/pitch variability, falling Fo/pitch contour, slow voice onsets/tone attacks, and micro-structural irregularity
Tenderness	slow speech rate/tempo, low voice intensity/sound level, little voice intensity/ sound level variability, little high-frequency energy, low Fo/ pitch level, little Fo/pitch variability, falling Fo/pitch contours, slow voice onsets/tone attacks, and micro-structural regularity

Note. Fo refers to the fundamental frequency of the voice.
Based on Juslin, P. N., & Laukka, P. (2003). *Communication of emotions in vocal expression and music performance: Different channels, same code?* Psychological Bulletin, 129, 770–814. Copyright © 2003, American Psychological Association.

of basic emotions that served important functions throughout evolution (Juslin, 1998):

- basic emotions in vocal expressions can be recognized cross-culturally, even in traditional cultures (Bryan & Barrett, 2008)
- basic emotions in vocal expression are perceived categorically (Laukka, 2005)
- categorical perception of emotions is not necessarily driven by language (Sauter, LeGuen, & Haun, 2011)
- spontaneous ("natural") vocal expressions convey basic emotion categories to the same extent as posed ("acted") expressions (Juslin, Laukka, & Bänziger, 2018)
- it is notoriously difficult to "retrain" a participant to express a specific basic emotion with a different expressive pattern (Clynes, 1977, pp. 44–45)
- there is a similar pattern of age-related differences in recognition of emotions from vocal expression and music performance (Laukka & Juslin, 2007; see also Lima & Castro, 2011)
- congenitally *amusical* individuals with deficits in processing acoustic and structural attributes of music are significantly worse than matched controls at decoding basic emotions in vocal expressions (Thompson, Marin, & Stewart, 2012)
- basic emotions are easier to communicate than complex emotions in music (Gabrielsson & Juslin, 1996; cf. Senju & Oghushi, 1987)
- basic emotions in music can be recognized cross-culturally (Fritz et al., 2009)
- basic emotions are correctly recognized in both speech and music even when free response formats are used (Juslin, 1997c; Kaiser, 1962)
- basic emotions in music show high cross-cultural agreement, whereas non-basic emotions show low cross-cultural agreement (Laukka, Eerola, Thingujam, Yamasaki, & Beller, 2013)

- basic emotions such as *sorrow, anger, love, joy,* and *fear* are explicitly part of a number of non-Western theories of musical emotions (e.g., Becker, 2004, p. 58)
- the decoding of basic emotions in music is very quick (Bigand et al., 2005; Peretz, Gagnon, & Bouchard, 1998)
- the decoding of basic emotions in music does not require musical training (e.g., Juslin, 1997a)
- the expression of basic emotions in music does not require musical training (Yamasaki, 2002)
- even children (3–4 years old) are able to decode basic emotions in music with better than chance accuracy (e.g., Cunningham & Sterling, 1988)
- even children are able to use voice-related cues to express basic emotions in their songs (Adachi & Trehub, 1998)
- the ability to decode basic emotions in music performances is correlated with measures of emotional intelligence (Resnicow, Salovey, & Repp, 2004)
- there are cross-cultural similarities in cue utilization for acoustic features shared between vocal expression and musical expression (Balkwill & Thompson, 1999; Laukka et al., 2013)
- the decoding of basic emotions in music involves many of the same brain regions as perception of basic emotions in vocal expression (Escoffier, Zhong, Schirmer, & Qui, 2013; Paquette, Takerkart, Saget, Peretz, & Belin, 2018)

Despite this body of evidence of links between musical and vocal expression of emotion, there are objections to the vocal link to emotion in the literature. Thus, for example, Stephen Davies (2001) argues that instrumental music does not generally *sound* much like a voice, which may well be true (Schubert, 2018).

But that is not how the semblance of iconic coding "works": the music does not need to be similar in *all* respects for it to suggest vocal emotion (a road sign or a map does not need to include every detail in order to be comprehensible). The crucial aspect is that the expressive modulations (the changes in speed, dynamics, pitch contour, and timbre) used by musicians to express emotions are like those that occur in the voice when a speaker is expressing the same emotions. Evidence shows that such emotion-processing may occur subconsciously (Juslin, Harmat, & Laukka, 2018; Pell & Skorup, 2008).

Furthermore, the objection to the voice hypothesis can only apply to instrumental music; the majority of the music heard in the world features singing, in which case the role of the voice is beyond question. How could an artist sing a song about *despair* expressively without borrowing expressive features from emotional speech?[2]

11.3 Is Music a Super-Expressive Voice?

As explained earlier, it is not necessary for iconic sources to work that we consciously hear the similarities between the music and emotion in voices, since the perceptual processing is mostly implicit in nature. However, sometimes, it appears, musicians really *do* want us to think of the music as a "voice." Miles Davis noted that "people tell me my sound is like a human voice and that's what I want it to be" (Davis, 1990, p. 389). Many performers of blues music were attracted to the vocal qualities of the slide guitar (Erlewine, Bogdanow, Woodstra, & Koda, 1996). Eric Clapton claims that his original interests and intentions in guitar playing mainly revolved around quality of tone, "the way the instrument could be made to echo or simulate the human voice."[3]

Consider the range of expressive effects used by musicians. String bending on the electric guitar may fulfill the purpose of making the tones sound more like a human voice; "it's more like a violin or a voice; you just gliss up to it,"

[2] Sometimes, the link between musical expression and emotions in the voice becomes perhaps *too* salient—as when John Lennon came under the influence of Dr Arthur Janov's primal scream therapy, and practised it wholesale on his first (proper) solo album, *Plastic Ono Band* (1970).

[3] Retrieved from the IMDb database; see <https://m.imdb.com/name/nm0002008/quotes>

says blues guitarist B.B. King.[4] The use of such *portamento* (pitch sliding from one note to another) is obviously a common feature of singing (Dibben, 2014). Another feature is vibrato, which gives warmth to an instrument's tone, and enhances its similarity to the human voice. We have shown in our laboratory that vibrato rate and depth varies depending on the emotion the performer intends to express (Juslin, Friberg, Schoonderwaldt, & Karlsson, 2004).

One reason why singing musical phrases is such good practice for instrumentalists (Dubal, 1985, p. 221) may be that it helps a performer to connect with more fundamental principles of vocal expression of emotion. We also know that principles from vocal rhetoric was used by many composers throughout the eighteenth century (Cook & Dibben, 2010).

However, to the extent that we hear musical notes as "voices," these voices might be of a *special* kind. I have proposed that in terms of how the brain processes these musical notes, musical expression of emotions could be conceived as a kind of "super-expressive" voice.

> What I want to suggest to the reader is that what makes a certain performance on, say, the violin, so expressive is the fact that it sounds a lot like the human voice, whereas at the same time it goes far beyond what the human voice can do (e.g., in terms of speed, pitch range, onsets, and timbre). In effect, musical instruments are processed by the brain module as "super-expressive" voices. The "attention" of the module is gripped by the musical instrument's voice-like, animate character, and we then become moved by the extreme "turns" taken by this "voice", as it were. For example, if the voice sounds tender when it has slow voice onsets and high pitch, a musical instrument may sound extremely tender in virtue of its even slower tone onsets and higher pitch. (Juslin, 2000b, p. 283).

Slightly similar ideas were proposed by Sperber and Hirschfield with respect to face perception (Sperber & Hirschfield, 2004). Masks, cosmetics, and caricatures might work as "super-stimuli" for the fusiform face area of the brain, leading to a heightened affective response.

[4] Quoted in an article by Jas Obrecht (2010), retrieved from: <http://jasobrecht.com/b-b-king-live-at-the-regal/>.

The fascination with the *Castrati*, opera singers who were castrated before reaching puberty to preserve their high voices (particularly between 1650 and 1750), might be related to this "super-natural" quality of a voice—in this case combining the high notes of women or boys with the lung power of men (e.g., Beyer, 2011). The same thing can perhaps explain the wonder of the high C's in opera tenors. (A young Luciano Pavarotti was dubbed "the king of the high C's" after his successful performances of Donizetti's aria "Pour Mon Ãme" at the Metropolitan in New York during the 1972–1973 season.)

Consider, then, that musical instruments may simulate such voice-like features—but so much *faster, louder*, and *higher* in pitch. If these emotions are processed by an independent module in the brain (as findings suggest; Peretz, 2010), which simply responds to expressive patterns regardless of where they happen to occur, it is perhaps no wonder that we are so intrigued. In Chapter 20, focusing on the arousal of felt emotions, I will describe a mechanism called *contagion*, which is particularly sensitive to voice-like patterns of expression (Juslin, 2000b).

Our fascination with "super-expressive" or "super-natural" voices can perhaps explain why musicians like to play around with the so-called *vocoder*, an electronic device that can be used to create "singing" that sounds half-human and half-machine.[5] (Imagine a robot that sings, or simply listen to the song "Around the World" by the electronic duo Daft Punk.) We seem to have a fascination with voices that do *not* quite sound like voices, and with non-voices that *do* sound quite like voices. (Are we searching for the voice of angels?)

I propose that most of the emotion-feature links summarized in Table 8.1 are likely to derive from iconic relationships since they can be accounted for in terms of formal similarities with other forms of nonverbal expression, in particular the voice. These relationships enable basic emotions to be communicated reliably in music—even cross-culturally—if musicians wish to

[5] The vocoder was initially developed to reproduce the human voice on a synthesizer. The electronic instrument inventor Robert Moog is credited as having developed the first solid-state unit specifically for use in music.

do so. Due to its ancient origins, this kind of coding has the most *uniform* impact on musical expression.

Yet the notion that basic emotions are privileged in musical expression does *not* imply that other emotions cannot be conveyed in music. Music can convey more complex emotions to listeners under some circumstances, but there is lower listener agreement with regard to such emotions (Laukka et al., 2013). Part of the reason is that complex emotions are coded differently. They involve intrinsic and associative coding (in addition to iconic coding). Let us now look at these additional ways of conveying emotion.

CHAPTER 12

FURTHER LAYERS

Intrinsic and Associative Expression

12.1 Intrinsic Coding: The "Will" of the Tones

Intrinsic signs gain their meaning from being embedded in a formal system. A good example is language, where the meaning of a sentence is dependent on syntactic rules of the language. Because music can also be regarded as having a syntax of sorts (a set of rules that govern the combination of structural elements into sequences), several authors have argued that musical features may obtain emotional meaning from their place in the syntax of a piece (Dowling & Harwood, 1986; Meyer, 1956; Narmour, 1991).

Note that the meaning derives from *internal* relationships between various parts of the music, rather than from relationships between the music and extra-musical events. Consider a simple example: a performer may use *syncopation* in a performance (a shifting of the normal accent to a normally unaccented beat) to create tension. This expressive feature gains its impact only with reference to other events in the same rhythmic sequence. How can this type of intrinsic meaning contribute to musical expression?

Here, it may be helpful to bring in the concept of *tonality* from music theory. The term has different meanings in different contexts, but I will use it to refer to the arrangement of pitches and/or chords of a musical work, scale, or musical system into a "hierarchy" of perceived relations, stabilities, attractions, and directionality.

Some notes in the music may be regarded as more "important"—they occur more frequently than others, or are perceived as more "stable." For instance, the tonic is regarded as "stable," non-diatonic notes are regarded as "unstable." Musical notes close to the perceptual stability point seem to reduce *tension*, whereas notes distant from this point seem to increase it.[1]

Furthermore, when notes that differ in terms of their "stability" are combined into sequences, there is a sense of "direction" or "purpose" to these musical relationships. Thus, for example, a seventh scale degree moving to tonic is called a "leading tone" because it appears to lead to the "goal" of the tonic, which is perceived as more stable than the "restless" leading tone (Huron, 2006).

Music theory often features references to tonal and harmonic *motion* (Lerdahl & Krumhansl, 2007), even gravitational *forces* between musical tones and chords. A series of chords often implies motion in a certain direction (Larson & VanHandel, 2005).

The influential music theorist Heinrich Schenker talked about "the will of the tones" to capture the impression that musical notes seem to "yearn" for their resolution. For example, V7 chords "yearn" to resolve to I chords—either because this is what listeners commonly expect based on their previous experiences (Huron, 2006) or because this is the "ideal" resolution harmonically (Bashwiner, 2014). Either way, "the will of the tones" gives rise to subtle changes in perceived musical tension (Nielsen, 1987), which may be calculated and predicted based on musical features (Lerdahl, 1996).

Certain aspects of our perception of musical structure reflects "hardwired" principles of the human brain (e.g., the "gestalt laws"; Bregman, 1990). However, a great deal of our tonal perception is shaped by "statistical learning" (Huron, 2006) through "exposure" to the typical music within a specific cultural and historical context. Thus, intrinsic sources are expected to be more dependent on culture and learning than are iconic sources (Chapter 11). We can also expect musically trained listeners to be more sensitive to intrinsic sources than untrained listeners. Musicologists may be

[1] Distance can also be measured on other musical dimensions, such as meter: strong beats are "stable," weak beats are "unstable."

"over-sensitive" to them, or, more precisely, they may tend to over-estimate the extent to which ordinary listeners will detect and respond to certain musical relationships. Intrinsic sources of emotions are usually discussed in relation to the arousal of *felt* emotions (Dowling & Harwood, 1986; Meyer, 1956; Sloboda, 1991), and I will cover this in Chapter 24.

There is no doubt that intrinsic sources *can* arouse emotions in a listener (Steinbeis, Koelsch, & Sloboda, 2006), but the same kind of internal play between various parts of the musical structure may also, arguably, contribute to the *perceived* emotional expression. It may influence the perceived level of emotion intensity in a music performance (Sloboda & Lehmann, 2001; Timmers & Ashley 2007) or the perceived tension in a composition (Nielsen, 1987; see also Lindström, 2006).

In fact, my experience from pilot testing in our laboratory is that many of the musical events singled out by music theorists are too subtle to arouse *felt* emotion in regular music listeners. Either the listeners do not detect anything special about the event, or they simply register the emotional event *in the music*—that is, perception of emotion. Much of the so-called musical affect that music theorists talk about (cf. Lerdahl, 1991) may not concern felt emotion at all, but rather the affective intensity of the perceived musical expression, as intrinsically coded.[2]

I realize that this interpretation may seem controversial, since most theorists studying intrinsic sources apply it to *felt* emotion. Yet, I maintain as a working hypothesis that a fair number of the intrinsic events are probably more relevant to perceived than aroused emotion. I find it somewhat ironic that even the intra-musical patterns that "absolutists" focused on to get away from representation of emotion (Hanslick, 1854) may contribute to the perceived emotional expression of a piece of music.

Note that included among the musical features in Table 8.1 are some intrinsically coded features such as syncopations and (musical) consonance/dissonance. A classic example is the melodic interval known as *diabolus in*

[2] It seems unlikely that listeners' own emotions would change at the same rate and with the same level of detail.

musica—the augmented fourth, or the tritone (e.g., Cooke, 1959), linked to expression of *anger* (although the expressive impact of a musical interval is highly dependent on context; Thompson, 2015).

The precise role of intrinsic sources in musical expression of emotion remains to be properly investigated, though it seems unlikely that intrinsic sources can express discrete emotions by themselves without the content supplied by iconic or associative sources. A syncopation can enhance the musical tension locally, but does not specify whether this tension is reflective of, say, *anxiety, excitement,* or *anger*. Adding a non-diatonic note will not resolve the matter. Intrinsic sources cannot be grouped into patterns of features that convey specific emotions.

Perhaps a more fruitful way to conceptualize them would be to propose that the structural interplay of tension and release helps to *qualify* specific emotions conveyed by iconic and associative coding. Intrinsically coded features could make a "local" musical event sound slightly more positive, tense, or intense than a previous event.

Such a "modulatory" role does not suggest that intrinsic sources are unimportant. Far from it. Within the broad "emotional tone" set by iconic sources in a musical section, intrinsic sources provide *nuance, direction,* and a sense of *purpose*. By contributing dynamically shifting levels of tension, valence, and uncertainty, intrinsic sources may help to express more complex and time-dependent emotions.

Musicologist David Huron offers some interesting unpublished data regarding general "qualia" that music listeners sensed while *imagining* each scale degree (Huron, 2006). For instance, the tonic was described as "stable" and "home," the mediant as "bright" and "lifted," the subdominant as "descending" and "tentative," the dominant as "strong" and "muscular," and the leading tone as "unstable" and "restless."

There were many discrepancies between listeners, however, as acknowledged by Huron. To be clear, the participants were asked to report how each scale degree made them "feel," but I am strongly inclined to think that they really described the *perceived* quality of the interval: hearing the dominant interval will hardly make *you* feel "muscular."

Huron analyzed the verbal responses to find an underlying structure, and found that seven semantic categories could account for most of the descriptions: *certainty/uncertainty* (e.g., abrupt, inevitable), *tendency* (e.g., downward), *completion* (e.g., unfinished, resolved), *mobility* (e.g., flow, drifting), *stability* (e.g., unstable, solid), *power* (e.g., bold), and *valence* (e.g., satisfying, harsh) (Huron, 2006).

These qualia dimensions may help to refine and qualify emotional nuances such that broad emotion categories conveyed by iconic sources are turned into more complex emotions. To illustrate, a musical event expressive of *tenderness* (Table 8.1) might turn into the (closely related) emotion of *longing* momentarily as a result of a melodic interval with "pointing" or "restless" qualia. Similarly, tonal closure may convey a momentary sense of relief or "a glimmer of hope" amidst an overall expression of *anxiety* or *despair*. Such musical events contribute to a sense of narrative or "affective trajectory" (for examples see Hatten, 2010; Spitzer, 2013).

I must emphasize that most of the expressive possibilities discussed in this section are still a matter of speculation; they seem plausible but have not been tested empirically. There is no doubt that intrinsic sources influence how we experience music and that music theorists have a proper understanding of how this contributes to musical tension. What remains to be shown is the extent to which these processes contribute to our perception of specific emotions in music. We need to move from plausible speculation to confirmed causal effects.

12.2 Associative Coding: The Leitmotifs of Life

Finally, we will consider the notion of *associative* coding. A piece of music can be perceived as expressive of an emotion simply because something in the music (e.g., a melody, timbre) has been repeatedly associated with other meaningful stimuli or events in the past, either through chance or by design. In psychology this is usually referred to as *classic conditioning* (Lavond & Steinmetz, 2003).

As is often the case in science, classical conditioning was discovered by mere accident. In the 1890s, the Russian physiologist Ivan Pavlov was studying salivation in dogs in response to being fed. He noticed that his dogs would begin to salivate whenever he entered the room even when he was *not* bringing them food. How could this be?

The answer was that, because the food was always delivered by Pavlov, the dogs gradually learned to associate him (or a lab assistant, more generally) with "food," such that the mere sight of Pavlov would evoke the meaning food, which then triggered a salivation response. This basic principle underlies a great deal of learning in humans also, perhaps more than we like to think!

Music occurs frequently in all kinds of contexts in everyday life (Juslin, Liljeström, Västfjäll, Barradas, & Silva, 2008), which provide rich opportunities for developing associations—probably *more* so than in other arts. Hence, music listening commonly gives rise to various sorts of associations, some of which may involve emotional meaning (Pike, 1972).

Sometimes, these associations are purely personal: Sociologist Tia DeNora describes the case of "Lucy," who associates Franz Schubert's *Impromptus* with her father who used to play these on the piano while she was falling asleep in the evenings (DeNora, 2010). Other times, the associations were intended by the composer. A well-known example is opera composer Puccini's use of the first phrase from the American national anthem "The Star Spangled Banner" in *Madame Butterfly* to suggest feelings of patriotism in the American protagonist (Dowling & Harwood, 1986).

In contrast to the iconic sources discussed earlier, these conditioned responses are in a sense arbitrary: there is no similarity in form between the emotion and the structural features. For example, organ music may be perceived as expressive of *solemnity* and *spirituality* because it has been heard repeatedly and most frequently in a church by the average Western listener. Listeners from a different culture may not have the same association upon hearing this type of music.

In contrast to the intrinsic sources discussed earlier, associative sources are not dependent on the subtle interplay between different parts of the musical structure. Musical structure is still involved, of course, since some musical feature (e.g., a melodic theme, a rhythm, a phrase, a timbre) must serve as the "retrieval cue" for the association—as in Puccini's quote of a phrase from "The Star Spangled Banner."

Conditioned responses may also arouse *felt* emotions (*evaluative conditioning*; Chapter 21). In the present context, however, an associative source only suggests, or refers to, an emotion or the concept of an emotion, without actually arousing the emotion in the listener. (We may think of the notion of sadness, without feeling sad.) It can be a challenge sometimes to distinguish these processes (section 4.8), but physiological responses typically "give away" the fact that the listener is experiencing a felt emotion, rather than just perceiving an emotion.

In the "politics" of music and emotion, associative sources have not fared well. They have usually been regarded as "aesthetically irrelevant" by music researchers and theorists (e.g., Hanslick, 1986), yet this does not seem to be how the composers view them. Dowling and Harwood observed that "every composer from Bach to Brahms as well as from Telemann to Tchaikovsky has used elements having strong extra-musical associations" (Dowling & Harwood, 1986, p. 205).[3] This is just one of many "tools" used by composers to achieve their expressive aims.

The truth is that "associative sources" are very important for musical expression of emotions. A simple illustration of how they may add complexity to musical meaning is provided by a performance by Jimi Hendrix at the legendary Woodstock Festival on August 18, 1969 (captured on film). Toward the end of his concert, Hendrix suddenly launched into his very own interpretation of the American national anthem (see Figure 12.1).

At one level, his performance could be heard simply as a "sonic assault"—admired or abhorred for its distorted, sustained notes and wild amplifier feedback. However, associative sources revealed a much deeper (and more disturbing) meaning to the listeners in attendance. The performance

[3] Hinting at the "politics" of musical emotions, however, Dowling and Harwood apparently felt the need to explain that "there is nothing morally wrong with that" (Dowling & Harwood, 1986, p. 205).

Figure 12.1 Jimi Hendrix performing at the Woodstock Festival 1969.
Illustration by Costis Chatzidakis.

occurred at a time when the United States had been involved in the controversial war in Vietnam for several years, at great loss of life. A national anthem typically suggests "patriotism" to listeners, but this interpretation managed to communicate something more complex. How?

Interspersed within the notes of the melody were other events: the sounds of war. Through a creative use of "twang bar," feedback, distortion, "hammer-ons," and "pull-offs," Hendrix was able to create sounds that listeners immediately associated with jet planes, falling bombs, and human screams. At one point, he even inserted a musical quote of "Taps" (a bugle call, played at military funerals by the US armed forces). Hendrix also performed the piece in a slower tempo than usual, giving the rendition a more sad and mournful quality.

Through this combination of associative and iconic sources, Hendrix managed to convey a far more complex and ambivalent emotion than what he could have done using only iconic sources. Someone from a non-Western culture would have heard only a frightening level of noise—and it *was* noisy—but for someone familiar with the broader context, the musical performance was ultimately a powerful statement of "anti-war sentiment" (made by a man who served in the 101st Airborne)—a musical expression of "mixed emotions": *sadness, horror, patriotism,* and *regret.*

Some emotions would not be possible to express at all in music were it not for associative sources. Consider the emotion category of *nostalgia–longing.* It is part of Hevner's adjective circle (Figure 7.2), and was amongst the top 10 emotions expressed in music, as rated by at least one of the listener samples in Table 6.1. Yet, there is no distinct pattern of iconically coded musical features that expresses this emotion. Nor can intrinsically coded features specify *nostalgia* through local changes in musical tension.

If we briefly consider popular songs about *nostalgia,* it is clear that there are no distinct musical features which occur consistently across them; for instance, compare the music of "Yesterday" by the Beatles with "Summer of '69" by Bryan Adams, or "Caroline No" by the Beach Boys with "Sitting on the Dock of the Bay" by Otis Redding, or "Heroes" by David Bowie with "A Case of You" by Joni Mitchell. They are not very similar in terms of their musical features, are they?

Because *nostalgia* is often regarded as a bittersweet emotion (Wildschut, Sedikides, Arndt, & Routledge, 2006), one could argue that its expression should involve musical features that combine positive and negative valence (e.g., shifting between major and minor chords), perhaps in combination with features suggestive of a moderate level of activity or arousal (e.g., a slow tempo, soft loudness). However, this will, in all likelihood, express only *sadness* and *tenderness,* which is not quite the same thing. A mixture of *sadness* and *tenderness* certainly seems compatible with *nostalgia* (and this is arguably the strategy taken in much film music), yet something more is ultimately required to convey the distinct emotion of *nostalgia* off-screen.

If it is true that *nostalgia–longing* lacks a natural, iconic musical pattern, why is this the case? The most probable reason is that there is no distinct iconically coded expression of *nostalgia* in the voice or in body language.

From this point of view, it is not surprising that Rigg observed a markedly lower recognition accuracy for *longing* than for *joy* in his listening tests (Rigg, 1937).

How, then, could music express *nostalgia*? First, we may note that *nostalgia–longing* as an emotion is by definition linked to memory: the term "longing" suggests that we yearn for something that we know and have encountered, but that is not present in the here and now. *Nostalgia* may be regarded a special form of *longing*, longing for something in the past which is now gone.

The link to memory rules out the possibility that *nostalgia* can expressed by mere intrinsic coding. Instead, the trick is to insert musical features or events that will reliably evoke associations of events or things from the past—conditioning is a simple form of memory. It may be a short musical quotation from a well-known piece with a strong cultural impact or a signature lick from a solo by a well-known musician.

Some instrumental timbres are strongly associated with specific time periods in pop music. For me, the sound of the Moog synthesizer is strongly associated with early 1970s music, so that when I hear its sound in new tracks, it gives the music a *nostalgic* expression. Someone unfamiliar with earlier uses of the Moog may not get this impression.[4]

Associations might also involve cultural or geographical settings. By inserting material from the folk music of his birth country (the Czech Republic) into compositions, Antonín Dvořák was able to suggest a feeling of *longing* to many listeners. In this case, the associations were forged in the past.

However, composers could also create such associations during the actual piece of music. Associative coding plays a crucial role in composer Richard Wagner's *leitmotif* strategy, whereby specific melodic themes can be associated with specific characters or events in a musical drama to great expressive effect. The method was, arguably, pioneered by Hector Berlioz, who used a specific phrase repeatedly (the "*idée fixe*") to suggest a protagonist's romantic

[4] Think of the use of the flute in pop from the late 1960s and early 1970s—you rarely hear the flute in today's hits.

Figure 12.2 Recurring motive ("*idée fixe*") in "Symphonie Fantastique" by Hector Berlioz.

fixation with a woman in his "Symphonie Fantastique" (see Figure 12.2). Needless to say, the protagonist in the program was himself.

The leitmotif method might be used to express *nostalgia*. By reinserting a musical theme previously associated with "happy times" in a later scene of a more reflective character, the composer can suggest nostalgic reminiscence of happier days to the listener. Something of that sort occurs in Giuseppe Verdi's opera *La Traviata*, where the hero and the heroine recall earlier days by singing musical phrases associated with previous events.

I suspect that associations forged over long time-periods in everyday life will tend to be more powerful for an individual listener than the associations created within a composition, but the latter have the obvious advantage that they will be shared among most listeners to the work.[5]

Perhaps we should make a distinction here between "communal" and "personal" associations. Communal associations are those that are shared by most people within a large group (albeit *not* necessarily across cultures). Included in this category are those expressive meanings that are purely conventional. Throughout the history of music, there are a number of examples of systems for emotional communication built on conventions (Benestad, 1978).

[5] In discussing associative sources, the reader may wonder if autobiographical memories of specific events should also be covered, but I will save my discussion of such memories for Part III. The reason for this is that I believe that a *single* exposure to a musical feature concurrently with a specific event is unlikely to forge a lasting association of emotional meaning, unless the event was experienced with strongly *felt* emotion (Chapter 22).

A nice example is the "Doctrine of Affections" of the Baroque era (Buelow, 1983), which held that music (mostly vocal music) should express "affects," in the sense of idealized emotional states. Each piece should only express one "affect." Various treatises (e.g., Mattheson, 1739) postulated systematic principles for how each "affect" should be expressed most effectively.

Although some of the principles given can be accounted for in terms of iconic coding (e.g., intense joy—or euphoria—should be expressed by "a rapidly rising sequence of thirds"), other principles seem purely associative. For example, the idea that patterns of falling notes convey "sighs" (Pogue & Speck, 1997) could hardly be replicated in listening tests featuring modern listeners, who are unfamiliar with the conventions. Allegedly, though, the principles *did* work at the time.

Through conventional coding, music might achieve a more precise and complex expression, but its recognition will depend on having the required knowledge and/or experience. Hence, expression based on conventional coding will necessarily be less universal and more context- and listener-dependent than expression based on iconic coding.

In modern society, the richest source of conventional, emotional meaning is probably film music, because it prioritizes clear communication of emotional meaning over originality of expression. The music fulfills specific "functions" in movies (Cohen, 2010), and those functions are more easily served if composers follow conventions. Hence, there are clearly some culture-specific musical "clichés" used in film music. In older soap operas, comedies, and crime movies, mere insertion of a saxophone implies that things are about "heat up" on the screen (saxophone phrase → sexual desire). Some of the conventions build on iconic or intrinsic coding, others are purely conventional but they work just the same within our culture.

Imre Lahdelma and Tuomas Eerola suggest that the minor triad, the minor seventh, and especially the major seventh chord all suggest *nostalgia–longing* to listeners (Lahdelma & Eerola, 2016). If that is the case, I think they do so mainly because they have been featured in music used in movies at nostalgic moments. There is no plausible psychological process that can explain how those chords could *intrinsically* convey *nostalgia*. Rather than claiming that they reliably convey *nostalgia* in any general sense, I would submit that they are "consistent" with an expression of nostalgia, albeit not "sufficient" in the absence of conventional associations.[6]

Personal associations are those that are completely unique to individual listeners, and that bring a richer and more personal side to the expressive contents conveyed through iconic and/or intrinsic sources. These are connotations reflecting the individual life history of the listener. A good example is the previously mentioned case of Lucy, whose hearing of the Franz Schubert *Impromptus* brings connotations of "comfort" mainly because her father used to play these pieces at the piano while she was falling asleep after dinner (DeNora, 2010). Some of these "idiosyncratic" impressions are beyond systematic modeling, but could still explored in terms of in-depth interviews (Barradas, in press).

Ironically, considering that music theorists often regard associative sources as aesthetically irrelevant, music analyses in what we could call the "hermeneutic" tradition are also clearly concerned with associative coding, whether in terms of style-specific conventions or more personal associations of the analyst. Robert Hatten thus admits that the hermeneutic approach involves "hypothetical 'leaps of faith', constructing potential meanings" (Hatten, 1994, p. 2).

In principle, there are no limits to what might possibly be linked to a musical feature through association or convention: musical expression of emotions through this type of coding can be developed infinitely. However, it may only do so for individuals having the required learning history or knowledge about the conventions. Further research is clearly needed to understand exactly how associate sources contribute to the perception of emotions in music.

[6] Personally, I find it hard to *not* hear Ennio Morricone's theme from the movie *Cinema Paradiso* (1988) as expressive of *nostalgia–longing*, but I am quite certain that my impression was conditioned not only by my watching the movie itself but also by conventions set by similar uses of film music in the Western world.

12.3 Codings Combined: A Multiple-Layer Model

Having reviewed different types of coding, we are ready to consider how they may *combine* to produce musical expression of emotions, both basic and complex emotions (Juslin, 2013b).

Figure 12.3 shows how musical expression of emotion may be conceived. The *x*-axis shows the degree of cross-cultural specificity, from the most universal to the most culture-specific. On the *y*-axis are the types of emotions expressed, from the most basic to the most complex.

In this two-dimensional space, there are three layers of musical expression of emotion which correspond to the three types of coding reviewed earlier. The idea is that upper layers tend to build upon lower layers. As one moves along the "diagonal," the emotional expression of the music becomes more complex, as well as more culture-specific.

The "core" layer of expression (bottom) consists mainly of iconically coded basic emotions based on vocal expression and human gesture (Chapter 11). This layer explains universal recognition of basic emotions in musical expression (Fritz et al., 2009). Whenever we observe strong listener agreement in empirical studies, it is mostly thanks to iconic coding which

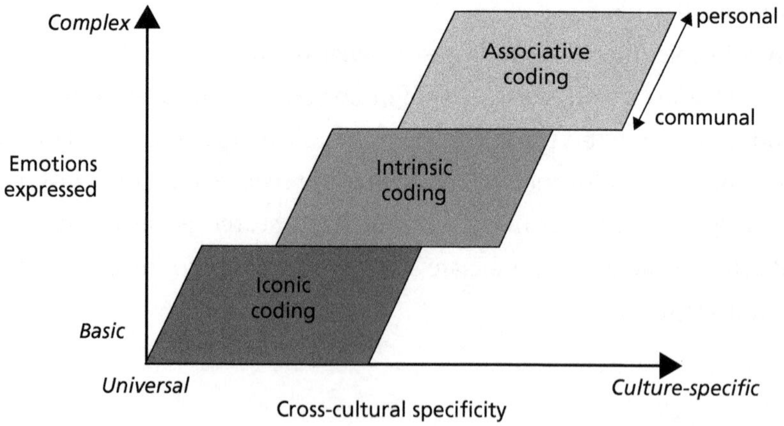

Figure 12.3 Multiple-layer model of emotional expression.

due to its characteristics tends to render emotional expressions broad (some might say imprecise), yet robust and reliable (see Chapter 10).

However, this "core" layer can be extended, qualified, or even modified by two additional layers in terms of intrinsic and associative coding, enabling music listeners to perceive more complex emotions. These are less cross-culturally invariant than the basic emotions.

The intrinsically coded expression may add dynamically changing contours (e.g., variations in tension, arousal, or intensity), which help to shape more time-dependent emotional expressions, typically within the broad category set by the "core" layer. Such contours may help to convey, say, a moment of more intense *despair* within a section that generally expresses *sorrow*.

Associative coding adds an even richer level of complex emotions, but with low levels of cross-cultural and inter-individual agreement. This layer can, furthermore, be divided into a *communal* subsection and an *idiosyncratic* (deeply personal) subsection (Figure 12.3). The communal subsection refers to the common associations of a particular social group, based upon shared experiences (e.g., group identity) or musical conventions of a particular genre. At the final, idiosyncratic layer of expression, listeners can perceive just about *any* emotion in the music, through unique and deeply personal associations.

To illustrate this further in a musical piece, the *overall* emotion category or broad "emotional tone" (e.g., *sadness*) might be specified by iconically coded features (e.g., slow tempo, minor mode, low and often falling pitch contour, legato articulation); this basic emotion category is given "expressive shape" by intrinsically coded features (e.g., local structural features such as syncopations, dissonant intervals, and melodic appoggiaturas), creating "tension" and "release," which contribute to more time-dependent and complex nuances of the same emotion category (e.g., *despair* versus *hopelessness*). To this we add a final and more personal layer of expression (e.g., that the listener associates the piece with a particular person, event, or physical location).

Most listeners will probably agree about the first layer. Some would agree about the second—perhaps especially musicians, who have the knowledge and the motivation to pay attention to more subtle details of the musical structure. Few would, of course, agree about the final layer.

Consider "Serenade for Strings in E major" by Antonín Dvořák, which premiered in Prague in 1876. The piece, composed for violins, viola, cellos, and double basses, consists of five movements, most of which use a simple "A–B–A" form. I believe that most listeners would tend to hear *melancholy* in the second movement, *tenderness* in the fourth movement, and *joyfulness* in the final movement. Throughout each movement, there are also patterns of tension and release, peaks and valleys, which reflect the shifting levels of intrinsically coded musical tension.

I also expect that listeners from the Western part of the Czech Republic will additionally hear snippets of Böhmish folk music (e.g., a Böhmish two-step), which evoke further associations of a more "national" character. This will contribute to a more complex expression—a sense of *nostalgia*, mixed with the aforementioned emotions. The associative layer of expression adds depth to the overall tone provided by the iconic layer. Further emotional depth may be added by more idiosyncratic associations of a very personal nature (e.g., associating the piece with a specific village visited in your home country where you enjoyed the best Czech beer you ever drank).

A useful analogy may be to compare the multiple layers of emotional expression to color perception. According to a common system, colors are analyzed in terms of three aspects: *hue* (wavelength), *brightness* (brilliance), and *saturation* (purity). We can think of these as corresponding to iconic, extrinsic, and associative coding, respectively.

To illustrate, iconic coding provides the emotional "hue" (e.g., you feel blue); intrinsic coding contributes to dynamic changes in the "brightness" or "intensity" of the color; and associative coding offers "saturation" or "depth" to the color: the more personal associations you bring to a musical event, the more "saturated" the perceived expression will be, and the more deeply it will resonate with your life.

The relative importance of the three layers of musical expression could vary as a function of the musical style, the historical context, and the artist, as well as listener characteristics. Specific pieces of music may also involve different types of coding. Depending on whether we select pieces of music that rely on iconic or associative sources, the degree of listener agreement or communication accuracy will obviously vary.

Conceived in this manner, it is easy to see how perception of emotional expression in music might lead to *both* agreement (Juslin, 1997a) and disagreement (Huber, 1923); cross-cultural similarities (Fritz et al., 2009) and differences (Gregory & Varney, 1996); a shared meaning (Sloboda & Juslin, 2001, p. 95) and deeply personal meaning (Gabrielsson & Lindström Wik, 2003)—sometimes, perhaps, even within the same study or piece of music. Further, one may conceive of "mixed emotions" resulting from distinct emotional meanings at different layers, somewhat akin to what Annabel Cohen refers to as "emotional polyphony" (Cohen, 2010, p. 882).

This can help us to explain how the best music created may go some way toward conveying the complexity and ambiguity that are typical of the emotions experienced in the real world. Still, I submit that iconic sources are most powerful (Table 8.1) because associative sources are too individual and intrinsic sources are too indeterminate.

12.4 Can the Model Account for Previous Findings?

Roger Brown studied listeners' ability to decode emotions in pieces of different styles and genres in classical music (Brown, 1981). In a first task, he chose 12 music excerpts and asked musicians and non-musicians to sort them into six broad emotion categories. In a second task, they were instead asked to identify 6 pairs out of 12 other musical excerpts that represented "variations on sadness"; that is, variants *within* the same broad emotion category.

While listeners were quite successful in the first task, they were not in the second until Brown supplied his own descriptions of the six sadness categories. However, non-musicians were still unsuccessful. Brown concluded that if the different expressions are not too similar (as in the first task), the emotion categories could be identified even by listeners not highly knowledgeable about classical music. However, if pieces are close in expression (the second task), "the agreement on synonymous pairs can only be achieved by listeners highly conversant with the traditions involved" (Brown, 1981, p. 264).

I think we could re-interpret these results as follows: the recognition of broad basic emotion categories was based on iconic coding, which does not require musical expertise; whereas the recognition of more complex or subtle nuances within these emotion categories was based on associative (or intrinsic) coding, which requires knowledge of musical conventions (or music theory).

Similarly, in a cross-cultural study of perception of emotions by Petri Laukka and co-workers, it was found that decoding of basic emotions was quite robust, regardless of whether the music was familiar or not, presumably because it is based on iconic coding (Laukka, Eerola, Thingujam, Yamasaki, & Beller, 2013). Decoding of complex emotions was more limited as it merely occurred for some listener groups and/or for familiar musical cultures. These complex emotions are more likely to be based on associative coding, such as social conventions.

A decomposition into distinct types of coding may also help to account for both similarities and differences between emotional speech (Juslin & Scherer, 2005) and musical expression (Gabrielsson & Juslin, 2003). Iconic coding of basic emotions will tend to be similar across the two channels (Juslin & Laukka, 2003), but associative and intrinsic sources of emotion will diverge, because the distinct functions of speech and music in human life will shape the conventions underlying their use differently.

One major implication of the "multiple-layer model" of musical expression of emotions is that completely shared emotional meaning among listeners—involving all layers—is probably rare and occurs only under *special circumstances*: it requires not only that two listeners come from the same culture and have generally similar background (e.g., musical training), but also that they probably need to have some shared experiences with the music. This may occur when close friends follow a specific artist as "fans" for a number of years, or when family members share a history with certain music. Yet even then, the perceived meaning will not overlap completely.

The special circumstances probably apply more often in the distant origins of music, when so-called primitive societies consisted of small groups of people who performed music that was familiar and important to all members of the group. It could be argued that emotional meaning in music is far less shared in today's postmodern society, than it used to be in the lives of our forefathers. Musical meaning, just like everything else, has been individualized in the Western world.

Nonetheless, based on current theory and evidence, I think there are some prototypical emotions frequently expressed in music, which are linked to the "functions" of music in our evolutionary past. They are coded somewhat differently, but in pre-modern societies this made less of a practical difference.

As a guiding principle for my selection, I have assumed that the most important emotion categories are those at the intersection between: (i) the emotions categories that are most *feasible* to express through music (in particular the basic emotions) and (ii) the emotion categories that people most *want* to express, which is presumably a subset of the basic emotions, plus some complex emotions linked to important functions of music such as religious worship, social belonging, and sensual seduction.

Based on these premises, I propose the following list of seven "prototypical" emotions which have been—and continue to be—expressed often in music: *happiness* (festive songs), *sadness* (mourning), *love–tenderness* (lullabies and tender love songs), *anxiety* (existential fears in life), *nostalgia* (social/cultural identity), *anger* (protest and war songs), *spirituality–solemnity* (religion), and *sexual desire* (mating). In my view, these emotions form the core of musical expressivity.

I will leave it to you to come up with relevant examples of each emotion category from your personal music collection.

CHAPTER 13

DEVIATION FROM THE EXACT

The Role of the Performer

I suggested previously that iconic sources of emotion may be particularly important for the shared meaning in music. We also saw that some musical features (e.g., tempo) may have a stronger influence on listeners' perception than others. These features are usually under the performer's control. Moreover, the "super-expressive voice" theory suggests that musicians enhance the expressive impact through means such as glissando, string bending, and vibrato.

A plausible case could therefore be made that emotional expressivity is most salient in the *performance* of music. Consider that even a potentially beautiful piece of music can lack true expressiveness if it is performed in a "dead-pan" manner. We may still appreciate the "clever construction" or "originality" of the work, but it does not become truly "moving" until there is a performer who makes the notes "come alive" somehow.

Daniel Leech-Wilkinson argues that the role of the performance has been "disastrously underestimated" (Leech-Wilkinson, 2013, p. 52); he emphasizes that to understand the emotional power of music, "we must consider experiences of performances, not the content of scores" (p. 44).

Thus, we now turn our focus to the performance, the topic with which I began my own studies of music and emotion several years ago (Juslin, 1998). Being a musician myself, long before I considered taking a psychology course, my initial interest focused on how a musician can achieve an expressive performance, and why we perceive it as expressive at all.

13.1 "The Unlimited Resources for Instrumental Art"

What does it really mean to perform a piece of music? What is it that a performer is "adding" to make a musical score "come alive," and sound musical and expressive? We know that if we program a computer to play a piece exactly as notated—or in perfectly timed intervals if the music is non-notated—the music will sound strikingly dull. This question has intrigued researchers for quite some time; some readers may be surprised to hear that studies of performance have been conducted for more than a century (see Gabrielsson, 1999, 2003).

In this field, the notion of expression has often been used in a narrower manner than how we have encountered it earlier in Part II. Researchers have usually investigated performances by measuring many acoustic features and relating these measures to a musical notation. In this context, *expression* refers to the systematic variations or "deviations" in timing, dynamics, timbre, and pitch that form the so-called microstructure of a performance and differentiate it from another version of the same piece. The term "microstructure" suggests that some of these deviations might be quite small.

How small a "deviation" can listeners detect? This depends very much on the circumstances, although some clues are provided by a study conducted by musicologist Eric Clarke (1989). Using short tonal and atonal sequences, he observed that in a strictly metronomic sequence, listeners could usually detect a note lengthening of only 20–30 milliseconds (ms). In a sequence with some *rubato*, the lengthening had to be roughly 50 ms to be detected. We are better at detecting a small decrease in tempo than an increase (Kuhn, 1974). Detection is also context-dependent: it is more difficult to detect note lengthening when it is expected to occur, for instance at the end of a musical phrase (Repp, 1992; see section 13.3).

The variations are small, but that does not mean they are unimportant. On the contrary, these variations are what make people go through all kinds of trouble to hear a human performance, rather than the "dead-pan" renditions of a computer. These variations make possible novel and insightful interpretations of familiar pieces.[1] In addition, the variations also hold the secret to why we prefer one musician over another. (Why does the guitarist around the corner not sound exactly like Jimi Hendrix, even if he plays the same licks?)

One of the true pioneers in this field is the Iowa-based researcher Carl Emil Seashore. He directed a large research group which produced groundbreaking results. One of Seashore's discoveries was that a musician never performs a piece of music exactly as notated; there are always various "systematic variations" or "expressive deviations" from what seems prescribed by the musical notation. While some variations could be accidental, most of them appear to be highly systematic and replicable—and indeed *intentional*. These variations are, according to Seashore, key to musical expressivity.

> The unlimited resources for vocal and instrumental art lie in artistic deviation from the pure, the exact, the perfect, the rigid, the even, and the precise. This deviation from the exact is, on the whole, the medium for the creation of the beautiful—for the conveying of emotion. (H. G. Seashore, 1937, p. 155)

Notice that Seashore does not really explain *why* or *how* the variations are important. This was apparent to Leonard Meyer: "because Seashore advances no theory or attempts no explanation of the relationship between deviation and affective aesthetic experience, his viewpoint lacks substance and plausibility" (Meyer, 1956, p. 203). I would not go *that* far, but it is clear that Seashore's account is incomplete. Fortunately for us, modern research has been able to explain what the variations do and why, but the road leading there was not always straight.

[1] It is very common that performers *change* their interpretation of familiar pieces over the course of a career as a result of new insights or influences, meetings with new musicians, audiences, or going to new places, or just to avoid boredom and keep themselves challenged.

13.2 Expression: Not Just a Matter of "More" or "Less"

The task of explaining performance expression is not an easy one. Look at Figure 13.1. It shows deviations in timing from a "mechanical" (i.e., nominally correct) performance in a professional rendition of Mozart's Piano Sonata in A major (K 331), taken from a classic study by Alf Gabrielsson (1987).

The researcher's task is to explain the *origins* and *functions* of these highly intricate patterns of variability in the acoustic parameters. The problem, as pointed out by Bill Thompson and co-workers is that "using measurements of actual performances alone, it is difficult to separate the effects of

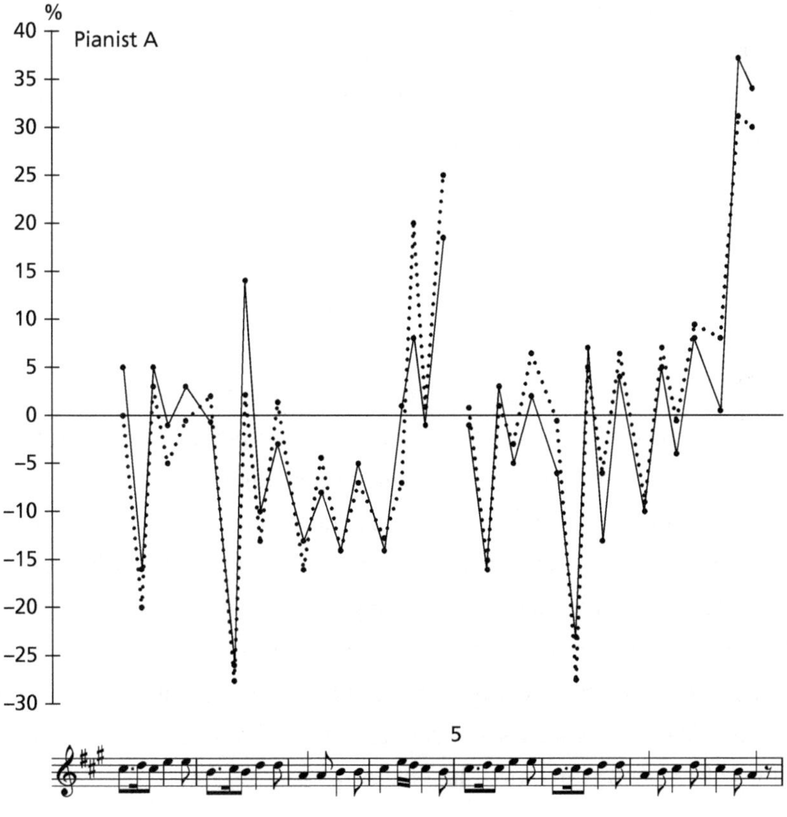

Figure 13.1 Deviations in timing from mechanical performance in a rendition of Mozart's Piano Sonata in A major.
Reproduced with permission of the Royal Swedish Academy of Music. © 1987.

combined, though psychologically distinct, expressive actions" (Thompson, Sundberg, Friberg, & Frydén, 1989, p. 64). That is, we cannot deduce simply from looking at these zig-zag patterns what the origins and functions of these patterns are.

Most researchers simply resorted to a purely descriptive approach, summarizing variations in terms of "means" and "standard deviations." This arguably lead to an approach to expression in performance that I call "the single-factor view." It refers to the tendency to regard performance expression as a single entity—a homogenous category.

According to this view, performance expression is this mysterious quality of which there is simply more or less, without specifying what is meant by the term; the expression is simply "appropriate," "exaggerated," or "lacking. However, there is no consideration of *what* is expressed, or *how* it is expressive, which implies that there is only one way of performing expressively. If this was true, why would anyone bother to listen to different interpretations of a piece?

13.3 All Variations Are Not Created Equal: The GERMS Model

It is important to realize that the expressive variations in a performance are not all the same kind. A psychological approach suggests that performance expression is best conceived of as a multi-dimensional phenomenon, which can be de-composed into different components that make distinct contributions to the aesthetic impact of a given performance. Expressive features serve different—and sometimes opposing—functions (Clarke, 1989).

Which are the expressive components "hidden," as it were, in the musical patterns? Drawing on previous research, I have argued that expression derives from five main sources, collectively referred to as the GERMS model (Juslin, Friberg, & Bresin, 2002; Juslin, 2003):

- *Generative rules* (G) that mark the structure in a musical manner (Clarke, 1988). Through variation in musical features such as timing, dynamics, and articulation, the performer is able to communicate group boundaries (Gabrielsson, 1987), metric accents (Sloboda, 1983), and harmonic structure (Palmer, 1996) to the listener. One robust finding is that tempo variation has a tendency to be determined by the phrase structure. Phrase endings are usually marked with a decrease in tempo, and the amount of slowing reflects the depth of embedding in the hierarchical structure (Todd, 1985).

Generative features may increase the emotional impact of the music, but they do so primarily by enhancing the expression that is *inherent* in the structure of the piece. For example, we saw earlier that dissonance can be used to convey the tension of negative emotions. A performer might decide to emphasize a dissonant feature of the structure through a dynamic accent. C. P. E. Bach notes that "dissonances are generally played more loudly and consonances more softly, because the former stimulate and exacerbate the emotions, while the latter calm them" (Watson, 1991, p. 23).

Part of the expression thus reflects the *structure* of the piece performed. However, this aspect is strongly dependent on stylistic conventions and on the individual performer's interpretation of the structure (Juslin, 2003).

- *Emotional expression* (E) that serves to convey emotions to listeners (Juslin, 1997a). By manipulating "overall" features of the performance such as tempo, timbre, and loudness, a performer is able to give the performance a certain emotional character. As Henry Shaffer has pointed out: "a performer can be faithful to the structure and at the same time have the freedom to shape its moods" (Shaffer, 1992, p. 265).

Usually, the performer will attempt to support the emotional expression suggested by piece-specific features (e.g., melody, harmony) or by composers' intentions, but by "contradicting" the expression of the composition, a performer may be able to express conflicting, mixed, or complex emotions—the kind of emotions you experience when you don't know what type of pizza to order.

Most studies of emotional expression to date have focused on basic emotions (Adachi & Trehub, 1998; Balkwill & Thompson, 1999; Bresin & Friberg, 2000; Gabrielsson & Juslin, 1996; Kotlyar & Morozov, 1976; Scherer & Oshinsky, 1977). However, we have examined more complex emotions at our Uppsala laboratory. Thus, Table 13.1 shows patterns of musical features used by professional performers to express 12 basic and complex emotions.

Table 13.1 Musical features used to express 12 basic and complex emotions by professional performers.

	Musical Feature						
Emotion	**Tempo**	**Sound level**	**Articulation**	**Timbre**	**Attack**	**Vibrato extent**	**Vibrato rate**
Anger	∧	∧	=	∧	∧	∧	=
Contentment	∨	=	∧	=	∨	∨	∨
Curiosity	=	=	∨	=	∨	∧	=
Disgust	=	∧	∨	=	∧	=	∧
Fear	=	∨	∨	∨	∧	=	∧
Happiness	∧	∧	∨	=	∧	∨	=
Jealousy	∧	∧	=	∧	=	∧	∨
Love	∨	=	∧	=	∨	=	∨
Pride	=	∧	=	∧	∧	=	∧
Sadness	∨	∨	∧	∨	∨	∨	∨
Shame	∨	∨	∨	∨	=	=	∧
Tenderness	∨	∨	∧	∨	∨	∨	=

Note. ∧ indicates a high value, ∨ indicates a low value, = indicates a medium value. A high value indicates (respectively for each cue) fast (vs. slow) tempo, high (vs. low) sound level, legato (vs. staccato) articulation, much (vs. little) high-frequency energy in the spectrum, fast (vs. slow) attack velocity, large (vs. small) vibrato extent, and fast (vs. slow) vibrato rate.
Reprinted from Juslin, P. N., Friberg, A., Schoonderwaldt, E., & Karlsson, J. (2004). *Feedback-learning of musical expressivity*. In A. Williamon (Ed.), Musical excellence: Strategies and techniques to enhance performance (pp. 247–270). By permission of Oxford University Press.

These data hint at part of the difficulty in conveying more complex emotions reliably to listeners. Note that many of the feature levels are quite similar for certain clusters of emotions. For instance, the three emotions *sadness, tenderness,* and *shame* are virtually indistinguishable in terms of sound level and tempo. (If musical features do not clearly separate complex emotions, listeners could hardly differentiate between them either.)

- *Random fluctuations* (R) that reflect human limitations in motor precision (Gilden, 2001). Studies have consistently shown that even when expert performers attempt to play perfectly even time intervals (e.g., in a tapping task), there are still small and involuntary fluctuations in timing in their performances.

Intriguingly, the random fluctuations are not "completely" random. Research indicates that long time intervals (slow tempi) yield proportionally *larger* variations than short intervals; that a performed interval which is shorter than the mean is typically followed by one that is longer than the mean (producing characteristic zig-zag patterns in timing); and that there is also a more long-term "drift" over time—as when a drummer's energy is flagging (Madison, 2000).

These aspects, which can be simulated by computer algorithms (Juslin et al., 2002), have been explained in terms of two sources: a central (albeit imperfect) "time-keeper" mechanism in the brain, and "noise" caused by tiny delays in the motor system (Wing & Kristofferson, 1973; see also Gilden, 2001). These sources lead to tempo drift and ziz-zag patterns, respectively.

Practice instills precision. Yet, from an aesthetic point of view, random variations contribute to the "living" character of music, that slight *unpredictability* that makes every performance absolutely unique. Accounts suggest that pianist-composers such as Franz Liszt and Frédéric Chopin performed their pieces differently each time (Cook, 1998). Musicians cannot exactly replicate their timing patterns in a music performance, even when instructed to do so, though differences between renditions are usually very small (Gabrielsson, 1999).

A *slight* unevenness in the performance of a difficult passage can even enhance the extent to which it sounds "impressive," as if this minor imperfection reminds us of how minor the mariginals are and how exceptional the feat really is. Perhaps this is why some musicians prefer a high degree of spontaneity when they are recording. When performances become "too perfect," they lose some of the "unpredictability" and vitality.

- *Motion principles* (M) which hold that tempo changes should follow natural patterns of human movement, such as gestures. The term *biological motion* (e.g., Johansson, 1973) is used to refers to the dynamic patterns of movement that are characteristic of biological organisms (e.g., humans), compared to movement by physical objects.

In music, such patterns may be of two kinds. First, performers may intentionally (though not necessarily consciously) try to recreate such patterns. Patrick Shove and Bruno Repp suggest that an aesthetically pleasing performance is "one whose expressive microstructure satisfies basic constraints of biological motion" (Shove & Repp, 1995, p. 78).

For instance, consider the shaping of final ritardandi in music performance. My two Swedish colleagues, Anders Friberg and Johan Sundberg (1999), were able to show that final ritardandi follow a mathematical function highly similar to that of runners' decelerations. Music slows down by using the same tempo curve as a sprinter who stops running. This was also the ritardando function preferred by listeners in a test comparing various mathematical functions.

A second kind of biological motion is *non-intentional* patterns of variability which reflect anatomical constraints of the body, in connection with the motor-requirements of specific musical instruments (e.g., Penel & Drake, 1999). To illustrate: some phrases require larger movements on a piano keyboard or guitar fretboard, which could produce subtle effects on timing patterns. Moreover, every performer has a unique sonic "fingerprint" in terms of his or her minor deviations.

- *Stylistic Unexpectedness* (S) that reflects a performer's deliberate attempt to *deviate* from stylistic expectations regarding performance conventions to add tension and unpredictability to the performance (Meyer, 1956, p. 206). This component is the least investigated of all components thus far.

If the preceding four components (structure, emotion, precision, gesture) might suffice to produce a performance with acceptable expression, this component is, perhaps, needed to create a truly *special* performance. Bruno Repp (1997) provides some examples of expert performances featuring bold and unexpected patterns of expression.

The pianist Alfred Cortot might be a good example. Daniel Barenboim (1999) suggests that Cortot "looked for anything that was extraordinary," something that was not "smelling of normality." Daniel Leech-Wilkinson (2013) conducted an interesting analysis of Cortot's performance of Chopin's Etude No. 1 in A major, Opus 25, in a recording from 1934, and discovered some peculiar expressive features.

For example, instead of emphasizing key points of the structure such as the beginning of a new structural unit by slowing down (as expected based on the G-component), he *sped* up. Instead of emphasizing an important note by lengthening, he rather unexpectedly emphasized a less important note *before* the important one (Leech-Wilkinson, 2013). It is debatable as to whether this is the optimal way to the clarify structure, but it *does* enhance the expressive intensity of the performance—a novel and original interpretation.

Our expectations depend strongly on learning and cultural context; expressive patterns that were once "shockingly unusual" may be heard as "commonplace" today. This means that the S-component has hardly any of the "universal appeal" of the E-component which is based on iconic coding of emotion; the S-component is instead linked to stylistic evolution and novelty (see Chapter 29 for further discussion).

13.4 Lessons from The GERMS Model

Some of these components of expression, when used effectively, may contribute not only to the expression of music but could also actually move us (*arouse* emotion). Sometimes, the difference is subtle. Strong and convincing emotional expressions ("E") could be "contagious." Unexpected deviations from style conventions ("S") could shock us. We will soon move on to discuss such emotional reactions and others (in Part III).

Importantly, *all* of these components of expression have their origin in psychological abilities and mechanisms from outside the music domain. Each component may be explained in terms of its "adaptive function." The G-component is linked to our capacity for syntactic processing (particularly linguistic phonology; see Lerdahl, 2013), without which human language would not be possible. The E-component is linked to our evolutionarily ancient abilities to communicate basic emotions nonverbally, conveying important information to conspecifics as well as being able to infer their future behaviors (Juslin, 2001). The R-component is linked to our imperfect ability to synchronize our actions with other individuals for various purposes (Clayton, 2016), such as hunting or moving heavy objects. The M-component is linked to our perceptual ability to distinguish animate objects from inanimate objects—and even to infer the precise nature of the animate object—based on sound patterns, which may have great survival value (Hodges & Sebald, 2011). Finally, the S-component is linked to our ability to develop schematic expectations for sequences of events (Huron & Margulis, 2010), even if we may wish to deviate from them.

Psychological experiments have demonstrated that it is possible to manipulate separate expressive components so as to produce distinct effects on listeners' ratings of the expression of a synthesized performance.

Unsurprisingly, perhaps, the E-component has the strongest influence on the overall expressivity of the music (Juslin, Friberg, & Bresin, 2002).

By distinguishing different components of expression, we could explain individual differences among performers more satisfactorily. Different performers may be characterized in terms of the relative weights they give to different aspects of expression. Some performers might give priority to motor precision (R), over emotional expression (E). Clarifying the structure (G) may be essential for a classical pianist, but may be less important for a blues guitarist.

Table 13.2 summarizes hypothesized characteristics of each of the five components that can guide research (Juslin, 2003). One implication of the GERMS model is that at some stages of learning, different aspects of expression will need to be taught separately because they have distinct characteristics.

13.5 Playing Expressively—It's All About Passion

Some scholars prefer to consider expression in a *general* sense. Thus, it could be interesting to look at what "playing expressively in general" might involve. It is probably true that musicians do not always deliberately aim for a specific expression, they just try to play "expressively." This, of course, does not preclude that the actual *playing* is still expressive in a *particular* way.

As explained in the Preface, I have been a guitarist for 30 years, mainly in the genres of blues, jazz, and rock. My impression is that most solos in these genres do not explicitly aim for the expression of discrete emotions. Thus, for example, jazz playing is often rather "absolutist" in nature; the main focus is on the note patterns as such. Blues and rock playing is more clearly "referentialist". Rock guitar solos commonly have an "angry" touch, in terms of aggressive note attacks, heavy vibrato, distortion, pentatonic scales—and *loudness*!

The best blues playing is clearly emotional (think of B.B. King, Albert Collins, Eric Clapton, and Albert King) and is often reminiscent of the

Table 13.2 Hypothesized characteristics of the GERMS components of music performance.

	Component				
Characteristic	G	E	R	M	S
Origin of pattern	Generative transformations of the musical structure	Emotion-specific patterns of acoustic cues deriving from vocal expression	Internal timekeeper and motor delay variance reflecting human limitations	Biological motion; distinct patterns of movement typical of human beings	Deviations from expected performance conventions
Nature of pattern	Local expressive features related to the structural interpretation	Mainly overall levels of multiple uncertain, partly redundant cues that are compensatory	Semi-random patterns, 1/f noise and white noise; very small in magnitude, irregular	Dynamic, non-compensatory patterns; smooth and global	Local; not predictable from the structure
Salient brain regions	Left hemisphere (adjacent to Broca's area)	Right hemisphere (the basal ganglia)	Lateral and medial parts of the cerebellum, plus the motor cortex	Left hemisphere (the superior temporal sulcus)	Anterior cingulate cortex
Perceptual effects	Clarifies structure; affects the inherent expression of a piece	Expresses emotions and moods (mainly in broad categories of emotion)	Generates a "living" and natural quality	Yields expressive form that is similar to human gestures	Heightens tension and unpredictability
Knowledge dependence	Medium	Low	None	Low	High
Aesthetic contribution	Beauty, Order, Coherence	Recognition, Arousal, Personal expression	Unevenness, Novelty	Balance, Unity, Recognition	Novelty, Arousal
Under voluntary control	Yes, mostly	Yes	No	Yes, partly	Yes

Adapted from Juslin, P. N. (2003). *Five facets of musical expression: A psychologist's perspective on music performance.* Psychology of Music, 31, 273–302. Copyright © 2003 by Society for Education, Music, and Psychology Research.

human voice, but what is its *expression*? It differs depending on the artist, the song, and the solo (guitarist Buddy Guy occasionally seems to aim for expression of "pure madness"). Still, it seems that the most expressive guitar playing aims for an emotional expression that is actually not that different from what, say, a classical violinist might seek. How can we characterize this expressive quality?

One clue comes perhaps from a listening experiment I conducted in the 1990s (Juslin, 1997b). Listeners were asked to rate 108 music performances, which varied systematically with regard to features such as tempo, sound level, articulation, timbre, and tone attacks on emotion scales such as *sad, happy, angry, tender, fearful,* and *expressive*. I explored the relationships between the ratings on the different scales, using a statistical technique called cluster analysis.

What I found was that the kind of expression in music that listeners found most *expressive* featured a *tender* or *sad* quality. These findings can, in turn, be related to those of the expression mark experiment presented in section 7.3. The expression mark *espressivo* co-varied strongly with the emotion terms *despair* (typically considered belonging to the *sadness* category) and *desire* (typically considered belonging to the *love* category, to which *tenderness* also belongs).

What I think we may tentatively conclude is that often when a musician aims for "expressive playing" *in general*, the resulting expression will tend to have a quality of "passionate desire" or "love." Imagine trying to desperately persuade and seduce a resistant lover. The musical features will be reminiscent of those used to express *sadness* and, in particular, *love–tenderness* (see Table 8.1). (Many of these features are common in pieces from the Romantic era, a period that emphasized expression of emotions; Pogue & Speck, 1997).

Love may be a common expression in music (Kreutz, 2000; Levitin, 2006; see Chapter 6), but love is not always harmonious, and this comes across in the expression of a great deal of music. The most expressive guitar solos in blues appear to vary along a dimension that ranges from "tender pleading" to "aggressive frustration." Imagine, again, that you would try to desperately persuade or seduce a resistant lover and that you weren't successful. Such playing involves emotional contrasts between soft, "pleading," *tender* notes with string bending, and explosive cascades of notes with "aggressive" attack and heavy vibrato, expressive of *frustration*. Blues playing at its best, to me, sounds like an intense lovers' quarrel.

In summary, this part of the book has shown that listeners find music expressive of emotions, and that musicians may even communicate certain emotions to listeners with some reliability. There are three distinct "layers" of musical expression of emotions. Each layer corresponds to a specific type of coding of emotional meaning. The "core" layer is based on iconically coded basic emotions, and it can explain findings of universal recognition of emotions in both speech and music. This core layer can be extended, qualified, and sometimes even modified by two additional layers based on intrinsic and associative coding, respectively, which enable listeners to perceive more complex emotions in music. The additional layers are less cross-culturally invariant, though, and they depend more on the social context and the listener.

We may refer to the three layers (i.e., Iconic-Intrinsic-Associative) as the ICINAS framework. It is through the *combined* forces of these different sources that musical expression of emotions is able to resonate so deeply with our own experience. The "emotional polyphony" of music can mirror the complexity and ambiguity of emotions we experience in life, to the point that music seems almost to express the inexpressible.

However, perceiving the music as expressive of emotions is often only the first step towards a fulfilling music experience; clearly, what most listeners strive for is to be "moved," to experience a *felt* emotion in response to the music. This, then, is the topic I turn to in Part III.

PART III

AROUSAL OF EMOTION

CHAPTER 14

BEYOND PERCEPTION

When Music Moves Us

Music arouses strong emotional responses in people, and they want to know why.
—(Dowling & Harwood, 1986, p. 202)

In 2007, my partner Susanne and I visited Parc Güell, a beautiful park composed of gardens and architectural elements located on Carmel Hill in Barcelona, designed by the renowned architect Antoni Gaudí, champion of Catalan modernism. A few minutes after arriving, a busker started to play "Romance", an old (possibly Spanish) guitar piece from the seventeenth century, on a gut-string guitar.

The remarkable thing was what happened next. With amazement I noticed that Susanne had tears in her eyes *within seconds* of hearing the first phrase of the music. "*This*," I thought, "is the power of music." An instrumental piece can move us beyond imagination. With this brief anecdote, we have arrived at the topic that many readers will find most fascinating: music can *arouse* deep and profound emotions.

When I defended my doctoral thesis in Uppsala (Juslin, 1998)—a dissertation focusing on the expression and communication of emotion in music performance—one of the criticisms leveled at my work by a professor was this: "Why have you focused on perception of emotions? Is not the arousal of emotions more important?"

At the time I was annoyed by his comment. "What is the point of criticizing a thesis on a specific subject for not being a thesis on something *else*? Shouldn't criticism focus on whether the thesis achieved the aims it set out to achieve?" I still believe this is true to some extent, but the reviewer made a valid point. Perhaps the *felt* emotions are really the most important, the very thing that "drives" our engagement with music. Perceiving emotion in music is all very well, but music experience would be a rather "cold" exercise without the affect it arouses.

A study by Emery Schubert (2007) suggests that the way music makes the listener *feel* is more important in determining his or her enjoyment than perceiving an emotion the music is communicating. Enjoyment *is* a feeling, so it could hardly be any other way. (It is perhaps not a coincidence that my own research eventually took a turn in this direction, from perception to felt emotion.)

14.1 Emotion: A Catalyst for Embarking on a Musical Career?

In Part II, we explored the notion that music is heard as expressive of emotions by listeners. Often, however, musicians wish to accomplish more than simply to communicate a certain emotional character to the listener. They also wish to *arouse* emotions in the listener.

The violinist Yehudi Menuhin settles for no less a goal than "to move an audience" (Menuhin, 1996, p. 413). Similarly, singer Antwon The Swan from the Red Hot Chili Peppers notes that "the whole reason we started playing music is cos we loved making people feel certain ways and our music is very heavily based on emotion and just the feel you get when you listen to it" (Driver, 2001, p. 349). Guitarist Keith Richards explains his views on song writing:

> What is it that makes you want to write songs? In a way you want to stretch yourself into other people's hearts. You want to plant yourself there, or at least get a resonance, where other people become a bigger instrument than the one you're playing. It becomes almost an obsession to touch other people. To write a song that is remembered and taken to heart is a connection, a touching of bases. A thread that runs through all of us. A stab to the heart. (Richards, 2010, p. 278)

This wish to "move" the audience becomes more understandable, perhaps, if we consider that strong emotional experiences with music are often a key factor influencing subsequent career choice to become a musician (Sloboda, 1989).

In Boyd and George-Warren's interview study, several artists recalled being struck with unforgettable force by a particular musician or type of music. It might be "a certain song, the shape or sound of a particular instrument, a specific feeling or attitude emanating from a particular musician" (Boyd & George-Warren, 2013, p. 138); "they were deeply touched by a form of music or individual artists who stirred within them the longing to write and perform their own sound" (p. 133).

For some musicians, it was a song that had a decisive effect. Singer and songwriter Graham Nash (from The Hollies and Crosby, Stills, Nash, & Young) remembers hearing the Everly Brothers at a school dance:

> It paralyzed me. It had to stop what I was doing, which was walking across the dance floor. And I stopped because I was so shocked musically. Right at that moment, something inside of me said, "I want to make people feel what I feel at this moment." (Smith, 1988, p. 294)

For others, it was a specific solo. Woodie Shaw, for example, cites the opening trumpet solo by Lee Morgan in "Moanin'" by Art Blakey and the Jazz Messengers, as his biggest influence.[1] For others, it might be the sensuous timbre of a musical instrument. A participant in John Sloboda's study of early memories with music recalled, "the music was a clarinet duet, classical ... I was astounded at the beauty of the sound. It was liquid, resonant, vibrant. It seemed to send tingles through me" (Sloboda, 2005, p. 183).

Such early emotional experiences with music appear to plant a seed for embarking on a musical career. However, even for that sizable portion

[1] For me, it was hearing the first notes of Eric Clapton's opening blues solo in the Billy Myles song, "Have You Ever Loved a Woman?", from the Derek and the Dominos album *Layla and Other Assorted Love Songs* (see Chapter 23) that made me become serious about learning to play the electric guitar as a young teenager.

of the Western population that does not aim for a musical career, emotion still seems to be a main motivation for engaging with music. For example, in one survey study, the most commonly self-reported motive for listening to music was to express, release, and influence emotions (Juslin & Laukka, 2004).

14.2 Aims and Questions

It is often regarded as one of the great mysteries in life that music, which consists seemingly only of "abstract tone sequences," is able to arouse such strong emotions: "Music is and will remain a mystery," argues a participant in Alf Gabrielsson's study (Gabrielsson, 2011, p. 445). Researchers, too, find emotional reactions to music puzzling, for a reason that is perhaps best captured by yet another paradox regarding music and emotion:

PARADOX 4: Music, an abstract form of art which appears removed from our concerns in everyday life, may arouse emotions, biologically evolved reactions related to human survival.

Can we resolve this paradox? I think we can, but doing so may require that we abandon some common conceptions about music and emotion, which have prevented a deeper understanding (see Chapter 17).

Does music really arouse emotions? If so, how do we know? Which emotions does it evoke? Are these emotions different from other emotions? In which settings do emotions occur? Why and how does music arouse emotions? Why do "live" concerts tend to conjure up stronger emotions than recorded music? Why do different listeners react differently to the same piece of music? Are the emotions aroused by music the same across cultures? In this Part, I will address these questions and more.

I will present eight psychological mechanisms (principles) through which music can arouse emotions in listeners, as well as a framework that may help us to understand the mechanisms. In doing so, I will connect with the themes of this book. We will see that emotional responses to music are intrinsically social in nature; that they involve "implicit" psychological processes in the form of multiple emotion mechanisms, many of an ancient evolutionary origin; and that they are influenced by various factors in the music, the listener, and the context.

CHAPTER 15

DOES MUSIC AROUSE EMOTIONS? HOW DO WE KNOW?

Many researchers consider emotional reactions to music to be of major importance, yet the notion that music arouses emotions has been the subject of controversy—much more so than the notion that music is heard as expressive of emotions.

15.1 The Case Against Arousal of Emotions: Meet The "Cognitivist"

Philosopher Peter Kivy introduces an important distinction between "cognitivists" and "emotivists" (Kivy, 1990). The "cognitivist" argues that music does not arouse emotions in listeners, it only expresses emotions which are perceived by listeners. The "emotivist," by contrast, argues that music may also arouse felt emotions in listeners. (Curiously, Kivy himself is often branded a "cognitivist," despite having declared himself an "emotivist"; Kivy, 2001, p. 85.)

In my estimation, the "emotivists" outnumber the "cognitivists" by a long way, though I could be wrong. Those who question the proposition that emotional reactions to music exist are sometimes dismissed as nutjobs, but in science we should be wary of self-evident truths.[1]

[1] It is possible that those scholars who reject the idea that music arouses emotions belong to a group of people who do not actually experience such emotions; that is, they might be relying on their own introspection when taking a stand on this issue (see section 3.5 and the Kivy–Radford debate).

What, then, are the typical arguments of the "cognitivist"? One argument is that listeners mistake the emotions expressed in the music for their own. Another argument is that because emotions depend on appraisals of events in terms of their consequences for our goals and concerns in life (Chapter 4), an emotional reaction to music does not "make sense." (Music does not seem to have any implications for our life goals.) One final argument is that the behavior manifestations characteristic of emotions seem to be missing in music listeners.

All these charges should be taken seriously. Therefore, although we might be convinced that music can arouse emotions, we should take a step back and consider the basic question: *are there emotional reactions to music?* This question is not trivial, because it raises important issues about the measurement of emotions.

In Part I, I defined emotion partly in terms of various "components" that together constitute an "emotion episode." Any attempt to answer the question of whether music can arouse emotions should proceed from this definition. To what extent might listening to music produce reactions in the different components of emotion? Let us examine the components, one by one: feeling, expression, psychophysiology, neural activation, action tendency, and regulation. To make them easier to remember, I shall refer to them jointly as the FEPNAR components.

15.2 "I Feel Good (Like I Knew That I Would)": Self-Reported Feelings

The most obvious form of evidence concerns *subjective feeling*; that is, the experiential or phenomenological aspect of emotions. This is what we usually have in mind when we talk about "emotions" in everyday life. (Take a moment to imagine how you *feel* when you are, say, *anxious*, as opposed to *relaxed.*) This is the most important component, if you ask lay people (Nielsen & Kaszniak, 2007), and many music researchers also regard it as essential (Zentner & Eerola, 2010).

To gain access to listeners' subjective feelings, researchers rely on the method of communication par excellence in humans: language. In a wide range of investigations, including listening experiments (Pike, 1972), surveys (Gabrielsson, 2011), diary studies (Sloboda, Ivaldi, & O'Neill, 2001), and in-depth interviews (DeNora, 2000), people have reported that they experience feelings using checklists, adjective ratings, or free description (see Chapter 5).

We saw in Part II that most studies of emotion perception in music have relied on self-reporting, and the same is arguably true for studies of aroused emotions—but often additional measures are used. If listeners can simply report what they feel, do we really need any other measure? Although it may seem unlikely that people are mistaken about their own feelings, many researchers believe that verbal self-reports of emotions can be unreliable sometimes.

First, listeners might confuse emotions expressed in the music with emotions they feel themselves. As Leonard Meyer argues, "it may well be that when a listener reports that he felt this or that emotion, he is describing the emotion which he believes the passage is supposed to indicate, not anything which he himself has experienced" (Meyer, 1956, p. 8). Indeed, it may be difficult sometimes to distinguish between perception and arousal of emotions. (Are we only perceiving sadness in the music, or are we perhaps feeling a little sad ourselves also?)

Second, we may report an emotion just because we think this is *expected* by the investigator, a phenomenon referred to as *demand characteristics* (Orne, 1962). Let us say you participate in a study where an experimenter plays a piece of music that has a sad expression (as denoted by features such as minor mode, slow tempo, low average pitch, and legato articulation), and tells you to "report how you feel"; you may then be inclined to report that you feel sad even if you are not really experiencing that emotion.

There is nothing malicious about this; quite the opposite, you are perhaps only trying to be "helpful" to the researcher, or show that you understand what he or she is seeking. Even so, the consequence is that the self-report is not a valid indicator of your feeling state. This is only one example of a more general problem, referred to as *reactivity*. Asking listeners to report their emotional experiences may *alter* those same experiences.

Third, there is a common misconception that we can directly access subjective feelings via verbal self-reports. The truth is that self-reports must necessarily involve a combination of "raw" feeling and reflective awareness. More precisely, we can only access our immediate emotional experience (i.e., *primary awareness*) as "filtered" through a cognitive overlay of reflective thought and evaluation (i.e., *secondary awareness*; cf. Lambie & Marcel, 2002).[2]

The balance between raw feeling and reflective consciousness depends partly on how much "in the grip of an emotion" you are at a particular moment (Nielsen & Kaszniak, 2007).[3] However, because self-reports *invariably* depend on reflective thought, they will be influenced by folk psychology (common lay beliefs) and hyperbole.

To illustrate, consider the following description of a feeling by the conductor Bruno Walter, upon hearing Richard Wagner's "Tristan and Isolde":

> From the first sound of the cellos my heart contracted spasmodically . . . Never before had my soul been so deluged with floods of sound and passion, never before had my heart been so consumed by yearning and sublime bliss. (Goulding, 1995, p. 148)

We can hardly take this self-report as a direct reflection of the raw feeling. Furthermore, because self-reports usually depend on verbal language, they involve the same problems as discussed regarding perception of emotion (section 7.2), such as individual differences in verbal fluency or emotion vocabulary and cross-cultural differences in terminology.

Individual differences between listeners' self-reports may not reflect only language, however. Because self-reports involve reflective cognition, we can

[2] Many researchers believe that other mammals also have "raw" feelings (primary awareness), but that they lack reflective awareness of their feelings (Panksepp, 1998).

[3] Notably, during moments of *flow* (Harmat, Ørsted Andersen, Ullén, Wright, & Sadlo, 2016), we appear to disconnect momentarily from our awareness of the self as "object," but the moment we become aware of being in flow, the disconnection will disappear.

also encounter error variance due to individual differences in what is called *emotional awareness.*

Carol Gohm and Gerald Clore present evidence of four trait dimensions of emotional experience: *attention to emotion* (e.g., the extent to which individuals monitor or value their emotions), *clarity* (e.g., the ability to identify and distinguish their emotions), *intensity* (e.g., the strength with which individuals experience emotions), and *expression* (e.g., the extent to which individuals express emotions) (Gohm & Clore, 2000). Some of the dimensions clearly reflect varying degrees of emotional awareness, but others reflect the fact that different listeners may not actually *experience* emotions in the same way. (We cannot blame self-reports for the latter problem, of course.)

In any case, because of the problems associated with verbal self-reports of feelings, many researchers have relied on additional types of evidence of emotion, and doing so partly avoids these problems.

15.3 "With Every Heartbeat": Psychophysiological Measures

Have you ever experienced—at a specific moment during a "live" concert, or while listening to your favorite music—that your heart is "beating with excitement." This type of response belongs to a second category of measures, which we call "psychophysiological."

Psychophysiology is the branch of psychology that is concerned with the physiological bases of psychological processes (Andreassi, 2007). As noted in Chapter 4, emotions are almost by definition embodied phenomena: it is hard to imagine having an emotion without any kind of physiological response.

If you look back at the quotation by Hector Berlioz that opened the book, you will find that it features several references to physiological responses. If we look past the hyperbole of his description, the strong somatic component suggests he may have been describing a genuine emotion.

Physiological responses are sometimes mentioned in self-reports. For example, listeners in Gabrielsson's study of strong experiences mention "sweating," "changed breathing," "heart palpitations," "burning cheeks," "trembles," and "tensioning of muscles" (Gabrielsson, 2011, p. 375). Yet physiological responses as a source of evidence are more useful when "objective" measures (e.g., readings of skin conductance) can be obtained.

Note that this emotion component is less subject to demand characteristics than verbal self-reports of feeling, because it is not usually possible to control autonomic responses by will power. You may wish to be "a good participant" by responding in the "expected" or "intended" way, but for the most part you cannot really determine your physiological response patterns.

In my opinion, physiological measurement should routinely be used whenever it is practically feasible, because it may help us to distinguish *felt* emotion from mere *perception* of emotion. In the former case, we would expect to discover changes in physiological measures, as part of the emotional response, whereas in the latter case, we would not expect such changes *unless*, say, the listener was running like a madman to a concert.

Several experiments have shown that music listening can give rise to physiological responses similar to those shown to other "emotionally competent" stimuli. This may include changes in heart rate, skin temperature, electrodermal response, respiration, and hormone secretion (for a review, see Hodges, 2010; see also Chanda & Levitin, 2013).

The results are inconsistent or contradictory across studies, however. One reason is that most physiological studies did not control whether the listeners experienced an emotion (and, if so, which emotion). Intermingled in these studies are (i) listeners who experienced one emotion, (ii) listeners who experienced another emotion, and (iii) listeners who experienced no emotion at all. No wonder there are inconsistencies in the results. However, the lion's share of the evidence confirms that music *does* cause physiological responses, and the effects can be quite large (e.g., Lundqvist, Carlsson, Hilmersson, & Juslin, 2009).

Not only does music produce physiological responses in listeners, the responses also seem to be reflective of the pieces heard or more precisely the experience of them. For instance, different pieces of music may produce distinct patterns of physiological response (Krumhansl, 1997), such that it is feasible to *discriminate* between pieces based on physiological variables (Nyklíček, Thayer, & Van Doornen, 1997). Intense subjective feelings involve higher levels of autonomic arousal (Rickard, 2004), while *electromyographical* (EMG) measures of facial muscles may reveal the valence of the feeling, positive or negative (Witvliet & Vrana, 2007).

If physiological responses can inform us about emotions experienced by music listeners, why can't we just use these measures, instead of having to rely on self-reporting (which is subject to demand characteristics)? One problem is that there is no simple one-to-one mapping between psychophysiological responses and experienced emotions (Larsen, Berntson, Poehlmann, Ito, & Cacioppo, 2008). Physiological measures may be influenced by a variety of factors (apart from any emotion), such as time of day, temperature of the laboratory room, individual characteristics, etc. Thus, we cannot (yet) determine precisely which emotion—if any—a listener is experiencing simply by looking at physiological indices.

What we can do is to point in the approximate direction. We can distinguish emotions to some extent by locating them in one of the four "quadrants" of the *circumplex* model (Russell, 1980; Figure 4.1). To illustrate: if listeners report that they experience *happiness*, their physiological responses should indicate *high arousal* and *positive valence*. This pattern should be evident in measures of autonomic activity and facial expressions, respectively, as shown in the previous literature (Andreassi, 2007; for examples, see Juslin, Harmat, & Eerola, 2014).

Just as with "uncertain cues" used in musical communication (Chapter 10), single indices of psychophysiology cannot distinguish specific emotions. Still, prospects look promising since multivariate approaches become more common. In a thoughtful review, Donald Hodges concludes that "though the issue is not entirely settled, there is mounting evidence that multivariate approaches may lead to the discovery of distinct patterns of psychophysiological activity that can differentiate among various emotions" (Hodges,

2010, p. 296). I agree. The crucial point is that by obtaining physiological patterns which are consistent with verbal self-reports, we can draw more valid conclusions about experienced emotions.[4]

15.4 The Thrill of It All: Music and Goosebumps

There is a particular kind of psychophysiological response to music that has been variously referred to as "thrills," "chills," or "frisson" (Huron, 2006; Panksepp, 1995; Sloboda, 1991). David Huron and Elisabeth Hellmuth Margulis define "chills" as "a pleasant tingling sensation associated with flexing of hair follicles, resulting in gooseflesh (technically called piloerection) accompanied by a cold sensation, and sometimes producing a shiver" (Huron & Margulis, 2010, p. 591).

Think about your own music experiences; perhaps you have experienced goosebumps or shivers down your spine at a certain moment of the music (e.g., the climax of a guitar solo). These bodily reactions appear to be intense but relatively short lived—lasting from less than a second to about ten seconds (Huron & Margulis, 2010).

The chill response appears to be quite rare, however, even in "peak" experiences with music. Less than 10% of the reports in Gabrielsson's 2011 study mentions "chills" or "gooseflesh." Estimates of the percentage of individuals who experience chills to music range from 35% (Konečni, Wanic, & Brown, 2007) to 90% (for musicians in Goldstein, 1980). On average, only about half the studied population appears to have experienced the phenomenon in relation to music, which is remarkable.

Chills seem more frequent in females, amongst musicians, in people who are *not* "sensation seekers," and in response to *sad* (as opposed to *happy*) music

[4] Some researchers have a tendency to be distrustful about physiological measures: if the measures do not produce clear effects, the researchers question the measures. In fact, what they should be worrying about is whether the *self-reports* are accurate. My experience is that emotions *do* produce physiological responses; if we fail to detect such responses, the most plausible reason is that the listeners are not experiencing emotions.

(Grewe, Nagel, Kopiez, & Altenmüller, 2007; Goldstein, 1980; Panksepp, 1995). Participants generally experience more chills to self-selected music (Nusbaum, Silvia, Beaty, Burgin, Hodges, & Kwapil, 2014) than to music selected by an experimenter (Konečni et al., 2007), although this tendency does not seem to reflect mere familiarity (Guhn, Hamm, & Zentner, 2007). Contributing to the mystique of chill responses is that they are not perfectly reproducible when playing the same musical event on different days, even in individuals with high chill susceptibility (Altenmüller et al., 2013).

Chill experiences are not confined to music, or to positive emotional experiences, for that matter. Huron and Margulis suggest that they may occur when viewing disgusting pictures; in response to hearing fingernails scratching a blackboard; during orgasm; when experiencing a sudden insight, a dentist's drill, or physical contact with another person (Huron & Margulis, 2010).

The fact that chills can be either pleasant or unpleasant suggests that the response is not itself an emotion category, since emotions are partly defined by a positive or negative valence. Rather, it is a physiological symptom which may occur together with different emotions, like *surprise, fear, sadness*, and *awe* (Huron, 2006; Juslin, Harmat, & Eerola, 2014; Konečni, 2005; Sloboda, 1991).

Listeners are often able to specify the moments in the music where the chills tend to occur (Sloboda, 1991). Correlates of chills include "a rapid large change of loudness" (especially an increase); "a broadening of the frequency range"; "an abrupt change of tempo or rhythm" (e.g., a syncopation); "the entry of one or more instruments or voices"; "new or unprepared harmony"; or "the return of a theme or motive." Examples of musical excerpts that listeners have cited as chill-inducing may be found in Huron and Margulis (2010), Panksepp (1995), and Sloboda (1991), but the effectiveness of specific pieces of music tends to be different depending on the listener.

A variety of theories have been proposed to account for musical chills, for instance that they involve a distress response to a perceived "separation call" in the music (Panksepp, 1995); a contrastive valence response linked to musical expectancies (Huron, 2006); or a response to what is heard as the piercing sound of hunting predators or the shrieking call of conspecifics attacked by a predator (Owren & Randall, 2001). I am not sure what music these last authors have in mind (Axl Rose?). In any case, none of these theories have been tested to date. I believe that several different mechanisms can account for the symptom of chills, some of which may be related to the above theories (Chapters 18–24).

I have experienced chills to music numerous times in my life, but they seem to become rarer as I get older. As music experiences accumulate, something really special may be needed to obtain the same kind of reaction. The change may indeed have to do something with age. It is known that psychophysiological responsivity tends to decline with age more generally. Thus, we may be less prone to experience chills as we get older.

I remember one piece of music which repeatedly gave me chills as a teenager. I was sixteen when I bought Luciano Pavarotti's album *In Concert* (1986) (Figure 15.1). There is some background that probably contributed to my experience of the music.

In Modena, it was not Luciano who was the star in the family; he was mainly known as "the baker's son." The baker in question was Luciano's father, also a fabulous singer, but riddled with stage fright; never embarking

Figure 15.1 Opera singer Luciano Pavarotti, once dubbed 'the king of the high C's'. *Illustration by Costis Chatzidakis.*

on a musical career, but who sang regularly in his local village. Thus, in Modena, Pavarotti was always in the shadow of his father. There are several examples in the literature of artists who have found it difficult to succeed on their "home turf." This, then, was the context for my hearing of the music.

The piece in question was "Nessun Dorma", which has now been played ad nauseum (it did not yet seem that way in the 1980s). As perhaps many readers will recognize, this is a tenor aria from Giacomo Puccini's opera, *Turandot*. What gave me chills was, unsurprisingly, the final climax. After a short build-up, Pavarotti—or his character, Calaf—sings: "*Dilegua, o notte! Tramontate, stelle! Tramontate, stelle! All'alba vincerò! Vincerò! Vincerò!*" ("*Vanish, o night! Set, stars! Set, stars! At dawn, I will win! I will win! I will win!*"). Pavarotti is full of energy and confidence—almost overshooting the final notes (*Vincerò!*), a sustained B4, followed by the final note, an even longer A4.

The circumstances—that Pavarotti is in good form; that he stands before his home audience; and that he is actually singing "I will win, I will win"; the beautiful melody; the expectations associated with the build-up in the strings just before the final phrases—all conspired to give me chills. The roar of the audience during the final sustained note really brought it home for me (*Bravo!*); *this*, I thought, is what musical triumph sounds like!

15.5 "Singing in the Brain": Neural Activation

I explained earlier that physiological responses have the advantage that they are not strongly affected by demand characteristics. This is true also for that special part of our body that we call the brain.

Several studies have shown that listeners' responses to music involve brain regions which are known from previous studies to be involved in emotional reactions; these include both ancient structures in subcortical areas ("deeper" in the brain) and new structures in cortical areas (more "superficial"). The structures implicated in emotional reactions to music go by names such as the amygdala, the hippocampus, the striatum, the cingulate cortex, the insula, the pre-frontal and orbitofrontal cortex, the cerebellum, the frontal gyrus, the parahippocampal gyrus, and the brainstem (Blood & Zatorre, 2001; Brown, Martinez, & Parsons, 2004; Koelsch, Fritz, von Cramon, Müller, & Friederici, 2006; Menon & Levitin, 2005; for a review, see Juslin & Sakka, in press).

It may be argued that these findings provide independent support for the "emotivist" position that music arouses emotions, but results also make it perfectly clear that "there is not a single, unitary emotional system underlying all emotional responses to music" (Peretz, 2010, p. 119). The relevant brain regions are widely distributed. In "the age of the brain," it may be tempting to think that brain research holds the key to explaining musical emotions: we can simply look inside the brain to see what is going on. The truth is, of course, more complicated.

First, the results so far are fairly inconsistent in that different studies tend to report different patterns of activation. This may partly reflect methodological problems. In a review, Isabelle Peretz points out that brain-mapping "cannot disentangle correlation from causation," and that data from brain imaging studies tend to be "over inclusive" (Peretz, 2010, p. 114). What this means is that brain studies have a poor precision when it comes to pinpointing the regions responsible for particular psychological processes (let alone the nature of these psychological processes).

One strategy is to search for brain areas that are consistently activated across studies. In their extensive overview, Stefan Koelsch and his coworkers suggest that a special network consisting of the amygdala, the hippocampus, the para-hippocampus, the temporal poles, and (perhaps) the pre-genual cingulate cortex may play a consistent role in emotional processing of music (Koelsch, Siebel, & Fritz, 2010). However, few brain regions are consistently activated across studies (Juslin & Sakka, in press). One reason for this might be a lack of conceptual precision.

Note that emotions might be analyzed along many different dimensions in a brain study. First, one can distinguish brain regions in terms of whether they involve *perception* or *arousal* of emotion (Wager et al., 2008). Not all brain studies of music have taken this distinction into consideration, but our review indicates that only for arousal of emotions have several studies reported changes in the amygdala, the striatum (including nucleus accumbens), and the hippocampus. At least some of these regions might thus distinguish arousal of emotions from mere perception (Juslin & Sakka, in press).

Second, one can also try to distinguish brain regions in terms of *specific emotions* (Damasio et al., 2000; Murphy, Nimmo-Smith, & Lawrence, 2003; Panksepp, 1998; Phan, Wager, Taylor, & Liberzon, 2002; Saarimäki et al., 2016). The experience of *fear* could activate a different brain region than the experience of *joy*. However, the notion of emotion-specific brain activation remains controversial. Studies of emotions have not yet found evidence that specific emotions may be consistently localized to distinct brain regions (Lindquist et al., 2012).

Finally, one can analyze brain regions in terms of distinct *psychological processes* or *brain functions* (Cabeza & Nyberg, 2000)—exploring what the brain is "doing" and "why." This is where psychology becomes crucial; brain activation per se is pure physiology and does not tell us anything about what the brain is doing, unless it is linked to some kind of behavioral data (psychology). The coupling of precise psychological predictions with brain imaging is the neuroscientific approach that holds most promise when it comes to explaining emotional reactions to music (Juslin & Zentner, 2002).

In my view, the search for a single network that is consistently activated in emotional reactions to music is futile. In Chapter 25, I will show how psychological theory can help to make sense of results from brain studies in a more principled approach. Which brain network is activated depends on which psychological mechanism produced the emotion in question.

15.6 "Cry Me A River": Emotional Expression

One reason that philosopher Peter Kivy remained skeptical towards the possibility that music can arouse what he calls emotions of the "garden variety" (e.g., *sadness, happiness*) was that reactions to music do not involve "the behavioral manifestations" of such emotions (Kivy, 1999). However, is this really true?

Let us consider one common type of behavioral manifestation: *expressive behavior*. Do people express emotions when they listen to music? Yes, it is perfectly clear that music listening makes people smile, laugh, cry, and furrow their eyebrows—as shown by both measurements of facial muscles in the laboratory (Witvliet & Vrana, 2007) and informal observation of listeners during "live" concerts, where facial, vocal, and bodily expressions of emotions are common. (Look at pictures of audiences taken during rock concerts.)

Crying is a particular form of expressive behavior that appears to occur quite commonly in response to music. William Frey conducted a survey study of crying in general, and found that 63 out of 800 crying episodes reported were caused by music (Frey, 1985). About 24% of the listeners in Gabrielsson's 2011 survey study mention "tears" or "crying." Females do so to a greater degree (28%) than males (18%)—consistent with gender differences in expressivity documented in emotion research more generally (Brody & Hall, 2008).

We tend to associate tears and crying with *sadness*, but crying is a complex phenomenon that might occur together with other feelings such as *joy* and *relief*. Many listeners report the experience of crying to music as pleasurable and rewarding rather than aversive (Gabrielsson & Lindström Wik, 2003). Listeners often cry when they feel "moved" (section 16.3)—as in the anecdote from Parc Güell that opened this part of the book. Later in Part IV, I will hypothesize that this response may result from a kind of "emotional overflow," which occurs when several psychological mechanisms are activated simultaneously and produce conflicting "outputs."

Expressive behavior is a distinct marker of emotion. As John Sloboda observes, "it is very difficult to be mistaken about whether you cried or not to a piece of music" (Sloboda, 1992, p. 39). Yet, some emotional expressions might be subtle and hard to detect. It has long been known from experimental studies conducted in Uppsala that even when no facial expression can be clearly observed visually, there may still be small expressive movements in the face in reaction to an emotional stimulus, which can be recorded through electromyography (Dimberg & Thunberg, 1998). Such subtle expressions may also be recorded during music listening (Juslin et al., 2014, 2015) to confirm that an emotion occurs.

15.7 "I'd Like to Move It": Action Tendencies

The late "grandfather" of emotion psychology in Europe, Nico Frijda, liked to define emotions in terms of different modes of "action readiness" (Frijda, 2016): that is, each emotion seems to prepare us for a certain type of action. However, Frijda also explained that states of action readiness do not *always* instigate action—they may remain states of preparation. Thus, researchers often refer to them as "action tendencies."

To illustrate: we may tend to run away when scared, but through "willpower," we can stay put. In other words, our action tendencies can be controlled or suppressed to some extent. (In modern society, this may indeed be the most common outcome!) However, emotions might also lead to a change of priorities (Oatley, 1992) with more long-term effects on behavior. Perhaps you won't run up and kiss an artist during an exceptional performance, but you might buy or download the artist's albums for years to come.

Music anthropologist Judith Becker notes that the image of the music listener typically conveyed in psychological studies in the Western world is that of an individual person who is physically still, listening "respectfully" to the music, attentively and silently, for instance at a symphony concert (Becker, 2001). Becker observes that this is *not* how most people in the world relate to music. It may not even be typical of many Western listeners.

A psychological experiment is not representative of a typical listener context. Neither is the average concert of classical music. In fact, adopting a broader perspective, it becomes clear that concert audiences in most musical genres are far from passive.[5] Many musical contexts (e.g., rock concerts)

[5] This was also arguably the case back in the day, when "classical music" was just "music," and audiences were less "still," "silent," and "respectful" than during today's classical music concerts.

encourage overt actions in listeners, such as moving, jumping, dancing, or clapping one's hands (e.g., Gabrielsson, 2011, p. 376). At least *some* of these actions surely reflect emotional engagement with the musical event.

Music can also influence people's action tendencies in other ways. For instance, it can affect people's tendencies to help other people (Fried & Berkowitz, 1979), to consume products (North & Hargreaves, 2008), or to move—overtly or covertly. Even when listeners may *seem* to sit still, electromyographic measures can reveal spontaneous muscle contractions, as if we literally cannot sit still when we hear a musical rhythm (Harrer & Harrer, 1977).

In fact, the most typical behavior tendency in response to music is to move in coordination—in *sync*—with the music. This is related to a mechanism called *entrainment*, which is further discussed in Chapter 19. Dancing, then, is an action tendency of special significance for experiences of music, perhaps particularly in non-Western cultures (Rouget, 1985).

Some scholars have argued that emotional reactions to music differ from other emotions in that they do not lead to *immediate* goal-directed or adaptive behavior (Zentner, Grandjean, & Scherer, 2008). On reflection, the same is true of most non-musical emotions in everyday life too; it is just not the case that every time we experience an emotion, we immediately carry out some adaptive behavior.

On the contrary, we frequently experience emotions without an urgent need to act, as when a memory is evoked, when we "catch" the happy emotion of a smiling stranger, or when we are engaged in mental imagery. Only certain emotions prompt direct action, regardless of whether they are caused by music or not. Even emotions that do evoke action tendencies are often regulated. Arguably, only a child, drunk, or imbecile will act on every emotion felt.

The same is arguably true in a musical setting also. Action tendencies are commonly ignored or regulated (see section 15.8). This is, presumably, why Carol Krumhansl found that physiological responses occurring while people listened to music under laboratory conditions ("still" and "silent") were rather similar to those observed by other scientists when participants experienced emotions to a non-musical event in a situation involving behavioural suppression (Krumhansl, 1997).

At the same time, it is quite clear that strong emotional reactions to music sometimes *do* cause immediate behavior, such as leaving a dreadful concert, buying a CD, or hugging a performer; and peak experiences with music sometimes lead to major life decisions, which have powerful long-term influences on behavior (Gabrielsson, 2011).

15.8 "Can't Stop the Feeling": Emotion Regulation

Have you ever experienced being so moved by music that you were embarrassed? (You are not alone.) How did you handle the situation? Did you try to calm down by distracting yourself with thoughts or by taking deep breaths? If so, this is a perfect example of emotion regulation.

James Gross defines emotion regulation as the process of "shaping which emotions one has, when one has them, and how one experiences or expresses these emotions" (Gross, 2014, p. 6). People use various strategies (e.g., distraction, venting, reappraisal) based on goals (e.g., to reduce stress), which result in various emotional outcomes (e.g., calm relaxation).

There is evidence that this process occurs in music experience. Listeners attempt to regulate their emotional reactions to music, for example, with regard to what is deemed "appropriate" responses in a social context (Becker, 2004). Several reports in Gabrielsson's survey illustrates this phenomenon. For example, one woman notes: "I was ashamed that I found it so hard to control myself, but the emotions were so strong" (Gabrielsson, 2011, p. 121).

An emotional episode does not *necessarily* involve regulation: if you are among close friends or with your family, you may not bother to hide your emotional reaction. Yet the fact that we observe attempts at regulation provides additional support for the "emotivist" view, because these would hardly occur if there were no emotions to regulate in the first place.

However, there are strong cross-cultural differences in how emotions are regulated and why (Becker, 2004). For example, listeners attending a

Portuguese Fado house openly cry during the performances and do not seem to be ashamed; it is an expected and perfectly appropriate response (Barradas, in press). Various cultures differ in terms of "display rules" for emotions (Ekman, 1973), "culturally valued emotions" (Mesquita, Vissers, & De Leersnyder, 2015), and "ideal affect" (Tsai, 2007). Hence, regulation is arguably the component *most* subject to cultural influence.

Whether regulation should be regarded as part of the emotional episode or as something that happens afterwards is open for debate. As we will see later, listeners do not only try to regulate the emotions aroused by music, they also commonly *use* music to regulate their emotions to other life events (Baltazar & Saarikallio, 2016; Sakka & Juslin, 2018b).

15.9 What Is Synchronization and Why Does It Matter?

I have reviewed different types of evidence that music can arouse emotions. Perhaps you are familiar with "the duck test," which is a humorous way of referring to abductive reasoning. "If it looks like a duck, swims like a duck, and quacks like a duck—then it probably *is* a duck." The same kind of reasoning is often used to conclude that music arouses emotions. If listeners report feelings, if they cry and laugh, if they show physiological responses, if they have action tendencies, and if they seem to be involved in regulation, then they probably *are* experiencing emotions! This seems fair enough.

Still, it could be argued that many of the studies cited have looked at only *one* of the components (e.g., only at feelings or only at physiological responses), and that this should not count as evidence if emotions are defined as featuring *all* these components (cf. Chapter 4). Klaus Scherer and Marcel Zentner have proposed the rather conservative criterion that an emotional response to music should involve "evidence of a *synchronized* response of all or most organismic subsystems" (Scherer & Zentner, 2001, p. 363, emphasis added). The subsystems correspond to the FEPNAR components discussed earlier in this chapter.

Why should such synchronization occur? Again, an evolutionary perspective will be helpful. It can be assumed that a synchronized response serves to prepare us for appropriate behavior during a critical event. Robert Levenson notes more specifically that "behaviors such as withdrawal, expulsion, fighting, fleeing, and nurturing each make different physiological demands" (Levenson, 1994, p. 124). One function of emotions is to create the optimal physiological milieu to support the specific behavior that is required.

To illustrate, *fear* is associated with a motivation to flee and brings about sympathetic arousal consistent with this action: increased cardiovascular activation, greater oxygen exchange, and increased glucose availability. Hence, it is no coincidence that emotions involve simultaneous responses in a number of sub-components: These represent a synchronized effort to deal with the emotion-inducing event.

If we could show that synchronization can occur during music listening, this would strengthen the case for the "emotivist" position (cf. section 15.1). This is, in fact, what has been found. We measured self-reported feelings, facial muscle activity (EMG), and physiological responses in 32 participants while they listened to brief pieces of pop music, composed with either a *happy* or *sad* expression. (Newly composed music was used in order reduce individual differences due to personal memories associated with the music.)

The results showed a synchronized response in the experiential, expressive, and physiological components: For example, *happy* music produced more zygomatic facial-muscle activity (i.e., smiling), higher skin conductance, lower finger temperature, more felt *happiness,* and less felt *sadness* than did *sad* music (Lundqvist, Carlsson, Hilmersson, & Juslin, 2009).

Quite clearly, a "cognitivist" would have a hard time explaining why listeners react to the music with a synchronized response in multiple emotion components if they are not experiencing an emotion. If the synchronized reactions are not emotions, then what are they and why do they occur? Personally, I find it difficult to think of a plausible rival hypothesis.

In the best of all possible worlds, synchronization would always occur reliably in studies of emotion. In reality, it does not, for all kinds of reasons.[6] One reason is that synchronization is easiest to detect during strong emotions. A great deal of music listening features fairly weak affective responses (Sloboda et al., 2001), and in these cases synchronization might not be observed. However, judging from my own experience at the Uppsala laboratory, when truly effective stimuli are used, some degree of synchronization *does* tend to occur quite reliably (see section 25.9).

In cases where synchronization has *not* been observed, researchers have been inclined to interpret this as evidence that musical emotions do not generally involve synchronization (see Grewe et al., 2007). However, a more parsimonious and plausible explanation is that these particular studies simply *failed* to arouse strong emotion in listeners. It is not obvious that emotions will be easily aroused in artificial laboratory environments featuring unfamiliar music and/or music selected by the researcher. The aforementioned "demand characteristics" of the laboratory situation may lead the listener to report an emotion, when in fact there is none.

Why, then, are some researchers so quick (too quick) to conclude that emotional reactions to music do not involve a synchronized response? It is because they cannot see why music as a stimulus should *require* a synchronized response (in contrast to, say, a bear chasing us in the woods). This way of framing the problem rests on a mistaken assumption, as I will show in Chapter 17. Being able to show that synchronization occurs in a study is useful because it enables the researcher to distinguish arousal of emotions from mere perception of emotions, which is still an occasional problem in the field.[7]

In summary, in my estimation there is little doubt that music can arouse emotions just as "real" as other emotions experienced in life. The different

[6] Note that synchronization is not always successfully demonstrated in general emotion studies. Fair or not, we seem to place greater demands on studies of musical emotions than we do on studies of non-musical emotions!

[7] Indeed, it could be the case that some failures to observe synchronization between components of emotion in previous studies is due to the fact that the studies merely observed perception of emotion.

types of evidence are too strong to explain away. This should not tempt us to think that music *always* arouses emotions, or that it arouses *all* types of emotions to the same extent, in *all* people equally. However, as Philip Ball notes, "no one can doubt that some music is capable of exciting some emotion in some people some of the time" (Ball, 2010, p. 257).

Where does this leave us with respect to the conflict between "cognitivists" and "emotivists"? At the end of the day, even the seemingly sternest critics of the notion of musical arousal of emotions—Hanslick, Stravinsky, Kivy, and Konečni—have conceded that music *can* arouse emotions in listeners. Peter Kivy states: "I never denied, nor do I deny now that the simple, unadorned statement is true that 'music arouses emotions'" (Kivy, 2001, p. 85).

Eduard Hanslick argues that "music works more rapidly and intensely upon the mind than any other art. With a few chords, we can be transported into a state of mind that a poem would achieve only through lengthy exposition … The other arts persuade, but music invades us" (Hanslick, 1986, p. 50).

CHAPTER 16

THE PREVALENCE OF EMOTIONAL REACTIONS

16.1 How Often Does Music Arouse Emotions?

Having offered evidence that music can arouse emotions in listeners, the next question is how often music arouses emotions. Think about your own experiences with music. Clearly, not all emotions occur equally often, do they? In fact, not all occasions may even involve an emotion.

The term *prevalence* is used to refer to the relative frequency of occurrence of a certain phenomenon, such as emotional reactions to music, in the population of interest. I have borrowed this term from epidemiology (Juslin, Liljeström, Västfjäll, Barradas, & Silva, 2008), but you can rest assured, it is not a sickness to experience emotions in response to music.

Prevalence of emotions is usually measured through self-report. Although it could be difficult to report the causes of emotions reliably, the feelings themselves can be reported quite well. Prevalence data are important because they describe the phenomena that any theory of music and emotion must be able to explain.

First, let us consider the *overall* prevalence of both music and emotions. How can we get a good estimate of how prevalent music is in daily life? The psychological experiment is *not* useful for this purpose, due to its artificial context. A questionnaire which asks listeners to estimate how often they encounter music could be more useful. In a survey study featuring a randomized and statistically representative sample of the Swedish population,

78% of the responders said that they listen to music at least once every day (Juslin, Liljeström, Laukka, Västfjäll, & Lundqvist, 2011)—a first indication that music is common in our daily lives.

However, such aggregated estimates of prevalence are known to be prone to certain biases in memory. A better way to obtain estimates of prevalence is to measure music experiences as they occur naturally and spontaneously in daily life. This goal can be achieved by means of *the experience sampling method* (Hektner, Schmidt, & Csikszentmihalyi, 2007).

Participants are given a small computer or a phone app that they carry with them at all waking hours over a one to three week period. During each week, the device emits sound signals at predetermined or—preferably—randomized intervals. Each time the participant hears the sound signal, he or she should immediately respond to a set of questions administered by the device about current (or recent) events, which may or may not have involved music (Juslin et al., 2008). A specialized mobile app for music experience was designed by William Randall and Nikki Rickard (2013).

One advantage of the method is that it enables us to explore musical events as they unfold in their natural and spontaneous context. Another advantage is that it renders possible repeated measurements over time so that we may obtain a better sense of whether the emotions occur in specific patterns (e.g., on certain days of the week).

Preliminary findings from several studies (Juslin et al., 2008; see also North, Hargreaves, & Hargreaves, 2004; Sloboda, Ivaldi, & O'Neill, 2001) show that music, in some form, occurs in about 30–40% of the episodes sampled randomly in everyday life. However, the music does not *always* arouse an emotion. Preliminary data indicate that we are only moved by the music in 55–65% of the episodes featuring music (Juslin & Laukka, 2004; Juslin et al., 2008; Juslin, Barradas, Ovsiannikow, Limmo, & Thompson, 2016). In other words, a lot of the time music *fails* to arouse any emotion. In section 25.5 I will discuss various reasons why music does not always arouse emotions.

Musical emotion episodes are most prevalent in the *evening*, followed by the *afternoon*, and then the *morning*. Moreover, they are more common during *weekend days*, than during *workdays* (Juslin et al., 2008). These patterns mainly reflect patterns of work versus leisure, with music listening occurring more frequently during leisure time.

However, there are large individual differences in overall prevalence. In one study, listeners were asked to estimate roughly how much of the total time spent listening to music they feel emotions (Juslin & Laukka, 2004). The estimated proportions ranged from 5% of the time to 100%, although responses were roughly normally distributed, with most estimates clustering around the average (55%).

Individual prevalence of emotional reactions to music is correlated with individual prevalence of music listening: the more you listen to music, the more you tend to experience emotions to music (Juslin et al., 2008). However, the two are only moderately correlated, which shows that other factors might also influence prevalence.

Females and musically trained individuals experience emotions to music more frequently than do males and untrained listeners. Further, people who score high on the "big five" personality traits "Openness to Experience" and "Extraversion" have a higher overall prevalence than people who score low (e.g., Juslin et al., 2008, 2011) and might also experience emotions more intensely (Liljeström, Juslin, & Västfjäll, 2013; McCrae, 2007).

16.2 Which Emotions Does Music Arouse?

Having looked at the overall prevalence of musical emotions, we will now look at the prevalence of *specific* emotions. This issue was initially mostly a matter of speculation among researchers, often based on personal experience and sometimes slipping into the treacherous territory of debating what people *ought to* experience, rather than what they actually *do* experience. However, over the last ten years or so, a large number of empirical studies have addressed the question. The results accumulated to date suggest the following three conclusions:

1. Music arouses mostly positive emotions

I want you to think of your own experience. Is it not true that when you listen to music and become moved that positive emotions are far more frequent? If not, after all, why would you pursue this activity in the first place? In this respect, at least, music listening may not be very different from other activities that we enjoy—we enjoy them because they are interesting and make us feel good.[1]

Does the evidence bear out these impressions? Indeed, at least two studies have shown that emotion categories usually regarded as "positive" by researchers are significantly more common than emotion categories usually regarded as "negative" (Juslin et al., 2008, 2011). Around 70% of the reports in Alf Gabrielsson's study involve positive emotions (Gabrielsson, 2011). John Sloboda and co-workers report that music listening in everyday life typically tips the affective valence in a positive direction (Sloboda et al., 2001).

I should acknowledge that people in the Western world tend to experience more positive than negative emotions *in general*, that is, even in a non-musical context (Diener & Diener, 1996). Even so, musical emotion episodes feature significantly more positive emotions than do non-musical emotion episodes, as revealed by experience sampling data (Juslin et al., 2008).

These results are hardly surprising. Would researchers devote so much attention to exploring the potential benefits of music for health and subjective well-being (MacDonald, Kreutz, & Mitchell, 2012) if music did not make us feel good? However, because music evokes mainly positive emotions, we should arguably devote more time to understanding positive emotions. Our knowledge about positive emotions is under-developed because

[1] To be fair, I know some people who hardly ever listen to music. The reason for this abstinence is perhaps not that they experience *negative* emotions every time they listen to music. (Some people just feel they "don't have time to listen to music" in their everyday life.) However, I suspect that they are "unmoved" by music, or at least not moved to a sufficient extent to motivate further listening. Other activities might be more tempting.

most research in the general emotion field has focused on negative emotions such as anxiety (Oatley, Keltner, & Jenkins, 2006).

Possible reasons for this "bias" is that positive emotions are fewer and less well differentiated, and that they do not generally create problems for people. One further reason might be that positive emotions seem more difficult to explain from an evolutionary perspective. However, Barbara Fredrickson argues that positive emotions are *also* functional and constitute products of evolutionary selection pressures (Fredrickson, 1998). She discusses four positive emotions which, as it happens, are all common in response to music (Juslin et al., 2008): *joy, interest, contentment,* and *love.*

- *Joy* is associated with the urge to be playful, which itself is linked to both physical and intellectual skills and creativity.
- *Interest* is associated with the urge for rewarding exploration, increasing one's knowledge of the world.
- *Contentment* is associated with an urge to savor and integrate one's recent events and experiences.
- *Love* is associated with the urge to be close to the "target" of one's affection (a romantic partner, family, or friends), which serves to build and solidify one's social resources.

Positive emotions tend to "broaden our mindset" in ways that are beneficial to health and creative problem-solving (Fredrickson, 1998). Put more bluntly, then, through the largely positive emotions it arouses, music may help us to be playful and creative, to explore the external world, to reflect and make sense of our experiences, and to connect with persons and things we love. No wonder that music has mental health benefits (Hanser, 2010; Helsing, Västfjäll, Bjälkebring, Juslin, & Hartig, 2016).

2. Music may arouse both basic and complex emotions

You may recall from Chapter 4 that some researchers distinguish between basic and complex emotions. (The former are considered innate and biologically adaptive, whereas the latter are considered more dependent on learning and cultural context.) Initially, some authors claimed that music does not arouse basic emotions (e.g., Kivy, 1990; Scherer, 2003); but since then, a large number of studies have shown that music can arouse both basic emotions (e.g., *sadness, interest, happiness, surprise*) and complex emotions (e.g., *pride, nostalgia, awe*; Gabrielsson, 2011; Juslin & Laukka, 2004; Juslin et al., 2008, 2011; Juslin, Harmat, & Eerola, 2014; Juslin, Barradas, & Eerola, 2015; Juslin, Barradas, Ovsiannikow, Limmo, & Thompson, 2016; Sloboda, 1992).

As we will see in Chapter 25, which emotion will occur in a given event is to a large extent determined by which underlying *mechanism* (if any) is activated. Most mechanisms may arouse a number of different emotions. Still, there is a sense in which each mechanism can be related to its own "family" of emotions (see Chapter 25). Thus, the finding that music arouses both basic and complex emotions will be easier to understand once we consider how music can evoke emotions through both basic and complex mechanisms.

3. Certain emotions occur more frequently and consistently than others

In a series of studies conducted over many years, we have explored the prevalence of specific emotions in reaction to music. We have used a type of *method triangulation* to obtain more or less "representative" samples of listeners, situations, and pieces of music, respectively. Figure 16.1 presents some examples of results from each of these types of studies. What is striking to me is the overall similarity of pattern across methods. This suggests that there is *some* level of stability in the estimates—they are hardly random.

Based on these and other studies (Juslin & Laukka, 2004; Sloboda, 1992; Wells & Hakanen, 1991; Zentner, Grandjean, & Scherer, 2008), I tentatively propose a set of broad emotion categories which recur across different studies: *calm–relaxation, happiness–elation, nostalgia–longing, interest expectancy, pleasure–enjoyment, sadness–melancholy, arousal–energy, love–tenderness, pride–confidence, admiration–awe,* and *spirituality–transcendence*. The precise ordering varies between studies and probably varies to some extent depending on musical genre and cultural context also (Juslin et al., 2016a). Note that the emotions that music commonly arouses appear to be slightly different from those that music commonly expresses express (see section 6.3).

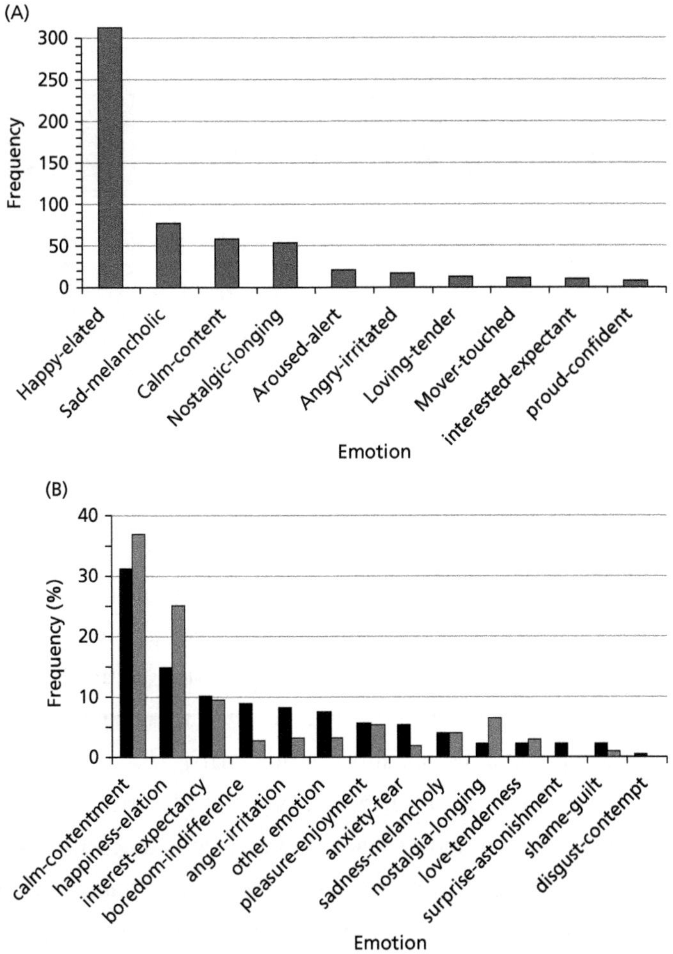

Figure 16.1 Prevalence of emotional reactions to music in studies featuring representative samples of listeners (A), situations (B), and pieces of music (C), respectively.

A) Reproduced from Juslin, P. N., Liljeström, S., Laukka, P., Västfjäll, D., & Lundqvist, L.-O. (2011). *Emotional reactions to music in a nationally representative sample of Swedish adults: Prevalence and causal influences*. Musicae Scientiae, 15, 174-207. (Special Issue on Music and Emotion). Copyright © 2011, © SAGE Publications

B) Reproduced from Juslin, P. N., Liljeström, S., Västfjäll, D., Barradas, G., & Silva, A. (2008). An experience sampling study of emotional reactions to music: Listener, music, and situation. Emotion, 8, 668-683.

C) Data from https://link.springer.com/content/pdf/10.1007%2Fs10919-017-0268-x.pdf

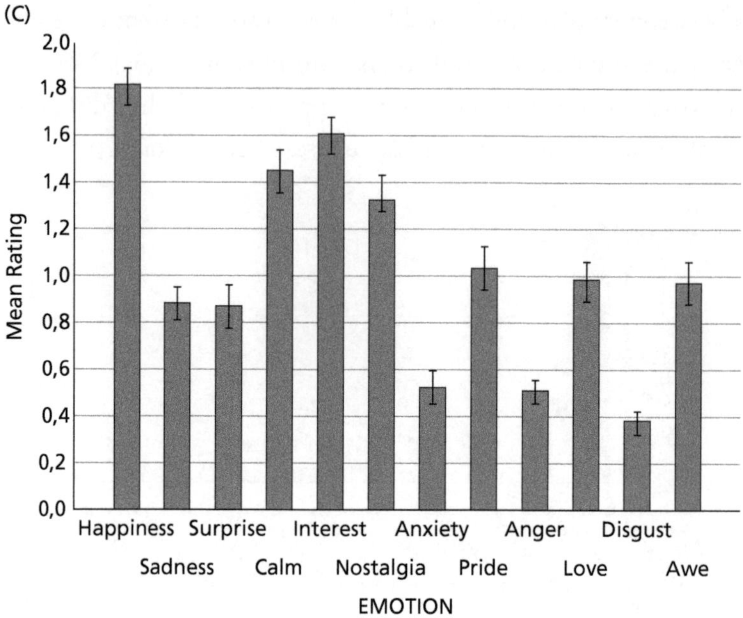

Figure 16.1 (Continued)

Another notable finding is that music may arouse "mixed" emotions (e.g., both *happiness* and *sadness*) just like other emotional events (Oatley & Duncan, 1994). Although some scholars argue that music arouses mostly "mixed emotions," actual data so far suggest that they occur in a minority of the musical emotion episodes—for instance 13% in Gabrielsson's research (2001) and 11% in Juslin and colleagues' study (2011).

Why do "mixed" emotions occur in response to music? My hypothesis is that they occur when at least two different mechanisms provide conflicting emotional outputs (e.g., that one arouses *sadness* whereas the other arouses *happiness*). This possibility will be further explained when we look at the actual mechanisms involved in the arousal of emotions (Chapter 17).

In summary, then, music can arouse a wide range of emotions. It can evoke anything from mere *arousal* and basic emotions, such as *happiness* and *sadness*, to complex emotions, such as *nostalgia, pride,* and *awe*. A striking example of just how varied responses to music can be is given in Table 16.1;

Table 16.1 Positive and negative emotions reported in strong experiences with music, ordered from low to high arousal.

Emotion	Frequency	Percent
Positive		
Peace, calm, harmony, stillness	106	11.1
Safety, warmth	44	4.6
Humility, insignificance	9	0.9
Wonder, admiration, reverence, respect	31	3.3
Solemnity, patriotism	19	2.0
Contentment, satisfaction, gratitude	86	9.0
Enjoyment, delight, sweetness, beauty	260	27.3
Joy, happiness, bliss	370	38.8
Elation, excitement, tension	92	9.7
Love, sexual feelings	39	4.1
Perfection, everything fits	32	3.4
Feeling proud, powerful	31	3.3
Euphoria, as if intoxicated, rapture, ecstasy	80	8.4
Negative		
Feel tired, faint, exhausted, "empty'	80	8.4
Feel lonely, abandoned, small, insignificant	6	0.6
Longing	9	0.9
Melancholy, unhappiness, sadness	82	8,6
Confusion, nervousness, tension, worry	52	5.5
Frustration, disappointment	14	1.5
Embarrassment, shame	14	1.5
Discomfort, (psychic) pain, envy, jealousy	30	3.1
Anxiety, fear, dread, despair	36	3.8
Anger, rage, hate	8	0.8
Shock, horror, terror, chaos, panic, unbearable	18	1.9

Reproduced from Gabrielsson, A. (2010). Strong experiences with music. In P. N. Juslin & J. A. Sloboda (Eds.), *Handbook of music and emotion: Theory and research*. Oxford: Oxford University Press. By permission of Oxford University Press.

it shows all the emotions that Alf Gabrielsson encountered in his study of "peak" experiences (Gabrielsson, 2010). *This* is what a theory of music and emotion must be able to explain.

16.3 Does Music Arouse "Unique" and "Music-Specific" Emotions?

Readers may be excused for thinking that none of the conclusions cited earlier are surprising. What *is* surprising, perhaps, is that until recently, many of these conclusions were still controversial. Many scholars preferred to conceive of responses to music in terms of a narrower range of "music-unique" emotions.

Are musical emotions different from other emotions? There is no simple "yes" or "no" answer to this question, because our answer will depend on what we mean: "different" in what sense?

Clearly, *one* unique thing about emotions aroused by music is that they are aroused by *music*! The *contexts* in which musical emotions occur might also have some peculiar characteristics, though it is difficult to generalize across cultures (Becker, 2004). In addition, emotional reactions to music may be *positively biased*, as compared to the average valence for emotions in general.

However, when people suggest that musical emotions are different from other emotions, they typically have something else in mind. Some scholars maintain that music (or "art" in general) may arouse "unique" emotions not experienced in everyday life. For example, music educator Keith Swanwick claims that "emotions in 'life' ... and emotions we might experience as a result of engaging with music are not the same" (Swanwick, 1985, p. 29).

Here, I need to briefly introduce the term "aesthetic emotions," which has been used in two different ways. Some scholars use this term to refer to *all* emotional responses to artworks (e.g., in music, theater, or painting), without implying that the emotions themselves are of a peculiar kind.

(According to such a use of the term, which I do not endorse, *all* emotions reviewed in section 16.2 are "aesthetic emotions," simply because they involve music.)

The term has also been used more narrowly to refer to a peculiar type of emotion believed to be aroused *only* when perceivers are engaged with artworks; this idea reflects the long-lasting impact of philosopher Immanuel Kant, who likes to distinguish *aesthetic pleasure* from other types of pleasure. Aesthetic pleasure, he argues, is the result of "disinterested" perception and a concern with "pure form". This use of the term, just like the notion of music-unique emotion, implies that there are emotions had when, and *only* when, we perceive a work of art, an idea that has not found much favor in modern aesthetics (Neill, 2003).

Is there evidence that music can arouse "unique" emotions that do not occur in other contexts? Scherer and Zentner (2008) suggest that states like *wonder, tenderness, nostalgia,* and *tension* are aesthetic emotions "unique" to music. However, a review of empirical findings shows that these states also occur in several everyday contexts that do not involve music or even works of art more generally.[2] If there exist "music-unique" emotions, their nature remains to be specified.

However, I will argue in Part IV that the term *aesthetic emotion* retains its usefulness if we define aesthetic emotions as states caused specifically by an evaluation of aesthetic properties of an artwork; for instance, admiration for the skill of an artist or the beauty of a composition. In other words, aesthetic emotions should be distinguished by their *causes,* rather than by their being "unique" states. To illustrate: we might admire someone for being able to eat a lot of hot dogs, but this does not make it an aesthetic emotion. If we admire the beauty of a composition such as J. S. Bach's *Arioso* from Cantata BWV 156—Adagio, the term aesthetic emotion would seem more appropriate.

So far, we have not managed to come up with any "music-unique" emotions, and yet the search for such emotions continues. Some researchers

[2] Other terms proposed by music analysts, such as *cognitive irony* (Narmour, 1990), cannot be seriously regarded as proper emotions.

have suggested that the experience of "being moved" is something unique to music (Scherer & Zentner, 2001), quite apart from the type of emotions we experience in everyday life. Yet, this hypothesis does not hold up on closer examination.

First, people often report being moved also in a non-musical context; parents become moved when their children take their first steps, or when they get married. Second, it is not clear that the phrase always refers to a unique affective state. After all, the term *emotion* literally means "to move" (Plutchik, 1994), so to say that one is moved may simply imply that one is feeling emotional, without specifying in what way (Robinson, 2005).

Even when the phrase "feeling moved" *is* used to denote a particular state, it may not be quite what some scholars have in mind. A rare series of studies by Winfried Menninghaus and co-workers analyzed the concept of being moved based on a questionnaire (Menninghaus et al., 2015). The authors concluded that the great majority of eliciting scenarios were linked to social relationships or critical life events such as death, birth, marriage, and separation. (So far, it sounds a lot like the types of events that would arouse an "ordinary" emotion.) The authors concluded that the most common emotions in episodes of feeling moved were *happiness* and *sadness*—not exactly the most "exotic" of emotions. In fact, these states are often considered "basic" by emotion researchers (section 4.8).

All things considered, it is ironic for those scholars who suggest that we should focus on the state of feeling moved rather than on traditional basic emotions that the former states seem to consist of the latter. However, an interesting conclusion in Menninghaus and colleague's study was that episodes of feeling moved often included both positive and negative affect, making it a "mixed" emotion (Menninghaus et al., 2015). Of course, mixed emotions occur in non-musical contexts too, and perhaps even more frequently (31% of the episodes in Oatley & Duncan, 1994).

As a last resort, some scholars have looked at the phenomenon of chills, arguing that *this* is the quintessential musical response, but as noted earlier (see section 15.4), we experience chills in many non-musical contexts. David

Huron argues that the chill response is related to the *fear* system in the brain—not exactly a "music-unique" emotion (Huron, 2006).

Indeed, when we compare musical emotions with non-musical emotions, we tend to rely on caricatures of both: the music connoisseur experiencing the most sophisticated and complex emotional state imaginable versus the primitive fear of a person running away from a bear in the woods. Neither of these scenarios is common in everyday life.

If we look at more representative examples of both musical and non-musical emotions, the similarities between the two become more apparent than their differences. By emphasizing differences—which is easy enough, if we look only at "surface appearances"—researchers have looked in the wrong direction for the *causes* of emotional reactions to music (see Chapter 17).

My conclusion is that the notion of a unique set of emotions aroused only by music can be rejected on empirical grounds. In fact, just a moment's reflection will show that this idea is untenable. If I claim that music arouses a unique set of emotions, why stop there? Is there a unique set of emotions for the visual arts? For sculpture? For sports? For politics? For war? Surely, there is something special about the emotions we experience in these other contexts too. Following this trajectory, we will end up with an endless list of unique emotions. The problem is that our emotion mechanisms evolved long before most of these human activities even existed.

Fortunately, for all concerned, there is no need to travel down that road. With such a wide range of "normal" emotions, we will have no problem describing the *happiness, nostalgia, awe, interest,* or *pleasure* that we experience when listening to music. But what should we make of the characteristic frequency distribution for music that is skewed towards positive emotions?

This is merely one example of a more general principle, that there are different frequency distributions across the spectrum of emotions as a function of the precise context sampled (e.g., music, sports, politics, or intimate relationships). Indeed, the distribution of emotions could differ to some degree even for different genres of music: We may experience more *nostalgia* in response to fado than we do to speed metal, yet observing that music arouses some emotions more frequently than others is a far cry from postulating "unique" emotions.

Why, then, have some authors been so prone to advocate such a proposition? Why does the issue create so much commotion? I believe there are two plausible explanations. First, as in the discussion of music as communication (Chapter 7), the issue appears to reflect the "politics" of music and emotion. Somehow, the question of which emotions music arouses is transformed into the question of which emotions music *ought to* arouse. Unique and sublime works of art ought to arouse unique and sublime emotions, correct?

The second explanation is that we easily confuse the unique nature of our musical experience *as a whole* with the notion that the experience must involve a "unique" set of emotions (Juslin et al., 2010). Recall from section 4.2 that music experience comprises several different aspects, of which emotion is only one. We do not have to invent a new set of emotions to account for the unique nature of music experience; there are so many other aspects of our experience that may carry the burden of explanation. Much of what makes music experiences unique are non-emotional aspects—like the conscious perception of musical structure, and its subtle, dynamic changes over time. Referring to such qualia as "emotions" is doing a disservice to the field. Perhaps there are more promising ways of capturing what is special about music experiences.

16.4 Collective Emotions, Refined Emotions, Meta-Musical Emotions

Music not only arouses emotions at the individual level but also at the *interpersonal* and *intergroup* level. Such "collective emotions" have been rarely investigated in the emotion field generally (for a review, see Von Scheve & Salmela, 2014)—and even less in musical contexts. When people attend concerts or make music together, their emotions are in part influenced by the emotions of *other* people present (see Becker, 2004, for some examples from field work).

Such emotions can be considered part of *dynamic social systems* and may involve collective emotion regulation (Parkinson, Fischer, & Manstead, 2005). Consider the collective wave of emotion spreading across the audience in a stadium when Bruce Springsteen plays the first notes of "Born to Run". To capture such social processes in music experiences, and their role in collective action (Garofalo, 2010), remains a major challenge for future research in this field.

People who love music (like you and me, presumably) tend to develop a special relationship to their emotional experiences with music, like someone with an interest in wine or literature may do as well. Nico Frijda and Louise Sundararajan (2007) propose the concept of *refined emotions* to capture this phenomenon (inspired partly by Chinese poetics).

The concept does *not* refer to a special subset of emotions, for example that *anger* is coarse, whereas *love* is refined. Instead, it refers to a special "mode" of experiencing all the ordinary emotions which is characterized by an attitude of detachment, restraint, self-reflexivity, and savoring. It is a kind of "emotional connoisseurship," if you like.

This mode of experiencing emotions seems to be relevant in a musical context, where we may savor and reflect upon the emotion the music arouses (Barradas, in press). Yet it may also occur in relation to religion, poetry, and gourmet food. The essence of the notion of refined emotions lies in the secondary awareness of the "raw" feeling (primary awareness) experienced. Refined emotions differ from both "peak" experiences (Gabrielsson, 2011) and "flow" states (Harmat, Ørsted Andersen, Ullén, Wright, & Sadlo, 2016), which are considerably less detached and self-aware.

If we allow a generous definition of musical emotions, we may also consider emotions that occur not only during actual listening to music, but also when imagining future experiences of music listening (e.g., longing for a record release), or recalling past experiences of music (e.g., a concert). We have previously referred to these as "meta-musical emotions" (Juslin & Sloboda, 2010), emotions only indirectly related to music, such as experiencing excitement over one's record collection or the arrival of a new instrument. Several times, I have dreamt that I am in a record store and stumble upon a fantastic recording I have never found before. I am thinking to myself "I cannot believe I have missed this amazing album!"—only to wake up and realize with some disappointment that the record does not exist. Nico Frijda emphasizes the role of anticipation:

> Anticipation of feelings can be a cause of action: some actions appear to have no other aim than to obtain certain feelings. They include actions like ... paying dearly to go to concerts. (Frijda, 2016, p. 617)

Note that all these subsets involve emotions of the regular kind, which are aroused through the same kind of mechanisms as other emotions. They only involve special modes and contexts. It can be fitting, then, to look closer at the mechanisms underlying emotional responses to music. I will argue in Chapter 32 that much of the richness of our emotion experiences with music comes from the combined effects of many mechanisms. How, exactly, do the mechanisms work? We have arrived at what is often regarded as the greatest mystery of them all.

CHAPTER 17

HOW DOES MUSIC AROUSE EMOTIONS?

Of all the problems concerning music and emotion discussed by philosophers since the time of the ancient Greeks, none is probably more intriguing than the question of how music arouses emotions. In fact, this is arguably the single most important question in the field. It is also a question with far-reaching implications for other issues concerning music and emotion.

Which emotions does music arouse? Which brain regions are involved in this process? When do musical emotions develop? Are they universal or culture-specific? What is the relationship between perceived and aroused emotions? Are musical emotions somehow unique?

The answers to these questions are all linked to the "how" question. They cannot be answered satisfactorily without understanding the psychological processes through which emotions come into being. Oddly, the issue has not received as much attention from researchers as you might expect, as indicated by literature searches (Juslin & Västfjäll, 2008).

How could this neglect of underlying mechanisms occur? There may be a number of reasons, but I can think of one in particular. Eric Clarke, Nicola Dibben, and Stephanie Pitts describe a transformation of the musicology field that occurred in the early 1990s, whereby music psychology emerged from psychology departments and moved into music departments (Clarke, Dibben, & Pitts, 2010). This was, in many ways, a positive development, but it meant that many of the studies of music and emotion published over the last two decades were carried out by scholars who were not trained in psychology.

One consequence has been that the intervening psychological processes were ignored in favor of a search for direct links between musical features and emotions. If such an approach is incomplete when investigating perception of emotions (see Part II), it is even less satisfactory when investigating arousal of emotions.

17.1 The Crux of the Matter

Why is the issue so perplexing? Part of the puzzle is that the conditions of emotion elicitation in music and outside music appear so different (Krumhansl, 1997)—at least superficially. Typically, an emotion is aroused when an event, object, or person is judged as having the capacity to influence the goals or plans of the perceiver (Oatley, 1992).

For example, in the unlikely event that I see you buy this book at the local bookstore, I may judge this event as having a positive impact on my goal: to raise enough money to buy a new electric guitar. This emotion approach, pioneered by Magda Arnold and Richard Lazarus, is referred to as *appraisal theory* (for an excellent introduction see Scherer, 1999).

However, when we listen to music, only rarely has the music per se implications for our goals or plans in life.[1] Although a jazz saxophonist may really be "killing it" in a solo on stage, we do not feel that our life is threatened. (This is, of course, what the paradox mentioned at the beginning of Part III is all about: music arouses emotions, even though it does not seem to have any serious life consequences.)

The paradox has met with different responses. Some scholars have argued that because emotions to music do not seem to involve emotionally

[1] Here a distinction must be made between goals in intentional uses of music (e.g., using music to relax) and goals being directly involved in the emotion induction process per se; see section 25.4 for further discussion.

relevant beliefs, these may not be "real" emotions: "The lack of an explanation in ordinary, 'folkpsychological' terms for the purported arousal of the garden-variety emotions seems convincing if not, perhaps, absolutely conclusive evidence that no such arousal takes place" (Kivy, 1990, p. 152).

Others have argued that the problem could be our theories. "Explaining emotional responses to instrumental music is a real problem for appraisal theories, and may be a real threat to the generality of appraisals as elicitors of emotion" (Ellsworth, 1994, p. 195). From this point of view, then, the challenge is to formulate an alternative explanation, which makes more sense in a musical context. What could such an account look like?

Before taking a closer look at various accounts, we should perhaps first ask ourselves what *is* an explanation? Briefly, it is a statement made to clarify something, specifying the reason for or cause of something, thereby making it understandable. I will suggest that previous attempts to explain musical emotions have succeeded to different degrees in this task. We might divide these attempts into three categories, which I have named tongue in cheek after a well-known movie by Sergio Leone.

17.2 Previous Accounts: "The Good, The Bad, and The Ugly"

Let us begin with the less promising road taken. In the "ugly" category, I will identify two approaches. The first one is not an account at all. It *rejects* an account of musical emotions altogether, stating that emotional reactions to music either cannot be explained or should not be explained. It argues they are and should remain inexplicable. Jean-Michel Pilc suggests that musical emotions "cannot be explained"; "by analyzing them, we just destroy them ... let's preserve the mystery" (Pilc, 2012, p. 74).

Statements of this kind are surprisingly common in the broader literature and also amongst music listeners. ("Music is and will remain a mystery," notes a participant in a survey study; Gabrielsson, 2011, p. 445.) I have to respect this opinion in other people and yet, from a scientific perspective,

I have to disagree with it. It *is* possible to explain emotional reactions to music, and to do so can have great value, because the research could have implications for physical health and subjective well-being (e.g., Västfjäll, Juslin, & Hartig, 2012). Moreover, analyzing emotional reactions to music will not "destroy" them. As I will explain in section 17.4, many of the mechanisms involved are completely impervious to such knowledge.

The second approach that I attribute to the "ugly" category is more subtle. This approach seems to be *intended* as an "account" or "explanation," even if it is not. This approach basically suggests that music influences emotions "directly." To illustrate: Jenefer Robinson claims that "happy music affects us directly", and that the music affects us "because of a direct response" (Robinson, 2005, p. 392).[2] What is wrong with this approach? After all, it sounds rather direct.

Whenever you hear the word "directly" in accounts of behavior, you should be wary. What does it *mean* that something influences you "directly"? The use of the word "directly" only goes to show that no explanation has yet been provided. Clearly, *something* has to happen in the central nervous system of a listener for an emotion to occur, and it is that "something" (information processing) that needs to be explained.

The notion that objects and events "directly" cause our emotions is sometimes referred to as the "nativist fallacy" (Silvia, 2012). It appears to be particularly common in music research, perhaps because we often think of music as abstract sequences of notes, devoid of meaning. Yet, if no meaning was involved, no emotion would be aroused. Our emotional response is the ultimate "proof" that there is meaning in music. The task is then to explain *how* and *why* the mind finds music meaningful to such an extent that it warrants an emotional response.

Let us move on to the "bad" account category, which is a *bit* better than the "ugly" category. Here I can also identify two approaches. The first states that correlations between surface features of the music (e.g., tempo) and

[2] To be fair, Robinson also reviews some of the mechanisms postulated by music psychologists (Robinson, 2005).

aroused emotions constitute an account. We might call this "the causal factors approach". At first sight, it seems like a perfectly legitimate way to explain musical emotions to claim that we are affected by features of the music, so if we pinpoint the musical features that co-vary with the aroused emotion, we have provided an explanation.

Correlations between musical features and aroused emotions may, indeed, be the *first* stage towards an account, but such correlations alone do not constitute an explanation. Why not? First, there is hardly any musical feature that will invariably arouse a certain emotion.[3] The emotion depends equally on factors in the listener and the context (section 2.3). An approach that focuses simply on musical surface features will lead to overly simple conclusions, such as that "fast tempo evokes positive emotions" (Gomez & Danuser, 2007, p. 380). (We found several examples in our experiments in Uppsala where a piece with fast tempo may arouse a negative emotion.)

There is another more crucial reason why mere correlations between surface features of the music and aroused emotions do not constitute an explanation: they simply move the burden of explanation from one level (e.g., "Why does 'Adagio for Strings' by Samuel Barber arouse *sadness*?") to another level ("Why does a slow tempo (occasionally) arouse *sadness*?"). The causal factors approach confuses description with explanation (Juslin, Harmat, & Eerola, 2014; see also Davies, 2001). The approach is useful to map causal factors that may influence or moderate emotions, but it does not offer an explanation of *why* the effects occur. When intended that way, it is yet another example of the "nativist fallacy."[4]

The second approach in the "bad" category occurs, occasionally, in brain research. Imaging studies of musical emotions are only in their infancy (Peretz, 2010), but they involve exciting developments (Koelsch, 2014). Unfortunately, the findings from brain research are often misunderstood or

[3] The closest we get is a *brainstem reflex* to an "extreme" value in some acoustic feature (see Chapter 18).

[4] Music theorists often fall in this trap, arguing that, say, "this piece is sad because of its falling semitones."

over-interpreted. Perhaps we are swayed by the expensive tools that neuroscientists are using.

To illustrate: *a lot* was made of the finding that enjoyment of music appears to involve the same "pleasure center" in the brain as other forms of pleasure, such as food, sex, and drugs. (This includes dopamine-rich areas of the brain like the nucleus accumbens; see, for example, Blood & Zatorre, 2001.) But where did they *expect* musical pleasures to occur? In our feet? It would have been more remarkable if musical pleasures involved a different and unique part of the brain (which, of course, it did not).

Mapping what brain regions are activated when we experience an emotion can certainly be a worthwhile activity. The problems begin when basic findings (e.g., that the pleasure center is activated when we experience pleasure) are interpreted as an "explanation". Such an approach implies that the cause of emotions is whatever part of the brain is activated: "Why does music arouse emotions? Because a brain region called nucleus accumbens is activated."

Having found that certain brain regions are active when listeners feel pleasure while they hear music, Salimpoor and colleagues wrote that their results "help to explain why music is of such high value across all human societies" (Salimpoor, Benovoy, Larcher, Dagher, & Zatorre, 2011, p. 257). In fact, by that time we already knew that music arouses pleasure in listeners. The question is *why* music activates the pleasure center, and this issue remained unanswered by their findings. In essence, this approach confuses explanation with manifestation of one and the same phenomenon at different levels (e.g., subjective versus neurological).

Most psychologists believe in some version of philosopher Baruch Spinoza's double aspect theory according to which mental (psychological) and physical (brain, body) processes are aspects of the same underlying reality (Eysenck, 1994). According to this perspective, it is tautological to say that the experienced pleasure is "caused" by pleasure centers in the brain; they are two sides of the same coin.

What is required to make progress? This brings me to the "good" category. I believe that real progress in the study of musical emotions can only be achieved by understanding the psychological processes that "mediate" between musical features and aroused emotions.

Psychologists distinguish between "moderator" and "mediator" variables. Moderators specify when a certain effect will hold; for instance, that the effect will be stronger when a moderator variable takes a certain value. (One example is social context: listeners may experience more intense emotions when they listen together with friends than when they listen alone; Liljeström, Juslin, & Västfjäll, 2013). Mediators, in contrast, address *how* or *why* the effects occur in the first place; the cause of the observed effects (Baron & Kenny, 1986).

A theory of emotion causation needs to explain both why a specific event arouses an emotion (*elicitation*) and why the aroused emotion is of a specific kind (*differentiation*) (Moors, 2009). I will refer to the psychological process through which this is achieved as *the mechanism*.

17.3 What Does a Mechanism Account Entail?

Because the idea of a mechanism is crucial in the following chapters and because it is often misunderstood, it may be helpful to describe the concept a little further. Broadly speaking, a mechanism refers to those causal processes through which an outcome is brought into being.

Mechanisms may be defined differently depending on the scientific discipline. Nevertheless, Peter Hedström and Petri Ylikoski (2010) discuss four ideas that are shared by most definitions:

- A mechanism is identified by the kind of effect or phenomenon it produces. A mechanism is always a mechanism *for* something.
- A mechanism is an irreducibly causal notion. It refers to the entities of a causal process that produces the effect of interest.
- The mechanism has a structure. A mechanism-based explanation seeks to disclose this structure.

- Mechanisms form a hierarchy: although a mechanism at one level presupposes the existence of certain entities, with characteristic properties and activities, it is expected that there are lower-level mechanisms which can explain these properties and activities. However, their explanation is a separate issue.

A mechanism-based explanation describes the causal process selectively, "it does not aim at an exhaustive account of all details but seeks to capture the crucial elements of the process by abstracting away the irrelevant details" (Hedström & Ylikoski, 2010, p. 53). This could sound easy but, as acknowledged by these researchers, "sometimes finding underlying mechanisms is the hardest part of the scientific work" (Hedström & Ylikoski, 2010, p. 56).

In the present context, a mechanism account comprises a functional description of what the mind is "doing," in principle (e.g., "retrieving a memory") when an emotion is aroused. This description of the process at a psychological level must not be confused with the separate issue of where in the brain the process is "implemented." (The fact that an area of the brain is activated does not tell us much unless this information is combined with a psychological theory about what the brain area is doing and why.) Similarly, a process description must not be confused with the phenomenological experience it seeks to explain (Dennett, 1987).

The use of the term "mechanism" does not imply that human beings are "machines" or that emotional reactions to music are completely determined by musical features. A psychological mechanism depends on both incoming and stored information, which is processed in dynamic interaction with an environment (Frijda, 2008). Usually, it is the context that turns (or fails to turn) "causal potential" into "causal outcome." That is why musical emotions depend on the music, the listener, and the context (cf. section 2.3).

The following chapters will largely be devoted to a discussion of the multiple mechanisms that music can engage, but in order truly to appreciate the nature of these mechanisms, we must first resolve the fourth paradox of music and emotion (presented in section 14.2).

17.4 Emotions Have a Logic of Their Own

Recall the paradox: on the one hand, we have "music," an abstract form of art that seems distant from our concerns in everyday life and is regarded as a "harmless" leisure activity (Pinker, 1997). On the other hand, we have "emotions," evolved mechanisms that served functions in human survival throughout evolution (Plutchik, 1994; Ch. 9). How are these seemingly non-commensurable phenomena linked together?

I have previously argued that failure to resolve this paradox is largely due to an assumption, which seems implicit in much reasoning about music and emotion (Juslin, 2013a). We can call it "the assumption of realism." Because we are aware that music is something of no serious consequence to our crucial life goals, our emotion mechanisms should *not* respond to music; that is, we seem to assume that the mechanisms are "realistic" in how they function.

Thus, for instance, Peter Kivy suggests that "music provides neither the objects nor, therefore, the belief-opportunities that would make it possible for musical works to arouse such emotions as anger, sadness, joy" (Kivy, 1990, p. 165). As a matter of fact, because such responses seem so "implausible," some scholars have simply concluded that music cannot arouse such emotions.

There is only one problem: the evidence that I reviewed in section 16.2 indicates that music *can* arouse these emotions, as well as many others. What we have here is a good example of the limitations of introspection (one of the themes from section 2.3): the conscious mind does not seem to give us impressions that are consistent with the empirical findings.

However, the dilemma can be resolved by following the lead of Blaise Pascal, who noted that "[t]he heart has its reasons, which reason does not know" (Pascal, 1958, p. 78, fragment 277); that is, emotions have a logic or rationality of their own, quite apart from conscious thought. To explain emotional reactions to music, we need to uncover the underlying logic of our mechanisms through experimentation and psychological theory.

If we reject the assumption of realism, we may proceed to develop another kind of theory of emotion, which allows for the following proposition.

Many of the mechanisms do *not* actually have access to, or take into consideration, information about whether the object of attention is "music" or not; the mechanisms will react to certain information in an event, wherever it may occur (Juslin, 2013a).

A plausible case can be made that our conscious awareness that a stimulus is "music" comes rather late in psychological processing, such that most emotion mechanisms will react to certain features without knowing to which these features belong. In addition, it is not as if we can turn off these ancient mechanisms just because we happen to be listening to music.

We should be thankful that this is the case. It is precisely the possibility that some emotion-provoking features are treated as "real" at some levels of the brain, even though at other levels they are discounted as "music," that makes it possible for us to derive such rich emotions from music. It may explain why musical events arouse emotions that do not seem to "make sense" in a musical context, such as fear (Gabrielsson, 2001).

To understand the underlying mechanisms and why they work as they do, we need to step back and consider the roots of our emotions. It is time to reconnect with one of the primary themes of this book (cf. section 2.3): evolutionary perspectives.

17.5 "Should I Stay or Should I Go?": The Evolutionary Basis of Emotions

The focus here is on psychological mechanisms. The only known process which is capable of creating psychological mechanisms is evolution through natural selection (Buss, 2014). Some scholars like to make a distinction between *proximal* and *ultimate* explanations (Mayr, 1982): Proximal explanations concern the mechanism of a behavior. Ultimate explanations are about how the mechanism came to exist.

I can imagine some readers frowning at this. Where is the *art*? Stay with me—we will get to the aesthetics (Part IV). Where are the *cultural* influences? Yes, music as an art form is shaped by its social, political, religious, and economic context. I will consider cultural differences in the coming chapters. First, however, we need to consider the *foundation*: the emotional architecture upon which both art and culture build. We must go back to our evolutionary origins and ask what the brain does, and why.

All living organisms tend to share some fundamental characteristics (Frijda, 2016). First, they are autonomous systems; second, they can produce self-initiated movements; third, their movements can show direction: they move towards some things and away from other things.[5]

To determine the direction of movement—whether to approach or avoid an object—the organism needs to have some type of *evaluative* process. This, then, is a forerunner of our emotions. Evolutionary psychologists argue that emotions originally developed in order to guide action or, rather, to choose between behavioral alternatives. ("Should I stay or should I go?" as The Clash sang.)

Subjective feeling (cf. section 15.2)—particularly the complex form of reflective awareness that we have as humans—developed much later. The rich consciousness that modern humans have the luxury of possessing is not actually needed in order to have something that for all practical purposes functions as an emotion. This is key to understanding the limits of introspection (section 3.5). Many emotion systems developed *before* reflective consciousness appeared on the scene and do not depend on it for their proper functioning. This is partly the reason why to this day we can often experience emotions elicited by inputs of which we are consciously unaware, contributing to the apparent "irrationality" of emotions.

To be able to choose between actions based on an evaluation process, an organism needs to be sensitive to its environment. Complex organisms have specialized senses to perceive the external world, but can also perceive aspects of their internal milieu, so-called *interoception* (Craig, 2008). Perception is not just an "objective" registering of external objects and

[5] Remarkably, even bacteria—which are among the smallest living organisms—fulfill these basic requirements; they move towards higher concentrations of glucose and away from toxic substances.

events: it is augmented by information from previous encounters with the same or similar objects and events. Thus, we perceive the object's *meaning* for us—what it may "afford" us, whether good or bad (cf. Gibson, 1979).

Accordingly, an evolutionary perspective on human perception of sounds suggests that the survival of our ancient ancestors depended upon their abilities to detect patterns in sounds, derive meaning from them, and adjust their behavior accordingly (Hodges & Sebald, 2011; Juslin, 2013a). The perceived meaning of events is related to "concerns," some of which are innate or "hardwired," others which are culturally learned or more fleeting in nature. Often, we have many concerns simultaneously, some of which may be contradictory. It has thus been proposed that emotions serve to prioritize certain concerns over others (Oatley, 1992).

All of the mechanisms that I will describe in Chapters 18–24 have in common that they serve to guide, direct, or motivate behavior, but they do so in different ways, and with different degrees of specificity and flexibility (cf. Chapter 25). These differences between the mechanisms reflect their evolutionary origins, the way in which they developed initially.

17.6 Which are the Mechanisms, and When did they Evolve?

The human brain did not develop from scratch. It is the result of a long evolutionary process, during which newer brain structures were gradually imposed on older structures (Gärdenfors, 2003; Lane, 2000; Streidter, 2005). Brain circuits are laid out like the concentric layers of an onion, functional layer upon functional layer. One consequence of this arrangement, which is the result of natural selection rather than design, is that emotions can be triggered at multiple levels of the brain (Juslin, 2015).

Proceeding from this view, I have proposed that there are a number of induction mechanisms which developed gradually and in a particular order during evolution, from simple reflexes to complex judgments. They have in common that they might be triggered by "a musical event," broadly defined as *music, listener,* and *context.* I will refer to the mechanisms jointly in terms of the BRECVEMA model (Juslin, 2013a), named after their first letters:

- *Brainstem reflex*: a hardwired attention response to subjectively "extreme" values of basic acoustic features, such as volume and speed (e.g., Davis, 1984); you may become *startled* and *surprised* by the loud beginning of a rock song.
- *Rhythmic entrainment*: a gradual adjustment of an internal body rhythm, such as heart rate, towards an external rhythm in the music (e.g., Harrer & Harrer, 1977); you may experience *excitement* when your body is drawn into the captivating rhythm of a piece of techno music.
- *Evaluative conditioning*: a regular pairing of a piece of music and other positive or negative stimuli leading to a conditioned association (e.g., Blair & Shimp, 1992); you may feel *happy* when you hear a piece of music that has repeatedly occurred previously in a festive context.
- *Contagion*: an internal "mimicry" of the perceived voice-like emotional expression of the music (e.g., Juslin, 2000b); you may experience *sadness* when you hear a slow and highly expressive performance on the cello or violin.
- *Visual imagery*: inner images of an emotional character conjured up by the listener through a metaphorical mapping of the musical structure (e.g., Osborne, 1980); you may become *relaxed* when you indulge in mental images of a landscape suggested by a piece of "new-age" music.
- *Episodic memory*: a conscious recollection of a particular event from the listener's past that is "triggered" by the music (e.g., Baumgartner, 1992); you may experience *nostalgia* when a song evokes a vivid personal memory from the time you met your current life partner.
- *Musical expectancy*: a response to the gradual unfolding of the syntactical structure of the music and its expected or unexpected continuations (e.g., Meyer, 1956); you may feel *anxious* due to the uncertainty created by a musical phrase without a clear tonal centre.

- *Aesthetic judgment*: a subjective evaluation of the aesthetic value of the music, based on an individual set of weighted criteria (Juslin, 2013a); you may take *pleasure* in the extraordinary beauty of a classical composition.

In addition to these eight mechanisms, music can also arouse emotions through the default mechanism for induction of emotions, *cognitive goal appraisal* (Lazarus, 1991). You may become *annoyed* when a neighbor plays music late at night, blocking your goal of going to sleep. But as explained earlier, appraisal tends to be of less importance in a musical context.

I will provide more elaborate explanations and examples of each mechanism. However, we will first explore the origin of each mechanism. They are listed above in accordance with the approximate order in which the brain functions have been hypothesized to have appeared during evolution. I should acknowledge that scholars may differ somewhat when it comes to the exact sequence (Gärdenfors, 2003; cf. Donald, 1991, 2001; Joseph, 2000), but the overall picture is similar (Figure 17.1).

First came simple *sensations* and an ability to direct one's *attention* (as reflected in brainstem reflexes), along with *physical coupling* processes

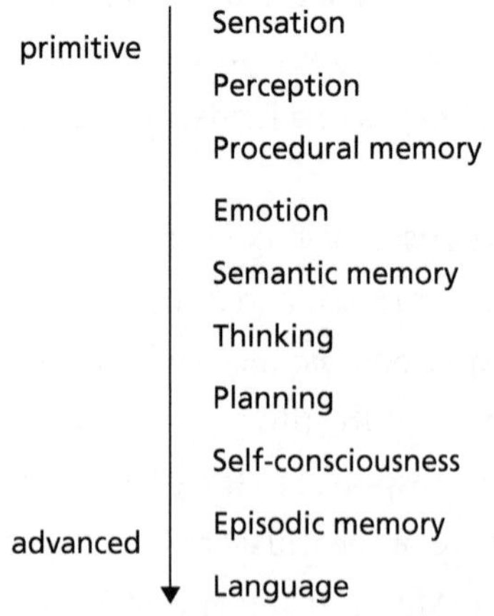

Figure 17.1 Hypothesized evolutionary development of different brain functions.

(as reflected in rhythmic entrainment). Both occur, in some form, even in very simple organisms.[6]

Then came *perception* (sensory impressions that are interpreted), which is crucial for all remaining mechanisms, followed by a basic capacity for *learning associations* among events (as reflected in evaluative conditioning). Perception and conditioning can be observed even in flies, worms, snails, and fish (LeDoux, 2000).

The ability to *respond empathically* to vocal expressions of emotions of conspecifics (as reflected in emotional contagion) is a somewhat later development associated with social mammals and the "the limbic system" of the brain (Ploog, 1992).[7]

Later still is the development of *inner imagination* (as reflected in visual imagery), which requires a type of mental representations that are detached from direct sensory stimulation (see Gärdenfors, 2003) and appeared along with the development of the neocortex of the brain.

Such representations enable "time travel" in an organism, such as the ability to imagine future events or the ability to *recall specific events* from one's life (as reflected in episodic memory). Episodic memories also require *self-consciousness*: perceptions of an inner world and a sense of self which is separate from the external world.

A conception of time and an inner world are essential to the ability to *plan* (e.g., sequences of action) and *narrate* (e.g., to order elements into a coherent story), which paves the way for the development of a complex *language*. Language presupposes the previous brain functions, and also requires the capability for *syntactic processing*[8] (as reflected in musical expectancy) to be able to handle a complicated grammar (Schoenemann, 1999).

The approximate time in evolution when artistic sensibility and aesthetic activities appeared has been much debated by scholars. If we adopt a *wide*

[6] Notably, I am talking about "inner" entrainment here, not the kind of "external" entrainment that occurs when we synchronize our movements with a beat.

[7] The term *empathy* refers in the present context simply to a process through which an organism comes to feel the same emotion as another organism (e.g., by means of motor mimicry).

[8] Recall that "syntax" refers to a set of rules which govern the combination of structural elements into sequences.

time-frame, language and art seem to have developed at about the same time. The answer to the question of "which one came first" depends on how we define both language and art. Both are symbolic behaviors which seem to have existed in some rudimentary form even in Neanderthals, but they really took off with the advent of modern humans approximately 200,000 years ago.

Many linguists and biologists believe that language occurred well before cave art—the most familiar form of prehistoric art. Fossil and DNA evidence of speech adaptations support the presence of some form of Neanderthal language. For instance, the FOXP2 gene, believed to be responsible for language acquisition, has been found also in Neanderthals, who shared a common ancestor with humans nearly a million years ago (Johansson, 2013). However, sign language rather than spoken language may have been the original language (Corballis, 2002).

There is some tentative evidence that artistic activities date back as far as 500,000 years ago (e.g., collecting objects of beauty), and at least 200,000 years ago, axes and other tools were shaped more beautifully than was needed for any practical purpose (Hodges & Sebald, 2011). Pre-historic bone flutes were found in France and Slovenia, estimated to be 53,000 years old (Gray, Krause, Atema, Payne, Krumhansl, & Baptista, 2001).

Yet if push comes to shove, I think that some form of proto-language, perhaps a combination of non-verbal gestures and vocal expressions, appeared before aesthetic activities developed.[9] Hence, I think it makes sense to place *aesthetic judgment* last in the list of mechanisms, in particular if we adopt anything like a modern conception of artistic behavior (see Part IV).

17.7 Two Mechanisms Are Better Than One

The first question that might arise in this context is this: why would evolution equip us with such a multitude of emotion mechanisms? Would not

[9] Aesthetic judgments may not be linked to a single brain function. Brain functions employed may depend on the criteria for aesthetic value involved (Chapter 29). However, judgments of beauty appear to involve relatively more "recent," cortical brain structures (Jacobsen, Schubotz, Höfel, & v. Cramon, 2006).

just one mechanism be sufficient? The most plausible explanation is that all mechanisms have contributed, in their own unique way, to our adaptation. (Note that more evolved species tend to preserve structures responsible for basic behaviors to the extent that they have been adaptive, or at least not maladaptive.)

Imagine for a moment that you are attempting to design an organism which would be able to survive in an uncertain and potentially dangerous environment. Would you rather spread your bets across various options for danger detection, or would you prefer to place all bets on a single solution? Evolution does not work in terms of a pre-conceived "design", but the evolutionary process has clearly favored organisms with multiple solutions, our emotions included.

Different mechanisms rely on different types of *mental representation* which help to guide future action. A representation is a physical state that conveys some meaning or information about the state of the world within a processing system (Fox, 2008). The representations are *intentional*, in the sense used by philosopher Franz Brentano (1973): they are always *about* something, although the "beliefs" of each mechanism need not be consciously available (Brentano, 1973). The representations of the mechanisms may be associative, analogical, as well as sensori-motoric (see section 25.1).

Each mode of representation can have both strengths and weaknesses concerning its utility in tracking significant aspects of the environment. Simple representations enable mechanisms to accomplish "quick and dirty" processing in response to an urgent threat. In some cases, it may be better to do *something* than to get caught up in time-consuming thinking.

In contrast, more complex representations enable mechanisms to accomplish more sophisticated, but relatively slow, processing of environmental cues. In some cases, it is preferable to do exactly the right thing rather than to just act quickly. Figure 17.2 offers a humorous illustration of the distinct strategies to handle danger.

An emotional system that relies on multiple modes of information brings a certain advantage. If one mechanism fails to react to a critical event, another mechanism might pick up the slack. This is an example of *functional*

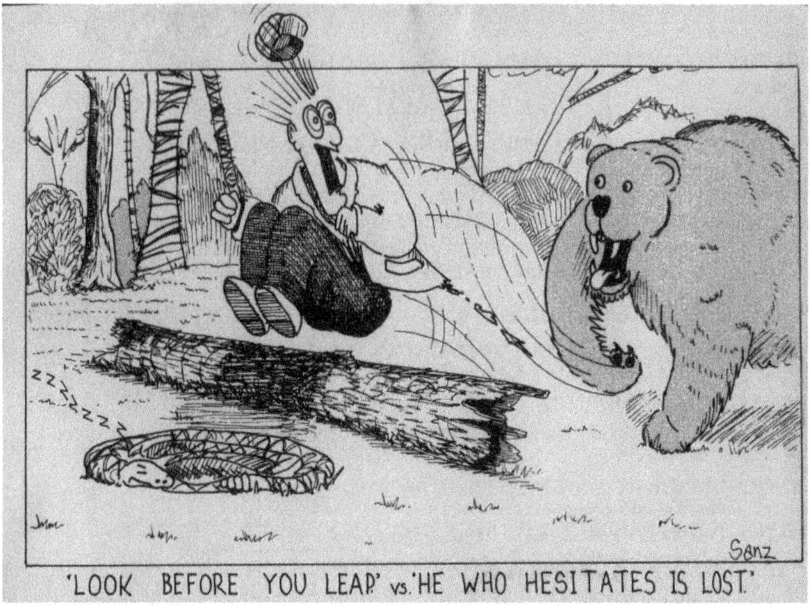

Figure 17.2 The perils of "quick and dirty" and "slow and accurate" processing, respectively.
Reproduced from Eysenck, M. W., *Perspectives on Psychology*, p.4. Hillsdale, NJ: Erlbaum. Cartoon by Sanz. © 1994–Psychology Press.

redundancy, or the fact that the same behavioral function can be achieved through many different processes in the central nervous system (Brunswik, 1956; Norris, Coan, & Johnstone, 2007). However, a potential drawback of a system featuring many mechanisms at various levels is that it can produce *conflicting outputs* under some conditions—hence the occurrence of "mixed" emotions (section 32.2). In the following chapters, we shall explore how musical events might engage each of our emotion mechanisms in unique ways.

CHAPTER 18

JUMPING AT SHADOWS

Brainstem Reflex

It is finally time to take a closer look at each of the mechanisms that can arouse emotions, as applied in a musical context. The BRECVEMA model (see section 17.6; Juslin, 2005, 2013a; Juslin & Västfjäll, 2008; Juslin, Liljeström, Västfjäll, & Lundqvist, 2010) will serve as the backdrop for an in-depth discussion of eight mechanisms in Chapters 18–24. Chapter 25 will then show how these mechanisms can be described in terms of a set of predictions that may serve to guide future research and applications. We will start with primitive mechanisms and gradually move on to more sophisticated ones. This chapter introduces a mechanism that involves a close link between perception and motor behavior.

18.1 Why You Should Not Fall Asleep During Concerts

Imagine yourself sitting at an evening concert of classical music, quietly enjoying yourself. The music is soft, consonant, and harmonious. You drift to sleep, only to be awakened by a loud chord that makes you jump out of the chair with your hair standing on end!

Something like this happened to the unexpecting audience at the premiere of Franz Joseph Haydn's Symphony No. 94 in G major. In the second movement, marked *Andante*, a *forte* kettledrum stroke occurs at the end of the *pianissimo* repeat of the first section. "That will make the ladies scream," the composer himself is supposed to have quipped after finishing this part of the composition (Watson, 1991, p. 152).

I have yet to hear screams in listening tests that use this famous piece, but the excerpt may certainly startle listeners of any gender, if appropriately calibrated (Juslin, Barradas, & Eerola, 2015). To startle listeners is a fairly easy trick, one I can't help pulling on students in my music psychology course. (It never fails!) It turns out I am not the only one who enjoys this trick. "People everywhere delight in startling one another," argues Ronald Simons (1996, p. 3) in an entertaining treatise on the topic; "an ancient game," according to American writer Kurt Vonnegut (1976, p. 204).

The startle response is only the most prototypical example of a more general mechanism I term *brainstem reflex*. This refers to a process whereby an emotion is aroused in a listener because an acoustic feature—such as sound intensity or roughness of timbre—exceeds a certain cut-off value for which the auditory system has been designed by natural selection to quickly alert the brain. It is a kind of "override" system (section 4.8), which is activated when an event seems to require first-priority attention (Simons, 1996).

Our perceptual system is constantly scanning the immediate environment in order to detect potentially important changes or events. Brainstem mechanisms are responsive even during sleep (Raloff, 1983). Sounds that meet certain criteria will induce an increased activation of the central nervous system, in the early stages of auditory processing.

All other things being equal, sounds that are very sudden, loud, dissonant, or feature fast or accelerating temporal patterns may induce *arousal, surprise*, or an *unpleasant* feeling in listeners (Berlyne, 1971; Burt, Bartolome, Burdette, & Comstock, 1995; Foss, Ison, Torre, & Wansack, 1989; Juslin, Harmat, & Eerola, 2014; Juslin et al., 2015). A listener in Alf Gabrielsson's study remembers hearing "an extremely quick thing, a movement that starts straight off without forewarning and just charges along. Wow, what a boost!" (Gabrielsson, 2011, p. 425).

Brainstem reflexes are said to be "hard-wired": they are quick, automatic, and unlearned. For instance, the playing of a sound with sharp attack at the sound level of 115 decibels behind a listener *will* reliably induce a startle response, *surprise,* and an associated increase in arousal (Levenson, 2007). We cannot help but respond to this stimulus—it's in our genes.

18.2 Why Do We Have Brainstem Reflexes?

The brainstem reflex is the mechanism that comes closest to depending (purely) on acoustic features, as opposed to learning and memories. However, even here, some degree of habituation or sensitization might occur over time (Simons, 1996).[1] We still need to explain *why* these particular features (e.g., a loud sound, sensory dissonance), rather than others, arouse a response. "Because they are arousing," you might say. But why? "Because they are extreme," you might respond. "Extreme" according to whom? Why are they perceived as "extreme"?

Those individuals in our ancient past who reacted with *arousal* and *fear* to sounds that increased rapidly in volume or tempo, or that were low-pitched, loud, and noisy had a greater survival rate than those who did not. This is because these features are correlated with things like looming objects that are about to hit us, or a large predator that is about to attack us. Hence, individuals who treated these features as "urgent" survived to procreate. Their behavior tendencies became part of our genetic makeup and continue to influence how we react to simple acoustic characteristics even today.[2]

Thus, for example, the perceived *pleasantness* and *unpleasantness* of sensory consonance and dissonance reflects how the hearing system divides frequencies into critical bandwidths: if the frequency separation of two tones is either very small or larger than the critical bandwidth, the tones will be

[1] *Habituation* refers to a non-associative learning process whereby gradual decreases in response occur with repeated presentation of the same stimulus (Andreassi, 2007, p. 32). We get used to the sensory stimulation. *Sensitization* is the opposite, in which repeated administration of a stimulus results in an amplified response.

[2] One example is arousal reactions to deep, grumbling bass tones, which may be linked to earthquakes or the threatening growl of a large animal (for the latter, try the beginning of Górecki's Symphony No. 3, I. *Lento*).

heard as consonant; if the separation is about one-quarter of a critical band, the tones will be heard as maximally dissonant (Plomp & Levelt, 1965).[3]

One example of a musical excerpt that might trigger a brainstem reflex to sensory dissonance (enhanced by loudness) is the first movement (*Adagio*) of Gustav Mahler's Symphony No. 10. It is the moment in the music (about seven minutes into the movement) where the reinstated theme culminates in a shattering dissonance, an organ-like chord. More than one listener in Alf Gabrielsson's study of strong experiences with music mentioned this section as a source of a negative affect:

> There it was. A chord so heart-rending and ghost-ridden that I had never experienced before. Not unlike a huge organ where you pull out every organ stop at random. A dissonance that pierced my very marrow. (Gabrielssson, 2001, p. 439)

The emotional power of the excerpt has been confirmed in listening tests (e.g., Juslin et al., 2015). But why do we perceive sensory dissonance as "unpleasant" in the first place, thus prompting us to *avoid* rather than approach it? The answer may be that sensory dissonance is suggestive of "danger" in a natural environment. For instance, it occurs in the threat and warning calls of many species of animals (Ploog, 1992)—including humans (Juslin & Laukka, 2003)—and might also be a cue to physical destruction.

Thus, dissonance may have been selected by evolution as a primary reinforcer of behavior (Rolls, 2007). The term *reinforcer* refers to a stimulus that enhances the probability that a specific behavior will occur in the future. A *primary* reinforcer does so without any special training or experience, because it is biologically based. A *secondary* reinforcer, in contrast, acquires its power via a history of association with a primary reinforcer or other secondary reinforcers (section 21.1).

Not all sounds that are primary reinforcers evoke negative affect: A breathy voice of the opposite gender may sound positively "sexy" to a

[3] *Sensory* dissonance should not be confused with *musical* dissonance, which occurs in a sequence of notes. The latter aspect is much more subject to learning and cultural and historical influences.

perceiver (something that is commonly exploited in certain types of pop music). However, all primary reinforcers are related to biological needs in some way.

All this suggests that brainstem reflexes are not unique to humans. In fact, they are the most ancient of our emotion-arousing mechanisms, and are universal in mammals, reptiles, birds, and amphibians. The esteemed emotion researcher Robert Plutchik notes that "the brain stem structures are surprisingly uniform from fish to man" (Plutchik, 1994, p. 271). Accordingly, the startle response may be the one reaction to musical sound that you can share with a fish! (For a refreshing wake-up signal, try the first 20 seconds of "Harmonielehre: Part 1" by John Adams.)

For brainstem reflexes to be adaptive, it is crucial that they respond rapidly. Studies indicate that the rapidity of the human startle, as indexed by the jaw muscles, may be 14 milliseconds (Davis, 1984), which is quite extraordinary. The phrase "brainstem reflex" is fitting because it highlights that the process can occur very early in the auditory processing, for example in the inferior colliculus of the brainstem (Brandao, Melo, & Cardoso, 1993).

A warning signal can be emitted in the brain before any elaborate classification of the sound event has taken place. We respond to the stimulus, even before knowing what it is. This may explain why the aroused affect is usually rather coarse. The arousal of more specific emotion categories requires more knowledge about *what kind* of threat or opportunity is imminent.

To simplify: we may characterize the mechanism metaphorically, in terms of how it behaves. Brainstem reflexes appear to adhere to the following principle: "I do not yet know what I am hearing, but *anything* that features so-and-so acoustic characteristics warrants immediate and undivided attention." If something *very* loud is quickly approaching, no matter what it is, it is most likely a source of concern that requires urgent attention.

This "quick-and-dirty" approach of the brainstem reflex comes at a price. Most responses to potentially important events tend to be "false alarms". Thus, for instance, Haydn's audience in the introductory example was not in serious trouble, after all. Evolutionary psychologists explain this in terms of a "cost–benefit asymmetry": Basically, the cost of getting killed even once is so much higher than the cost of responding to 100 "false alarms." From this point of view, it is easier to understand why brainstem reflexes such as the startle response remain in the behavior repertoire of highly evolved species like human beings: they continue to serve us well, on the whole.

The precise physiological processes underlying brainstem responses are still not completely understood, though evidence indicates that they occur in close connection with the so-called reticular system of the brainstem and the intralaminar nuclei of the thalamus, which receive inputs from the auditory system (Kinomura, Larsson, Gulyás, & Roland, 1996).

As explained by Rhawn Joseph, the brainstem subserves a number of sensory and motor functions, including auditory perception and the mediation and control of attention, emotional arousal, heart rate, breathing, and movement (Joseph, 2000). While the reticular system may be activated and inhibited by "higher" brain regions such as the amygdala, hypothalamus, and orbitofrontal cortex, it can also be activated independently of these regions in a reflex-like manner so that attention is directed at potentially important sensory stimuli (Tranel, 2000).

For instance, research indicates that the reticulospinal tract is required for the acoustic startle response because lesions in this tract abolish the response (Boulis et al., 1990). Yet although the neural circuitry that mediates the acoustic startle is located entirely within the brainstem, the system can be modulated by higher neural tracts (Miserendino, Sananes, Melia, & Davis, 1990).

18.3 Do Brainstem Reflexes Play a Role in Music?

Musical sounds, just like any other type of sound, might trigger brainstem reflexes. Haydn's "Surprise" symphony mentioned at the beginning of this chapter is only the most well-known example. Another example that might be effective—given a sufficient sound intensity—is the beginning of "Infernal Dance of all Kashchei's Subjects," a section of the ballet and orchestral concert work "The Firebird," composed by Igor Stravinsky. The excerpt begins with a loud drum and brass chord. One further example is the fourth movement, *Allegro con spirito,* of Symphony No. 2 in D major, composed by Johannes Brahms, where a loud section breaks in suddenly in bar 23 with the full orchestra. (All excerpts have been found to produce *surprise* and autonomic *arousal* in listening experiments; Juslin et al., 2015.)

Ronald Simons provides further examples from opera: a sudden trumpet call interrupts a slow, dreamy, soothing passage in Rossini's overture to "William Tell"; and a diminuendo is followed by a crash in von Weber's overture to "Oberon" (Simons, 1996, p. 81). Simons notes that evoking a brainstem reflex is a particularly useful technique in opera in which audience members can be startled by a musical event at the same time as a character in the opera is startled by some event onstage.

Samuel Rous, in the *Victrola Book of the Opera,* describes a scene from Giuseppe Verdi's opera, "Aida" (Figure 18.1):

> The scene is serene, soft, and gentle. Aida waits there for her lover. Suddenly, unexpectedly, and portentously she catches sight of her father. She cries out: "Ciel! Mi padre!" The accompanying music is sudden and loud, and the audience is startled right along with the heroine. (Rous, 1929, p. 32)

Figure 18.1 Poster for Giuseppe Verdi's opera *Aida.*
Illustration from Pexels. *Licensed under the Creative Commons Zero license (https://creativecommons.org/publicdomain/zero/1.0/).*

Not all brainstem responses involve a startle, of course. More generally, climaxes in music tend to involve marked increases in tempo, loudness, and pitch. Daniel Berlyne (1971) cites Richard Wagner's Prelude to "Tristan and Isolde" as an example of an arousing effect created by the repetition of a motif at successively higher and higher pitches. Maurice Ravel's piece "Bolero" is essentially one long *crescendo*, ending in a climax. (It may remind some people of something else.)

One listener remembers hearing the final movement of Mahler's Symphony No. 8: "when the choir "pulls along" the orchestra and soloists in a crescendo that accelerates right up to the last notes where the concert hall's magnificent organ joins them in a fortissimo, I am no longer in a concert hall, I am on Mount Tabor!" (Gabrielsson, 2011, p. 425).

These are only a few examples of musical events that might arouse brainstem reflexes, but I can see an objection coming miles away: "This is hardly a musically relevant response." (Tell that to Stravinsky!) Are brainstem reflexes that involve music merely a curiosity, or a joke, as perhaps suggested by the Haydn anecdote? Not quite: brainstem reflexes appear to contribute to music experiences on a regular basis.

Indeed, a brainstem reflex is probably the first emotional response you ever experience to music! Brainstem reflexes to music occur even prior to birth. Researchers have found that playing loud music to a fetus produces heart-rate accelerations as well as a motor response (for a review, see Lecanuet, 1996). As pointed out by John Dewey: "vision arouses emotion in the form of interest. It is sound that makes us jump" (Dewey, 1934, p. 237).

Brainstem reflexes may be more common in some musical genres than others, and will also occur more frequently during "live" concerts (see section 25.7) because of the volume and the fact that we do not have any control over the beginning of musical events. The first note at a loud rock concert will commonly trigger a brainstem reflex, which enhances the excitement and physiological arousal upon hearing the following notes.

Sheer volume, it may be argued, is hardly musically important. (Many rock musicians would disagree!) On the other hand, there are few excellent pieces of music whose reception are not intensified by a high sound level.

Although brainstem reflexes may appear primitive and far removed from "music as art," I think they may contribute to even our most profound aesthetic experiences sometimes (see Gabrielsson, 2011, p. 425).

Imagine hearing for the first time ever a piece such as Johann Sebastian Bach's Toccata and Fugue in D minor, BWV 565, performed loudly in a colossal setting, such as the cathedral in Uppsala (cf. Konečni, 2005); your brainstem responses to the *loud* sound, the *dissonance* of the organ chords, and the *deep bass* notes would, arguably, intensify the feelings of *awe* you experience in response to the physical grandeur of the music as a result of other mechanisms (e.g., *aesthetic judgment*) described later.[4]

If you find it odd to think of aesthetic *awe* in the same context as brainstem reflexes, then note that some researchers have defined *awe* as "reverential or respectful fear"—usually in response to something physically vast (Haidt & Seder, 2009). Music, too, can give the impression of physical vastness, through wide frequency range, high sound level, powerful note attacks, and the added effect of large hall reverberation.

Paradoxically, considering that brainstem reflexes are experientially salient at the moment they happen, they can be easily forgotten during the course of listening to a piece of music, simply because so much else is usually happening at the same time, or soon thereafter. It is often the case that a brainstem reflex (e.g., to a loud sound) coincides in time with another event (e.g., a change of key) recruiting another mechanism (e.g., *musical expectancy*), such that the two events "reinforce" each other; but the other event could appear more "musically meaningful" in our ongoing conscious experience, which means that the effect of the brainstem reflex is "masked" and overseen. Yet, the brainstem reflex may provide an immediate "shot" of neurochemicals to the brain, enhancing the effect of the other musical event.

Ronald Simons (1996) claims that startle responses are easy to remember, but I wonder if this is true in the context of music. Although self-report

[4] I write "for the first time" simply because the piece mentioned here may be the most well-known piece of organ music ever written, such that hearing it *once again* may evoke all sorts of other responses (e.g., associations; see Chapter 21), which I do not want to focus on in the present chapter.

estimates of the prevalence of brainstem reflexes seem quite stable (at a relatively low level), even cross-culturally (Juslin et al., 2016a), I think it is telling that data from studies where listeners report probable causes of emotions in close proximity to the actual listening episode indicate a higher prevalence (Juslin, Liljeström, Västfjäll, Barradas, & Silva, 2008).

A brainstem reflex (e.g., a startle) may also lead to a *secondary* response (Levenson, 2007), such as *laughter, anxiety,* or *anger,* depending on how the surprising event is interpreted (or appraised) afterwards (cf. Lazarus, 1991; Chapter 25). Hence, although brainstem reflexes are quite uniform across cultures and individuals, one can expect some individual differences in terms of this secondary response. For example, we observed that listeners who suffered from depression reacted with more *anxiety* than healthy controls to a surprising musical event that involved a brainstem reflex (Sakka & Juslin, 2018a).

Brainstem reflexes can explain *arousing* and *surprising* effects of music and how mere sound can induce *pleasantness* and *unpleasantness,* but it is unclear how the mechanism can explain the induction of specific emotions, beyond *surprise* and *fear.* Brainstem reflexes are the first piece of the puzzle, but they represent only a small part of what our emotional experiences with music might contain. Thus, let us move on to the next mechanism.

CHAPTER 19

GET INTO THE GROOVE

Rhythmic Entrainment

Have you ever experienced being at a concert where you listen to a captivating rhythm with a salient beat and feel that you just cannot seem to sit still? You are gradually drawn into the rhythm of the music, and feel aroused as you "become one" with the music, the musicians on stage, and the other listeners at the event? Chances are that you experienced what researchers refer to as rhythmic entrainment.

If brainstem reflexes focus on music as sound and sensation, entrainment focuses on *rhythm*. This is a primary feature of life. After all, we live in a rhythmic environment (e.g., seasons of the year, periods of daylight and darkness), and our bodies are "symphonies of rhythm" (Strogatz, 2003, p. 1), as reflected in processes such as heart rate, brainwaves, and sleeping patterns. So crucial is rhythm to human life that lack of it may be a sign of illness (Hodges & Sebald, 2011).

Rhythm is also one of the most fundamental features of music (Gabrielsson, 2016). The music therapist Thayer Gaston refers to rhythm as "the organizer and energizer" (Gaston, 1968, p. 17). Rhythm confers structure to the music and brings the musical notes to life. Gaston observes that most people disregard music to which they cannot keep a beat, and that the favorite music of adolescents almost always contains "a driving beat." Its repetitive structure enables listeners to enter into "sync" with the music. This is key to the second of our eight mechanisms.

Rhythmic entrainment refers to a process whereby an emotion is evoked by a piece of music because a powerful, external rhythm in the music influences some internal bodily rhythm of the listener (e.g., heart rate), such that the latter rhythm adjusts toward and eventually "locks in" to a common periodicity (Clayton, Sager, & Will, 2005).

For example, while lying on a sofa, you might listen to a piece of music with a marked pulse somewhat faster than your current heart rate. Eventually, your heart rate increases and aligns with the rate of the music. The adjusted heart rate then spreads to other emotion components (Chapter 15) such as feeling through *proprioceptive feedback* (signals from sensory receptors in muscles, joints, and skin which help to regulate the pattern of muscle activation during movement; Grey, 2010), thus inducing increases in arousal. The entrainment process may also often give rise to external movements, such as head bobbing and foot stamping, but this is not presumed to be required: bodily rhythms may entrain to music without movement.

The basic idea here is that emotions may be aroused not only "top-down" (central evaluative processes in the brain influencing the body) but also "bottom-up" (a change in physiological response can influence brain processes). To illustrate: a raised pulse and quickened breathing can create a feeling of *excitement* in the absence of any cognitive appraisal of an event.

19.1 What Are the Characteristics of Entrainment?

The mechanism of entrainment is not unique to music. The phenomenon was discovered in 1665 by the scientist Christian Huygens. He observed that two pendulum clocks with close but unsynchronized periods, mounted on the same wall, would eventually synchronize their strokes. The different amounts of energy transferred between the moving pendulums, due to the initially asynchronous movement periods, cause a negative feedback loop. This feedback drives an adjustment process, in which the difference in energy amount is gradually reduced to zero until both moving bodies move in synchrony (Thaut, McIntosh, & Hoemberg, 2015).

Mere observation of synchronous variation in two variables, however, does not necessarily imply entrainment (Clayton, Sager, & Will, 2005); for instance, transient sync could arise by chance (Strogatz, 2003). Entrainment refers to synchronization that is caused by a certain process.

The foremost expert on entrainment in music today, Martin Clayton, explains that there are two components required in entrainment (Clayton et al., 2005): first, there must be (at least) two autonomous oscillators. (Oscillators are entities that cycle automatically at more or less regular time intervals.)

Autonomy means that they should both be able to oscillate, even if they are separated. Thus, the definition does not include mere resonance. The body of an acoustic guitar will begin to oscillate in tune with a plucked string, but as soon as the string stops oscillating, so does the body. Hence, these are not two autonomous oscillators.

Second, the two oscillators must *interact* in some way. They need to be coupled. "Two or more oscillators are said to be coupled if some physical or chemical process allows them to influence one another" (Strogatz, 2003, p. 3). (In the case of the pendulum clocks examined by Huygens, the transmitting medium was the vibrating wall.) The coupling may be "strong" or "weak"; that is, oscillators can entrain more or less strongly.

There are also two aspects of entrainment: (i) *period* entrainment (that the oscillators have the same frequency), and (ii) *phase* entrainment (that the focal points occur at the same time). But it is period entrainment that "drives" the process (Thaut et al., 2015). In real-life situations, it is not uncommon for two periodic processes to lock frequency but remain out of phase (Clayton et al., 2005).

If mere demonstration of synchrony between two variables is not sufficient to prove the presence of entrainment, how can we make sure that we are observing genuine entrainment? Critical in establishing entrainment is to identify disturbances (perturbations and transitions) during the synchronization process. More specifically, we should be able to observe a stabilization of the period relationship, and the reassertion of this stability following a perturbation (Clayton, 2012).

For example, Michael Thaut and co-workers demonstrated that finger and arm movements entrain to the period of a metronome and stay locked to this frequency even when subtle tempo changes are introduced that are not consciously perceived by the listener (Thaut et al., 1998).

As implied by the last example, entrainment is not limited to pendulum clocks mounted on a wall. Entrainment is found throughout nature: it seems to be evidenced in some way or other by all animals and plant species, highlighting its importance. Yet it may be especially salient in humans. Marie Riess Jones assumes that human beings are inherently rhythmical creatures with tunable perceptual rhythms that can entrain to time patterns of the external world (Jones & Boltz, 1989).

19.2 How May Entrainment Be Reflected in a Musical Setting?

While many types of behavior, such as speech, exhibit rhythmical aspects, none does perhaps more so than musical behavior. Hence, it comes as no surprise that synchronized behavior, as a possible sign of entrainment, has been documented in a variety of musical contexts in every culture. Anthropologists and ethnomusicologists such as Alan Lomax (1962), John Blacking (1973), and Charles Keil and Steven Feld (1994) have revealed the important role of rhythmic processes in military drills, religious rituals (e.g., shamanism), and dancing (Becker, 2004; McNeill, 1995).

Martin Clayton (2016) argues that entrainment is particularly noticeable in activities where rhythmic coordination will make physical work (e.g., moving a heavy object) more efficient. It has further been suggested that entrainment is crucially involved in early mother–infant interaction (Dissanayake, 2000) for emotion regulation and bonding. Hence, the rhythmical aspects of music may offer some clues to the evolutionary origin and function of music.

Most music listening in everyday life in the modern Western world involves pre-recorded music (e.g., Juslin, Liljeström, Västfjäll, Barradas, &

Silva, 2008). In such a context, the entrainment process may be termed "asymmetrical": listeners entrain to external sounds that they cannot themselves influence (Clayton, 2012). ("Symmetrical" entrainment, however, may occur between members of a musical ensemble.)

Wiebke Trost and Patrik Vuilleumier (2013) argue that there are various "levels" of entrainment: perceptual, motor, physiological, and social. However, it seems to me that they are confounding the underlying *mechanism* of entrainment (the gradual mental coupling of oscillators) with its *manifestation* as "internal" (perception, psychophysiology) or "external" (motor behaviors, social behaviors) synchronization. Indeed, Wiebke Trost, Carolina Labbé, and Didier Grandjean have subsequently admitted that neural entrainment may be the basis of all observed entrainment effects (Trost, Labbé, & Grandjean, 2017, p. 106). Internal and external synchronization (as different manifestations of entrainment) might occur in social or solitary settings. Hence, the social aspect is not another "level," but rather a context variable.

I submit that manifestation of entrainment at the *physiological* level is most promising when it comes to explaining how entrainment may lead to the arousal of emotions, since we know that autonomic arousal might affect emotions from the bottom up (Levenson, 2014). The process is likely to be rather slow, due to natural constraints of the cardiovascular system (Trost et al., 2017).

Even if we disregard the slow physiological response of the proprioceptive feedback, oscillators do not synchronize instantaneously; and the period takes longer to adjust than the phase (Clayton et al., 2005). This means that entrainment is a slower induction process than a brainstem reflex, and that experimental designs that aim to test the mechanism must allow a sufficient amount of time for a potential entrainment effect to occur.

Sometimes, however, two oscillators do not synchronize, at all. Under what conditions will rhythmic entrainment to music occur in such a way that emotion is aroused? We don't know for certain. The entrainment-inducing properties of music that will influence affect presumably depend on the music having a marked pulse—as evident in, say, techno music, march music, and certain types of film music (Juslin, 2013a). The pulse should also be close to the "natural" heart or respiration rate of the listener. For two oscillators to entrain, their periodicities need to be fairly close to each other (Aschoff, 1979).

Failure to adhere to this principle can explain why a study by Carolina Labbé Rodriguez did not observe (strict) entrainment of heart rate and respiration to musical rhythm. The author concedes that such period and phase synchronization "would have been unlikely" (Labbé Rodriguez, 2015, p. 166) with the tempi selected (e.g., 128 beats per minute—far from a resting heart rate), begging the question why the tempi were selected in the first place. But rhythms need not entrain only in "unison." They can also involve subdivisions and hierarchical relationships (Clayton et al., 2005). This means that documenting entrainment may require the use of more sophisticated statistical techniques, like the models developed in *dynamical systems theory* (for examples, see Lesaffre, Maes, & Leman, 2017).

19.3 Does Entrainment Involve Sensori-Motoric Representations?

Like brainstem reflexes (section 18.1), entrainment involves a close link between auditory perception and motor responses. This is partly because the motor system is responsible not only for producing a rhythm but also involved in the perception of rhythms (Clayton et al., 2005). This may explain our strong urge to move in response to musical grooves and beats.

So strong is our tendency to move when we hear rhythmic music that even when suppressing overt motor response to music, many listeners are engaging in subliminal physical action (as revealed by electromyographical measures of muscle activity; see Fraisse, Oleron, & Paillard, 1953; Harrer & Harrer, 1977). Photographer Pattie Boyd reports anecdotally that when she was married to guitarist Eric Clapton, she observed him tapping his feet to inner music whilst he was asleep (Boyd, 2008).

How is the psychological mechanism of rhythmic entrainment implemented physiologically? Most scholars hypothesize that entrainment to auditory cues involves multiple, linked neural oscillators in the brain (Jones, 2009). An alternative theory assumes that the process through which a regular isochronous pulse is activated while one listens to music—*beat induction*—is mediated by "somato-topic body maps" with crucial input from the vestibular system, leading to a sense of inner motion (Todd & Lee, 2015). Both approaches have in common a focus on sensori-motoric representations.[1]

Which brain areas, exactly, are involved in rhythmic entrainment? This question remains yet to be explored fully, but preliminary studies have obtained evidence of neural oscillation patterns to rhythmic stimulation in early auditory areas, motor areas (sensorimotor cortex, supplementary motor area), the cerebellum, and the basal ganglia (e.g., Fujioka, Trainor, Large, & Ross, 2012; Tierney & Kraus, 2013; Trost el al., 2014), perhaps primed early on by reticulospinal pathways in the brain stem (Rossignol & Jones, 1976).

The cerebellum might be particularly important in "active" entrainment (when coordination of motor responses is involved; Grahn, Henry, & McAuley, 2011; cf. Table 13.2). During "passive" entrainment to auditory stimulation, the caudate nucleus of the basal ganglia may be the key area (Trost et al., 2014), with the cerebellum assuming less importance. Considering that entrainment seems to involve early auditory processing and subcortical brain areas, it is not surprising that people can rarely verbalize and report the nature of their entrainment process (Jones & Boltz, 1989).

19.4 Is There Really Evidence of Entrainment in Music?

There is little doubt that rhythmic entrainment—manifested "internally" or "externally"—may occur in response to music. What remains to be

[1] Patel and Iverson (2014) argue that the exceptional ability for motor entrainment shown by humans (and some non-human animals) depends on the evolution of *vocal learning*, which brought with it enhanced dorsal auditory pathway connections between auditory regions and motor planning regions via the parietal cortex.

demonstrated fully is that this mechanism is able to arouse *emotions* in music listeners. Previous studies have mainly explored whether musical rhythms may influence bodily rhythms per se.

Gerhart Harrer reported that music listeners tended to synchronize either their heart rate or their respiration rate to the music, and that one could "drive" the pulse with appropriate music (Harrer & Harrer, 1977). (The latter effect is often sought after in film music that seeks to create excitement and tension in viewers; think of *Jaws*.) Early studies such as this one have an anecdotal character and do not report the data in sufficient detail to enable us to conclude that proper entrainment has been obtained.

What is required to show more conclusively that entrainment can arouse emotion is an experiment in which we can observe (i) that a physiological rhythm aligns its period or a subdivision with a musical rhythm; (ii) that this synchronization is re-established after a disturbance; and (iii) that the change in physiological rhythm causes a change in experienced emotion. I am not currently aware of any study that has demonstrated entrainment based on these criteria.

Because entrainment can be elusive, some researchers have relaxed the requirements and used a "softer" definition, according to which it is sufficient to show that the physiological response moves in the "right direction"—for instance that the heart rate of a listener accelerates *towards* a faster musical rhythm, without adopting a similar period ("synchronization tendencies"; Labbé Rodríguez, 2015, p. 18).

Such a "soft" definition is problematic, however: if we do not demand a similar period and the reassertion of stability following a perturbation, how can we distinguish entrainment from just any change in physiological arousal? An increase in heart rate might simply reflect emotional arousal induced by another mechanism. It is the synchronization of the period and its stability that *defines* rhythmic entrainment.

A number of studies suggest that respiration rate and heart rate can change *towards* the tempo of music (Etzel, Johnsen, Dickerson, Tranel, & Adolphs, 2006; Khalfa, Roy, Rainville, Dalla Bella, & Peretz, 2008; Nyklicek, Thayer, & Van Doornen, 1997) or the simple rhythmical pattern of a metronome

(Haas, Distenfeld, & Axen, 1986). But are these genuine instances of entrainment (as defined earlier), or do they merely reflect overall changes in arousal due to some other induction mechanism?

In the face of difficulties of obtaining objective evidence of entrainment, Carolina Labbé and Didier Grandjean (2014) devised a self-report scale aimed to capture "subjective entrainment" in listeners. However, it remains unclear whether ratings on the scale bear any relationship to *actual* entrainment as defined above. In fact, I doubt that listeners are able to report in a valid manner whether their internal bodily rhythms are entrained to an external rhythm or not.[2] The burden of proof lies with the scale developers.

19.5 Which Types of Affect Might Entrainment Induce?

At the present stage of investigation, it seems plausible that the process may regulate *arousal* levels in listeners (see section 4.7). It may also arouse some secondary—and mainly positive—emotions of a social character (Juslin, 2013a).

When we spontaneously think of rhythmic entrainment, we may tend to think of its arousing effects, for instance, how the funky grooves of certain James Brown songs excite our bodies, or the moments after the "drop" in electronic dance music where the beat is especially salient. Still, entrainment may also potentially reduce levels of arousal. It all depends on whether our bodily processes are entraining to a faster or slower rhythm.

Consider lullabies, which are used in every culture to calm infants and help them fall asleep. Johannes Kneutgen found that when soothing lullabies were played for infants, their breathing rhythms became synchronized with the slow musical rhythm (Kneutgen, 1970). In short, entrainment may

[2] The finding that subjectively rated entrainment was correlated with feelings of *nostalgia* in a listening test confirms my suspicion that whatever the scale is measuring, it is not physiological entrainment. How could entrainment explain the induction of *nostalgia*—an emotion that is virtually by definition related to memory?

be a source of both *excitement* and *calm*, two common emotional reactions during musical events (see section 16.2). Although mainly documented anecdotally, the former emotion could turn into a kind of "trance"—as described in ethnographic studies (Becker, 2004; Rouget, 1995) and commonly observed during "rave parties" (Gauthier, 2004).

In addition, entrainment could contribute to certain valenced states, primarily positive ones. I prefer to conceive of these states as "secondary responses." For example, it has often been suggested that entrainment between individuals can create a strong sense of "social bonding" (Levitin, 2010) and "feeling connected" (Juslin, 2013a).

Interpersonal synchrony, it seems, can serve as a cue for prosocial behavior: when we move together in time, we become more likely to trust and cooperate with one another, and to like and help each other, and these effects extend even to infants (Cirelli, Wan, & Trainor, 2016). Do we perhaps experience feelings of intimacy and social connectedness even when we are entrained to musical rhythms during passive listening to music?

Whereas being in "sync" with music may be a source of pleasure, the opposite—failing to synchronize with the music—may be frustrating, even annoying. This might happen with music featuring a complex time signature where we simply fail to grasp the metrical structure and/or the beat. Or it can happen when we are moving, but are unable to move in "sync" with the music. (Have you ever tried to walk while listening to music that features a gradual accelerando?)

One would expect musicians to be more sensitive to rhythmical aspects than other listeners. Curiously, a study that measured "implicit synchrony" (spontaneous synchronization during walking) found that musicians that had never met before spontaneously synchronized their movements earlier amongst themselves than participants in a control group, but not better than people sharing a romantic relationship (Preissman et al., 2016).

Although not strictly an emotion, the subjective feeling or qualia of "a strong urge to dance" is arguably also related to the entrainment mechanism. While entrainment could happen even if a music listener is sitting perfectly still, one may hypothesize that the process is reinforced by self-movements (as entrainment manifested at different levels may influence each other; e.g., Trost et al., 2017). A listener who attended a salsa concert featuring special syncopations and a "rhythmic carpet" notes that "I experienced those more intensely when my body could take part" (Gabrielsson, 2011, p. 427).

For the sake of conceptual precision, we may want to distinguish the emotion caused by the (inner) rhythmic entrainment process per se from the emotion caused by any movement that may or may not occur in connection with the entrainment process. For instance, when music listening involves dancing, some of the pleasure experienced by the listener might simply be due to endorphins released in the body as a result of prolonged physical activity. This effect may enhance the positive emotion produced by the entrainment process itself, but should be properly regarded as a secondary response.

Similarly, Neil Todd and Christopher Lee (2015) hypothesize that moving to music may be rewarding in itself due to its stimulation of the vestibular system and its brain connection to the limbic system of the brain, which is implicated in emotions (Joseph, 2000); they further suggest that this stimulation, and the drive to dance from vestibular reflexes, is enhanced by loud and bassy notes, due to the low-frequency sensitivity of the vestibular apparatus. This could help to explain why the music at raves and discos is so loud: feeling the acoustic vibrations of the pulse is pleasurable and helps us synchronize with the beat (see also Figure 19.1).[3]

Self-reports from listening experiments (Juslin et al., 2018) and cross-cultural survey studies (Juslin et al., 2016a) suggest that rhythmic entrainment *could* be a frequent source of emotion in what we, for lack of a better word, refer to as "popular music." Some scholars even appear to take the entrainment mechanism for granted (e.g., "Rhythmic entrainment is an important component of emotion induction by music"; Trost et al.,

[3] Recent studies confirm that loud bass may play a role in the synchronization of dance (Van Dyck, Moelants, Demer, Deweppe, Coussement, & Leman, 2013).

Figure 19.1 Dancing, a common manifestation of rhythmic entrainment to music. Photo by Tim Gouw, from Pexels. *Licensed under the Creative Commons Zero license (<https://creativecommons.org/publicdomain/zero/1.0/>).*

2014, p. 55). However, as hinted at earlier, there is an urgent need for experimental studies proving that internal entrainment (as defined here) can have a causal role in arousing emotional reactions to music. Until then, the precise role of entrainment will remain somewhat uncertain.

CHAPTER 20

MIRRORING THE EXPRESSION

Contagion

Contagion is something that you have probably experienced numerous times in everyday life, outside a musical context. Have you ever noticed that when you have a casual conversation with someone who is depressed, you tend to walk away from the encounter feeling somewhat depressed yourself? Or that when you encounter a cheerful stranger, your mood lifts a little too? There is reason to believe that something similar may happen when we listen to music.

Emotional *contagion* refers to a process whereby an emotion is induced by a piece of music because an independent region of the brain reacts to certain acoustic features *as if* they were coming from a human voice that expresses an emotion, which leads the listener to mirror the emotional expression internally (Juslin, 2000b).[1] For instance, the music may have a *sad* expression (e.g., slow tempo, low pitch, low sound level, dull timbre) which arouses *sadness* in the listener.

The contagion mechanism is strongly related to the emotional expression of the music, which I discussed in Part II. We saw that listeners commonly perceive discrete emotions in pieces of music. There is also evidence that often when listeners perceive a discrete emotion in a piece, it also *arouses* the same emotion in them (Juslin, Harmat, & Eerola, 2014; Juslin, Barradas, & Eerola, 2015; Kallinen & Ravaja, 2006; Lundqvist, Carlsson, Hilmersson, &

[1] My use of the term contagion is similar to what Hatfield and colleagues refer to as "primitive" contagion (Hatfield, Cacioppo, & Rapson, 1994, p. 3), in order to distinguish it from higher-level types of cognitive empathy, which are not necessarily emotional.

Juslin, 2009). "The music was a very sad song ... the music made me very sad," notes a listener in a study by John Sloboda (1989, p. 37).

In fact, exploratory self-report data from experience sampling studies (Juslin, Liljeström, Västfjäll, Barradas, & Silva, 2008) and cross-cultural surveys (Juslin, Barradas, Ovsiannikow, Limmo, & Thompson, 2016) suggest that the emotional expression is a common source of emotional reactions to music. In Alf Gabrielsson's study of "strong experiences with music," it was the single most commonly reported cause by the participants (Gabrielsson, 2011).

We should of course keep in mind the limitations of self-report when it comes to establishing causes of aroused emotions (see Chapter 3). Yet, even these preliminary findings suggest that the notion of contagion is worth exploring further.

20.1 Where Does the Notion Come from?

The idea of emotional contagion is hardly new. It was not initially suggested with respect to music, but rather as a general explanation of emotional empathy. Theodor Lipps (1903) was probably the first scholar to propose a mechanistic account of empathy where the perception of an emotional gesture in another person directly induces the same emotion in the perceiver through *mimicry* (Preston & de Waal, 2002). Mimicry is the action of mimicking someone or something—in this case, an emotional expression.

In a landmark publication, Elaine Hatfield and colleagues defined contagion as "the tendency to automatically mimic and synchronize facial expressions, vocalizations, postures, and movements with those of another person's and, consequently, to converge emotionally" (Hatfield, Cacioppo, & Rapson, 1994, p. 5). Studies by clinical observers, neuroscientists, primatologists, social psychologists, and sociologists have confirmed that people "catch" the emotions of others when perceiving their emotional expressions, and that this process assists them in understanding the feelings of others (Hatfield, Bensmana, Thornton, & Rapson, 2014).

Most investigations of emotional contagion to date have concentrated on *facial expressions.* My colleague in Uppsala, Ulf Dimberg, was able to show that people exposed to pictures of facial expressions of emotions spontaneously activate the same face muscles, even when the pictures are processed outside of awareness; they further report feeling these same emotions (Dimberg, Thunberg, & Elmehed, 2000). People find it nearly impossible to suppress such mirroring reactions (Dimberg, Thunberg, & Grunedal, 2002).

To show that facial mimicry is related to arousal of emotions, scholars have manipulated the facial expressions of participants in different ways—for instance, tricking them into adopting a facial expression or arranging things so that participants will unconsciously mimic others' expressions. (One study famously asked subjects to hold a pencil in the mouth in such a way that their zygomaticus muscles, used during smiling, would be activated; Strack, Martin, & Stepper, 1988). Such manipulations of subjects' expressions really spark changes in their emotional experience: People tend to feel emotions consistent with the expression they have adopted, and have difficulty experiencing emotions inconsistent with the expression (Hatfield et al., 2014).

Evidence of emotional contagion is not limited to facial expressions, however. There are also studies indicating that expressions in the *voice* are contagious, producing mirroring emotional reactions in the listener (Hietanen, Surakka, & Linnankoski, 1998; Neumann & Strack, 2000). Skyler Hawk and his co-workers found that both hearing and reproducing vocalizations of *anger, disgust, happiness,* and *sadness* produced specific facial responses and self-reported emotions congruent with these vocalizations (Hawk, Fischer, & Van Kleef, 2012).

Using an audio platform which allowed them to (covertly) manipulate the emotional tone of the auditory feedback given to subjects talking in an experiment, Jean-Julien Aucouturier and his co-workers were able to show that this influenced both self-reported emotion and skin conductance level (arousal) in the direction of the emotions targeted in the manipulations (Aucouturier, Johansson, Hall, Segnini, Mercadié, & Wanatabe, 2016). (The participants were unaware of the manipulations.)

20.2 How Might Contagion Occur in Music?

The psychological process of emotional contagion has been thoroughly documented for a variety of non-verbal channels, but how could the notion of contagion be applied to *music*? The most obvious way in which musical events can produce contagion effects is through the non-verbal expressions (face, body) shown by performers during a "live" concert (Figure 20.1).

That this may occur is supported by an experimental study, indicating that participants who watched a video-taped singer's music performance produced spontaneous matching of facial muscles to the singer's facial expressions (Chan, Livingstone, & Russo, 2013). Contagion at "live" concerts may also involve the emotional expressions of fellow members of the audience (producing *collective emotions*; section 16.4), for instance, sharing the *joy* and *excitement* at watching one's idols in the flesh. (These phenomena should perhaps be properly regarded as "context effects" rather than effects of the music per se.)

However, the idea here is that the *music* itself might produce a kind of emotional contagion, even when listening in the absence of any visual

(a) (b)

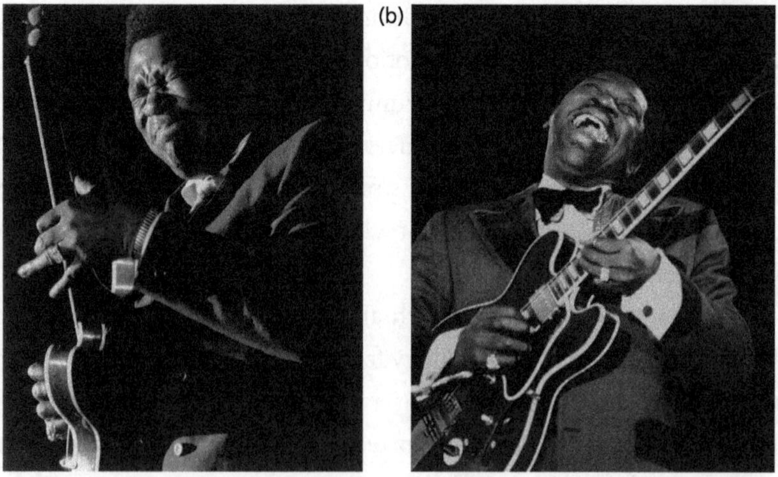

Figure 20.1 Non-verbal expression of emotion in the blues performer B. B. King.
Photo by Tom Copi/Michael Ochs Archives/Getty Images. Photo by Dan Farrell/NY Daily News Archive via Getty Images.

impression. How could that be? If we are listening to an expressive singer, there is no real mystery. To achieve an expressive performance, the singer might "borrow" voice cues from emotional speech, such as vibrato, sighs, screams, moans, or a "crying" voice. Can instrumental music also produce contagion?

Recall from section 11.2 that music often features expressive acoustic patterns similar to those that occur in emotional speech, in terms of changes in pitch, tempo, loudness, timbre, and temporal patterns (Juslin & Laukka, 2003). I have thus argued that we get emotionally aroused by voice-like expressive modulations in music via a process in which a neural mechanism responds quickly and automatically to certain sets of stimulus features as if they belonged to a human voice, which leads us to "mirror" the perceived emotion internally (Juslin, 2000b).

Furthermore, I have argued that musical sounds could sometimes be even *more* emotionally evocative than the human voice. According to the previously mentioned "super-expressive voice" theory (Juslin, 2000b, 2001; see section 11.3), what makes a particular performance of music on, say, the violin, so expressive is that it sounds a lot like the human voice, whereas at the same time it goes far *beyond* what the human voice can do in terms of speed, intensity, and timbre.

For example, if human speech is perceived as excited when it has a fast rate, loud intensity, and bright timbre, a musical instrument might sound *extremely* excited by virtue of its even higher speed, increased intensity, and brighter timbre. This possibility should render music a particularly potent source of contagion, sometimes even more so than emotional speech.

I propose that the musical instruments that resemble the human voice most closely will be most effective when it comes to arousing emotion in listeners through contagion. Some of the most commonly suggested candidates in the literature include the oboe, the clarinet, the cello, and the violin: "there are in the music of the violin ... accents so closely akin to those of certain contralto voices that one has the illusion that a singer has taken her place amid the orchestra," notes Marcel Proust (Watson, 1991, p. 236; for some empirical support, see Mores, 2009).

The key to such striking vocal similarities may not be just the musical instrument's timbre or register, but rather whether it enables the required types of expressive contours to occur in the performance.

Because the contagion mechanism is responsive to subtle musical features which convey the emotional expression (e.g., pitch contours, timing patterns), it will depend particularly on the *performer's* contribution to the music (see Chapter 13). Individual musicians clearly differ in their ability to achieve a "singing" quality on their instrument, and this aspect might be key to "touching" the listener. To illustrate: we may admire the beauty of a composition to some degree even if it is performed in a "dead-pan" manner by a computer, but the piece may not become truly "moving" unless it is performed expressively, so as to be emotionally "contagious" too.

20.3 Why Are Some Scholars Sceptical of Contagion Theory?

The contagion theory has not been without its critics. Thus, for instance, philosopher Jenefer Robinson notes that, although the contagion mechanism may have some plausibility, it has limited application because "it applies only to music that *sounds like* vocal expression" (Robinson, 2005, p. 388). She is perhaps forgetting that most music heard today *is* vocal music, where the chances of contagion via the voice are plentiful, in particular when the singer is truly expressive.

From Maria Callas and Billie Holiday to Janis Joplin and Adele, listeners have been deeply moved by expressive voices. For instance, listen to the beginning of Jeff Buckley's version of "Corpus Christi Carol" on his 1994 album, *Grace*. Recall too the fascination with the high voices of the Castrati (see section 11.3), or the widest vocal range of any human being, achieved by the American singer Tim Storms on August 1, 2008 (9 octaves and 11 semitones).

Yet, the claim here is that also voice-like features of, say, a violin or cello may arouse basic emotions through a contagion effect. Listen, for example, to Concerto for Two Violins in A minor, Opus 3 No. 8, II. *Larghetto e Spiritoso*, written by Antonio Vivaldi and performed by Accademia Ziliniana. After the brief introduction, a solo line played with intense vibrato on the violin begins—first approximately in the range of the human voice, but then moving into "super-voice" territory, higher up—and is soon joined by a second violin in a moving, vocal-like duet. If you are like me, you cannot resist the strong impression of someone, *something*, "singing." (And the piece has proved to be effective in listening tests; see Juslin et al., 2015).

Even so, some scholars have argued that music does not sound much like vocal expression, except in special cases (Davies, 2001). A cello, for instance, does not sound like a human voice to such an extent that we may confuse the two (Schubert, 2018). Why should we react to a musical instrument as if it were a vocal expression of emotion if we can so clearly distinguish between the two things perceptually?

Here we need to recall the onion metaphor (see section 17.6), according to which the brain consists of several layers, some of which may work independently of others. One plausible explanation of the contagion effect of music is that expressions are processed by a domain-specific and autonomous *module* of the brain (cf. Fodor, 1983) which reacts to certain features in the acoustic stimulus independently of its context (Juslin, 2001).

The key aspect is that the module does not "know" the difference between vocal expressions and other acoustic expressions. It will react in the same way (say, detecting *sadness*) as long as certain features (e.g., slow speed, low pitch, low dynamics, dull timbre) are present in the auditory stimulus. In all likelihood, the module evolved before musical sounds were created on Earth so the "problem" of confusing vocalizations and musical sounds would not have entered into the equation at this evolutionary stage.

20.4 Is There Any Support for A Modular Account?

I acknowledge that a modular view of information processing has been the subject of some debate, yet even some of its most ardent critics have admitted that special-purpose modules can exist at more primitive, subcortical levels of the brain where much of the processing of emotions occurs (e.g., Panksepp & Panksepp, 2000). If we consider Jerry Fodor's (1983) list of features, it is clear that a modular theory of emotion perception in music receives support:

- *modules are fast*: judgments of musical emotions are quick (Peretz, Gagnon, & Bouchard, 1998)
- *modules are innately specified*: the ability to "decode" emotions from music develops early (Cunningham & Sterling, 1988), and the ability to discriminate between emotions develops even earlier, towards the end of the first year (Flom, Gentile, & Pick, 2008)
- *modules are autonomous*: perception of emotional expression can occur implicitly (Juslin, Harmat, & Laukka, 2018; Pell & Skorup, 2008)
- *modules are domain-specific*: there is evidence of brain dissociations between judgments of musical emotion and of musical structure (Peretz et al., 1998a) as well as between judgments of musical emotion and of musical familiarity (Peretz & Gagnon, 1999)
- *modules are hardwired*: it seems impossible to "re-learn" how to associate expressive forms with discrete emotions (Clynes, 1977, p. 45)
- *modules are automatic*: emotion induction through music is possible even if listeners do not attend to the music (Juslin & Liljeström, in press)
- *modules are capsules of information*: we appear to respond to music performances as if they were expressions of emotion (Witvliet & Vrana, 2007), despite knowing that music does not literally have any emotions to express (cf. Davies, 2001).

There is also evidence that decoding of basic emotions in music performances involves many of the same brain regions as perception of basic emotions in vocal expressions (Escoffier, Zhong, Schirmer, & Qui,

2013; Paquette, Takerkart, Saget, Peretz, & Belin, 2018). This is the first step in supporting the contagion mechanism, demonstrating that our brains have a tendency to process emotions in speech and music in a similar way.

A second step is to show that some form of "mirroring" reaction also occurs. Exactly how the psychological process of contagion is implemented physiologically is not yet clear. Early contagion theories tended to assume that so-called afferent physiological feedback from mimicking muscles lead to the arousal of a "matching" emotion. This is the essence of the facial feedback hypothesis, advocated by scholars such as Charles Darwin, Silvian Tomkins, Ross Buck, and James Laird (Adelmann & Zajonc, 1989).

One might also envision emotional effects of *vocal* feedback. When subjects are "tricked" into reproducing voice patterns associated with discrete emotions, using a cover story to hide from the subjects that the focus is on their emotions, they also tend to *feel* these emotions as a result (Hatfield, Hsee, Costello, & Denney, 1995; Rueff-Lopes, Navarro, Caetano, & Silva, 2014).

However, perhaps the mirroring response need not take the form of actual movements, but merely the activation of brain regions associated with such movements? More recently, researchers have proposed that the process may rather be implemented by means of "mirror neurons" in the brain. Studies in the 1990s discovered neurons in the monkey's pre-motor cortex, which discharged both when a monkey carried out an action and when it merely observed another individual performing a similar action (di Pellegrino, Fadiga, Fogassi, Gallese, & Rizzolatti, 1992).

There is at least *some* evidence indicating that a mirror neuron system exists also in humans. For example, several studies show that when individuals watch or hear an action carried out by another individual, the motor cortex becomes active in the absence of overt motor activity (Rizzolatti & Craighero, 2004). Observation and imitation of facial expressions activate the same pre-motor areas (Wild, Erb, Eyb, Bartels, & Grodd, 2003). Jane Warren and colleagues found that a network of pre-motor cortical regions were involved in processing of affective nonverbal vocalizations (Warren et al., 2006).[2]

In view of findings that emotions in speech may activate mirror neurons, and that emotional expression in music seems to involve similar acoustic patterns for basic emotions as speech, it does not seem too far-fetched that expressive music could activate mirror neurons as well.

Direct evidence of an activation of mirror neurons in connection with emotional reactions to music has to my knowledge not yet been presented. However, an imaging study by Stefan Koelsch and colleagues found that music listening activated brain areas related to a circuitry which serves the formation of premotor representations for vocal sound production, even though no singing was observed among the participants (Koelsch, Fritz, Cramon, Müller, & Friederici, 2006). The authors conclude that this could reflect a mirror function mechanism, and their findings offer tentative support to the hypothesis that listeners may "mirror" the emotional expression of music internally.

20.5 Why Do We Experience Emotional Contagion?

In view of the strong action–perception link that seems to exist for emotional expression, it may be instructive to consider the evolutionary origin of vocal expression of emotions more generally.

The German clinical psychiatrist, primate behavior researcher, and anthropologist Detlev Ploog has described the transformation of the larynx—from a pure respiratory organ (e.g., in lungfish) to a respiratory organ with a limited vocal capability (in amphibian, reptiles, and lower mammals), and to the sophisticated instrument that humans use to sing or speak in an expressive manner (Ploog, 1992).

[2] I should acknowledge that some authors argue that the notion of "mirror neurons" has been seriously oversold in the field of neuroscience, and that imitative behavior may be better explained in other ways (Hickok, 2014).

Vocal expression is particularly important in social mammals. Social grouping evolved as a means of cooperative defense, although this meant that some kind of communication had to develop to enable sharing of tasks, space, and food (Plutchik, 1994). Vocal communication provided a means of social coordination.

Paul MacLean has argued that the limbic system of the brain—a key region of emotions—underwent an enlargement with mammals, and that this development was associated with increased sociality, as evident in play behavior, infant attachment, and vocal signaling (MacLean, 1993). (What is music, if not a kind of play with vocal sounds that help us stay socially connected?)

Biologists shy away from using words such as "emotion" in connection with animal behavior, yet it would seem that most animal vocalizations involve motivational states that are closely related to emotions (Marler, 1977), as inferred from the situations in which the vocalizations occur. Detlev Ploog reports a small number of vocal expressions in squirrel monkeys, linked with crucial life events: warning calls ("alarm peeps"), threat calls ("groaning"), desire for social contact calls ("isolation peeps"), and companionship calls ("cackling") (Ploog, 1981). These could be considered forerunners of vocal expressions of basic emotions in humans (Chapter 11).

Given phylogenetic continuity of vocal expression and cross-species similarities in the types of situations that generate expressions, it is perhaps not surprising then that there is evidence of cross-species universality of vocal expression. Eugene Morton noted that "birds and mammals use harsh, relatively low-frequency sounds when hostile, and high-frequency, purer tone-like sounds when frightened, appeasing, or approaching in a friendly manner" (Morton, 1977, p. 855). Notice that somewhat similar links were described for music in Table 8.1 of this book.[3]

Why, then, did emotional contagion evolve in the first place? Did it have any evolutionary function? Indeed, it may have been adaptive to rapidly

[3] These findings are intriguing because they suggest the possibility of "cross-species contagion," as when we are emotionally moved by the cries of a dog, which appear sufficiently similar to human cries to arouse a mirroring response.

have one's emotions cohere with those of one's conspecifics. Consider a scenario where members of a group suddenly express *fear* and run away. An individual who is immediately "smitten" by the *fear* can react more quickly so as to avoid, say, an approaching predator than one who must first scan the environment on its own to locate the threat, appraise the situation, and decide on the suitable course of action.

One may object that there are many examples in modern society where such "group contagion" of emotions has negative consequences; just think of riots, panicking crowds, and lynch mobs. Yet, such examples do not preclude that contagion was mostly adaptive in its original context.

More broadly, many scholars have assumed that contagion serves to facilitate group cohesion and social interaction (Darwin, 1972; Preston & deWaal, 2002). Social benefits might involve enhanced empathy, rapport, and bonding. (In support, contagion *does* seem to create affiliation and liking amongst people; Lakin, Jefferis, Cheng, & Chartrand, 2003.) Music has commonly served—and continues to serve—that same function. Indeed, some scholars have argued that this emotion-coordinating feature may explain the origins of music (Roederer, 1984).

The ancient evolutionary origin may explain some characteristics of the contagion mechanism; for example, that it is seemingly universal, has a high degree of modularity and automaticity, that it may induce emotions very quickly, and that it is uncontrollable and largely inaccessible to conscious awareness (Dimberg et al., 2002; Hatfield et al., 2014; Neumann & Strack, 2000).

Contagion seems to develop early, but not quite as early as brainstem reflexes. Precursors of emotional contagion via facial and vocal expressions have been observed as early as the first year of development (Soussignan & Schaal, 2005). Marvin Simner investigated vocal mimicry in newborns, two to four days old, and found that they began to cry when they heard the cry of another newborn (Simner, 1971). In an attempt to make sure that the infants were responding to the distress of the other infant rather than simply to the noise, he played a synthetic cry that was similarly noisy to the infants. This did *not* make them cry. I am not aware of any study that has tried to explore emotional contagion through music in infants.

20.6 Which Emotions Can Contagion Arouse?

Contagion will involve the arousal of an emotion in the listener more or less identical to that expressed in the music. (If the music is *sad*, you will become *sad*; if the music is *happy*, you will become *happy*.) Yet because the contagion mechanism is linked to the human voice, we may assume that contagion will mainly occur for emotions that have a distinct vocal profile.

Exactly which emotions can be conveyed in the voice is under debate (Keltner, Tracy, Sauter, Cordaro, & McNeil, 2016), but the current best bet is that they correspond to the basic emotions (Chapters 4 and 11). Most complex emotions do not have a unique vocal profile that may give rise to contagion. Because the expression of complex emotions involves other types of coding that are not based on iconic similarity (see Chapter 12), I submit that contagion cannot arouse complex emotions without the help from other induction mechanisms.

Yet, although the immediate effects of the contagion mechanism could be limited to basic emotion categories and their nuances, it might also involve "secondary responses." Manfred Clynes suggests that when we hear a convincing emotional expression, this is perceived as "sincerity" by the listener, who may thus feel *sympathy* for the performer (Clynes, 1977).

This highlights a classic distinction in non-verbal behavior between *spontaneous* ("genuine") and *posed* ("acted") emotional expression. We have recently shown in Uppsala that listeners are able to distinguish the two types of vocal expression of emotion (Juslin, Laukka, & Bänzinger, 2018) —even at an implicit level, as revealed by arousal reactions (Juslin, Harmat, & Laukka, 2018).

On the assumption that singers (and other instrumentalists) usually aim to express emotions in the most naturalistic and convincing manner possible, I hypothesize that contagion effects will be stronger the more the singer's or performer's emotional expression resembles an "authentic" expression, as opposed to a "fake" expression (Korb, With, Niedenthal, Kaiser, & Grandjean, 2014). The same notion presumably underlies the common (albeit still untested) presumption that, "a musician cannot move others unless he too is moved" (Bach, 1778/1985, p. 152). Having said that, I think performers can, to a considerable extent, be trained to approximate authentic expressive patterns in the absence of felt emotions (Juslin, Friberg, Schoonderwaldt, & Karlsson, 2004), although the skill may come easier to some than others. The greatest performers seem to have a knack for giving the music exactly the right expressive shape.

Personally, I have always been quite prone to emotional contagion. Thus, if a public speaker becomes nervous, so do I. If someone is speaking with a sad or happy voice, I tend to "catch" these emotions. In fact, my original interest in music and emotion probably sprung from my tendency to become strongly moved by the expressive, voice-like quality of certain instrumental passages, particularly on the electric guitar.

Sometimes the emotional impact of the human voice becomes even more striking when it is featured in a "machine-like" context. For instance, consider the best-selling "club-album" *Play* by the artist Moby, released in 1999. In many songs on the album, Moby features samples of voices from indigenous black music from the 1920s and 1930s (recorded by Alan Lomax) in newly composed backing tracks, consisting of "ambient beats," created with synthesizers and drum machines. Moby received some criticism for this, but he explained: "my main interest in these old vocals was more my emotional response to them, as opposed to where they came from" (Irvin & McLear, 2003, p. 658). The samples *are* moving, indeed, but the end result may not be everyone's cup of tea.

20.7 How Can Contagion Be Distinguished?

I have argued that contagion might contribute to a sense of social intimacy and bonding. This is reminiscent of the effect of the entrainment mechanism discussed above. Both mechanisms rely on sensori-motoric representations. Thus, it could be tempting to regard them as basically the same mechanism (Thompson & Quinto, 2011).

Many discussions of how music could influence groups of people (McNeill, 1995) seem to conflate entrainment and contagion, and the two mechanisms may often function together, achieving a common goal in human social activities. They may even share neural resources, at some level of the brain. Yet, although we are still in the early stages of exploring both phenomena scientifically, I think there is already reason to believe that entrainment and contagion need to be distinguished conceptually.

For entrainment to occur, a strong pulse or rhythm is necessary and sufficient. For contagion to occur, a strong pulse is hardly sufficient, neither is it required. The focus is more on voice-like aspects. (A vocal affect expression can be contagious, without having a marked rhythm.) Furthermore, entrainment appears to be a slower induction process (Clayton, 2012) than contagion (Dimberg & Thunberg, 1998). Only contagion can arouse a whole range of discrete emotions. Entrainment mainly regulates the level of arousal, apart from positive (secondary) responses.

The two processes also appear to be implemented physiologically in different ways (oscillator neurons and/or vestibular networks for entrainment versus mirror neurons for contagion). However, I hypothesize that when entrainment occurs, it may tend to enhance the effect of the contagion mechanism also, since contagion depends partly on temporal aspects of expression (Table 8.1).

We have made some preliminary attempts to capture the emotional contagion mechanism in experimental settings in Uppsala, using both synthesized music examples and excerpts from the existing repertoire. Recall from Chapter 13 that music performances which express *sadness* are perceived as particularly "expressive" by listeners (Juslin, 1997b).

To maximize the chances of inducing emotional contagion in listeners, we have selected examples which include a *sad* expression and solo voices performed on the cello or violin; such as "Vocalise," Opus 34, No. 14, by Sergei Rachmaninoff, arranged for cello and piano; "Prayer," from Jewish Life No. 1, by Ernest Bloch, composed for cello and piano; and the (aforementioned) Concerto for Two Violins in A minor, Op. 3 No. 8, II. *Larghetto e Spiritoso*, by Antonio Vivaldi (Juslin et al., 2014, 2015).

Our series of experiments indicated that listeners reacted to such musical excerpt as predicted; that is, they experienced *sadness* at the *sad* expression, as indicated by self-reports of feelings, autonomic responses, and facial expressions. They also pointed to the emotional expression as the probable cause of their emotion (see section 25.9 for further examples of such experiments).

In conclusion, it seems plausible that listeners' emotions to music sometimes reflect social modular responses to the emotion-specific acoustic patterns of the music. Indeed, this may perhaps partly explain the documented tendency of some listeners to use music as a "social companion" to reduce feelings of loneliness (Juslin & Laukka, 2004). After all, what better reaffirmation that "you are not alone" than hearing a deeply expressive voice of emotion?

The mechanisms discussed in Chapters 18–20 are the most ancient and "visceral" mechanisms, and can be fruitfully conceived of as "embodied cognition" (Shapiro, 2011). They have in common their close link between perception and motor behavior. (Brainstem reflexes literally make us jump; entrainment and contagion involve "inner" motor responses, which may also be manifested "externally" as, say, clapping, foot stomping, or motor mimicry.)

However, there are also mechanisms featuring mental representations which seem "detached" from immediate sensory stimulation and motor behavior, and that expand the range of emotional reactions we can have when listening to music. These mechanisms will be explored next.

CHAPTER 21

RING MY BELL

Evaluative Conditioning

So far we have explored three psychological mechanisms that can arouse musical emotions. Brainstem reflexes and, in particular, rhythmic entrainment and contagion, may all produce strong emotional reactions in listeners, yet there is still something "impersonal" about those responses; in a sense, they may belong to "anyone." The three mechanisms tend to influence different listeners in much the same way (apart from the moderating effect of trait variables), and they all focus very much on "the here and now".

In Chapters 21–23, I will ponder three mechanisms that add more personal significance to your responses: *evaluative conditioning, episodic memory*, and *visual imagery*. They help to render your emotional responses uniquely yours. They show how specific pieces of music fit into the larger scheme of your personal life, and enable you to "travel" mentally in space and time. (Do you remember yesterday, when all your troubles seemed so far away?)

They can do so because they rely on mental representations that are more "detached" from the immediate context (Gärdenfors, 2003) than the sensori-motoric representations discussed earlier. They reflect events that happened previously or that may happen in the future. They are all in some sense dependent on memory, and may even share neural resources in the brain, but they also have some unique characteristics. In this chapter, we will consider the most ancient of the three mechanisms.

21.1 What Is Evaluative Conditioning?

Some of our emotional reactions to music seem to be based on relatively simple associations. *Evaluative conditioning* refers to a process whereby an emotion is aroused by a piece of music just because this stimulus has been paired, repeatedly, with other positive or negative stimuli, which are not necessarily logically connected to the music in any way.[1] It is a special form of classic conditioning that involves the pairing of an initially neutral conditioned stimulus (CS) with an affectively valenced, unconditioned stimulus (US). After the pairing, the CS acquires the ability to arouse the same affective state as the US in the perceiver (De Houver, Thomas, & Baeyens, 2001).

To illustrate: perhaps you have visited your best friend repeatedly during a certain time period. Invariably, you have a lot of fun together, which makes you *happy*. As it happens, a certain piece of music has been playing in the background during nearly every visit, without you paying much attention to it. Over time, through repeated co-occurrences, the music may eventually come to arouse *happiness* even in the absence of the social interaction. You will simply hear the piece somewhere and it will make you feel *happy*, without you being able to explain why.[2]

As you will recall, we have encountered conditioned responses previously when discussing perception of emotions (see section 12.2). The difference is that, in the present context, the association arouses a felt emotion rather than just evoking the concept of the emotion. That is, we do not just perceive the music as expressive of the emotion, we actually come to *feel* that emotion ourselves. This distinction may be particularly difficult to make when it comes to associations, but remember that a multi-component approach to measuring emotions can help us to distinguish between the cases—between "hot" and "cold" cognition (Chapter 15).

[1] As Randolph Nesse observes, emotion mechanisms "may use any cue correlated with the relevant situation, even if it is not reliably or causally connected" (Nesse, 2009, p. 160). This is particularly true of conditioning.

[2] Such seemingly inexplicable responses to music appear to be quite common. A listener in Gabrielsson's study reports how "tears run down my cheeks. I have no idea why" (Gabrielsson, 2001, p. 438).

Conditioned responses may be both a curse and a blessing. Simply consider the story of Gustav Mahler. (You may have heard the beautiful *Adagietto* of his Fifth Symphony.) Mahler grew up in difficult family circumstances. His father abused his mother. After a particularly severe incident, Mahler fled the house only to encounter a man playing a happy drinking song on a barrel organ outside on the street. During psychotherapy sessions with Freud, Mahler apparently realized that incidents such as this one had made him associate happy music with tragedy (Pogue & Speck, 1997).

This is only an extreme example of a process that is quite common in everyday life. We all experience conditioned responses on a daily basis. If I say "beer," you might think "fun" (or "hangover" depending on your learning history). But some of these associations are special, in that they involve a strong *emotional valence.*[3] Evaluative conditioning has some peculiar characteristics, with crucial consequences for music experience.

21.2 What Are the Characteristics of Evaluative Conditioning?

First, evaluative conditioning can occur even if the participant is unaware of the contingency of the two stimuli (Field & Moore, 2005; Hammerl & Fulcher, 2005). An association may be both established and arouse emotions without awareness (e.g., Martin, Stambrook, Tataryn, & Beihl, 1984; Öhman & Mineka, 2001). Indeed, there is even some indication that attention can hamper effects of the process (De Houver, Baeyens, & Feld, 2005), perhaps because conscious attention activates "higher-level" mechanisms (e.g., cognitive goal appraisal; section 25.4), which may reduce the impact of "lower-level" mechanisms. Gregory Razran found in a series of studies that affective attitudes towards various pieces of music, paintings, and

[3] Evaluative conditioning is also sometimes referred to as *affective learning, emotional conditioning,* or *preference conditioning.*

photographs could be modified by free lunches—at least as long as the participants were *unaware* of this aim to condition them (Razran, 1954).

Second, evaluative conditioning seems to be more resistant to extinction than other forms of classic conditioning (LeDoux, 2002). *Extinction* refers to a process whereby post-acquisition presentations of the conditioned stimulus (say, a piece of music) without the unconditioned stimulus (a happy event) leads to a gradual elimination of the previously acquired response (De Houver et al., 2001). The resistance to extinction of evaluative conditioning may simply reflect the effect emotions have on the encoding of memories: emotional events are generally better remembered than non-emotional events (Reisberg & Heuer, 2004). This characteristic implies that once a piece of music has been strongly linked with an emotional outcome, this association could be quite persistent (Bolders, Band, & Stallen, 2012).

Third, evaluative conditioning appears to depend on automatic, unintentional, and effortless processes (De Houver et al., 2005; LeDoux, 2002), which involve sub-cortical brain regions such as the amygdala and the cerebellum (Balleine & Killcross, 2006; Johnsrude, Owen, White, Zhao, & Bohbot, 2000; Sacchetti, Scelfo, & Strata, 2005). These characteristics might help to explain why conditioned reactions can be induced so quickly, without conscious awareness or voluntary control. "I was simply moved without wanting or expecting to be," observes Thomas Turino, in his description of a musical event which evoked powerful emotional associations in him (Turino, 2008, p. 225).

A non-musical example—although featuring a musician—is supplied by Keith Richards from the Rolling Stones (Figure 21.1), who describes how certain sounds from his childhood in the United Kingdom during the Second World War still exert a powerful effect upon him:

> Even now when I'm walking down a hotel and someone's watching a World War II movie on TV in their room and an air-raid siren goes off and catches me unawares, it puts my hair up, zzzzzschouooooupe! 'Shit, there's bits of me that remembers more than my memory does. My hairs have memories'. (Driver, 2001, p. 377)

Figure 21.1 Keith Richards of the Rolling Stones, striking a pose, playing a riff.
Illustration by Costis Chatzidakis.

Although dear Keith may be mistaken about the precise physical location of his memories, his anecdote fits well with the evaluative-conditioning mechanism. For his fans, the chills and the gooseflesh (cf. section 15.4) will instead occur at the precise moment Keith is beginning one of his iconic introductory "riffs" (just think of "Satisfaction"), which immediately evokes positively valenced feelings associated with the ensuing hit song. This affectively laden "aha! moment" is a common response to music. (However, it may also involve a negative association, if the song is a dreaded one.)

Interestingly, scholars have observed that rates of conditioning are faster when using *acoustic* CSs, relative to other types of CSs (Lavond & Steinmetz, 2003). In addition, evaluative conditioning seems to be faster than (non-affective) classical conditioning. In a so-called eye-blink conditioning paradigm, it can take 25–50 trials to create a conditioned response (Lavond & Steinmetz, 2003), whereas in evaluative (affective) conditioning, the learning can be much quicker (LeDoux, 2000). In other words, the stronger your initial emotional response is, the quicker you will establish an emotional association.

However, the timing of the delivery of the CS and US used in conditioning is critical (Lavond & Steinmetz, 2003)—which may explain why the cerebellum is involved in conditioning, just like in another strongly time-dependent process that we encountered earlier, rhythmic entrainment (section 19.3). Specifically, if a piece of music does not occur in close temporal proximity to the emotional event, no emotional learning will take place.

21.3 Has Conditioning with Music Been Investigated?

While conditioning seems to be generally acknowledged as a powerful source of emotion in music (e.g., Berlyne, 1971, p. 33; Dowling & Harwood, 1986, pp. 204–205; Hanslick, 1986; Sloboda & Juslin, 2001, pp. 94–95; Turino, 2008), few studies so far have actually examined evaluative conditioning involving music. There are several possible reasons for this neglect.

First, the associations are often highly personal and idiosyncratic (see Gabrielsson, 2011). Different listeners have different learning histories (with some notable exceptions). This may appear to render conditioned responses difficult to study. Such an impression is not necessarily correct, however; there are well-established paradigms for conditioning (Lavond & Steinmetz, 2003) that may be used to demonstrate conditioning with music in a controlled experimental setting. You can create emotional associations to a piece of music during the course of an experiment.

It may be more difficult to explore conditioned responses in field studies. However, common cultural experiences may sometimes lead to shared associations. One example is the negative emotions experience by many Jews after the Second World War on hearing the music of Richard Wagner due to members of the Nazi party in Germany loving his music (Sloboda & Juslin, 2001; Turino, 2008). Such shared emotional associations to music could be investigated further in future research.

Another reason for the neglect of conditioned responses is that they do not seem to be related to the music as such: the music mainly acts as a conditioned stimulus. Hence, such responses are often regarded as "irrelevant" to the music and consequently unworthy of study (Hanslick, 1986). However, as explained in section 12.2, several famous composers rely on conditioning in their works, and affective associations can have powerful effects in real-world contexts (Turino, 2008). If evaluative conditioning is a strong and frequent source of musically aroused emotions in everyday life, the mechanism clearly needs to be part of any credible framework.

Perhaps the real reason for the lack of relevant research is that most scholars simply take the phenomenon for granted. Yet even if we are very confident that evaluative conditioning can function well in a music setting, we still need to work out the details and ramifications of the process.

Precisely which feature of a musical stimulus that best serves as the conditioned stimulus as well as its degree of *generalization* and *discrimination* are issues that need to be tested. The melody (or theme) of the music could be particularly effective in classical music. In popular music, certain "hooks," "licks," or "grooves" could be similarly effective. However, studies of *fear* conditioning have demonstrated that even a simple tone can be effective in establishing a strong association (LeDoux, 2002).

Yet the low status of evaluative conditioning (recall the "politics" of music and emotion) can explain why one of the few relevant studies—probably the best one—was actually conducted on dogs. Dogs are social animals, and may show a distressed response if they are left alone or being separated from their owner.

In a rare experimental study, Linda Bernardini and Alberto Niccolini explored the possibility of evoking positively valenced conditioned responses in dogs showing symptoms of separation problems by listening to music (Bernardini & Niccolini, 2015). Fourteen dogs were conditioned over twenty days. Three times a day, they would listen for twenty minutes to a piece of music chosen by the owner, in a calm environment and in the presence of the owner.

Four days after the conditioning period, each dog was subjected to three experimental tests, consisting in being alone for five minutes in an unknown environment (different for each test), in silence, or listening to the music chosen by the owner, or a never-heard piece of classical music (an excerpt from "The Goldberg Variations" by J. S. Bach, performed by Glenn Gould).

The dog's behavior was video-taped and observation of the sessions revealed that there was significantly less "barking" and "scratching the door" when the dog was listening to the music previously heard together with the owner, compared to both the Bach excerpt and a period of silence. The conditioned piece had a calming effect on the dog, it seems.[4]

That the findings were obtained with dogs should not be a cause of concern in the present context. After all, who does not love dogs? More importantly, the basic processes studied involve parts of the brain that work in pretty much the same manner in all mammals. (The most commonly used animal in psychological studies of conditioning is probably the rat.)

Much suggests that music could have a similarly calming influence on humans in everyday life. (Recall that *calm* is a common emotional response to music; section 16.2.) By listening to our favorite music via headphones while traveling in a foreign and potentially stressful environment, we can regain a sense of personal control, familiarity, safety, and relaxation.

[4] Several studies suggest that music can have a calming effect on animals, but most of these were not conducted under controlled experimental settings. Also, the extent to which various animals "enjoy" music remains unclear.

There is some indirect evidence of evaluative conditioning featuring music in humans also. Elizabeth Blair and Terrance Shimp (1992) found that when participants were originally exposed to a piece of music in an unpleasant situation, they later held a less favorable affective attitude toward a product presented together with the music than participants who had not been pre-exposed to the same conditioning. The negative emotion of the initial event became associated with the music, and this negative state was subsequently re-evoked during the product evaluation.

It should really not come as a surprise that conditioning has attracted interest in consumer research and among advertisers. As pointed out by Thomas Turino, verbal statements about things usually call forth an analytical state of mind: they invite the perceiver to assess the truth or falsity of the claim being made (Turino, 2008). (This is *not* what advertisers want!)

Emotional associations, in contrast, partake of the things they signify; hence, they seem more natural, real, *unquestionable*. (You cannot argue with a piece of music.) Instead of trying to appeal to us with rational arguments (which in many cases are severely lacking), advertisers try to appeal "directly to our emotions" through conditioned responses. We can hardly resist such processes unless we switch off our technical devices (TVs, phones, computers), because the conditioning mechanism works implicitly and automatically.

Further evidence of conditioned responses comes from a study by Klas Hellström and Petri Laukka (2012). Thirty-seven listeners participated in an experiment consisting of two phases, conditioning and evaluation. In the conditioning phase, short musical excerpts previously rated as "neutral" in a pilot study were paired with positive and negative pictures from a large database (the International Affective Picture System). One musical excerpt was consistently presented together with a negative picture, whereas another excerpt was consistently presented together with a positive picture.

In the evaluation phase, the conditioned excerpts were featured in an affective priming task where the participants were instructed to rate, as quickly as possible, the valence of positive and negative words. Each word was preceded by the primed music excerpts. Reaction times were recorded in each trial.

Because previous research has shown that response latencies are facilitated when prime and target share the same valence, the authors predicted that positive words should be evaluated faster if they were preceded by a positively conditioned piece of music than if preceded by a negatively conditioned one. Negative words, in contrast, should be evaluated faster if they were preceded by a negatively conditioned piece than if preceded by a positively conditioned one.

The expected effect occurred for the positive words, but for some reason the negative words did not work. The researchers acknowledge that conditioning is known to be affected by a range of procedural characteristics, which may explain the results.

21.4 Which Emotions Might Conditioning Arouse?

It seems uncontroversial that evaluative conditioning may induce both positive and negative affect. Beyond that affective dimension, most studies so far have mainly reported evidence that involves basic emotions (cf. Joseph, 2000; LeDoux, 2002; Olatunji, Lohr, Sawchuk, & Westendorf, 2005), which I discussed in Chapters 4 and 11. This seems consistent with the ancient origins of the mechanism (Gärdenfors, 2003) and with the low-level brain regions involved (Lane, 2000). However, it cannot be ruled out that evaluative conditioning may arouse more complex emotions also.

For example, how can we come to experience a feeling of *nostalgia* to a piece of music we have never heard before? (Nostalgia as a feeling is most typically associated with personal memories of specific events; see section 22.4.) I recall experiencing strong *nostalgia* when I heard the first track on the album *Forever Changes* by the group Love, even though I had never heard it before. One plausible explanation might be that a piece features some aspect (e.g., a timbre), which has been subconsciously associated with previous nostalgic events. (Consider the use of, say, Glenn Miller's

"Moonlight Serenade" in many movies to suggest the mood and associations of the 1930s.)

However, precisely which emotions evaluative conditioning involving music might arouse remains to be systematically tested. What we *do* know is that the evoked affect can vary in intensity, from mild affect to intense emotions. Most of our conditioned responses may, in fact, involve low intensities.

One phenomenon related to a mild form of positive affect is referred to as *the mere exposure effect* (also sometimes referred to as *the familiarity principle*). It is the tendency for people to develop a preference for things just because they are familiar with them. To illustrate: when choosing what music to listen to, you may sometimes have a tendency to select music you are already familiar with. Edward B. Titchener describes "the glow of warmth" we feel in the presence of something familiar (Titchener, 1910).

The mere-exposure effect is most strongly associated with Robert Zajonc (2001). He suggests that the phenomenon could be regarded as a form of conditioning, if one assumes that the absence of aversive events constitutes the "unconditioned stimulus." In other words, stimuli that we have encountered repeatedly without suffering negative consequences will eventually produce a positively valenced response.[5] This helps to account for a tendency of some listeners to make less-than-adventurous choices of music. Similar to effects reported in evaluative conditioning studies (De Houver et al., 2005), mere-exposure effects can occur even when the relevant stimuli are inaccessible to the subject's awareness (Zajonc, 2001).

21.5 What Is the Role of Conditioning in Everyday Life?

A remarkable aspect of conditioned responses is that they may begin very early on. So-called post-natal behavior effects of pre-natal exposure are

[5] We will consider the role of familiarity further when discussing aesthetic judgments of music in Part IV.

consistent with evidence that the evaluative conditioning mechanism is functional even prior to birth (for a review, see Hepper, 1996).

For example, one study used the theme song from the British TV series *Neighbours* and could show that a pre-natal conditioning procedure featuring this music produced a post-natal different reaction to the piece as compared to music not used in the conditioning phase (Hepper, 1988). It seems that the forging of emotional associations to sounds begins even before we are born.

Music often occurs in situations where music listening is not the *only* or the primary activity. People play music while they are cleaning the house, having people over for dinner, doing the dishes, studying for an exam, or training at the gym (Juslin & Laukka, 2004; Juslin, Liljeström, Västfjäll, Barradas, & Silva, 2008, Juslin, Liljeström, Laukka, Västfjäll, & Lundqvist, 2011; Sloboda & O'Neill, 2001). In such circumstances, where the music occurs in the background of other activities, subtle conditioning processes outside awareness may easily occur. Hence, it appears plausible that evaluative conditioning can account for many of our emotional responses to music in everyday life, probably more than we like to think.

It is easy to overlook the importance of conditioning in musical emotions, given its largely implicit nature and the apparently simple processes that underlies it, but I think it would be a grave mistake to do so. Ethnomusicologists and music anthropologists would probably be the first to point out how much of our responses to music are conditioned by the context we inhabit (e.g., Becker, 2004). Indeed, conditioning is a perfect example of how the social and cultural context helps to shape our emotional responses to music in subtle ways.

Thomas Turino notes that emotional associations are both powerful and direct, and continually take on new layers of meaning, while still retaining the old ones—what he refers to as "semantic snowballing" (Turino, 2008). He describes how the civil rights movement used pre-existing tunes, associated with the church and labor movements, setting new lyrics to the songs focusing on civil rights. The emotional power of the revised songs derived from the old associations with religious righteousness and progressive politics, but equally from the new layers of meaning in the lyrics.

Over time, a piece of music could continue to mean more and more (and different) things. As compared to the sensori-motoric mechanisms outlined in the previous chapters, the emotional effect of conditioned responses is more fluid, unstable, and unpredictable. This may be one reason why we sometimes no longer enjoy a piece of music that once used to give us pleasure: our emotional associations to the piece may simply have changed, reflecting the fact that we have gained further experience or knowledge of the music, ourselves, or the world. Responses that involve other induction mechanisms may be more persistent over time.

At the end of the day, a great deal of our musical emotions, as well as our musical preferences (see section 31.3) reflect our individual learning history: the mere statistics of repeated pairings of certain types of music with certain types of emotional contexts. After all, one of the aspects that distinguish human beings from most other species is our unique capacity for *learning*. Let us embrace this aspect of musical affect. Why is Pavlov's hair so soft? Classical conditioning!

CHAPTER 22

BLAST FROM THE PAST

Episodic Memory

It will hardly have escaped your attention that a piece of music may serve as a powerful trigger, or "retrieval cue," of memories from your personal life (Janata, Tomic, & Rakowski, 2007). "A favourite song I had not heard for some time . . . it brought back certain memories," notes a listener in Sloboda and O'Neill (2001, p. 419).

Indeed, fiction, poetry, and movies contain a large number of examples of personal memories evoked by music. For example, in the short story *The Dead* by the Irish author James Joyce, there is a moment where the character, Gretta Conroy, begins to cry when she hears the song "The Lass of Aughrim" because it evokes a melancholic memory from her youth. John Davies refers to this effect as the "Darling, they are playing our tune" phenomenon (Davies, 1978).

22.1 What Is Episodic Memory? What Does It Do?

Episodic memory refers to a process whereby an emotion is induced in a listener because the music evokes a personal memory of a specific event in the person's life. When the memory is evoked, so too is also the emotion associated with the event. The emotion can be intense, perhaps because the physiological response pattern to the original event is stored in memory, together with the experiential content, as proposed in the theory of Peter Lang (1979).

In everyday life, we often think of memory as a unitary thing, but there are different types of memory. Having carefully studied amnesic patients and animals for several years, psychologists and neuroscientists came to the conclusion that there are multiple memory systems in the brain, with partly distinct neurological substrates.

Conditioning, reviewed in the previous chapter, is a simple and ancient form of memory (often called *procedural memory*), which concerns simple associations. Conditioned responses are examples of "non-declarative memory," an implicit type of memory expressed via performance rather than recollection (Squire, 2004).

Semantic memory contains general information about the world; that electric guitars have strings, or that the diatonic scale consists of seven notes. Semantic memory is "declarative"—we can recollect and verbalize the memory. In contrast to conditioned responses, semantic memories are not tied to a particular stimulus; they can be voluntarily accessed even in its absence by means of active recall.

This is true also for *episodic memory*, which refers to memory for personally experienced events, including information about the spatial and temporal context. You may remember attending a certain "live" concert in a specific city at a particular time. This type of memory emerges fairly late during child development (e.g., compared to conditioning), and is also sensitive to aging and disease, such as dementia.

Endel Tulving has arguably offered the most influential theory of episodic memory (Tulving, 2002). He emphasizes the unique phenomenology of this kind of memory. Episodic memories are not simply remembered, they are *relived* in the sense of a "mental replay." They involve the experiencing self and a subjective sense of time. When retrieving an episodic memory, you have the impression of traveling mentally back in time to the recalled event. You can revisit the event, as it were, to retrieve information (e.g., what did the venue of the concert look like? With whom did you attend this event? What did the musicians look like? When did the singer fall asleep on stage?).

We do not remember *all* events, of course. Emotion serves as a marker for episodic memory: we tend to remember "special" events, as cued by our emotional responses (Allen, Kaut, & Lord, 2008). (Some scholars say that the most important function of memory is *forgetting*, avoiding encoding all the irrelevant information that temporarily passes through our brains.) That emotions serve as "contextual cues" for memories is a perfect example of how cognition and emotion are interdependent and difficult to separate (Pessoa, 2013).

The role of emotion is apparent in musical contexts too. Listeners are more likely to retrieve a spontaneous memory when they are cued by a song that moves them emotionally (Schulkind, Hennis, & Rubin, 1999). Carol Krumhansl found that listeners had more frequent and specific memories to pieces of music that aroused strong emotional responses in them (Krumhansl, 2017). There is also evidence that the emotional expression of the music can influence the response time to access a memory, as well as the valence of the evoked memory (Sheldon & Donahue, 2017).

Episodic memory, as defined here, is a relatively recent phenomenon, from an evolutionary perspective (Gärdenfors, 2003). Episodic memory requires detached mental representations (i.e., representations of events or objects that are not currently sensed in the external world) and a sense of self, tying together the individual episodes. Self-awareness, found only in a few higher-order animals, is thought to be closely tied to the development of the frontal lobe of the brain.[1]

For a long time, scholars believed that episodic memory is unique to humans, but carefully conducted experiments have suggested that a few other species also manifest signs of an episodic memory (Dere, Zlomuzica, Huston, & De Souza Silva, 2008). Of course, we do not know if these species *experience* memories in quite the same way as humans.

Episodic memory is an important aspect of what it means to be human. Just think of all the science fiction movies, where scientists plant personal

[1] The anthropologist Kenneth Oakley distinguishes between three levels of consciousness in evolution: the first is *awareness*, which involves sub-cortical and old parts of the brain, and includes basic processes such as sensation and conditioning; the second level is *consciousness*, which involves part of the cortex and the hippocampus, and includes such processes as perception and mental imagery; the third level is *self-awareness*, which involves the more recently developed frontal lobe, and includes processes such as episodic memory and self-reflection (Oakley, 1985).

memories in androids, cyborgs, and replicants to give them a sense of "personal identity." Episodic memories give us a sense of who we are, where we come from, and perhaps even where we are going. Episodic memory enables us to anticipate the future and thus to be better prepared for upcoming events. Although memories seem to direct our attention backward in time, like all mechanisms discussed here they ultimately serve to guide future behavior.

22.2 How Are Episodic Memories Distinguished?

In earlier research, most authors have sorted both conditioning and episodic memory under a common label such as "memory-based" or "associative" mechanisms (see Dowling & Harwood, 1986; Gabrielsson, 2011; Scherer & Zentner, 2001; Sloboda & Juslin, 2001). To be fair, the two types of memory *do* co-occur to some degree in music experiences (Juslin, Harmat, & Eerola, 2014; Juslin, Barradas, & Eerola, 2015). However, the two mechanisms also differ in important ways.

Episodic memories focus on single events, whereas conditioning involves multiple pairings over time. Episodic memory always involves a conscious recollection of the previous event in time that preserves much contextual information, whereas in evaluative conditioning, we often have no recollection of the events that brought about the affective association. Unlike conditioning, episodic memory seems to be organized in a hierarchical structure, with three different levels: life-time periods, general events, and event-specific knowledge (Conway & Rubin, 1993). The two kinds of memory also have partly different process characteristics and brain substrates (see section 25.1). Hence, there is every reason to treat episodic memory as a separate mechanism.

Like conditioned responses, episodic memories to music are often regarded as external to the music. However, while frequently sneered upon by "music snobs," episodic memories could be one of the most common, powerful, and subjectively important sources of emotions during music listening in everyday life (Juslin, Liljeström, Västfjäll, Barradas, & Silva, 2008; Liljeström, Laukka, Västfjäll, & Lundqvist, 2011; Juslin et al., 2016a; Sloboda, 1992; Sloboda & O'Neill, 2001).

For instance, in a survey study featuring a representative sample of the Swedish population, episodic memory was the mechanism rated as most common of all by the participants (Juslin et al., 2011). In the same study, memory-related causes occurred in 24% of the 706 emotion episodes reported. Notably, even in the peak experiences with music investigated by Gabrielsson, which mainly feature "special" musical events where the *music* occupies central stage, 12% of the reports still involved memories (Gabrielsson, 2011).[2]

It is not surprising that pieces of music are closely intertwined with memories and associations in everyday life. Musical events do not occur in an "aesthetic vacuum" (Sloboda, 2010); music accompanies most important human activities. "We dance, drive, argue, laugh, and make love to albums; their music enters our lives, our souls" (Lydon, 2005, p. 9). Some people may have a fond memory associated with Mendelssohn's "Wedding March" in C major, for instance.

Many of the memories focus on music per se and could have serious consequences. A retrospective memory study by John Sloboda has indicated that strong and positively valenced childhood memories of musical events may be important in determining which individuals will pursue a high level of involvement in music later in life (Sloboda, 1989).[3]

This last point illustrates that episodic memories are not necessarily "musically irrelevant." Episodic memories may also involve previous events that are directly tied to the music at hand (e.g., memories of previous recordings or "live" performances of the piece, of having performed the piece oneself, of having read about the artist's creative intention, etc.).

[2] If these estimates do not seem high to you, remember that there are several mechanisms that may be involved, which means that each mechanism can only be involved in so many cases. The *most* frequent source of emotion may not occur in more than, say, 35% of all musical-emotion episodes (e.g., *contagion* in Juslin et al., 2008).

[3] Sadly, the opposite is also true: negative childhood experiences with music may prevent people from engaging further with music in life.

Even absolutists would have a hard time arguing that such memories are aesthetically irrelevant, because they may enrichen and deepen a listener's understanding and appreciation of the music at the moment of reception. Besides, it is not as if we can "turn off" memories which come to us unbidden. They alert us to the wider personal context of the music heard.

22.3 What Do We Know About Episodic Memories in Music?

Only a handful of studies have investigated episodic memories evoked by music. The first study was conducted by Hans Baumgartner (1992). Seventy-three undergraduate students in United States filled out a questionnaire, which aimed to assess how readily people can bring to mind episodic memories associated with a piece of music, and also to examine the characteristics of these episodes, including the emotions aroused.

The results showed that the participants could easily bring to mind instances of music-evoked memories. (Only two participants failed to recall a specific instance.) A significant result was that 64% of the recalled memories involved *social* relationships of some kind, relating to past or current romantic partners (e.g., the first date, sexual experiences) or time spent with friends during parties, concerts, special events, and vacations. Why do most memories tend to be social? One possible explanation is that emotional events are easier to recall than non-emotional events (Reisberg & Heuer, 2004) and that most emotional events involve social interactions (Ekman, 1992).

The memories reported in Baumgartner's study were quite vivid, and most memories were strongly emotionally charged (70% scored the maximum value on intensity) (Baumgartner, 1992). Listeners tended to "re-live" the original experience, and this often involved imagery (see Chapter 23). Overall, 84% of the events were positively valenced (which may reflect a "positivity bias" in memory recall: see Kennedy, Mather, & Carstensen, 2004), but memories of past romantic involvements were just as likely to be negative as positive. As acknowledged by Baumgartner, his data do not enable him to draw conclusions about the prevalence of episodic memories evoked by music (Baumgartner, 1992).

A more recent study by Petr Janata and co-workers (Janata et al., 2007) comes somewhat closer to addressing this issue. In a listening test, 329 participants (undergraduate students between the ages of 18 and 29 years) listened to short excerpts of 30 pieces of music. The pieces were randomly selected for each listener from a larger corpus of 1,515 songs from the Billboard Top 100 Pop and R&B lists on the Apple iTunes Music Store. Songs were selected so that the tunes were on the charts in the years during which the listeners were between 7 and 19 years old.

Subjects listened to each segment and answered questions about the familiarity of the song, autobiographical salience, and affective response to the song. If the song evoked memories, additional forms were presented to capture the nature of the contents. Results indicated that 54% of the songs were rated as *somewhat* or *very familiar*, and 29% of the songs evoked an autobiographical memory in the listener. Not all songs that were familiar evoked a memory, but among songs that *did* evoke a memory, 88% were familiar. [4] In strong agreement with Baumgartner's seminal findings, most of the memories had a strong social component (e.g., friends, romantic partners, and close family).

There were also wide individual differences. Some participants reported memories for fewer than 10% of the songs; others did so for over 50% of the songs. Some of the variation may simply reflect chance, considering the modest sample of songs (30) and that stimuli were randomly selected for each listener. Yet, this factor can hardly explain all of the variance. Rather, these findings reflect that we have now left behind the sensori-motoric mechanisms, which tend to produce quite uniform responses in listeners, and moved on to mechanisms which involve an increasing degree of diversity.

[4] Schulkind and colleagues report a slightly higher estimate of memory prevalence (~ 40%) in their study, but also use a different stimulus-selection method (Schulkind, Hennis, & Rubin, 1999).

The diversity in reaction is also seen in the wide range of emotions evoked by the memories in the study by Janata and colleagues (2007). The top 10 emotions (if we disregard "feeling youthful," which may not be an emotion proper, as defined here; Chapter 4) were *happiness, nostalgia, excitement, energy* (a correlate of *arousal*), *contentment, love, joy, calm, inspiration*, and *sadness*. Most emotions were positively valenced.

We should be aware that although the musical excerpts were sampled from a larger corpus of music in the Janata study, the resulting stimulus selection for each listener still falls short of having ecological validity in relation to the listeners' usual listener environment, where self-chosen and familiar music seems to be more common (e.g., Juslin et al., 2008).

To estimate the prevalence of emotional episodic memories, they need to be measured alongside other potential mechanisms in a field setting. In a series of studies in Uppsala, we have estimated the prevalence of different mechanisms using a number of methods including survey studies, experience sampling, and experiments (Juslin & Laukka, 2004; Juslin et al., 2008, 2011, 2016a, 2018). One conclusion was that *episodic memory* is consistently rated or reported as one of the top three most frequent sources of emotions during music listening in everyday life.

However, the prevalence of episodic memory appears to depend partly on the culture studied. In the previously mentioned cross-cultural web-survey study, featuring 668 participants from six countries categorized as "individualist" (Australia, Sweden, United States) or "collectivist" (Brazil, Kenya, Portugal), both semantic (aggregated) and episodic data indicated that the mechanism *episodic memory* was significantly more frequent in "collectivist" cultures. (Conversely, there were no significant differences concerning mechanisms such as *brainstem reflex* and *rhythmic entrainment*; Juslin et al., 2016a.)

In the episodes where emotions were thought to have been caused by *episodic memory* (45% of the total), the emotional tone of the memory was "mixed" in 47%, "positive" in 28%, and "negative" in 25% (overall). However, there was a difference between the culture categories: negative memories were more common in collectivist episodes (40%) than in individualist episodes (6%). In contrast, positive memories were more common in individualist episodes (50%) than in collectivist episodes (11%).

22.4 Nostalgia Is Not What It Used to Be

Although music-evoked memories could arouse a wide range of emotions, as indicated by earlier studies, *nostalgia* appears to be particularly important (Sloboda & O'Neill, 2001). *Nostalgia* has been defined as "sentimental longing or wistful affection for the past" (*New Oxford Dictionary of English*, 1998). It is usually regarded as a "bittersweet" emotion that occurs when reminiscing about fond and personally meaningful memories from one's past.

Some listeners actively use music to remind them of valued past events, a kind of nostalgic function (Sloboda & O'Neill, 2001). Sociologist Tia DeNora found in an interview study that for many of the listeners music helped them to recall former partners and, along with these memories, "emotionally heightened moments" in their lives (DeNora, 2000, p. 63).

It has been suggested that the experience of *nostalgia* may serve psychological functions. The Norwegian scholar Even Ruud was a pioneer in the study of music and identity (Ruud, 1997), and argued that emotional memories involving music promote a strong sense of self identity, contributing to four aspects of mental health: *vitality, agency, belonging*, and *meaning*. Episodic memories evoked by music help us maintain a coherent identity, amid the constant flux of events (Bluck, Alea, Habermas, & Rubin, 2005).

In the cross-cultural study mentioned earlier, *nostalgia* was more frequent in "collectivist" cultures than in "individualist" cultures; "collectivist" cultures also attached greater overall importance to musical *nostalgia*. How can this be explained? It has been hypothesized that "collectivist" cultures show greater resistance to change and modernity than "individualist" cultures. *Nostalgia* could serve the function of preserving social identity by reliving one's past (Shaw & Chase, 1989).

My former student, Gonçalo Barradas, examined how induction mechanisms are manifested within a collectivist cultural setting with great potential for deeply felt emotion: fado music in Portugal (Barradas, in press). This is a kind of urban folk music which originated in the streets of Lisbon in Portugal, and is known for its emphasis on loss, memory, *sadness*, and *nostalgia*—*saudade* in Portuguese (Elliott, 2010).

Barradas conducted 34 interviews with listeners to obtain in-depth information on how the cultural context might shape both listening motives and emotions. The results revealed that listeners strived for music experiences that would arouse culturally valued emotions; music-induced *nostalgia*, in particular, was regarded as important, and contributed to an enhanced sense of wellbeing. A 43-year-old male explained how "certain fado songs take me to my childhood, they make me nostalgic" (Barradas, in press, p. 11).

Some memories evoked by fado were *sad*, but were regarded as valuable in contributing to maturation and personal growth. *Sad* and *nostalgic* memories were used to reflect upon and overcome past experiences, enabling listeners to reappraise their past, and to reinforce their sense of self and connectedness with others.

Several artists in popular music trade to a considerable degree on musical nostalgia, and the real-life implications of music-induced nostalgia is the stuff of legends. There is the story of when a singer at a prison concert sang "Home, sweet home," and the inmates were so deeply moved by the music that seven of them escaped the same night, and were re-arrested in their respective homes the next day (Watson, 1991, p. 41).

Listeners who are initially in a negative state (e.g., *sadness*) may be more prone to experience *nostalgia* to music. Thus, the tendency to experience (intense or prevalent) *nostalgia* is linked to personality traits such as neuroticism (e.g., Barrett, Mesquita, Ochsner, & Gross, 2010). Hence, *nostalgia* may also occur as a "secondary" response to *sadness* induced by music (see Juslin et al., 2014, 2015). A study by Liila Taruffi and Stefan Koelsch found that *nostalgia* was the most frequently experienced response to music with a *sad* expression (76%), even more frequent than *sadness* (45%) (Taruffi & Koelsch, 2014). We may thus hypothesize that *sad* music has a tendency to evoke *nostalgic* memories.

22.5 How Is Episodic Memory Reflected During Development?

Episodic memory as an induction mechanism shows some noteworthy developmental trends. Emotions aroused by episodic memory develop much later than those aroused by brainstem reflex, rhythmic entrainment, contagion, and conditioning. Due to *childhood amnesia,* we do not remember much from the first years of our lives. Children's ability to recall and converse about episodic memories develops slowly across the pre-school years (Fivush & Sales, 2004). Episodic memory is also the type of memory that begins to decline first as a result of aging (Tulving, 2002).

Both developmental trends should, in principle, be readily observable in listeners' emotional reactions to music that involve the episodic memory mechanism. Matthew Schulkind and his co-workers reported that older listeners retrieved fewer episodic memories from music overall than young listeners in a listening test, consistent with the expected memory decline (Schulkind et al., 1999).

Even so, a striking finding is that music may (sometimes) trigger episodic memories in elderly people whose memories are otherwise inaccessible (Bruhn, 2002). Concetta Tomaino describes how music therapists working with people suffering from late-stage Alzheimer's disease have noted dramatic changes when the patients hear personally preferred pieces of music: they may suddenly be able to verbalize fragmented information about their past (Tomaino, 2002).

One important characteristic of episodic memory more generally is the common finding that people tend to recall more memories from their youth and early adulthood (15–25 years of age) than from those periods that precede or follow it. This is referred to as *the reminiscence bump,* and has been obtained with music (Schubert, 2016). The effect may be explained by the fact that many self-defining experiences tend to occur at this stage of life development (Conway & Holmes, 2005). It is a time when we do a lot of things for the very first time.

Music plays an important role in adolescents' lives, particularly for the development of a self-identity (Laiho, 2004). For instance, a participant in the study by Alf Gabrielsson recalled that "as a teenager, I lived in music, my entire existence was interpreted with the help of music" (Gabrielsson, 2011, p. 446).

Given such tendencies, one could expect episodic memories associated with music to be particularly emotionally vivid and occur frequently with regard to music from young adulthood, as indeed seems to be the case. Matthew Schulkind and colleagues found that older adults preferred, knew more about, and had stronger emotional responses to music popular during their youth than to music popular later in life (Schulkind, Hennis, & Rubin, 1999).[5] I predict that emotional responses to music due to episodic memory more frequently involve events from one's youth and early adulthood than from other periods in one's life (except for very recent events).

We may also expect episodic memory to become a richer source of emotion as we get older.[6] (After all, a four-year-old will have precious little to be *nostalgic* about!) With increasing age, music becomes increasingly a "sonic rear-view mirror." Songs become a kind of retrospective road map to the "milestones" in our lives. Paradoxically, it could be the case that we approach music in the most "absolutist" manner (cf. section 5.3) as small children before we have forged so many extrinsic associations with pieces of music.

22.6 How Are Songs Linked to Episodic Memories?

For us to create associations or episodic memories, the pieces of music need to recur, and we tolerate an awful lot of repetition when it comes to pieces of music, as noted by Elizabeth Margulis (2014). Just think about it for a minute: we only watch a movie or read a book that we like a couple of times, whereas we may hear songs and albums *hundreds* of times. In fact, we could

[5] People also tend to show the greatest liking for music that was popular during their youth (Holbrook & Schindler, 1989; Krumhansl, 2017), suggesting that there may be a "critical period" during which basic norms for musical value are formed, with long-lasting effects on aesthetic judgments and preferences (see Part IV).

[6] That is, before episodic memory decline sets in!

hear certain loved songs on a greater number of occasions than we meet some of our close friends.

We saw earlier that our responses to music have a strong *social* component, as reflected in entrainment and contagion processes. Sometimes, it seems that our relationships to particular songs are treated by the mind in the same way that we treat friends.

Consider the excitement when we "get to know" a new song that we have looked forward to "meet." With every replay, we discover and understand new aspects of its "personality". Some songs are "easy to get to know," but do not offer much "depth." Other songs are "an acquired taste", but if we give them a chance and really try to get to know them, we may be rewarded with rich experiences and novel insights.

Sometimes, we fall in love with a song; we may have passionate affair with the song, but eventually it cools off, and we may even get bored with it. Later we may be surprised to have ever enjoyed the "company" of certain songs; we have simply grown apart. Or we may feel as meeting a long-lost friend, recalling those good times we enjoyed together. Some songs we do not "meet" very often, but we love them, and feel reassured that "they are there for us," should we need them.

Some songs are more like "superficial acquaintances"; clearly they are not close friends and we do not particularly like to have them around, but for one reason or another, we just keep on encountering them regularly throughout our lives until they become part of our life story, whether we like it or not. Songs, just like people, are forever linked to specific time periods of our life, and they really do serve, quite literally, as the soundtrack of our lives.

Singer and songwriter, Elton John, reflects on the important role of songs in people's lives:

> I am only just beginning to realize how songs affect people. Stupid that it's taken me so long. I've always had periods in my life where certain records at certain times played a very strong role. The times when I'm really miserable, or not in love. Or times I was in love with someone, and it was really disastrous. I will play a particular song for that moment probably a million

> times. At certain times, "How sweet it is to be loved by you", "My sweet lord", and "Brown sugar" have meant a great deal in my life. But for so long I never thought songs could be like that. And I'm a songwriter. (Smith, 1989, p. 281)

Why did Odysseus, king of Ithaca and the main protagonist and hero of Homer's epic, weep in response to the song of the great bard, Demodocus? Because the music mattered to him; "it connected him with his past and reminded him of significant events in his personal history" (Bicknell, 2009, p. 149). That is no small thing.

CHAPTER 23

SEEING IN THE MIND'S EYE

Visual Imagery

Which member of the Beatles had the biggest nose? Chances are that you will answer this question by visualizing the members and searching these images for relevant information.

We saw previously that episodic memories may involve imagery. In Hans Baumgartner's (1992) study, for instance, the recollection was often accompanied by imagery associated with the original experience. Similarly, in the investigation by Petr Janata and his co-workers (2007), images occurred 31% of the time (25% of these were rated as *very vivid*). Even in listening experiments that attempt to *selectively* activate the memory mechanism, imagery will often co-occur to some extent with memories (e.g., Juslin, Barradas, & Eerola, 2015, Table 7). This is only to be expected; episodic memories are often represented in the form of images.

Imagery may also occur in the absence of a specific memory (Juslin, Liljeström, Västfjäll, Barradas, & Silva, 2008): we can imagine novel visual events that we have never witnessed or experienced and that we *could* not possibly have experienced. I can imagine myself playing a tuba on top of the Eiffel Tower, but clearly that has never happened, nor will it ever happen.

Of course, my ability to imagine this scenario is dependent on previous memories of having seen myself, a tuba, and the Eiffel Tower, but the brain is able to create new images based on such memory fragments, and such images may have a strong effect. Hence, there is reason to consider imagery as a distinct emotion mechanism in music too.

23.1 How Might Visual Imagery Occur in Music Listening?

Visual imagery refers to a process whereby an emotion is evoked in the listener because he or she conjures up inner images (e.g., a beautiful landscape or an inspired artist) while listening to the music. "Sitting by the river, listening to the quiet lap of water ... that is what it conjures up," noted a musician in describing a piece of music in Persson (2001, p. 280). Images might come about in three ways, which have in common the interaction between musical structures and evoked images.

First, mental imagery may occur when listeners conceptualize the musical structure through a non-verbal mapping between the metaphorical "affordances" of the music and image schemata grounded in bodily experience (Lakoff & Johnson, 1980). For instance, if the music features a melody with rising pitch, a listener might imagine that he or she is flying higher and higher in the air. In other words, the musical structure helps to shape a narrative of images unfolding in the listener over time (Juslin & Västfjäll, 2008).

This illustrates the fact that visual imagery is more strongly influenced by the precise structure of the music than is episodic memory, for which some aspect of the music, such as a theme, mainly serves a "retrieval cue" for the memory. Both *iconic* (e.g., gradual changes in "acoustic cues") and *syntactic* sources ("the will of the notes") of musical expression (cf. Part II) may shape the mental images.

Links between musical features and visual images may involve conceptual metaphors of an emotional character (cf. Kövecses, 2000): rising pitch contour ("happiness is up"), staccato articulation ("happiness is light"), and fast tempo ("happiness is vital"). The links might also involve force dynamics linked to the "vitality affects" discussed in section 6.6: an explosive *crescendo* could be reimagined as the aggressive action of a "virtual agent" in the narrative. Some forms of music analysis appear to come close to this type of imagery (Spitzer, 2004).

Examples of imagery or metaphor mentioned by participants in Alf Gabrielsson's study include: "notes swirling around like snowflakes in the air," a solo voice "reminiscent of the movements of a bird up and down in the air," a musical segment coming "in waves roughly like a swell out at sea," and musical notes "dancing around like a whirlwind" (Gabrielsson, 2011, pp. 356–357). Gabrielsson notes that the visual images are highly individual and vary in richness of detail, but note that the reports involve different pieces of music.

A second type of imagery might occur when listeners bring to a listening experience certain types of knowledge or myths about the circumstances surrounding the creation of the piece or about the artist in question. Visual imagery based on such information might be mapped upon the music and influence how one experiences it. Is the song just a commercial product created by an efficient but impersonal team of songwriters, or is it a sincere cry for help from a deeply moved artist in the midst of a personal crisis?

It is very easy to offer examples of pieces of music whose emotional impact has been enhanced by myths or knowledge about the circumstances of their creation. (Think of Mozart's "Requiem", composed close to his death, or Eric Clapton's "Tears in Heaven," composed after his son died.) A personal example of this kind of mental imagery is provided later in the chapter. In some cases, the images evoked enhance emotions already felt from activation of other mechanisms (Band, Quilter, & Miller, 2001–2002); in other cases, the images themselves seem to be responsible for the emotion (Juslin et al., 2008).[1]

Third, a music listener can create images based on how certain aspects of the music mirror aspects of the listener's current life experience. Thus, sociologist Tia DeNora describes how listeners "find themselves" in music structures. Music is a mirror that allows one to "see one's self", but it is also a "magic mirror" since its specific properties may come to *configure* the image reflected through its perceived structures (DeNora, 2000, p. 70).

[1] Note that visual imagery could either trigger emotions, or be triggered by emotions. That the "causal arrow" may go in either direction is a complication that we need to keep in mind when conducting empirical studies.

The observation that listeners may experience musical structure as metaphorically conveying important aspects of what is happening in their own lives forms the basis of some therapeutic uses of music. Helen Bonny developed a method, *guided imagery and music* (GIM), where a "traveler" is invited to share his or her emotional images, as they are experienced in real time during a pre-programmed sequence of music (Toomey, 1996–1997).

These GIM programs come with suggestive titles, such as *transitions, serenity, positive affect,* and *expanded awareness.* Frances Goldberg explains that the music exerts its influence by "providing focus, emotional support, structure for the experience, and dynamic movement to the images." The music may serve "both as a catalyst for creative image formation and as a container for the gestalt of feelings and images" (Goldberg, 1992, p. 4).

The evoked visual images offer a starting point for discussion of relevant emotional "themes" between therapist and client. For example, Nicki Cohen has described a GIM therapy session with a client, Jodie, whose visual imagery included "witnessing a processional with a cross, the powerful image of a mother holding her child, and the child looking at the world across the mother's shoulder"; Jodie later described her feeling as "held safe while looking forward" (Cohen, 2015, p. 148). (The piece in question? Bach's "Air on the G String.")

We chose to label the mechanism *visual imagery* initially (Juslin & Västfjäll, 2008), because we regarded it as unlikely that listeners can be engaged in auditory imagery at the same time as they are listening to music. (This is because auditory imagery and auditory perception are recruiting many of the same brain regions.) However, I do not rule out the fact that mental imagery during music listening may involve other modalities, it is just that visual images seem to dominate.

23.2 Why Do We React Emotionally to Images?

People appear to react to such mental images much in the same manner as they would to the corresponding stimuli in the "real" world; for example, responding with positive emotions to nature scenes or babies, or with negative emotions to accidents or cruelty to animals.

You may object: "The images are not real, so why in the world would we react emotionally to them?" The answer is that these images are treated as "real" by *some* parts of your brain. Mental imagery is a form of "mental simulation," and it is so good that it may fool your body. Just consider the power of sexual fantasies, or that simply imagining a frightening event can be enough to make you scared. (The mere *image* of climbing the Eiffel Tower with my tuba makes my hair stand on hand!)

This provides some clues to the origin and function of mental imagery, which is a relatively recent development from an evolutionary perspective (Gärdenfors, 2003). By creating an inner world through mental simulation, you can foresee the consequences of various actions. Through simulation you can test dangerous ideas in your mind before you carry them out in the physical world. Hence, your (bad) ideas can die instead of you. But for the simulations to influence your behaviors, their consequences need to be taken seriously—hence the emotion involved!

Mental images can be regarded as "internal triggers" of emotional responses (Plutchik, 1984). Different imagery contents are associated with different emotions (Lyman & Waters, 1989) and distinct patterns of physiological response (Schwartz, Weinberger, & Singer, 1981). This supports the contention that mental imagery involves "real" emotions. There is evidence that imagery evokes stronger emotional responses than does verbal processing (Holmes, Mathews, Mackintosh, & Dalgleish, 2008). Thus, mental imagery is often used as a mood-induction technique in psychological studies (Gerrards-Hesse, Spies, & Hesse, 1994).

Mental imagery is usually defined as an experience that resembles perceptual experience, but that occurs in the absence of relevant sensory stimuli. Creating an image requires the ability to *suppress* the sensations one has for the moment so that they do not come into conflict with the detached representation. Peter Gärdenfors argues that the suppression of information coming in from the real world is probably managed by the frontal lobe, a "modern" part of the brain in charge of "executive functions" (mental processes required for the "cognitive control" of various behaviors), which play a key role in attention, short-term memory, planning, and fantasizing (Gärdenfors, 2003).

Visual imagery also appears relatively late during our *ontogenetic* (life history) development. In accordance with theories of symbolic development (e.g., Piaget, 1951), it may be assumed that visual imagery develops during the pre-school period when children create increasingly complex symbolic representations of the external world (for empirical evidence, see Kosslyn, Margolis, Barrett, Goldknopf, & Daly, 1990). Mental imagery is crucially involved in both play and creative thought.

23.3 Do the Images Really Involve a Pictorial Format?

For a long time, the notion of mental imagery was controversial in psychology. For example, during the "imagery debate" (Kosslyn, Thompson, & Ganis 2006), researchers discussed whether mental imagery involves a distinctively pictorial representation of events, as argued by Stephen Kosslyn, or a mere "propositional" representation, as argued by Zenon Pylyshyn.

The issue was partly resolved by a mental rotation experiment published in a classic *Science* article. The researchers Roger Shepard and Jacqueline Metzler (1971) presented participants with two-dimensional line drawings of groups of three-dimensional block objects and asked them to determine whether each object was the same as a second figure, which in some cases was a rotation of the first object.

If participants solved this mental task by decomposing objects into propositions—as Pylyshyn claimed—we would expect that the *time* it takes to decide whether the object is the same or not is independent of how much the object has been rotated. Instead, it was found that decision time increased linearly with the angular difference in the portrayed orientations of the two objects, implying that the participants manipulated the mental images as topographic and topological wholes rather than as propositions.[2]

Supporting a pictorial view is that many of the brain regions that are activated during visual perception are similarly activated when a person is involved in visual imagery. Specifically, imagery will activate spatially mapped regions of the occipital cortex, the visual association cortex, and—for image generation—left temporo-occipital regions (Ganis, Thompson, Mast, & Kosslyn, 2004). The visual cortex may also show enhanced activation during music listening (Thornton-Wells et al., 2010), a finding that appears puzzling until the possibility of listeners visualizing images during music listening is raised.

23.4 What Is the Evidence for Imagery in Music?

Musical stimuli may be effective in stimulating visual imagery, perhaps even more so than other stimuli (Quittner & Glueckauf, 1983). Francis Goldberg notes that music does not only evoke images, "it encourages images to move and evolve" (Goldberg, 1992, p. 2). She further notes that more vivid imagery tends to co-occur with stronger emotional experiences during GIM therapy sessions.

Evidence of imagery during music experience comes from a seminal study by John Osborne, which examined how listeners reacted to synthesizer music under relaxed conditions (Osborne, 1980). The listening test took place in a carpeted room with subdued lighting. The participants were asked to lie down on the floor and undertook a brief relaxation exercise prior to the start of the test. Then they were instructed to put their attention completely into the music played, and to become "completely involved with the music." After the music stopped, the participants were asked to describe

[2] Later, Stephen Kosslyn suggested that the images themselves are quasi-pictorial representations whereas the generative, long-term structure of imagery is propositional (e.g., like a TV set whose output is a picture, but whose mechanisms for generating this picture are better expressed in discrete symbols of electronics).

in detail the responses they had, including thoughts, emotions, images, and bodily sensations. Their descriptions were analyzed by two independent scorers.

The results showed that mental images that came to mind during the music were significantly more frequent than the other response categories (thoughts, emotions, and bodily sensations), which were not significantly different from each other. (Notably, 43% of the listeners did not experience any emotion.) Images consisted primarily of idiosyncratic narratives, but Osborne also observed some recurrent themes, such as natural scenes (e.g., sun, sky, ocean) and out-of-body experiences (e.g., floating above the Earth).

Most images (77%) had a negative valence, featuring themes such as *fear* and *loneliness*, though the results were perhaps reflective of the genre of music (e.g., the band Tangerine Dream; "spacey, synthesized electronic music with simple structure, some free form, and much repetition"; Osborne, 1980, p. 134).[3] Imagery evoked by music may also produce a positive state of deep relaxation, with possible health benefits such as reduced cortisol levels (McKinney, Antoni, Kumar, Tims, & McCabe, 1997).

Visual imagery was rather dominant in Osborne's study, but this result may partly reflect the fact that the conditions—the listening context—were particularly conducive to the production of images in the minds of the listeners. Imagery may be relatively more common during attentive and immersive music listening, when alone, and perhaps at home, with eyes closed or lights turned down. Visual imagery appears to be less common in other listening contexts.

To illustrate: only 10% of the reports in Alf Gabrielsson's study of "peak experiences" with music included imagery (73% of the reports featured cases of "live" music, where visual impressions are often salient and may prevent visual imagery) (Gabrielsson, 2011). The corresponding estimate of

[3] It has been argued that certain musical characteristics are particularly effective in stimulating vivid imagery, such as repetition, predictability in melodic, harmonic, and rhythmic elements, and slow tempo (McKinney & Tims, 1995). However, I am not aware of any study that has systematically compared different types of music.

prevalence of imagery in emotion episodes sampled randomly in a variety of everyday settings by Juslin and colleagues (2008) was 7%.

23.5 Are There Individual Differences in Imagery?

The relatively modest overall prevalence of visual imagery is not only explained by *context* factors, but also by *individual* factors. When I first discussed visual imagery at conferences, I was immediately struck by how the responses of other scholars to the notion varied: some clearly recognized the phenomenon and attributed great importance to it, while for others it did not seem to strike a resonance at all.

One explanation is that there *are*, in fact, wide individual differences between people in their overall tendency to experience imagery: some experience it frequently whereas others hardly experience it at all. Although some of this variation might be due to different listening styles (see the kinds of context factors cited above), there are also differences with regard to the *ability* to generate visual images as measured for instance by the Vividness of Visual Imagery Questionnaire (VVIQ) developed by David Marks (1973). Subjectively reported variations in imagery vividness are correlated with individual differences in the ability to accurately recall information presented in pictures (Rodway, Gillies, & Schepman, 2006). Moreover, self-reported imagery vividness correlates with activation of the visual cortex in brain imaging studies (Cui, Jeter, Yang, Montague, & Eagleman, 2007).

Many of the mechanisms considered earlier have in common that they involve "involuntary" responses that we cannot really control or evoke at will. A special feature of imagery is that the listener is to some extent able to influence the emotions aroused by the music. Although images could come into the mind unbidden, in general a listener can conjure up, manipulate, and dismiss images at will.

Reed Larson suggests that music offers a medium for adolescents through which they might conjure up strong emotional images around which a temporary sense of self may cohere (Larson, 1995). The music is like a "fantasy ground" for exploring possible selves during the process of resolving a personal identity in late adolescence (see also DeNora, 2010). Studies indicate that adolescent males, in particular, use music to create a "cool" and "trendy" image, which is "acted out" during listening, even when they are alone (North, Hargreaves, & O'Neill, 2000).

23.6 How May Extra-Musical Information Influence Imagery?

Sometimes, visual imagery is influenced by the lyrics of the music or by a "story" associated with the music. Jonna Vuoskoski and Tuomas Eerola (2015) exposed some listeners to a sad description as well as a description of a nature scene before listening to a mournful-sounding piece of music. Results showed that listeners with the sad scenery experienced a more intense sadness than those presented with the music but no description, presumably because mental imagery stimulated by the scenario enhanced their responses to the music.

My Australian colleague Bill Thompson suggests that what we know about an artist or about the circumstances surrounding the creation of his or her music can strongly affect a listener's reception of the music. Is our emotional response to Jeff Buckley's song "The Last Goodbye" on the *Grace* album from 1994 intensified if we know that he drowned soon after recording this album? (On the title song, Buckley sings "it's my time coming, I'm not afraid, afraid to die.")

I would like to share a personal story to illustrate the potential role of such mental imagery. For me, the circumstances that surrounded the creation of the *Layla* album by Derek and the Dominos featuring Eric Clapton (see Figure 23.1) clearly stimulated my imagery when I heard this music as a young teenager and an aspiring guitar player.

Coincidentally or not, Eric Clapton's best album is also his most emotionally expressive. It is also a perfect example of the "love theme" in musical expression (Levitin, 2006). Clapton fell in love with Pattie Boyd,

Figure 23.1 Eric Clapton on stage with Derek and the Dominos, December 1970. *Photo by Elliott Landy/Redferns/Getty Images.*

the wife of his best friend (George Harrison). *Layla* is a "concept album" of sorts featuring original songs about unrequited love and blues songs that could also apply to the same theme, such as "Have You Ever Loved a Woman?" ("Something deep inside of you/Won't let you wreck your best friend's home"). As in the case of the classical composer Hector Berlioz and his groundbreaking "Symphonie Fantastique," *Layla* was written with the explicit aim to seduce a woman. (Both composers were ultimately successful in their pursuit.)

With the *Layla* album, Clapton transformed his skill and stylistic knowledge of the blues into something deeper and far more personal. When Clapton's songs became more personal, his guitar playing changed to some extent. The change in sound can be attributed, in part, to a switch of guitars from Gibson guitars to a Fender Stratocaster. More importantly, however, he also developed a more emotionally expressive style of playing—perfectly in keeping with the tone of the album—that makes full use of techniques such as string bending, flageolet harmonics, vibrato, and powerful note attacks.

The romantic lyricism of songs like "Bell Bottom Blues," "Have You Ever Loved a Woman?" and "Layla" on the original album, and "Why Does Love Got to Be So Sad?," "Presence of the Lord," and "Let it Rain" on the "live" album ("In Concert") were all enhanced by the image of this brilliant guitar player, desperately in love with his best friend's wife, on a steady decline from drug use, but still playing and singing his heart out until the bitter end. How I listened to the music—alone, in the dark, at high volume, fully immersed in the music, empathizing with the playing and the emotions—enhanced the power of my imagery.

The fact that my imagery reflected the "true" circumstances of the making of the album is, in a sense, not so important. The imagery would have been just as powerful in my listening experience if it was all based on a myth. Indeed, myth and legend may have strong effects on music experience through mental imagery. Why would artists otherwise spend so much time and energy on creating their own powerful image?

Note, however, that myth and legend do not influence the imagery associated with popular music only. It has been a huge part of how the music of composers such as Mozart and Beethoven has been received over the years by their audiences. Simply consider the "mad artist" syndrome, according to which artists suffer from elevated levels of psychopathology (Jamison, 1993): they are "mad, but creative," unlike the rest of us, who are "sane, but uncreative".

Musicologist Nicholas Cook notes that one of the common myths about Beethoven is the notion that he was a "misunderstood genius" whose music was not appreciated in his own day (Cook, 1998). This myth contributes to his "authenticity" as one who refuses to pander to popular taste and whose music is only later recognized as being of "intrinsic" and "eternal" aesthetic value.

Cook argues that Beethoven's deafness has come to occupy a special role in the myth-making literature surrounding his life and work, painting a highly dubious picture of someone who is alienated from society and whose experience of deafness is somehow conveyed in the music.

Cook and Dibben cite a review of the Ninth symphony by music critic Franz Joseph Frölich, where this symphony is interpreted as "the expression of Beethoven's struggle with deafness and his ultimate transmutation of suffering into joy," such that for instance the first movement is the expression of "tender longing, heroic strength, pathos, and a vision of joy" (Cook & Dibben, 2010, p. 49).

The image of a heroic and successful struggle against adversity may or may not be a true reflection of the state of affairs surrounding the creation of the piece. Regardless, the images may influence our emotion upon hearing the work (often regarded as the best symphony ever). Cook and Dibben make a compelling case that what we *believe* to be true of the music, or its creator, will shape our experience of the music (Cook & Dibben, 2010). Unfortunately, the causal influence of this type of imagery on emotional reactions to music is yet to be investigated by psychologists.

In the foregoing chapters, I considered mechanisms whose emotions focus very much on the here and now (e.g., *surprise* from a brainstem reflex), or mechanisms whose emotions focus very much on the past (e.g., *nostalgia* from episodic memory). Emotions aroused by imagery might be construed as "omnidirectional" in that they could focus on the past, but more likely focus on current and imagined future events (Juslin, 2013a). In the next chapter, I will focus on an induction mechanism whose emotions are typically even *more* future-oriented.

CHAPTER 24

WHAT COMES NEXT?

Musical Expectancy

Previous chapters of this book have shown that musical events are far from being mere abstract notes patterns devoid of meaning for listeners. Could there still be a sense in which the patterns of musical notes *themselves* have an emotional impact on the listener? As noted in Chapter 5, some musicians and music theorists like to conceive of music in absolute terms, as "pure" and "autonomous" note patterns. One mechanism that appears to come close to this ideal is musical expectancy.

24.1 What Is Musical Expectancy?

Paris, May 29, 1913. It is the premiere of a new ballet at the Théâtre de Champs-Elysées featuring music by the composer Igor Stravinsky. Choreographer Sergei Diaghilev of the Ballets Russes told the composer to "surprise me." Diaghilev got what he asked for, to the point that the event caused a major riot. The work should perhaps have been called "Riot of Spring" rather than "Rite of Spring."

Members of the audience screamed, booed, hissed, and fought. (However, a few, including Claude Debussy, cheered.) The composer himself commented that the audience "were very naïve and stupid people."[1] It may be *the*

[1] Retrieved from Classic fM: <http://www.classicfm.com/composers/stravinsky/news/rite-and-the-riot/>.

most notorious premiere in the history of show business. However, exactly what happened that night is still a bit of a mystery. What remains beyond doubt is that Stravinsky's music was one of the culprits in the chaos that ensued.

The most well-known part of the revolutionary, avant-garde work is arguably "Les Augures Printaniers," a section characterized by a repetitive stamping chord in the horns and strings, featuring E-flat superimposed on a triad of E, G-sharp, and B. There is much in the section that might stimulate an emotional response: the sensory dissonance (brainstem reflex?); the strong pulse (rhythmic entrainment?); the breaking of artistic norms (aesthetic judgment?).

However, the most distinctive feature of the section is its *unpredictable* temporal structure. Musicologist David Huron claims that the irregular rhythmic accents that start the piece are 40 times more difficult to predict than a random sequence (Huron, 2006). A first-time listener—especially at that time in music history—could be excused for responding with confusion. The piece still induces *arousal* and *anxiety* in modern listeners who are not highly familiar with it (Juslin, Barradas, & Eerola, 2015; Table 6, Figure 1).

Musical expectancy refers to a process whereby an emotion is aroused in a listener because a specific feature of the music violates, delays, or confirms the listener's expectations about the continuation of the music. Every time you hear a piece of music your expectations are raised, based on music you have heard before. For example, the sequential progression of E–F# may create the expectation that the music will continue with G#. In other words, some notes seem to *imply* other notes (Meyer, 1956; Narmour, 1990), and if these musical implications are not realized, if the listener's expectations are thwarted, an emotional response might be induced.

Musical expectancy, then, does not refer to *any* unexpected event that could occur regarding music. A simple form of unexpectedness (e.g., the sudden onset of a loud tone) would, instead, be a case of the brainstem reflex mechanism (Chapter 18). Similarly, more general surprising aspects of an event involving music—that a concert was better than the listener had expected—would instead be an example of a mechanism called "cognitive goal appraisal" (see section 25.4).

Musical expectancy refers to *those expectancies that involve relationships between different parts of the musical structure* (Meyer, 1956; Narmour, 1991). You may recall the discussion of intrinsic coding in Chapter 12 and Heinrich Schenker's talk about "the will of the tones", that "unstable" notes in the structure seem to "yearn" for their resolution to more stable notes.

Consider the so-called deceptive cadence. A cadence is usually defined in Western musical theory as any melodic or harmonic configuration that creates a sense of finality or resolution. The cadence will appear "deceptive" if the listener expects a dominant chord to resolve to the tonic (the common pattern), but instead it moves to a superdominant or submediant chord. To illustrate: in the key of C major, a deceptive cadence may be when the dominant (V) G major chord moves to the superdominant (VI) A minor chord; the expected resolution is suspended or interrupted, creating musical tension.[2]

During music listening, the unfolding structure will give rise to constantly changing levels of musical tension and uncertainty, and as explained in Chapter 12, these shifts may contribute to the emotions *perceived* in a piece of music. Often, I believe, that is "all" they will do; but occasionally, intrinsically coded events in the music will also *arouse* an emotion, due to their link to musical expectations.

The expectations usually operate at a subconscious level such that you will become aware of them only when something really unexpected happens. Indeed, the strongest emotions are arguably aroused when a listener's musical expectations are disrupted, rather than when they are confirmed (cf. Miceli & Castelfranchi, 2015).

Consider the classic recording "Peace Piece" by jazz pianist Bill Evans. This is a fairly simple improvisational piece from his 1958 album, which begins in a calm and harmonious manner, featuring a tender Cmaj7 to G9sus4

[2] A couple of deceptive cadences can be heard at the beginning of the final movement of Gustav Mahler's Ninth symphony.

two-chord progression. Just when you are so relaxed that you may be on the verge of falling asleep, Evans suddenly plays some very "odd" atonal notes (about 3.36 seconds into the music) that could make you fall of your chair, at least the first time you hear them. You may not have been aware that you expected to hear some notes rather than others, but you certainly did not expect *these* notes! How can we account for such a response?

24.2 Theoretical Foundations: Meet Leonard B. Meyer

The expectancy mechanism has been most extensively elaborated by musicologist Leonard B. Meyer in what is perhaps the most cited book on music and emotion (Meyer, 1956). Philosopher Peter Kivy referred to it as "the book that taught many of us for the first time that you can talk about music without talking nonsense" (Kivy, 1987, p. 153). Indeed, it is a milestone which came to foreshadow many theoretical issues debated in the following decades.

Meyer's work, like all works, built on previous ideas. He referred to theorists such as Henry Aiken, who had pondered the "delight in perception which results from the arousal and suspension or fulfillment of expectations which are the products of many previous encounters with works of art" (Aiken, 1950, p. 313). Still, Meyer was the first theorist to develop the notion of musical expectancy in a *convincing* way. The secret? He turned to psychology. Meyer was inspired by contemporary theories of perception (e.g., "gestalt theory") and emotions (e.g., John Dewey's "conflict theory").

It is noteworthy that Meyer seemed acutely aware of the crucial role of psychological theory: "given no theory as to the relation of musical stimuli to affective responses, observed behavior can provide little information as to either the nature of the stimulus, the significance of the response, or the relation between them" (Meyer, 1956, p. 10). Curiously, these thoughts were at odds with the dominant behaviorist school of psychology in the 1950s, which was only too happy to focus on simple stimulus–response relationships without considering intervening processes (like many current music and emotion studies, I might add; see section 17.2).

The primary hypothesis of Meyer's psychological analysis was that "emotion-felt is aroused when an expectation—a tendency to respond—activated by the musical stimulus situation, is temporarily inhibited or permanently blocked" (Meyer, 1956, p. 31). For example, a listener may expect a dissonant chord to resolve into a consonant one and this event may be delayed by a creative composer. Meyer submits that "every inhibition or delay creates uncertainty or suspense, if only briefly, because in the moment of delay we become aware of the possibility of alternative modes of continuation" (Meyer, 1956, p. 27); "the greater the buildup of suspense, the greater the emotional release upon resolution" (p. 28).

Meyer proposes that musical expectancies arise in two distinct ways (Meyer, 1956). First, they reflect primitive perceptual processes—the ways the mind is bent on grouping and organizing stimuli. This is captured in the "gestalt laws" of perception, where, for instance, movement in a particular direction creates expectation for further movement in that direction, "law of good continuation". (Figure 24.1 shows a number of examples of such "gestalt laws" for perceptual organization.) Meyer's student, Eugene Narmour, provides a detailed theoretical working out of such ideas in the context of melodic expectancies (Narmour, 1990, 1991).

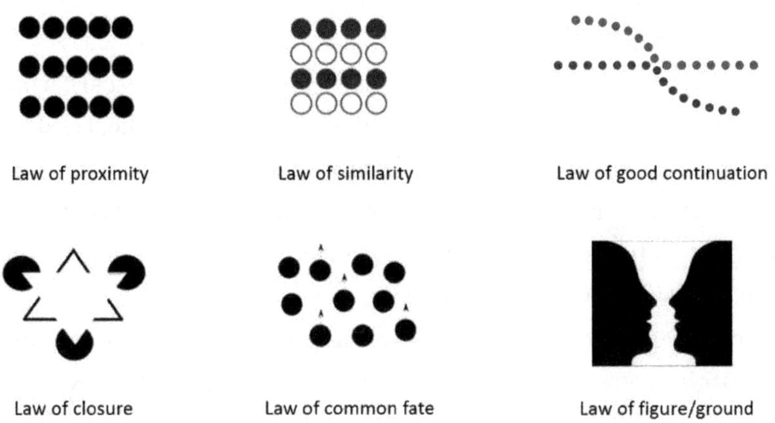

Figure 24.1 Examples of the gestalt laws of perception.

Second, there are expectations which are based on learned "schemata" for music sharing structural regularities. Some expectations relate to the entire body of tonal music. Others relate to specific styles and genres (e.g., AABA song form, sonata form). Meyer postulates that expectations are based on stylistic norms that are learned by mere exposure. Thus, expectations are usually style-specific (for evidence, see Carlsen, 1981; Krumhansl, Louhivuori, Toiviainen, Järvinen, & Eerola, 1999). Subsequent studies have indicated that learning may ultimately be more influential than the "gestalt laws" in shaping our musical expectations.

24.3 The Crucial Role of Learning and Prediction

Like conditioning, then (Chapter 21), the musical expectancy mechanism is notable for its strong dependence on individual learning: "Listeners ... anticipate most strongly the sound sequences to which they have been most frequently exposed" (Huron & Margulis, 2010, p. 578). To illustrate: it has been estimated that close to three-quarters of Western music is in the major mode. Consistent with this pattern, David Huron has found that listeners tend to assume that unfamiliar pieces are in major keys (Huron, 2006).

A general ability to detect syntactical violations can be observed fairly early in human development. Sebastian Jentschke and co-workers found evidence that 30-month-old children show neurophysiological responses (early right anterior negativity) to syntactically irregular musical harmonies (e.g., out of key chords) in simple chord sequences (Jentschke, Friederici, & Koelsch, 2014). However, their results also showed that harmonic integration (as reflected in the N5 brain response) had not quite yet developed. Indeed, many types of response due to musical expectancy depend on sufficient exposure to the relevant musical style.

Empirical evidence that musical expectancies depend a great deal on cultural learning comes from the fact that such responses are not shared by young children. John Sloboda observed that five-year-old children were unable to reject gross chordal dissonances as "wrong"; by the age of nine, however, they were overtly laughing at the "wrong" chords, and scoring almost at adult levels (Sloboda, 1989).

Another test in Sloboda's investigation concerned the ordering of musical chords that could be either "conventional" (ending with a cadence) or "scrambled" (ending without resolution). On this test, children did not achieve adult levels of performance until the age of 11, in accordance with what we might expect if the task requires exposure to the relevant musical style. Evidence of age differences have also been reported for sensitivity to tonal hierarchies (Krumhansl & Keil, 1982) and implied harmony (Trainor & Trehub, 1994).

An important question, however, is *why* we develop musical expectancies in the first place. David Huron and Elisabeth Margulis draw attention to the biological importance of expectation, arguing that "the ability to foretell the future confers obvious survival benefits even when the predicted future is just seconds away" (Huron & Margulis, 2010, p. 576). This is because we can react faster to events that are foreseen than to those that are completely unexpected (Jakobs, Wang, Dafotakis, Grefkes, Zilles, & Eickhoff, 2009), something that appears to hold true for musical sequences as well (Bharucha & Stoeckig, 1986). When listeners are asked to indicate whether the pitch goes up or down in a melody, they respond faster when the melodic contour conforms to their expectation (Aarden, 2003).

Why do we respond this way to *musical* patterns which, on the face of it, do not appear to have any implications for critical life goals? Again, presumably, the answer is that our brains will react to deviations from schematic expectations in *any* sequential pattern to which we are exposed. It does not have to be a musical pattern, but neither is music excluded. The mechanism reacts to any departure from statistically derived expectations, because this may signal that something is about to go wrong.[3] Researchers have observed that the brain may react to deviations from expectations "pre-attentively"; that is, even when the music is ignored by the listener (Koelsch, Schroger, & Gunter, 2002).

[3] This is, perhaps, why Huron and Margulis argue that, from a biological perspective, a surprising event always represents a kind of cognitive failure—a sign that we are not "on top of things" (Huron & Margulis, 2010).

24.4 Does Expectancy Build on Language–Music Parallels?

I believe that the musical expectancy mechanism, as defined here, depends on the evolutionary development of *semantic* memory, the ability to *plan* (e.g., sequences of action) and *narrate* (e.g., to order elements into a coherent story), and language-like *syntax processing* (Chapter 17). These are all relatively "recent" developments as compared to the first four mechanisms discussed in Chapters 18–21 (Gärdenfors, 2003). There is much to suggest that language and music "share" cognitive processes which are involved in the musical expectancy mechanism.

I explained in Chapter 11 that one similarity between (spoken) language and music seems to be that the prosodic aspects of speech ("tone of voice") are like emotionally expressive features of music performance (Juslin & Laukka, 2003). In this chapter we encounter another similarity, in terms of the hierarchical structure of language and music. Like language, music consists of perceptually discrete elements, organized into hierarchically structured sequences.

In a landmark publication, Fred Lerdahl and Ray Jackendoff (1983) developed the generative theory of tonal music (GTTM), which was an influential attempt to identify the "rules" of a musical grammar.[4] The theory describes how (experienced) listeners organize music in terms of four types of hierarchical structure: (i) grouping structure (e.g., motives, phrases, sections); (ii) metrical structure (e.g., "strong" and "weak" beats); (iii) time-span reduction (links between rhythm and pitch in units such as periods, theme groups, and sections); and (iv) prolongational reduction (e.g., tension-release patterns). It is by engaging with (some of) these structures that musical expectations arise. (Research suggests that lay listeners are often insensitive to formal aspects at a larger timescale; see Tillman & Bigand, 2004).

[4] In linguistics, *grammar* refers to the set of structural rules that govern the composition of clauses, phrases, and words in a natural language.

Researchers have found that violations of musical expectancy activate roughly the same brain regions that have been previously implicated in violations of syntax in language (Maess, Koelsch, Gunter, & Friederici, 2001). Aniruddh Patel has suggested that syntactical processing in both language and music share a common set of processes for syntactical integration localized in the Broca's area of the brain, which operate on distinct structural representations for music and language (Patel, 2008). The key role of such mental representations (Huron, 2006; Huron & Margulis, 2010) reveals the largely illusionary nature of an "absolutism" ideal, even for the musical expectancy mechanism. Responses to music never depend solely on the notes. Leonard Meyer, in common with many of his disciples, posited an "ideal" listener to avoid having to deal with individual differences evident in actual behavioral responses: "Granted listeners who have developed reaction patterns appropriate to the work in question, the structure of the affective response to a piece of music can be studied by examining the music itself" (Meyer, 1956, p. 32).

The problem with this approach becomes clear if we consider the origins of the expectations: they are learnt. "Because listeners have different listening backgrounds, predictability must be listener-specific" (Huron & Margulis, 2010, p. 578).

24.5 What is the ITPRA Theory?

A more recent model, which explicitly allows for the possibility that different listeners might bring various mental representations and predictive frameworks to the same piece of music is Huron's ITPRA theory, which proposes five different—and supposedly neurologically distinct—expectation systems (*Imagination, Tension, Prediction, Reaction, Appraisal*), which operate across domains, but that can be applied to musical events also (Huron, 2006; see Figure 24.2).

The five systems are grouped into *pre-outcome* and *post-outcome* phases. In the *pre-outcome* phase, an individual might consciously *imagine* different

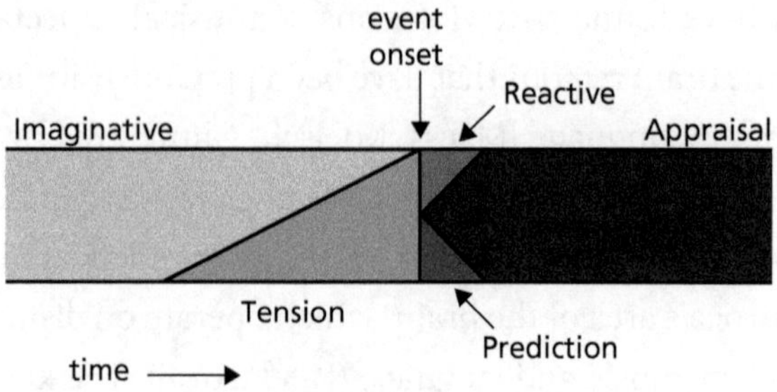

Figure 24.2 David Huron's ITPRA theory of expectancy.
Huron, David, Sweet Anticipation, figure: ITPRA Theory of Expectancy, © 2006 Massachusetts Institute of Technology, by permission of The MIT Press.

possible outcomes and "vicariously" experience some of the feelings that would be expected for each outcome. As the anticipated event approaches, arousal states (*tension*) are fine-tuned so that ensuing behaviors are optimized.

After an event has occurred, three processes are initiated. The accuracy of the pre-event prediction is assessed (*prediction response*). Positive feelings are evoked when the outcome is expected, and negative feelings are evoked when the outcome is surprising. At the same time, a "quick and dirty" *reaction response* is generated. Finally, the *appraisal response* represents a slower assessment of the situation, taking into account complex social and situational factors.

The most original aspect of the ITPRA model is the hypothesis that for a given musical event (e.g., the onset of a chord), the listener's overall feeling is a mixture of the feelings generated by the imagination, tension, prediction, reaction, and appraisal responses to the expectation, all occurring within a few seconds. (This seems to imply that all expectancy-based emotions will be "mixed emotions", but Huron mainly discusses individual emotions, such as surprise.)

The ITPRA model is bold, to say the least. Twelve years after it was introduced, I am still not aware of any attempt to test the theory (either by its originator or someone else), and questions remain whether it is even *possible* to test the model.

For instance, how would you be able to demonstrate the occurrences of all the rapid, short-lived, but distinct response stages during music listening? How does the model specify which events we will react to? Or do we respond to every single event in the music? Since expectations appear to be computed *all the time* during listening (Vuust & Kringelbach, 2010), how may the ITPRA model explain the finding that we do not experience emotions to music all the time? What is the nature of the mixed emotions aroused by the successive response stages?

24.6 How Do We Distinguish Expectancy from Other Mechanisms?

Another potential criticism of the ITPRA model is that it is over-reaching in its attempt to cram in all different kinds of response under the broad umbrella of musical expectancy. David Huron suggests that *surprise* may be the prototypical emotion aroused via expectancy (Huron, 2006). We encountered another mechanism hypothesized to arouse *surprise* in music listeners in Chapter 18 (brainstem reflex). Because they often arouse the same emotion, it is perhaps tempting to treat the two mechanisms as similar.

Both tend to involve "local" musical events that seem surprising to the listener. The difference between the two mechanisms is that musical expectancy relies on schematic expectations built up by the previous syntactical structure, whereas brainstem reflexes involve hardwired responses to "extreme" acoustic features of the music (e.g., a very loud note) which are not systematically related to the foregoing structure.

Curiously, theorists do not seem to agree about which condition will produce the strongest surprise. Meyer argues that "surprise is most intense where no special expectation is active", which is precisely the case with a brainstem reflex (Meyer, 1956, p. 29). There is nothing in the foregoing structure that leads the listener to expect such a sudden event. In contrast, Huron claims that events will be most surprising when they are "set up" by previous events (Huron, 2006, p. 270). Further research is needed to resolve this issue.

Anyhow, it is crucial not to confound psychologically distinct emotion-induction processes. The "trick" to distinguish mechanisms is not to lose track of their underlying mental representations. As explained by Maria Miceli and Christiano Castelfranchi, a system (mechanism) may perform seemingly anticipatory behaviors that are *not* based on anticipatory representations (Miceli & Castelfranchi, 2015). The system may simply react to a stimulus with a behavioral response (e.g., a conditioned response), which happens to be functional in preparing the organism for an upcoming event.

Still, this does not necessarily require an anticipatory representation of the event (e.g., a prediction). Sensori-motoric representations only react to what is in front of our nose. Brainstem reflexes, for instance, are merely "re-active" mechanisms triggered by a present stimulus. There are no anticipatory representations involved.[5] In contrast, musical expectancy involves genuinely anticipatory (i.e., predictive) mechanisms. Therefore, an emotion like *hope* cannot be aroused by a brainstem reflex or contagion, but can certainly be aroused by musical expectancy.

24.7 Does Musical Expectancy Really Arouse Emotions?

There is no doubt that musical structure evokes expectancies, and there are several quite sophisticated theories laying out how and why such expectancies occur. In contrast, there is surprisingly little evidence that such expectancies actually cause *emotional reactions* in music listeners. Somehow, this part is often taken for granted.

One problem could be that expectancy theories of musical emotion can be difficult to test. For example, a piece of music could produce several different

[5] Some examples provided by Huron appear to involve mere brainstem reflexes, rather than schematic expectations (Huron, 2006, p. 325).

expectations at various hierarchical levels of the music, and these expectations may be different for different listeners. This makes it difficult to understand exactly what the listener is responding to in a musical event, at least if we are using "real" pieces of music (as opposed to simpler musical stimuli).

John Sloboda notes that there are some issues that need to be resolved before strong predictions can be made about emotional responses on the basis of structural analysis (Sloboda, 2005, Ch. 13). For instance, almost every note in a piece of music confirms or violates *some* expectancy, so how do we know which are the crucial ones? To predict actual emotional responses, Sloboda argues, we need somehow to take into account the density of eliciting events, the positioning within the compositional architecture, and the so-called asynchrony of levels (that an event may simultaneously confirm a musical expectation on one level while violating it on another). None of these factors has yet been investigated, unfortunately.

Although the complexity of musical expectancy highlighted by these ideas can seem daunting, there are some promising preliminary findings. A seminal study by John Sloboda that sought to study emotional responses to music—in particular "chills" (see section 15.4)—provided some self-report data consistent with the expectancy mechanism (Sloboda, 1991).

Eighty-three participants—most of them musicians—were required to mention specific pieces of music to which they could recall having experienced various physical manifestations associated with emotions. Having identified these pieces (coming primarily from classical music), they were then asked to specify the exact location within the music that induced these responses. Most participants reported whole pieces or movements, but about a third of the participants were able to locate their reaction within a theme or smaller unit.

The results showed that musical events associated with "tears" (crying, lump in the throat) commonly contained melodic appoggiaturas and melodic or harmonic sequences; events associated with "shivers" (goose pimples, shivers down the spine) usually contained a new or unprepared harmony; and events associated with "heart reactions" (racing heart) contained syncopations or prominent events occurring earlier than anticipated. Sloboda argued that some of these results reflect schematically based musical expectations.

Sloboda's (1991) findings suggest that Meyer's (1956) theory is highly plausible. More direct evidence that expectations play a role in arousing emotion comes from an experimental study reported by Nikolaus Steinbeis, Stefan Koelsch, and John Sloboda (2006). To study the effect of harmonic expectancy violations, they recorded subjective measures of *tension* and *emotion*, as well as electrodermal activity, heart rate, and electro-encephalogram (EEG) in 12 musicians and 12 non-musicians.

Steinbeis and colleagues focused on harmony, because harmonic violations could be easily quantified in music-theoretically justifiable terms with reference to the "Circle of Fifths" (Steinbeis, Koelsch, & Sloboda, 2006). Stimuli consisted of three matched versions of six Bach chorales which differed only in terms of one chord, which was harmonically either *expected*, *unexpected*, or *very unexpected* (see Figure 24.3).

Figure 24.3 Experimental manipulations of the musical expectancy mechanism. Version A is an excerpt of the original composition by Bach, with a harmonically unexpected event (indicated by the dashed square); Versions B and C are identical to the original, apart from the harmonic events enclosed within boxes, which were rendered to be either harmonically more expected than the original (Version B) or less expected than the original (Version C).
Reproduced from Steinbeis, N., Koelsch, S., & Sloboda, J. A. (2006). *The role of harmonic expectancy violations in musical emotions: Evidence from subjective, physiological, and neural responses.* Journal of Cognitive Neuroscience, 18, 1380–393. © 2006 *Massachusetts Institute of Technology.*

The results indicated that tension, emotionality, and electrodermal activity increased with an increase in harmonic unexpectedness in a dose–response relationship. The EEG analyses focused on *event-related potentials* (ERPs): scalp-recorded brain responses (voltage fluctuations) that are time-locked to specific sensory, cognitive, or motor events. Analysis of ERPs revealed an early negativity (EN) response to both the *unexpected* and *very unexpected* harmonies, taken to reflect the detection of the unexpected event, and this response was significantly larger in amplitude to the *very unexpected* chords than to the *unexpected* chords.[6] Moreover, these EN responses peaked earlier for musicians than for non-musicians.

Both groups also showed a P3 component in response to the *very unexpected* chords, although this effect was considerably larger for musicians. The P3 (P300) wave is an ERP component believed to reflect processes linked with stimulus evaluation and categorization. Differences between musicians and non-musicians in the processing of musical expectancies are what we would expect if the expectations reflect stylistic learning (Meyer, 1956).

Our own studies at Uppsala University have also explored musical expectancy as an induction mechanism. To confound listeners' expectations, we have selected musical excerpts featuring unexpected melodic, harmonic, and/or rhythmic sequences, often with unresolved uncertainty.

For example, our stimuli include one excerpt from Alban Berg's Lyric Suite, Three Pieces for String Orchestra, Part III: *Adagio Appassionato*, composed in 1926. The piece follows (but does not strictly adhere to) Schoenberg's "twelve-tone practice," which abandons harmonically conceived tonality. The unassuming listener will experience his or her expectations being repeatedly thwarted by the musical patterns. Statistical analyses confirm that the musical excerpt features a low degree of "key clarity." Listening tests show that pieces like this may arouse *anxiety*, in

[6] The early left anterior negativity is a polarization of the electrical field, which appears very early in processing of auditory stimuli (*circa* 150–200 ms) and that may be related to the coarse processing of syntactic information.

accordance with Meyer's (1956, p. 27) predictions, as well as autonomic arousal and corrugator muscle activity ("frowning") in listeners (Juslin, Barradas, & Eerola, 2015).

24.8 Which Emotions Does Musical Expectancy Arouse?

Although the role of musical expectancies has proved difficult to verify in non-experimental studies and has been tested in only a few experimental studies, it appears plausible that some of our emotional responses to music *do* reflect disruptions of style-specific expectations. But what types of emotions might be aroused by such events?

Meyer discussed emotions in an approach characteristic of psychology in the 1950s; that is, as *undifferentiated arousal* (Duffy, 1941). However, although Meyer seems to accept this idea at the beginning of his book, he then seems unable to *stick* to the idea in the rest of the book. He admits that mere arousal through interruption of musical expectancies has little value; to be meaningful, the arousal needs to be followed by a satisfying resolution.

Thus, at various places Meyer argues that the musical play with expectations may lead to the induction of more specific emotions, such as *anxiety* (Meyer, 1956, p. 27), *hope* (p. 29), and *disappointment* (p. 182). Similarly, Huron's more recent book suggests that musical expectancies can arouse *surprise, anticipation, awe,* and *boredom* (Huron, 2006, p. 356). However, neither Meyer nor Huron offers empirical evidence that musical expectations will arouse these emotions in listeners.

In their recent book on expectancy and emotions more generally, Miceli and Castelfranchi posit a "family" of expectancy-related emotions (Miceli & Castelfranchi, 2015). Thus, for example, they argue that that *anticipatory* emotions may involve *anxiety, hope,* and *trust*; and that *invalidated* anticipatory representations arouse *surprise, disappointment,* and *relief.*

However, our experience sampling study suggests that about 76% of all music heard in everyday life is familiar to the listener (Juslin, Liljeström,

Västfjäll, Barradas, & Silva, 2008). In those cases where the music is familiar to the listener, one can reasonably expect many expectations to be "correct". What happens with our emotions *then*?

Miceli and Castelfranchi argue that validated expectations arouse "confirmation emotions" that bear little distinctive features, except that they will tend to be *less intense*. This "dilution effect", they note, will apply to either positive confirmed expectations or negative confirmed expectations (Miceli & Castelfranchi, 2015). Most frequently, perhaps, when expectations are confirmed, the result is only a mild form of *satisfaction* or *contentment* (the latter is a common response to music in everyday life, according to some studies; Juslin et al., 2008). Confirmation brings a sense of "cognitive security".[7]

What would happen, then, if you encountered a piece of music that is completely and utterly predictable at every level, down to the timing of each individual note? You would probably be able to submit a paper to the International Interdisciplinary Boredom Conference. (Yes, such a thing really exists.)

As far as music is concerned, most of the above ideas are speculative. Prevalence data from recent studies (Chapter 16) suggest that many of the above emotions *do* occur in reaction to music, but perhaps not as often as expected. For instance, evidence from a number of studies reveal that *anxiety, hope, disappointment, surprise, anticipation, awe,* and *boredom* occur only rarely in listeners' emotions to music (Juslin & Laukka, 2004; Juslin et al., 2008; Zentner, Grandjean, & Scherer, 2008), even when open-ended response formats are used (Juslin, Liljeström, Laukka, Västfjäll, & Lundqvist, 2011).

24.9 What is Wittgenstein's Dilemma?

We have seen that thwarted musical expectations *can* arouse emotions in listeners, but that this may not be very common. Could it be the case that

[7] Miceli and Castelfranchi's analysis thus contrasts with Huron's (2006), which holds that confirmed expectations will tend to arouse *pleasure*—a rather more intense state.

we are rarely surprised by a piece of music simply because we have heard it before?

Philosopher Ludwig Wittgenstein (1966) put his finger on a potential problem in a musical expectancy account of emotional reactions to music. If we are very familiar with a piece of music, why do we want to hear it again? After all, it holds no surprises for us. Expressed differently, if musical expectation really *is* the key to emotional reactions, how is it that we continue to experience emotions to pieces of music we know well?

First, many of the violations of expectations may occur on a subconscious level (Dowling & Harwood, 1986), involving a module for music processing that is "denied" conscious access (cf. Fodor, 1983), as suggested by Ray Jackendoff (1992). If this module is "sealed" from other parts of the system, then it may be possible that however well one knows the piece, *surprise* can still occur within the module, because this processor is always hearing the piece "for the first time."

Such a modular reaction is based on what neuroscientist Jamshed Bharucha refers to as *schematic* expectation (how music *in general* goes), which he distinguishes from *veridical* expectation (how a *specific* piece of music goes) (Bharucha, 1994). A piece you know very well may still be very unusual compared to how *most* pieces sound.

Look at Figure 24.4. You will presumably have the perceptual impression that one of the two horizontal lines is longer than the other. If I inform you that the two lines are, in fact, of the same length, you would think that this "knowledge" will change how you perceive them. Yet, your perceptual

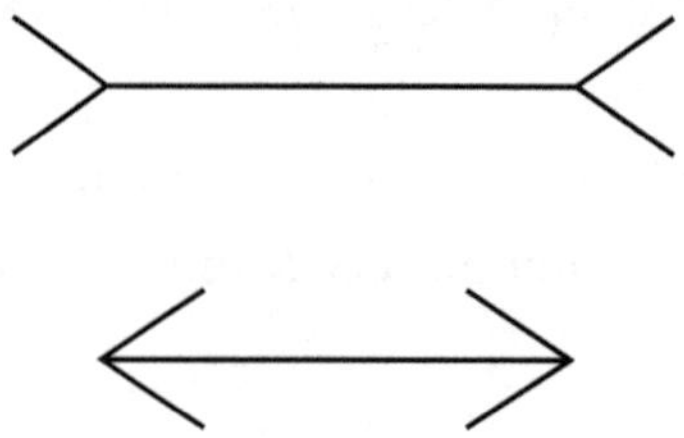

Figure 24.4 The Müller–Lyer illusion, as an example of 'modular' processing.

impression remains because the perceptual process occurs at a low, modular level of the brain, unsusceptible to higher-level knowledge. In a similar way, patterns of musical notes could remain "surprising" to our brain, time after time, at a perceptual level.

But *do* we really react with the same amount of *surprise* when hearing a piece which was rather "shocking" the first time again? This is debatable. One possibility is that the "surprisingness" (Berlyne, 1971) of pieces of music *does* diminish with repeated exposure, but that continued emotional responses to the music reflect other mechanisms, such as contagion and memories, which remain much the same throughout repeated listening to the same piece.

Ultimately, observations that most listening involves familiar music, and that the emotions associated with thwarting musical expectations are rare, may simply reflect the fact that listeners are not surprised by music very often. Some commentators suggest that Meyer's theory overestimates the role of novelty in music experience (Davies, 1994).

24.10 Musical Expectancy: A Critical Appraisal

The expectancy mechanism has had a privileged status in music research (Huron & Margulis, 2010), presumably due to its very strong focus on details of the musical structure. However, looks can be deceptive: even this mechanism depends heavily on the listener and the context. Schematic expectations rely on memory representations, which reflect individual exposure to musical patterns that are characteristic of a particular cultural context. Notice how difficult it is to form musical expectations when you listen to music from a completely foreign culture.

The elevated status of musical expectancy seems partly related to a specific *way* of listening to music. According to Eric Clarke and colleagues, it involves regarding music as a form of "sonic play" in which listeners "take pleasure in appreciating cleverly wrought structures" (Clarke, Dibben, & Pitts, 2010, p. 67).

This strong emphasis on musical expectancy might reflect in part the training of music theorists who spend much of their time analyzing musical scores. Perhaps they sometimes forget that not all listeners hear music in the same way as music theorists. As I explained in section 12.1, my impression from pilot studies is that many subtle musical events singled out by music analysts as "significant" tend to pass the ordinary listener by without arousing any emotions.

Peter Vuust and Morten Kringelbach submit that the musical expectancy mechanism is important because the brain is constantly involved in prediction (Vuust & Kringelbach, 2010). However, *all* human cognition and behavior is future-oriented. Profound as this may seem, it could hardly be any other way: it simply reflects the fact that time moves in a forward direction. After all, cognition can hardly be geared towards changing past events.

It may well be true that the brain is constantly computing expectancies at some level, but that does not necessarily make them important in the *present* context, if those expectancies fail to arouse emotions in listeners. That is, the "importance" of a mechanism should be measured in terms of its "output" (the prevalence and intensity of emotions aroused), and here the evidence is still meagre.

Preliminary estimates of the prevalence of mechanisms, based on self-report indices from questionnaire studies (Juslin et al., 2011, 2016a), experience sampling studies (Juslin et al., 2008), and experiments (Juslin, Sakka, Barradas, & Liljeström, 2018) suggest that musical emotions are rarely aroused by expectancy. However, listeners may not be able to report all causal mechanisms in a valid manner, given the often implicit nature of the mechanisms.

It is more difficult to "explain away" the findings that emotions related to expectancy are not so prevalent in listeners' music experiences. If the musical expectancy mechanism is really of such significance, would we not expect to see more of its impact on listeners' emotions? One could counter this with the argument that musical expectancy does not arouse what we call "emotions" here, but that would just reinforce my point and exclude it from the current discussion.

The precise role of musical expectancy in the musical arousal of emotions remains somewhat unclear. This is reflected by the fact that although some scholars regard this mechanism as the most fundamental (Vuust & Kringelbach, 2010), others exclude it completely from their analysis (Levinson, 1997; Scherer & Zentner, 2001). I believe that it *is* important, but more so in some contexts than in others. Effects in studies so far have generally been quite modest compared to those of other mechanisms (Juslin, Harmat, & Eerola, 2014; Steinbeis et al., 2006).

We need studies that connect current models of musical expectancy with systematic listening tests to demonstrate clearly that expectancies *do* lead to aroused emotions, as shown by multi-component measurements (e.g., subjective feeling, physiology, expression). If such studies do reveal (heaven forbid!) that the musical expectancy mechanism does *not* really arouse frequent or intense emotions, this must be accepted.

However, if musical expectations generally fail to shock us, I believe that there is a possible saving grace: these patterns do *not* mainly arouse emotions by being surprising or not to the listener, but by offering *pleasure* through the way they influence *aesthetic judgment* via such criteria as originality, wittiness, and beauty. This topic will be discussed at length in the final part of the book. Beforehand, though, we must first take stock of the seven mechanisms outlined thus far.

CHAPTER 25

PREDICTIONS, IMPLICATIONS, COMPLICATIONS

We have now looked at seven psychological mechanisms through which music might arouse emotions. In this chapter, I will widen the perspective and consider some of the implications of this multi-mechanism framework. I will explain why we need to distinguish between the mechanisms in both research and applications.

I shall also address some more general questions raised by the previous chapters. With such a large number of mechanisms, why doesn't music *always* arouse emotions? Why do different listeners react differently to the same piece of music? How does the context influence musical emotions? Why do "live" concerts tend to arouse more intense emotions than recorded music? Are emotional reactions to music similar across different cultures?

25.1 What Are the Unique Characteristics of The Mechanisms?

We have seen that psychological theories can offer plausible accounts of musical emotions. However, in order to be truly useful, the "mechanism schemes" laid out in the preceding chapters must be made more explicit and detailed, and their assumptions must be supported by relevant evidence.

The question then naturally arises: what are the unique characteristics of each mechanism? If we only had some hypotheses that might guide both researchers and practitioners. A problem is that most studies so far have not investigated specific mechanisms.

Fortunately, since the mechanisms are not actually unique to music, we may obtain valuable clues from research in *other* domains. Hence, by synthesizing theory and research in various domains outside music, my colleague Daniel Västfjäll and I were able to present the first set of hypotheses that may help music researchers to distinguish among the various mechanisms (Juslin & Västfjäll, 2008). Table 25.1 offers an "updated" version of these from Juslin (2013a).

Evolutionary *order* refers to the approximate order in which the seven brain functions can be hypothesized to have appeared during evolution (Gärdenfors, 2003). For instance, brainstem reflexes developed long before episodic memory (Chapter 17).

Survival value of brain function specifies the most important benefit that each brain function originally brought to those organisms that possessed this function. Thus, for example, visual imagery allowed humans to "simulate" important events internally by means of mental images, in the absence of direct sensory input. This meant that overt and potentially dangerous actions could be evaluated internally before they were implemented in the world.

Information focus broadly specifies the type of information that each induction mechanism is processing. For instance, musical expectancy focuses on syntactic information (Meyer, 1956), whereas contagion focuses on emotional motor expression (Juslin, 2000b).

Mental representation describes the mode of mental representation utilized by the respective mechanism. Each psychological mechanism represents a unique form of input that can guide decision making regarding future behavior. For instance, evaluative conditioning involves associative representations, whereas musical expectancy involves schematic representations (Chapter 17).

Key brain regions are those brain regions that have been most consistently associated with each mechanism in previous imaging studies. For instance,

Table 25.1 Theoretical predictions of the BRECVEM framework (adapted from Juslin, 2013a).

Mechanism	**Survival value of brain function**	**Information focus**	**Ontogenetic development**
Brainstem reflex	Focusing attention on potentially important changes or events in the close environment	Extreme or rapidly changing basic acoustic characteristics	Prior to birth
Rhythmic entrainment	Facilitating motor coordination in physical work tasks	Periodic pulses in rhythms, especially around 2Hz	Prior to birth (perception only)
Evaluative conditioning	Being able to associate objects or events with positive and negative outcomes	Co-variation between events	Prior to birth
Contagion	Enhancing group cohesion and social interaction, e.g., between mother and infant	Emotional motor expression, especially vocal expression	First year
Visual imagery	Permitting internal simulations of events that substitute for overt and risky actions	Self-conjured visual images	Pre-school years
Episodic memory	Allowing conscious recollections of previous events and binding the self to reality	Personal events in particular places and at particular times	3–4 years
Musical expectancy	Facilitating symbolic language with a complex semantics	Syntactic information	5–11 years

Mechanism	**Key brain regions**	**Cultural impact/ learning**
Brainstem reflex	The inferior colliculus, the reticulospinal tract of the reticular formation, and the intralaminar nuclei of the thalamus	Low
Rhythmic entrainment	Networks of multiple oscillators in the early auditory areas, the cerebellum, motor regions, and the caudate nucleus of the basal ganglia	Low
Evaluative conditioning	The lateral nucleus of the amygdala and the interpositus nucleus of the cerebellum	High
Contagion	Right inferior frontal regions (including the frontal gyrus), right anterior superior temporal sulcus, "mirror neurons" in pre-motor regions, and the basal ganglia (for identification)	Low
Visual imagery	Spatially mapped regions of the occipital cortex, the visual association cortex, and (for image generation) left temporo-occipital regions	High
Episodic memory	The medial temporal lobe, in particular the hippocampus, the medial pre-frontal cortex, the prenucleus, the entorhinal cortex, and the amygdala (all predictions apply to memory retrieval)	High
Musical expectancy	The left perisylvian cortex, "Broca's area," the dorsal region of the anterior cingulate cortex, and the orbitofrontal cortex	High

(*continued*)

Table 25.1 Continued

Mechanism	**Induced affect**	**Induction speed**	**Degree of volitional influence**
Brainstem reflex	Arousal, surprise Secondary responses: e.g., anxiety, laughter	High	Low
Rhythmic entrainment	Arousal increase/decrease (calm, excitement) Secondary responses: "social bonding", joy	Low	Low
Evaluative conditioning	Basic emotions (Complex emotions?)	High	Low
Contagion	Basic emotions Secondary response: sympathy	High	Low
Visual imagery	All possible emotions	Low	High
Episodic memory	All possible emotions, but in particular nostalgia and longing	Low	Medium
Musical expectancy	Anticipation, anxiety, hope, surprise, disappointment, interest, relief, tension	Medium	Low

Mechanism	Availability to consciousness	Modularity	Dependence on musical structure
Brainstem reflex	Low	High	Medium
Rhythmic entrainment	Low	High	Medium
Evaluative conditioning	Low	High	Low
Emotional contagion	Low	High	Medium
Visual imagery	High	Low	Medium
Episodic memory	High	Low	Low
Musical expectancy	Medium	Medium	High

Adapted from *Physics of Life Reviews*, 10, Juslin, P. N., *From everyday emotions to aesthetic emotions: Toward a unified theory of musical emotions*, pp.235–266.

visual imagery has been associated with activation of the visual cortex of the brain (Cui, Jeter, Yang, Montague, & Eagleman, 2007).

In principle, musical emotions can be expected to involve three classes of brain regions: (i) regions activated simply because music is *perceived* (e.g., the primary auditory cortex); (ii) regions usually involved in the *conscious experience of emotions*, regardless of the cause of the emotion (e.g., the rostral anterior cingulate and the medial pre-frontal cortex; Lane, 2000, pp. 356–358; the periaqueductal grey; Panksepp, 1998); and (iii) regions selectively involved in information processing that differs depending on *the mechanism* that caused the emotion.

Thus, although musical emotions may involve several brain regions (Koelsch, 2014), the hypotheses in Table 25.1 focus on the last type of regions: those that can help researchers to *discriminate* between various mechanisms. The hypotheses are not meant to imply that each mechanism is located in a separate region. Rather, each mechanism may involve a network of dynamically interacting regions (Bressler & Menon, 2010).

Cultural impact and learning refers to the relative extent to which each mechanism is affected differently by music that differs from one culture to another. For example, brainstem reflexes mainly reflect "hardwired" reactions to simple features that are not affected much by learning, whereas musical expectancy reflects learned schemata for styles of music that differ from one culture to another and that make listeners from different cultures react differently to a piece of music.

Ontogenetic development focuses on the approximate time in development when respective mechanism could begin to have a noticeable effect on musical emotions. For instance, brainstem reflexes to music are functional even prior to birth (Lecanuet, 1996), whereas reactions which involve musical expectancy may not develop fully until between the ages of 5 and 11 (Sloboda, 1989). There is a tendency for mechanisms to develop ontogenetically in roughly the same order as they developed phylogenetically (see *evolutionary order*).

Induced affect specifies which affective states might be expected to be aroused depending on the mechanism. For example, whereas emotional contagion might be expected to arouse only basic emotions which have more or less distinct non-verbal expressions, visual imagery could be expected to arouse all possible human emotions. As we have previously suggested, there is a link between the types of emotions that can be aroused and the types of brain regions involved in the induction process (Juslin & Västfjäll, 2008, Table 4).

As illustrated in Figure 25.1, Richard Lane suggests that at a brainstem level, responses are limited to autonomic activation (i.e., *arousal*); at a limbic level, responses are limited to discrete (basic) emotions; and at "higher" paralimbic or pre-frontal levels, responses may involve more complex "blends" (mixed emotions) (Lane, 2000, pp. 362–363). This hierarchy is broadly consistent with the current framework.

Temporal focus of affect specifies whether the emotions aroused by respective mechanism are oriented mainly toward the present (e.g., *surprise* for brainstem reflex), toward the past (e.g., *nostalgia* for episodic memory), or toward to the future (e.g., *anxiety* for musical expectancy). This is related to the extent of "time travel" enabled by the mechanism. More recent ones tend to enable more "time travel" than more ancient ones (cf. *evolutionary order*).

Induction speed refers to how much "processing time" a mechanism requires, relative to other mechanisms, for an emotion to occur in a specific

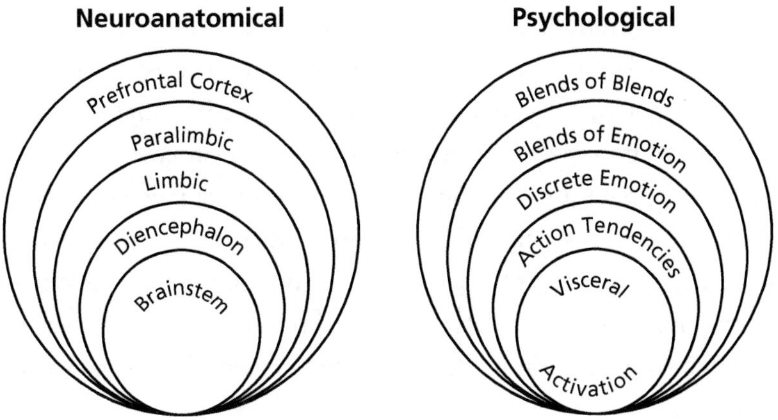

Figure 25.1 Links between brain levels and types of emotions.
From Lane, 2000.

situation. For example, brainstem reflexes can induce emotions very quickly (in less than a second), whereas musical expectancy can be expected to require more time (a number of seconds), since some of the musical structure must unfold in order for a musical expectation to occur that can be confirmed or violated.

Degree of volitional influence refers to the extent to which the listener him- or herself may actively influence the induction process (e.g., through focus of attention, active recall, self-activation). For instance, emotional reactions that involve evaluative conditioning could be involuntary and seemingly "automatic" (Martin, Stambrook, Tataryn, & Beihl, 1984), whereas reactions that involve visual imagery can be strongly influenced by the listener (Larson, 1995).

Availability to consciousness states the extent to which at least *some* aspects of the induction process are available to the listener's consciousness, so that the listener can be able to explain his or her response. For example, if a piece of music evokes an episodic memory, the listener will have a conscious recollection of the previous event and some inkling of the reasons (e.g., the appraisal) that made this event evoke the emotion that is now re-experienced. Conversely, conditioned responses can be aroused outside conscious awareness (Öhman & Soares, 1994).

Modularity refers to the extent to which the induction process of the mechanism may function as an independent and information-encapsulated "module," which may be activated in parallel with other psychological processes (Fodor, 1983). Contagion could be described as highly "modular" because it can be activated independently of other processes (see Juslin & Liljeström, in press), and is not influenced by the information of other modules (e.g., we may react to music as an expressive voice, even if we know, at some cognitive level, that the music is not really a voice). Conversely, imagery is highly dependent on attentional resources which are easily distracted by competing stimuli that may interfere with the image-generation process (Kosslyn, Thompson, & Ganis, 2006).

Dependence on musical structure refers to the degree to which the induction process depends on the exact structure and style of the music heard. At one extreme, the structure of the music is not important as such, it simply functions as a "retrieval cue." This is the case for evaluative conditioning and episodic memory. At the other extreme, the precise unfolding pattern of the musical structure strongly determines the nature of the induced emotions. This is the case for musical expectancy. However, *all* mechanisms relate to musical structure in their own way, whether through a melodic theme, a voice-like timbre, a rhythmic pattern, or an unusual chord.

25.2 What Can We Learn from the Framework?

The present framework has several implications for this field. I will focus here on only two of these. One major conclusion we can draw from the previous section is that *musical emotion is not a unitary phenomenon.*

Consider some of the questions that scholars have asked in the past: which emotions may music arouse? How early do musical emotions develop? Is the listener active or passive in the causal process? How much time does it take for music to arouse an emotion in a listener? Are musical emotions innate or learned responses? Are such emotions cross-culturally invariant?

For all these questions, the answer depends on the precise mechanism concerned (Table 25.1). We cannot answer these questions in a *general* sense without first making clear which type of musical emotion (read "mechanism") we are considering. In fact, many previous disagreements in the field can be resolved by realizing that different scholars have (without being aware of it) studied different mechanisms.

This realization brings us to a second major implication for studies of musical emotions: for data to contribute in a cumulative way to our knowledge, researchers need to specify—as far as possible—the mechanism involved in each case, otherwise studies will lead to results that are inconsistent or that cannot be given a clear interpretation (Juslin & Västfjäll, 2008).

This may be illustrated by brain imaging studies of music and emotion. Studies have revealed changes in blood flow in a number of brain areas such as the amygdala, the hippocampus, the striatum, the cingulate cortex, the insula, the orbitofrontal cortex, the cerebellum, the visual cortex, the frontal gyrus, the motor cortex, and the brainstem (Juslin & Sakka, in press).

However, different areas have been implicated in different studies, for reasons that are unclear. The problem is that neuroscientists have tended to study musical emotions in a simple one-to-one fashion (see Figure 25.2a); that is, they play musical extracts that are supposedly "emotional" to listeners, and then look at what emotions were aroused and what brain areas were affected.

The complicating factor is that real-word events are often *multiply mediated*: they may have more than one cause. Thus, when we play a musical extract for a listener, any of a number of induction mechanisms could be activated (see Figure 25.2b), and depending on which one(s), the outcome may be completely different, whether in terms of the felt emotion, brain regions activated, or any other process characteristics (Table 25.1).

It is in this light we should view results from imaging studies of music and emotion: the fact that different studies have reported different patterns of brain activation may, at least in part, reflect different induction mechanisms. This may explain why some studies have reported an activation of, say, visual cortex or motor regions, whereas others have reported an activation of hippocampus or Broca's area. We cannot expect the same brain

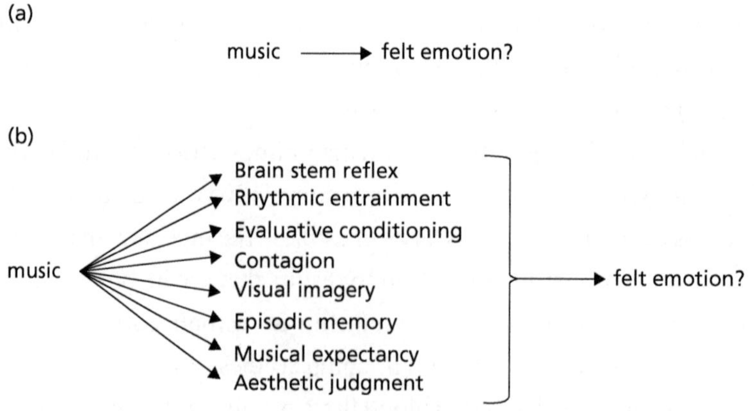

Figure 25.2 Single versus multiple mediation of musical emotions.

regions areas to be active regardless of what the brain is doing. And we don't know what the brain is doing, unless we are controlling the underlying mechanism.

Although many neuroscientists continue to go about their business as usual and pay little attention to psychological mechanisms, some scholars seem to have taken the framework to their hearts (see Koelsch, 2012).[1] One of the few brain imaging studies that explicitly adopted a mechanism approach is the study by Petr Janata, which explored neural correlates of autobiographical memories evoked by music (Janata, 2009).

The theoretical framework outlined in the previous chapters has some important implications for the relationship between perception and arousal of emotion: Whether a piece of music that *expresses* a specific emotion will *arouse* the same emotion, a different emotion, or no emotion at all is not a simple issue but depends on the precise mechanism involved.

For instance, if an emotion is aroused by, say, episodic memory, this state may be completely independent of the expression of the piece. In contrast, if an emotion is aroused by contagion, the state will clearly reflect the expression. Thus, we must not presume that felt emotions will always be the same as perceived emotions. This is far from the case. In a study by Paul Evans and Emery Schubert, felt and perceived emotion matched in only 61% of the instances (Evans & Schubert, 2008).

Which mechanism is the most important? This question was raised by some researchers upon learning about the present framework. Indeed, some scholars have been quick to propose some kind of "hierarchy", though they emphasize different mechanisms depending on their focus and background. Musicologists tend to embrace the musical expectancy mechanism since it is highly reflective of the musical structure (Vuust & Kringelback, 2010). Others argue that contagion (Gardiner, 2008) or conditioning (Bezdek & Gerrig, 2008) are the most important.

[1] Stefan Koelsch has largely adopted the BRECVEMA framework, though he does not refer to it as such (e.g., Koelsch, 2012, pp. 212–216).

I remain reluctant to consider any mechanism more important than the others. To assign a higher "value" to some of the mechanisms because they are more commonly studied in musicology is questionable.[2] Rather, the criterion should be the mechanisms' impact on listeners' emotions, and then the picture becomes complicated. No-one would presumably argue that brainstem reflexes are the most important, although without them we would not be here today, so in that narrow sense, they are, of course, *extremely* important! But apart from them, the relative prevalence and importance of specific mechanisms is likely to *vary* depending on numerous factors: the listener, the musical genre, the piece, the context, and so on.

From this point of view, arguing about which mechanism is the most important *in general* seems futile. It is more feasible, perhaps, to consider the relative importance of different mechanisms for specific pieces, artists, genres, or historical periods. For instance, Frederic Kiernan argues that the BRECVEMA framework may be applied historically to explain how specific features of musical structure became "emotionally significant" in particular historical periods (Kiernan, 2017).

25.3 Are There Further Induction Mechanisms?

The BRECVEMA framework—as it currently stands—features eight mechanisms (including *aesthetic judgment*; see Part IV). I am confident that these account for the lion's share of emotions aroused by music in everyday life, yet I do not rule out the possibility that further mechanisms will eventually be discovered by researchers. This is, after all, work in progress.

A few additional mechanism proposals have already been made in the literature. However, so far these are either (i) unwittingly examples of one of the mechanisms already featured in the framework, (ii) mechanisms less

[2] Musicologists have, in the past, tended to limit their structural analyses to aspects of musical expectancy, but I encourage them to *expand* their analyses to other mechanisms also. What features of the structure are important in establishing a conditioned response? What features of the structure facilitate some images rather than others?

relevant in musical settings, or (iii) not mechanisms at all. Let us briefly consider some of these proposals.

Glenn Schellenberg suggests that "mere exposure" is an additional mechanism that helps to explain our emotional responses to music (Schellenberg, 2008). Clearly, however, this term refers to a phenomenon, not a mechanism per se (Zajonc, 2001). It refers to the observation that we tend to develop a preference for things merely because they are familiar to us. As explained in Chapter 21, the phenomenon can be explained by one of the existing mechanisms in the BRECVEMA framework, *evaluative conditioning*. Mere exposure thus conceived is simply a side-effect of associative learning. Moreover, mere exposure is arguably more relevant to explaining music *preference* (e.g., what we like) than emotions proper (section 31.3).

An even simpler form of learning—not included in the framework—is *habituation* (mentioned in Chapter 18). As you may recall, this is a non-associative learning process whereby gradual decreases in response occur with repeated presentation of the same stimulus. While this could, perhaps, be considered a basic mechanism, habituation is unable to explain how music arouses emotions. Quite the opposite, it may explain why a piece of music will *fail* to arouse equally strong emotions upon repeated playbacks: we simply "get used" to its emotional effect.

Some authors have suggested that *semantic content* may constitute an additional mechanism (Clarke, Dibben, & Pitts, 2010; Fritz & Koelsch, 2008), but it is important to note that (mere) emotional meaning (i.e., semantic content) is not sufficient to *arouse* an emotion; the content must also be *processed* in some way for an aroused emotion to occur (e.g., contagion, evaluative conditioning, episodic memory), otherwise we are merely talking about *perception* of emotions, again (Part II).

Eric Clarke and co-workers do acknowledge the role of evaluative conditioning—a form of associative learning—and yet they feel the need to propose an additional mechanism called "semantic associations" (Clarke et al., 2010, p. 85), which would seem to be either exactly the same thing as evaluative conditioning or a case of "associative sources" of *perceived* emotions, in which case it is not an induction mechanism.

What about *lyrics* of songs? In the previous discussion of mechanisms, I did not mention lyrics (although they were discussed in relation to expression of emotion in section 6.3). Laboratory studies show that lyrics *may* have an effect on emotions, though the precise outcome varies markedly across studies (e.g., Mori & Iwanaga, 2013; Sousou, 1997; Stratton & Zalanowski, 1994).

Studies featuring representative samples of listeners (Juslin, Liljeström, Laukka, Västfjäll, & Lundqvist, 2011) or situations (Juslin, Liljeström, Västfjäll, Barradas, & Silva, 2008) suggest that emotions during music listening are sometimes caused by lyrics or, perhaps, a special combination of music and lyrics. In these samples, lyrics was not a frequent source of emotion (accounting for only 4% of the emotions in the latter study).

However, the importance of lyrics may vary from one genre to another and from one song to another. We found in a cross-cultural study that a listening motive to *listen to lyrics* was more common in "collectivist" countries, such as Brazil and Kenya, than in "individualist" countries, such as Sweden and the United States (Juslin et al., 2016a). Moreover, Gonçalo Barradas found that when *fado* music listeners in Portugal experienced *sadness* and *nostalgia*, these emotions were often linked to song lyrics (Barradas, in press; see also Batcho, 2007).

Lyrics have been somewhat neglected in music and emotion research, perhaps because most previous research has focused on classical music, which is mainly instrumental. Lyrics might play a more prominent role in popular music: "Popular musicians are loved, and even worshipped, not only for their abilities to write songs and perform them publicly, but for their ability to "speak" to their audiences" (Lull, 1992, p. 3).

Should lyrics, then, be regarded as an additional mechanism? Not really. Lyrics should rather be conceptualized as a "musical feature" (like tempo), even though it is clearly a *special* type of musical feature. Like other musical features, lyrics do not influence emotions "directly," the effect is again necessarily "mediated" by psychological mechanisms. Hence, at least some of the mechanisms I have described earlier may help to explain the emotional effects of lyrics.

A set of lyrics may evoke powerful associations (evaluative conditioning) or significant memories (episodic memory); they make describe things, events, or people that stimulate mental images (visual imagery); they may carry an important "message" or simply be beautiful (aesthetic judgment).

A moving example of the special combination of music and lyrics (and visuals, if the video is also considered) is the song "Hurt," as performed by country singer Johnny Cash. The song was written by Trent Reznor, leader of the band Nine Inch Nails, but was later covered by Cash on his album *American IV: The man comes around* (2002). The song was written in a moment of loneliness and desperation, features references to addiction and self-harm, and was interpreted by some people as looking at how to find a reason to live in the midst of depression and pain. Recorded just seven months before Cash died, his frailty is evident in the trembling voice, resonating perfectly with the subject matter, and the accompanying video, which adds further layers of emotional associations.

Some authors suggest that music lyrics can serve important functions for music listeners by helping them to explore feelings, ideas, and memories, and to overcome everyday problems (Hargreaves, Miell, & MacDonald, 2002). Hence, although not exactly a mechanism, lyrics may clearly play a role in music's emotional impact.

25.4 What Is the Role of Cognitive Goal Appraisal?

Are there other examples of induction mechanisms then that may be relevant in music? One additional mechanism already mentioned is *cognitive goal appraisal*. You will recall from Chapter 17 that this is often considered the "default" mechanism for induction of emotions in everyday life. The basic idea is that an emotion is aroused when an event, object, or person is evaluated as having implications for a perceiver's life goals, plans, or motives in terms of goal congruence, coping potential, and compatibility with norms (Scherer, 1999).

The term "appraisal" may be confusing, because it can be used both in a "broad" sense and a "narrow" sense. If you use the term broadly, then *all* mechanisms are, in a sense, "appraisal."[3] However, used in this manner, we are forced to lump together quite *different* processes (e.g., contagion, episodic memory, rhythmic entrainment). Hence, I now prefer the "narrow" sense of the term, which reserves "appraisal" for cases where a *goal representation* is implicated in the induction process; this is, after all, the essence of appraisal theory (Smith & Kirby, 2009).

The notion of goals can *also* be confusing. Other mechanisms in the BRECVEMA framework also involve goals, surely? A brainstem reflex suggests a "life-preservation goal", doesn't it? As noted by Maria Miceli and Christiano Castelfrenchi, one should make a distinction between a "goal" being embedded in an organism's design by evolution and a *goal proper* which is an internal representation which is used as a set point in a control system (Miceli & Castelfranchi, 2015).

BRECVEMA mechanisms (Chapters 18–24) may be functional in realizing design-embedded goals, but they do not involve internal goal representations of the results to be achieved. The cognitive goal appraisal mechanism, in contrast, involves high-level mental representation of concurrent goals, plans, and motives. Events will be evaluated by the appraisal mechanism in relation to these goals proper.

Can a piece of music have goal implications? I gave you a simple example earlier: Imagine lying in your bed, late at night, trying to sleep. You have an important meeting the next day and you are eager to get a good night's sleep. Suddenly, you hear an all-too familiar sound through the walls of your apartment. Oh no! Your neighbor is at it again, playing his piano "around midnight." It takes only a few seconds for you to get really *annoyed*.

As illustrated by this example, there is no doubt that music *can* arouse emotions via cognitive goal appraisal. (Hence, I have frequently listed this

[3] This is how I used the term initially, calling a project Appraisal in Music and Emotion (AMUSE). Similarly, Mitch Waterman seems to use the term "appraisal" in this broad sense in his study (Waterman, 1996).

as an additional mechanism, alongside the others.) If this was the *typical* route to musical emotions, however, we would hardly be puzzled by our responses. The mystery is precisely the observation that we are moved by music, even though the musical notes are irrelevant to our plans or goals in everyday life.

How is appraisal different from other mechanisms? (Proper) goal representations are believed to be located in the prefrontal cortex, a "higher" and more "modern" part of the brain which is linked to executive functions and conscious experience. This is significant because it explains why goal appraisal fails to play an important role in musical emotions.

Low-level mechanisms such as brainstem reflex and contagion can be "fooled" into reacting to "mere" music (because of their "modular" circuits; section 25.1), but high-level appraisal cannot. There is no way you are going to believe that a piece of music is going influence your chances of getting a new job. At *this* level of the brain, we simply *know* that the music does not have such goal implications.

However, music is used to achieve various goals in everyday life, surely? Indeed, listeners use music to get energized, to relax, and to evoke precious memories (e.g., DeNora, 2000; Juslin & Laukka, 2004; Lamont, Greasley, & Sloboda, 2016). This might seem to suggest that goal appraisal is involved.

Here we need to distinguish between two different senses in which goals could be involved in music: (i) using music to *achieve* a goal (e.g., to get distracted) (which is common in emotion regulation using music; see Baltazar & Saarikallio, 2016); and (ii) a goal being involved in the actual process (or mechanism) through which the music *arouses* the desired emotional state.

To illustrate, a listener may become content because he or she succeeds in achieving her goal of relaxing (goal appraisal), but the relaxation per se—the effect of the musical event—is produced by another mechanism (e.g., visual imagery). Similarly, a listener may succeed in achieving the goal to evoke nostalgic memories, but the induction mechanism responsible for such nostalgia is likely to be episodic memory, not goal appraisal.

Experience-sampling data from our laboratory suggest that goal appraisal is the least commonly occurring mechanism (Juslin et al., 2008).

Self-reports must, of course, be treated with caution, but because goal appraisal is a high-level process, with current goals and motives being salient in consciousness, this is clearly one mechanism where we could expect people to be able to report occurrences reliably. Even so, goal appraisal occurred in only 2% of the musical emotion episodes.

25.5 Why Do Listeners React Differently to the Same Music? And Why Does Music Not Always Arouse Emotions?

It has long been recognized that there are individual differences between listeners in reactions to music (Sloboda, 1996). Leonard Meyer observes that "the same stimulus may excite emotion in one person but not in another" (Meyer, 1956, p. 13). For instance, listening to heavy metal music may arouse *anger* in some listeners but *joy* in others (Gowensmith & Bloom, 1997; Thompson, Geeves, & Olsen, 2018).

Fortunately, the present framework may help to explain individual differences in responses. Many of the mechanisms described earlier (e.g., evaluative conditioning, episodic memory, musical expectancy) depend on various types of memory representations, which differ from one person to another. Because of differences in their learning history, different listeners do not, in a sense, hear the "same" music.

The mechanisms are also influenced by trait characteristics to some extent. For example, listeners high in empathy may show more intense contagion responses than those low in empathy (Eerola, Vuoskoski, & Kautiainen, 2016), and listeners with trait anxiety may respond with stronger brainstem reflexes to startling events (Ray et al., 2009).

Moreover, listeners could have different music preferences (Rentfrow & McDonald, 2010) as well as different motives for listening to music (Juslin & Isaksson, 2014), both of which may have a powerful effect on musical emotions. (How often do you thoroughly enjoy a piece of music from a genre you really hate?) As we will see in next part of this book, different listeners rely on different criteria when they judge the aesthetic value of songs (Juslin, Sakka, Barradas, & Liljeström, 2016).

It is also easy to forget that many of these individual variables fluctuate over time. When you hear a piece of music several times across a given time period such a week, not only is the context likely to be different from one occasion to the next, your physical and mental state is unlikely to be exactly the same. All things considered, it is really more surprising that listeners' responses to music are as *similar* as they are.

There is another riddle to solve: with so many induction mechanisms, why doesn't music *always* arouse emotions? We saw earlier that music appears to arouse an emotion only about 50% of the total time spent listening (Juslin & Laukka, 2004; Juslin et al., 2008, 2011, 2016a). Why is this the case? Based on the BRECVEMA framework, we may assume that if a musical event *fails* to feature information relevant for any of the mechanisms, then consequently no emotion will be aroused in the listener.

To illustrate, if you listen to a piece of music that does *not* include any extreme sound event (Brainstem reflex); a quite pronounced or catchy rhythm (Entrainment); a passionate and voice-like expression (Contagion); structural aspects that invite metaphorical analogies to external events (Visual imagery); unexpected melodic, harmonic, or rhythmic sequences (Musical expectancy); an aesthetic quality such as vast beauty (Aesthetic judgment); or has been linked with emotionally laden life events (Evaluative conditioning, Episodic memory); or (less plausibly) have crucial implications for your goals in life (Appraisal), then chances are slim that the piece will arouse an emotion in you.[4]

Yet, even when a musical event features information relevant to a specific mechanism (for instance, a melodic theme linked to an emotional episodic memory), the music can *still* fail to arouse an emotion. Here, it is useful to employ psychologist James Gibson's notion of "affordances": musical events "afford" certain emotions for a listener, but do not guarantee them (Gibson,

[4] Such supposedly "neutral" pieces of music are, however, surprisingly difficult to find (see Juslin, Barradas, & Eerola, 2015).

1979). To see why, recall that a "musical event" was broadly defined as the joint information in the *music*, the *listener*, and the *situation* (see Chapter 3). Thus far, the discussion has centered around musical aspects and listener aspects. Let us now consider the role of the situation.

25.6 Are Induction Mechanisms Influenced by Context?

There was a time in human history not so long ago when musical events tended to be tied very much to specific times and places. Before the advent of recorded music, music tended to be performed at certain occasions for specific purposes such as weddings, funerals, and festivities. Although music is still linked to ceremonies and special occasions, what is remarkable about our modern world is that all kinds music are available, at all times, and at all places. Never before has music been heard in such a wide range of contexts.

A common misunderstanding of the notion of mechanisms is that it implies that our reactions to music are determined merely by musical features, perhaps in relation to individual factors. In fact, it is often the context that will ultimately determine whether a mechanism is activated or not: it is the context that turns causal potential into causal outcome. Thus, I have repeatedly emphasized the role of the social context in responses to music (e.g., Juslin & Laukka, 2004).

To support this point, think whether you would experience the same piece of music in the same way in a shopping mall as in a concert? Think about how your attention may be focused differently or how your intentions and expectations may differ. Your affective reaction is likely to depend strongly on what "function" the music serves in a particular context (Sloboda & O'Neill, 2001).

If you find yourself in a stressful situation, music might be used to relieve stress; if there is a special occasion, music might be used to evoke nostalgic memories; and if you attend an evening concert, music might be the focus of aesthetic contemplation and appreciation. Various aspects of the context help to determine *which* mechanism is activated.

25.6 ARE INDUCTION MECHANISMS INFLUENCED BY CONTEXT?

The aforementioned experience sampling method (ESM) has helped scholars to explore the ways in which music is experienced in everyday life, including when and where emotions occur. Settings have been studied in terms of three main variables: *activities, locations,* and *social conditions.*

Survey (Juslin et al., 2011) and ESM data (Juslin et al., 2008) indicate that the most common activities during musical emotion episodes are (focused) music listening, travel, movie or TV watching, work/study, social interaction, and relaxation. However, in a random sample of 573 musical emotion episodes from everyday life, only a minority (15%) of the episodes included focused music listening (Juslin et al., 2008). How might this impact on the emotion process?

If music is used as "background," with all attention focused on other activities, it suggests that some attention-dependent mechanisms (e.g., visual imagery) are already out of the equation. In contrast, more "modular" mechanisms (section 25.1) can still be activated. We observed in an experimental study that emotional reactions to musical excerpts selected to target the mechanisms *brainstem reflex, contagion,* and *musical expectancy,* respectively, were not changed or diminished in a group of listeners who performed a counting task (designed to require the listener's full attention), as indicated by (retrospective) self-reports of feelings and (concurrent) psychophysiological responses (Juslin & Liljeström, in press).

Researchers have also investigated the contexts in which musical emotions occur in terms of the physical *location.* A few studies suggest that listeners are particularly prone to experience emotions to music "at home" and "outdoors" (Juslin et al., 2008; North, Hargreaves, & Hargreaves, 2004; Sloboda, Ivalidi, & O'Neill, 2001). These kinds of results will, of course, partly reflect where listeners spend most time overall.

Yet, musical emotions can occur in a variety of locations, indicating that they are not really dependent on a particular location, with the exception of special concert experiences. This may seem to suggest that the context is not so important after all. However, as noted earlier, the context may influence *which* emotions are induced. For instance, consider the influence of *social* context; that is, whether other people are present or not in the musical event.

In an ESM study featuring 483 adolescents, Robert Thompson and Reed Larson (1995) found interactions between listening context and musical genre: "hard rock" aroused positive emotions across several contexts, but negative emotions when heard in the presence of family members. "Soft rock" aroused more positive emotions in the company of friends than when heard alone. The authors concluded that intimate companionship transformed themes of *longing* and *nostalgia* in this music into a more positive, "binding" experience.

In our own ESM study (Juslin et al., 2008), featuring a Swedish adult sample, we found that some emotions, such as *happiness–elation, pleasure–enjoyment,* and *anger–irritation,* often occur in a social setting (during social interaction, amongst friends); others, such as *calm–contentment, nostalgia–longing,* and *sadness–melancholy,* often occur in a solitary setting.

The context is so influential that one can *predict* specific emotions to some degree based on contextual factors, in the absence of detailed information about the music (Juslin et al., 2011). That the prevalence of specific emotions varies depending on the context highlights the need to use representative samples of situations to obtain valid estimates of emotion prevalence.

25.7 Why Do "Live" Concerts Produce More Intense Emotions than Recorded Music?

One type of social context that may hold a particular significance is the "live" concert. In 1877 Thomas Edison invented the gramophone; before then, *all* music was in a sense "live music." Public concerts began to be organized professionally by musicians themselves when the systems of court and ecclesiastical patronage broke down in seventeenth century (Harbor, 2013).

Consider how much things have changed. In the ESM study by Juslin and co-workers, only 7% of the musical emotion episodes sampled during a two-week period involved "live" music (Juslin et al., 2008). "Live" music has become so rare that some listeners do not seem to know what "live" music sounds like anymore.

At the same time, research suggests that some of our most *intense* experiences of music occur during concerts (e.g., Lamont, 2011). In Gabrielsson's study, 73% of the peak experiences involved "live" music (Gabrielsson, 2011). People are clearly willing to invest a lot of time, energy, and money to attend concerts and music festivals (see Figure 25.3).

Scholars suggest a number of reasons for the continued attraction of concerts, including the prospect of interacting with the musicians (or seeing the musicians interacting on stage), the intimacy of the venue, the proximity to the performers (e.g., eye contact), shared experience with other audience members, and opportunities to become fully immersed in a performance (Burland & Pitts, 2014). There are, in fact, several aspects that could enhance the intensity of emotional reactions during a "live" concert:

- Higher volume

Brainstem reflexes (Chapter 18) are likely to occur more often at "live" concerts than during listening to recorded music, in both classical and pop

Figure 25.3 Many emotionally intense music experiences occur during "live" concerts.
Licensed under the Creative Commons Zero license (<https://creativecommons.org/publicdomain/zero/1.0/>).

music. Sublime pieces of music that are already impressive will get an additional "boost" when they are played at concert level and hit us physically, enhancing our sense of *awe* at the music.

- Multimodal experience

We saw earlier that vocal expressions or voice-like tones in the music may be "contagious," that the listener may become "smitten" by the emotional expressivity of a real or imagined voice (Chapter 20). This effect may be further enhanced in a "live" setting when we can also watch facial expressions and movements of performers (Chan, Livingstone, & Russo, 2013).

- Low control over music

In contrast to most listening to recorded music, where the order of songs is usually known or even decided by the listener (unless using the "shuffle" function on your music device), "live" concerts will often involve a set list that is unknown to the concert goer. This lack of control makes it more likely that the listener will experience surprises or strong "aha!" moments when recognizing an unexpected song choice, which evokes emotional associations (Chapter 21).

- Complete focus on music performance

As explained in section 25.1, some of the mechanisms that underlie emotional reactions to music require full attention on the music in order to produce any effect. Yet, many musical events in everyday life seem to involve other activities than focused music listening (Juslin et al., 2008; Sloboda et al., 2001). We might expect listeners who are fully immersed in the music performance at a concert (Radbourne, Johanson, & Glow, 2014) to experience richer emotions, as a result of a potentially wider range of mechanisms being activated (Chapter 32).

- Shared emotions

During "live" concerts, listeners are immersed in a group of people with shared aims and interests whose behaviors could influence those of other audience members. This may lead to both group entrainment and social contagion, secondary effects that could enhance the emotional experience of the music (Gabrielsson, 2011).

Not all concert experiences represent an improvement on home listening, though. Tickets are often expensive, yet concerts can be disappointing (e.g., poor sound system or acoustics, too loud music, uninspired performance, disturbing audience members, "wrong" choices of songs, uncomfortable seats, a blocked view; e.g., Pitts, 2014).

Concerts can also be disappointing in other ways. In June 2015, the Foo Fighters rushed on stage in Stockholm to an ecstatic crowd. "It's gonna be a long night!" singer Dave Grohl shouted. A few minutes later he fell off stage and broke a leg and was forced to stop the gig. (To his credit, however, he returned to the stage and finished the gig sitting in a wheelchair while medics attended to his broken leg!) Events such as these are unique to "live" concerts.

"Live" concerts can, of course, be experienced second-hand through "live albums." However, these are usually "hit-or-miss" affairs. Most "live" albums lack the atmosphere of real concerts and are instead more characterized by off-key singing, aimless jamming, editing, or so much overdubbing that the performance is more or less a studio recording. Only a small proportion of all "live albums" have become true classics; and they all lack the most crucial feature: the *social* nature of concert attendance, including the experiencing of "collective emotions."

25.8 Are Musically Aroused Emotions Cross-Culturally Invariant?

If we widen the perspective further, matters of context also pertain to the *cultural* context. Why should musical emotions vary as a function of culture? One reason is that the *values* within a culture could influence listeners' motives for engaging with music, the frequency with which they engage in musical activities associated with particular emotion-induction mechanisms, and the emotions resulting from those activities.

To illustrate, in cultures where, for example, dancing is highly valued, the mechanism of rhythmic entrainment may play a crucial role in emotional responses to music, inducing feelings of positive *arousal*. In cultures where traditional songs are usually played to honor important events in life, the mechanism of episodic memory could play a key role, arousing feelings of *nostalgia*. In cultures where musical works are mainly regarded as objects for aesthetic contemplation, the mechanism of aesthetic judgment may play an important role, evoking feelings of *awe*.

Cross-cultural reviews of music and emotion tend to focus on the "surface features" of music (Higgins, 2012), but note that diversity on the level of surface features of the music does *not* necessarily mean that there is diversity on the level of underlying mechanisms. For example, although music that evokes *nostalgia* in people in one culture may sound different from music that evokes *nostalgia* in listeners in a different culture, this does not rule out that the emotion is evoked for the same reason in both cultures—for instance, "bittersweet" episodic memories.

Hence, when it comes to mechanisms, it seems feasible to adopt a version of *moderate universalism*: an account of the arousal of emotions can be cross-culturally valid at the level of mechanisms, despite cross-cultural diversity in musical "surface features" and felt emotions (Juslin, 2012).

The truth is that we still know little about whether emotional reactions to music are invariant across cultures. Ethnographic studies carried out by anthropologists have revealed a number of cross-cultural differences in musical emotions in countries like Brazil (Seeger, 1987), Liberia (Stone, 1982), New Guinea (Feld, 1982), Peru (Turino, 1993), and India (Viswanathan & Cormack, 1998), but such studies tend to focus on how the emotions are conceptualized and interpreted by listeners, rather than on how the underlying psychological mechanisms work.

I concur with Judith Becker (2001) in her findings that every culture has its own "habitus of listening" —that is, its own tacit "mode" or "style" of listening to music that seems completely "natural," and that listeners learn through unconscious imitation of those around them. The "habitus" involves answers to questions such as "what is music listening?," "what emotions are appropriate?," and "how is the event framed?" Listeners develop dispositions to listen with a particular focus. Such inclinations do not rule out the possibility that the same mechanisms are at work in different cultures.

We recently conducted a web-survey study in a first attempt to estimate the prevalence of (i) specific emotional reactions, (ii) psychological mechanisms, and (iii) listening motives across cultural contexts (Juslin et al., 2016a). Specifically, 668 participants from six countries categorized as either "individualistic" (Australia, Sweden, United States) or "collectivistic" (Brazil, Kenya, Portugal) completed a web survey featuring 22 items which measured musical emotions in general ("semantic estimates"), the most recent emotion episode involving music ("episodic estimates"), and individual trait variables.

Results clearly showed that there *were* cross-cultural differences, but differences were fewer and smaller than expected, considering the enormous heterogeneity of music across different societies (e.g., Clayton, 2016). (This is similar to previous findings that suggest that for emotions, in general, cross-cultural similarities tend to be larger than cross-cultural differences; e.g., Scherer, 1997). However, some notable differences were, for instance, that *nostalgia–longing, spirituality–transcendence*, and *happiness–elation*, and the mechanism *episodic memory*, were more prevalent in "collectivist" cultures. Conversely, *sadness–melancholy* and the mechanism *musical expectancy* were more prevalent in "individualist" cultures.

Differences were at least partly explainable with respect to cultural context. To illustrate, the feeling of *spirituality–transcendence* was most prevalent in Kenya, where music and religion are closely intertwined (Kigunda, 2007). The two most frequently preferred musical styles there—gospel and hip-hop—are used by churches to evangelize youth (Kagema, 2013).

Figure 25.4 presents some results from this study for emotions and mechanisms, respectively. With the usual reservation about limitations of

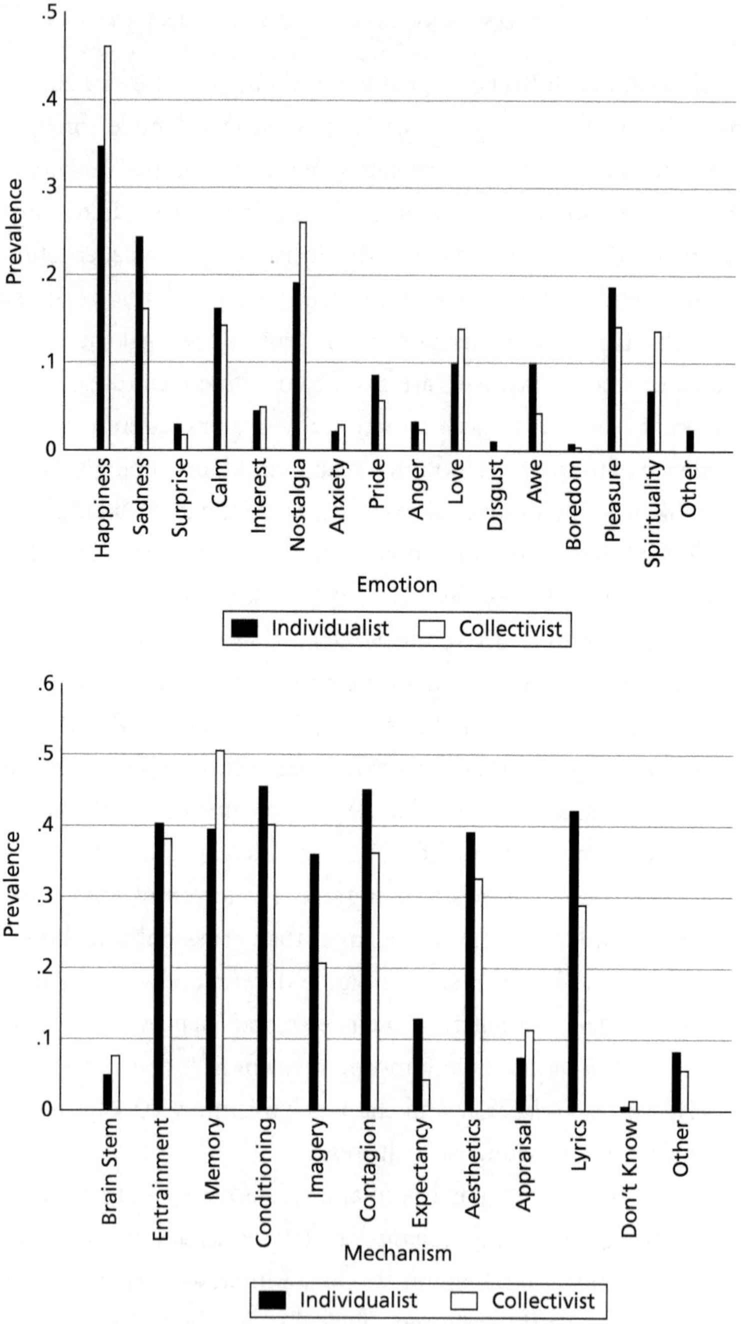

Figure 25.4 Prevalence of emotions and induction mechanisms in "individualist" and "collectivist" cultures, respectively.
Reproduced from Juslin, P. N., Barradas, G. T., Ovsiannikow, M., Limmo, J., & Thompson, W. F. (2016). Prevalence of emotions, mechanisms, and motives in music listening: A comparison of individualist and collectivist cultures. Psychomusicology: Music, Mind, and Brain, 26, 293–326. Copyright © 2016 American Psychological Association.

self-reports of causes, these data suggest that essentially the same psychological mechanisms occur across different cultures, even though the relative prevalence can vary. This is at least consistent with the idea that the mechanisms are products of evolution.

You may recall that one of the predictions in Table 25.1 concerned the degree of *cultural impact*. The influence of culture will most likely differ depending on the mechanism involved in a specific episode. For example, we would expect to find less cross-cultural diversity for brainstem reflexes than for statistically learned musical expectancies. However, such differences among mechanisms are difficult to test in a survey. This raises a more general question, namely how to measure and distinguish mechanisms empirically.

25.9 How Can Specific Mechanisms Be Investigated?

Speculating about possible causes is all very well, but if we want to be serious, we also need to *test* the theories to see whether they are correct. We need to translate the general principles of the mechanism framework into concrete research practices.

Most findings concerning mechanisms to date come from *field studies* that rely on self-report (e.g., Baumgartner, 1992; Janata, Tomic, & Rakowski, 2007; Juslin et al., 2008, 2011, 2016a, 2018). As much as they are useful in exploring the prevalence of musical emotions and their occurrence in different contexts, field studies also have a serious drawback: they do not enable us to draw strong conclusions about cause and effect, because there are too many confounding variables in the real world.

Another problem is that listeners can only report those psychological processes of which they are consciously aware. This means that implicit processes (e.g., many of the mechanisms) can only be studied by means of indirect methods, which are much easier to apply in a laboratory.

I argue that when it comes to testing theories about mechanisms, there is just no substitute for experiments. We must actively manipulate particular mechanisms so as to produce immediate behavioral effects in listeners. Being able to *predict* and *control* aroused emotions in terms of specific mechanisms is the ultimate evidence of a valid process description.

Teasing out the unique effects of different mechanisms in empirical research is somewhat tricky, however. Pieces of music often include information relevant to more than just one mechanism. Thus, in order to separate the effects of individual mechanisms, we need to be able to "activate" as well as "suppress" specific mechanisms in each case by manipulating aspects of the *music*, the *listener*, and the *situation*. This manipulation can be done in at least three principal ways (Juslin, 2013a):

First, one can select or manipulate pieces of music in such a way as to provide the information required for a certain mechanism to be activated, while excluding or removing other information (*the principle of information selection*). One possibility is to attempt to find existing pieces of music that feature information relevant to a particular mechanism. Use of "real" music makes it easier to arouse an intense emotion in listeners, but at the cost of reduced experimental control. To establish stronger causal conclusions, one can instead manipulate musical features by using synthesis, selecting a suitable "carrier" piece which is subsequently computer-edited, adding or removing various musical features relevant for certain mechanisms (Juslin et al., 2014).

Second, one can design the experimental test procedure in such a way that it will prevent the type of "information processing" required for a mechanism to be activated (*the principle of interference*). To illustrate: one can, for instance, give listeners a task that recruits attentional resources to such an extent that visual imagery—also dependent on these resources—will be made impossible. Modular mechanisms can still be activated (Juslin & Liljeström, in press).[5]

Third, one can manipulate characteristics of the listener. This could be done, for instance, by creating specific memories during the test procedure

[5] Another possibility may be to use a neurochemical interference strategy. For instance, it has been shown that blocking of a particular class of amino acid receptors (NMDA) in the lateral amygdala of the brain interferes with the acquisition of evaluative conditioning responses (Miserendino, Sananes, Melia, & Davis, 1990).

prior to presenting the "target" stimulus (*the principle of procedural history*), to enable study of memory-based mechanisms such as evaluative conditioning (Hellström & Laukka, 2015). One may create certain episodic memories in one participant group but not in another (contrast) group and then compare their responses.

In recent experiments (Juslin et al., 2014, 2015), we have manipulated four mechanisms, using both "synthesized" and "real" musical excerpts, which included "extreme" acoustic events (brainstem reflex), voice-like emotional expressions (contagion), unexpected musical sequences (musical expectancy), or were associated with emotional life events for many Swedish listeners (episodic memory), respectively. We relied on multiple measures in order to draw more valid conclusions about aroused emotions than would be possible from a single measure (see Chapter 15).

The results enabled us to draw the following conclusions. First, the experimental conditions aroused emotions in listeners largely in accordance with our predictions. The listeners' self-reports indicated, for example, that the brainstem reflex condition aroused the highest levels of *surprise*, and that the episodic memory condition aroused the highest levels of *nostalgia*.

Second, additional measures in terms of facial expression and autonomic response confirmed that listeners experienced *felt* emotions (as opposed to simply perceiving emotions expressed in the music), and the physiological patterns were consistent with the emotion ratings.

Third, the results did *not* just reflect commonly studied "surface features" of the music, such as tempo, sound level, or timbre. For example, contrary to such music-emotion correlations, the tempo could be faster in a piece that aroused *sadness* in listeners than in a piece that aroused *happiness*. This is because listeners' responses were driven by mechanisms (e.g., whether a particular memory was evoked), rather than by "surface features" per se.

In these studies we attempted to manipulate mechanisms one at the time. This is required to really understand how (or indeed if) each mechanism "works." In the "real" world, however, mechanisms could, of course, co-occur in response to a single piece of music. In fact, much of the richness of our emotional experiences with music is arguably due to complex interactions between different mechanisms (discussed further in Chapter 32).

These preliminary investigations suggest that a rigorous way forward is possible. Even so, the studies only scratch the surface of what needs to be done in order to properly evaluate a multi-mechanism framework. Much work remains to design clever experiments that enable us to study each mechanism, and although results look promising, there is more to the story.

For one thing, these studies were designed to maximize experimental control and to minimize the influence of contextual factors. Still, emotions aroused were not as neatly differentiated as one would like. "Hidden in the data," so to speak, are *individual differences* between listeners which cannot be avoided, even in a highly controlled context. Different listeners may activate distinct mechanisms to the same music (e.g., memory for one listener, contagion for another).

Hence, the common assumption that different listeners will react in the same way to a given piece of music is dubious, to say the least, casting doubts on attempts to use pieces of music as if they were medical pills. Note, however, that the BRECVEMA framework may be helpful in *explaining* individual differences between listeners, because it is precisely at the mechanistic level that such differences emerge.

Individual differences present a genuine challenge for the field of music and emotion, in my estimation. As neuroscientist Richard Davidson notes, "the fact of individual differences is the most salient characteristic of emotion" (Davidson, 2012, p. 7). Music researchers, it appears, have yet to understand the consequences of this condition. Doing so requires adopting a "statistical-ideographic" approach (Brunswik, 1956), where responses are first modeled on an individual level before they are aggregated. Such an "ideographic" approach will be illustrated in the next part of the book.

In this part, I have outlined a multi-level framework that explains emotional reactions to music in terms of a set of psychological mechanisms, which developed gradually and in a specific order during evolution. Together, these seven mechanisms are able to account for a wide range of affective responses—from *arousal* and startle responses to *happiness, sadness, contentment,* and *nostalgia.*

If you recall my list of mechanisms in Chapter 17, however, you might notice that there is one mechanism we have not actually dealt with yet: aesthetic judgment. One limitation of the seven mechanisms presented in previous chapters is that they do not appear able to explain emotions that relate specifically to the aesthetic value of music. Hence, one further mechanism needs to be added to the framework to account for what I call aesthetic emotions. Because this mechanism is arguably the most elusive of them all, it has generously received its own part of the book: Part IV.

PART IV

AESTHETIC JUDGMENT

CHAPTER 26

AESTHETICS

The Hard Problem?

The business of music should in some measure lead to the love of the beautiful.
—Plato, *The Republic*

26.1 There Is No Accounting for Taste—Or Is There?

You have probably heard the phrase a billion times: there is no accounting for taste. Aesthetic judgments seem too subjective, idiosyncratic, and unreliable to be investigated in a systematic manner. But is this view correct? What *is* the nature of aesthetic judgments? This, dear reader, may be the most difficult of all issues in the study of musical affect.

We are virtually surrounded by aesthetic judgments when engaging with musical events. Those judgments are made public in all sorts of ways: through applause, booing, or cheering at concerts ("the throwing of oranges seems to have been a more or less recognized means of expressing disappointment in the eighteenth century," according to Percy Scholes; Watson, 1991, p. 387.) Aesthetic judgments are also reflected in the buying of concert tickets and CDs, and in reviews of music by both critics and lay people. Reviews, in particular, tend to lay bare the implicit assumptions and expectations of listeners' aesthetic judgments.

When I read critical reviews of classical music concerts in daily newspapers in Sweden these days, the reviewers tend to be respectful of the composer and the musicians. What they write is frequently nonsense, but the tone is respectful. This was not always the case. Slonimsky's *Lexicon of Musical Invective* offers striking examples of "critical assaults" throughout history (cf. Figure 26.1).

"The art of composing without ideas has decidedly found in Brahms one if its worthiest representatives" (Slonimsky, 1969, p. 73, on Symphony No. 4).

"*American Scene* by Roy Harris proved to be not only monumental but colossal—a colossal failure" (Slonimsky, 1969, p. 107).

Figure 26.1 The music critic—feared and revered.
Illustration by Costis Chatzidakis.

"We must seriously pose the question as to what extent [the] musical profession can be criminal" (Slonimsky, 1969, p. 54, on Alban Berg's "Wozzeck").

"It seems too much like a sheer nothing, on the grandest possible scale ... It may be the Music of the Future, but it sounds remarkably like the Cacophony of the Present" (Slonimsky, 1969, p. 116, on Liszt's "Faust Symphony").

"Mahler had not much to say in his Fifth Symphony and occupied a wondrous time saying it" (Slonimsky, 1969, p. 121).

"*An American in Paris* is nauseous claptrap, so dull, patchy, thin, vulgar, long-winded and inane, that the average movie audience would be bored with it ... This cheap and silly affair seemed pitifully futile and inept" (Slonimsky, 1969, p. 105).

"The rambling cacophonies from Mr. Bloch's pen ... produced no effect except boredom ... Are there not enough horrors assailing the world at present without adding those of unnecessary dissonances?" (Slonimsky, 1969, p. 67, on Ernest Bloch's "Three Jewish Poems").

Yes, critical music reviews from the past can certainly make for amusing reading,[1] but aesthetic judgment is a serious matter. Aesthetic judgments occur in all kinds of situations and are of crucial importance to composers, performers, and listeners alike. For example, aesthetic judgments of music performance are usually made when applying for admission to a music conservatoire, or when musicians audition for a new job in an orchestra or a band. Aesthetic judgments have to be made by producers of records, and consumers are often guided by reviews that involve aesthetic judgments, and that may have a strong impact on sales and download numbers. In short, aesthetic judgments have consequences.

In addition, aesthetic judgments are also frequently at work when you engage attentively with music, and help to shape your music experience. This

[1] Artists in popular music are hardly spared. When Bob Dylan released the album *Self-portrait*, after a string of classic albums such as *Highway 61* and *Blonde on Blonde*, music critic Greil Marcus famously began his album review in the *Rolling Stone* magazine (June 8, 1970) with a question: "What is this shit?"

means that no account of musical affect can be complete without having addressed the role of aesthetic judgments.

So far, I have used the term "aesthetic judgment" as if it were perfectly clear what is meant by it, but this is not the case. Even scholars within the field of aesthetics acknowledge that they are "still a long way from sharing a cohesive account" (Schellekens, 2011, p. 224).

When lay people think about an aesthetic judgment, they frequently have a certain image in mind: they think of a connoisseur of fine art, an expert with considerable knowledge, skill, and taste who is carefully contemplating a serious work of art in order somehow, mysteriously, to assess its "true value." Surely, only experts are able to make proper judgments of aesthetic value?

Yet, at the same time, we have probably all found that experts sometimes disagree about the value of an artwork, or that they may be the victims of "prestige effects" (e.g., their judgments may be biased by irrelevant information in the context; section 31.2). Sometimes it is not even clear what *is* an artwork and what is not (and who decides?). At times, the art world looks like a big hoax.[2] What are we to make of all these impressions? Could psychology contribute to our understanding of these phenomena, particularly in the case of music?

26.2 Aims and Outline

In Part IV, we will look closer at the nature of aesthetic judgment. Are listeners' judgments of music reliable? What criteria do listeners rely on in such judgments? Are there individual differences in how these criteria are weighted? Could individual differences be explained by expertise? Which aesthetic criteria tend to be most influential? How are aesthetic judgments affected by contextual factors? How do aesthetic judgment, preference, and emotion relate to one another? Why do we sometimes like music that we

[2] Melchionne argues that "our taste is often incoherent, the practice of criticism is largely arbitrary, and creative practices something of a free-for-all" (Melchionne, 2011, p. 1).

judge as being of poor quality? Why do we respond to aesthetic objects *as if* they were real although we know they are not? How can aesthetic judgments be studied? Are aesthetic judgments related to moral judgments? Can negative emotions be enjoyable in art, and if so, why? How are aesthetic judgments related to the other emotion mechanisms?

We will address these ancient issues from a modern psychological perspective, taking several cues from philosophical aesthetics (e.g., Levinson, 2003). The focus will be on music and value, and how aesthetic judgments of music might influence preferences and emotions.

It makes sense to discuss this topic in the final part of the book. First, the aesthetic judgment mechanism is the most recent addition to the BRECVEMA framework (Juslin, 2013a). Second, if this framework is broadly correct, aesthetic judgment is also the most recent mechanism to develop throughout evolution. Third, theories and findings suggest that the sense of aesthetic value develops relatively late during child development (Swanwick, 2001).

It can further be argued that our aesthetic responses *integrate* the other mechanisms—and more—into a more complete and fulfilling experience. For some commentators, an aesthetic response remains the "ideal" response to a musical work. Some scholars suggest that one of the aims of music education should be to cultivate attitudes that predispose students towards aesthetic appreciation and sensitivity (Reimer, 1968). May it even be the case that the health benefits of music are maximized when the music experiences are not just emotional, but also profoundly aesthetic in a deeper sense?

Finally, aesthetic judgment is the mechanism in most urgent need of further research. Most psychologists are reluctant to explore aesthetics (Jacobsen, 2006), despite renewed interest with the arrival of the field of *neuroaesthetics* (Brattico & Pearce, 2013; Huston, Nadal, Mora, Agnati, & Cela-Conde, 2015; Shimamura, 2012).

I should explain at the outset that this Part will offer relatively less firm empirical evidence than the previous Parts of this book simply because there are fewer relevant studies. Disagreement about conceptual issues and a general lack of relevant data makes this aspect of musical affect the most challenging to explore.

Nonetheless, I believe it is possible to offer some preliminary observations regarding how aesthetic judgments can be conceptualized psychologically, and how they might relate to perceived and aroused emotions, as dealt with in Parts II and III. Personally, I find these research directions quite promising—and that is at least a start.

First, I will review seminal work in experimental aesthetics to illustrate how psychologists have tended to approach this complex topic. Then, having found this early work wanting, I will propose a novel approach which integrates notions from philosophical aesthetics with modern psychological theory, including a preliminary model which can offer a useful way forward. I will explain how preferences and emotions may be related to aesthetic judgment. Finally, I will consider how all the mechanisms considered so far in this book may *combine* with aesthetic judgments to produce the rich and holistic experiences that we have come to expect from our most treasured musical events in life (Gabrielsson, 2011).

In the process, I will reconnect with some of the themes in the book. I will show that aesthetic judgments are affected by various factors in the music, the listener, and the context (an "interactionist" view on aesthetics); that such judgments could be subject to strong social influences; and that there are limits to introspection, even in the case of aesthetic judgments. We will also see, once again, how musical affect involves multiple mechanisms.

Although I will devote much of Part IV to characterizing the nature of aesthetic judgment and its relationship to emotions, I should give a preliminary working definition of what I take to be an aesthetic response to avoid confusion and also to help to set the context for the subsequent discussion.

26.3 What May a Working Definition of Aesthetic Response Look Like?

First, I should explain that there are (at least) two distinct and broad uses of the term *aesthetic response* in the literature. Some authors have used the term to denote *all* reactions to anything remotely related to art—whether it is music, theater, film, or painting—regardless of the nature of the response. (According to this view, *everything* discussed in this book is "aesthetic" by definition.)

To illustrate: if you were to experience *surprise* when hearing a sudden, loud sound in a piece of music (e.g., through a brainstem reflex), this would be called an aesthetic response simply because it was a response to music. This broad use of the term does not exclude *any* affective response, which means that it cannot help us de-compose the different kinds of responses that might occur when we listen to music.

Hence, I will instead use the term in a second, more "narrow" sense to denote a *special* class of affective responses to music. (I shall defend this narrow use of the term later.) Expressed simply, *an aesthetic response occurs to the extent that an aesthetic judgment is being made.* Aesthetic responses, then, are responses that include but are not necessarily limited to some kind of aesthetic judgment.[3]

Aesthetic experience, in turn, simply refers to *consciously perceived* aspects of the aesthetic response. Aesthetic experiences of music can also include any number of regular aspects of music experience, such as perception, cognition, and emotion (Gabrielsson, 2011; Table 4.1). The only difference is that an aesthetic judgment has now been added to the mix.

With this definition of aesthetic experience, I do not intend to say that listeners cannot have intense, emotional, or valuable experiences of music without making an aesthetic judgment. (For instance, in Alf Gabrielsson's studies of strong experiences with music, there are many strong experiences that make no mention of aesthetic properties of the music.) It only states that responses to music that involve an aesthetic judgment might be distinct in certain ways, and that it can therefore be helpful for researchers to consider them separately. After having read Part IV, you can consider whether it makes sense to make this distinction, but for now I simply ask you to accept this premise.

[3] Note that whether we prefer to use the term "broadly" or "narrowly" is not really an issue that can be resolved empirically. However, I will try to show that a narrow use of the term is more heuristic in the study of musical affect.

To repeat, then, aesthetic responses are those that include some type of aesthetic judgment. The term *aesthetic judgment,* in turn, is used to refer to the process by which the value of a piece of music "as art" is determined, based on one or more subjective criteria that relate to properties of the artwork, either its form or its content. To illustrate, you may judge Johan Sebastian Bach's "The Well-Tempered Clavier" (BWV 846–893) as an aesthetically valuable piece of music, based on the perception of the *beauty* of its form. The nature of the aesthetic judgment process (henceforth just *aesthetic judgment*) will be further elaborated in section 30.2.

Aesthetic judgments can produce *outcomes,* in the form of preferences (liking) and emotions. In the BRECVEMA framework (Chapter 17), aesthetic judgment is considered a mechanism that may arouse emotions, alongside several other mechanisms. I will argue later that a lot of confusion has arisen in this field because aesthetic judgments *may* arouse emotions, but *need not* do so.

Why is there a tendency to think that aesthetic judgments *must* involve emotions? The most plausible reason is that when we try to recall an aesthetic experience, we tend to bring to mind events that were emotional, because emotional events are, in general, better remembered (Reisberg & Heuer, 2004). By contrast, we are less likely to recall events that involved aesthetic judgment, but that did *not* arouse emotions. As a result, in our mind, we tend to equate aesthetic judgment with emotions (as some philosophers have done; see Schellekens & Goldie, 2011). This is a gross oversimplification, as I intend to show later.

Aesthetic judgments are not unique in being partly independent from emotions. The same is true for other mechanisms discussed in Part III. To illustrate this, episodic memories may arouse emotions, but they also commonly occur without emotions. (If asked, you may recall where and when you had lunch yesterday, but your episodic memory of that event is unlikely to evoke any emotion unless the event was special in some way.) We are reminded, yet again, of the overlap between systems that serve "cognition" and "emotion," respectively, in the brain (Pessoa, 2013).

26.3 A WORKING DEFINITION OF AESTHETIC RESPONSE

We will soon look closer at these complex phenomena, but first I shall briefly review how psychologists have *traditionally* approached aesthetic responses, quite differently from the above conceptualization. This survey will serve to illustrate the need for a novel approach, which is presented in the following chapters.

CHAPTER 27

TRADITIONAL APPROACHES TO AESTHETICS

Although empirical aesthetics might be regarded as one of the oldest subfields in psychology (Fechner, 1876), psychologists have generally been reluctant to study aesthetic responses (Lazarus, 1991). When they *have* done it, their approach has frequently deviated from that of classical aesthetics.

Thus, for example, whereas most philosophers tend to discuss aesthetic responses in terms of rare and complex "peak" experiences which involve sublime works of art, psychologists have instead focused on more mundane responses to artworks, such as preference for simple stimulus features (e.g., Hargreaves & North, 2010). Ideas from philosophical aesthetics have, on the whole, not been very influential on the work of psychologists (Silvia, 2012).

27.1 Empirical Aesthetics: Meet Daniel Berlyne

The most important contribution to the field was made by Daniel Berlyne, who launched the "new empirical aesthetics." Although some of the research presented in his two books (Berlyne, 1960, 1971) is now dated, his work is still worthwhile reading and is full of insight.

In accordance with the prevailing zeitgeist of the 1960s, Berlyne mainly focuses on the notion of autonomic arousal as opposed to discrete emotions. He argues that art influences its perceivers largely by manipulating their arousal. At the basis of Berlyne's theoretical framework is the idea that every organism strives to keep itself at some moderate level of arousal. Berlyne posits that listeners prefer music that gives them some *optimum* level of arousal. If the arousal potential of the music is too high, listeners will reject the music. Similarly, if the arousal potential is too low, listeners will also reject the music—they will be bored to death, figuratively speaking.

For example, you may find a children's song to be so simple that it is boring. On the other hand, you may find a piece of avant-garde jazz or a piece from the new Vienna School of classical music so unpredictable and complex that it is stressful to hear. You will find a more "optimal" level of complexity by listening to pieces such as "All Blues" by Miles Davis and "Kashmir" by Led Zeppelin, thus resulting in a moderate level of arousal.

Accordingly, Berlyne suggests that listeners' preferences are related to arousal in the form of an inverted U-shaped curve, sometimes referred to as the Wundt curve (Figure 27.1). The variables that mediate the arousal potential of the stimulus include "psychophysical variables" (e.g., speed), "ecological variables" (e.g., associations), and "collative variables" (information characteristics of the stimulus, such as complexity). To illustrate: music that

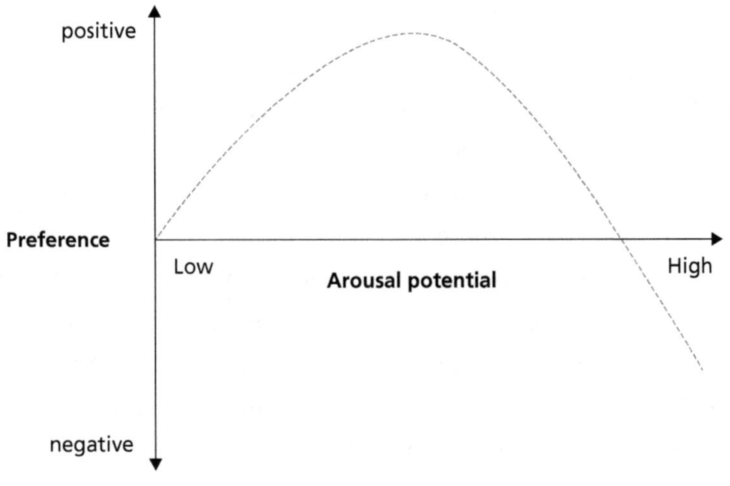

Figure 27.1 Inverted U-shaped curve describing the relationship between arousal potential and preference (liking).

is complex, fast, or unpredictable will tend to be more arousing than music that is simple, slow, or predictable.[1]

Why is moderate arousal preferred? The reason, according to Berlyne, is that the fibers of the reticular activating system associated with arousal pass through both pleasure and displeasure centers on their way to higher brain areas. However, the pleasure center has a lower threshold level and a lower asymptotic level than the displeasure center, therefore a moderate level of cortical arousal will be preferred to either extreme. (Note that Berlyne focuses on preferences rather than emotions.)

Berlyne's model has received some support in empirical studies. One example is a study by Paul Vitz (1966), which focused on complexity, as conceptualized in terms of "information theory" (Shannon & Weaver, 1949). The notion of *redundancy* may be used to describe the amount of information in a given stimulus: the less redundancy in the stimulus, the more information it contains; the more information it contains, the higher the complexity.

This applies also to stimuli that extend in time, like music. A stimulus that contains a great deal of redundancy is one whose continuation is easy to predict from its structure. Such a stimulus may be said to have a low level of complexity. In the experiment by Vitz, complexity was varied by controlling variability along such dimensions as pitch, volume, and duration in brief tone sequences. As predicted by Berlyne's theory, listeners preferred moderate levels of stimulus complexity to either extreme.

One might, of course, object that the music stimuli used in the Vitz experiment are relatively simple as compared to "real" music. Can the same results be obtained with more "ecologically valid" music? One example is the study by Michael Burke and Mark Gridley, in which they asked musically trained and untrained listeners to report liking for a selection of piano works such as Debussy's "The Girl with the Flaxen Hair" and Boulez's Piano Sonata No. 1. (Burke & Gridley, 1990). Burke and Gridley also asked seven professors of music to rate the complexity of each piece. They then plotted

[1] Some of these effects can readily be explained by the BRECVEM mechanisms discussed previously throughout Part III.

listeners' preferences against the professors' ratings of complexity. Again, they found an inverted U-curve: preferences were highest for pieces of intermediate complexity.

27.2 How Is Preference for Complexity Influenced by Familiarity?

Several studies have indicated that preference for complexity might be moderated by other factors such as *familiarity* with the stimulus. Thus, for instance, Herbert Krugman asked his participants whether they preferred (and listened) to jazz or classical music (Krugman, 1943). Then he exposed them to their disliked category of music once a week for eight weeks. The results showed that for a majority of the subjects, their liking increased for the previously disliked category of music after exposure, and some listeners decided they liked this category even *better* than the one they preferred at the start.

Helen Mull adopted a more short-term approach (Mull, 1957). She was curious to know whether repeated listening to works by unfamiliar composers might increase liking of the music. To test the hypothesis, Mull played examples of such works by Arnold Schoenberg and Paul Hindemith to 16 music students five times in close succession. Results showed that this exposure enhanced the listeners' liking as compared to base ratings.

Russell Getz claims that the maximum effect of repetition will be reached around the sixth or eighth repetition (Getz, 1966), but this is likely to depend both on the music and on the listener. David Hargreaves found that listeners' ratings of preference for avant-garde jazz did not increase over several repetitions (Hargreaves, 1982). Even so, American composer Roger Sessions submits that "the key to the understanding of contemporary music lies in repeated hearing: one must hear it until it sounds familiar" (Watson, 1991, p. 84).

But why do our preferences change even if the level of complexity stays the same? How can familiarity effects be explained? William Gaver and

Georger Mandler propose a distinction between two aspects of complexity (Gaver & Mandler, 1987). *Physical complexity* refers to the redundancy of information in the stimulus, an objective feature of the stimulus that remains invariant as long as the stimulus itself remains invariant. *Psychological complexity* is the product of both the physical complexity and the listener's knowledge of its structure.

The psychological complexity could change with repetition because the listener's knowledge about the structure increases. Indeed, knowledge is crucially involved in the appreciation of art. It enables perceivers to form expectations, which help them to interpret the artwork and direct attention to its salient features (Gombrich, 1969). This can explain why experts sometimes prefer more complex artworks than novices (Hare, 1974).

Thus, although many of the variables investigated by Berlyne can be quantified objectively, studies suggest that it is the *subjective* experience of these variables that counts rather than their objective nature. For instance, depending on your knowledge and/or familiarity with a piece, *you* may find this music fairly simple whereas *I* find the same music rather complex. Psychological complexity is a far better predictor of preferences than the objective complexity.

We can now understand how mere repetition can increase preference. Increased exposure to a piece or style of music provides the listener with more opportunities for understanding the piece or style, increasing the listener's knowledge of the structure. With each increase in knowledge comes greater familiarity (and confirmed expectations!), and hence increased preference.

Note, however, that the effects of familiarity do not reflect just interactions with complexity. Familiar music can also enable a larger number of mechanisms for arousal of emotions to be activated (e.g., evaluative conditioning and episodic memory). Thus, we may prefer familiar music partly because it is more likely to arouse (positive) emotions than is unfamiliar music. This is certainly true, up to a point: repeated listening to a piece may also lead us to like the piece *less*. According to Berlyne, "simple music" (i.e., music with a low level of physical complexity) should be liked less with exposure to it, whereas "complex music" should be liked more (Berlyne, 1970).

Ronald Heyduk explored this interaction of complexity with familiarity in influencing music preference (Heyduk, 1975). Four piano pieces were constructed, each representing different degrees of physical complexity in terms of their chordal and rhythmic characteristics (e.g., syncopation). Each piece was judged by listeners on a "likeability" scale. Results indicated that most listeners had some initial level of preferred complexity. Each listener then listened to one of the pieces an additional 16 times (!).

Heyduk assumed that *psychological complexity* (the product of both the physical complexity and the listener's knowledge of its structure) would decrease with exposure. He also assumed that the effect of exposure would depend on the listener's initially preferred complexity level. Indeed, Heyduk found that if the repeated piece was of a psychological complexity far higher than the preferred level of the listener, as shown by his or her initial ratings, liking of the music increased as a function of repeated exposure.

However, if the repeated piece was of a complexity much lower than the preferred level, liking of the piece decreased with repeated exposure. The results show that the preferred level of complexity is different for different people. Heyduk thus concludes that "repeated exposure effects are a function of both situational and individual factors" (Heyduk, 1975, p. 84).[2]

Most studies reviewed thus far have used simple and, arguably, artificial experimental stimuli. Can similar effects be obtained with more "ecologically valid" stimuli from the "real" world? The answer comes from a study by musicologist Tuomas Eerola, which featured the 12 UK albums by the Beatles (Eerola, 1997). Eerola used computer techniques to score each of the songs with regard to objective complexity, and calculated an "overall complexity" score for each album. He then compared that score with the number of weeks the album stayed in the charts.

[2] This shows, once again, that we cannot understand responses to music by analysing *only* the music (Chapter 2).

Results revealed that albums of a relatively low musical complexity, such as *Please Please Me*, peaked early in the charts, but then failed to sustain this early popularity. More complex albums like *Abbey Road* and *Sgt Pepper's Lonely Hearts Club Band*, which took longer to peak when first released, received higher levels of continued sales and higher critical acclaim.

Another example is provided by Dean Keith Simonton's studies of the *melodic originality* of music compositions (Simonton, 2010; discussed in Box 7.1). Simonton found that objective indicators of a classical work's relative impact and popularity are related to its arousal potential—as indexed by melodic originality—in roughly the same way proposed by Berlyne.

His analysis featured 15,618 themes which define the classical repertoire. Objective ratings gauged the frequency that a composition is likely to be heard in the concert hall, opera house, or recording studio. The relationship between this measure and estimates of melodic originality was neither linear positive nor linear negative but curvilinear. The most popular compositions were those that have moderate levels of melodic originality, whereas the most unpopular compositions were those with the highest levels of originality. Compositions with low originality had more middling popularity. This is perhaps because although classical music varies in originality, it is seldom completely derivative and boring as other types of music can be.

27.3 Do We Prefer (Proto)Typical Artworks?

Berlyne's approach received some support, but some scholars felt that it was insufficient to account for aesthetic responses. A rival approach was thus proposed by Colin Martindale. His basic hypothesis is that people's aesthetic likes and dislikes are based on "preference for prototypes" (Martindale, 1984).

Prototype theory has its origin in the work by psychologist Eleanor Rosch (1978). It suggests that membership in a certain category, for instance *birds*, is determined by resemblance to prototypical exemplars; the prototype itself is an abstract schema that consists of a set of weighted features representing the exemplar of a category of instances. In the *bird* category, for example, robins are presumably more prototypical than are penguins, because the latter lack the key feature of being able to fly. The idea is that we classify our everyday experiences by comparing them to prototypes for those types of experience.

Martindale's theory states that, other things being equal, we prefer prototypical stimuli in art. This idea was partly inspired by the notion of *neural networks*. Martindale and Moore conceive of the mind as consisting of interconnected cognitive units, each of which holds the representation of a different object. Units coding more prototypical stimuli are activated more frequently, since these stimuli are experienced more frequently than atypical ones (Martindale & Moore, 1988). Thus, they propose that "aesthetic preference is hypothetically a positive function of the degree to which the mental representation of a stimulus is activated. Because more typical stimuli are coded by mental representations capable of greater activation, preference should be positively related to prototypicality" (Martindale & Moore, 1988, p. 661).

Martindale and Moore (1989) examined this idea with regard to listeners' liking for themes in classical music, and found that 51% of the variance was accounted for by typicality measures, whereas only 4% was accounted for by complexity, suggesting that complexity may not be as important as Berlyne (1971) thought in the context of other stimulus variables (see also Juslin & Isaksson, 2014, for further evidence that complexity per se may not be very important).

However, David Hargreaves and Adrian North maintain that both theories could be correct and that they may, in fact, be complementary (Hargreaves & North, 2010). Furthermore, complexity and typicality are not independent of one another. To illustrate, what is "typical" for a specific style of music could in part be its complexity level. (Pieces of jazz fusion are usually more complex than pieces of disco pop.)

Why do listeners prefer "typical" themes? The explanation is that more typical stimuli produce greater neural activation, and that such neural activation in itself is pleasurable for the listener. I have never found this explanation convincing, and the above findings can indeed be explained differently.

One might argue that preference for typical music is *confounded* with familiarity: is it simply that prototypical musical themes are perceived as more familiar and therefore are more liked? Perhaps familiar stimuli are just easier to process perceptually. According to the "perceptual fluency theory" (Reber, Schwarz, & Winkielman, 2004; see section 29.1), we like stimuli that are easy to process.

Finally, as noted by Paul Silvia, typicality can be difficult to specify in a more general sense, because an artwork may be "typical" or "atypical" on a range of different categories (Silva, 2012). In short, questions abound when it comes to interpreting our (apparent) preference for typicality.

27.4 New Empirical Aesthetics: A Critical Appraisal

Let us now take stock of what empirical aesthetics has contributed to our understanding of aesthetic responses to music. One of the criticisms that may be leveled at both Berlyne and Martindale is that they focus almost exclusively on "stimulus properties," with little or no consideration of *contextual* factors. As we will see later, aesthetic responses can clearly be affected by the context.

More recent studies by David Hargreaves and his co-workers offer a much more dynamic view, conceptualized in terms of their *reciprocal feedback model* (Hargreaves, MacDonald, & Miell, 2005). Like Tia DeNora (2000), they suggest that listeners choose music according to "arousal state goals" which might change over time, depending on the "functions" of the music in a specific context. Music is used as a "resource" to achieve various goals, sometimes to *increase* arousal, sometimes to *decrease* it. What counts as "optimal" arousal (cf. Berlyne, 1971) depends on the goal. This approach, then, is more context sensitive and uses "ecologically valid" music stimuli; in short, real music (for a good overview, see North & Hargreaves, 2008).

However, like Berlyne, Hargreaves and colleagues focus primarily on *arousal*, rather than on more nuanced states (e.g., *awe*). Does art really *aim* at manipulating arousal? At first glance, it can seem so: many artworks that are considered "great" have (or at least had on their premiere) an arousing effect. Surely artworks that leave us bored cannot be successful?

Yet the aim of an artist is seldom merely to arouse an "optimum" level of arousal in listeners; this sounds more like the aim of the Muzak company, which offers piped music to shops and elevators. Certainly, pieces of music can provide just the right amount of arousal, but an artist probably *aims* for something else, such as to create something beautiful or expressive.

Similarly, a listener's aesthetic experience cannot be reduced to a certain amount of arousal. When we seek out an aesthetic experience with music, we expect more than this. All things being equal, we may indeed like stimuli that evoke a moderate degree of arousal, but all things are most definitely not equal. That is the problem. We attend concerts in order to admire the skill of a musician; react with wonder at the wittiness of a composition; are shocked by the novelty of a piece; or derive pleasure from the beauty of a harmonic progression. In Berlyne's model, the focus is merely on an optimum level of arousal. Yet, mere arousal does not amount to much by way of an aesthetic experience; if this was the case, we would be content with the arousal induced by a brainstem reflex (Chapter 18).

While listeners admittedly sometimes choose music to achieve an optimum level of arousal for a particular context or activity (Hargreaves & North, 2010), listeners might also simply select a piece of music and let their arousal (or valence, for that matter) go wherever the music takes it. That is, the main aim is to explore the *music*, and any changes in arousal that may occur are secondary to that aim. In addition, when we engage more *deeply* with music, it seems, we can experience it in a slightly different way, and this has not been addressed in empirical aesthetics so far.

What scholars in empirical aesthetics have in common is that they tend to define an aesthetic response in a very broad manner as *any* response a person may have to a work of art. (According to this view, getting annoyed by the loud music played by a neighbor might qualify as an "aesthetic response.") Such a definition fails to distinguish the *special* nature of some experiences, which involve regarding an artwork with a focus on aesthetic properties in what is commonly called "an aesthetic attitude" (Fenner, 1996; see Chapter 28).

Berlyne and Martindale explored *some* aspects that could play a role in aesthetic experiences, such as emotional arousal and style, but left out many other aspects (e.g., beauty) that may be regarded as equally important (Chapter 29). It can also be argued that the "collative" variables studied by Berlyne (e.g., uncertainty, novelty, complexity) are perhaps in a sense *one* variable. Factor-analytic research suggests that they are based on the same underlying factor (Silvia, 2012). Finally, some of the variables explored in the Berlyne approach (e.g., speed) may not even be considered important or relevant as criteria for judgments of aesthetic value by music listeners.

Recall that aesthetic judgment was defined as the process through which the value of a piece of music "as art" is determined, based on one or more subjective criteria relating to properties of the artwork, either its form or its content. I might easily rate my liking for tone sequences with fast versus slow speed, but this task does not necessarily require a judgment of aesthetic value. We do not normally assess the aesthetic value of a piece of music based on its tempo unless, perhaps, we are dealing with the genre of "speed metal"!

The complicating factor, as I intend to show, is that whereas aesthetic judgments always lead to preferences (like or dislike), preferences are not always based on aesthetic judgments. We can like a piece of music for any number of reasons (e.g., just because it helps us fall asleep) which may have nothing to do with aesthetic properties of the music. Thus, whether studies in empirical aesthetics have looked at aesthetic judgment, as defined here, is open for debate.

I will stick my chin out and say that although they are studies of preference, they are not, generally, studies of aesthetic judgment. We have no reason to doubt the findings from studies in empirical aesthetics, but they are more relevant to an understanding of preferences for music in a non-aesthetic context of everyday music listening (Sloboda, 2010; Chapter 31).

27.4 A CRITICAL APPRAISAL

My view of the work by Daniel Berlyne and his followers is that they have made pioneering efforts to understand preferences for various stimulus properties. Still, it must be said that neither preference (liking) nor aesthetic judgment (as defined previously) can be explained merely in terms of manipulation of arousal level. These theories seem too limited in scope to be able to explain those aspects of our experiences that seem distinctly aesthetic. Paul Silvia is even more blunt: "showing contrived stimuli to abject beginners and measuring how much they like it strikes me as a poor paradigm for arts research" (Silvia, 2012, p. 270).

CHAPTER 28

WHAT'S SPECIAL?

Adopting the Aesthetic Attitude

Is there anything uniquely aesthetic? If so, what is it? There is no universal agreement on the answers to these questions (Schellekens, 2011), which we will grapple with repeatedly in the following sections. However, one "hint" was provided in Chapter 27: that an aesthetic experience may involve a special mode of music listening, which differs in some respects, at least, from other modes. Following a long and not entirely uncontroversial tradition in aesthetics, I will refer to this as *the aesthetic attitude*. Is there such a thing, and if so, what distinguishes it?

28.1 What's in an Aesthetic Attitude?

Perhaps, a good starting point may be to look for cases that no-one with a straight face would argue are instances of "aesthetic experience" of music (casting aside the over-general use of the term; section 26.3). In Part III, I outlined several mechanisms that may arouse emotions in music. We saw that we can be emotionally affected by a piece of music without even consciously attending to the sounds, if this music has become associated with a certain emotion via evaluative conditioning (Chapter 21). Technically speaking, this is an emotional response to music. Still, no-one would presumably argue that this is an *aesthetic* experience.

If we rule out *this* case as an example of "aesthetic response," we have already conceded that that there are some responses that are "more aesthetic" than others. The "only" question, then, is how to make the distinction—where to draw the line. One may propose a range of different answers to this question, most of which will not lead to a clear distinction.

In my view, the most promising way to distinguish aesthetic responses from other responses is to define them in terms of an aesthetic judgment, as triggered by an aesthetic attitude. The latter means that the listener's attention is focused on the music and that one or more criteria for aesthetic value are brought to bear on the music, whether explicitly or implicitly (Juslin, 2013a). (A *criterion* is usually defined as something such as a standard, which is used as a reason for making a judgment or decision.)

Why do we react *differently* to a piece of music in the concert hall than we do hearing the same piece in a shopping mall? To put it more broadly, why do we react differently to a can of beans at a museum of modern art than we do at a shopping mall? It is because in one of these contexts we adopt an aesthetic attitude, which brings with it a certain frame of mind and particular dimensions of evaluation (discussed in more detail in Chapter 29).

Let me briefly illustrate the difference with two hypothetical cases. In the first case, you sit at home, studying for a test. To try to keep yourself motivated, you put on some rhythmic music in the background. Your focus is mainly on the book you are reading, although you might be stamping your feet. As time passes, you notice that the background music has enhanced your energy level and made you more cheerful.

In the second case, you put on a piece of music in order to listen to it carefully. As you listen, you pay attention to the form of the music and its content; you evaluate the skill of the performer, the beauty of the harmonic progression, or the originality of the rhythmic pattern. You conclude that this is an excellent piece, and you experience a sense of wonder. Only in this case did you adopt an aesthetic attitude.

Not all philosophers agree that there is such a thing as a uniquely aesthetic attitude, but we should remember that philosophers often rely on their own introspection to form their views (section 3.5). My view is that there are individual differences in this regard: some listeners rarely experience events or objects with an aesthetic attitude; others may do so very frequently, even in many contexts that may not ordinarily be considered "aesthetic." We can find aesthetic pleasure in sport, for instance.[1]

For some listeners, especially those with little interest in music, an aesthetic attitude toward the music may be quite rare or non-existent. (There is probably a large percentage of "everyday music listening" which does not involve an aesthetic attitude; Sloboda, 2010.) For others, particularly those who have a deep and/or professional interest in music, an aesthetic attitude may be the predominant listening mode. Individual differences of this kind might explain some of the controversies in the field; many scholars approach the subject based on their own way of engaging with music.

How can we be sure that there is such a thing as an aesthetic attitude? Is there evidence that our perception of an event or object can change depending on the attitude we adopt towards it, or that there is a change in brain activity? Indeed, a brain imaging study suggests that the brain's activity changes when people view paintings with an aesthetic attitude compared to when they view the same paintings merely to extract certain visual information (Cupchik, Vartanian, Crawley, & Mikulis, 2009). In other words, our brains *do* seem to process stimuli differently when they are perceived as aesthetic. We have no reason to believe that the same is not true for music. In fact, certain pieces of music (e.g., John Cage's *4'33"*) make no sense at all without adopting an aesthetic attitude!

It may be tempting here to link the aesthetic attitude to certain kinds of music (e.g., classical) rather than others (e.g., pop), and perhaps some moderate correlations of this kind do indeed exist. Yet, there are plenty of dinner parties where classical music is being played and where there is not an aesthetic attitude in sight. Similarly, there are many discerning "pop connoisseurs" who regularly adopt an aesthetic attitude when listening to music (Frith, 1996).

Few music psychologists have adopted the position that aesthetic responses are distinct or that they involve an aesthetic attitude. Therefore, to

[1] This is the reason why some philosophers like to make a distinction between the subfields of *philosophy of art* and *aesthetics*: aesthetic responses are not necessarily limited to works of art (Gracyk, 2012).

investigate these notions in more detail, and to understand the kind of perceptual dimensions that may come into play, we will have to turn to a neighboring field for guidance.

28.2 Back to the Foundation: Philosophical Aesthetics

I have previously suggested that our aesthetic responses to music are characterized by the inclusion of a process of aesthetic judgment, triggered by an aesthetic attitude (Juslin, 2013a). The nature of aesthetic judgments is traditionally investigated within the field of aesthetics, the branch of philosophy devoted to conceptual and theoretical inquiry into art and aesthetic experience (for an excellent overview, see Levinson, 2003). Still, it is fair to say that several hundred years of philosophical work has failed to yield a consensus that can guide empirical research in a straightforward way. (That is not really the main aim of philosophy in any case.)

Part of the problem is defining "art," with some scholars arguing that the concept is inherently open, and so resistant to definition (Weitz, 1956). As soon as someone attempts to delimit the concept of art, it is not long before an artist will attempt to revolt against that definition. (How would *you* define art?) However, as noted in Chapter 4, we should not get too hung up on finding the perfect definition first; this could be the end result rather than the starting point.

Definitions aside, common conceptions of "aesthetic experience" emphasize its focus on the object's *form* (e.g., elements of art, design principles, and physical materials) and/or *content* (e.g., the semantic content, including what the artist intends or what the audience perceives). Can a focus on the music's form and content thus serve as a defining feature of the aesthetic judgment process? Not really: *all* the mechanisms described in Part III engage, in one way or another, with the form and/or content of the music; thus, this is not unique to an aesthetic appreciation. What *is* the unique aspect?

Philosopher Jerrold Levinson notes that "aesthetic properties are perceptual properties relevant to the aesthetic value of the object that possesses them"

(Levinson, 2003, p. 6). Similarly, philosopher Malcolm Budd notes that "for you to experience a work with (full) understanding your experience must be imbued with an awareness of (all) the aesthetically relevant properties of the work—the properties that ground the attribution of artistic value" (Budd, 1995, p. 4).

In other words, the aesthetic attitude may be conceived as bringing a focus on the properties of music that are regarded as relevant for its value as art. Not every conceivable feature of the musical event is relevant to its "aesthetic status" (e.g., Gopnik, 2012). To illustrate: when you make an aesthetic judgment of a guitar solo by Mark Knopfler, the color or shape of his Gibson Les Paul guitar is, presumably, not a feature you will consider relevant for assessing the *aesthetic* value of the *notes* emanating from his guitar.

Aesthetic judgments are based on properties of the music and of the listener and context. In philosophers' terminology, we say they exhibit a *supervenient* relationship. This occurs when the existence of one thing depends on the presence or particular arrangement of certain other things. To illustrate: an aesthetic judgment may depend on certain properties, such as beauty, which in turn may depend on low-level musical features, such as order and symmetry. What, then, are the relevant properties?

28.3 What Properties Distinguish Art?

A natural point of departure for a consideration of aesthetic aspects of a given music experience is to take stock of writings within the field of aesthetics. Theorists have proposed a large number of properties that can help to distinguish and define art. The only property for which there is a fairly strong consensus is that an artwork must involve an *artifact* of some kind—it must be a product of human activity. Musical compositions and performances clearly fulfill this requirement.[2]

[2] But what if a piece of music is generated by a *computer* according to some elaborate algorithm: could that still be considered art?

28.3 WHAT PROPERTIES DISTINGUISH ART?

What other features might distinguish art? A review of European concepts of art put forward from ancient Greece to modernity suggests that the following notions have been influential (Juslin, 2013a; for extensive overviews, see Levinson, 2003; Scruton, 1997):

- art as possessing formal properties such as *beauty* (Kant, 2000), *complexity* (Berlyne, 1971), *wittiness* (Levinson, 2003), or the *sublime* (Lyotard, 1994)
- art as *expression* (e.g., "clarifying an emotion"; Collingwood, 1938)
- art as *originality* (e.g., "modernism"; Kraus, 1986)
- art as *good taste* (e.g., "the absence of extremes"; Fechner, 1876)
- art as *artistic skill* (e.g., "fashioning objects that are admired"; Sparshott, 1982)
- art as *reception* (e.g., "feelings in the audience"; Tolstoy, 1960)
- art as conveying a *message* ("implicitly advancing some proposition"; Levinson, 2001)
- art as defined by *institutions* ("art is what art schools, museums, and artists define as arts"; Dickie, 1974)
- art as *representation* of nature ("mimesis"; Plato, 1923)
- art as *intention* ("art is something produced with the intention of giving the capacity to satisfy aesthetic interest"; Beardsley, 1982)
- art as *historical development* (e.g., "an object that a person intends to be seen as a work of art"; Levinson, 1990)

Note that some of these notions of art focus on properties of the work itself; others focus more on the social-historical context of the artwork or the perceiver. Moreover, many of the notions involve attempts at a *functional* definition of art, specifying what purpose art serves (e.g., to express emotions, imitate nature, or convey messages).

However, the purpose of art is constantly changing (Hodge, 2017). A problem, then, is that "different artworks are correctly valued for performing very different functions, and therefore there cannot be a unifying functional definition of art" (Gracyk, 2012, p. 108). Thus, it has proved difficult to formulate a classic definition of art in terms of a set of necessary and sufficient conditions.

There have been few attempts to integrate different theories into a common framework. Just as with old theories of music and emotion, art theories tend to be "monolithic" (section 2.3). Most theories also have a normative ("prescriptive"), as opposed to descriptive, focus, which presents another problem for psychological application. They aim to capture what art *is* or *ought* to be in a universal sense.

Ruth Lorand concludes that attempts to develop a normative aesthetics have in general been found wanting or ineffective (Lorand, 2007). What seems to be lacking is a minimum level of consensus among judges of art in the relevant community (Eggerman, 1975; Hogan, 1994). Considering that perceivers cannot even agree about the aesthetic value of mere rectangles (McManus, Cook, & Hunt, 2010), how could they agree about such an infinitely more complex artwork as a symphony?

Fortunately, however, because psychology is *descriptive*, it does not have to grapple with the thorny issue of "objective" aesthetic value; in other words, we do not have to resolve the issue what art *really* is (in a universal sense). It is sufficient to describe and explain actual aesthetic judgments made by music listeners in a specific context. This project is arguably more feasible (see Chapter 31).

Are any of the theories of art just cited relevant to understanding ordinary music listeners? Is your music experience affected by aesthetics? Your answer may depend on your interest in art and the extent to which you are familiar with these theories. It has been argued that such theories *do* influence our everyday experiences of art, however, reflecting that criteria for aesthetic value are, to a considerable extent, *socially constructed*. This is partly why aesthetic norms change so much over time.

Blake Gopnik submits that scholars need to pay attention to what "art experts" say because they determine to a large extent what counts as the salient features and effects of works of art, even for lay consumers of art (Gopnik, 2012). I believe that an effective psychological theory, one that can account for listeners' actual responses, must take *their* criteria as a point of departure, rather than the criteria embraced by art theorists. Can theories of art be reconciled with how "ordinary" music listeners conceive of this matter? This is where our journey must involve empirical data again.

28.4 Do Listeners Think of Music as "Art"? On What Grounds?

Postulating that aesthetic responses require an aesthetic attitude is all very well, but we may have ignored one important requirement: do listeners really consider music "art" in the first place? If not, then the whole enterprise of developing a theory of aesthetic judgment for music would appear to be poorly guided.

We made a first attempt to investigate everyday conceptions of music as art in a survey study conducted in Uppsala (Juslin & Isaksson, 2014). Do "regular" music listeners consider music "art"? If so, what are the most important criteria for regarding a piece of music as "art"? What is the role of emotions in such judgments? These issues are related to the distinction between "high" and "low" culture in society (DiMaggio, 1987). What distinguishes music as one of the "fine arts" from music as "mere entertainment" or a commercial commodity?

A 13-item questionnaire was administered to 72 Swedish participants (18–43 years old) who studied either psychology or music at a conservatory level. In response to the item "do you consider music art?", 35% of the listeners answered "always," 46% responded "often," 18% responded "sometimes," and only 1% responded "never." Surprisingly, the tendency to consider music "art" was not influenced by music education. Psychology students and music students were equally inclined to consider music art, although music students rated aesthetic value as more important for their choice of music in everyday life than psychology students.

The 99% of the participants who considered at least *some* music to be "art" were asked to rate the relative importance of different aesthetic criteria with respect to music. The list of criteria was largely based on the notions outlined in section 28.3, and also featured aspects that have been investigated in the "new empirical aesthetics" (Berlyne, 1971).

Before reading any further, think about it: which criteria for aesthetic value of music are most crucial, in your view? Now compare these with the listeners' responses in the survey study. Figure 28.1 presents some results in terms of mean ratings across listeners and some examples of ratings by individual listeners.

Three things are apparent from the results. First, there seems to be no *single* aesthetic criterion that may account for listeners' aesthetic judgments of music.

Second, some criteria (e.g., *expressivity, emotional arousal, originality, skill, message,* and *beauty*) are rated as far more important than others, overall. Note that some of the variables studied in the "new empirical aesthetics", such as *familiarity* and *complexity*, are *not* in general rated as important by music listeners. These results make sense: Although familiarity with a piece might increase liking per se (Peretz, Gaudreau, & Bonnel, 1998), it may not be an important factor when judging specifically the *aesthetic* value of the music.

Similarly, mere complexity might not be sufficient for a high rating. To illustrate: consider a purely *random* pattern of musical notes. The pattern has a low level of redundancy (i.e., high complexity), yet few listeners would consider this pattern aesthetically valuable. This could help to account for the common rejection of modernist composers, whose music is perceived by many casual listeners as "just random notes." (Listen to the beginning of Piano Sonata No. 1: II. *Leggiero e legato*, by Carl Vine.)

Third, note that different listeners tend to emphasize different criteria (Figure 28.1). Hence, although listeners overall rated the expression and arousal of emotion as the most important criteria, certain listeners did not consider these criteria important *at all*. This suggests that it may be impossible to define art in terms of a set of necessary and sufficient conditions, at least from a psychological perspective. A psychological approach must accommodate the fact that there are *individual differences* in how criteria for aesthetic value are weighted.

From these findings, then, we can tentatively conclude that with regard to aesthetic judgments of music, listeners generally embrace a definition of art

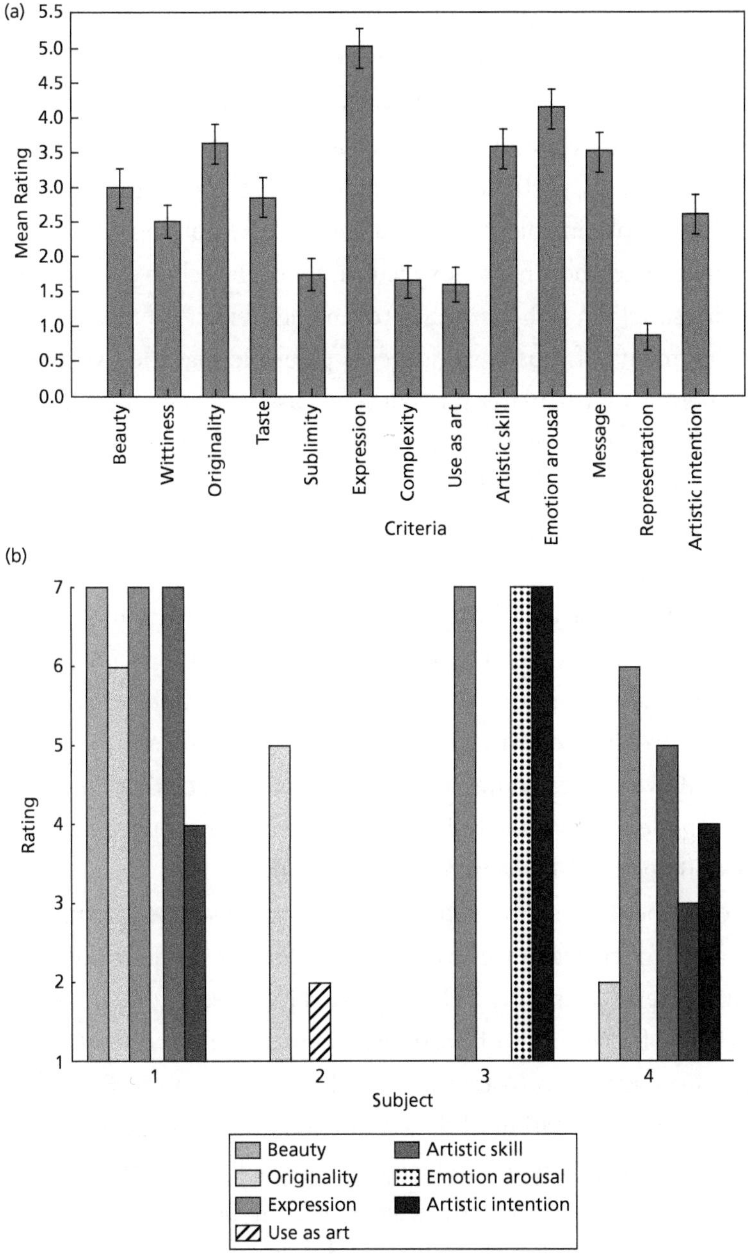

Figure 28.1 Average and individual ratings of criteria for aesthetic value of music.
Adapted from Juslin, P. N, & Isaksson, S., "Subjective criteria for choice and aesthetic value of music: A comparison of psychology and music students", Research Studies in Music Education, Vol.36, pp.179-198. Copyright © 2014, © SAGE Publications.

in terms of *multiple attributes* or *clusters*, rather than a single attribute that is a necessary and sufficient condition (for a discussion, see Stecker, 2003). Thus, the empirical data appear consistent with a so-called cluster approach to art criteria advocated by philosophers such as Denis Dutton (2006) and Berys Gaut (2000). That is, partly unrelated criteria may be sufficient, either alone or together, for placing pieces of music into the category of (good) "art."

We must remember that an explicit rating of the relative importance of criteria *in general* is not the same as proven *causal* effects of these criteria on actual judgments of music, yet it seems plausible that the two are partly related, perhaps particularly for "engaged" listeners (Greasley & Lamont, 2016), who seem to be better able to articulate their subjective criteria than lesser engaged listeners. (This difference may, of course, in part be due to engaged listeners *making* aesthetic judgments more frequently than lesser engaged listeners.)

I believe we must remain open to the possibility that many listeners have a limited insight when it comes to their own criteria for judgments (Melchionne, 2011), and that their implicit judgment policies will have to be *inferred* through experimentation (section 31.1). Vincent Bergeron and Dominic McIver Lopes argue that "we should be skeptical of the somehow compelling idea that we are fully aware of the reasons for our aesthetic responses" (Bergeron & McIver Lopes, 2012, p. 71).

Some independent support for the criteria just discussed stems from recent analyses of critical reviews of music performances from publications. A study by Elena Allesandri and co-workers included a content analysis of 100 reviews of recordings of Beethoven sonatas, published in *Gramophone* between 1934 and 2010 (Alessandri, Williamson, Eiholzer, & Williamon, 2015). Using a combination of data reduction and thematic analysis, they managed to extract "themes" which overlapped significantly with criteria proposed in philosophical aesthetics as well as in the survey study by Juslin and Isaksson (e.g., *novelty, style, emotion*, and *technical skill*).

Now it is time to have a closer look at these criteria for aesthetic value.

CHAPTER 29

AESTHETIC CRITERIA

Meet the Usual Suspects

In order to make an aesthetic judgment, we need some criteria on which to base the judgment. Which criteria underlie listeners' aesthetic judgments of music? There is a paucity of research on this matter. However, based on proposals from philosophical aesthetics and on preliminary research findings, I believe that listeners' criteria will tend to include—but not be limited to—eight broad dimensions.

29.1 Beauty: In the Eyes of the Beholder?

Of all the criteria for aesthetic value suggested over the years, none has probably occupied a more central position than beauty. Aesthetics has sometimes been (narrowly) *defined* as "the study of beauty, and its opposite, ugliness" (Huron, 2016, p. 233). Older theories posited that "all art aims at beauty." Yet today, beauty forms only a small part of the domain (Gracyk, 2012).

Clearly, not all art is beautiful. As a visit to any museum of modern art will confirm, artists do not always *intend* to create something beautiful (Chatterjee, 2012); they might seek to provoke, confront, confuse, or disgust the perceiver (Silvia, 2012), not the wisest approach if, as an artist, you seek popularity. Then again this is arguably not the main goal of most artists.[1]

[1] David Huron discusses the "contrarian aesthetic" of modern composers like Schoenberg, Prokofiev, and Stravinsky, who intentionally aim for psychological disruption, unease, disturbance, and irritation (Huron, 2006, pp. 350–353).

Ruth Lorand admits that the notion of beauty has receded or even disappeared from contemporary aesthetic theory, yet she claims that it is as relevant now as it was at the time of Plato and Kant, simply because it has never ceased to be of interest in everyday life. "Given the great attention, time, energy and resources that are dedicated to creating, achieving or preserving beauty in various aspects of life, it is quite clear that beauty is vital and significant ... Beauty has never been in exile as far as experience is concerned" (Lorand, 2007, p. 1).

This may be particularly true in the case of music. Eva Istok and coworkers asked more than 300 university students in Finland to write as many adjectives as they could to describe the aesthetic value of music (Istok et al., 2009). Analyses of their verbal associations indicated that "beautiful" was the most commonly used word, appearing in roughly two-thirds of the responses.[2] However, because the study relies heavily on recall memory, one can argue that certain criteria of potential importance may not have sprung to the participant's mind.

When listeners do not have to recall potential criteria on their own, beauty is not as dominant. For instance, in the survey study by Juslin and Isaksson described in Chapter 28, listeners were asked to rate the importance of specific criteria. Beauty came only sixth in the ratings (Juslin & Isaksson, 2014). Nonetheless, it was rated highly by *some* listeners. Indeed, Gabrielsson's study of peak experiences features several mentions of musical beauty: "it was so wonderfully beautiful that tears came to my eyes" (Gabrielsson, 2011, p. 142).

Donald Hodges offers a list of examples of pieces of music which many listeners have regarded as beautiful (Hodges, 2017, pp. 46–47). His list features pieces like "Flower Song" from *Lakme* by Leo Delibes; "Aria" from "Goldberg Variations" by J. S. Bach; and 4th movement (*Adagietto*) from Symphony No. 5 by Gustav Mahler.

[2] One can also discern responses related to other criteria, such as skill, emotional arousal, novelty, and wittiness (Istok et al., 2009).

But what, exactly, *is* beauty, and how can it be explained? Hodges observes: "we recognize beauty when we see or hear it, or we are aware when it is absent. However, defining beauty is elusive" (Hodges, 2017, p. 39). The analysis is complicated by the different uses of the word. The word is often over-used in the sense in which "beautiful" applies to everything that is good about a work. However, there is also a more precise use of the term, which I shall focus on here. Beauty may be conceptualized as a perceptual quality, namely, the experience of a work as extraordinarily "pleasing to the senses."

I do *not* regard beauty as an emotion, however; it is a perceptual impression that may often, though not always, arouse an emotion in the perceiver (see section 30.4). The perception of astounding beauty may arouse *pleasure* or *wonder*, yet the object of perception *can* be separated from its emotional effect.

To illustrate: if I were to show you pictures of two scenes or people, one of which is far more beautiful than the other, you can certainly make a judgment and select the more beautiful of the two, *even* if I were to stamp on your foot so hard that the only thing you actually *feel* during the perceptual judgment task is pain. We can, in principle, assess beauty in a "detached" manner, separate from any affective response.

This point is worth making since some authors seem inclined to equate beauty with pleasure (Vuoskoski & Eerola, 2017). Yet beauty does not necessarily or exclusively evoke pleasure, and nor is pleasure induced only by the perception of beauty. After all, all positive emotions are virtually by definition regarded as pleasurable, and positive emotions can just as well derive from, say, an episodic memory.

Is beauty an "objective" feature of an object? If so, we would expect a high level of agreement between judgments of beauty across times and places. This does not appear to be entirely true, at least in the extreme. Is it the case that beauty is in the eye of the beholder? This does not seem to be entirely correct either. There is far more agreement than we would expect if beauty impressions are entirely subjective. Could there be some truth to both of these views?

Most modern analyses of beauty adopt an *interactionist* perspective of beauty, compatible with the psychophysical principle discussed earlier (section 6.2). According to this view, beauty emerges from a relationship between the perceiver and the perceived object, rather than from merely "objective" features of the object *or* merely "subjective" features of the perceiver.[3] In other words, perception of beauty in music is always influenced by *both* "subjective" aspects (e.g., social norms, individual experience) and "objective" aspects (e.g., musical features that appear to us in a certain way due to how our perceptual machinery has evolved biologically).

Focusing on the latter, which perceptual features are associated with beauty? Scholars have tried to link beauty to characteristics such as symmetry, balance, proportion, clarity, order, and the absence of extremes (Eysenck, 1981; Hodges, 2017; Reber, 2008). Most of these features seem perfectly applicable to music also, yet I am not aware of any study that has explored which features are heard as beautiful in music. This represents a formidable future project—capturing the musical correlates of perceived beauty.

Evolutionary accounts of the origins of beauty tend to emphasize its role in mate selection, arguing that attractive features (e.g., symmetry) may have served as clues to genetic health. An alternative approach (the "costly signal theory") holds that artistic behavior displays the vigor of the creator. Making art requires considerable time and effort, so if an individual can afford to waste resources on this maladaptive indulgence, this is a clear sign of fitness (Chatterjee, 2012).

A more straightforward attempt to explain why perceptual features are linked to beauty is the "perceptual fluency hypothesis," which states that the more fluently the perceiver can process an object, the more positive is the reaction (Reber, Schwarz, & Winkielman, 2004). All the features mentioned earlier (e.g., order, symmetry, balance) have in common that they enhance perceptual fluency.

[3] This account rejects claims that aesthetic value could be "objectively defined" (Bicknell, 2009, pp. 141–142).

Perceptual fluency effects may reflect innate principles for stimulus organization (Bregman, 1990), shared by many art forms. Leonard Meyer (1956) argues that beautiful music satisfies our innate preferences for gestalt principles (cf. Figure 24.1). However, fluency effects may also reflect cultural influences in terms of repetition and implicit learning. If so, beauty could be partly related to familiarity and prototypicality (Chapter 27), which both could enhance a perceiver's processing fluency. The fluency hypothesis could perhaps also explain what David Huron refers to as "the prediction effect": the idea that listeners generally prefer to have their expectations confirmed (Huron, 2006).

Perceptual fluency cannot be the whole story, however. If beauty is just a matter of perceptual fluency, then we should find very simple children's songs or extremely trivial pop songs the most beautiful of all. I doubt that this is true for most people. Clearly, something more is required. Perhaps the notion of perceptual fluency needs to be augmented by notions such as Hans Eysenck's proposal that beauty involves some optimum combination of "order *x* complexity" (Eysenck, 1981).

Another suggestion is that listeners are responding to the beauty in the music's "expressive character" (Bicknell, 2009, p. 108), which suggests that beauty is sometimes conflated with another criterion: expression. Manfred Clynes suggests that authentic emotional expression "is experienced as 'sincerity'" (Clynes, 1977, p. 60) and that such purity of expression "also turns out to be beautiful" (p. 54).[4] Can music be truly beautiful if it completely lacks expression?

29.2 Put Some Expression into It!

A recurrent idea in the literature is that art is expressive (Levinson, 2003). In other words, it may express, represent, signify, or refer to something else

[4] Yet, even the beauty of expression could be related to perceptual fluency, because the closer to the "ideal" form (cf. Clynes, 1977) an emotional expression is, the more fluently the emotion recognition process might proceed.

beyond itself; and that "something"—the "content" or "meaning"—is regarded by many scholars as a key aspect of aesthetic value.

You will note that this is the third time in the book we encounter musical expression. In Part II, I explained that music may *express* emotions that are *perceived* by listeners. In Part III, I proposed that the emotional expression in the music can also *arouse* emotions in listeners through the mechanism of contagion (Chapter 20). Here, I suggest that expression is one of the criteria on which listeners base *aesthetic judgments*: to be aesthetically valuable, music should be heard as expressive.

I should perhaps clarify that my use of this term differs from the way some philosophers have used it. Expression has been a key feature of many theories of art throughout history, but it appears that what philosophers refer to as "expression theories" might include theories that focus on the *arousal* of felt emotions (Gracyk, 2012, Ch. 2). In contrast, I will use the term expression only to refer to the *perception* of emotion in music. This corresponds to what Theodore Gracyk refers to as "expression as cognitive recognition" (Gracyck, 2012, p. 39). (Emotional arousal is treated as a separate criterion in section 29.4.)

Musical expression is based on a large number of musical features, which are shaped by both composer and performer. These have been extensively mapped in previous studies (see Table 8.1). Clearly, the perceived expression of the music can play a role when listeners attach aesthetic value to a piece. First of all, the listener may assess the *extent* to which a piece is expressive: some pieces of music are more expressive than others.

If the listener is assessing a performance, he or she may also assess whether the expression seems *appropriate* for the piece in question. This might concern both the types of expressive variation and their extent. Emery Schubert argues that there exists a quantifiable boundary of acceptable deviation in expression: too little variation sounds dull, too much sounds comical (McPherson & Schubert, 2004).[5]

[5] Mozart explains in a letter to his father that "the passions, whether violent or not, should never be expressed as to reach the point of causing disgust"; rather, the music should "flatter and charm" the ear (Watson, 1991, p. 95).

Finally, the listener might assess whether the expression seems *convincing* and *sincere*. When an artist's expression is perceived as insincere, it might arouse *anger* in the audience, as noted by Gracyk (2012). I presume that when listeners judge expression as a criterion for aesthetic value, they typically rate whether the music in question features a sufficient amount of sincere and musically appropriate emotional expression. (A contagion response may aid the listener in this decision; see Chapter 20.)

Gary McPherson and Emery Schubert include "expression" as one of the main criteria by which music performances are formally assessed (e.g., in educational settings) (McPherson & Schubert, 2004). "Sub-dimensions" include "the understanding of the emotional character of the work" or "the projection of the mood and character of the work." The authors point out that there are *norms* against which expressive variations are evaluated, norms that depend on style and cultural and historical context (see also Leech-Wilkinson, 2006, 2013).

The case can be made that expression is a more important criterion than beauty for listeners. For instance, interviews suggest that audiences prefer the most expressive performers (e.g., Boyd & George-Warren, 2013). In the survey study by Juslin and Isaksson (2014), expression was rated as *the* most important criterion of aesthetic value of music, by both musicians and non-musicians.[6] Clearly, not all good music is beautiful (in the traditional sense of the word), but is there any good music that completely lacks expression? Expression might be the *bona fide* indicator that an artwork is truly an artifact, a product of human activity.

29.3 Novelty: What's New?

Music that is beautiful and expressive passes the test of time, but there is still something missing: artists commonly strive to create something *new* in

[6] It could be that the very process of recognizing or inferring an emotion in music is pleasurable. Aristotle discusses this impulse as humanity's "desire to know." In Chapter 4 of the *Poetics*, he identifies it with the pleasure human beings find in all "mimesis"—the pleasure of learning and inference.

their works. Indeed, most definitions of creativity involve some reference to "novelty" or "originality," frequently combined with the requirement that it should be valuable or useful (Simonton & Damian, 2012).

The composer Antonio Salieri—a contemporary of Mozart—was by all accounts a decent composer, but Mozart was so much more *innovative* (Pogue & Speck, 1997). "All great artists are innovators," insists cellist Pablo Casals (Watson, 1991, p. 86).

Some degree of novelty is probably expected in most art contexts, but the desire to create something new, even at the expense of other criteria represented here, arguably reached a peak during the 1950s with the modernistic avant-garde and its obsession with anything new and original (Dahlstedt, 1990). This movement pushed the boundaries of aesthetic norms, and intentionally so.

Composers of the twentieth century who are often regarded as avant-garde or modernist include Alban Berg, John Cage, Charles Ives, Philip Glass, Gyorgy Ligeti, Meredith Monk, Arnold Schoenberg, Karlheinz Stockhausen, Igor Stravinsky, Edgard Varèse, Anton Webern, and Iannis Xenakis. Some of their works can be challenging for newcomers. Artists pay a price for novelty; many are derided or vilified when they first present their works.

Yet, even if we turn to various forms of popular music, many classic or groundbreaking albums involve drastic departures from what came before. This is true of John Coltrane's *Love Supreme*, Marvin Gaye's *What's Going On*, and Miles Davis' *Bitches Brew*. Singer and songwriter Jackson Browne describes hearing a key track on the Beatles' *Sgt Pepper* album for the very first time:

> I remember hearing "A day in the life" on the radio. It was off a Beatles acetate, before the Sgt. Pepper album even came out. Nothing before had prepared me for this incredible song. It was a milestone, and it changed everything. (Smith, 1989, p. 313)

Daniel Berlyne argues that a novel artwork is interesting because it falls between the perceiver's existing categories, thereby creating uncertainty and conflict between competing categorizations and interpretations (Berlyne,

1960). He also distinguishes between "short-term novelty" (e.g., contrasts with recent experience), "long-term novelty" (e.g., novelty within longer timespans), and "complete novelty" (e.g., encountering a new object).

All three kinds may readily be observed in music: novelty within a piece (e.g., modulation to a new key); novelty from a music-historical perspective (e.g., insertion of a slow rather than a fast final movement in a symphonic work); and entirely novel styles or instruments (e.g., the introduction of the piano forte). Moreover, one novel development tends to "breed" other novel developments. For instance, the introduction of the electronic microphone lead to a new, more intimate singing style ("crooning"), which arguably helped to express and arouse a novel set of intimate emotions compared to the "shouting" style of the past.

Novelty is special as a criterion of aesthetic value in that it involves an "expiration date": what is novel at one point in time can obviously not remain novel for all eternity. Works that rely *exclusively* on novelty for their effect will therefore lose their magic over time, and age less well than works which rely (equally) on other aesthetic criteria. We can still appreciate their novelty or originality from a historical point of view, but it is an intellectual appreciation—they do not shock us anymore.

Survey data suggest that novelty/originality retains a role in aesthetic judgments for today's music listeners (Juslin & Isaksson, 2014), although it may not be the most important criterion (cf. Figure 28.1). As Eric Clarke observes, not all music performance takes creativity as its goal. It appears more plausible to describe music performance in terms of a continuum from "interpretation" to "innovation," with the balance between the two depending on genre (Clarke, 2012).

The same applies to music composition, but here the demands for novelty are clearly greater. One aspect of novelty that has been operationalized and tested is the aforementioned notion of melodic originality (Simonton, 2010). Recall from Chapter 27 that melodies scoring high in melodic originality sound more "novel," "unpredictable," and "interesting" to listeners.

However, because of habituation (Chapter 18), each generation of composers will feel compelled to produce work that overcomes habituation to a given level of originality. Even individual composers tend to increase their use of melodic originality as their careers progress, with the notable exception of the years immediately preceding death. During this time, a composer's compositions tend to show declining levels of melodic originality. Dean Keith Simonton refers to this tendency as the "swan-song phenomenon" (Simonton, 2010).

"Art demands of us that we shall not stand still," asserted Beethoven (Watson, 1991, p. 83), but are there limits to this development? I believe there are. Ultimately, music builds on our mental faculties, a psychological foundation that cannot be completely overruled by cultural evolution.

Consider the music written by Anton Webern. The composer suggested of his music that "in fifty years one will find it obvious, children will understand it and sing it" (Watson, 1991, p. 211).[7] That did not happen and I believe it will *never* happen. The challenge is to be able to compose novel music which remains within the boundaries of acceptability from a purely perceptual and cognitive information-processing perspective (e.g., "the gestalt laws").

As far as aesthetic judgment in music experience is concerned, it is the listener's subjective sense of novelty that is decisive for the outcome (Chapter 27). This, in turn, is influenced to a great extent by knowledge and experience (Hargreaves & North, 2010). Moreover, what is rated as novel in one historical or cultural context will not necessarily be rated as novel in a different context. This serves to highlight the fact that aesthetic judgments are historically situated.

29.4 Emotion: If it Doesn't Move You …

I devoted a great deal of space in Part III to discussing arousal of emotions. Now, we encounter this phenomenon again, albeit in the context of criteria

[7] Webern belonged to the circle of the Second Viennese School and made frequent use of atonality and twelve-tone technique in his compositions.

for *aesthetic value* of music. Indeed, it has often been argued that art should arouse emotions in the perceiver (Shimamura, 2012).

The value of emotional experience is implicit in the ancient idea that art may bring *catharsis,* "the purification of the soul through affective experience" (Cook & Dibben, 2010, p. 47). It is also explicit in the idea that "we enjoy art for its own sake" (Aiken, 1950). The transferring of emotions from artist to audience is a key aspect of Tolstoy's theory (Tolstoy, 1960), and Jenefer Robinson argues that a good criterion for successful Romantic expression is the arousal of "appropriate emotions" in the listener (Robinson, 2005, p. 380). Similarly, emotional arousal was an important aspect of Daniel Berlyne's theory, which assumes that works of art are typically designed to "arouse" the perceiver somehow (Berlyne, 1971).

Whatever the merits of these theories, it would seem that most people *do* prefer artworks that arouse emotions in them. Theodore Gracyk suggests that "many visitors to art museums are put off by artworks that they find detached, 'cold', or 'intellectual' rather than emotional" (Gracyk, 2012, p. 25).

Perhaps emotion is particularly important in the case of music, an art form that at first glance seems less conceptual than, say, visual art. Plato famously proclaimed that "the excellence of music is to be measured by pleasure" (Watson, 1991, p. 386). As you will recall from section 28.4, *emotional arousal* was the second highest rated criterion for aesthetic value in a survey study of music listeners (Juslin & Isaksson, 2014). Would you judge a piece of music that consistently fails to arouse any emotion in you as aesthetically valuable?

On closer examination, however, the relationship between emotion and aesthetic judgment is not so simple. Some theories more or less equate aesthetic judgment with emotion (Schellekens & Goldie, 2011), but as I have suggested, aesthetic judgments may, in fact, occur without any emotion, and we saw in Part III that emotional arousal does not require aesthetic judgments.

As I will describe in Chapter 30, the relationship is further complicated by the possibility that felt emotion can be both a *criterion* on which to base aesthetic judgments and an *outcome* of such judgments. We may rate a piece as aesthetically valuable because it arouses an emotion, and we may also come to experience an emotion as a result of having rated the music as aesthetically valuable.

Add to this the aforementioned individual differences between listeners. We need to acknowledge the fact that some listeners regard the emotions aroused by a piece of music—if any—as irrelevant to its aesthetic value (for an example, see data in Figure 28.1). Eduard Hanslick does not deny music's ability to arouse strong emotions in listeners, but he questions whether this is indicative of its artistic value (Hanslick, 1986).

For example, you may argue that the goal of music composition is to create something novel, expressive, or beautiful; and that aroused emotions are just a by-product, if the composer is successful. In conclusion, then, the relationship between emotions and aesthetic judgments is a complex one, which will be further discussed in Chapter 30.

29.5 Skill: Faster, Faster!

Artistic behavior is commonly regarded as a trained ability or mastery of a medium, like the efficient use of a language to convey meaning (e.g., feelings, thoughts, observations; Breskin, 2010). The review of the live performance by Niccolo Paganini at the beginning of Chapter 5 clearly involves assessment of skill.

Humans cultivate, recognize, and admire technical artistic skills (Dutton, 2009), and this form of appreciation applies to *musical* skills as much as to any other art form. For example, many of the listeners in Alf Gabrielsson's study of peak experiences referred to qualities of the performance, such as "a jazz trumpeter's virtuoso solo," in explaining their response (Gabrielsson, 2011, p. 437). As noted by John Sloboda, we may marvel at the speed with which a pianist is able to play a difficult passage or we may admire a brilliant composer's use of the medium (Sloboda, 1999).

Andreas Lehmann offers historical and psychological perspectives on skills in music performance (Lehmann, 2006). He argues that the (seemingly effortless) display of star pianists, violinists, and rock guitarists involves some of the most exacting skills of which the human brain and body is capable. Lehmann cites anecdotal evidence of famous musicians trying to outperform each other in veritable "play offs" (such as Mozart versus Clementi).

Some music performances have gone beyond what contemporaries considered possible at the time, and the complexity of technical skills has tended to increase over time (at least in some genres of music), because musical instruments have been optimized, new playing techniques have been developed, and musical training has become more widely accessible and efficient. Lehmann is not quite certain that virtuosity is related to the aesthetic enjoyment of a piece of music (Lehmann, 2006, p. 4), although he acknowledges that "mastery of technical problems is prerequisite for the production of expressive interpretations" (Lehmann, 2006, p. 19).

Skill of execution was traditionally viewed as inseparable from art. Rembrandt was admired by his contemporaries for his virtuosity. In *mannerism*, a court style driven by a need to compete with each other, artists would often upset the harmony of the art for the sake of effect and virtuosity (Hodge, 2017).

Critics of modern art sometimes focus on the apparent lack of skills required in the production of works such as Marcel Duchamp's "readymades." (Consider "Fountain": a porcelain urinal.) Similarly, music listeners might question whether John Cale's (silent throughout) 4'33" requires skill. Does it?

The emphasis on skill in artistic endeavor is so ingrained that many people tend to discount those works that were not difficult to create (that did not require special artistic skills): "I could have done that myself!" Yet skill is only one of many criteria for evaluating art; works that do not require special technical skills could still be novel or convey a message, for instance. Technical skills are commonly disregarded in "pop art."

In music, the notion of skill has arguably broadened from its original focus on composing and physically performing music to include also production skills and "recycled" music played by machines. Any piece of music considered "a great work of art" is likely to invite an attribution of great skill to its creator. (Who could write Mass in B minor, BWV 232, without possessing an extraordinary amount of musical skill?)

Musical skills may be discernible in isolation from other criteria (e.g., "technical abilities") or may be more or less "inferred" from other criteria in hearing the music (e.g., the ability to perform *expressively*, or to write *beautiful* melodies). The latter is illustrative of the fact that aesthetic criteria are not independent: I noted earlier (Chapter 13) that a potentially beautiful composition may not be truly heard as such unless it is performed expressively, which in turn will require some technical skill.

29.6 Message: But What Does It Mean?

Art often implies the conveying or communicating of an idea or intention (Levinson, 2001). The artist may intend to convey a certain message and the perceiver may perceive a certain message. Some scholars argue that the value of an artwork depends on whether the intended message is detected by a perceiver (Reber, 2008), but others would probably dispute this. In any case, we should recall from section 5.6 that an artwork's potential to convey referential information to the perceiver is separate from the question of whether the artwork was made with a particular intention or not.

To illustrate: a listener could judge the aesthetic value of a piece of music in terms of it having a certain "message," regardless of whether the music was, in fact, composed with that message in mind. The listener's imagination will reign supreme, as far as the response is concerned. By all accounts, some of our oldest artworks (e.g., prehistoric cave paintings) involved a focus on conveying concepts or messages, perhaps to "a higher being" (Shimamura, 2012). Messages in art frequently concern life, society, and nature, and are typically implied rather than explicitly stated (Hodge, 2017)—perhaps particularly in instrumental music, which is often regarded as a non-representational art (Scruton, 1997).

Whenever we search for the underlying meaning of the music (for an example, see Cook & Dibben, 2010, p. 49), we are effectively applying a *conceptual* approach to art (Shimamura, 2012). A listener's subjective sense of understanding of the musical message might lead to a feeling of "cognitive mastering" (Leder, Belke, Oeberst, & Augustin, 2004) or an appreciation of the "wittiness" of a work (Levinson, 2003). But appreciation of conceptual aspects of art may require some knowledge about art history and style. Conceptual artworks can be regarded as statements *about* art which make us think and question the very definition of art. Thus, conceptual art is frequently controversial or political (Hodge, 2017).

Many of the messages conveyed in music are obviously more straightforward, such as emotions. The notion of music as communication is controversial amongst music theorists (Chapter 7), but evidence from survey studies indicate that many performers and listeners *do* conceive of music as a form of communication (Juslin & Laukka, 2004; Lindström, Juslin, Bresin, & Williamon, 2003).

The precise content of the communicative process, the "message," remains a matter of debate (Cross, 2012), but the point is that many listeners will judge the aesthetic value of a piece of music in terms whether they may discern a specific idea, message, or concept in the piece. In some cases, this process is informed by knowledge about the piece or artist involved. Studies show that providing information about an artwork may strongly affect the way it is perceived (Crozier & Chapman, 1981), sometimes in a way that may bias the evaluation (Chapter 31).

There is a quite widespread practice of providing program notes before classical concerts, based on the assumption that the extra-musical information will positively affect the music experience. Yet research suggests that the effect on the listener's reception of the music is not necessarily beneficial. In fact, prefacing an excerpt with a text description may reduce enjoyment of the music (Margulis, 2010), perhaps because program notes conflict with the listener's personal interpretation of the music.

If a piece of music contains lyrics, this may further contribute to a listener's assessment of the message criterion. Examples of the role of lyrics in strong experiences with music are given in Gabrielsson (2011, pp. 432–435). Recall that lyrics can be regarded as special kind of "musical feature" that activates various mechanisms, including aesthetic judgment. Some artists, such as Nobel prize winner Bob Dylan, are judged highly because of their lyrics, which are interpreted as carrying crucial messages or making important statements (Garofalo, 2010).

29.7 Style: If It Ain't Got That Swing ...

Style refers to the distinct manner in which an act is performed or an artifact made—or *ought* to be performed and made (Gombrich, 1998). Artistic objects and performances satisfy "rules of composition" which place them in a recognizable style. Style is a crucial aspect of art and its history, and this is true also for music (Meyer, 1956).

How does a style develop? An artist often tries to create something novel (see the novelty criterion). In doing so, the artist will (implicitly or explicitly) establish a new set of "rules." If other artists see these "rules" as valid for themselves, they will apply these in their works. The resulting artworks then take on that "style," whether it is Baroque, Rococo, Romanticism, Impressionism, Expressionism, Cubism, or Fauvism (i.e., the style of Raoul Dufy, whose painting "The Red Violin" features on the cover of this book).

Some styles begin when artists intentionally break with accepted "rules," perhaps as a reaction against a previous style. *Neo-classicism*—embracing order, restraint, and clarity of form—was a reaction to the frivolous sensuality of Rococo. Similarly, *Romanticism* was a reaction against neo-classicism, characterized by strong emphasis on passions, sentiment, and individuality (Hodge, 2017). Other styles or movements are defined only in retrospect, when time has lapsed and works can be put into historical perspective. Style appreciation depends heavily on knowledge, which may be explicit or implicit in nature (e.g., statistical learning; section 24.3).

In music, style serves crucial functions for listeners. Composing music within the boundaries of a style creates *coherence*; it helps to place the music within a specific historical and social *context*; and it gives the listener a *frame of reference* for understanding the music. A piece of music that does not adhere consistently to any style may appear disjointed and incoherent.

Musical style is related to the *preference for prototypes* theory discussed in section 27.3. More specifically, studies found that listeners appreciate those musical themes the most that are prototypical of a particular style (Martindale & Moore, 1989). This suggests that one criterion for aesthetic value could be whether the music heard adheres to the norms of its musical style. (A slow ballad performed on ukulele may not go down well on a "speed-metal" album.)

Music styles are necessarily fuzzy categories: classification is somewhat arbitrary, style categories often overlap, and categories come and go over time (Hargreaves & North, 2010; Chapter 31). Nonetheless, I believe that different musical styles have different "affordances" for listeners in terms which aesthetic criteria are emphasized, and hence which affective states are evoked. Miles Davis: "styles in music produce certain kinds of feeling in people. If you want someone to feel a certain way, you play a certain style" (Davis, 1990, p. 388).

Preferences for specific styles might affect one's aesthetic judgment not only with regard to the aesthetic criteria considered important. Helmut Leder and colleagues suggest that the classification of an artwork as belonging to a non-preferred style might terminate further aesthetic processing (Leder et al., 2004).

Applied to music, this suggests that if you hear a piece of music from a style you do not like (say, "goth"), your aesthetic processing may stop before you have given the piece full or fair consideration. Such prejudice can tend to reinforce one's negative view of the style. Music education may play a role in overcoming such skepticism. Still, it remains plausible that the aesthetic judgments of listeners are affected not only by the perceived adherence to a given style, but also by whether the style *itself* is a preferred one or not.

The concept of style might also be applied at the *individual* level, with crucial implications. Leder and co-workers argue that "nowadays, an artist's success is mainly due to a recognizable and distinctive artistic style" (Leder et al., 2004, p. 491). Dean Keith Simonton notes that listeners with deep experience of classical music will eventually learn to identify distinctive styles of specific composers, by relying on *minor encoding habits* (Simonton, 2010). These are distinctive ways of constructing thematic material which might tell experts if they are listening to Mozart or Haydn, even if they listen to a composition they have never heard before (Paisley, 1964).

It would appear that there is a trade-off between developing a distinct individual style (which might also contribute to novelty), and adhering to stylistic norms suggested by preference for prototypes. Preliminary data from our laboratory suggest that for most listeners, originality is more important for aesthetic judgments than prototypicality (see Juslin, Sakka, Barradas, & Liljeström, 2016), which offers some support to Leder and colleagues' (2004) claim about the importance of a distinctive style.

29.8 Sensing Overwhelming Greatness: The Sublime

The meaning of the term *sublime* is complex and has changed over time (Bicknell, 2009). It has sometimes been used more or less interchangeably with beauty, but certain authors have argued that the sublime and the beautiful are different qualities, even though they often occur together (Burke, 1958; Kant, 2000). I will adopt the latter view here.

The sublime refers to a certain aesthetic quality that induces *awe* in the perceiver—a sense of being overwhelmed or overpowered. It is evoked by "a particularly magnificent, large, or powerful object or event," which might be "natural" (e.g., mountains, thunderstorms, the raging sea) or made by humans (e.g., a building, works of art) (Bicknell, 2009, p. 9). This experience is linked with feelings of insignificance before this extraordinary object or event.

Many scholars link the quality of the sublime to fear (e.g., Huron, 2006), as long as the object of terror is not too proximate. Edmund Burke considers it an overwhelming emotion, evoked by a glimpse of infinite perfection of the divine, a sort of delightful horror (Burke, 1958). Jonathan Haidt and Patrick Seder define awe as "reverential or respectful fear" in response to "vastness" (Haidt & Seder, 2009, p. 6), often something physically huge such as "galaxies of innumerable stars; the vast, seemingly unending expanse of the ocean; or the earth-shaking power of an erupting volcano" (Shimamura, 2012, p. 8); but it may also concern things with vast power, genius, or complexity. Certain pieces of music are sublime and can arouse feelings of *awe* and *wonder*, if the listening conditions are optimal.

Certain people prefer to listen only to the most sublime pieces of music ever composed. Others do not appear to appreciate being "overwhelmed" by music. Hence "the sublime" is not rated highly as a criterion by every music listener (Figure 28.1). The sublime may be linked to musical aspects such as complexity, volume, and beauty. In general, it appears agreed that experiences of awe to sublime artworks are rare (Huron, 2006; Juslin, 2011; Konečni, 2005). Such unusual experiences may still help to motivate music listeners to seek out new aesthetic experiences, perhaps in the hope of having another experience of similar intensity.

Thus far, I have discussed eight criterion candidates for aesthetic value. There is something to be said for each one of them. Music lacking in expression is not art at all; music without beauty is not pleasing to the ears; music without novelty is not interesting; music without skills is mediocre; music that does not arouse emotions fails to produce an embodied experience; music that lacks stylistic unity is incoherent; music without a message or intention is empty; and music that is not sublime won't change your life. In contrast, music that manages to cover *all* these criteria is *very* likely to be judged as aesthetically valuable.

Perhaps we should not expect pieces of music to fulfill the various criteria equally often. Presumably, many pieces are judged as expressive and skillfully performed; most pieces also conform more or less to a well-defined style; some of them are perceived as beautiful or emotion arousing; a few of them are innovative or carry an important message. But very few are truly sublime.

CHAPTER 30

A NOVEL APPROACH TOWARDS AESTHETIC JUDGMENT

Having defined aesthetic experience and reviewed some of the aesthetic criteria by which we might evaluate music, we are ready to consider a more complete description of the judgment process. This will pave the way for my explanation of how aesthetic judgments may produce both preferences and emotional states.

30.1 Why a Novel Approach Is Needed

The previous chapters suggest that a new approach to aesthetics is needed. Philosophers have failed to reach a consensus about the aesthetic properties that define art. Music psychologists have used an overly broad definition of aesthetic response, and have neglected crucial criteria such as beauty, focusing mostly on arousal. Both have largely ignored individual differences.

What we need, then, is an approach that recognizes a uniquely aesthetic mode of reception, and that captures all relevant criteria of the judgment process. We must further abandon the normative approach (what art *ought to* be), in favor of a descriptive and empirical approach (what art *is* to most people), which is to say a psychological approach. A dominant feature of aesthetic judgment is its diversity, something that a normative approach is not well-equipped to handle.

Diversity may spell serious trouble for a psychological approach too, but as will soon become apparent (section 31.1), a psychological approach is able to *model* such individual differences in terms of individual sets of criteria for aesthetic value. Hence, aesthetic responses are in *some* ways, at least, more amenable to investigation in psychology than in philosophy.

In what follows, I propose a novel approach that takes philosophical aesthetics as its point of departure, but adopts a descriptive (as opposed to normative) and empirical (as opposed to speculative) perspective, and takes individual differences explicitly into consideration instead of ignoring them.

We need a preliminary psychological model that may guide our exploration. As mentioned earlier, I regard aesthetic judgment as one of the psychological mechanisms through which music may arouse emotions. Thus, before describing the model, it may be useful to situate the mechanism within the broader BRECVEMA framework.

To begin with, I assume that the aesthetic judgment mechanism is a more *recent* addition to the human behavioral repertoire than the other mechanisms; whereas these latter mechanisms have a long evolutionary history (and may be shared with other animals), current notions of "art" and "the artist" are quite modern concepts that would not have been recognized by our human ancestors (Dahlstedt, 1990).

Plato and Aristotle, for example, had no word for art in their vocabulary, and it is doubtful whether da Vinci used this concept. It was only as recently as 1736 that French philosopher Charles Batteux made an attempt to distinguish the "fine arts" (corresponding to our modern conception) from the "technical" or "mechanical" arts (Gracyk, 2012).

Of course, what could today be regarded as "artistic behavior" existed long before then, but the products of such behavior were arguably not approached in the same way as they are now. Prehistoric art from around 500,000 years ago was most likely part of religious rituals—perhaps to evoke hunting success (Hodge, 2017)—rather than being regarded as "art for art's sake." Moreover, even those behaviors are recent, compared to the long evolutionary history of our other emotional mechanisms (section 2.3).

One consequence of the relatively recent development of aesthetic judgment, as compared to other mechanisms, is that it relies to a greater extent on "higher" cognitive functions, domain-relevant knowledge, and a more fluid, individualized process, which changes across time and context. This means that aesthetic judgments are strongly influenced by cultural factors.

Although there may exist *some* universals that set constraints on what we initially find beautiful (e.g., symmetry in faces), "the arts are about particularity, and the particularity of art history is inherently unpredictable in terms of broad universals" (Sheridan & Gardner, 2012, p. 281). Aesthetic and stylistic norms change over time in society (Jacobsen, 2006), as any overview of art history will show. This is because art is heavily influenced by its social, political, religious, and economic environment (Hodge, 2017). This applies to music too and makes it difficult to pin down a definitive account of music listeners' aesthetic judgments constant for all times and places.

However, I think we should make a distinction between the *contents* of aesthetic judgments and the *judgment process* per se. To illustrate: although the precise criteria used to evaluate artworks may differ across contexts, the judgments may still involve the same psychological constraints and processes. Moreover, it can be assumed that *within* a given cultural context, we will find at least modest agreement also about the contents of aesthetic judgments. What we need, then, is a model and analytic methods which enable us to accommodate both similarities and differences between judges.

30.2 How Can Judgments Be Conceptualized? A Preliminary Model

Figure 30.1 presents a preliminary model of aesthetic judgment in music experience, which might help to conceptualize the process (Juslin, 2013a). Consistent with Helmut Leder and co-workers' model for aesthetic appreciation in the visual arts (see Leder, Belke, Oeberst, & Augustin, 2004), it is suggested that the aesthetic judgment process begins with an implicit or explicit pre-classification of the music as "art," which will lead the listener to adopt an aesthetic attitude. As you will recall (Chapter 28), this means that the listener's attention is focused on the music, and that one or more criteria are brought to bear on the music as standards for evaluation.

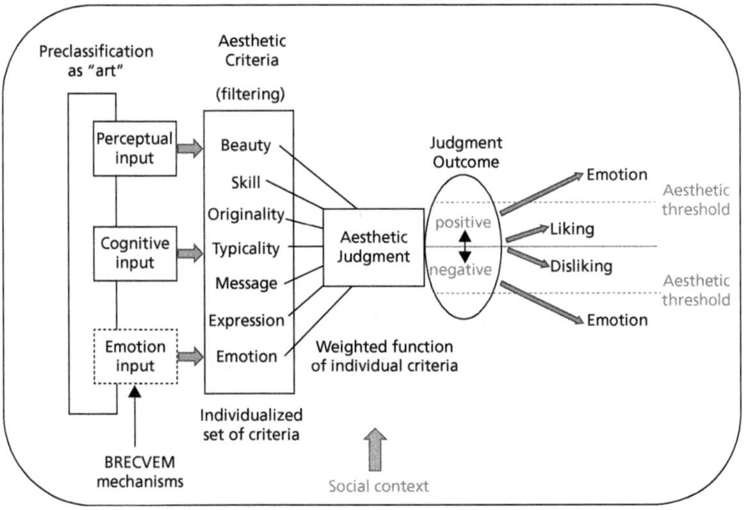

Figure 30.1 Preliminary model of aesthetic judgment in music experience.
Adapted from Physics of Life Reviews, 10, Juslin, P. N., "From everyday emotions to aesthetic emotions: Toward a unified theory of musical emotions", pp.235–266. Copyright © 2013 Elsevier B.V.

As observed by Leder and colleagues, the borders between what was considered an artwork once and what is called art today are constantly changing (Leder et al., 2004, p. 490). Thus, it is not self-evident when an aesthetic attitude is "called for"; the impetus can come from various sources. An aesthetic framing might serve as a cue that the music in question deserves an aesthetic attitude.

For instance, if a piece of music is performed in a prestigious concert hall, you might be more likely to adopt an aesthetic attitude towards it. As Theodore Gracyk notes, "artworks are typically designed to be occasions for aesthetic judgment" (Gracyk, 2012, p. 169). The setting will (in more or less subtle ways) let you know if the musical event *is* such an occasion. This is yet another example of how the context may influence which mechanism is activated by a musical event.

Another possibility is that the music *itself* has some perceptually salient feature (e.g., novelty or extraordinary beauty), which draws the listener's attention to its aesthetic potential. You might be listening in a superficial manner to a piece of background music but suddenly hear something *special* in the music (e.g., a unique skill) which then triggers an aesthetic attitude. If the music arouses an intense emotion, this may be suggestive of aesthetic value for some listeners, and may thus elicit further aesthetic processing (Juslin & Isaksson, 2014).

In general, it can be expected that some pieces of music will invite an aesthetic attitude to a greater extent than other pieces (because of certain formal features), but there is no guarantee that an aesthetic judgment will be initiated. This will depend on several factors, including the listener's attention and knowledge, the characteristics of the situation, etc. (If you hear music on TV during a commercial break while you are making coffee, you are unlikely to adopt an aesthetic attitude even if the music is your personal favorite among Beethoven's 32 piano sonatas.)

We are more likely to be drawn into an aesthetic experience if we are deeply engaged with the music than if the music merely occurs in the background and is of secondary importance (as in many everyday listening situations; see Sloboda, Ivaldi, & O'Neill, 2001). The same piece of music may create vastly different responses in the listener depending on whether it is rated as "art" or not. To illustrate: we may like a simple "pop" song, but once we adopt an aesthetic attitude and assess it in terms of its *aesthetic* merits, our liking for it may wane. Perhaps this can account for the changes in music preferences that may occur as a result of music education.

Although I believe that aesthetic judgments are often made explicitly (in particular amongst music experts), I suggest that the judgment process may also be largely implicit sometimes. The defining feature is whether the listener's aesthetic criteria have been brought to bear on the music, not whether the evaluation was made at a conscious level. It is commonly found that people are unable to (correctly) explain the basis of their own judgments or preferences (Nisbett & Wilson, 1977), illustrating once more the perils of trusting introspection.

This seems to present us with a problem: how can we empirically determine that an aesthetic judgment occurs? One straightforward solution is simply to *ask* listeners to make an aesthetic judgment (Juslin, Sakka,

Barradas, & Liljeström, 2016). However, if the aim is to explore the extent to which such judgments occur spontaneously, such a strategy is not possible. Just like when we need to tease out the effects of different mechanisms for arousal of emotions (section 25.9), careful experimentation offers a solution: implicit aesthetic judgments may be *inferred* from data in experiments that manipulate musical events in a systematic manner and measure outcomes (Chapter 31).

Let us now return to the preliminary model of aesthetic judgment in music experience. Once an aesthetic attitude has been adopted, perceptual and cognitive analyses of the music will proceed, providing "inputs" to the aesthetic judgment process (Figure 30.1). This can be construed as a continuously ongoing process. Like other affective responses to music, aesthetic processing can be affected by a number of factors in the *artwork*, the *perceiver*, and the *situation* (Jacobsen, 2006). Information related to each factor is channeled through the *perception*, *cognition*, and *emotion* of the listener:

- *Perceptual* inputs are sensory impressions based on "low-level features" of the music that are regarded as mandatory in the process (Jacobsen, 2006; Juslin, 2013a; Shimamura, 2012).[1] These impressions occur early both in the judgment process and in our ontogenesis. They are assumed to be based largely on our biology and are relatively uniform among listeners, since they reflect basic principles of perceptual organization (e.g., Bregman, 1990). Typical low-level features may be symmetry, order, proportion, harmony, balance, and figure-ground contrast (Arnheim, 1974; Ramachandran & Hirstein, 1999).
- *Cognitive* inputs involve higher-order concepts that are more knowledge-based than the perceptual-sensory inputs. The

[1] Although one can envisage making aesthetic judgments of merely imagined music, the process of auditory imagery would still involve many of the same brain regions for sensory processing, as would actual music (Zatorre & Halpern, 2005).

knowledge is organized in terms of "schemata," or socially determined memory representations, which store domain-specific knowledge about music (e.g., information concerning the musical style, the composer, or the performer, and music history). Both the nature and extent of cognitive input will vary depending on the level of expertise of the listener, but even provision of information at the moment of reception can strongly affect listeners' aesthetic judgments (Crozier & Chapman, 1981; cf. section 31.2). Some researchers claim that stylistic knowledge and a sense of the art-historical context is required to have a genuinely aesthetic appreciation (Bullot & Reber, 2013).

- *Emotional* inputs may or may not occur in any instance of aesthetic judgment. If the music arouses an emotion through one of the BRECVEM mechanisms described in Part III, this response will "inform" the judgment process to the extent that the listener includes in his or her set of aesthetic criteria at least one criterion that *could* be informed by the reaction (e.g., *emotion arousal*; see section 29.4). However, I will argue that emotional input is not needed for an aesthetic judgment to take place or to produce an outcome; that is, aesthetic judgments could proceed in a purely "intellectual" manner (based on perceptual-cognitive inputs only). The possibility that emotional inputs are optional could help to explain the ongoing debate concerning whether aesthetic judgments are necessarily emotional or not.

Some philosophers have proposed that an aesthetic response *ought* to be a "detached" and "distanced" consideration of an artwork that does *not* let emotions "cloud one's judgment". Jeanette Bicknell argues that "a listener who is often deeply moved by music is not necessarily a good judge of that music's merit" (Bicknell, 2009, p. 123). "What ought to be" is a normative issue, however, and falls outside the purview of a psychological approach. I argue that aesthetic judgments *are* frequently influenced by emotional inputs from other mechanisms, whether we like it or not.

30.3 What Happens with the Inputs? Enter the Criteria

Whether the perceptual, cognitive, and emotional inputs will have an effect on the resulting judgment depends on the listener's criteria for aesthetic value (Figure 30.1). I presume that judgments involve individual sets of subjective criteria, and also a relative weighting of the criteria. Listeners may differ in terms of *how many* criteria they use, *which* criteria they use, and how the criteria are *weighted* in the judgment process (Juslin et al., 2016b). Hence, when two listeners hear the same piece of music, their aesthetic judgments may produce vastly different outcomes.

I explained earlier that scholars have proposed a large number of potential criteria for considering something "art" or even "good art," but do listeners really make us of *all* these criteria in their real-life judgments? Here, again, it may be constructive to take stock of what we know about psychological processes. A large body of research on memory and human judgment suggests that there are certain limitations concerning the amount of information we can process at any point in time. (Such cognitive limitations help to account for the fact that we only use a quite small number of discrete pitches in melodies.)

Based on studies of cognitive judgments which involve multiple "cues" (Brehmer & Brehmer, 1988), and limitations with regard to "working memory" (Cowan, 2010), I assume that judges tend to use a relatively small number of criteria (one to four) which might include *beauty, expressivity, originality, emotional arousal, skill, message*, and *typicality* (Juslin et al., 2016b). The listener's subjective criteria function as filters in the judgment process. They determine which of the perceptual, cognitive, and emotional inputs will influence the judgment process.

To take a simple example: a particular piece of music may afford a listener the possibility of aesthetic appreciation in terms objective features (e.g., order, symmetry) that are correlated with perceived beauty (Reber, 2008). Whether this impression is rated highly depends on the individual listener's criteria for aesthetic value. Some listeners may regard the perception of beauty as essential to the value of a piece of music. Still others may regard it as peripheral at best. It is not that some listeners fail to *detect* the perceptual features, it is simply that the features are "discounted" in their aesthetic judgment.[2]

I do not assume that the aesthetic criteria are independent of one another, but rather that they (like most variables in the "real" world; Brunswik, 1956) are more or less correlated with one another, positively or negatively. For example, conformity to *style* rules might be positively correlated with *beauty*, since "prototypicality" might influence perceptual fluency, but might be negatively correlated with *novelty*, which often involves the breaking of stylistic "rules."

The implication of these intercorrelations is that an artwork cannot be all things to all people all the time. A work cannot satisfy all criteria equally. Yet because music is considered to be the temporal art par excellence, music is probably better able to *alternate* between satisfying different demands at various moments in time, than, say, a visual work of art. In addition, all of the criteria above involve some *unique* variance that can be measured in listening tests (Juslin et al., 2016b).

Which criteria a listener applies to a piece of music might depend on expertise, such as having a musical education. Gerald Cupchik and Janos Laszlo argue that naïve perceivers adopt a more "direct" mode of reception, whereas experts adopt a more "cognitive" reception (Cupchik & Laszlo, 1992). In terms of my model, this suggests that non-experts rely to a greater degree on basic sensory and perceptually based criteria such as *beauty*, whereas experts rely to a greater degree on knowledge-based criteria such as *style* (requiring art-historical knowledge) and *message* (a conceptual approach).

An aesthetic judgment can be initiated by a salient percept with regard to any of the criteria, but once the evaluation of one criterion has begun, other criteria might be evaluated as well. The assessment of specific criteria occurs continuously, but judgment outcomes will be produced at certain

[2] Sometimes, beauty has been disregarded because it is seen as serving the wrong social values (Lorand, 2007).

points in time, "cued" by particularly significant moments in the music such as the ending of a piece or improvisation or the moment when a decision has to be made about buying a CD or downloading a track. Audience applause at a live concert may serve as a contextual trigger of the listener's evaluation (and so may booing).

I submit that judgment outcomes can be subject to updating, as new "evidence" occurs during continued listening. A brilliant music performance may begin to deteriorate half-way through. Research in event perception could offer clues to how the "segmentation" of events culminates with judgment outcomes at important event boundaries (Tversky & Zacks, 2013). But how do preferences and emotions come into the picture?

30.4 How Do We Go from Aesthetic Judgment to Preference and Emotion?

Figure 30.2 shows, in a simplified and schematic fashion, different overall outcomes of the aesthetic judgment process as it relates to preference and emotions. If the judgment process indicates that, on balance, the music is "good," this will result in liking (positive preference). Conversely, if the process indicates that, on balance, the music is *not* "good," it will result in

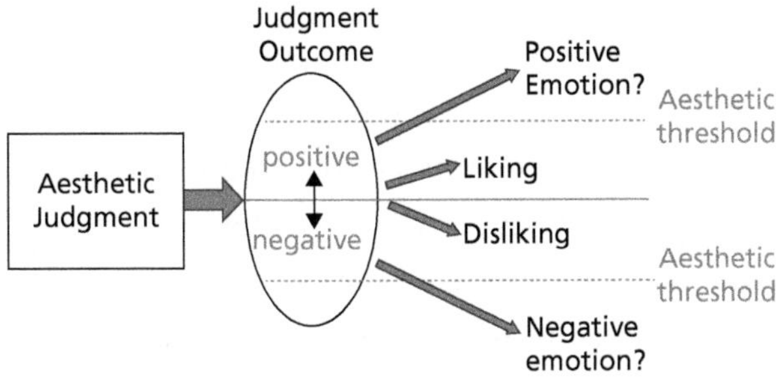

Figure 30.2 Affective outcomes of the judgment process.
Adapted from Physics of Life Reviews, 10, Juslin, P. N., "From everyday emotions to aesthetic emotions: Toward a unified theory of musical emotions", pp.235–266. Copyright © 2013 Elsevier B.V.

dislike (negative preference).[3] In both these cases, no emotion is necessarily aroused (unless, of course, one of the *other* emotion mechanisms happens to be activated quite independently during the course of listening).

If, however, the result of the judgment process is that the music is judged as *extraordinarily* good or bad, overall or according to at least one of the criteria, an emotion will be aroused in addition to the preference, with valence determined by the outcome of the judgment process. We like a competent performance—but we *marvel* at an exceptional one!

The present model assumes that aesthetic judgments will arouse emotions when at least one of the evaluative criteria reaches a certain level. This idea is consistent with Gustav Fechner's concept of "aesthetic threshold" (Fechner, 1876). Thus, for example, a piece of music judged as merely pleasing to the ears will simply be registered as that, without arousing an emotion; but a piece judged as extraordinarily beautiful will indeed arouse an emotional response, such as *wonder*. The precise aesthetic threshold may differ between individuals in ways that could be tested.

In sum, the present model postulates that an aesthetic judgment could lead to both liking (i.e., preference) and emotion. Liking (or disliking) is a mandatory outcome, whereas emotion is a possible additional outcome. Because emotion is not mandatory in this judgment process, the present model differs from previous views that have defined aesthetic experience as "intense" (see Konečni, 1982; Price, 1986). According to my model, an aesthetic experience could also be relatively calm and contemplative if the outcome of the judgment process is merely "liking."

"Is preference not just another word for aesthetic judgment?" I have heard some people ask. Not if you ask me. Preference is an *affective outcome*, just like a mood or an emotion, which should be distinguished from its *causal mechanisms*. Aesthetic judgment is just one of many causal processes that may influence preferences. Music preferences can be based on all sorts of reasons, most of which may have little to do with "art." You may like a piece of music

[3] Recall from section 2.4 that *preference* is defined as a more low-intensity affective evaluation of an event, object, or person, which may be longer-lasting than the more intense state of an *emotion*.

simply because it helps you to fall at sleep at night or because it helps you to study. These examples can hardly be construed as aesthetic judgments.

For obvious reasons, my focus here is on the *emotions* that can occur as a result of aesthetic judgments. Although aesthetic judgments may produce a variety of emotions (like the other mechanisms covered in Part III), such judgments will tend to produce some emotions more often than others. These states are referred to by some authors as "the appreciation emotions" (Haidt & Seder, 2009). Presumably, different emotions are associated with different criteria for aesthetic value.

A few examples might suffice to illustrate this point. Novelty in the music may *surprise* the listener (Berlyne, 1971). This is followed by *interest*, if the music is comprehensible (Silvia, 2012). "Cognitive mastering" of a complex musical structure may lead to *satisfaction* (Leder et al., 2004). Beautiful music might induce *pleasure* (Bicknell, 2009). Skills in performance may arouse *admiration* or *envy* in the listener (Hodges & Sebald, 2011), or, if they are really exceptional, *wonder*. If music featuring both beauty and physical grandeur is heard in a "colossal" performance setting such as a medieval cathedral, it could arouse *awe* (Konečni, 2005, p. 37).

Emotions such as these are met with approval even by Peter Kivy, a philosopher who seems very sceptical towards other types of musical emotions (Kivy, 2001; e.g., those discussed in section 16.2). Not all aesthetic judgments evoke positive emotions, however. Roger Scruton argues that an artwork could "fail" in two ways: it may fail to interest us, which I would regard as a failure to invite an aesthetic attitude, or it may invite an interest of which we disapprove, which I would interpret as a completed aesthetic judgment process, resulting in a primarily negative outcome (Scruton, 1997).

A frequent misunderstanding among lay people is the belief that all art aims to evoke positive emotions, and that artworks that do *not* evoke positive emotions are somehow failures (Silvia, 2012). In fact, many artworks seem intended to arouse negative emotions. For example, in the conceptual art (or anti-art) movement Dada, artists posed difficult questions about society, the role of artists, and the purpose of art, and often aimed to arouse *shock*, *outrage*, and *offense* in the viewer (Hodge, 2017). Similarly, modernist composers created pieces of music that were almost certain to induce negative emotions, by persistently transgressing musical expectations of listeners (Huron, 2006; see Juslin, Harmat, & Eerola, 2014, for some empirical data).

Some of the negative states include what researchers have termed "moral emotions"; that is, emotions that involve norms about right or wrong (Buck, 2014). Moral emotions are characteristic of aesthetic judgments, because they do not generally occur as a result of the other mechanisms (discussed in Part III), with the exception of cognitive goal appraisal. The reason is that aesthetic judgments are more strongly focused on *norms*, both individual and social.

In fact, a sizeable proportion of the affect evoked by music throughout history may be "moral outrage" as a result of aesthetic judgments based on norms—from the premiere of Igor Stravinsky's "Rite of Spring" in Paris in 1913 and the audience reception to Bob Dylan's shift from acoustic troubadour to loud electric guitarist in 1966; to the Beastie Boys' UK tours of the 1980s, which provoked the following review by Ivor Key: "they are loud, talentless and disgusting" (Driver, 2001, p. 471).

Some empirical evidence that aesthetic judgments are linked to moral judgments comes from brain imaging studies. Thomas Jacobsen and his colleagues investigated aesthetic judgments of the beauty of geometrical shapes varying, for instance, in symmetry. They found that such judgments involved a brain network that partially overlapped with one underlying judgments of moral cues in previous brain research (Jacobsen, Schubotz, Höfel, & v. Cramon, 2006).

30.5 Aesthetic Emotions versus Everyday Emotions

In the previous section, I briefly mentioned "appreciation emotions" and "moral emotions" as two subsets of emotions that have been found to occur in aesthetic contexts involving music. I will subsume both of these under a broader heading. Emotions that were aroused by aesthetic judgments will be referred to as "aesthetic emotions." Recall from section 16.3 that the notion of "aesthetic emotions" has been used in two different ways: one view considers *all* emotions to art to be "aesthetic" regardless of their underlying cause. In contrast, I will reserve this term for emotions that were caused by an aesthetic judgment.

The argument is *not* that the associated emotion is unique to art, but rather that the *origin* of the reaction—the causal process—is of a particular kind. Those emotions that are *not* caused by aesthetic judgments (see Part III) will be referred to as "everyday emotions", because their causes (their intentional objects) do not differ, in principle, from those of other emotion-arousing events or objects in everyday life.

Note that because the distinction is based on the underlying causal process rather than on the resulting emotion per se, the same emotion (e.g., *interest*) might be an "everyday emotion" or an "aesthetic emotion" depending on how it was aroused. Similarly, *pleasure* could be caused by an aesthetic judgment, but is not necessarily so.

One thing that complicates the picture and invites misunderstanding is that emotions can (i) simply co-occur with aesthetic judgments (being activated independently through one of the BRECVEM mechanisms) or (ii) be the direct *result* of an aesthetic judgment. Only the latter would be called "aesthetic emotions" using my terminology. The context of the music listening may determine which of these types of emotions will occur (see section 30.2).

Since some of the mechanisms responsible for arousal of emotions are implicit by nature, it is possible that listeners occasionally *misattribute* an emotion evoked by one of the BRECVEM mechanisms—an "everyday emotion"—to an aesthetic judgment on a conscious level that only happens to occur at the same time. This will create the false impression of an "aesthetic emotion" when there is, in fact, only an "everyday emotion" and an *independent* aesthetic judgment.

So far I have suggested that aesthetic judgment is a causal mechanism capable of producing two types of affective outcome: preference and emotion. In the absence of emotions aroused by the (other) BRECVEM mechanisms, *preference, emotion,* and *aesthetic judgment* will be consistent with each other. To illustrate: you may encounter a piece of music that you rate as being extremely valuable aesthetically, due to its novelty and beauty. As a consequence, you will experience positive emotions (e.g., *wonder*) and you will like the piece (preference).

Consider, however, the possibility that a piece that is judged as being of low aesthetic value by the listener nonetheless arouses a positive emotion, through a psychological mechanism such as evaluative conditioning. In such a case, emotion and aesthetic judgment will end up as contradictory, with ambivalent feelings as a result (discussed further in Chapter 32). It is not obvious whether such a scenario will result in *like* or *dislike*; it might depend on how much emphasis a listener puts on the specifically *aesthetic* value of music, as opposed to just any affect the music might evoke.

I submit that for "engaged" music listeners (Greasley & Lamont, 2016), including musicians, music preferences will mainly reflect aesthetic judgments of music; for less "engaged" music listeners, however, I believe that music preferences will commonly be based on other factors (including positive emotions induced through the BRECVEM mechanisms), effectively bypassing an aesthetic judgment as defined here (e.g., "I prefer this music because it makes me feel good"). Recall that preferences may be based on any number of reasons, of which emotion and aesthetic judgment are two distinct possibilities, yet preference requires neither of these processes (section 31.3).

30.6 Are Aesthetic Judgments, Preferences, and Emotions Independent?

The present model assumes that aesthetic judgment, preference, emotion are independent to some extent (Juslin, Liljeström, Västfjäll, & Lundqvist, 2010). This partial independence is reflected in numerous ways. First, as Part III should have made clear, it is perfectly possible for music to arouse an emotion in a listener without the listener making an aesthetic judgment. Thus, for example, a piece of music may subconsciously arouse *sadness* in a listener who does not even attend to the sound merely because the music has repeatedly been paired with sadness-evoked stimuli in the past (evaluative conditioning).

Second, it is perfectly possible to like a piece of music heard on the radio without the music arousing an emotion (with a synchronized response in experience, physiology, and expression; Chapter 15). We may simply prefer the piece heard at this moment over a piece heard earlier. Such a preference need not involve an aesthetic judgment. The music in question (e.g., a pop song) may not generally be considered "art," and hence does not invite an "aesthetic attitude."

Finally, an aesthetic judgment may occur without emotion. Members of a jury in a piano performance contest repeatedly make assessments of the aesthetic merit of various expressive interpretations, but the circumstances may not be optimal for arousing emotions. Of course, if a judge rates a performance *very* favorably, he or she may not be able to avoid becoming moved by it (recall the principle of "aesthetic threshold" from section 30.4). Even the sternest professional critic will ultimately surrender emotionally in the face of greatness.

In a real-life context, aesthetic judgment, preference, and emotion often influence each other. Obviously, we tend to like music that we regard as aesthetically valuable and that manages to arouse positive emotions in us. However, the causal arrow may point in different directions. We may rate the music as aesthetically valuable *because* it managed to arouse an emotion, or we may respond with an emotion because of how highly we value the music (e.g., its beauty) aesthetically. We may react with an emotion simply because we happened to come across a piece of music that we already like, and so forth (Juslin et al., 2010).

Is there some empirical evidence to support my assumption of partial independence? A dissociation between aesthetic judgments and preferences was obtained by David Hargreaves and co-workers. In their study, both musically trained and untrained listeners gave higher ratings of *quality* to classical pieces than to popular pieces, yet the same pattern was not found in their ratings of *liking*. In other words, preferences could not be fully accounted for by aesthetic judgments of quality (Hargreaves, Messerschmidt, & Rubert, 1982).

Similarly, evidence of a dissociation between aesthetic judgments and arousal of emotion was obtained in a study by Sam Thompson, which investigated listeners' responses during a concert (Thompson, 2006). Results showed that listeners were able to differentiate between the perceived *quality* of the performance and their own *emotions*. Their enjoyment of the musical event was better predicted by their "emotional engagement" than by the perceived "quality" of the performance, suggesting (again) that aesthetic judgments are not the primary determining factor for liking for most people. It may be sufficient, or even more important, that the music arouses positive emotions.

Finally, a study from my own laboratory, which will be described fully in Chapter 31, found that listeners' individual ratings of *aesthetic value, liking*, and *emotion intensity* for 72 pieces of music from different musical genres were only moderately correlated (Juslin et al., 2016b). *Aesthetic value* was more strongly correlated with *preference* than with *emotion intensity*, as could be expected from the model outlined above. (Only *some* aesthetic judgments arouse an emotion, but *all* influence preferences). To understand the model as well as its implications more fully, we need to adopt a broader perspective on aesthetic judgments.

CHAPTER 31

AESTHETICS AND AFFECT IN BROADER PERSPECTIVE

In this chapter, I will broaden the perspective taken earlier and discuss some questions raised by the model outlined in Chapter 30. Are aesthetic judgments reliable? Do listeners' ratings generally agree with regard to a given piece of music? How is aesthetic judgment influenced by the social context? What role does music preference play in emotional responses? Should we distinguish between utilitarian and aesthetic uses of music? To address these issues, we first need to be able to measure aesthetic judgments somehow.

31.1 How Can Aesthetic Judgments Be Investigated?

Previous research in empirical aesthetics suggests that there are individual differences between judges, and that judges are sometimes unable to account for the criteria they use to rate a work of art in a complete or reliable way. How, then, could we capture these judgments scientifically? Here, we may benefit from a previously untapped potential to rely on well-established analytic techniques in cognitive science referred to as *judgment analysis* (Cooksey, 1996).

Key to this approach is a powerful statistical technique called *multiple regression analysis,* which is used to estimate relationships amongst variables. For instance, one can predict the unknown value of one variable ("the dependent variable") from the known values of two or more other variables ("the independent variables," the predictors).

Judgment analysts use multiple regression models to capture how individual raters combine multiple differentially weighted bits of information ("cues") to arrive at an overall judgment. In a typical experiment we could ask listeners to rate the aesthetic value of pieces of music which vary with respect to various aesthetic dimensions (e.g., novelty, expressivity).

Although one can objectively manipulate these aesthetic properties in musical examples, we saw earlier that what matters is the *subjective* perception by listeners (e.g., perceived beauty) rather than objective features (section 27.2). Therefore, it makes more sense to use subjective impressions of aesthetic criteria—as rated by listeners—as statistical predictors.

In such regression analyses, the goal is to examine how well ratings of aesthetic criteria may predict the overall rating of aesthetic value. Results will show whether judgments are systematic (a high multiple correlation is interpreted as a high degree of consistency in the responses of the rater; Cooksey, 1996); they will also show how many and which criteria are used by listeners, their relative importance, and how they are combined into judgments (e.g., whether there are "additive" or "multiplicative" effects of criteria).

The beauty of this analytic technique is that listeners' judgment strategies may be extracted in the statistical analysis independently of any conscious awareness of criterion use that listeners may have. Using this method, we do not have to give each listener an exhaustive definition of what "aesthetic value" refers to (which would prejudge the thing we are investigating). Rather, a definition can be *empirically* derived by modeling how the listener's judgments are actually made: the definition is revealed by the listener's overall judgments and their covariation with the ratings of individual criteria.

The typical focus on individual judges in judgment analysis is crucial for its use in the present context, because a common feature of aesthetic judgments is the large variability. As noted by Paul Silvia, a theory of aesthetics needs to account for the fact that different perceivers have different reactions to the same artwork (Silvia, 2012). Hence, we must adopt an "idiographic" approach where listener judgments are first modeled at the individual level before they are summarized.

Multiple regression models have been successfully applied to ratings of emotional expression in music (Juslin, 2000a), but have only been used to capture aesthetic judgments of music in one study published so far (Juslin, Sakka, Barradas, & Liljeström, 2016). This study may serve to illustrate the feasibility of the proposed approach.

We used a *stratified random sampling* procedure to select 72 pieces of music, from 12 genres. These pieces were divided across two groups of participants (N = 44), who judged each piece regarding seven aesthetic criteria (e.g., beauty, originality, expressivity) as well as the overall aesthetic value. Both individual (*idiographic*) and averaged (*nomothetic*) regression analyses were conducted on the listeners' judgments.

Results indicated that regression models provided a good fit to listeners' judgments (mean variance accounted for = 76%), suggesting that the process is systematic and mainly additive. Some criteria (e.g., originality) made a larger contribution to prediction than others overall. However, there were large individual differences between listeners regarding what criteria they used. In fact, the nomothetic regression model did not adequately capture the "judgment policies" of individual listeners.

Table 31.1 shows some data from the study in terms of the weighting of different aesthetic criteria by individual listeners. Note that Listener 1 appears to rely heavily on expressivity, whereas Listener 4 puts more weight on artistic skill. Listener 6 emphasizes originality and the extent to which the music arouses emotion (unlike Listeners 1 and 4).

Perhaps it may be possible to distinguish distinct types of judges, such as "expressionists" (valuing expressivity), "modernists" (novelty), "stylists" (prototypicality), and "hedonists" (arousal of emotion). "I am more pleased with what moves me than with what astonishes me," notes composer François Couperin, apparently emphasizing emotions over novelty in art (Watson, 1991, p. 135). Further research is needed to understand how and why such individual differences in aesthetic judgment develop.

Scientia non est individuorum ("science does not deal with individual cases"), yet these findings illustrate that it is feasible to account for individual differences while remaining objective. There *is* "accounting for taste"—at least, in

Table 31.1 Examples of idiographic regression models of aesthetic judgments by six listeners.

Listener	R	Predictors/Criteria						
		Beauty	Originality	Expressivity	Skill	Emotion	Message	Typicality
1.	.95	.13	−.09	.65*	.28*	.09	.02	.17*
2.	.89	.05	.32*	−.31	.44	.43	.24	−.16
3.	.64	.35	.06	.05	.15	.06	.29	.13
4.	.96	.33*	.06	.13	.60*	−.08	−12	−.03
5.	.91	.35*	.23*	−.03	.40*	.31*	−19	.04
6.	.97	.04	.59*	.45*	.12	−.28*	.10	.16*

Note. R refers to the multiple correlation of the regression model, which indicates the extent to which overall aesthetic judgments could be predicted based on a linear combination of the criteria for aesthetic value. Criterion data indicate the relative weight of the criteria for each listener in the judgment process (* indicates that a beta weight was statistically significant).

Data from Juslin, P. N., Sakka, L., Barradas, G., & Liljeström, S. (2016). No accounting for taste? Idiographic models of aesthetic judgment in music. *Psychology of Aesthetics, Creativity, and the Arts*, 10, 157–170.

the sense that aesthetic judgments are systematic and can be explained by distinct weighting schemes for subjective criteria of aesthetic value.

31.2 Are Aesthetic Judgments Reliable? Bias and Context

Because aesthetic judgments have important consequences in certain contexts (Chapter 26), it is relevant to ask whether individual judges agree or not in their judgments. The previous section showed that listeners may differ with respect to how they use various criteria, and this leads us to believe that they also differ with respect to their *overall* judgments. Here, we have to distinguish between *inter-judge* reliability (do different listeners make similar judgments?) and *intra-judge* reliability (does the same listener make similar judgments over time?).

Duane Lundy examined the inter-judge reliability among professional music critics (Lundy, 2010). His study featured 5,161 randomly chosen albums in popular music covering nine genres (pop, rock, alternative, heavy metal, electronica/dance, rap/hip-hop, soul/funk, folk, and blues) and ratings by 352 critics (compiled from books of reviews), resulting in a total of 15,220 album ratings. All ratings were converted to a standard scale from 0 to 100.

Pairs of critics who had rated at least 30 of the same albums were compared in order to obtain an estimate of consensus. As could be expected, *exact* agreement was low: the average critic pair gave exactly the same rating for only 27% of the albums (range: 6–67%). However, Lundy argues that correlation is a much better index, because it effectively taps into a similar *pattern* of ratings of two judges across albums. Using this index, Lundy found that 87% of the critic pairs showed statistically significant and positive correlations. In contrast, no significant negative correlations were found. The average correlation was moderately sized ($r = .49$).

Lundy concludes that these results support the view that there is something stable in aesthetic judgments across individuals, time, and place, "in contrast to the idea that aesthetic judgments are hopelessly idiosyncratic" (Lundy, 2010, p. 255). I agree that there is *some* stability, perhaps particularly among professional music critics. (Still, an average correlation of .49 means that only 24% of the variance on average is shared between critics. Hence, there is still quite a lot of diversity.) Lundy suggests that experts show higher levels of agreement than non-experts, but few studies have looked at the reliability of lay listeners.

One estimate comes from our previously mentioned study (Juslin et al., 2016b), in which 44 listeners rated the aesthetic value of 72 pieces of music from different genres in a listening test. To estimate the agreement amongst the listeners, we computed the intraclass correlation coefficient. Results indicated that there were large individual differences between the listeners in their aesthetic judgments, as indicated by low correlations (.18–.24). These results suggest that ordinary listeners diverge in their judgments even more than professional critics (for some support, see Lundy & Smith, 2016).

I observed in section 31.1 that music listeners' judgments are highly systematic: they can be predicted accurately based on a linear combination of the criteria rated. At the same time, we find that there are large individual differences. Usually, we associate high systematicity with high inter-judge agreement, but these aspects are apparently separated here.

As suggested by the model provided in Chapter 30, the explanation is that individual judges apply their criteria systematically but that they rely on different sets of criteria and/or different weighting of the criteria. How can we explain the fact that experts often show higher levels of agreement? [1]

One possibility is that experts are more consistent in how they apply their "judgment policies." However, we saw in section 31.1 that even lay listeners are quite consistent, suggesting that internal consistency cannot be the whole story. Another possibility is that the judgments by experts are less influenced by various biases or context factors (discussed later in this section). A perceiver who knows little about art may be more inclined to

[1] I write "often" here, because this is not always the case: Harald Fiske reports that inter-judge reliability in assessing music performance is unrelated to performing ability of the judge (Fiske, 1977).

judge it based on "secondary" cues, such as whether the artist is famous or not.

Perhaps there is also a more direct explanation. Some clues are provided by studies of music performance evaluation (the kind that occurs in music education). Such judgments involve many of the criteria for aesthetic value mentioned earlier (e.g., technical skill, expression, originality of interpretation). Estimates of inter-judge reliability vary a lot across studies (McPherson & Thompson, 1998), but may relatively high under some circumstances.

More specifically, it has been found that the use of a formal rating scale may increase inter-judge reliability by forcing the judges to rely on the same set of evaluative dimensions (criteria). I hypothesize that the same thing may account for differences between experts and lay listeners. Experts tend to rely on more similar (although not identical) sets of criteria than do lay listeners.

Few studies have looked at the *intra-judge* reliability of aesthetic judgments. In the visual domain, Lea Höfel and Thomas Jacobsen (2003) conducted an experiment to explore the temporal stability and consistency (i.e., reliability) of aesthetic judgments of the beauty of graphic patterns. In a first session, non-artist psychology students were asked to judge 252 patterns. In a second session, the same participants were asked to categorize 80 of the same patterns again.

Owing to external circumstances, the time span between the two sessions varied from one day to 14 months, which made it possible to investigate the temporal stability. When the time span was only a few days, the two judgments were relatively stable; but with longer time spans, the judgments differed significantly, highlighting the "fluid" nature of aesthetic judgments.[2]

In a rare study, Harald Fiske explored intra-judge reliability when experienced musicians judged a set of music performances (Fiske, 1983).

[2] Höfel and Jacobsen also found that when the same stimulus was repeated within the same listening session, judgment consistency increased, but primarily because the participants could now *remember* the stimulus.

Unbeknownst to them, some of the performances were repeated in the set so that the raters provided two judgments for these performances. Fiske discovered *very* low correlations between the first and second set of judgments of the same performances, suggesting that judges apply their criteria inconsistently.

A more plausible explanation perhaps is that there were strong order effects in the test, which affected impressions of each criterion (Kroger & Margulis, 2016). Imagine that the *first* time you hear a music performance it is preceded by an excellent performance. Due to the contrast between the two performances, you will not rate the performance highly. If, however, when you hear the same performance a *second* time, it is preceded by a mediocre performance, suddenly the target performance may sound rather good.

Perhaps there are other sources of variability that can explain the inconsistency in judgments. One could expect criterion use to vary depending on the *context* of the judgment. The previous model (Figure 30.1) presumes that aesthetic judgments of music are *mostly* influenced by the outcomes of evaluations of specific criteria, but as Gary McPherson and Emery Schubert note, any music evaluation is affected by other factors which impact on the reliability of the evaluation (McPherson & Schubert, 2004).

For example, contextual factors such as visual impressions, audience support, and stereotyping may all influence aesthetic judgments of music. Such extraneous variables can influence which criteria become the focus of attention, among other things. To illustrate: a musician who has an expressive body language will direct more attention to the expressive aspects of his or her performance than one who is not. We may perceive a guitar solo as more skillful if it is heavily applauded by other listeners during a concert.

A number of studies have demonstrated so-called prestige effects: that aesthetic judgments are affected by what we know, or *think* we know, about artists or their works. A classic example is a study by George Duerksen, which indicated that students rated technical and musical aspects of a recorded piano performance lower when told that the performer was a student than when told that it was a famous musician (Duerksen, 1972).

Should "prestige variables" be considered "criteria" for aesthetic judgment? Because they are presumably not part of what the judge *intentionally* (whether explicitly or implicitly) aims to base his or her judgment on, I am inclined to think not; they are better regarded as contextual factors that "bias" the judgment. However, we cannot rule out that some listeners do consider "fame" a valid criterion of aesthetic value.

31.3 Music Preferences: It's Only Rock "N" Roll, But I Like It!

So far, I have focused mostly on aesthetic judgment as a mechanism that renders musical experiences into aesthetic experiences, and that may produce both preferences and emotions. The main focus of this book is on emotion. Yet, because preferences are related to emotions, I will briefly consider them here (for a more extensive review, see Greasley & Lamont 2016).

Recall from section 2.4 that in comparison to emotions, preferences are frequently defined as more long-term affective evaluations of objects or persons, with a lower felt intensity. In the music domain, it is common to add a time dimension to the concept of preference.

For instance, Harry Price suggests that *preference* involves an act of choosing, esteeming, or giving advantage to one thing over another ("I prefer to listen to Samuel Barber's Second Essay this evening"), whereas *taste* involves a listener's long-term "commitment" to preferences (e.g., "I generally like classical music") (Price, 1986).

Not all researchers adhere to this terminology, however, and in practice it may be difficult to separate the two concepts operationally. However, I believe that most studies have purported to examine preferences of a more long-term nature ("taste") rather than short-term preferences, and to concentrate on relatively broad genres or styles of music (Russell, 1997).

Studies of music preferences are concerned with our *differential* liking for different types of music. When people say that they love music, what they really mean is that they love the kind of music that they like. If you browse through music in general, you will fairly soon find that there is a lot of music you do not like at all, and that hardly any music leaves you completely "neutral."

Long-term preferences are reflected by what music people choose to listen to, what recordings they choose to buy, and what concerts they choose to attend. In empirical studies, preferences are measured in terms of verbal self-report or time spent listening to various types of music in controlled settings (operant listening tests).

Note that different measures yield different results: John Geringer reports a moderate correlation ($r = .50$) between verbal self-reports and listening measures of music preferences (Geringer, 1982). To some extent, this probably reflects the problem of choosing "representative" exemplars of particular musical styles in an operant listening test: the preferences depend not only on style, but also on the particular piece and artist chosen. However, it may also reflect a more serious problem, the fact that self-reported preference cannot always be taken at face value. Listeners may sometimes report preferring a high-prestige genre when they really prefer to listen to other genres.

Another major problem concerns the categorization of types of music. Music preference is often discussed and studied in terms of styles or genres. Such categorization is necessarily imperfect. Music may be described in many different ways and at different levels. These categories change over time and new genres appear constantly. Studies frequently contrast "popular music" with "classical music", even though differences *within* these categories are virtually as large as those between them. (Popular music features such disparate entities as love ballads, heavy metal, and reggae.)

Understandably, many musicians express resistance against music genre labels: "I hope the music we make can't be labeled. My whole point about music is that labeling is limiting. It prejudices people. My whole crusade at the moment is confounding stereotypes... I have a single called "Englishman in New York," which has a jazz section in it, and then a hip-hop section" (Sting, in Smith, 1988, p. 410).

My personal view is that in talking about different types of music, genre labels are the least bad of the available alternatives. "Music" as a superordinate category is so diverse that we require some means to be more specific; the level of individual "songs" or "artists," on the other hand, is too specific to be useful in most analyses; "sub-genres" such as "Bristol jungle," "Kraut rock," or "Jump blues" are problematic because they are usually comprehensible only to those who are listening to them. Hence, the intermediate level of "genres" (e.g., jazz, rock, folk) is, despite its limitations, arguably the most feasible level to explore links between preferences and other variables (Rentfrow & McDonald, 2010).[3]

Despite various problems with studies of music preference, some reasonably robust findings have emerged from these studies. Preferences for musical genres are related to demographic variables such as gender, age, social class, and ethnic group, as well as various subcultures, life styles, and values (Greasley & Lamont, 2016; Rentfrow & McDonald, 2010; Russell, 1997).

Note, however, that these results are correlational, which means that it is not possible to draw conclusions about the *cause* of the links. In fact, the few models outlined so far (e.g., LeBlanc, 1982) tend to consist of long lists of variables that might potentially influence music preference, albeit without closer specification of the underlying processes.

There is, arguably, no end to the reasons listeners could offer to explain their preference for a piece of music, and many of the reasons may be highly personal and idiosyncratic. However, it would perhaps not be out of order in the present context to claim that a fair deal of listeners' preferences are based on (positive) emotions.

31.4 How Is Preference Related to Emotion and Choice?

How does music preference interact with emotion in music listening? Quite often, I would say, music preference is the *beginning* as well as the *end* of an

[3] By the way, note how useful genre labels are even for those who tend to resist them: Consider the Sting quotation, and how easily we understand his reference to a "jazz" section and a "hip-hop" section in a song. Or when James Brown "warns" his fellow musicians on one of the live cuts on the *Sex Machine* album, "Don't play so much jazz," I think they know *exactly* what he means.

emotional episode. It influences which musical events we are exposed to in everyday life, while at the same time it becomes "updated" on the basis of the outcome of such musical events.

To illustrate: music preferences influence which musical "affordances" we expose ourselves to, because if we like a certain genre or artist, we will actively seek out situations and contexts where we can experience the music and its associated characteristics; the situations and their characteristics will influence what mechanisms of emotion induction can be activated, including aesthetic judgment.

Emotions clearly influence preferences: we like music that makes us feel good! Hence, if you decide to listen to a song that you have previously liked very much, and that song now fails to "deliver", that lack of positive emotion and the resulting disappointment may lead you to "downgrade" your preference for that song.

But preferences also influence emotions. Listeners tend to choose to listen to types of music they like, and this may contribute to both more intense and more positive emotions (Blood & Zatorre, 2001; Liljeström, Juslin, & Västfjäll, 2013). Several factors may explain the positive role of music choice.

First, self-chosen music is likely to be more *familiar* to the listener than other-chosen music. In Chapter 27, I explained that familiarity in itself may enhance a listener's liking (North & Hargreaves, 1995). Familiar music also enables a greater number of mechanisms for arousal of emotions to be activated, such as memory-based mechanisms like evaluative conditioning and episodic memory. Episodic memory seems to be one of the most common sources of emotion from music (see Juslin, Liljeström, Västfjäll, Barradas, & Silva, 2008; Juslin, Liljeström, Laukka, Västfjäll, & Lundqvist, 2011; Sloboda & O'Neill, 2001; Taruffi & Koelsch, 2014).

Second, self-chosen music may offer a greater sense of "control" over the situation, which is conducive to experiencing positive emotions (Fox, 2008). When we are able to listen to music of our own choice through headphones, even novel and stressful settings may become more comfortable. The grind of the daily commute may be turned into one's favorite time of the day, thanks to listening to preferred music.

31.4 HOW IS PREFERENCE RELATED TO EMOTION AND CHOICE?

The music encountered in everyday life consists of a mixture of self-chosen music and music that listeners simply happens to hear. Even though a case could be made that we have greater control over the music we hear today than ever before (due to portable music players with an extensive memory), we are still exposed to music that others have chosen and that we do not necessarily like, which may arouse negative emotions (e.g., Juslin et al., 2008).

When listeners may decide for themselves, they choose music differently depending on the context in which the music will be consumed. Music choice is strongly related to motives and functions of music listening. These motives and functions may vary over time (Sloboda, Ivaldi, & O'Neill, 2001). Yet, some criteria for music choice could be more important than others overall.

This issue was investigated in a survey study featuring 72 participants (36 psychology students and 36 music students) in Sweden (Juslin & Isaksson, 2014). The listeners were asked to rate the relative importance of a large set of criteria for their music choice, based on findings from previous studies of the goals, functions, and motives for music listening (see Juslin & Laukka, 2004; Juslin et al., 2008, 2011; North, Hargreaves, & O'Neill, 2000; Roe, 1985; Schäfer & Sedlmeier, 2010; Sloboda et al., 2001).

Figure 31.1 shows the results from the listeners' ratings. The results reveal that there is no single criterion that can account for music choice. Instead, a whole range of criteria play a role. Still, it is clear that listeners rated the expression and arousal of emotions as the most important criteria for their music choice. Indeed, that the music arouses emotions was the single most important criterion out of 18 possible factors.

Familiarity, in contrast, was not rated highly. Although familiarity with a piece of music may indeed increase liking (e.g., Peretz, Gaudreau, & Bonnel, 1998), it might not be an important variable when listeners choose music in everyday life. The mere fact that a piece of music is familiar is not sufficient motivation to choose to listen to it. After all, there is plenty of music that is familiar to us but that we nevertheless dislike.

Further analyses suggested that listeners' ratings of the relative importance of criteria in music choice were predictive of their preferences for

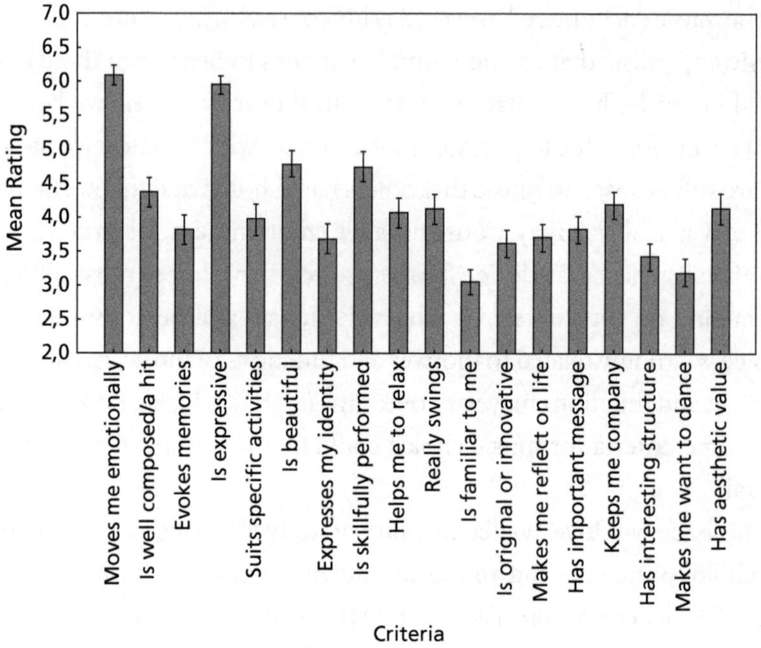

Figure 31.1 Listeners' ratings of criteria for music choice.
Adapted from Juslin, P. N, & Isaksson, S., 'Subjective criteria for choice and aesthetic value of music: A comparison of psychology and music students.', Research Studies in Music Education, Vol.36, pp.179-198. Copyright © 2014, © SAGE Publications.

specific genres. For example, preference for classical music was associated with tendencies to choose music that "is skillfully performed," jazz with tendencies to choose music that "really swings," and pop music with tendencies to choose music that "makes me want to dance."

What subjects in this study did not know was that the criteria were divided into "intrinsic" factors and "extrinsic" factors. The common feature to the nine items that measured "intrinsic" criteria was that they focused on the music "itself," what the music "is" or "has" (e.g., that it is well-composed, expressive, beautiful, skillfully performed, or original; that it really "swings"; or has an important message, an interesting structure, or aesthetic value).

In contrast, the common feature to the nine items that measured "extrinsic" criteria was that they focused more on "external" effects of the music and the ulterior functions it may serve for the listener (e.g., that the music can help the listener to relax, evoke valuable memories, express identity, get company, or reflect on life; or that it suits particular activities or is conducive to dancing).

This distinction between "intrinsic" and "extrinsic" criteria was based on seminal literature on musical aesthetics (Hanslick, 1986; Kant, 2000; Meyer, 1956), and reflects the historical conflict between those who have argued that the value of music resides primarily in the music itself (e.g., absolute music, formalism) and those who have argued that the value of music is largely due to its effects and its benefits for society (e.g., expressionism).

As was expected, there were significant differences between psychology students and music students in the relative weighting of the criteria. In particular, psychology students tended to rate "extrinsic" criteria (e.g., "suits specific activities"), as opposed to "intrinsic" criteria (e.g., "has interesting structure"), higher than did the music students. This is consistent with a tendency amongst musicians to consider music in "absolute" terms, and not as a "background" to other activities (DeNora, 2000, p. 61). These results lead us naturally to the recurrent debate about different uses of music.

31.5 Utilitarian versus Aesthetic Uses of Music: A False Dichotomy?

In much of the literature, one detects a conflict between appreciating "art for art's sake" and using music for various purposes. The latter may actually be more common, if we consider musical activities in the world as a whole (Hodges & Sebald, 2011).

Earlier, I contrasted "everyday emotions" with "aesthetic emotions," but the two categories are not meant to differ in a normative way: aesthetic emotions are not necessarily "better" or more "musical" than everyday emotions, they only have different causes and induction mechanisms.

Other authors, however, *do* appear to make a normative distinction. Some theorists advocate the notion of "aesthetically warranted emotions" (Hatten, 2010; Robinson, 2005). This notion is fraught with difficulties: "aesthetically warranted" according to whom? Who decides? Experts? The problem is that even experts often disagree about how artworks should be interpreted.

Understandably, psychologists take a different view. "There is no one way to listen to a piece of music, and no one emotion appropriate to it," as noted by John Sloboda (2005, p. 218). Yet the idea that some uses of music and their associated responses are more valuable than others is common amongst some musicians.

A clear example of such an "elitist" view is provided by composer Arnold Schoenberg, who is reported to have stated that, "if it is art it is not for all, and if it is for all it is not art" (Watson, 1991, p. 97). Similarly, composer John Cage complains about listeners who "misuse [music] as a means of distraction, entertainment, or acquisition of 'culture'" (Watson, 1991, p. 91). So what are we to make of statements like these? Some clues come from another composer, Igor Stravinsky:

> Most people like music because it gives them certain emotions such as joy, grief, sadness, and image of nature, a subject for daydreams or - still better - oblivion from "everyday life". They want a drug – dope ... Music would not be worth much if it were reduced to such an end. When people have learned to love music for itself, when they listen with other ears, their enjoyment will be of a far higher and more potent order, and they will be able to judge it on a higher plane and realise its intrinsic value. (Stravinsky, 1975, p. 163)

My personal interpretation of Stravinsky's quotation is that music can arouse much more than just "everyday emotions." If listeners engage with music in terms of aesthetic judgments, they will be rewarded with a more fulfilling experience of the music.

Recall the distinction between "absolutism" and "referentialism" made in section 5.3. Perhaps the apparent "snobbery" of some composers really only reflects the wish or longing for music to be "just" music; to let the music occupy center stage and not be a means for something else—a communicative symbol, tool, commodity, or intervention. If so, it is easy to feel sympathy for such a wish. Nonetheless, it is arguably impossible for music to be perceived as "absolute," to be heard *only* as patterns of notes.

The BRECVEMA framework can help to explain a frequent idea among philosophers of art and some musicians, the one that an aesthetic response should be a "detached" or "distanced" consideration of an art object which does not let emotions "come in the way." This view can be understood as a consequence of the possibility that emotions induced by the BRECVEM mechanisms may influence an aesthetic judgment, and so potentially "bias" that judgment.

Even if aesthetic judgment *itself* would arouse an emotion, that emotion would be a more "true" reflection of the listener's aesthetic criteria than a judgment only inflected by emotions from the other mechanisms—at least, if the listener does not view "emotion" as one of the key criteria for his or her aesthetic judgment. This is presumably why some music theorists are so keen to focus on "aesthetic emotions", as defined here.

However, this issue is also partly related to the distinction between "high" and "low" culture (DiMaggio, 1987). In times past there was no distinction between "classical" and "popular" music, there was just "music." Brahms made his living playing in sailors' bars in Hamburg; Vivaldi got fired from his job; Beethoven was involved in physical fights; and Mozart was really just a young composer expected to offer pleasant entertainment on Saturday evenings (Pogue & Speck, 1997).

When did all this change? Philosopher Theodore Gracyk suggests that the project of defining art was partly inspired by a social distinction introduced in the eighteenth century between uncultured past-times and cultured ones which were obviously superior (Gracyk, 2012). Basically, definitions of art "arouse within a social project of disentangling the proper enjoyments of the lower and upper classes" (Gracyk, 2012, p. 146).

Hence, many accounts of aesthetic responses are motivated by the goal of "elevating" art. In the case of music and emotion, there is a tendency to distinguish between "aesthetic" and "refined" emotions to great works of art and "basic" and "vulgar" emotional responses to trivial pop music. Sociologist Pierre Bourdieu argues that this divide between "fine art" and "popular art" is a mechanism for perpetuating social divisions in modern society (Bourdieu, 1984).

Eric Clarke and his co-workers point out that a culturally dominant attitude among some listeners to classical music is that the music is a form of "sonic play" or "acoustical chess" (Clarke, Dibben, & Pitts, 2010, p. 67). (This is clearly a form of aesthetic attitude towards the music; see Chapter 28.) They further suggest that this development towards decontextualized "functionlessness" is sometimes regarded as one of the crowning achievements of Western art music; that music could aspire to lofty ideals, having become free from practical concerns.

However, the "functionlessness" of art is, after all, an illusion. The idea that music should be an object of aesthetic contemplation is just another kind of "function" or "purpose." (Recall that most definitions of art are functional; they focus on what function the art is supposed to fulfil.) There is a common notion that music served important functions *once*, but that music is now only an abstract art form. This view is not quite accurate: for most people in everyday life, music never stopped being functional (Sloboda & O'Neill, 2001).

We need to acknowledge the manifold affordances of music (Clarke et al., 2010). For some people, music is a subtle art form; for others, it is a form of healing. The two aspects are not necessarily mutually exclusive. Music can be an artwork and serve other functions as well. What if the most aesthetically satisfying music also offers the best healing? Can music even be truly sublime, without having a healing effect upon us? Reports of peak experiences with music clearly suggest that they have such effects (Gabrielsson, 2011). Aesthetic experiences may leave us with feelings of optimism, vigor, wonder, gratitude, and reverence for life.

Perhaps there is a deeper reason for this connection between aesthetics and health benefits. John Callender observes that psychotherapy often focuses on judgments of self, and that such self-judgments take the form of "aesthetic judgments"; they typically have a moral character (Callender, 2005). Concepts of beauty commonly center on aspects such as harmony, unity, internal coherence, and proportion; mental disorders tend to involve a loss of internal coherence and meaning, as well as feelings that seem out of proportion.

31.5 UTILITARIAN VERSUS AESTHETIC USES OF MUSIC

If it is true—as Leslie Greenberg argues—that our emotions are the primary generators of personal meaning (Greenberg, 2012), could music listening help us to explore, reflect upon, and make sense of our emotions, so as to regain a sense of internal coherence, harmony, unity, and self-identity? Might aesthetic experiences serve to integrate different aspects of our mental life—perceptual, cognitive, and emotional—into a more coherent whole?

To serve this purpose, works of art would need to be sufficiently complex. Indeed, it is often argued that the greatest artworks feature multiple layers of meaning. As I have tried to show, music has the potential to achieve this. In the next chapter of this book, I will consider how all the available sources of emotion in music combine, in order to induce more complex emotions—experiences whose emotional ambiguity seem to reflect so well the ambivalence of life itself.

CHAPTER 32

THE LAST CHORUS

Putting It All Together

> Who is there that, in logical words, can express the effect music has on us? A kind of inarticulate unfathomable speech, which leads us to the edge of the infinite and lets us for moments gaze into that.
>
> —Thomas Carlyle (Watson, 1991, p.35)

From a historical point of view, it may seem extremely arrogant to think that we can explain the mystery of the emotional power of music, this classic riddle which has confused thinkers from Plato to Darwin. Still, these strange animals that we call human beings have performed heart transplants, created the Internet, mapped out their own genome, and built rockets which travelled to the moon. Surely we should be able to say something articulate about emotional responses too?

In their landmark publication in the field of musicology, *A generative theory of tonal music*, Fred Lerdahl and Ray Jackendoff explained why they did not address the problem of emotion in music: "like most contemporary music theorists, we have shied away from affect, for it is hard to say anything systematic beyond crude statements such as observing that loud and fast music tends to be exciting" (Lerdahl & Jackendoff, 1983, p. 8).[1]

Having read the previous 31 chapters, I think you will agree that we have a little more than this to say about musical emotions these days. Before I become self-congratulatory about the field's advances, I should reiterate that

[1] They acknowledge that musical affect is "crucial to artistic concerns" (Lerdahl & Jackendoff, 1983, p. 249).

much work remains to fully explore and understand the manifold mechanisms involved. Still, even *now* it is possible to suggest ways of explaining how these mechanisms could produce some of the most complex and rewarding emotions we experience with music.

32.1 Explaining the Richness of Music Experience

Psychological explanations might sometimes appear "too simple." Surely the immensely rich and complex emotions we experience in reaction to music cannot be explained by a relatively small set of simple mechanisms, such as conditioning?

However, as observed by philosopher Derek Matravers, this way of thinking ultimately rests on a fallacy: "that the explanation of a phenomenon must match that phenomenon in *gravitas*" (Matravers, 1998, p. 225). In other words, even a very simple process may produce a very complex outcome. Imagine the complexity possible if we combine *many* such processes.

As previously explained in Chapter 2, many problems in our previous attempts to understand musical emotions have come from a tendency to propose "monolithic" theories (Budd, 1985). As I will attempt to demonstrate in this chapter, the richness of our emotion experiences with music most likely comes from the *combined* effects of several mechanisms.

To understand this, we need to look at all the available emotion sources. I explained in Part II that music can *express* a wide range of emotions through iconic, intrinsic, and associative sources (ICINAS); and in Part III that music can *arouse* emotions through brainstem reflexes, rhythmic entrainment, evaluative conditioning, contagion, visual imagery, episodic memory, and musical expectancy (BRECVEM). Here in Part IV, I have added one final mechanism, aesthetic judgment, which could help to integrate the other sources of emotion.

We saw in section 25.6 that music commonly occurs in a variety of everyday contexts where other concerns (e.g., talking to friends, cooking dinner, worrying about your mortgages, driving in heavy traffic, attending to your children) will take priority. Such circumstances are not optimal in order for musical arousal of emotion to take place, and so musical events often *fail* to arouse an emotion.

What happens if *all* different sources of musical emotion, perceived and felt, combine in a real-world listening context under circumstances that *are* beneficial for emotions to occur? The truth is that our knowledge about this is still rather limited, partly due to the enormous challenges of investigating the emotion-induction process in a controlled manner in "field settings."

In the following sections, I will formulate some hypotheses about how different phenomena of music and emotion can be explained by the previously described theoretical frameworks. I will focus in particular on how a musical event can arouse *complex emotions,* and on how listeners may *differ* in their emotional response to such an event.

It is important to remember that even if two listeners may react with the same emotion to a piece of music, their music experiences may still differ to some extent, due to other aspects (different perceptual impressions, thoughts, and reflections). In fact, more than one mechanism may arouse the same emotion but with different foci of attention. To illustrate: two listeners could both become *happy* upon hearing a specific song, yet one focuses on the happy expression of the music, whereas the other focuses on the cheerful lyrics.

Furthermore, because of the dynamic nature of music, we may expect different emotion-inducing events to follow each other in quick succession during a piece. One listener in Alf Gabrielsson's study describes "a series of conflicting emotions: fright, sorrow, hate, love, anger, and, finally, an internal piece that words cannot describe" (Gabrielsson, 2011, p. 143).

In other words, part of the richness comes from *emotional contrasts* over time, the dynamics of responses to longer pieces of music, which could arouse much more complex, ambiguous, and temporally shifting emotions. Some of these shifts involve "the law of affective contrast" proposed by John Gilbert Beebe-Center (1932), which holds that a shift in adaptation level may lead to an enhanced emotional response (see also Huron, 2006).

As observed in Parts II and III, which source or mechanism will be activated depends on several factors in the *music* (e.g., what information is available in the music?), the *listener* (e.g., is the listener's attention focused on the music?) and the *situation* (e.g., which are the circumstances of the listening context?). Thus, specific sources of emotion may be expected to correlate with specific music genres, listener states, listener activities, and listening situations in complicated ways that we are only beginning to explore.

Yet, even if we limit ourselves, for the time being, to a particular situation, with a particular listener, at a particular moment, there is still plenty of opportunity for a complex emotion to occur. How?

32.2 When Mechanisms Interact: Mixed Emotions

One prediction that could be made based on the BRECVEMA framework, with its range of partly independent mechanisms, is that music should be able to arouse *mixed emotions*; that is, combinations of various emotions. This is because more than one mechanism could be activated simultaneously at different levels of the brain (Juslin, 2013a).

For example, a piece of music could make a listener *happy* due to the happy expression of the piece (through contagion), but at the same time make the listener *sad* because the piece reminds him or her of a sad event in the past (through episodic memory). Thus, the result will be a "bittersweet" combination of both *happiness* and *sadness*. Jerrold Levinson suggests that because life itself has a mixed character with happiness and sadness, good things and bad, music that reflects this bittersweet or poignant quality will tend to move listeners the most (Levinson, 2015).

As noted in section 16.2, instances of mixed emotions are commonly reported in studies. It is fair to argue, however, that previous theories of emotion have largely been unable to explain convincingly why or how mixed emotions occur. Indeed, a single-mechanism theory such as Klaus Scherer's "component process theory" would clearly have a hard time explaining how two emotions can occur at the same time; the theory presupposes a single outcome (Scherer, 2001).

In contrast, the BRECVEMA framework predicts that mechanisms at various brain levels will produce *conflicting outputs* because they rely on different mental representations (section 17.7). In short, different types of "evidence" will yield different responses which are not necessarily in agreement.

From an evolutionary view, this might be construed as a "flaw" in the cognitive design. From an aesthetic perspective, though, it could be construed as an advantage. It may be argued that the greatest works of art tend to feature several "layers" of meaning which are occasionally in conflict. It would appear that music is well positioned to achieve such ambiguity, not only in the expression of emotions (see section 12.3), but also in the arousal of emotions.

Listeners in Gabrielsson's study provide several examples: "it was painful and pleasant at the same time," reports a middle-aged woman who has listened to Franz Schubert's posthumous string quartet (Gabrielsson, 2011, p. 143). An elderly man recounts a childhood experience where "melancholia and anguish gripped me, but I also felt some form of joy" (Gabrielssson, 2011, p. 140). Another participant, who had listened to "Barcarolle" by Offenbach, explains that "it was so wonderfully beautiful that tears came to my eyes. I felt sad and happy at the same time" (Gabrielssson, 2011, p. 142).

The final example is interesting because it corresponds to the common description of "feeling moved" (Menninghaus et al., 2015): a combination of *happiness* and *sadness* along with tears (see section 16.3). You will recall the anecdote that opened Part III: I described how my partner Susanne was moved to tears *within a few seconds* of hearing "live" music at Parc Güell in Barcelona. This type of experience, *being moved to tears by music*, is by no means uncommon (Frey, 1985; Sloboda, 1991), although some individuals may be more prone to this phenomenon than others. Why does it occur? Sometimes, listeners cry simply because the music makes them sad, but in most of the episodes something else is going on which does *not* appear to be mere sadness.

I hypothesize that the experience of tears during music listening may be conceptualized as a sign of "emotional overflow," resulting from the combined (and perhaps conflicting) outputs from more than one mechanism.

Figure 32.1 Surprising musical event in "Verklärte Nacht" by Arnold Schoenberg.
Used by permission of Belmont Music Publishers, Los Angeles.

It is a sense of being "overwhelmed" by emotion; a type of mental "short-circuit" and "emotional surrender," which may tend to occur in peak experiences (Gabrielsson, 2011). (It could also occur after particularly intense events that do not involve music, such as surviving a near-fatal accident.) The hypothesis could be tested by composing musical stimuli that *effectively* and *simultaneously* trigger more than one mechanism at the same time, and that target opposing affective outcomes.

Not all multi-mechanism responses need to be contradictory, however. They might equally often *reinforce* each other, as for instance in the case of the respondent "Lucy" in a study by Tia DeNora, whose feelings of *calm* evoked by listening to Schubert's "Impromptus" came both from the "musical calm" (perhaps contagion) and from the personal associations and episodic memories linked to this music, which were comforting (DeNora, 2000).

Similarly, a stylistically unexpected event in a piece of music may be reinforced by the adding of a brain stem reflex event involving sound intensity. One example is the onset of a harmonically unexpected D-major chord at the beginning of measure 229 in Arnold Schoenberg's piece "Verklärte Nacht", which is accompanied by an abrupt change in loudness, specified in the musical score as a change from *pianissimo* to *forte*: see Figure 32.1.

32.3 Interactions Between Aesthetic Judgment and Other Mechanisms

Although aesthetic judgments may occur independently of other mechanisms, it seems likely that they often influence each other in more or less

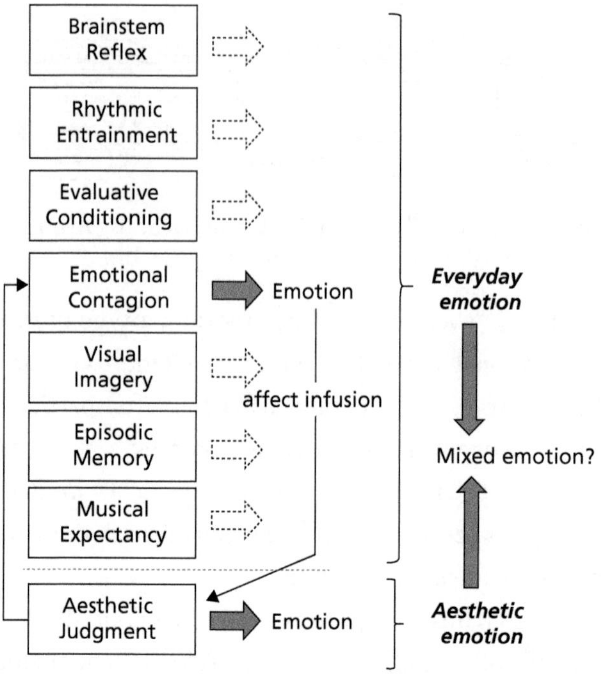

Figure 32.2 Interactions between aesthetic judgment and other mechanisms.
Reprinted from *Physics of Life Reviews*, 10 (3), Patrik N. Juslin, From everyday emotions to aesthetic emotions: Towards a unified theory of musical emotions, pp. 235-66, doi.org/10.1016/j.plrev.2013.05.008 Copyright © 2013 Elsevier B.V. with permission from Elsevier.

subtle ways. For example, an emotion aroused by one of the BRECVEM mechanisms (Part III) might influence, "bias," or "inform" an aesthetic judgment indirectly related to the mechanism (see Figure 32.2) by highlighting some features of the music, rather than others.[2]

Imagine hearing a piece of music and having to make an aesthetic judgment about it. Activation of the contagion mechanism, which reflects the emotional expression of the music, may inform your rating of the "expression" criterion. Activation of the expectancy mechanism, which primarily reflects stylistic deviations, may inform your ratings of the "novelty" and "style" criteria (cf. Chapter 29).

[2] This is one example of a more general principle called "affect as information": the notion that people often *use* feelings to guide their beliefs and judgments (Forgas, 1995).

Moreover, the activation of *any* of the seven BRECVEM mechanisms, along with the ensuing emotion, may inform your rating of the "emotion" criterion (i.e., suggesting an aesthetic value in terms of being able to arouse emotion), at least if emotion is part of your set of subjective criteria. It is in this sense that aesthetic judgments may reflect and "integrate" the outcomes of other emotion mechanisms.

Another possible effect of emotions on aesthetic judgment is that a positive emotion could make the listener process the music more "holistically," whereas a negative emotion could make him or her process it more "analytically" (cf. Leder, Belke, Oeberst, & Augustin, 2004), as may be expected from the "broaden and build theory" of Barbara Fredrickson (1998; section 16.2). This may have an effect on the number or type of aesthetic criteria that are brought to bear on a piece of music.

It is also likely that aesthetic judgments may influence the activation of other induction mechanisms. If the listener adopts an aesthetic attitude to a piece of music, his or her criteria for aesthetic value and their relative weighting may have a bearing on whether the music will arouse emotions through one of the *other* mechanisms, by influencing the listener's attention during the actual listening to the music. For example, the aesthetic framing of a concert with classical music may invite an aesthetic attitude that makes the listener focus on the criterion "expression," which then will increase the chance that the contagion mechanism is activated.

Moreover, one can envisage "everyday emotions" and "aesthetic emotions" to occur together and "reinforce" each other in some circumstances, but to more or less "interfere" with each other in others. Thus, for instance, an extremely negative aesthetic judgment of a piece of music might "overrule" a potential (positive) emotion aroused by other mechanisms, at least for mechanisms that involve "higher" cognitive processes. Some "lower-level" mechanisms may be "immune" to such quality judgments, enabling some special kinds of affective states.

One peculiar form of mixed emotion that may be explained within the present framework is what I call "guilty pleasures" in music listening (Juslin, 2013a). This phenomenon occurs when you experience a positive emotion to a piece of music that you consider having a low aesthetic quality.

On the face of it, this seems to go against the model of aesthetic judgment I proposed in the previous chapter, yet I see this all the time amongst friends and relatives, and have experienced it myself too. (I am not thinking here of the fact that some music may be perceived as so utterly bad that it is comical, though that is of course another possibility!) You can actually enjoy, and even like, music that you do not admire *at all*.

I have some friends who have a special relationship to the song "Barbie Girl" by Aqua. Quite clearly they think the song is plain silly and completely lacking in aesthetic merit, yet they repeatedly request the song at parties, and thoroughly enjoy it—partly because it carries positive emotional associations to past experiences of having fun and generally mucking about. But they tend to apologize when they ask for the song to be played.

Similarly, when I hear certain songs that were in my parents' record collection when I grew up in Sweden in the 1970s, I don't know whether to laugh or cry. On the one hand, they are associated with a warm sense of *nostalgia*. On the other hand, I know that the songs themselves usually sound ridiculous. The odd mix of feelings derives from a combination of episodic memory and aesthetic judgment. My secondary response to these initial feelings is a sense of awkwardness over feeling so good about something so bad, hence the term "guilty pleasures."

This phenomenon is somewhat related to a type of experience reported by Jeanette Bicknell and others, where one is "seeing through" a manipulative attempt to arouse emotions in "cheap art" and still cannot help but being emotionally affected by it (Bicknell, 2009). (Recall from Part III that many of the emotion mechanisms are "modular" in nature: they function independently of other mental processes and of conscious will.)

Without wishing to imply that film music is generally "cheap art," there are certain musical clichés used in movie soundtracks which we recognize as such and find rather corny. ("OK, here comes the tear-jerking strings—right on cue.") Nonetheless, we cannot help but reacting in the expected or intended way, which can be annoying (if you think about it too much).

Both phenomena, "guilty pleasures" and "giving in to clichés," reflect the same cause: Simply put, mechanisms of a more "implicit" nature (e.g., conditioning and contagion) can be "immune" to negative judgments regarding aesthetic value. We cannot turn off the low-level responses of our mammalian brain just because more sophisticated parts of our intellectual machinery find certain musical notes to be "trivial," "banal," or "clichéd." Hardwired responses or years of statistical learning cannot be undone at will.

Our ancient mechanisms may account for those immediate and involuntary effects that music can have on emotions—independently of rational thoughts, aesthetic judgments, or willpower. As noted by Franz Liszt: "Music does not lie to the feelings" (Watson, 1991, p. 38).

I do not wish to argue that listeners cannot *at all* influence their emotional experiences. As discussed in Part III, some mechanisms (e.g., visual imagery) may be affected by the listener considerably. (The listener's influence on the induction process is discussed in section 32.6.) However, recall from Chapter 21 that evaluative conditioning might create positive associations to *any* kind of music. Such "low-level emotional learning" goes on all the time, whether we are aware of it or not. So, be careful with what kind of music you surround yourself with, unless you seek those guilty pleasures!

32.4 Emotional Responses to Fiction

So far I have largely described phenomena whose value for aesthetic experiences with music might appear debatable. Are there also more positive consequences of multiple mechanisms?

Indeed, a multi-level theory could help to explain a recurrent issue in philosophical discourse regarding emotions often referred to as "the paradox of fiction." The dilemma is this: why do we react to fictive events *as if* they were real, even though we know they are not? Why do we respond emotionally to fictional characters in an opera or a movie, or to the emotional expression in music? After all, nothing is really at stake in these events.

Again, the key is that our emotions might be induced at multiple levels of the brain, some of which are implicit and independent of other psychological processes. Accordingly, emotional reactions to fiction (e.g., theater, movies, music) may be treated as "real" at *one* level in the brain, while at the same time they are "discounted" at other, higher levels. This can explain the lack of action undertaken: we do not storm the stage to intervene in the events of an opera, for instance.[3] Fiction, in effect, runs effective "simulations" on our ancient mechanisms, relying on mechanisms like evaluative conditioning, contagion (e.g., "mirror neurons"), and imagery.

This type of "disconnect" between mechanisms at different levels of the brain could also help to explain the *refined emotions* that were discussed in section 16.4. Remember that this term refers to a special mode of experiencing all our "ordinary" emotions, which is characterized by attitudes of detachment, restraint, self-reflexivity, and—particularly—savoring.

Just like we may savor the taste of a well-tempered 2005 Châteauneuf-du-Pape from Chateau Rayas, we may savor sublime emotions experienced while listening to music. This listening mode may be particularly common when we adopt an aesthetic attitude towards the music.

What makes such *aesthetic distancing* possible is that emotion processing at lower brain levels is discounted at higher levels, which enables us to adopt a more reflective stance toward our emotions. Does this mean that emotions we experience during an opera are "real"? Both "yes" and "no": they are treated as "real" by parts of your brain, which will trigger some common "symptoms" of emotions (e.g., psychophysiological reactions); but the responses are partly "inhibited" by higher cognitive processes (to varying degrees in different people).

The present explanation of mixed emotions requires that more than one mechanism may be activated at the same time. This remains to be clearly demonstrated—even though there are self-report data which suggest a

[3] It should be noted that such inhibition of action occurs frequently also in non-fictional emotion episodes, for instance when there is a 'false alarm' or when social norms prohibit certain behaviors (see section 15.7).

co-activation of mechanisms. The problem is not unique to emotional reactions to music; it remains unclear to what extent emotions in general may reflect the output from several mechanisms simultaneously (cf. Izard, 1993).

Philosopher Jenefer Robinson (2005) speculates, in her review of psychological research, that all mechanisms can be activated simultaneously, but I consider this to be highly unlikely. The simultaneous activation of all mechanisms would be possible only if they did not share *any* of the "neural resources" required for the induction process. This is almost certainly not the case. The co-activation of two mechanisms is most plausible when the mechanisms occur at distinct levels of the brain (e.g., sub-cortical versus cortical), and where one of the mechanisms has a high degree of modularity (section 25.1).

The possible co-activation of different psychological mechanisms—at least those that do not interfere with each other's information processing—implies that an important task for future research is to explore possible *interactions* between various mechanisms. Indeed, if we wish to capture the complexity of our musical emotions, this is really where we should be at work.[4]

32.5 Can We Enjoy Negative Emotions? The Case of "Pleasurable Sadness"

The possible co-activation and interaction of various mechanisms could help us to explain a particular phenomenon which has long been recognized, but that has received new attention recently amongst music researchers. It is commonly referred to as "pleasurable sadness."

In 1621, Robert Burton pointed out in his book, *Anatomy of Melancholy*, that, "many men are melancholy by hearing music, but it is a pleasing melancholy

[4] To achieve a *completely independent* manipulation of mechanisms can be difficult, given the strong interrelationships that exist between various musical features (cf. section 10.1). It is difficult to change one type of mechanism-relevant information in the music without changing another type of information to *some* extent.

that it causeth" (Watson, 1991, p. 42). Much later, Jerrold Levinson published an influential article on the pleasurable sadness sometimes experienced while listening to music (Levinson, 1982). We encounter yet another paradox of music and emotion, which needs to be resolved.

PARADOX 5: People tend to avoid experiencing sadness in everyday life, yet they seem to find the experience of sadness pleasurable in music listening.

First, many discussions on this topic are confusing because of a lack of precision. The paradox has often been formulated somewhat carelessly as "can sad music be pleasurable?" When authors use the phrase "sad music," it may refer to a number of different things: it may refer to "music perceived as sad," or "music that arouses sadness," or both: that "the music is perceived as sad and also arouses sadness" (as could happen with the contagion mechanism; Chapter 20). How we resolve the dilemma will, of course, depend on exactly what we mean when we use this phrase.

First, let us look at some of the ways in which the apparent paradox of pleasurable sadness may be (and indeed has been) addressed. Recall that the philosopher Peter Kivy denied (at least initially) that music arouses the "garden variety" emotions such as happiness, sadness, and anger (Kivy, 1990). In line with this view, he would presumably argue that listeners do *not* experience sadness at all. Instead, they simply perceive sadness *expressed* in the music, and then confuse emotions perceived with emotions felt. (If they experience any emotion, it is not sadness.) Scholars have long argued that this could be the case (Meyer, 1956). John Sloboda suggests that the distinction between perceived and aroused emotion may be particularly "blurred" in a musical context because "misattributions" do not bring us up against any of the constraints or contradictions provided by a real-life event (Sloboda, 1999).

Recent findings confirm that music with a sad expression (what *some* theorists call "sad music") may arouse many other emotions in the listener than sadness, such as *nostalgia, peacefulness,* and *wonder* (e.g., Juslin, Harmat, & Eerola, 2014; Taruffi & Koelsch, 2014; Vuoskoski, Thompson, McIlwain,

& Eerola, 2012). That is, there is no *necessary* link between perceived and felt sadness.

Referring to the BRECVEM framework described in Part III, we already know that any piece of music can arouse a number of different emotions, depending on which mechanism is being activated. It may, for instance, be the case that the music evokes a memory of a positive event, which then arouses *happiness* and *nostalgia*, regardless of the expression of the music.

It is really not so strange that music that arouses positive emotions is experienced as pleasurable (positive emotions are, by definition, pleasurable), even if the music features a sad expression (e.g., minor mode, slow tempo, legato articulation, and descending pitch contours). In this case, there is no "paradox" that needs to be explained.

Hence, Kivy may be right, in that some cases of supposed "pleasurable sadness" are no such thing: listeners just experience a pleasurable emotion when they hear a piece of music with a sad expression. However, Kivy's hypothesis cannot account for *all* cases of reported pleasurable sadness: there is now evidence that music with a sad expression can *arouse* genuine sadness in listeners, as indicated by self-report, facial expression, and psychophysiology (Juslin et al., 2014). These sad experiences are not necessarily pleasurable. Some listeners report that they *do* avoid music that makes them sad (Taruffi & Koelsch, 2014). But there is evidence that at least *some* sadness-arousing music is experienced as pleasurable (see Vuoskoski et al., 2012). In such cases, there really *is* a paradox. Or is there?

A different account, offered by David Huron, is that music-aroused sadness triggers adaptive physiological responses in the body (e.g., the release of prolactin), which counteract the painful nature of the sad emotion (Huron, 2011). The pleasure experienced is due to the consoling and comforting effect of hormones. Although there could be some truth to this notion, the account seems insufficient when it comes to explaining the paradox.

First, the physiological response is actually an "after-effect," and so there is no "pleasurable sadness," there is only pleasure *following* sadness. Compare it to a fear-inducing event: you could experience relief *after* the scary event, yet it would be misleading to call it "relieving fear." If the pleasure is only an "after-effect" of pure sadness, reducing the time lag between a brief exposure of the music and the self-report would allow only the "pure" sadness to occur, before the hormonal after-effect has emerged. As with Kivy's hypothesis, there is no "real" paradox here, only a sequence of events.

Second, if so-called pleasurable sadness is merely a hormonal "after-effect", why do we not try to experience sadness to any *other* event in everyday life in order to obtain a similar pleasurable "after-effect"? (We do not decide to watch a TV documentary of starving children so that we may obtain "pleasurable sadness.") Huron's account fails to address how music is *special* in this regard, which is what many theorists have argued (Levinson, 1982).

Emery Schubert offers a theory that is better able to account for the special nature of music and art generally (Schubert, 1996). He follows Daniel Berlyne's idea that "in stimulus situations classifiable as art, there are cues that inhibit the aversion system" (Berlyne, 1971, p. 93). Schubert proposes that an aesthetic context will activate a so-called node in the neural network of the brain that *inhibits* the displeasure center, which appears reasonable enough. However, then he argues that the pleasure felt arises from mere neural activation: "any activation is pleasurable" (Schubert, 1996, p. 18).

This sounds unacceptably vague to me: why would mere neural activation produce pleasure? The originator of this notion of "cognitive hedonics," Colin Martindale, seems to be aware of this when he acknowledges that "the reader may be concerned about the mechanism whereby activation of cognitive units engenders pleasure" (Martindale, 1984, p. 66). Thus, Martindale goes on to speculate about possible neurotransmitters involved. More promising are his hints elsewhere (Martindale, 1984, p. 50) that recognition memory might be involved (i.e., a proper mechanism).[5]

Still, the positive affect derived from "mere recognition" and activation of a cognitive concept node pales in comparison to the more intense sadness

[5] In later publications, Emery Schubert submits that contagion is the mechanism whose effect is inhibited.

experience it is supposed to replace. Think about it: we recognize things all the time, and yet we do not walk around experiencing pleasure all day long. Even if we assume that we *do* experience pleasure from mere activation of cognitive nodes, and that the "displeasure inhibition" idea is true, how, one wonders, would the listener *know* that what he or she is feeling is *sadness* in the first place? (If the felt sadness is inhibited, there is hardly any room for "pleasurable sadness" to occur in the listener's experience.)

More importantly, Schubert's account appears inconsistent with data from a study by Jonna Vuoskoski and co-workers, which shows that experienced sadness to pieces of music is rated as pleasurable to some extent, whereas experienced fear to pieces of music is rated as *only* unpleasant (Vuoskoski et al., 2012). If dissociation from displeasure takes place in an aesthetic context, Vuoskoski and colleagues ask, why isn't "scary" music somewhat pleasurable also?

The BRECVEMA framework offers another possible account, which might be more compatible with the above findings. The apparent paradox could be explained in terms of an interaction between two mechanisms, the contagion mechanism and the aesthetic judgment mechanism. According to this view, listeners *do* indeed experience genuine sadness (resulting from the contagion mechanism), but they *also* experience pleasure, which derives from the perceived beauty of the music (aesthetic judgment mechanism: cf. Figure 32.2).

Note that part of the beauty might reside in the expression of the music (Bicknell, 2009), and that there is indication that music with a *sad* expression is perceived as more expressive than music with other expressions (see Juslin, 1997b). It may be that music with a *sad* expression is generally both more expressive and more beautiful than music with other expressions, thus contributing to the particularly paradoxical response in the case of sadness.[6]

[6] While most people will perceive the beauty of the music, only those listeners who score high on the trait *empathy* may respond with strong sadness to the music through contagion, suggesting that we should find considerable individual differences in the prevalence of so-called pleasurable sadness.

If my proposal is correct, there is actually a mixed emotion of sadness and pleasure. It is not that the felt sadness per se is a source of pleasure, the sadness just happens to occur *together* with a pleasurable impression of beauty. It follows from the hypothesis that the "pleasurable sadness" postulated by scholars should dissolve once the listener is exposed to music that is sadness-arousing, albeit not aesthetically pleasing (Juslin, 2013a). Sadness-arousing capacity and aesthetic attractiveness need to be manipulated independently in order to dissociate the aesthetic judgment from the contagion. If a piece arouses sadness but is judged as "ugly" or "awful," the pleasure should disappear.

Note that simultaneous induction of pleasure and sadness could involve other mechanisms than just contagion. Alf Gabrielsson reports music experiences that involve beauty and "a touch of melancholy because of the fickleness of life" where, for instance, the sound of Zarah Leander's voice is felt to symbolize the past, reminding the listener of people and voices that fell silent long ago. Here, we might tentatively infer a combination of aesthetic judgment and memory. The result is "painful, but I enjoy it at the same time" (Gabrielsson, 2011, p. 142).

One attractive feature of these accounts is that they help to explain the "unique" context of music vis-a-vis other sadness-arousing phenomena in everyday life (e.g., "appreciating beauty"). They also enable predictions about *when* sadness will occur with pleasure, and when it will not. The account explains why not *all* sadness-evoking events involve the paradoxical state, and also why we do not seem to experience "pleasurable anxiety" during music listening: anxiety-inducing music is just not perceived as that beautiful, most of the time (Juslin et al., 2015).

In addition, by explaining so-called pleasurable sadness in terms of a mixture of two emotions, it avoids the quite problematic assertion that an emotion which is *by definition* negative in valence (sadness) is "experienced as positive," in which case the experienced state arguably fails to meet one basic criterion for sadness. Better then to postulate that the sadness occurs *together* with another emotion aroused by a different mechanism.

32.6 Can We Create the Ultimate "Peak" Experience?

Several times throughout this book I have mentioned "peak" experiences. The humanistic psychologist Abraham Maslow explored such experiences in general, and concluded that they happen most frequently during sexual intercourse or when listening to music, sometimes, when doing both at the same time (Maslow, 1968). However, empirical data suggest that "peak" experiences with music are not common, on the whole. For some listeners, they occur only once, or a couple of times during a lifetime (Gabrielsson, 2011). Some people never experience it.

There are some people, though, that may have such experiences more frequently than others, for a variety of reasons. They may have a deep interest in music; they may have special traits such as *openness to experience* (McCrae, 2007) or *auditory style* (Brodsky, Sloboda, & Waterman, 1994); they may be adolescents or young adults (musical interest seems to peak at this age generally); or they may just be fortunate. Reaching "peak" experiences with music may require that all beneficial circumstances coincide. Perhaps we can also improve the prospects of having such an experience somehow, through our own behaviors.

Not listening to crappy music could be a good start! It simply cannot be true that every piece of music on earth "affords" a "peak" experience to the same extent, all individual differences notwithstanding. Some pieces of music recur in reports of strong experiences (Gabrielsson, 2011, p. 410), including certain compositions by Bach, Beethoven, and Mozart. It is not simply a question of genre, though. As Miles Davis notes, "good music is good no matter what kind of music it is" (Davis, 1990, p. 195).

What might be the ultimate piece of music for arousing strong emotions? This question is, of course, difficult to answer in a general way, but based on what has been covered in previous parts of this book, we can argue that in order to arouse maximum emotion in you, the music should include: extreme sound events (brainstem reflex), a quite pronounced and captivating rhythm (entrainment); a voice-like emotional expression (contagion); structures that invite metaphorical analogies to external events (visual imagery); unexpected melodic, harmonic, and rhythmic sequences (musical expectancy); aesthetic qualities such as beauty, originality, and skill (aesthetic judgment); and also have links to emotionally significant life events (evaluative conditioning, episodic memory); and—less plausibly—have implications for your life goals (cognitive goal appraisal).[7]

Accomplishing all this is, of course, a tall order. Perhaps it is no coincidence that many of the "peak" experiences with music involve works by some of the greatest composers and performers. I have not yet found any piece of music that features every one of the mechanisms that I have described in this book. Perhaps there are such pieces, or might I challenge a composer to compose one?

However, as I have tried to show repeatedly in the book, how we react to a piece never depends on the music alone, but also on listener characteristics and on the nature of the listening context. For instance, I think we can focus our *attention* in ways that will at least improve the chances of particular mechanisms being activated, provided that the music features information relevant for those mechanisms. We can switch focus over time while listening to a piece between *content* (e.g., contagion) and *form* (e.g., musical expectancy), *present* (e.g., brainstem reflex) and *past* (e.g., episodic memory) (Juslin, 2012).[8]

Hence, although we cannot exactly *decide* which emotions to have, philosopher Robert Solomon suggests that we may "practice" and "cultivate" emotions (Solomon, 2007). For instance, we can put ourselves in situations that we know will tend to invite the desired emotions, and we can focus on those aspects of these situations that are consistent with the desired

[7] This is an interesting thought exercise, but I am not sure that the "best" experience of music is necessarily one that is constantly packed with strong emotional reactions. Even "great music" does not always arouse emotions, and arousal of emotion is not necessarily what makes it great. This is, perhaps, really a philosophical issue: what would constitute the ultimate musical experience?

[8] Some musicologists have criticized the BRECVEMA model, arguing that it cannot account for how specific pieces of music arouse emotions. To me, this suggests a serious lack of imagination, and it is typically just an excuse for doing more music analysis, analysis of subtle musical features that do not actually arouse emotions in listeners.

emotions, rather than on those that are not. In a musical context, listeners may thus enhance the chances of responding emotionally through their own actions.

A few studies have illuminated this phenomenon. Emilie Gomart and Antoine Hennion cite in-depth interviews with music lovers and drug addicts showing how both engage in "techniques of preparation" to obtain the maximum effect (Gomart & Hennion, 1999). Listeners describe how they use specific "listening strategies" so as to be ready to respond emotionally in preferred or expected ways.

Similarly, Tia DeNora explains how listeners in her study routinely engaged in various practices of "tuning in," of producing a musical event that would be capable of moving them. DeNora observes that an event's

> emotional "effects" [were] achieved through an assemblage of musical practices: the choice of specific recordings, volume levels, material cultural and temporal environments of listening (e.g., choosing to listen in bed, in a rocking chair, in the bath in the evening, the morning, while preparing to go out), and the pairing and compiling of musical works, memories, previous and current contexts of hearing such that the respondents could often be conceived as—and spoke of themselves as—disk jockeys to themselves. (DeNora, 2010, p. 171)

The studies by Gomart and Hennion and DeNora remind me of own adolescent experiences of music. Although I would often listen to music with my best friend, the most intense experiences occurred when I was alone. I would choose a specific favorite track, dim the light in my room leaving only just enough light to be able to look at an album cover; I would listen at a very loud volume (my mother said she used to hear the music from blocks away when she came home from work); I would often engage in mental imagery related to the music, vividly imagining myself *being* the musician playing, and feeling every musical note in my body. I would become completely absorbed by the music, clearly approaching a "peak" experience, which would come to an abrupt end when someone entered the room to tell me to turn the volume down, with me probably looking like a complete imbecile. It is amazing to me, now, to think of the level of dedication and engagement I had. What I was doing, even though I did not really reflect on it at the time, was to try to achieve a "peak" experience with music on a regular basis. Suddenly, the description of the music experience by Hector Berlioz that began this book does not seem so outlandish anymore.

CHAPTER 33

CODA

Final Outlook

I have explained in previous parts of the book that many psychological processes are crucially involved in emotional reactions to music (e.g., conditioning, visual imagery, episodic memory, contagion, expectancy monitoring). From this point of view, the belief that we could ever understand our emotional responses to music just by looking at the musical notes appears absurd. Yet, this is still how many scholars in the domain continue to approach the topic.

In contrast, I have emphasized the roles of a range of psychological mechanisms that may be engaged by "a musical event". I refer to them jointly as the ICINAS-BRECVEMA framework. One of the finest compliments I have ever received came from a colleague who said that the framework was the first theoretical account of the matter that made sense to her "both as a musician and as a scientist." Be that as it may, many details and boundary conditions of the mechanisms remain to be investigated in future research. How might this be achieved?

Ultimately, when it comes to making true progress in the field, I do not think there is any substitute for *systematic experimentation* to tease out those psychophysical relationships that exist between musical features, the social context, and listener responses, as mediated by a range of mechanisms. More specifically, we need field studies in "ecologically valid" settings to demonstrate the plausibility of responses, followed by experimental studies in more "controlled" settings to establish that presumed causal relationships really do hold.

This will not be easy. The challenges are enormous. Then again, being a researcher is not meant to be easy. Without systematic experiments which actively *manipulate* specific mechanisms, we will arguably continue to fumble in the dark. I believe that the theoretical framework described here features a lifetime's worth of hypotheses to test, time I unfortunately do not have. I can only hope that other scholars will find at least some of the ideas promising enough to put them to the test.

Such empirical testing will lead to corrections, extensions, or amendments in the framework I have laid out. However, it can be argued that, ultimately, the usefulness of a theoretical framework is not decided by whether it is 100% correct, but rather by the amount of fruitful research it stimulates, so as to bring us closer to the answers we seek.

Thus, what does the future hold for the field of music and emotion? If there is anything we have learnt, it is that we are poor at making such predictions. When leading researchers in the field were asked to nominate key issues for future research, no-one appeared to expect that scholars would be so preoccupied with the phenomenon of "pleasurable sadness" (section 32.5) ten years later (Juslin & Sloboda, 2010, pp. 946–952).

If I had my way, future work in the domain would attempt to manipulate more "proactively" mechanisms in various applied settings, such as music education and music therapy. There remains unfulfilled potential in applying musical emotions effectively to enhance physical health and subjective well-being.

As I write this chapter, theories of *embodied cognition* (Lesaffre, Maes, & Leman, 2017) and *constructed emotion* (Barrett, 2017) are all the latest rage in the field. These perspectives have their merits, but they are not as "revolutionary" as their proponents would have you believe, and they are hardly "game changers" in the study of music and emotion.

Theories of embodied cognition have been described by some authors as the next paradigm shift in cognitive science, but Stephen Goldinger and co-workers note that the basic principles of the paradigm are either unacceptably vague ("cognition is influenced by the body") or offer nothing new ("cognition exists to guide action," "perception and action are intimately linked") (Goldinger, Papesh, Barnhart, Hansen, & Hout, 2016).

The central claim of theories of embodiment is that all or at least some cognitive processes can do without mental representations. My focus on mental representations might suggest that my framework is wholly inconsistent with theories of embodiment. However, emotions may actually be regarded as a form of embodied cognition, since they involve the whole body; they aim to guide action; there is a continuous interaction between perceiver and ecology; and sensori-motoric links play a key role in *some* of the low-level mechanisms such as entrainment. My framework is only incompatible with a "strong" version of embodied cognition, which rejects *all* types of mental representation. Such a version is unable to account for most cognitive phenomena (Shapiro, 2011).[1] I fail to see how an embodied account on its own could explain the wide range of emotional responses to music described in this book.

Similarly, the theory of constructed emotion (Barrett, 2017) highlights the role of emotional learning and emphasizes the large individual differences in emotion (consistent with the present framework). However, the notion that our emotional experiences are "constructed in the moment by interacting parts of the brain" is trivial: how else could they occur?

The larger claims, that we enter the emotional world largely as "clean slates" and that emotions (just like money) are "a product of human agreement" (Barrett, 2017, p. xiii), are most certainly misleading. There are definitive constraints to *how* and *what* we learn emotionally, and those constraints are key to understand emotions in a musical context also.

Indeed, the greatest lesson of my 20-year quest to unravel the mysteries of our responses to music is that the relationship between music and emotion depends essentially on evolution. Most writing on music, particularly in the humanities, focuses on the cultural and historical context of music, and I concur with Kathleen Higgins that culture is implicated on every level

[1] Students of psychology will recall a previous school of thought in psychology that tried to explain cognitive phenomena without mental representations and that failed miserably: behaviorism.

of the relationship between music and emotion (Higgins, 2012). Music is, after all, a cultural artifact.

Yet, if it were not also the case that music can engage ancient and universal mechanisms, we could hardly explain the deep, universal appeal of music across geographical, historical, and cultural barriers. It is through such mechanisms that music can help to reduce intergroup hostility via cross-cultural musical collaboration (DeNora, 2010) or increase understanding across cultures (Clarke, DeNora, & Vuoskoski, 2015).

Much attention has been devoted to the question of whether the abilities that underlie music are uniquely human or not (Patel, 2018). However, when it comes to the mechanisms that underlie musical emotions, they may owe just as much to the evolution of social mammals as to any uniquely human faculties. As I have tried to show, this could be part of the secret of our responses to music.

With social mammals developed vocal signaling, play, and attachment (which are, arguably, key aspects of music also), and with them came increasing numbers of emotion mechanisms that are still at work today when we listen to music. As I have argued, it is only by "fooling" some of these mechanisms that music can have such strong emotional impact.

Indeed, because music engages so *fully* with our emotions, it can sometimes reveal the nature of our "emotional machinery" more clearly than the stimuli normally used to study emotions in psychology. The fact that music appears to be so abstract—meaning that our "post hoc" rationalizations for emotions cannot be made to fit easily—may actually help us to think more clearly about the true causes of our emotions.

Evolutionary perspectives on music and emotion commonly presume that the emotions aroused (and by implication their underlying mechanisms) must be shaped by the (putative) adaptive functions of music. In this book, I have suggested that the opposite is more likely: that music is tailored to have the maximum effect on already existing and ancient emotion mechanisms.

We may conceive of music as an ingenious form of "reverse engineering" of our many time-tested mechanisms for detecting emotional meaning in sounds, being based sometimes on the explicit knowledge of music composers, songwriters, and performers, but more often rooted in intuition, partly based on what sonic patterns move the creator of those sounds him or herself.

I suggested in Chapter 1 that emotional reactions to music tell a story about who we are, both as individuals (in terms of our life history, memories, traits, and preferences) and as a species (in terms of our innate disposition to use sounds as sources of information in our inferences about possible danger, emotional states of other individuals, and future events). Not only that: each mechanism tells its unique story about what kind of thing music could aspire to be, what promise it holds for us.

Is music mainly a matter of sound and sensation (brainstem reflex)? Or is its key function to enable us to synchronize physiological patterns and movements, such as dancing (rhythmic entrainment)? Does it offer an interpretative landscape of affective associations reflecting our life history (evaluative conditioning)? Does it function to create social cohesion (contagion)? Does it stimulate our imagination and enable us to travel mentally in space and time (visual imagery)? Is it key to our sense of personal identity and social belonging (episodic memory)? Is it an artistic play with sonic architecture and musical style (musical expectancy)? Or is it a source of aesthetic pleasure and wonder (aesthetic judgment)? Perhaps it mostly functions as a means of communication of emotions (Part II). Music can be all those things, and more.

Although our experiences of music are based on the same evolved brain mechanisms as other experiences of emotion in everyday life, the *unique* thing about music is that it is deliberately created to simultaneously activate mechanisms at various levels of the brain in ways that few other events or objects in our daily lives can. Hence, one answer to the question "why does music move us?" is "because we *want* music to move us and have designed it so that it will do so with the maximum effect" (Juslin, 2016).

We have come to the end of this journey, this attempt to unlock the secrets of musical affect. Have I explained musical emotions? I will let you be the judge of that, but the least I will claim is that I have shown that musical emotions are *explicable*: that they *can* be explained in principle. (But that would not be an enticing book title, would it?) I have offered a number of plausible explanations of musical emotions that may be systematically tested in rigorous experiments.

It is quite likely that some researchers will put down this book in protest at the various claims I have made. It is "part of the game" that researchers will want to present their "own" accounts. This book, then, is clearly not the "final word" on this difficult topic. (As Virgil Thompson notes, "nobody is ever patently right about music"; Watson, 1991, p. 382.) However, I believe there is now more agreement than disagreement about most of the questions I have discussed. I will stick my neck out and argue that any serious account of musical emotions will have to follow some of the lines I have sketched out in this book.

Whether we like to conceive of music as "sounding architecture" or "the most expensive of noises," "a safe kind of high" or "the speech of angels," it is clear that the striking beauty of music offers comfort to those of us who occasionally experience the unbearable sadness of life. Yet however fascinating, intriguing, or important the emotions evoked by music may be, they will always, ultimately, and irrevocably be secondary to the music itself. Let the music begin.

APPENDIX

THE LENS MODEL EQUATION AND ITS USE IN MODELING MUSICAL COMMUNICATION

The lens model equation (LME) was originally presented in an influential article by Hursch, Hammond, and Hursch (1964) in the context of studies of *cognitive judgment*. The aim of these studies was to relate the judge's "cognitive system" to a statistical description of the judgment task (Cooksey, 1996). However, I have shown that the LME can also be used to describe musical communication (Juslin, 2000a; Juslin, Karlsson, Lindström, Friberg, & Schoonderwaldt, 2006).

The LME (Eq. 1) embodies the fact that the communication accuracy, or achievement (r_a), is a function of two additive components. The first component is usually called the *linear* component, because it represents that component of the achievement which can be attributed to the linear regression models of the performer and the listener. The linear component shows that achievement is a function of *performer consistency* (R_e), *listener consistency* (R_s), and *matching* (G). Performer consistency refers to the multiple correlation of the performer model (i.e., performer's intention and cues) and listener consistency refers to the multiple correlation of the listener model (i.e., listener's judgment and cues). Both these indices reflect the degree to which the regression models fit the cue utilization and are usually interpreted as measures of consistency of the cue utilization. If $R = 1.0$, then the cue utilization is perfectly consistent. Matching (G) is a measure of the extent to which the cue weights of performers and listeners are similar to each other—that is, whether they use the same code. This index is obtained by correlating the predicted values of the performer's regression model with the predicted values of the listener's regression model. The resulting correlation is conceptually interpreted as the extent to which the performer's cue weights and the listener's cue weights would agree if both regression models were perfect (i.e., $R_e = R_s = 1.0$).

$$r_a = GR_eR_s + C\sqrt{(1-R_e^2)}\sqrt{(1-R_S^2)} \qquad \text{(Eq, 1)}$$

If the communication under study is unsuccessful, we might ask whether this is because (i) the performer uses a different code than the listeners (indicated by a low *G* value), (ii) the performer is applying the code inconsistently (indicated by a low R_e value), or (iii) the listeners apply their code inconsistently (indicated by a low R_s value). These three factors set the upper limit of achievement (Hursch et al., 1964). By analyzing each of them separately, it becomes possible to see how the communicative process can be improved (Juslin, 1998; Juslin et al., 2006).

The second component of the LME is typically called the *unmodeled* component of the communicative process. It includes both unsystematic and systematic variance not accounted for by the linear component. This includes effects of inconsistent cue utilization, order effects, distractions, memory intrusions, omission of relevant cues, or "configuration cue utilization" (i.e., the use of specific patterns of cue values). $(1—R^2_e)$ and $(1—R^2_s)$ refer to the residual variance of the regression models of performers and listeners, respectively. *C*, or *unmodeled matching*, represents the correlation between the residuals of the performer's model and the residuals of the listener's model. If *C* is high, it may indicate (i) a common reliance on acoustic cues in the performance not included in the regression models, (ii) chance agreement between the random model errors, (iii) cue interactions common to both models, or (iv) non-linear cue function forms common to both models (Cooksey, 1996). However, studies indicate that the unmodeled matching of the cue utilization makes a fairly small contribution in music performance (Juslin & Madison, 1999), which means that most of the variance is explained by the additive combination of the cues.

REFERENCES

Adachi, M., & Trehub, S. E. (1998). Children's expression of emotion in song. *Psychology of Music, 26*, 133–153.

Adelmann, P. K., & Zajonc, R. B. (1989). Facial efference and the experience of emotion. *Annual Review of Psychology*, 40, 249–280.

Adorno, T. W. (1976). *Introduction to the sociology of music* (Trans. E. B. Ashby). New York, NY: Seabury.

Aiken, H. D. (1950). The aesthetic relevance of belief. *Journal of Aesthetics, 9*, 301–315.

Alessandri, E., Williamson, V. J., Eiholzer, H., & Williamon, A. (2015). Beethoven recordings reviewed: A systematic method for mapping the content of music performance criticism. *Frontiers in Psychology, 6*, 57.

Allen, R. E. (1992). *The concise Oxford English dictionary.* Oxford: Clarendon Press.

Allen, P., Kaut, K., & Lord, R. (2008). Emotion and episodic memory. In E. Dere, A. Easton, L. Nadel, & J. P. Huston (Eds.), *Handbook of episodic memory* (pp. 115–132). Amsterdam: Elsevier.

Altenmüller, E., Kopiez, R., & Grewe, O. (2013). A contribution to the evolutionary basis of music: Lessons from the chill response. In E. Altenmuller, S. Schmidt, & E. Zimmerman (Eds.), *Evolution of emotional communication: From sounds in nonhuman mammals to speech and music in man* (pp 313–335). Oxford: Oxford University Press.

Andreassi, J. L. (2007). *Psychophysiology: Human behaviour & physiological response* (5th ed.). Hillsdale, NJ: Erlbaum.

Aarden, B. (2003). *Dynamic melodic expectancy.* Ph.D. dissertation, School of Music, Ohio State University.

Arnheim, R. (1974). *Art and visual perception.* Berkeley, CA: University of California Press.

Aschoff, J. (1979). Circadian rhythms: influences of internal and external factors on the period measured in constant conditions. *Zeitschrift für Tierpsychologie, 49*, 225–249.

Ashley, R. (2014). Expressiveness in funk. In D. Fabian, R. Timmers, & E. Schubert (Eds.), *Expressiveness in music performance: Empirical approaches across styles and cultures* (pp. 154–169). Oxford: Oxford University Press.

Aucouturier, J.-J., Johansson, P., Hall, L., Segnini, R., Mercadié, L., & Wanatabe, K. (2016). Covert digital manipulation of vocal emotion alters speakers' emotional states in a congruent direction. *Proceedings of the National Academy of Sciences, 113*, 948–953.

Bach, C. P. E. (1778/1985). *Essay on the true art of playing keyboard instruments* (Transl. and ed. by W. J. Mitchell). London: Eulenburg Books.

Balkwill, L.-L., & Thompson, W. F. (1999). A cross-cultural investigation of the perception of emotion in music: Psychophysical and cultural cues. *Music Perception, 17*, 43–64.

Ball, P. K. (2010). *The music instinct: How music works and why we can't do without it.* London: Bodley Head.

Balleine B. W., & Killcross, S. (2006). Parallel incentive processing: An integrated view of amygdala function. *Trends in Neuroscience, 29,* 272–279.

Baltazar, M., & Saarikallio, S. (2016). Toward a better understanding and conceptualization of affect self-regulation through music: A critical, integrative literature review. *Psychology of Music, 44,* 1500–1521.

Band, J. P., Quilter, S. M., & Miller, G. M. (2001–2002). The influence of selected music and inductions on mental imagery: Implications for practitioners of Guided Imagery and Music. *Journal of the Association for Music and Imagery, 8,* 13–33.

Barenboim, D. (1999). Contribution to: *The art of piano: Great pianists of the 20th century* (TV documentary). New York, NY: WNET Channel 13.

Baron, R. M., & Kenny, D. A. (1986). The moderator-mediator variable distinction in social psychological research: Conceptual, strategic and statistical considerations. *Journal of Personality and Social Psychology, 51,* 1173–1182.

Barradas, G. T. (in press). Understanding nostalgia and sadness in fado music: A qualitative approach to the psychological mechanisms underlying musical emotions. In A. C. Ferreira (Ed.), *Music, sound, and mind.* Rio de Janeiro, Brazil: Editora da ABCM.

Barrett, F. S., Grimm, K. J., Robins, R. W., Wildschut, T., Sedikides, C., & Janata, P. (2010). Music-evoked nostalgia: Affect, memory, and personality. *Emotion, 10,* 390–403.

Barrett, L. F. (2006). Emotions as natural kinds? *Perspectives on Psychological Science, 1,* 28–58.

Barrett, L. F. (2017). *How emotions are made.* Boston, MA: Houghton-Mifflin Harcourt.

Barrett, L. F., Mesquita, B., Ochsner, K. N., & Gross, J. J. (2007). The experience of emotion. *Annual Review of Psychology, 58,* 387–403.

Bashwiner, D. (2014). Tension. In W. F. Thompson (Ed.), *Music in the social and behavioral sciences: An encyclopedia* (pp. 1113–1115). London: Sage.

Batcho, K. I. (2007). Nostalgia and the emotional tone and content of song lyrics. *American Journal of Psychology, 120,* 361–381.

Baumgartner, H. (1992). Remembrance of things past: Music, autobiographical memory, and emotion. *Advances in Consumer Research, 19,* 613–620.

Beardsley, M. (1982). *The aesthetic point of view: Selected essays.* Ithaca, NY: Cornell University Press.

Becker, J. (2001). Anthropological perspectives on music and emotion. In P. N. Juslin & J. A. Sloboda (Eds.), *Music and emotion: Theory and research* (pp. 135–160). Oxford: Oxford University Press.

Becker, J. (2004). *Deep listeners: Music, emotion, and trancing.* Bloomington, IN: Indiana University Press.

Beebe-Center, J. G. (1932). *The psychology of pleasantness and unpleasantness.* New York, NY: Van Nostrand.

Beedie, C. J., Terry, P. C., & Lane, A. M. (2005). Distinctions between emotion and mood. *Cognition and Emotion, 19,* 847–878.

Behne, K.-E., & Wetekam, B. (1993). Musikpsychologische Interpretationsforschung: Individualität und Intention. *Jahrbuch der Deutschen Gesellschaft für Musikpsychologie, 10*, 24–37.

Benestad, F. (1978). *Musik och tanke. Huvudlinjer i musikestetikens historia från antiken till vår egen tid [Music and thought. Main lines in the history of musical aesthetics from antiquity to our time]*. Stockholm: Rabén & Sjögren.

Bergeron, V., & McIver Lopes, D. (2012). Aesthetic theory and aesthetic science: Prospects for integration. In A. P. Shimamura & S. E. Palmer (Eds.), *Aesthetic science: Connecting minds, brains, and experience* (pp. 63–79). Oxford: Oxford University Press.

Berio, L., Dalmonte, R., & Varga, B. A. (1985). *Two interviews* (translated and edited by David Osmond-Smith). New York, NY: Marion Boyars.

Berliner, P. F. (1994). *Thinking in jazz: The infinite act of improvisation*. Chicago, IL: University of Chicago Press.

Berlyne, D. E. (1960). *Conflict, arousal, and curiosity*. New York, NY: McGraw Hill.

Berlyne, D. E. (1970). Conflict, arousal, and hedonic value. *Perception and Psychophysics, 8*, 279–286.

Berlyne, D. E. (1971). *Aesthetics and psychobiology*. New York, NY: Appleton Century Crofts.

Bernardini, L., & Niccolini, A. (2015). Does music calm the dog? *Dog Behavior, 2*, 13–17.

Berry, J. W., Poortinga, Y. H., Breugelmans, S. M., Chasiotis, A., & Sam, D. (2011). *Cross-cultural psychology: Theory and applications* (3rd ed.). Cambridge: Cambridge University Press.

Beyer, R. (2011). *The greatest music stories never told*. New York, NY: Harper-Collins.

Bezdek, M. A., & Gerrig, R. J. (2008). Musical emotions in the context of narrative film. *Behavioral and Brain Sciences, 31*, 578–579.

Bharucha, J. (1994). Tonality and expectation. In R. Aiello (Ed.), *Musical perceptions* (pp. 213–239). Oxford: Oxford University Press.

Bharucha, J., & Stoeckig, K. (1986). Reaction time and musical expectancy: Priming of chords. *Journal of Experimental Psychology: Human Perception and Performance, 12*, 403–410.

Bicknell, J. (2009). *Why music moves us*. New York, NY: Palgrave-Macmillan.

Bigand, E., Vieillard, S., Madurell, F., Marozeau, J., & Dacquet, A. (2005). Multidimensional scaling of emotional responses to music: The effect of musical expertise and of the duration of the excerpts. *Cognition and Emotion, 19*, 1113–1139.

Blacking, J. (1973). *How musical is man?* Seattle, WA: University of Washington Press.

Blair, M. E., & Shimp, T. A. (1992). Consequences of an unpleasant experience with music: A second-order negative conditioning perspective. *Journal of Advertising, 21*, 35–43.

Blood, A. J., & Zatorre, R. J. (2001). Intensely pleasurable responses to music correlate with activity in brain regions implicated in reward and emotion. *Proceedings of National Academy of Sciences, 98*, 11818–11823.

Bluck, S., Alea, N., Habermas, T., & Rubin, D. C. (2005). A tale of three functions: The self-reported uses of autobiographical memory. *Social Cognition, 23*, 91–117.

Bolders, A. C., Band, G. P. H., & Stallen, P. J. (2012). Evaluative conditioning induces changes in sound valence. *Frontiers in Psychology: Emotion Science, 3*, 106.

Boulis, N. M., Kehne, J. H., Miserendino, M. J. D., et al. (1990). Differential blockade of early and late components of acoustic startle following intrathecal infusion of 6-cyano-7-nitroquinoxaline-2,3-dione (CNQX) or D, L-2-amino-5-phosphonovaleric acid (AP-5). *Brain Research, 520*, 240–246.

Bourdieu, P. (1984). *Distinction: A social critique of the judgement of taste* (Trans. R. Nice). London: Routledge.

Boyd, J., & George-Warren, H. (2013). *It's not only rock'n'roll: Iconic musicians reveal the source of their cretaivity.* London: John Blake.

Boyd, P. (2008). *Wonderful tonight: George Harrison, Eric Clapton, and me.* New York, NY: Three Rivers Press.

Brandao, M. L., Melo, L. L., & Cardoso, S. H. (1993). Mechanisms of defense in the inferior colliculus. *Behavioral Brain Research, 58*, 49–55.

Brattico, E., & Pearce, M. (2013). The neuroaesthetics of music. *Psychology of Aesthetics, Creativity, and the Arts, 7*, 48–61.

Bregman, A. S. (1990). *Auditory scene analysis: The perceptual organization of sound.* Cambridge, MA: MIT Press.

Brehmer, A., & Brehmer, B. (1988). What have we learned about human judgment from thirty years of policy capturing? In B. Brehmer & C. R. B. Joyce (Eds.), *Human judgment: The SJT view* (pp. 75–114). Amsterdam: Elsevier.

Brentano, F. C. (1973). *Psychology from an empirical standpoint* (trans. A. C. Rancurello, D. B. Terrell, & L. McAlister). London: Routledge. (Original work published 1874)

Bresin, R., & Friberg, A. (2000). Emotional coloring of computer-controlled music performance. *Computer Music Journal, 24*, 44–62.

Breskin, V. (2010). Triad: Method for studying the core of the semiotic parity of language and art. *Signs—International Journal of Semiotics, 3*, 1–28.

Bressler, S. L., & Menon, V. (2010). Large-scale brain networks in cognition: Emerging methods and principles. *Trends in Cognitive Sciences, 14*, 277–290.

Brodsky, W., Sloboda J. A., & Waterman, M. G. (1994). An exploratory investigation into auditory style as a correlate and predictor of music performance anxiety. *Medical Problems of Performing Artists, 9*, 101–112.

Brody, L. R., & Hall, J. A. (2008). Gender and emotion in context. In M. Lewis, J. M. Haviland-Jones, & L. F. Barrett (Eds.), *Handbook of Emotions* (3rd ed., pp. 395–408). New York, NY: Guilford Press.

Brown, R. (1981). Music and language. In *Documentary report of the Ann Arbor Symposium. National symposium on the applications of psychology to the teaching and learning of music* (pp. 233–265). Reston, VA: Music Educators National Conference.

Brown, S., Martinez, M. J., & Parsons, L. M. (2004). Passive music listening spontaneously engages limbic and paralimbic systems. *Neuroreport, 15*, 2033–2037.

Bruhn, H. (2002). Musical development of elderly people. *Psychomusicology, 18*, 59–75.

Brunswik, E. (1956). *Perception and the representative design of psychological experiments.* Berkeley, CA: University of California Press.

Bryan, G. A., & Barrett, H. C. (2008). Vocal emotion recognition across disparate cultures. *Journal of Cognition and Culture, 8*, 135–148.

Buck, R. (2014). *Emotion: A biosocial synthesis.* Cambridge, UK: Cambridge University Press.

Budd, M. (1985). *Music and the emotions. The philosophical theories.* London: Routledge.

Budd, M. (1989). Music and the communication of emotion. *Journal of Aesthetics and Art Criticism, 47*, 129–138.

Budd, M. (1995). *Value of art: Pictures, poetry and music.* London: Allen Lane/Penguin.

Buelow, G. J. (1983). Johann Mattheson and the invention of the Affektenlehre. In G. J. Buelow & H. J. Marx (Eds.), *New Mattheson studies* (pp. 393–407). Cambridge: Cambridge University Press.

Bullot, N. J., & Reber, R. (2013). The artful mind meets art history: Toward a psycho-historical framework for the science of art appreciation. *Behavioral and Brain Sciences, 36*, 123–137.

Bunt, L., & Pavlicevic, M. (2001). Music and emotion: Perspectives from music therapy. In P. N. Juslin & J. A. Sloboda (Eds.), *Music and emotion: Theory and research* (pp. 181–201). Oxford: Oxford University Press.

Burke, E. (1958). *A philosophical enquiry into the origin of our ideas of the sublime and beautiful.* London: Routledge & Kegan Paul.

Burke, M. J., & Gridley, M. C. (1990). Musical preferences as a function of stimulus complexity and listeners' sophistication. *Perceptual and Motor Skills, 71*, 687–690.

Burland, K., & Pitts, S. (Eds.). (2014). *Coughing and clapping: Investigating audience experience.* Farnham: Ashgate.

Burland, K., & Windsor, W. L. (2014). Moving the gong: Exploring the contexts of composition and improvisation. In K. Burland & S. Pitts (Eds.), *Coughing and clapping: Investigating audience experience* (pp. 101–114). Farnham: Ashgate.

Burt, J. L., Bartolome, D. S., Burdette, D. W., & Comstock, J. R. (1995). A psychophysiological evaluation of the perceived urgency of auditory warning signals. *Ergonomics, 38*, 2327–2340.

Buss, D. M. (2014). *Evolutionary psychology: The new science of the mind* (4th ed.). Boston, MA: Pearson/Allyn & Bacon.

Cabeza, R., & Nyberg, L. (2000). Imaging cognition II: An empirical review of 275 PET and fMRI studies. *Journal of Cognitive Neuroscience, 12*, 1–47.

Callender, J. S. (2005). The role of aesthetic judgments in psychotherapy. *Philosophy, Psychiatry, & Psychology, 12*, 283–296.

Campbell, I. G. (1942). Basal emotional patterns expressible in music. *American Journal of Psychology, 55*, 1–17.

Carlsen, J. C. (1981). Some factors which influence melodic expectancy. *Psychomusicology, 1*, 12–29.

Carreras, J. (1991). *Singing from the soul: An autobiography.* Seattle, WA: YCP Publications.

Casals, P. (1970). *Joys and sorrows.* London: MacDonald.

Chan, L., Livingstone, S., & Russo, F. A. (2013). Automatic facial mimicry of emotion during perception of song. *Music Perception, 30*, 361–367.

Chanda, M. L., & Levitin, D. J. (2013). The neurochemistry of music: Evidence for health outcomes. *Trends in Cognitive Sciences, 17*, 179–193.

Chatterjee, A. (2012). Neuroaesthetics: Growing pains of a new discipline. In A. P. Shimamura & S. E. Palmer (Eds.), *Aesthetic science: Connecting minds, brains, and experience* (pp. 299–317). Oxford: Oxford University Press.

Cirelli, L. K., Wan, S. J., & Trainor, L. J. (2016). Social effects of movement synchrony: Increased infant helpfulness only transfers to affiliates of synchronously-moving partners. *Infancy, 21*, 807–821.

Clapton, E. (2007). *Clapton: The autobiography*. New York, NY: Three Rivers Press.

Clarke, E. F. (1988). Generative principles in music performance. In J. A. Sloboda (Ed.), *Generative processes in music. The psychology of performance, improvisation, and composition* (pp. 1–26). Oxford: Clarendon Press.

Clarke, E. F. (1989). The perception of expressive timing in music. *Psychological Research, 51*, 2–9.

Clarke, E. F. (2005). *Ways of listening*. Oxford: Oxford University Press.

Clarke, E. F. (2012). Creativity in performance. In D. J. Hargreaves, D. Miell, & R. A. R. MacDonald (Eds.), *Musical imaginations: Multidisciplinary perspectives on creativity, performance, and perception* (pp. 17–30). Oxford: Oxford University Press.

Clarke, E. F., DeNora, T., & Vuoskoski, J. (2015). Music, empathy, and cultural understanding. *Physics of Life Reviews, 15*, 61–88.

Clarke, E. F., Dibben, N., & Pitts, S. (2010). *Music and mind in everyday life*. Oxford: Oxford University Press.

Clayton, M. (2012). What is entrainment? Definition and applications in musical research. *Empirical Musicology Review, 7*, 49–56.

Clayton, M. (2016). The social and personal functions of music in cross-cultural perspective. In S. Hallam, I. Cross, & M. Thaut (Eds.), *The Oxford handbook of music psychology* (2nd ed., pp. 47–59). Oxford: Oxford University Press.

Clayton, M., Sager, R., & Will, U. (2005). In time with the music: The concept of entrainment and its significance for ethnomusicology. *European Meetings in Ethnomusicology, 11*, 3–75.

Clynes, M. (1977). *Sentics: The touch of emotions*. New York, NY: Doubleday.

Clynes, M. (1991). On music and healing. In D. Campbell (Ed.), *Music: Physician for times to come* (pp. 121–145). Wheaton, IL: Quest Books.

Cochrane, T. (2013a). Composing the expressive qualities of music. In T. Cochrane, B. Fantini, & K. R. Scherer (Eds.), *The emotional power of music* (pp. 23–40). Oxford: Oxford University Press.

Cochrane, T. (2013b). On the resistance of the instrument. In T. Cochrane, B. Fantini, & K. R. Scherer (Eds.), *The emotional power of music* (pp. 75–83). Oxford: Oxford University Press.

Coenen A. (2010). Subconscious stimulus recognition and processing during sleep. *Psyche, 16*, 90–97.

Cohen, A. J. (2010). Music as a source of emotion in film. In P. N. Juslin & J. A. Sloboda (Eds.), *Handbook of music and emotion: Theory, research, applications* (pp. 879–908). Oxford: Oxford University Press.

Cohen, N. (2015). The floating leaf: Adapted Bonny method sessions for musician with brain damage. In D. Grocke & T. Moe (Eds.), *Guided Imagery & Music (GIM) and music imagery methods for individual and group therapy* (pp. 141–151). London: Jessica Kingsley Publishers.

Collingwood, R. G. (1938). *Principles of art.* Oxford: Clarendon Press.

Compton, T. (1988). McCartney or Lennon: Beatle myths and the composing of the Lennon-McCartney Songs. *Journal of Popular Culture, 22,* 99–131.

Conway, M. A., & Holmes, E. (2005). Autobiographical memory and the working self. In N. Braisby & A. Gellatly (Eds.), *Cognitive psychology* (pp. 507–543). Oxford: Oxford University Press.

Conway, M. A., & Rubin, D. C. (1993). The structure of autobiographical memory. In A. E. Collins, S. E. Gathercole, M. A. Conway, & E. M. Morris (Eds.), *Theories of memory* (pp. 103–137). Hillsdale, NJ: Erlbaum.

Cook, N. (1998). *Music: A very short introduction.* Oxford: Oxford University Press.

Cook, N. (2014). Implications for musicology. In D. Fabian, R. Timmers, & E. Schubert (Eds.), *Expressiveness in music performance: Empirical approaches across styles and cultures* (pp. 331–334). Oxford: Oxford University Press.

Cook, N., & Dibben, N. (2010). Emotion in culture and history: Perspectives from musicology. In P. N. Juslin & J. A. Sloboda (Eds.), *Handbook of music and emotion: Theory, research, applications* (pp. 45–72). Oxford: Oxford University Press.

Cooke, D. (1959). *The language of music.* London: Oxford University Press.

Cooksey, R. W. (1996). *Judgment analysis: Theory, methods, and applications.* New York, NY: Academic Press.

Corballis, M. C. (2002). *From hand to mouth: The origins of language.* Princeton, NJ: Princeton University Press.

Cowan, N. (2010). The magical mystery four: How is working memory capacity limited, and why? *Current Directions in Psychological Science, 19,* 51–57.

Craig A. D. (2008). Interoception and emotion: A neuroanatomical perspective. In M. Lewis, J. M. Haviland-Jones, & L. F. Barrett (Eds.), *Handbook of emotions* (3rd ed., pp. 272–292). New York, NY: Guilford.

Cross, I. (1999). Is music the most important thing we ever did? Music, development and evolution. In S. W. Yi (Ed.), *Music, mind, and science* (pp. 10–39). Seoul: Seoul National University Press.

Cross, I. (2012). Music as an emergent exaptation. In N. Bannan (Ed.), *Music, language, and evolution* (pp. 263–276). Oxford: Oxford University Press.

Cross, I. (2016). The nature of music and its evolution. In S. Hallam, I. Cross, & M. Thaut (Eds.), *The Oxford handbook of music psychology* (2nd ed., pp. 3–17). Oxford: Oxford University Press.

Cross, I., & Tolbert, E. (2016). Music and meaning. In S. Hallam, I. Cross, & M. Thaut (Eds.), *The Oxford handbook of music psychology* (2nd ed., pp. 33–46). Oxford: Oxford University Press.

Crozier, W. R., & Chapman, A. J. (1981). Aesthetic preferences, prestige, and social class. In D. O'Hare (Ed.), *Psychology and the arts* (pp. 242–278). Brighton: Harvester.

Cui, X., Jeter, C. B., Yang, D., Montague, P. R., & Eagleman, D. M. (2007). Vividness of mental imagery: Individual variability can be measured objectively. *Vision Research, 47*, 474–478.

Cunningham, J. G., & Sterling, R. S. (1988). Developmental changes in the understanding of affective meaning in music. *Motivation and Emotion, 12*, 399–413.

Cupchik, G. C., Vartanian, O., Crawley, A., & Mikulis, D. J. (2009). Viewing artworks: Contributions of cognitive control and perceptual facilitation to aesthetic response. *Brain and Cognition, 70*, 84–91.

Cupchik, G. C., & Laszlo, J. (1992). *Emerging visions of the aesthetic process: Psychology, semiology, and philosophy*. Cambridge: Cambridge University Press.

Dahlstedt, S. (1990). *Musikestetik [Music aesthetics]*. Uppsala: Department of Musicology, Uppsala University, Sweden.

Damasio, A. (1994). *Descartes' error: Emotion, reason, and the human brain.* New York, NY: Avon Books.

Damasio, A. R., Grabowski, T. J., Bechara, A., Damasio, H., Ponto, L. L. B., Parvizi, J., & Hichwa, R. D. (2000). Subcortical and cortical brain acitivity during the feeling of self-generated emotions. *Nature Neuroscience, 3*, 1049–1056.

Darwin, C. (1872/1998). *The expression of the emotions in man and animals* (3rd ed.). London: Harper-Collins.

Davidson, J. W., & Broughton, M. C. (2016). Bodily mediated coordination, collaboration, and communication in music performance. In S. Hallam, I. Cross, & M. Thaut (Eds.), *The Oxford handbook of music psychology* (2nd ed., pp. 573–595). Oxford: Oxford University Press.

Davidson, R. J. (1994). On emotion, mood, and related affective constructs. In P. Ekman & R. J. Davidson (Eds.), *The nature of emotion: Fundamental questions* (pp. 51–55). Oxford: Oxford University Press.

Davidson, R. J. (1995). Celebral asymmetry, emotion, and affective style. In R. J. Davidson & K. Hugdahl (Eds.), *Brain asymmetry* (pp. 361–387). Cambridge, MA: MIT Press.

Davidson, R. J. (2012). *The emotional life of your brain.* London: Penguin Books.

Davidson, R. J., Scherer, K. R., & Goldsmith, H. H. (Eds.). (2003). *Handbook of affective sciences.* Oxford: Oxford University Press.

Davies, J. B. (1978). *The psychology of music.* London: Hutchinson.

Davies, S. (1994). *Musical meaning and expression.* Ithaca, NY: Cornell University Press.

Davies, S. (2001). Philosophical perspectives on music's expressiveness. In P. N. Juslin & J. A. Sloboda (Eds.), *Music and emotion: Theory and research* (pp. 23–44). Oxford: Oxford University Press.

Davis, M. (1990). *Miles: The autobiography*. London: Picador.

Davis, M. (1984). The mammalian startle response. In R. C. Eaton (Ed.), *Neural mechanisms of startle behavior* (pp. 287–342). New York, NY: Plenum Press.

Dawes, R. M., & Corrigan, B. (1974). Linear models in decision making. *Psychological Bulletin, 81*, 95–106.

De Houver, J., Baeyens, F., & Feld, A. P. (2005). Associative learning of likes and dislikes: Some current controversies and possible ways forward. *Cognition and Emotion, 19*, 161–174.

De Houver, J., Thomas, S., & Baeyens, F. (2001). Associative learning of likes and dislikes: A review of 25 years of research on human evaluative conditioning. *Psychological Bulletin, 127*, 853–869.

Dennett, D. C. (1987). *The intentional stance.* Cambridge, MA: MIT Press.

DeNora, T. (2000). *Music in everyday life.* Cambridge: Cambridge University Press

DeNora, T. (2010). Emotion as social emergence: Perspectives from music sociology. In P. N. Juslin & J. A. Sloboda (Eds.), *Handbook of music and emotion: Theory, research, applications* (pp. 159–183). Oxford: Oxford University Press.

Denski, S. W. (1992). Music, musicians, and communication: The personal voice in a common language. In J. Lull (Ed.), *Popular music and communication* (2nd ed., pp. 33–48). London: Sage.

Dere, E., Zlomuzica, A., Huston, J. P., & De Souza Silva, M. A. (2008). Animal episodic memory. In E. Dere et al. (Eds.), *Handbook of episodic memory* (pp. 155–184). Amsterdam: Elsevier.

Dewey, J. (1934). *Art as experience.* Oxford: Balch.

Dibben, N. (2001). What do we hear when we hear music? Musical perception and musical materials. *Musicae Scientiae, 5*, 161–194.

Dibben, N. (2002). Gender identity and music. In R. A. R. Mac-Donald, D. J. Hargreaves, & D. Miell (Eds.), *Musical identities* (pp. 117–133). Oxford: Oxford University Press.

Dibben, N. (2014). Understanding performance expression in popular music recordings. In D. Fabian, R. Timmers, & E. Schubert (Eds.), *Expressiveness in music performance: Empirical approaches across styles and cultures* (pp. 117–132). Oxford: Oxford University Press.

Dickie, G. (1974). *Art and the aesthetic: An institutional analysis.* Ithaca, NY: Cornell University Press.

Diener, E., & Diener, C. (1996). Most people are happy. *Psychological Science, 7*, 181–185.

DiMaggio, P. (1987). Classification in art. *American Sociological Review, 52*, 440–455.

Dimberg, U., & Thunberg, M. (1998). Rapid facial reactions to emotional facial expressions. *Scandinavian Journal of Psychology, 39*, 39–45.

Dimberg, U., Thunberg, M., & Elmehed, K. (2000). Unconscious facial reactions to emotional facial expressions. *Psychological Science, 11*, 86–89.

Dimberg, U., Thunberg, M., & Grunedal, S. (2002). Facial reactions to emotional stimuli: Automatically controlled emotional responses. *Cognition and Emotion, 16*, 449–472.

Dimery, R. (2005). *1001 albums you must hear before you die.* London: Cassell.

Di Pellegrino, G., Fadiga, L., Fogassi, L., Gallese, V., & Rizzolatti, G. (1992). Understanding motor events: A neurophysiological study. *Experimental Brain Research, 91*, 176–180.

Dissanayake, E. (2000). Antecedents of the temporal arts in early mother-infant interaction. In N. L. Wallin, B. Merker, & S. Brown (Eds.), *The origins of music* (pp. 389–410). Cambridge, MA: MIT Press.

Donald, M. (1991). *Origins of the modern mind: Three stages in the evolution of culture and cognition.* Cambridge, MA: Harvard University Press.

Donald, M. (2001). *A mind so rare: The evolution of human consciousness.* New York, NY: Norton.

Dowling W. J., & Harwood, D. L. (1986). *Music cognition*. New York, NY: Academic Press.
Downey, J. E. (1897). A musical experiment. *American Journal of Psychology*, *9*, 63–69.
Driver, J. (2001). *The mammoth book of sex, drugs & rock 'n' roll*. London: Constable Publishers.
Dubal, D. (1985). *The world of the concert pianist. Conversations with 35 internationally celebrated pianists*. London: Victor Gollancz.
Duerksen, G. L. (1972). Some effects of expectation on evaluation of recorded musical performance. *Journal of Research in Music Education*, 20, 268–272.
Duffy, E. (1941). An explanation of "emotional" phenomena without the use of the concept "emotion". *Journal of General Psychology*, 25, 283–293.
Dutton, D. (2009). *The art instinct: Beauty, pleasure and human evolution*. New York, NY: Bloomsbury Press.
Edwards, R. H. (1992). Model building. In R. Colwell (Ed.), *Handbook of research on music teaching and learning* (pp. 38–47). New York, NY: Schirmer Books.
Eerola, T. (1997). The rise and fall of the experimental style of the Beatles: The life span of stylistic periods in music. In A. Gabrielsson (Ed.), *Proceedings of the third triennial ESCOM conference* (pp. 377–381). Uppsala: Uppsala University.
Eerola, T. (2011). Are the emotions expressed in music genre-specific? An audio-based evaluation of datasets spanning classical, film, pop and mixed genres. *Journal of New Music Research*, 40, 349–366.
Eerola, T., Friberg, A., & Bresin, R. (2013). Emotional expression in music: Contribution, linearity, and additivity of primary musical cues. *Frontiers in Psychology: Emotion Science*, 4, 487.
Eerola, T., & Vuoskoski, J. K. (2013). A review of music and emotion studies: Approaches, emotion models and stimuli. *Music Perception*, 30, 307–340.
Eerola, T., Vuoskoski, J. K., & Kautiainen, H. (2016). Being moved by unfamiliar sad music is associated with high empathy. *Frontiers in Psychology*, *7*, 1176.
Eggerman, R. W. (1975). Is normative aesthetics a viable field for philosophical inquiry? *Journal of Value Inquiry*, 9, 210–215.
Eibl-Eibesfeldt, I. (1989). *Human ethology*. New York, NY: Aldine.
Ekman, P. (Ed.). (1973). *Darwin and facial expression*. New York, NY: Academic Press.
Ekman, P. (1992). An argument for basic emotions. *Cognition and Emotion*, *6*, 169–200.
Elliott, D. J. (2005). Musical understanding, musical works, and emotional expression: Implications for music education. *Educational Philosophy and Theory*, *37*, 93–103.
Elliott, R. (2010). *Fado and the place of longing: Loss, memory and the city*. Farnham: Ashgate.
Ellsworth, P. C. (1994). Levels of thought and levels of emotion. In P. Ekman & R. J. Davidson (Eds.), *The nature of emotion* (pp. 192–196). Oxford: Oxford University Press.
Erlewine, M., Bogdanow, V., Woodstra, C., & Koda, C. (Eds.). (1996). *The blues*. San Francisco, CA: Miller-Freeman.
Escoffier, N., Zhong, J., Schirmer, A., & Qui, A. (2013). Emotions in voice and music: Same code, same effect? *Human Brain Mapping*, 34, 1796–1810.

Etzel, J. A., Johnsen, E. L., Dickerson, J., Tranel, D., & Adolphs, R. (2006). Cardiovascular and respiratory responses during musical mood induction. *International Journal of Psychophysiology, 61*, 57–69.

Evans, P., & Schubert, E. (2008). Relationships between expressed and felt emotions in music. *Musicae Scientiae, 12*, 75–99.

Eysenck, H. J. (1981). Aesthetic preferences and individual differences. In D. O. Hare (Ed.), *Psychology and the arts* (pp. 76–101). Brighton: Harvester.

Eysenck, M. W. (1994). *Perspectives on psychology*. Hillsdale, NJ: Erlbaum.

Fabian, D., Timmers, R., & Schubert, E. (Eds.). (2014). *Expressiveness in music performance: Empirical approaches across styles and cultures*. Oxford: Oxford University Press.

Farga, F. (1969). *Violins and violinists* (2nd ed.). London: The Cresset Press.

Farnsworth, P. R. (1969). *The social psychology of music* (2nd ed.). Ames, IA: Iowa State University Press.

Fechner, G. T. (1876). *Vorschule der ästhetik*. Leipzig: Breitkopf and Hartel.

Feld, S. (1982). *Sound and sentiment: Birds, weeping, poetics, and song in Kaluli expression*. Philadelphia, PA: University of Pennsylvania Press.

Fenner, D. E. W. (1996). *The aesthetic attitude*. Atlantic Highlands, NJ: Humanities Press.

Field, A. P., & Moore, A. C. (2005). Dissociating the effects of attention and contingency awareness on evaluative conditioning effects in the visual paradigm. *Cognition and Emotion, 19*, 217–243.

Fisk, J. (Ed.). (1997). *Composers on music*. Boston, MA: Northeastern University Press.

Fiske, H. E. (1977). Relationship of selected factors in trumpet performance adjudication reliability. *Journal of Research in Music Education, 25*, 256–263.

Fiske, H. E. (1983). Judging musical performances: Method or madness? *Update: Applications of Research in Music Education, 1*, 7–10.

Fivush, R., & Sales, J. M. (2004). Children's memories of emotional events. In D. Reisberg & P. Hertel (Eds.), *Memory and emotion* (pp. 242–271). Oxford: Oxford University Press.

Flom, R., Gentile, D., & Pick, A. (2008). Infants' discrimination of happy and sad music. *Infant Behavior and Development, 31*, 716–728.

Fodor, J. A. (1983). *The modularity of the mind*. Cambridge, MA: MIT Press.

Folkestad, G. (2002). National identity and music. In R. A. R. MacDonald, D. J. Hargreaves, & D. Miell (Eds.), *Musical identities* (pp. 163–178). Oxford: Oxford University Press.

Fónagy, I., & Magdics, K. (1963). Emotional patterns in intonation and music. *Zeitschrift für Phonetik, Sprachwissenschaft und Kommunikationsforschung, 16*, 293–326.

Forgas, J. (1995). Mood and judgment: The affect infusion model (AIM). *Psychological Bulletin, 117*, 39–66.

Foss, J. A., Ison, J. R., Torre, J. P., & Wansack, S. (1989). The acoustic startle response and disruption of aiming: I. Effect of stimulus repetition, intensity, and intensity changes. *Human Factors, 31*, 307–318.

Fox, A. E., Lapate, R. C., Shackman, A. J., & Davidson, R. J. (Eds.). (2018). *The nature of emotion: Fundamental questions* (2nd ed.). Oxford: Oxford University Press.

Fox, E. (2008). *Emotion science*. Basingstoke: Palgrave Macmillan.

Fraisse, P., Oleron, G., & Paillard, J. (1953). Les effets dynamogeniques de la musique. Etude experimentale [Dynamic effects of music. Experimental study]. *Année Psychologique, 53*, 1–34.

Fredrickson, B. L. (1998). What good are positive emotions? *Review of General Psychology, 2*, 300–319.

Freud, S. (1914/1955). The Moses of Michelangelo. In *The standard edition of the complete psychological works of Sigmund Freud. Vol. XIII* (pp. 209–238). London: The Hogarth Press.

Frey, W. H. (1985). *Crying: The mystery of tears*. Minneapolis, MN: Winston.

Friberg, A., & Sundberg, J. (1999). Does music performance allude to locomotion? A model of final ritardandi derived from measurements of stopping runners. *Journal of the Acoustical Society of America, 105*, 1469–1484.

Fried, R., & Berkowitz, L. (1979). Music that charms ... and can influence helpfulness. *Journal of Applied Social Psychology, 9*, 199–208.

Frijda, N. H. (2008). The psychologist's point of view. In M. Lewis, J. M. Haviland-Jones, & L. F. Barrett (Eds.), *Handbook of emotions* (3rd ed., pp. 68–87). New York, NY: Guilford.

Frijda, N. H. (2016). The evolutionary emergence of what we call "emotions". *Cognition and Emotion, 30*, 609–620.

Frijda, N. H., & Scherer, K. R. (2009). Affect (psychological perspectives). In D. Sander & K. R. Scherer (Eds.), *The Oxford companion to emotion and the affective sciences* (p. 10). Oxford: Oxford University Press.

Frijda, N. H., & Sundararajan, L. (2007). Emotion refinement: A theory inspired by Chinese poetics. *Perspectives on Psychological Science, 2*, 227–241.

Frith, S. (1996). *Peforming rites: On the value of popular music*. Oxford: Oxford University Press.

Fritz, T., Jentschke, S., Gosselin, N., Sammler, D., Peretz, I., Turner, R., Friederici, A. D., & Koelsch, S. (2009). Universal recognition of three basic emotions in music. *Current Biology, 19*, 1–4.

Fritz, T., & Koelsch, S. (2008). The role of semantic association and emotional contagion for the induction of emotion with music. *Behavioral and Brain Sciences, 31*, 579–580.

Fujioka, T., Trainor, L. J., Large, E. W., & Ross, B. (2012). Internalized timing of isochronous sounds is represented in neuromagnetic beta oscillations. *Journal of Neuroscience, 32*, 1791–1802.

Gabriel, C. (1978). An experimental study of Deryck Cooke's theory of music and meaning. *Psychology of Music, 6*, 13–20.

Gabrielsson, A. (1987). Once again: The theme from Mozart's piano sonata in A major. A comparison of five performances. In A. Gabrielsson (Ed.), *Action and perception in rhythm and music* (pp. 81–103). Stockholm: Publications issued by the Royal Swedish Academy of Music (No. 55).

Gabrielsson, A. (1999). The performance of music. In D. Deutsch (Ed.), *The psychology of music* (2nd ed., pp. 501–602). San Diego, CA: Academic Press.

Gabrielsson, A. (2001). Emotions in strong experiences with music. In P. N. Juslin & J. A. Sloboda (Eds.), *Music and emotion: Theory and research* (pp. 431–449). Oxford: Oxford University Press.

Gabrielsson, A. (2002). Emotion perceived and emotion felt: Same or different? *Musicae Scientiae, Special Issue 2001–2002*, 123–147.

Gabrielsson, A. (2003). Music performance research at the millennium. *Psychology of Music, 31*, 221–272.

Gabrielsson, A. (2010). Strong experiences with music. In P. N. Juslin & J. A. Sloboda (Eds.), *Handbook of music and emotion: Theory, research, applications* (pp. 547–574). Oxford: Oxford University Press.

Gabrielsson, A. (2011). *Strong experiences with music: Music is much more than just music.* Oxford: Oxford University Press.

Gabrielsson, A. (2016). *Introduktion till musikpsykologin [Introduction to music psychology].* Department of Psychology, Uppsala University, Sweden.

Gabrielsson, A., & Juslin, P. N. (1996). Emotional expression in music performance: Between the performer's intention and the listener's experience. *Psychology of Music, 24*, 68–91.

Gabrielsson, A., & Juslin, P. N. (2003). Emotional expression in music. In R. J. Davidson, K. R. Scherer, & H. H. Goldsmith (Eds.), *Handbook of affective sciences* (pp. 503–534). Oxford: Oxford University Press.

Gabrielsson, A., & Lindström, E. (1995). Emotional expression in synthesizer and sentograph performance. *Psychomusicology, 14*, 94–116.

Gabrielsson, A., & Lindström, E. (2001). The influence of musical structure on emotional expression. In P. N. Juslin & J. A. Sloboda (Eds.), *Music and emotion: Theory and research* (pp. 223–248). Oxford: Oxford University Press.

Gabrielsson, A., & Lindström Wik, S. (2003). Strong experiences related to music: A descriptive system. *Musicae Scientiae, 7*, 157–217.

Ganis, G., Thompson, W. L., Mast, F., & Kosslyn, S. M. (2004). The brain's mind images: The cognitive neuroscience of mental imagery. In M. S. Gazzaniga (Ed.), *The cognitive neurosciences* (3rd ed., pp. 931–941). Cambridge, MA: MIT Press.

Gärdenfors, P. (2003). *How homo became sapiens: On the evolution of thinking.* Oxford: Oxford University Press.

Gardiner, M. F. (2008). Responses to music: Emotional signaling and learning. *Behavioral and Brain Sciences, 31*, 580–581.

Gardner, H. (1985). *The mind's new science. A history of the cognitive revolution.* New York, NY: Basic Books.

Gardner, H. (1983/1993). *Frames of mind: The theory of multiple intelligences.* New York, NY: Basic Books.

Garofalo, R. (2010). Politics, mediation, social context, and public use. In P. N Juslin & J. A. Sloboda (Eds.), *Handbook of music and emotion: Theory, research, applications* (pp. 725–754). Oxford: Oxford University Press.

Gaston, E. T. (1968). *Music in therapy.* New York, NY: Macmillan.

Gaut, B. (2000). 'Art' as a cluster concept. In N. Carroll (Ed.), *Theories of art today* (pp. 25–44). Madison, WI: University of Wisconsin Press.

Gauthier, F. (2004). Rave and religion? A contemporary youth phenomenon as seen through the lens of religious studies. *Studies in Religion, 33*, 397–413.

Gaver, W. W., & Mandler, G. (1987). Play it again, Sam: On liking music. *Cognition and Emotion, 1*, 259–282.

Geringer, J. (1982). Verbal and operant music listening preferences in relationship to age and musical training. *Psychology of Music, Special Issue*, 47–50.

Gerrards-Hesse, A., Spies, K., & Hesse, F. W. (1994). Experimental inductions of emotional states and their effectiveness: A review. *British Journal of Psychology, 85*, 55–78.

Getz, R. P. (1966). The effects of repetition on listening response. *Journal of Research in Music Education, 14*, 178–192.

Gibson J. J. (1979). *The ecological approach to visual perception.* Boston, MA: Houghton Mifflin.

Gilden, D. L. (2001). Cognitive emissions of 1/f noise. *Psychological Review, 108*, 33–56.

Goehr, A. (1992). Music as communication. In D. H. Mellor (Ed.), *Ways of communicating* (pp. 125–152). Cambridge: Cambridge University Press.

Gohm, C. L., & Clore, G. L. (2000). Individual differences in emotional experience: Mapping available scales to processes. *Personality and Social Psychology Bulletin, 26*, 679–697.

Goldberg, F. (1992). Images of emotion: The role of emotions in Guided Imagery and Music. *Journal of the Association of Music and Imagery, 1*, 5–18.

Goldinger, S. D., Papesh, M. H., Barnhart, A. S., Hansen, W. A., & Hout, M. C. (2016). The poverty of embodied cognition. *Psychonomic Bulletin & Review, 23*, 959-978.

Goldman, A. (1995). Emotions in music (a postscript). *The Journal of Aesthetics and Art Criticism, 53*, 59–69.

Goldstein, A. (1980). Thrills in response to music and other stimuli. *Physiological Psychology, 8*, 126–129.

Gomart, E., & Hennion, A. (1999). A sociology of attachment: Music amateurs, drug users. In J. Law & J. Hazzart (Eds.), *Actor network theory and after* (pp. 220–247). Oxford: Blackwell.

Gombrich, E. H. (1969). *Art and illusion.* Princeton, NJ: Princeton University Press.

Gombrich, E. H. (1998). Style. In D. Preziosi (Ed.), *The art of art history: A critical anthology* (p. 150). Oxford: Oxford University Press.

Gomez, P., & Danuser, B. (2007). Relationships between musical structure and psychophysiological measures of emotion. *Emotion, 7*, 377–387.

Goodwin, C. J. (2008). *A history of modern psychology* (3rd ed.). New York, NY: John Wiley.

Gopnik, B. (2012). Aesthetic science and artistic knowledge. In A. P. Shimamura & S. E. Palmer (Eds.), *Aesthetic science: Connecting minds, brains, and experience* (pp. 129–159). Oxford: Oxford University Press.

Goulding, P. G. (1995). *Classical music: The 50 greatest composers and their 1,000 greatest works.* New York, NY: Ballantine Books.

Gowensmith, W. N., & Bloom, L. J. (1997). The effects of heavy metal music on arousal and anger. *Journal of Music Therapy, 34*, 33–45.

Gray, P. M., Krause, B., Atema, J., Payne, R., Krumhansl, C., & Baptista, L. (2001). The music of nature and the nature of music. *Science, 291*, 52–54.

Gracyk, T. (2012). *The philosophy of art: An introduction.* Cambridge: Polity.

Grahn, J. A., Henry, M. J., & McAuley, J. D. (2011). FMRI investigation of cross-modal interactions in beat perception: Audition primes vision, but not vice versa. *Neuroimage*, *54*, 1231–1243.

Greasley, A., & Lamont, A. (2016). Musical preferences. In S. Hallam, I. Cross, & M. Thaut (Eds.), *The Oxford handbook of music psychology* (2nd ed., pp. 263–281). Oxford: Oxford University Press.

Greenberg, L. S. (2012). Emotions, the great captains of our lives: Their role in the process of change in psychotherapy. *American Psychologist*, *67*, 697–707.

Gregory, A. H., & Varney, N. (1996). Cross-cultural comparisons in the affective response to music. *Psychology of Music*, *24*, 47–52.

Grewe, O., Nagel, F., Kopiez, R., & Altenmüller, E. (2007). Listening to music as a re-creative process: Physiological, psychological, and psychoacoustical correlates of chills and strong emotions. *Music Perception*, *24*, 297–314.

Grey, M. J. (2010). Proprioceptive sensory feedback. In *Encyclopedia of life sciences*. Chichester: John Wiley & Sons. DOI:10.1002/9780470015902.a0000071.pub2.

Gross, J. J. (2014). Emotion regulation: Conceptual and empirical foundations. In J. J. Gross (Ed.), *Handbook of emotion regulation* (2nd ed., pp. 3–20). New York, NY: Guildford.

Guhn, M., Hamm, A., & Zentner, M. R. (2007). Physiological and musico-acoustic correlates of the chill response. *Music Perception*, *24*, 473–483.

Gundlach, R. H. (1935). Factors determining the characterization of musical phrases. *American Journal of Psychology*, *47*, 624–644.

Gutheil, E. A. (1952). Introduction. In A. Carpurso, V. R. Fisichelli, L. Gilman, E. A. Gutheil, J. T. Wright, & F. Paperte (Eds.), *Music and your emotions: A practical guide to music selections associated with desired emotional responses* (pp. 9–13). New York, NY: Liveright.

Haas, F., Distenfeld, S., & Axen, K. (1986). Effects of perceived musical rhythm on respiratory pattern. *Journal of Applied Physiology*, *61*, 1185–1191.

Haidt, J., & Seder, P. (2009). Admiration and awe. In D. Sander & K. R. Scherer (Eds.), *The Oxford companion to emotion and the affective sciences* (pp. 4–5). Oxford: Oxford University Press.

Hallam, S. (2010). Music education: The role of affect. In P. N. Juslin & J. A. Sloboda (Eds.), *Handbook of music and emotion: Theory, research, applications* (pp. 792–817). Oxford: Oxford University Press.

Hallam, S., Cross, I., & Thaut, M. (Eds.). (2016). *The Oxford handbook of music psychology* (2nd ed.). Oxford: Oxford University Press.

Halliwell, S. (1987). *The poetics of Aristotle: Translation and commentary*. London: Duckworth.

Hammerl, M., & Fulcher, E. P. (2005). Reactance in affective evaluative learning: Outside of conscious control? *Cognition and Emotion*, *19*, 197–216.

Hampson, P. (2000). A naturalistic empirical investigation of Deryck Cooke's theory of music and meaning. In C. Woods, G. Luck, R. Brochard, F. Seldon, & J. A. Sloboda (Eds.), *Proceedings of the sixth international conference on music perception and cognition* (CD-rom). University of Keele, UK.

Hanser, S. B. (2010). Music, health, and well-being. In P. N. Juslin & J. A. Sloboda (Eds.), *Handbook of music and emotion: Theory, research, applications* (pp. 849–877). Oxford: Oxford University Press.

Hanslick, E. (1986). *On the musically beautiful: A contribution towards the revision of the aesthetics of music* (Trans. G. Payzant). Indianapolis, IN: Hackett. (Originally published 1854)

Harari, Y. N. (2014). *Sapiens: A brief history of humankind.* New York, NY: Vintage Books.

Harbor, C. (2013). *The birth of the music business: Public commercial concerts in London.* Unpublished doctoral dissertation, University of London, UK.

Hare, F. G. (1974). Artistic training and responses to visual and auditory patterns varying in uncertainty. In D. E. Berlyne (Ed.), *Studies in the new experimental aesthetics: Steps toward an objective psychology of aesthetic appreciation* (pp. 159–168). Washington, DC: Hemisphere.

Hargreaves, D. J. (1982). Preference and prejudice in music: A psychological approach. *Popular Music and Society, 8,* 13–18.

Hargreaves, D. J. (1986). *The developmental psychology of music.* Cambridge: Cambridge University Press.

Hargreaves, D. J., MacDonald, R. A. R., & Miell, D. E. (2005). How do people communicate using music? In D. E. Miell, R. A. R. MacDonald, & D. J. Hargreaves (Eds.), *Musical communication* (pp. 1–25). Oxford: Oxford University Press.

Hargreaves, D. J., Messerschmidt, P., & Rubert, C. (1982). Musical preference and evaluation. *Psychology of Music, 8,* 13–18.

Hargreaves, D. J., Miell, D., & MacDonald, R. A. R. (2002). *Musical identities.* Oxford: Oxford University Press.

Hargreaves, D. J., & North, A. C. (2010). Experimental aesthetics and liking for music. In P. N. Juslin & J. A. Sloboda (Eds.), *Handbook of music and emotion: Theory, research, applications* (pp. 515–546). Oxford: Oxford University Press.

Harmat, L., Ørsted Andersen, F., Ullén, F., Wright, J., & Sadlo, G. (Eds.). (2016). *Flow experience: Empirical research and applications.* New York, NY: Springer.

Harrer, G., & Harrer, H. (1977). Music, emotion, and autonomic function. In M. Critchley & R. A. Henson (Eds.), *Music and the brain. Studies in the neurology of music* (pp. 202–216). London: William Heinemann.

Haslam, N. (1995). The discreteness of emotion concepts: Categorical structure in the affective circumplex. *Personality and Social Psychology Bulletin, 21,* 1012–1019.

Hatfield, E., Bensmana, L., Thornton, P. D., & Rapson, R. D. (2014). New perspectives on emotional contagion: A review of classic and recent research on facial mimicry and contagion. *Interpersona, 8,* 159–179.

Hatfield, E., Cacioppo, J. T., & Rapson, R. L. (1994). *Emotional contagion.* New York, NY: Cambridge University Press.

Hatfield, E., Hsee, C. K., Costello, J., Weissman, M. S., & Denney, C. (1995). The impact of vocal feedback on emotional experience and expression. *Journal of Social Behavior and Personality, 10,* 293–312.

Hatten, R. S. (1994). *Musical meaning in Beethoven: Markedness, correlation, and interpretation.* Bloomington, IN: Indiana University Press.

Hatten, R. S. (2010). Aesthetically warranted emotion and composed expressive trajectories in music. *Music Analysis, 29*, 83–101. (Special Issue on Music and Emotion)

Hawk, S. T., Fischer, A. H., & Van Kleef, G. A. (2012). Face the noise: Embodied responses to nonverbal vocalizations of discrete emotions. *Journal of Personality and Social Psychology, 102*, 796–814.

Hebb, D. O. (1949). *The organization of behavior.* New York, NY: Wiley.

Hedström, P., & Ylikoski, P. (2010). Causal mechanisms in the social sciences. *Annual Review of Sociology, 36*, 49–67.

Hektner, J. M., Schmidt, J. A., & Csikszentmihalyi, M. (2007). *Experience sampling method: Measuring the quality of everyday life*. London: Sage.

Hellström, K., & Laukka, P. (2015). Evaluative conditioning: A possible mechanism underlying listeners' emotional responses to music? *Speech, Music and Hearing Quarterly Progress and Status Report, 52*, 43.

Helmholtz von, H. L. F. (1863/1954). *On the sensations of tone as a psychological basis for the theory of music.* New York, NY: Dover.

Helsing, M., Västfjäll, D., Bjälkebring, P., Juslin, P. N., & Hartig, T. (2016). An experimental field study of the effects of listening to self-chosen music on emotions, stress, and cortisol levels. *Music and Medicine, 8*, 187–198.

Hepper, P. G. (1988). Fetal 'soap' addiction. *Lancet, 1*, 1147–1148.

Hepper, P. G. (1996). Fetal memory: Does it exist? What does it do? *Acta Pædiatrica Supplement, 416*, 16–20.

Hevner, K. (1935). Expression in music: A discussion of experimental studies and theories. *Psychological Review, 42*, 186–204.

Hevner, K. (1936). Experimental studies of the elements of expression in music. *American Journal of Psychology, 48*, 246–268.

Heyduk, R. G. (1975). Rated preference for musical composition as it relates to complexity and exposure frequency. *Perception and Psychophysics, 17*, 84–91.

Hickok, G. (2014). *The myth of mirror neurons: The real neuroscience of communication and cognition*. New York, NY: W. W. Norton & Company.

Hietanen, J. K., Surakka, V., & Linnankoski, I. (1998). Facial electromyographic responses to vocal affect expressions. *Psychophysiology, 35*, 530–536.

Higgins, K. (2012). Biology and culture in musical emotions. *Emotion Review, 4*, 273–282.

Hodge, S. (2017). *The short story of art.* London: Laurence King.

Hodges, D. A. (2010). Psychophysiological measures. In P. N. Juslin & J. A. Sloboda (Eds.), *Handbook of music and emotion: Theory, research, applications* (pp. 279–311). Oxford: Oxford University Press.

Hodges, D. A. (2017). *A concise survey of music philosophy.* New York, NY: Routledge.

Hodges, D. A., & Sebald, D. (2011). *Music in the human experience: An introduction to music psychology.* New York, NY: Routledge.

Höfel, L., & Jacobsen, T. (2003). Temporal stability and consistency of aesthetic judgments of beauty of formal graphic patterns. *Perceptual and Motor Skills, 96*, 30–32.

Hogan, P. C. (1994). The possibility of aesthetics. *British Journal of Aesthetics, 34*, 337–350.

Holbrook, M. B., & Schindler, R. M. (1989). Some exploratory findings on the development of musical tastes. *Journal of Consumer Research, 16*, 119–124.

Holmes, E., A., Mathews, A., Mackintosh, B., & Dalgleish, T. (2008). The causal effect of mental imagery on emotion assessed using picture-word cues. *Emotion, 8*, 395–409.

Huber, K. (1923). *Der ausdruck musikalischer elementarmotive*. Leipzig: Johann Ambrosius Barth.

Hudson, R. (1994). *Stolen time. The history of tempo rubato*. Oxford: Clarendon Press.

Huron, D. (2001). Is music an evolutionary adaptation? *Annals of the New York Academy of Sciences, 930*, 43–61.

Huron, D. (2006). *Sweet anticipation: Music and the psychology of expectation*. Cambridge, MA: MIT Press.

Huron, D. (2011). Why is sad music pleasurable? A possible role for prolactin. *Musicae Scientiae, 15*, 146–158.

Huron, D. (2016). Aesthetics. In S. Hallam, I. Cross, & M. Thaut. (Eds.), *The Oxford handbook of music psychology* (2nd ed., pp. 233–245). Oxford: Oxford University Press.

Huron, D., & Margulis, E. H. (2010). Musical expectancy and thrills. In P. N. Juslin & J. A. Sloboda (Eds.), *Handbook of music and emotion: Theory, research, applications* (pp. 575–604). Oxford: Oxford University Press.

Hursch, C. J., Hammond, K. R., & Hursch, J. L. (1964). Some methodological considerations in multiple-cue probability studies. *Psychological Review, 71*, 42–60.

Huston, J. P., Nadal, M., Mora, F., Agnati, L. F., & Cela-Conde, C. J. (Eds.). (2015). *Art, aesthetics and the brain*. Oxford: Oxford University Press.

Hutto, D. D., Robertson, I., & Kirchhoff, M. D. (2018). A new, better BET: Rescuing and revising Basic Emotion Theory. *Frontiers in Psychology, 9*, 1217.

Imberty, M. (1979). *Entendre la musique*. Paris: Dunod.

Irvin, J., & McLear, C. (2000). *The mojo collection: The ultimate music collection*. New York, NY: Canongate.

Istok, E., Brattico, E., Jacobsen, T., Krohn, K., Muller, M., & Tervaniemi, M. (2009). Aesthetic responses to music: A questionnaire study. *Musicae Scientiae, 13*, 183–206.

Izard, C. E. (1977). *The emotions*. New York, NY: Plenum Press.

Izard, C. E. (1993). Four systems for emotion activation: Cognitive and noncognitive processes. *Psychological Review, 100*, 68–90.

Jackendoff, R. (1992). Musical processing and musical affect. In M. R. Jones & S. Holleran (Eds.), *Cognitive bases of musical communication* (pp. 51–68). Washington, DC: American Psychological Association.

Jacobsen, T. (2006). Bridging the arts and sciences: A framework for the psychology of aesthetics. *Leonardo, 39*, 155–162.

Jacobsen, T., Schubotz, R. I., Höfel, L., & v. Cramon, D. Y. (2006). Brain correlates of aesthetic judgments of beauty. *NeuroImage, 29*, 276–285.

Jakobs, O., Wang, L. E., Dafotakis, M., Grefkes, C., Zilles, K., & Eickhoff, S. B. (2009). Effects of timing and movement uncertainty implicate the temporo-parietal junction in the prediction of forthcoming motor actions. *NeuroImage, 47*, 667–677.

Jamison, K. R. (1993). *Touched with fire: Manic-depressive illness and the artistic temperament.* New York, NY: Free Press.

James, W. (1884). What is an emotion? *Mind, 9*, 188–205.

Janata, P. (2009). The neural architecture of music-evoked autobiographical memories. *Cerebral Cortex, 19*, 2579–2594.

Janata, P., Tomic, S. T., & Rakowski, S. K. (2007). Characterization of music-evoked autobiographical memories. *Memory, 15*, 845–860.

Jentschke, S., Friederici, A. D., & Koelsch, S. (2014). Neural correlates of music-syntactic processing in two-year old children. *Developmental Cognitive Neuroscience, 9*, 200–208.

Johansson, G. (1973). Visual perception of biological motion and a model for its analysis. *Perception and Psychophysics, 14*, 201–211.

Johansson, S. (2013). The talking Neanderthals: What do fossils, genetics, and archeology say? *Biolinguistics, 7*, 35–74.

Johnson-Laird, P. N. (1992). Introduction: What is communication? In D. H. Mellor (Ed.), *Ways of communicating* (pp. 1–13). Cambridge: Cambridge University Press.

Johnson-Laird, P. N., & Oatley, K. (1989). The language of emotions: An analysis of a semantic field. *Cognition and Emotion, 3*, 81–123.

Johnson-Laird, P. N., & Oatley, K. (1992). Basic emotions, rationality, and folk theory. *Cognition and Emotion, 6*, 201–223.

Johnsrude, I. S., Owen, A. M., White, N. M., Zhao, W. V., & Bohbot, V. (2000). Impaired preference conditioning after anterior temporal lobe resection in humans. *Journal of Neuroscience, 20*, 2649–2656.

Jones, M. R. (2009). Musical time. In S. Hallam, I. Cross, & M. Thaut (Eds.), *The Oxford handbook of music psychology* (pp. 81-92). Oxford: Oxford University Press.

Jones, M. R., & Boltz, M. (1989). Dynamic attending and responses to time. *Psychological Review, 96*, 459–491.

Jørgensen, H. (1988). *Musikkopplevelsens psykologi [The psychology of music experience].* Oslo: Norsk Musikforlag.

Joseph, R. (2000). *Neuropsychiatry, neuropsychology, clinical neuroscience.* New York, NY: Academic Press.

Juslin, P. N. (1995). Emotional communication in music viewed through a Brunswikian lens. In G. Kleinen (Ed.), *Music and expression: Proceedings of the conference of DGM and ESCOM, Bremen, 1995* (pp. 21–25). Bremen, Germany: University of Bremen.

Juslin, P. N. (1997a). Emotional communication in music performance: A functionalist perspective and some data. *Music Perception, 14*, 383–418.

Juslin, P. N. (1997b). Perceived emotional expression in synthesized performances of a short melody: Capturing the listener's judgment policy. *Musicæ Scientiæ, 1*, 225–256.

Juslin, P. N. (1997c). Can results from studies of perceived expression in musical performances be generalized across response formats? *Psychomusicology, 16*, 77–101.

Juslin, P. N. (1998). A functionalist perspective on emotional communication in music performance. *Comprehensive Summaries of Uppsala Dissertations from the Faculty of Social Sciences 78*. Uppsala, Sweden: Acta Universitatis Upsaliensis.

Juslin, P. N. (2000a). Cue utilization in communication of emotion in music performance: Relating performance to perception. *Journal of Experimental Psychology: Human Perception and Performance, 26*, 1797–1813.

Juslin, P. N. (2000b). Vocal expression and musical expression: Parallels and contrasts. In A. Kappas (Ed.), *Proceedings of the 16th conference of the International Society for Research on Emotions* (pp. 281–284). Quebec City, Canada: ISRE Publications.

Juslin, P. N. (2001). Communicating emotion in music performance: A review and a theoretical framework. In P. N. Juslin & J. A. Sloboda (Eds.), *Music and emotion: Theory and research* (pp. 309–337). Oxford: Oxford University Press.

Juslin, P. N. (2003). Five facets of musical expression: A psychologist's perspective on music performance. *Psychology of Music, 31*, 273–302.

Juslin, P. N. (2005). *How does music arouse emotions?* Paper presented at the Thirteenth Conference of the International Society for Research on Emotions, Bari, Italy, 11–15 July 2005.

Juslin, P. N. (2011). Music and emotion: Seven questions, seven answers. In I. Deliège & J. Davidson (Eds.), *Music and the mind: Essays in honour of John Sloboda* (pp. 113–135). Oxford: Oxford University Press.

Juslin, P. N. (2012). Are musical emotions invariant across cultures? *Emotion Review, 4*, 283–284.

Juslin, P. N. (2013a). From everyday emotions to aesthetic emotions: Toward a unified theory of musical emotions. *Physics of Life Reviews, 10*, 235–266.

Juslin, P. N. (2013b). What does music express? Basic emotions and beyond. *Frontiers in Psychology: Emotion Science, 4*, 596.

Juslin, P. N. (2015). Resilience: mediated not by one, but many appraisal mechanisms. *Behavioral and Brain Sciences, 38*, 33–34.

Juslin, P. N. (2016). Emotional reactions to music. In S. Hallam, I. Cross, & M. Thaut (Eds.), *The Oxford handbook of music psychology* (2nd ed., pp. 197–213). Oxford: Oxford University Press.

Juslin, P. N., Barradas, G., & Eerola, T. (2015). From sound to significance: Exploring the mechanisms underlying emotional reactions to music. *American Journal of Psychology, 128*, 281–304.

Juslin, P. N., Barradas, G. T., Ovsiannikow, M., Limmo, J., & Thompson, W. F. (2016a). Prevalence of emotions, mechanisms, and motives in music listening: A comparison of individualist and collectivist cultures. *Psychomusicology: Music, Mind, and Brain, 26*, 293–326.

Juslin, P. N., Friberg, A., & Bresin, R. (2002). Toward a computational model of expression in music performance: The GERM model. *Musicae Scientiae, Special Issue 2001–2002*, 63–122.

Juslin, P. N., Friberg, A., Schoonderwaldt, E., & Karlsson, J. (2004). Feedback-learning of musical expressivity. In A. Williamon (Ed.), *Musical excellence: Strategies and techniques to enhance performance* (pp. 247–270). Oxford: Oxford University press.

Juslin, P. N., Harmat, L., & Eerola, T. (2014). What makes music emotionally significant? Exploring the underlying mechanisms. *Psychology of Music, 42*, 599–623.

Juslin, P. N., Harmat, L., & Laukka, P. (2018). The wisdom of the body: Listeners' autonomic arousal distinguishes between spontaneous and posed vocal emotions. *Scandinavian Journal of Psychology, 59*, 105–112.

Juslin, P. N., & Isaksson, S. (2014). Subjective criteria for choice and aesthetic value of music: A comparison of psychology and music students. *Research Studies in Music Education, 36*, 179–198.

Juslin, P. N., Karlsson, J., Lindström, E., Friberg, A., & Schoonderwaldt, E. (2006). Play it again with feeling: Computer feedback in musical communication of emotions. *Journal of Experimental Psychology: Applied, 12*, 79–95.

Juslin, P. N., & Laukka, P. (2000). Improving emotional communication in music performance through cognitive feedback. *Musicae Scientiae, 4*, 151–183.

Juslin, P. N., & Laukka, P. (2003). Communication of emotions in vocal expression and music performance: Different channels, same code? *Psychological Bulletin, 129*, 770–814.

Juslin, P. N., & Laukka, P. (2004). Expression, perception, and induction of musical emotions: A review and a questionnaire study of everyday listening. *Journal of New Music Research, 33*, 217–238.

Juslin, P. N., Laukka, P., & Bänziger, T. (2018). The mirror to our soul? A comparison of spontaneous and posed vocal expression of emotion. *Journal of Nonverbal Behavior, 42*, 1–40.

Juslin, P. N., & Liljeström, S. (in press). Emotional reactions to music: Mechanisms and modularity. In A. C. Ferreira (Ed.), *Music, sound, and mind.* Rio de Janeiro, Brazil: Editora da ABCM.

Juslin, P. N., Liljeström, S., Laukka, P., Västfjäll, D., & Lundqvist, L.-O. (2011). Emotional reactions to music in a nationally representative sample of Swedish adults: Prevalence and causal influences. *Musicae Scientiae, 15*, 174–207. (Special Issue on Music and Emotion)

Juslin, P. N., Liljeström, S., Västfjäll, D., Barradas, G., & Silva, A. (2008). An experience sampling study of emotional reactions to music: Listener, music, and situation. *Emotion, 8*, 668–683.

Juslin, P. N., Liljeström, S., Västfjäll, D., & Lundqvist, L.-O. (2010). How does music evoke emotions? Exploring the underlying mechanisms. In P. N. Juslin & J. A. Sloboda (Eds.), *Handbook of music and emotion: Theory, research, applications* (pp. 605–642). Oxford: Oxford University Press.

Juslin, P. N., & Lindström, E. (2010). Musical expression of emotions: Modeling listeners' judgments of composed and performed features. *Music Analysis, 29*, 334–364. (Special Issue on Music and Emotion)

Juslin, P. N., & Madison, G. (1999). The role of timing patterns in recognition of emotional expression from musical performance. *Music Perception, 17*, 197–221.

Juslin, P. N., & Sakka, L. (in press). Neural correlates of music and emotion. In M. H. Thaut & D. A. Hodges (Eds.), *The Oxford handbook of music and the brain.* Oxford: Oxford University Press.

Juslin, P. N., Sakka, L. S., Barradas, G. T., & Liljeström, S. (2016b). No accounting for taste? Idiographic models of aesthetic judgment in music. *Psychology of Aesthetics, Creativity, and the Arts, 10*, 157–170.

Juslin, P. N., Sakka, L. S., Barradas, G. T, & Liljeström, S. (2018). *An idiographic approach to modeling emotional reactions to music.* Manuscript submitted for publication.

Juslin, P. N., & Scherer, K. R. (2005). Vocal expression of affect. In J. A. Harrigan, R. Rosenthal, & K. R. Scherer (Eds.), *The new handbook of methods in nonverbal behavior research* (pp. 65–135). Oxford: Oxford University Press.

Juslin, P. N., & Sloboda, J. A. (Eds.). (2001). *Music and emotion: Theory and research.* Oxford: Oxford University Press.

Juslin, P. N., & Sloboda, J. A. (Eds.). (2010). *Handbook of music and emotion: Theory, research, applications.* Oxford: Oxford University Press.

Juslin, P. N., & Västfjäll, D. (2008). Emotional responses to music: The need to consider underlying mechanisms. *Behavioral and Brain Sciences, 31*, 559–575.

Juslin, P. N., & Zentner, M. R. (2002). Current trends in the study of music and emotion: Overture. *Musicae Scientiae, Special Issue 2001–2002*, 3–21.

Kagema, N. D. (2013). The use of gospel hip-hop music as an avenue of evangelizing the youth in Kenya today: A practical approach. *American International Journal of Contemporary Research, 8*, 161–169.

Kaiser, L. (1962). Communication of affects by single vowels. *Synthese, 14*, 300–319.

Kallinen, K., & Ravaja, N. (2006). Emotion perceived and emotion felt: Same and different. *Musicae Scientiae, 10*, 191–213.

Kaminska, Z., & Woolf, J. (2000). Melodic line and emotion: Cooke's theory revisited. *Psychology of Music, 28*, 133–153.

Kant, I. (1790/2000). *Critique of the power of judgement* (ed. P. Guyer, trans. P. Guyer & E. Matthews). Cambridge: Cambridge University Press.

Keil, C., & Feld, S. (1994). *Music grooves: Essays and dialogues.* Chicago, IL: University of Chicago Press.

Keltner, D., Tracy, J., Sauter, D. A., Cordaro, D. C., & McNeil, G. (2016). Expression of emotion. In L. F. Barrett, M. Lewis, & J. M. Haviland-Jones (Eds.), *Handbook of emotions* (4th ed., pp. 467–482). New York, NY: Guilford Press.

Kendall, R. A., & Carterette, E. C. (1990). The communication of musical expression. *Music Perception, 8*, 129–164.

Kennedy, Q., Mather, M., & Carstensen L. L. (2004). The role of motivation in the age-related positivity effect in autobiographical memory. *Psychological Science, 15*, 208–214.

Khalfa, S., Roy, M., Rainville, P., Dalla Bella, S., & Peretz, I., (2008). Role of tempo entrainment in psychophysiological differentiation of happy and sad music? *International Journal of Psychophysiology, 68*, 17–26.

Kiernan, F. (2017). *Is the BRECVEMA model useful for historians?* Paper presented at the 5th International Conference on Music and Emotion (ICME), December 2017, University of Queensland, Australia.

Kigunda, M. (2007). *Music and health in Kenya: Sound, spirituality, and altered consciousness juxtaposed with emotions.* Saarbrücken, Germany: Verlag Dr. Müller.

Kihlstrom, J. F. (2013). Unconscious processes. In D. Reisberg (Ed.), *The Oxford handbook of cognitive psychology* (pp. 176–186). Oxford: Oxford University Press.

King, B. B. (1996). *Blues all around me.* London: Hodder & Stoughton.

Kinomura, S., Larsson, J., Gulyás, B., & Roland, P. E. (1996). Activation by attention of the human reticular formation and thalamic intralaminar nuclei. *Science, 271*, 512–515.

Kivy, P. (1980). *The corded shell: Reflections on musical expression*. Princeton, NJ: Princeton University Press.

Kivy, P. (1987). How music moves. In P. Alperson (Ed.), *What is music? An introduction to the philosophy of music* (pp. 149–162). University Park, PA: Pennsylvania State University Press.

Kivy, P. (1990). *Music alone: Reflections on a purely musical experience*. Ithaca, NY: Cornell University Press.

Kivy, P. (1993). Auditor's emotions: Contention, concession and compromise. *Journal of Aesthetics and Art Criticism, 51*, 1–12.

Kivy, P. (1999). Feeling the musical emotions. *British Journal of Aesthetics, 39*, 1–13.

Kivy, P. (2001). *New essays on musical understanding*. Oxford: Oxford University Press.

Kleinen, G. (1968). *Experimentelle Studien zum musikalischen Ausdruck [Experimental studies of musical expression]*. Hamburg: Universität Hamburg.

Kleinginna, P. R., & Kleinginna, A. M. (1981). A categorized list of emotion definitions, with a suggestion for a consensual definition. *Motivation and Emotion, 5*, 345–371.

Kneutgen, J. (1970). Eine Musikform und ihre biologische Funktion. Ueber die Wirkungsweise der Wiegenlieder. *Zeitschrift für Experimentelle und Angewandte Psychologie, 17*, 245–265.

Koelsch, S. (2012). *Brain & music*. Oxford: Wiley-Blackwell.

Koelsch, S. (2014). Brain correlates of music-evoked emotions. *Nature Reviews Neuroscience, 15*, 170–180.

Koelsch, S., Fritz, T., von Cramon, D. Y., Müller, K., & Friederici, A. D. (2006). Investigating emotion with music: An fMRI study. *Human Brain Mapping, 27*, 239–250.

Koelsch, S., Schroger, E., & Gunter, T. C. (2002). Music matters: Preattentive musicality of the human brain. *Psychophysiology, 39*, 38–48.

Koelsch, S., Siebel, W. A., & Fritz, T. (2010). Functional neuroimaging. In P. N. Juslin & J. A. Sloboda (Eds.), *Handbook of music and emotion: Theory, research, applications* (pp. 313–344). Oxford: Oxford University Press.

Konečni, V. J. (1982). Social interaction and musical preference. In D. Deutsch (Ed.), *The psychology of music* (pp. 497–516). New York, NY: Academic Press.

Konečni, V. J. (1984). Elusive effects of artists' 'messages'. In W. R. Crozier & A. J. Chapman (Eds.), *Cognitive processes in the perception of art* (pp. 71–93). Amsterdam: North-Holland.

Konečni, V. J. (2005). The aesthetic trinity: Awe, being moved, thrills. *Bulletin of Psychology and the Arts, 5*, 27–44.

Konečni, V. J. (2012). Composers' creative processes: The role of life-events, emotion and reason. In D. J. Hargreaves, D. E. Miell, & R. A. R. Macdonald (Eds.), *Musical imaginations: Multidisciplinary perspectives on creativity, performance, and perception* (pp. 141–155). Oxford: Oxford University Press.

Konečni, V. J., Wanic, R. A., & Brown, A. (2007). Emotional and aesthetic antecedents and consequences of music-induced thrills. *American Journal of Psychology, 120*, 619–643.

Korb, S., With, S., Niedenthal, P. M., Kaiser, S., & Grandjean, D. (2014). The perception and mimicry of facial movements predict judgments of smile authenticity. *PLOS ONE, i9*, e99194.

Kosslyn, S. M., Margolis, J. A., Barrett, A. M., Goldknopf, E. J., & Daly, P. F. (1990). Age differences in imagery abilities. *Child Development, 61*, 995–1010.

Kosslyn, S. M., Thompson, W. L., & Ganis, G. (2006). *The case for mental imagery*. Oxford: Oxford University Press.

Kotlyar, G. M., & Morozov, V. P. (1976). Acoustic correlates of the emotional content of vocalized speech. *Soviet Physics. Acoustics*, 22, 370–376.

Kövecses, Z. (2000). *Metaphor and emotion*. Cambridge: Cambridge University Press.

Kratus, J. (1993). A developmental study of children's interpretation of emotion in music. *Psychology of Music, 21*, 3–19.

Kraus, R. E. (1986). *The originality of the avant-garde and other modernist myths*. Boston, MA: MIT Press.

Kreutz, G. (2000). Basic emotions in music. In C. Woods, G. Luck, R. Brochard, F. Seddon, & J. A. Sloboda (Eds.), *Proceedings of the sixth international conference on music perception and cognition, August 2000* (CD-rom). Keele University, UK.

Kroger, C., & Margulis, E. H. (2016). "But they told me it was professional": Extrinsic factors in the evaluation of musical performance. *Psychology of Music, 45*, 49–64.

Krugman, H. E. (1943). Affective responses to music as a function of familiarity. *Journal of Abnormal and Social Psychology, 38*, 388–392.

Krumhansl, C. L. (1997). An exploratory study of musical emotions and psychophysiology. *Canadian Journal of Experimental Psychology, 51*, 336–352.

Krumhansl, C. L. (2017). Listening niches across a century of popular music. *Frontiers in Psychology, 8*, 431.

Krumhansl, C. L., & Keil, F. C. (1982). Acquisition of the hierarchy of tonal functions in music. *Memory and Cognition, 10*, 243–251.

Krumhansl, C. L., Louhivuori, J., Toiviainen, P., Järvinen, T., & Eerola, T. (1999). Melodic expectation in Finnish spiritual folk hymns: Convergence of statistical, behavioral, and computational approaches. *Music Perception, 17*, 151–195.

Kuhn, T. L. (1974). Discrimination of modulated beat tempo by professional musicians. *Journal of Research in Music Education*, 22, 270–277.

Labbé Rodríguez, C. (2015). *Entrainment as a psychological mechanism of emotion induction in music listening*. Doctoral dissertation, University of Geneva, Geneva, Switzerland.

Labbé, C., & Grandjean, D., (2014). Musical emotions predicted by feelings of entrainment. *Music Perception, 32*, 170–185.

Lahdelma, I., & Eerola, T. (2016). Single chords convey distinct emotional qualities to both naïve and expert listeners. *Psychology of Music, 44*, 37–54.

Laiho, S. (2004). The psychological functions of music in adolescence. *Nordic Journal of Music Therapy, 13*, 47–63.

Lakin, J. L., Jefferis, V. E., Cheng, C. M., & Chartrand, T. L. (2003). The chameleon effect as social glue: Evidence for the evolutionary significance of nonconscious mimicry. *Journal of Nonverbal Behavior, 27*, 145–162.

Lakoff, G., & Johnson, M. (1980). *Metaphors we live by*. Chicago, IL: University of Chicago Press.

Lambie, J. A., & Marcel, A. J. (2002). Consciousness and the varieties of emotion experience: A theoretical framework. *Psychological Review, 109*, 219–259.

Lamont, A. (2011). University students' strong experiences of music: Pleasure, engagement and meaning. *Musicae Scientiae, 15*, 229–249.

Lamont, A., Greasley, A., & Sloboda, J. A. (2016). Choosing to hear music: Motivation, process, and affect. In S. Hallam, I. Cross, & M. Thaut (Eds.), The *Oxford handbook of music psychology* (2nd ed., pp. 711–724). Oxford: Oxford University Press.

Lane, R. D. (2000). Neural correlates of conscious emotional experience. In R. D. Lane & L. Nadel (Ed.), *Cognitive neuroscience of emotion* (pp. 345–370). Oxford: Oxford University Press.

Lang, P. J. (1979). A bio-informational theory of emotional imagery. *Psychophysiology, 16*, 495–512.

Langer, S. K. (1957). *Philosophy in a new key*. Cambridge, MA: Harvard University Press.

Larsen, J. T., Berntson, G. G., Poehlmann, K. M., Ito, T. A., & Cacioppo, J. T. (2008). The psychophysiology of emotion. In M. Lewis, J. M. Haviland-Jones, & L. F. Barrett (Eds.), *Handbook of emotions* (3rd ed., pp. 180–195). New York, NY: Guilford Press.

Larson, R. (1995). Secrets in the bedroom: Adolescents private use of media. *Journal of Youth and Adolescence, 24*, 535–550.

Larson, S., & Van Handel, L. (2005). Measuring musical forces. *Music Perception, 23*, 119–136.

Lartillot, O., Toiviainen, P., & Eerola, T. (2008). A Matlab toolbox for music information retrieval. In C. Preisach, H. Burkhardt, L. Schmidt-Thieme, & R. Decker (Eds.), *Data analysis, machine learning, and applications: Studies in classification, data analysis, and knowledge organization* (pp. 261–268). Berlin: Springer.

Laukka, P. (2005). Categorical perception of vocal emotion expressions. *Emotion, 5*, 277–295.

Laukka, P., Eerola, T., Thingujam, N. S., Yamasaki, T., & Beller, G. (2013). Universal and culture-specific factors in the recognition and performance of musical affect expressions. *Emotion, 13*, 434–449.

Laukka, P., & Juslin, P. N. (2007). Similar pattern of age-related differences in emotion recognition from speech and music. *Motivation and Emotion, 31*, 182–191.

Lavond, D. G., & Steinmetz, J. E. (2003). *Handbook of classical conditioning*. Boston, MA: Kluwer.

Lazarus, R. S. (1991). *Emotion and adaptation*. Oxford: Oxford University Press.

LeBlanc, A. (1982). An interactive theory of music preference. *Journal of Music Therapy, 19*, 28–45.

Lecanuet (1996). Prenatal auditory experience. In I. Deliège & J. A. Sloboda (Eds.), *Musical beginnings: Origins and development of musical competence* (pp. 3–34). Oxford: Oxford University Press.

Leder, H., Belke, B., Oeberst, A., & Augustin, D. (2004). A model of aesthetic appreciation and aesthetic judgments. *British Journal of Psychology, 95*, 489–508.

LeDoux, J. E. (2000). Cognitive-emotional interactions: Listen to the brain. In R. D. Lane & L. Nadel (Ed.), *Cognitive neuroscience of emotion* (pp. 129–155). Oxford: Oxford University Press.

LeDoux, J. E. (2002). Emotion: Clues from the brain. In J. T. Cacioppo et al. (Eds.), *Foundations in Social Neuroscience* (pp. 389–410). Cambridge, MA: MIT Press.

Leech-Wilkinson, D. (2006). Expressive gestures in Schubert singing on record. *Nordic Journal of Aesthetics, 33*, 51–70.

Leech-Wilkinson, D. (2013). The emotional power of musical performance. In T. Cochrane, B. Fantini, & K. R. Scherer (Eds.), *The emotional power of music* (pp. 41–54). Oxford: Oxford University Press.

Lehmann, A. C. (2006). Historical increases in expert music performance skills: Optimizing instruments, playing techniques, and training. In E. Altenmüller, M. Wiesendanger, & J. Kesselring (Eds.), *Music, motor control and the brain* (pp. 3–24). Oxford: Oxford University Press.

Lerdahl, F. (1991). Musical parsing and musical affect. *Music Perception, 9*, 199–229.

Lerdahl, F. (1996). Calculating tonal tension. *Music Perception, 13*, 319–363.

Lerdahl, F. (2013). Musical syntax and its relation to linguistic syntax. In M. A. Arbib (Ed.), *Language, music, and the brain* (pp. 257–272). Cambridge, MA: MIT Press.

Lerdahl, F., & Jackendoff, R. (1983). *A generative theory of tonal music*. Boston, MA: MIT Press.

Lerdahl, F., & Krumhansl, C. L. (2007). Modeling musical tension. *Music Perception, 24*, 329–366.

Lesaffre, M., Maes, P.-J., & Leman, M. (Eds.). (2017). *The Routledge companion to embodied music interaction*. London: Routledge.

Levenson, R. W. (1994). Human emotion: A functional view. In P. Ekman & R. J. Davidson (Eds.), *The nature of emotion: Fundamental questions* (pp. 123–126). Oxford: Oxford University Press.

Levenson, R. W. (2007). Emotion elicitation with neurological patients. In J. A. Coan & J. J. B. Allen (Eds.), *Handbook of emotion elicitation and assessment* (pp. 158–168). Oxford: Oxford University Press.

Levenson, R. W. (2014). The autonomic nervous system and emotion. *Emotion Review, 6*, 100–112.

Levinson, J. (1982). Music and negative emotions. *Pacific Philosophical Quarterly, 63*, 327–346.

Levinson, J. (1990). *Music, art, and metaphysics: Essays in philosophical aesthetics*. Ithaca, NY: Cornell University Press.

Levinson, J. (1997). Emotion in response to art. In M. Hjort & S. Laver (Eds.), *Emotion and the arts* (pp. 20–34). Oxford: Oxford University Press.

Levinson, J. (2001). Messages in art. In S. Davies (Ed.), *Art and its messages: Meaning, morality, and society* (pp. 70–83). University Park, PA: Pennsylvania State University Press.

Levinson, J. (2003). Philosophical aesthetics: An overview. In J. Levinson (Ed.), *The Oxford handbook of aesthetics* (pp. 3–24). Oxford: Oxford University Press.

Levinson, J. (2015). The expressive specificity of jazz. In J. Levinson (Ed.), *Musical concerns: Essays in philosophy of music* (pp. 131–143). Oxford: Oxford University Press.

Levitin, D. J. (2006). *This is your brain on music: The science of a human obsession.* New York, NY: Dutton.

Levitin, D. J. (2010). *The world in six songs: How the musical brain created human nature.* London: Aurum.

Liljeström, S., Juslin, P. N., & Västfjäll, D. (2013). Experimental evidence of the roles of music choice, social context, and listener personality in emotional reactions to music. *Psychology of Music, 41*, 577–597.

Lima, C. F., & Castro, S. L. (2011). Emotion recognition in music changes across the adult life span. *Cognition and Emotion, 25*, 585–598.

Lindquist, K. A., & Barrett, L. F. (2008). Emotional complexity. In M. Lewis, J. M. Haviland-Jones, & L. F. Barrett (Eds.), *Handbook of emotions* (3rd ed., pp. 513–530). New York, NY: Guilford.

Lindquist, K. A., Wager, T. D., Kober, H., Bliss-Moreau, E., & Barrett, L. F. (2012). The brain basis of emotion: A meta-analytic review. *Behavioral and Brain Sciences, 35*, 121–143.

Lindström, E. (2003). The contribution of immanent and performed accents to emotional expression in short tone sequences. *Journal of New Music Research, 32*, 269–280.

Lindström, E. (2006). Impact of melodic organization on perceived structure and emotional expression in music. *Musicae Scientiae, 10*, 85–117.

Lindström, E., Juslin, P. N., Bresin, R., & Williamon, A. (2003). "Expressivity comes from within your soul": A questionnaire study of music students' perspectives on musical expressivity. *Research Studies in Music Education, 20*, 23–47.

Lippman, E. A. (Ed.). (1986). *Musical aesthetics: A historical reader. Volume 1: From antiquity to the eighteenth century.* New York, NY: Pendragon Press.

Lipps, T. (1903). Einfühling, innere Nachahmung und Organempfindung. *Archiv für die Gesante Psychologie, 1*, 465–519.

Loewenstein, D., & Dodd, P. (Eds.). (2004). *According to the Rolling Stones.* London: Weidenfield & Nicolson.

Lomax, A. (1962). Song structure and social structure. *Ethnology, 1*, 425–451.

Lomax, A. (1968). *Folk song style and culture.* New Brunswick, Canada: Transaction Books.

Lorand, R. (2007). *In defense of beauty.* Online article retrieved January 15, 2013 from: <http://aesthetics-online.org/articles/index.php?articles_id=34>.

Lull, J. (1992). Popular music and communication: An introduction. In J. Lull (Ed.), *Popular music and communication* (2nd ed., pp. 1–32). London: Sage.

Lundqvist, L.-O., Carlsson, F., Hilmersson, P., & Juslin, P. N. (2009). Emotional responses to music: Experience, expression, and physiology. *Psychology of Music, 37*, 61–90.

Lundy, D. E. (2010). A test of consensus in aesthetic evaluation among professional critics of modern music. *Empirical Studies of the Arts, 28*, 243–258.

Lundy, D. E., & Smith, J. L. (2016). It's tough to be a critic: Professional versus nonprofessional music judgment. *Empirical Studies of the Arts, 35*, 139–168.

Lydon, M. (2005). Preface. In R. Dimery (Ed.), *1001 albums you must hear before you die* (pp. 6–9). London: Cassell.

Lyman, B., & Waters, J. C. (1989). Patterns of imagery in various emotions. *Journal of Mental Imagery, 13*, 63–74.

Lyotard, J.-F. (1994). *Lessons on the analytic of the sublime* (trans. E. Rottenberg). Stanford, CA: Stanford University Press.

MacDonald, R., Kreutz, G., & Mitchell, L. (Eds.). (2012). *Music, health, and well-being.* Oxford: Oxford University Press.

MacLean, P. (1993). Cerebral evolution of emotion. In M. Lewis & J. M. Haviland (Eds.), *Handbook of emotions* (pp. 67–83). New York, NY: Guilford Press.

Madison, G. (2000). On the nature of variability in isochronous serial interval production. In P. Desain & W. L. Windsor (Eds.), *Rhythm perception and production* (pp. 95–113). Lisse, The Netherlands: Swets and Zeitlinger.

Maess, B., Koelsch, S., Gunter, T. C., & Friederici, A. D. (2001). Musical syntax is processed in Broca's area: A MEG study. *Nature Neuroscience, 4*, 540–545.

Malloch, S., & Trevarthen, C. (Eds.). (2010). *Communicative musicality: Exploring the basis of human companionship.* Oxford: Oxford University Press.

Margulis, E. H. (2010). When program notes don't help: Music descriptions and enjoyment. *Psychology of Music, 38*, 285–302.

Margulis, E. H. (2014). *On repeat: How music plays the mind.* Oxford: Oxford University Press.

Markman, A. B., & Rein, J. R. (2013). The nature of mental concepts. In D. Reisberg (Ed.), *The Oxford handbook of cognitive psychology* (pp. 321–345). Oxford: Oxford University Press.

Marks, D. F. (1973). Visual imagery differences in the recall of pictures. *British Journal of Psychology, 64*, 17–24.

Marler, P. (1977). The evolution of communication. In T. A. Sebeok (Ed.), *How animals communicate* (pp. 45–70). Bloomington, IN: Indiana University Press.

Martin, D. G., Stambrook, M., Tataryn, D. J., & Beihl, H. (1984). Conditioning in the unattended left ear. *International Journal of Neuroscience, 23*, 95–102.

Martindale, C. (1984). The pleasures of thought: A theory of cognitive hedonics. *Journal of Mind and Behavior, 5*, 49–80.

Martindale, C., & Moore, K. (1988). Priming, prototypicality, and preference. *Journal of Experimental Psychology: Human Perception and Performance, 14*, 661–670.

Martindale, C., & Moore, K. (1989). Relationship of musical preference to collative, ecological, and psychophysical variables. *Music Perception, 6*, 431–455.

Maslow, A. H. (1968). *Towards a psychology of being* (2nd ed.). New York, NY: Van Nostrand.

Matravers, D. (1998). *Art and emotion.* Oxford: Oxford University Press.

Mattheson, J. (1739). *Der volkommene Capellmeister.* (Facsimile edition 1954, Bärenreiter Verlag, Kassel and Basel.)

Mayr, E. (1982). *The growth of biological thought.* Cambridge, MA: Harvard University Press.

McCrae, R. R. (2007). Aesthetic chills as a universal marker of openness to experience. *Motivation and Emotion, 31*, 5–11.

McKinney, C. H., Antoni, M. H., Kumar, M., Tims, F. C., & McCabe, P. M. (1997). Effects of Guided Imagery and Music (GIM) therapy on mood and cortisol in healthy adults. *Health Psychology, 16*, 390–400.

McKinney, C. H., & Tims, F. C. (1995). Differential effects of selected classical music on the imagery of high versus low imagers: Two studies. *Journal of Music Therapy, 32*, 22–45.

McManus, I. C., Cook, R., & Hunt, A. (2010). Beyond the golden section and normative aesthetics: Why do individuals differ so much in their aesthetic preferences for rectangles? *Psychology of Aesthetics and Creativity*, 4, 113–126.

McNeill, W. H. (1995). *Keeping together in time: Dance and drill in human history.* Cambridge, MA: Harvard University Press.

McPherson, G. E., & Schubert, E. (2004). Measuring performance enhancement in music. In A. Williamon (Ed.), *Musical excellence: Strategies and techniques to enhance performance* (pp. 61–82). Oxford: Oxford University Press.

McPherson, G. E., & Thompson, W. F. (1998). Assessing music performance: Issues and influences. *Research Studies in Music Education*, 10, 12–24.

Melchionne, K. (2011). A new problem for aesthetics. *Journal of Aesthetics and Art Criticism*, *68*, 131–141.

Menninghaus, W., Wagner, V., Hanich, J., Wassiliwizky, E., Kuehnast, M., & Jacobsen, T. (2015). Towards a psychological construct of being moved. *PLoS ONE*, *10*, e0128451.

Menon, V., & Levitin, D. J. (2005). The rewards of music listening: Response and physiological connectivity of the mesolimbic system. *Neuroimage*, *28*, 175–184.

Menuhin, Y. (1996). *Unfinished journey.* London: Methuen.

Merriam, A. P. (1964). *The anthropology of music.* Evanston, IL: Northwestern University Press.

Mesquita, B., Vissers, N., & De Leersnyder, J. (2015). Culture and emotion. In J. Wright & J. Berry (Eds.), *International encyclopedia of social and behavioral sciences* (2nd ed., pp. 542–549). Oxford: Elsevier.

Meyer, L. B. (1956). *Emotion and meaning in music.* Chicago, IL: Chicago University Press.

Miceli, M., & Castelfranchi, C. (2015). *Expectancy and emotion.* Oxford: Oxford University Press.

Minassian, C., Gayford, C., & Sloboda, J. A. (2003). *Optimal experience in musical performance: A survey of young musicians.* Paper presented at the Meeting of the Society for Education, Music, and Psychology Research, London, March 2003.

Miserendino, M. J. D., Sananes, C. B., Melia, K. R., & Davis, M. (1990). Blocking of acquisition but not expression of conditioned fear-potentiated startle by NMDA antagonists in the amygdala. *Nature*, *345*, 716–718.

Moors, A. (2009). Theories of emotion causation: A review. *Cognition and Emotion*, *23*, 625–662.

Mores, R. (2009). Human voice: A sparse, meaningful and capable representation of sounds. In M. M. Boone (Ed.), *Proceedings of the NAG/DAGA international conference on acoustics, Rotterdam, March 2009* (pp. 875–878). Berlin: German Acoustical Society.

Morey, R. (1940). Upset in emotions. *Journal of Social Psychology*, *12*, 333–356.

Mori, K., & Iwanaga, M. (2013). Pleasure generated by sadness: Effect of sad lyrics on the emotions induced by happy music. *Psychology of Music*, 42, 643–652.

Morton, E. S. (1977). On the occurrence and significance of motivation-structural rules in some bird and mammal sounds. *American Naturalist*, *111*, 855–869.

Mull, H. K. (1957). The effect of repetition upon the enjoyment of modern music. *Journal of Psychology*, 43, 155–162.

Murphy, F. C., Nimmo-Smith, I., & Lawrence, A. D. (2003). Functional neuroanatomy of emotions: A meta analysis. *Cognitive, Affective, & Behavioral Neuroscience, 3*, 207–233.

Narmour, E. (1990). *The analysis and cognition of basic melodic structures*. Chicago, IL: University of Chicago Press.

Narmour, E. (1991). The top-down and bottom-up systems of musical implication: Building on Meyer's theory of emotional syntax. *Music Perception, 9*, 1–26.

Nattiez, J.-J. (1990). *Music and discourse: Toward a semiology of music* (transl. by Carolyn Abbate). Princeton, NJ: Princeton University Press.

Neale, J. M., & Liebert, R. M. (1986). *Science and behavior*. Englewood Cliffs, NJ: Prentice Hall.

Neill, A. (2003). Art and emotion. In J. Levinson (Ed.), *The Oxford handbook of aesthetics* (pp. 421–435). Oxford: Oxford University Press.

Nesse, R. M. (2009). Evolution of emotion. In D. Sander & K. R. Scherer (Eds.), *The Oxford companion to emotion and the affective sciences* (pp. 159–164). Oxford: Oxford University Press.

Neumann, R., & Strack, F. (2000). Mood contagion: The automatic transfer of mood between persons. *Journal of Personality and Social Psychology, 79*, 211–223.

Niedenthal, P., & Brauer, M. (2012). Social functionality of human emotion. *Annual Review of Psychology, 63*, 259–285.

Nielsen, F. V. (1987). Musical 'tension' and related concepts. In T. A. Sebeok & J. Umiker-Sebeok (Eds.), *The semiotic web '86: An international yearbook* (pp. 491–513). Berlin: Mouton de Gruyter.

Nielsen, L., & Kaszniak, A. W. (2007). Conceptual, theoretical, and methodological issues in inferring subjective emotion experience: Recommendations for researchers. In J. A. Coan & J. J. B. Allen (Eds.), *Handbook of emotion elicitation and assessment* (pp. 361–378). Oxford: Oxford University Press.

Nielzén, S., & Cesarec, Z. (1981). On the perception of emotional meaning in music. *Psychology of Music, 9*, 17–31.

Nilsson, U. (2009). Soothing music can increase oxytocin levels during bed rest after open-heart surgery: A randomised control trial. *Journal of Clinical Nursing, 18*, 2153–2161.

Nisbett, R. E., & Wilson, T. D. (1977). Telling more than we can know: Verbal reports on mental processes. *Psychological Review, 84*, 231–259.

Norris, C. J., Coan, J. A., & Johnstone, T. (2007). Functional magnetic resonance imaging and the study of emotion. In J. A. Coan & J. J. B. Allen (Eds.), *Handbook of emotion elicitation and assessment* (pp. 440–459). Oxford: Oxford University Press.

North, A. C., & Hargreaves, D. J. (1995). Subjective complexity, familiarity, and liking for popular music. *Psychomusicology, 14*, 77–93.

North, A. C., & Hargreaves, D. J. (2008). *The social and applied psychology of music*. Oxford: Oxford University Press.

North, A. C., Hargreaves, D. J., & Hargreaves, J. J. (2004). The uses of music in everyday life. *Music Perception, 22*, 63–99.

North, A. C., Hargreaves, D. J., & O'Neill, S. A. (2000). The importance of music to adolescents. *British Journal of Educational Psychology, 70*, 255–272.

Nyklíček, I., Thayer, J. F., & Van Doornen, L. J. P. (1997). Cardiorespiratory differentiation of musically-induced emotions. *Journal of Psychophysiology, 11*, 304–321.

Nusbaum, E., Silvia, P., Beaty, R., Burgin, C., Hodges, D., & Kwapil, T. (2014). Listening between the notes: Aesthetic chills in everyday music listening. *Psychology of Aesthetics, Creativity, and the Arts, 8*, 104–109.

Oakley, D. A. (1985). Animal awareness, consciousness, and self-image. In D. A. Oakley (Ed.), *Brain and mind* (pp. 132–151). London: Methuen.

Oatley, K. (1992). *Best laid schemes: The psychology of emotions.* Cambridge, MA: Harvard University Press.

Oatley, K., & Duncan, E. (1994). The experience of emotions in everyday life. *Cognition and Emotion, 8*, 369–381.

Oatley, K., & Jenkins, J. M. (1996). *Understanding emotions.* Oxford: Blackwell.

Oatley, K., Keltner, D., & Jenkins, J. M. (2006). *Understanding emotions* (2nd ed.). Oxford: Blackwell.

Obrecht, J. (2010). *B. B. King: Live at the Regal.* Online article retrieved from the Jas Obrecht Archive: <http://jasobrecht.com/b-b-king-live-at-the-regal/>.

Öhman, A., & Mineka, S. (2001). Fears, phobias, and preparedness: Towards an evolved module of fear and fear learning. *Psychological Review, 108*, 483–522.

Öhman, A., & Soares, J. J. F. (1994). Unconscious anxiety: Phobic responses to masked stimuli. *Journal of Abnormal Psychology, 103*, 231–240.

Olatunji, B. O., Lohr, J. M., Sawchuk, C. N., & Westendorf, D. H. (2005). Using facial expressions as CSs and fearsome and disgusting pictures as UCSs: Affective responding and evaluative learning of fear and disgust in blood-injection-injury phobia. *Journal of Anxiety Disorders, 19*, 539–555.

O'Neill, S., Edelman, J., & Sloboda, J. A. (2016). Opera and emotion: The cultural value of attendance for the highly engaged. *Participations: Journal of Audience & Reception Studies, 13*, 24–50.

Orne, M. T. (1962). On the social psychology of the psychological experiment with particular reference to demand characteristics and their implications. *American Psychologist, 17*, 776–783.

Osborne, J. W. (1980). The mapping of thoughts, emotions, sensations, and images as responses to music. *Journal of Mental Imagery, 5*, 133–136.

Owren, M. J., & Rendall, D. (2001). Sound on the rebound: Bringing form and function back to the forefront in understanding nonhuman primate vocal signaling. *Evolutionary Anthropology, 10*, 58–71.

Paisley, W. J. (1964). Identifying the unknown communicator in painting, literature and music: The significance of minor encoding habits. *Journal of Communication, 14*, 219–237.

Palmer, C. (1996). Anatomy of a performance: Sources of musical expression. *Music Perception, 13*, 433–453.

Panksepp, J. (1995). The emotional sources of 'chills' induced by music. *Music Perception, 13*, 171–208.

Panksepp, J. (1998). *Affective neuroscience.* Oxford: Oxford University Press.

Panksepp, J., & Panksepp, J. B. (2000). The seven sins of evolutionary psychology. *Evolution and Cognition, 6*, 108–131.

Papoušek, M. (1996). Intuitive parenting: A hidden source of musical stimulation in infancy. In I. Deliége & J. A. Sloboda (Eds.), *Musical beginnings: Origins and development of musical competence* (pp. 89–112). Oxford: Oxford University Press.

Paquette, S., Takerkart, S., Saget, S., Peretz, I., & Belin, P. (2018). Cross-classification of musical and vocal emotions in the auditory cortex. *Annals of the New York Academy of Sciences, 1423*, 329–337.

Parkinson, B., Fischer, A., & Manstead, A. S. R. (2005). *Emotion in social relations: Cultural, group, and interpersonal processes.* Philadelphia, PA: Psychology Press.

Pascal, B. (1958/1670). *Pensées* (trans. W. F. Trotter). New York: E. P. Dutton. (Original work published 1670.)

Patel, A. D. (2008). *Music, language, and brain.* Oxford: Oxford University Press.

Patel, A. D. (2018). Music as a transformative technology of the mind: An update. In H. Honing (Ed.), *The evolution of musicality* (pp. 113–126). Cambridge, MA: MIT Press.

Patel, A. D., & Iversen, J. R. (2014). The evolutionary neuroscience of musical beat perception: The Action Simulation for Auditory Prediction (ASAP) hypothesis. *Frontiers in Systems Neuroscience, 8*, 57.

Pell, M. D., & Skorup, V. (2008). Implicit processing of emotional prosody in a foreign versus native language. *Speech Communication, 50*, 519–530.

Penel, A., & Drake, C. (1999). Seeking 'one' explanation for expressive timing. In S. W. Yi (Ed.), *Music, mind, and science* (pp. 271–297). Seoul: Seoul National University Press.

Peretz, I. (2001). Listen to the brain: A biological perspective on musical emotions. In P. N. Juslin & J. A. Sloboda (Eds.), *Music and emotion: Theory and research* (pp. 105–134). Oxford: Oxford University Press.

Peretz, I. (2010). Towards a neurobiology of musical emotions. In P. N. Juslin & J. A. Sloboda (Eds.), *Handbook of music and emotion: Theory, research, applications* (pp. 99–126). Oxford: Oxford University Press.

Peretz, I., & Gagnon, L. (1999). Dissociation between recognition and emotional judgment for melodies. *Neurocase, 5*, 21–30.

Peretz, I., Gagnon, L., & Bouchard, B. (1998a). Music and emotion: Perceptual determinants, immediacy, and isolation after brain damage. *Cognition, 68*, 111–141.

Peretz, I., Gaudreau, D., & Bonnel, A-M. (1998b). Exposure effects on music preference and recognition. *Memory & Cognition, 26*, 884–902.

Persson, R. S. (2001). The subjective world of the performer. In P. N. Juslin & J. A. Sloboda (Eds.), *Music and emotion: Theory and research* (pp. 275–289). Oxford: Oxford University Press.

Pessoa, L. (2013). *The cognitive-emotional brain: From interactions to integration.* Cambridge, MA: MIT Press.

Phan, K. L., Wager, T., Taylor, S. F., & Liberzon, I. (2002). Functional neuroanatomy of emotion: A meta analysis of emotion activation studies in PET and fMRI. *NeuroImage, 16*, 331–348.

Piaget, J. (1951). *Play, dreams, and imitation in childhood.* London: Routledge.

Pike, A. (1972). A phenomenological analysis of emotional experience in music. *Journal of Research in Music Education, 20*, 262–267.

Pilc, J.-M. (2012). *It's about music: The art and heart of improvisation.* Montrose, CA: Glen Lyon Books.

Pinker, S. (1997). *How the mind works.* New York, NY: W.W. Norton.

Pitts, S. E. (2014). Musical, social and moral dilemmas: Investigating audience motivations to attend concerts. In K. Burland & S. E. Pitts (Eds.), *Coughing and clapping: Understanding audience experience* (pp. 21–33). Farnham: Ashgate.

Plamper, J. (2015). *The history of emotions: An introduction.* Oxford: Oxford University Press.

Plato. (1923). *The republic* (trans. B. Jowett). New York, NY: Random House. (Original work published around 380 BC)

Plomp, R., & Levelt, W. J. M. (1965). Tonal consonance and critical bandwith. *Journal of the Acoustical Society of America, 37*, 548–560.

Ploog, D. (1981). Neurobiology of primate audio-vocal behavior. *Brain Research Reviews, 3*, 35–61.

Ploog, D. W. (1992). The evolution of of vocal communication. In H. Papousek, U. Jürgens, & M. Papousek (Eds.), *Nonverbal vocal communication: Comparative and developmental approaches* (pp. 6–30). Cambridge: Cambridge University Press.

Plutchik, R. (1984). Emotions and imagery. *Journal of Mental Imagery, 8*, 105–111.

Plutchik, R. (1994). *The psychology and biology of emotion.* New York, NY: Harper-Collins.

Pogue, D., & Speck, S. (1997). *Classical music for dummies.* Hoboken, NJ: John Wiley & Sons.

Porter, A. (1966). Essay on the sleeve of the LP Tchaikovsky, Symphony No. 6 in B minor opus 74, with the Vienna Philharmonic Orchestra (conductor: Jean Martinon). London Records, STS15018.

Powell, J., & Dibben, N. (2005). Key-mood association: A self perpetuating myth. *Musicae Scientiae, 9*, 289–311.

Pratt, C. (1931). *The meaning of music. A study in psychological aesthetics.* New York, NY: McGraw-Hill.

Preissmann, D., Charbonnier, C., Chagué, S., Antonietti, J. P., Llobera, J., Ansermet, F., & Magistretti, P. J. (2016). A motion capture study to measure the feeling of synchrony in romantic couples and in professional musicians. *Frontiers in Psychology, 7*, 1673.

Preston, S. D., & de Waal, F. B. M. (2002). Empathy: Its ultimate and proximate basis. *Behavioral and Brain Sciences, 25*, 1–72.

Price, H. E. (1986). A proposed glossary for the use of affective responses in music. *Journal of Research in Music Education, 34*, 151–159.

Qiu, R., Wang, H., & Fu, S. (2017). N170 reveals the categorical perception effect of emotional valence. *Frontiers in Psychology, 8*, 2056.

Quinto, L., Thompson, W. F., & Taylor, A. (2013). The contributions of compositional structure and performance expression to the communication of emotion in music. *Psychology of Music, 42*, 503–524.

Quittner, A., & Glueckhauf, R. (1983). The facilitative effects of music on visual imagery: a multiple measures approach. *Journal of Mental Imagery, 7*, 105–120.

Radbourne, J., Johanson, K., & Glow, H. (2014). The value of "being there": How the live experience measures quality for the audience. In K. Burland & S. Pitts (Eds.), *Coughing and clapping: Investigating audience experience* (pp. 55–68). Farnham: Ashgate.

Raffman, D. (1993). *Language, music and mind*. Cambridge, MA: MIT Press.

Raloff, J. (1983). Noise: The subtle pollutant. In *Science yearbook: New illustrated encyclopedia* (pp. 194–199). New York, NY: Funk and Wagnalls.

Ramachandran, V. S., & Hirstein, W. (1999). The science of art. *Journal of Consciousness Studies, 6*, 15–51.

Randall, W. M., & Rickard, N. S. (2013). Development and trial of a mobile experience sampling method (m-ESM) for personal music listening. *Music Perception, 31*, 157–170.

Ratner, L. G. (1980). *Classic music: Expression, form and style*. New York, NY: Schirmer.

Ray, W. J, Molnar, C., Aikins, D., Yamasaki, A., Newman, M. G., Castonguay, L., & Borkovec, T. D. (2009). Startle response in Generalized Anxiety Disorder. *Depression and Anxiety, 26*, 147–154.

Razran, G. (1954). The conditioned evocation of attitudes: Cognitive conditioning? *Journal of Experimental Psychology, 48*, 278–282.

Reber, R. (2008). Art in its experience: Can empirical psychology help to assess artistic value? *Leonardo, 41*, 367–372.

Reber, R., Schwarz, N., & Winkielman, P. (2004). Processing fluency and aesthetic pleasure: Is beauty in the perceiver's processing experience? *Personality and Social Psychology Review, 8*, 364–382.

Reimer, B. (1968). Performance and aesthetic sensitivity. *Music Educators Journal, 54*, 27–114.

Reisberg, D., & Heuer, F. (2004). Memory for emotional events. In D. Reisberg & P. Hertel (Eds.), *Memory and emotion* (pp. 3–41). Oxford: Oxford University Press.

Rentfrow, P. J., & Gosling, S. D. (2003). The do re mi's of everyday life: The structure and personality correlates of music preferences. *Journal of Personality and Social Psychology, 84*, 1236–1256.

Rentfrow, P. J., & McDonald, J. A. (2010). Preference, personality, and emotion. In P. N. Juslin & J. A. Sloboda (Eds.), *Handbook of music and emotion: Theory, research, applications* (pp. 669–695). Oxford: Oxford University Press.

Repp, B. H. (1992). Probing the cognitive representation of musical time: Structural constraints on the perception of timing perturbations. *Cognition, 44*, 241–281.

Repp, B. H. (1997). The aesthetic quality of a quantitatively average music performance: Two preliminary experiments. *Music Perception, 14*, 419–444.

Resnicow, J. E., Salovey, P., & Repp, B. H. (2004). Is recognition of emotion in music performance an aspect of emotional intelligence? *Music Perception, 22*, 145–158.

Richards, K. (2010). *Life*. London: Weidenfeld & Nicolson.

Rickard, N. S. (2004). Intense emotional responses to music: A test of the physiological arousal hypothesis. *Psychology of Music, 32*, 371–388.

Rigg, M. G. (1937). An experiment to determine how accurately college students can interpret the intended meanings of musical compositions. *Journal of Experimental Psychology, 21*, 223–229.

Rigg, M. G. (1942). The expression of meanings and emotions in music. In F. P. Clarke (Ed.), *Philosophical essays in honor of Edgar Arthur Singer, Jr* (pp. 279–294). Philadelphia, PA: University of Pennsylvania Press.

Rizzolatti, G., & Craighero, L. (2004). The mirror-neuron system. *Annual Review of Neuroscience, 27*, 169–192.

Roach, J. R. (1993). *The player's passion: Studies in the science of acting.* Ann Arbor, MI: University of Michigan Press.

Robertson, E. (1934). The emotional element in listening to music. *Australasian Journal of Philosophy, 12*, 199–212.

Robinson, J. (2005). *Deeper than reason: Emotion and its role in literature, music, and art.* Oxford: Clarendon Press.

Robinson, J., & Hatten, R. (2012). Emotions in music. *Music Theory Spectrum, 34*, 74–106.

Rodway, P., Gillies, K., & Schepman, A. (2006). Vivid imagers are better at detecting salient changes. *Journal of Individual Differences, 27*, 218–228.

Roe, K. (1985). Swedish youth and music: Listening patterns and motivations. *Communication Research, 12*, 353–362.

Roederer, J. (1984). The search for a survival value of music. *Music Perception, 1*, 350–356.

Rohwer, D. (2001). Instrumental music students' cognitive and performance understanding of musical expression. *Journal of Band Research, 37*, 17–28.

Rolls, E. T. (2007). Emotion elicited by primary reinforcers and following stimulus-reinforcement association learning. In J. A. Coan & J. J. B. Allen (Eds.), *Handbook of emotion elicitation and assessment* (pp. 137–157). Oxford: Oxford University Press.

Rosch, E. (1978). Principles of categorization. In E. Rosch & B. B. Loyd (Eds.), *Cognition and categorization* (pp. 27–48). Hillsdale, NJ: Erlbaum.

Rossignol, S., & Jones, G. (1976). Audio-spinal influence in man studied by the H-reflex and its possible role on rhythmic movements synchronized to sound. *Electroencephalography and Clinical Neurophysiology, 41*, 83–92.

Rouget, G. (1985). *Music and trance: A theory of the relations between music and possession* (Trans. B. Beibuyck). Chicago, IL: University of Chicago Press.

Rous, S. H. (1929). *The Victrola book of the opera* (8th ed.). Camden, NJ: Victor Talking Machine Company.

Rueff-Lopes, R., Navarro, J., Caetano, A., & Silva, A. (2014). A Markov chain analysis of emotional exchange in voice-to-voice communication: Testing for the mimicry hypothesis of emotional contagion. *Human Communication Research, 41*, 412–434.

Russell, J. A. (1980). A circumplex model of affect. *Journal of Personality and Social Psychology, 39*, 1161–1178.

Russell, J. A. (1991). Culture and the categorization of emotions. *Psychological Bulletin, 110*, 426–450.

Russell, P. A. (1997). Musical tastes and society. In D. J. Hargreaves & A. C. North (Eds.), *The social psychology of music* (pp. 141–158). Oxford: Oxford University Press.

Ruud, E. (1997). Music and identity. *Nordic Journal of Music Therapy, 6*, 3–13.

Saarikallio, S. (2012). Cross-cultural approaches to music and health. In R. MacDonald, G. Kreutz, & L. Mitchell (Eds.), *Music, health, and well-being* (pp. 477–490). Oxford: Oxford University Press.

Saarimäki, H., Gotsopoulos, A., Jaaskelainen, I. P., Lampinen, J., Vuilleumier, P., Hari, R., Sams, M., & Nummenmaa, L. (2016). Discrete neural signatures of basic emotions. *Cerebral Cortex, 26*, 2563–2573.

Sacchetti, B., Scelfo, B., & Strata, P. (2005). The cerebellum: Synaptic changes and fear conditioning. *The Neuroscientist, 11*, 217–227.

Sakka, L. S., & Juslin, P. N. (2018a). Emotional reactions to music in depressed individuals. *Psychology of Music. 46*, 862–880.

Sakka, L. S., & Juslin, P. N. (2018b). Emotion regulation with music in depressed and non-depressed individuals: Goals, strategies, and mechanisms. *Music & Science.* Advance online publication. doi:10.1177/2059204318755023.

Salimpoor, V. N., Benovoy, M., Larcher, K., Dagher, A., & Zatorre, R. J. (2011). Anatomically distinct dopamine release during anticipation and experience of peak emotion to music. *Nature Neuroscience, 14*, 257–262.

Sauter, D. A., Le Guen, O., & Haun, D. B. M. (2011). Categorical perception of emotional facial expressions does not require lexical categories. *Emotion, 11*, 1479–1483.

Schäfer, T., & Sedlmeier, P. (2010). What makes us like music? Determinants of music preference. *Psychology of Aesthetics, Creativity, and the Arts, 4*, 223–234.

Schellekens, E. (2011). Experiencing the aesthetic: Kantian autonomy or evolutionary biology? In E. Schellekens & P. Goldie (Eds.), *The aesthetic mind: Philosophy and psychology* (pp. 223–235). Oxford: Oxford University Press.

Schellekens, E., & Goldie, P. (Eds.). (2011). *The aesthetic mind: Philosophy and psychology.* Oxford: Oxford University Press.

Schellenberg, E. G. (2008). The role of exposure in emotional responses to music. *Behavioral and Brain Sciences, 31*, 594–595.

Schellenberg, E. G., Krysciak, A. M., & Campbell, R. J. (2000). Perceiving emotion in melody: Interactive effects of pitch and rhythm. *Music Perception, 18*, 155–171.

Schellenberg, E. G., & von Scheve, C. (2012). Emotional cues in American popular music: Five decades of the Top 40. *Psychology of Aesthetics, Creativity, and the Arts, 6*, 196–203.

Scherer, K. R. (1997). The role of culture in emotion-antecedent appraisal. *Journal of Personality and Social Psychology, 73*, 902–922.

Scherer, K. R. (1999). Appraisal theories. In T. Dalgleish & M. Power (Eds.), *Handbook of cognition and emotion* (pp. 637–663). Chichester: Wiley.

Scherer, K. R. (2000). Psychological models of emotion. In J. Borod (Ed.), *The neuropsychology of emotion* (pp. 137–162). Oxford: Oxford University Press.

Scherer, K. R. (2001). Appraisal considered as a process of multilevel sequential checking. In K. R. Sherer, A. Schorr, & T. Johnstone (Eds.), *Appraisal processes in emotion: Theory, method, research* (pp. 92–120). Oxford: Oxford University Press.

Scherer, K. R. (2003). Why music does not produce basic emotions: A plea for a new approach to measuring emotional effects of music. In R. Bresin (Ed.), *Proceedings of the Stockholm music acoustics conference 2003* (pp. 25–28). Stockholm: Royal Institute of Technology.

Scherer, K. R. (2013). The singer's paradox: On authenticity in emotional expression on the opera stage. In T. Cochrane, B. Fantini, & K. R. Scherer (Eds.), *The emotional power of music* (pp. 55–73). Oxford: Oxford University Press.

Scherer, K. R., & Oshinsky, J. S. (1977). Cue utilisation in emotion attribution from auditory stimuli. *Motivation and Emotion, 1*, 331–346.

Scherer, K. R., & Zentner, M. R. (2001). Emotional effects of music: Production rules. In P. N. Juslin & J. A. Sloboda (Eds.), *Music and emotion: Theory and research* (pp. 361–392). Oxford: Oxford University Press.

Scherer, K. R., & Zentner, M. (2008). Music-evoked emotions are different - more often aesthetic than utilitarian. *Behavioral and Brain Sciences, 31*, 595–596.

Scherer, K. R., Zentner, M. R., & Schacht, A. (2002). Emotional states generated by music: An exploratory study of music experts. *Musicae Scientiae, Special Issue 2001-2002*, 149–171.

Schermann, T. K., & Biancolli, L. (Eds.). (1972). *The Beethoven companion*. Garden City, NY: Doubleday.

Schimmack, U., & Grob, A. (2000). Dimensional models of core affect: A quantitative comparison by means of structural equation modeling. *European Journal of Personality, 14*, 325–345.

Schoenemann, P. T. (1999). Syntax as an emergent characteristic of the evolution of semantic complexity. *Minds and Machines, 9*, 309–346.

Schubert, E. (1996). Enjoyment of negative emotions in music. *Psychology of Music, 24*, 18–28.

Schubert, E. (2003). Update of the Hevner adjective checklist. *Perceptual and Motor Skills, 96*, 1117–1122.

Schubert, E. (2004). Modeling perceived emotion with continuous musical features. *Music Perception, 21*, 561–585.

Schubert, E. (2007). The influence of emotion, locus of emotion and familiarity upon preference in music. *Psychology of Music, 35*, 477–493.

Schubert, E. (2010). Continuous self-report methods. In P. N. Juslin & J. A. Sloboda (Eds.), *Handbook of music and emotion: Theory, research, applications* (pp. 223–253). Oxford: Oxford University Press.

Schubert, E. (2016). Does recall of a past music event invoke a reminiscence bump in young adults? *Memory, 24*, 1007–1014.

Schubert, E. (2018). Which nonvocal musical instrument sounds like the human voice? An empirical investigation. *Empirical Studies of the Arts*. Advance online publication. doi:10.1177/0276237418763657.

Schulkind, M. D., Hennis, L. K., & Rubin, D. C. (1999). Music, emotion, and autobiographical memory: They are playing our song. *Memory & Cognition, 27*, 948–955.

Schwartz, G. E., Weinberger, D. A., & Singer, J. A. (1981). Cardiovascular differentiation of happiness, sadness, anger, and fear following imagery and exercise. *Psychosomatic Medicine, 43*, 343–364.

Scruton, R. (1997). *The aesthetics of music.* Oxford: Oxford University Press.

Seashore, H. G. (1937). An objective analysis of artistic singing. In C. E. Seashore (Ed.), *Objective analysis of musical performance: University of Iowa studies in the psychology of music. Vol. 4* (pp. 12–157). Iowa City, IA: University of Iowa.

Seeger, A. (1987). *Why Suya sing: A music anthropology of an Amazonian people.* Cambridge: Cambridge University Press.

Senju, M., & Ohgushi, K. (1987). How are the player's ideas conveyed to the audience? *Music Perception, 4,* 311–324.

Serafine, M. L. (1980). Against music as communication: Implications for music education. *Journal of Aesthetic Education, 14,* 85–96.

Shaffer, L. H. (1992). How to interpret music. In M. R. Jones & S. Holleran (Eds.), *Cognitive bases of musical communication* (pp. 263–278). Washington, DC: American Psychological Association.

Shannon, C. E., & Weaver, W. (1949). *The mathematical theory of communication.* Urbana, IL: University of Illinois Press.

Shapiro, L. (2011). *Embodied cognition.* New York, NY: Routledge.

Shaver, P., Schwartz, J., Kirson, D., & O'Connor, C. (1987). Emotion knowledge: Further explorations of a prototype approach. *Journal of Personality and Social Psychology, 52,* 1061–1086.

Shaw, C., & Chase, M. (Eds.). (1989). *The imagined past: History and nostalgia.* Manchester: Manchester University Press.

Sheldon, S., & Donahue, J. (2017). More than a feeling: Emotional cues impact the access and experience of autobiographical memories. *Memory & Cognition, 45,* 731–744.

Shepard, R. N., & Metzler, J. (1971). Mental rotation of three-dimensional objects. *Science, 171,* 701–703.

Sheridan, K. M., & Gardner, H. (2012). Artistic development: Three essential spheres. In A. P. Shimamura & S. E. Palmer (Eds.), *Aesthetic science: Connecting minds, brains, and experience* (pp. 276–296). Oxford: Oxford University Press.

Shimamura, A. P. (2012). Toward a science of aesthetics: Issues and ideas. In A. P. Shimamura & S. E. Palmer (Eds.), *Aesthetic science: Connecting minds, brains, and experience* (pp. 3–28). Oxford: Oxford University Press.

Shove, P., & Repp, B. H. (1995). Musical motion and performance: Theoretical and empirical perspectives. In J. Rink (Ed.), *The practice of performance: Studies in musical interpretation* (pp. 55–83). Cambridge: Cambridge University Press.

Silvia, P. J. (2012). Human emotions and aesthetic experience: An overview of empirical aesthetics. In A. P. Shimamura & S. E. Palmer (Eds.), *Aesthetic science: Connecting minds, brains, and experience* (pp. 250–275). Oxford: Oxford University Press.

Simner, M. L. (1971). Newborns' response to the cry of another infant. *Developmental Psychology, 5,* 136–150.

Simons, R. C. (1996). *Boo! Culture, experience, and the startle reflex.* Oxford: Oxford University Press.

Simonton, D. K. (2010). Emotion and composition in classical music: Historiometric perspectives. In P. N. Juslin & J. A. Sloboda (Eds.), *Handbook of music and emotion: Theory, research, applications* (pp. 347–366). Oxford: Oxford University Press.

Simonton, D. K., & Damian, R. I. (2012). Creativity. In D. Reisman (Ed.), *The Oxford handbook of cognitive psychology* (pp. 795–807). Oxford: Oxford University Press.

Skinner, B. F. (1953). *Science and human behavior.* New York, NY: Macmillan.

Sloboda, J. A. (1983). The communication of musical metre in piano performance. *Quarterly Journal of Experimental Psychology, 35,* 377–396.

Sloboda, J. A. (1989). Music as a language. In F. Wilson & F. Roehmann (Eds.), *Music and child development: Proceedings of the 1987 biology of music making conference* (pp. 28–43). St. Louis, MO: MMB Music.

Sloboda, J. A. (1991). Music structure and emotional response: Some empirical findings. *Psychology of Music, 19,* 110–120.

Sloboda, J. A. (1992). Empirical studies of emotional response to music. In M. Riess-Jones & S. Holleran (Eds.), *Cognitive bases of musical communication* (pp. 33–46). Washington, DC: American Psychological Association.

Sloboda, J. A. (1996). Emotional responses to music: A review. In K. Riederer & T. Lahti (Eds.), *Proceedings of the Nordic acoustical meeting* (pp. 385–392). Helsinki: The Acoustical Society of Finland.

Sloboda, J. A. (1999). Music performance and emotion: Issues and developments. In S. W. Yi (Ed.), *Music, mind, & science* (pp. 354–369). Seoul: Seoul National University Press.

Sloboda, J. A. (2005). *Exploring the musical mind: Cognition, emotion, ability, function.* Oxford: Oxford University Press.

Sloboda, J. A. (2010). Music in everyday life: The role of emotions. In P. N. Juslin & J. A. Sloboda (Eds.), *Handbook of music and emotion: Theory, research, applications* (pp. 493–514). Oxford: Oxford University Press.

Sloboda, J. A., Ivaldi, A., & O'Neill, S. A. (2001). Functions of music in everyday life: An exploratory study using the experience sampling methodology. *Musicae Scientiae, 5,* 9–32.

Sloboda, J. A., & Juslin, P. N. (2001). Psychological perspectives on music and emotion. In P. N. Juslin & J. A. Sloboda (Eds.), *Music and emotion: Theory and research* (pp. 71–104). New York, NY: Oxford University Press.

Sloboda, J. A., & Juslin, P. N. (2010). At the interface between the inner and outer world: Psychological perspectives. In P. N. Juslin & J. A. Sloboda (Eds.), *Handbook of music and emotion: Theory, research, applications* (pp. 73–97). Oxford: Oxford University Press.

Sloboda, J. A., & Lehmann, A. C. (2001). Tracking performance correlates of changes in perceived intensity of emotion during different interpretations of a Chopin piano prelude. *Music Perception, 19,* 87–120.

Sloboda, J. A., & O'Neill, S. A. (2001). Emotions in everyday listening to music. In P. N. Juslin & J. A. Sloboda (Eds.), *Music and emotion: Theory and research* (pp. 415–430). Oxford: Oxford University Press.

Slonimsky, N. (1969). *Lexicon of musical invective: Critical assaults on composers since Beethoven's time.* Seattle, WA: University of Washington Press.

Small, C. (1999). Musicking: The meanings of performance and listening: A lecture. *Music Education Research, 1,* 9–21.

Smith, C. A., & Kirby, L. D. (2009). Goals. In D. Sander & K. R. Scherer (Eds.), *The Oxford companion to emotion and the affective sciences* (pp. 197–198). Oxford: Oxford University Press.

Smith, J. (1988). *Off the record: An oral history of popular music.* London: Sidgwick & Jackson.

Solomon, R. (2007). *True to our feelings: What our emotions are really telling us.* Oxford: Oxford University Press.

Sousou, S. D. (1997). Effects of melody and lyrics on mood and memory. *Perceptual and Motor Skills, 85*, 31–40.

Soussignan, R., & Schaal, B. (2005). Emotional processes in human newborns: A functionalist perspective. In J. Nadel & D. Muir (Eds.), *Emotional development* (pp. 127–159). Oxford: Oxford University Press.

Sparshott, F. (1982). *The theory of the arts.* Princeton, NJ: Princeton University Press.

Spencer, H. (1857). The origin and function of music. *Fraser's Magazine, 56*, 396–408.

Sperber, D., & Hirschfeld, L. A. (2004). The cognitive foundations of cultural stability and diversity. *Trends in Cognitive Sciences, 8*, 40–46.

Spitzer, M. (2004). *Metaphor and musical thought.* Chicago, IL: University of Chicago Press.

Spitzer, M. (2010). Mapping the human heart: A holistic analysis of fear in Schubert. *Music Analysis, 29*, 149–213. (Special Issue on Music and Emotion)

Spitzer, M. (2013). Sad flowers: Affective trajectory in Schubert's Trockne Blumen. In T. Cochrane, B. Fantini, & K. R. Scherer (Eds.), *The emotional power of music* (pp. 7–21). Oxford: Oxford University Press.

Squire, L. R. (2004). Memory systems of the brain: A brief history and current perspective. *Neurobiology of Learning and Memory, 82*, 171–177.

Starobinski, J. (2013). On nostalgia. In T. Cochrane, B. Fantini, & K. R. Scherer (Eds.), *The emotional power of music* (pp. 329–335). Oxford: Oxford University Press.

Stecker, R. (2003). Definition of art. In J. Levinson (Ed.), *The Oxford handbook of aesthetics* (pp. 136–154). Oxford: Oxford University Press.

Steinbeis, N., Koelsch, S., & Sloboda, J. A. (2006). The role of harmonic expectancy violations in musical emotions: Evidence from subjective, physiological, and neural responses. *Journal of Cognitive Neuroscience, 18*, 1380–1393.

Stern, D. (1985). *The interpersonal world of the infant. A view from psychoanalysis and developmental psychology.* New York, NY: Basic Books.

Stern, D. (2010). *Forms of vitality: Exploring dynamic experience in psychology, the arts, psychotherapy, and development.* Oxford: Oxford University Press.

Stone, R. (1982). *Let the inside be sweat: The interpretation of music events among the Kpelle of Liberia.* Bloomington, IN: University of Indiana Press.

Strack, F., Martin, L. L., & Stepper, S. (1988). Inhibiting and facilitating conditions of the human smile: A nonobtrusive test of the facial feedback hypothesis. *Journal of Personality and Social Psychology, 54*, 768–777.

Stratton, V. N., & Zalanowski, A. H. (1994). Affective impact of music vs. lyrics. *Empirical Studies of the Arts, 12*, 173–184.

Stravinsky, I. (1934). Stravinsky: As I see myself (interview with N. Cameron). *Gramophone, August 1934*. Retrieved from: <https://www.gramophone.co.uk/feature/stravinsky-as-i-see-myself>.

Stravinsky, I. (1975). *Stravinsky: An autobiography*. London: Calders and Boyars.

Stravinsky, I., & Craft, R. (1981). *Expositions and developments*. Berkeley, CA: University of California Press.

Striedter, G. F. (2005). *Principles of brain evolution*. Sunderland, MA: Sinauer Associates.

Strogatz, S. (2003). *Sync: The emerging science of spontaneous order*. New York, NY: Hyperion.

Swanwick, K. (1985). *A basis for music education*. Windsor: NFER-Nelson.

Swanwick, K. (2001). Music development theories revisited. *Music Education Research, 3, No. 2*, 227–242.

Tajadura-Jiménez, A., Larsson, P., Väljamäe, A., Västfjäll, D., & Kleiner, M. (2010). When room size matters: Acoustic influences on emotional responses to sounds. *Emotion, 10*, 416–422.

Taruffi L., & Koelsch S. (2014). The paradox of music-evoked sadness: An online survey. *PLoS ONE*, 9:e110490.

Thaut, M. H., McIntosh, G. C., & Hoemberg, V. (2015). Neurobiological foundations of neurologic music therapy: Rhythmic entrainment and the motor system. *Frontiers in Psychology, 5*, 1185.

Thaut, M. H., Miller, R. A., & Schauer, L. M. (1998). Multiple synchronization strategies in rhythmic sensorimotor tasks: Phase vs. period adaptation. *Biological Cybernetics, 79*, 241–250.

Thayer, R. E. (1996). *The origin of everyday moods: Managing energy, tension, and stress*. Oxford: Oxford University Press.

Thompson, R. L., & Larson, R. (1995). Social context and the subjective experience of different types of rock music. *Journal of Youth and Adolescence, 24*, 731–744.

Thompson, S. (2006). Audience responses to a live orchestral concert. *Musicae Scientiae, 10*, 215–244.

Thompson, W. F. (2015). *Music, thought, and feeling: Understanding the psychology of music* (2nd ed.). Oxford: Oxford University Press.

Thompson, W. F., & Balkwill, L.-L. (2010). Cross-cultural similarities and differences. In P. N. Juslin & J. A. Sloboda (Eds.), *Handbook of music and emotion: Theory, research, applications* (pp. 755–788). Oxford: Oxford University Press.

Thompson, W. F., Geeves, A. M., & Olsen, K. N. (2018). Who enjoys listening to violent music and why? *Psychology of Popular Media Culture*. Advance online publication: <http://dx.doi.org/10.1037/ppm0000184>.

Thompson, W. F., Marin, M. M., & Stewart, L. (2012). Reduced sensitivity to emotional prosody in congenital amusia rekindles the musical protolanguage hypothesis. *Proceedings of the National Academy of Sciences USA, 109*, 19027–19032.

Thompson, W. F., & Quinto, L. (2011). Music and emotion: Psychological considerations. In P. Goldie & E. Schellekens (Eds.), *The aesthetic mind: Philosophy and psychology* (pp. 357–375). Oxford: Oxford University Press.

Thompson, W. F., & Robitaille, B. (1992). Can composers express emotions through music? *Empirical Studies of the Arts, 10*, 79–89.

Thompson, W. F., Sundberg, J., Friberg, A., & Frydén, L. (1989). The use of rules for expression in the performance of melodies. *Psychology of Music, 17*, 63–82.

Thornton-Wells, T. A., Cannistraci, C. J., Anderson, A. W., Kim, C., Eapen, M., Gore, J. C., Blake, R., & Dykens, E. M. (2010). Auditory attraction: Activation of visual cortex by music and sound in Williams syndrome. *American Journal on Intellectual and Developmental Disabilities, 115*, 172–189.

Tierney, A., & Kraus, N. (2013). The ability to move to a beat is linked to the consistency of neural responses to sound. *Journal of Neuroscience, 33*, 14981–14988.

Tillman, B., & Bigand, E. (2004). The relative importance of local and global structures in music perception. *The Journal of Aesthetics and Art Criticism, 62*, 211–222.

Timmers, R., & Ashley, R. (2007). Emotional ornamentation in performances of a Handel sonata. *Music Perception, 25*, 117–134.

Titchener, E. B. (1910). *A textbook of psychology*. New York, NY: Macmillan.

Todd, N. (1985). A model of expressive timing in tonal music. *Music Perception, 3*, 33–58.

Todd, N. P. M, & Lee, C. S. (2015). The sensory-motor theory of beat induction 20 years on: A new synthesis and future perspectives. *Frontiers in Human Neuroscience, 9*, 444.

Tolstoy, L. (1960). *What is art?* (trans. A. Maude). Indianapolis, IN: Hackett Publishing Company. (Original work published 1898)

Tomaino, C. (2002). The role of music in the rehabilitation of persons with neurologic diseases. *Music Therapy Today (online), August*, <http://musictherapyworld.net>.

Tooby, J., & Cosmides, L. (1990). The past explains the present: Emotional adaptations and the structure of ancestral environments. *Ethology and Sociobiology, 11*, 375–424.

Toomey, L. (1996-1997). Literature review: The Bonny Method of Guided Imagery and Music. *Journal of the Association for Music and Imagery, 5*, 75–103.

Trainor, L. J., & Trehub, S. E. (1994). Key membership and implied harmony in Western tonal music: Developmental perspectives. *Perception and Psychophysics, 56*, 125–132.

Tranel, D. (2000). Electrodermal activity in cognitive neuroscience: Neuroanatomical and neuropsychological correlates. In R. D. Lane & L. Nadel (Ed.), *Cognitive neuroscience of emotion* (pp. 192–224). Oxford: Oxford University Press.

Trost, W., Frühholz, S., Schön, D., Labbé, C., Pichon, S., Grandjean, D., & Vuilleumier, P. (2014). Getting the beat: Entrainment of brain activity by musical rhythm and pleasantness. *Neuroimage, 103*, 55–64.

Trost, W., Labbé, C., & Grandjean, D. (2017). Rhythmic entrainment as a musical affect induction mechanism. *Neuropsychologia, 96*, 96–110.

Trost, W., & Vuilleumier, P. (2013). Rhythmic entrainment as a mechanism for emotion induction by music: A neurophysiological perspective. In T. Cochrane, B. Fantini, & K. R. Scherer (Eds.), *The emotional power of music* (pp. 213–225). Oxford: Oxford University Press.

Tsai, J. L. (2007). Ideal affect: Cultural causes and behavioral consequences. *Perspectives on Psychological Science, 2*, 242–259.

Tulving, E. (2002). Episodic memory: From mind to brain. *Annual Review of Psychology, 53*, 1–25.

Turino, T. (1993). *Moving away from silence: Music of the Peruvian Altiplano and the experience of urban migration*. Chicago, IL: University of Chicago Press.

Turino. T. (2008). *Music as social life: The politics of participation*. Chicago, IL: University of Chicago Press.

Turk, I. (Ed.). (1997). *Mousterian 'bone flute' and other finds from Divje Babe I cave site in Slovenia*. Ljubljana: Zalozba ZRC.

Tversky, B., & Zacks, J. M. (2013). Event perception. In D. Reisberg (Ed.). *The Oxford handbook of cognitive psychology* (pp. 83–94). Oxford: Oxford University Press.

van Dyck, E., Moelants, D., Demer, M., Deweppe, A., Coussement, P., & Leman, M. (2013). The impact of the bass drum on human dance movement. *Music Perception, 30*, 349–359.

Van Zijl, A. G. W., & Sloboda, J. A. (2011). Performers' experienced emotions in the construction of expressive musical performance: An exploratory investigation. *Psychology of Music, 39*, 196–219.

Västfjäll, D., Juslin, P. N., & Hartig, T. (2012). Music, subjective well-being, and health: The role of everyday emotions. In R. MacDonald, G. Kreutz, & L. Mitchell (Eds.), *Music, health, and well-being* (pp. 405–423). Oxford: Oxford University Press.

Viswanathan, T., & Cormack, J. (1998). Melodic improvisation in Karnatak music: The manifestation of raga. In B. Nettl & M. Russell (Eds.), *In the course of performance: Studies in the world of musical improvisation* (pp. 219–233). Chicago: University of Chicago Press.

Vitz, P. C. (1966). Affect as a function of stimulus variation. *Journal of Experimental Psychology, 71*, 74–79.

Vonnegut, K. (1976). *Slapstick or lonesome no more!* London: Jonathan Cape.

Von Scheve, C., & Salmela, M. (Eds.). (2014). *Collective emotions: Perspectives from psychology, philosophy, and sociology*. Oxford: Oxford University Press.

Vuoskoski, J. K., & Eerola, T. (2015). Extramusical information contributes to emotions induced by music. *Psychology of Music, 43*, 262–274.

Vuoskoski, J., & Eerola, T. (2017). The pleasure evoked by sad music is mediated by feelings of being moved. *Frontiers in Psychology, 8*, 439.

Vuoskoski, J., Thompson, W. F., McIlwain, D., & Eerola, T. (2012). Who enjoys listening to sad music and why? *Music Perception, 29*, 311–318.

Vuust, P., & Kringelbach, M. L. (2010). The pleasure of music. In M. L. Kringelbach & K. C. Berridge (Eds.), *Pleasures of the brain* (pp. 255–269). Oxford: Oxford University Press.

Wager, T. D., Barrett, L. F., Bliss-Moreau, E., Lindquist, K. A., … Mize, J. (2008). The neuroimaging of emotion. In M. Lewis, J. M. Haviland-Jones, & L. F. Barrett (Eds.), *Handbook of emotions* (3rd ed., pp. 249–267). New York, NY: Guilford Press.

Warren, J. E., Sauter, D. A., Eisner, F., Wiland, J., Dresner, M.A., Wise, R.J., Rosen, S., & Scott, S. K. (2006). Positive emotions preferentially engage an auditory-motor 'mirror' system. *Journal of Neuroscience, 26*, 13067–13075.

Waterman, M. (1996). Emotional responses to music: Implicit and explicit effects in listeners and performers. *Psychology of Music, 24*, 53–67.

Watson, D. (Ed.). (1991). *The Wordsworth dictionary of musical quotations*. Ware: Wordsworth.

Watson, D., & Tellegen, A. (1985). Toward a consensual structure of mood. *Psychological Bulletin, 98*, 219–235.

Watson, K. B. (1942). The nature and measurement of musical meanings. *Psychological Monographs, 54*, 1–43.

Wedin, L. (1972). Multi-dimensional study of perceptual-emotional qualities in music. *Scandinavian Journal of Psychology, 13*, 241–257.

Weitz, M. (1956). The role of theory in aesthetics. *Journal of Aesthetics and Art Criticism, 15*, 27–35.

Wells, A., & Hakanen, E. A. (1991). The emotional uses of popular music by adolescents. *Journalism Quarterly, 68*, 445–454.

Werner, D. (1984). *Amazon journey: An anthropologist's year among Brazil's Mekranoti indians*. New York, NY: Simon and Schuster.

Whissel, C. (1996). Traditional and emotional stylometric analyses of the songs of Beatles Paul McCartney and John Lennon. *Computers and the Humanities, 30*, 257–265.

Whissel, R., & Whissel, C. (2000). The emotional importance of key: Do Beatles songs written in different keys convey different emotional tones? *Perceptual and Motor Skills, 91*, 973–980.

Wiik, M. (2012). *Emotioner och föredragsbeteckningar i klassisk musik: Ett möte mellan psykologisk forskning och musikalisk praxis*. Unpublished master's thesis, Uppsala University, Sweden.

Wild, B., Erb, M., Eyb, M., Bartels, M., & Grodd, W. (2003). Why are smiles contagious? An fMRI study of the interaction between perception of facial affect and facial movements. *Psychiatric Research: Neuroimaging, 123*, 17–36.

Wildschut, T., Sedikides, C., Arndt, J., & Routledge, C. (2006). Nostalgia: Content, triggers, functions. *Journal of Personality and Social Psychology, 91*, 975–993.

Wing, A., & Kristofferson, A. B. (1973). Response delays and the timing of discrete motor responses. *Perception & Psychophysics, 14*, 5–12.

Wittgenstein, L. (1922). *Tractatus logico-philosophicus*. New York, NY: Harcourt, Brace & Company.

Wittgenstein, L. (1966). *Lectures and conversations on aesthetics, psychology, and religious belief*. Oxford: Basil Blackwell.

Witvliet, C. V., & Vrana, S. R. (2007). Play it again Sam: Repeated exposure to emotionally evocative music polarises liking and smiling responses, and influences other affective reports, facial EMG, and heart rate. *Cognition and Emotion, 21*, 3–25.

Woody, R. H. (2000). Learning expressivity in music performance: An exploratory study. *Research Studies in Music Education, 14*, 14–23.

Woody, R. H. (2002). Emotion, imagery and metaphor in the acquisition of musical performance skill. *Music Education Research, 4*, 213–224.

Woody, R. H., & McPherson, G. E. (2010). Emotion and motivation in the lives of performers. In P. N. Juslin & J. A. Sloboda (Eds.), *Handbook of music and emotion: Theory, research, applications* (pp. 401–424). Oxford: Oxford University Press.

Workman, L., & Reader, W. (2008). *Evolutionary psychology: An introduction*. Cambridge: Cambridge University Press.

Zajonc, R. B. (2001). Mere exposure: A gateway to the subliminal. *Current Directions in Psychological Science, 6*, 224–228.

Zangwill, N. (2004). Against emotion: Hanslick was right about music. *British Journal of Aesthetics*, 44, 29–43.

Zatorre, R. J., & Halpern, A. R. (2005). Mental concerts: Musical imagery and auditory cortex. *Neuron*, 47, 9–12.

Zentner, M. R., & Eerola, T. (2010). Self-report measures and models. In P. N. Juslin & J. A. Sloboda (Eds.), *Handbook of music and emotion: Theory, research, applications* (pp. 187–221). Oxford: Oxford University Press.

Zentner, M. R., Grandjean, D., Scherer, K. R. (2008). Emotions evoked by the sound of music: Differentiation, classification, and measurement. *Emotion*, 8, 494–521.

Yamasaki, T. (2002). Emotional communication in improvised performance by musically untrained players. In T. Kato (Ed.), *Proceedings of the 17th International Congress of the International Association of Empirical Aesthetics* (pp. 521–524). Osaka, Japan: International Association of Empirical Aesthetics.

Yang, Y.-H., & Chen, H. H. (2011). *Music emotion recognition*. Boca Raton, FL: CRC Press.

NAME INDEX

Tables and figures are indicated by an italic *t* and *f* following the page number.

Adams, Bryan - "Summer of '69" 177
Adams, John - "Harmonielehre: Part 1" 269
Adele 292
'Someone like you' 56
Aiken, Henry 346
Allesandri, Elena 432
Altenmüller, Eckart 4–5
Andersson, Benny 141
Antwon The Swan 206
Aristotle 56, 122*n*1, 439*n*6, 453
Arnold, Magda 248
Aucouturier, Jean-Julien 289

Bach, C.P.E. 193
Bach, Johann Sebastian 136–37*n*6, 356, 356*f*, 505
"Air on the G String" 333
Arioso from Cantata BWV 156 241
"Art of the Fugue, The" 66–67
"Goldberg Variations, The" 310, 434
Toccata and Fugue in D minor, BWV 565 273
"Well-Tempered Clavier, The" 408
Baker, Ginger 137
Baker, Janet 6–7
Balkwill, Laura-Lee 131, 132
Ball, Philip 229–30
Barber, Samuel 32
"Adagio for Strings" 251
Barenboim, Daniel 197
Barradas, Gonçalo 324–25, 378
Bartók, Béla 68
Batteux, Charles 453
Baumgartner, Hans 321–22, 330
B.B. King 116, 165–66, 199–201, 290*f*
"How Blue Can you Get?" 95, 135
Becker, Judith 224, 391
Beebe-Center, John Gilbert 490
Beethoven 69, 93, 101, 136–37, 341–42, 432, 442, 456, 485, 505
Cavatina (Opus 130) 81
'Eroica' symphony 56–57
Fifth Symphony - *Scherzo* 85
"Missa Solemnis" 121
Ninth Symphony 36, 342
Piano Sonata No. 8 in C minor, Opus 13 ("Pathétique") 80
String Quartet No. 14 in C-sharp Minor, Opus 131 110, 134
Berg, Alban 440
"To the memory of an angel" 102*n*1
Lyric Suite, Three Pieces for String Orchestra Part III 357–58
"Wozzeck" 403
Bergeron, Vincent 432
Berliner, P.F. 121
Berlioz, Hector 3, 178–79, 214, 507–8
"Symphonie Fanastique" 178–79, 179*f*, 339–40
Berlyne, Daniel 272, 410–13, 414–15, 416, 417, 418, 419, 420, 421, 440–41, 443, 502
Bernardini, Linda 310
Bernstein, Leonard 16
Bharucha, Jamshed 360
Bicknell, Jeanette 458, 496
Blacking, John 278

Blair, Elizabeth 311
Bloch, Ernest
  "Prayer" from Jewish Life No. 1 301
  "Three Jewish Poems" 403
Bonny, Helen 333
Boulez - Piano Sonata No. 1 412–13
Bourdieu, Pierre 485
Bowie, David - "Heroes" 177
Boyd, Jenny 116–17, 118–19, 121, 207
Boyd, Pattie 280, 339–40
Brahms, Johannes 485
  Symphony No. 2 in D major 270–71
  Symphony No. 4 402
Brauer, M. 44
Brentano, Franz 263
Bresin, R. 143
Britten, Benjamin 31
Browne, Jackson 30–31, 116, 440
Brown, James 283, 478–79*n*3
Brown, Robert 185–86
Brunswik, Egon 141, 148, 154
Buckley, Jeff
  "Corpus Christi Carol" 292
  "Last Goodbye, The" 339
Buck, Ross 295
Budd, Malcolm 11–12, 18, 30, 425–26
Burke, Edmund 450–51
Burke, Michael 412–13
Burland, K. 121
Burton, Robert 499–500

Cage, John 104, 440, 484
  4'33" 39, 424, 445
Callas, Maria 292
Callender, John 486
Campbell, Ivy 91
Carlyle, Thomas 488
Casals, Pablo 440
Cash, Johnny - "Hurt" 379
Cash, Rosanne 116
Castelfranchi, Christiano 354, 358, 359, 380
Chopin, Frédéric 195–96
  Etude, Opus 25, No. 1 in A major 197
Clapton, Eric 111, 116, 165, 199–201, 207*n*1, 280, 340*f*
  Layla album 339–41
  "Tears in Heaven" 332
Clarke, Eric 36, 37, 56, 189, 247–48, 361, 377, 441, 486
Clayton, Martin 277, 278
Clementi 444–45
Clore, Gerald 214
Clynes, Manfred 79, 299, 437
Cochrane, Tom 63
Cohen, Annabel 185
Cohen, Nicki 333
Collins, Albert 199–201
Coltrane, John 115*b*
  Love Supreme 440
Compton, T. 87
Cooke, Deryck 63, 125–27
Cook, Nicholas 15, 39, 75–76*n*3, 100, 341–42
Cortot, Alfred 197
Couperin, François 471
Cross, I. 6, 79
Cupchik, Gerald 460

Darwin, Charles 8, 295, 488
Davidson, Richard 46, 396
Davies, John 316
Davies, Stephen 130, 164
da Vinci, Leonardo 453
Davis, Miles 165, 449, 505
  "All Blues" 411
  Bitches Brew 440
Debussy, Claude 343–44
  "Beau Soir" 110
  "Girl with the Flaxen Hair, The" 412–13
  Sonata for Cello and Piano in D Minor, L.135 125
Delibes, Leo - "Flower song" from *Lakme* 434
DeNora, Tia 174, 324, 332, 418, 493, 507–8
Descartes, René 23
Dewey, John 272, 346
Diaghilev, Sergei 343

Dibben, Nicola 30–31, 247–48, 342
Dimberg, Ulf 289
Dowling, Jay 14*n*3, 157, 175, 205
Duchamp, Marcell 445
Duerksen, George 476
Dufy, Raoul 448
Duncan, E. 242
Dunckel, Jean-Benoit 117
Dutton, Denis 430–32
Dvořák, Antonín 178
  Serenade for Strings in E Major, Opus 22 125, 184
Dylan, B. 447–48, 464
  Self Portrait 403*n*1

Edison, Thomas 386
Eerola, Tuomas 132–33*n*5, 143, 180–81, 339, 415
Evans, Bill - "Peace Piece" 345–46
Evans, Paul 375
Eysenck, Hans 437

Farga, F. 62
Farnsworth, P.R. 118
Fechner, Gustav 462
Feld, Steven 278
Fiske, Harald 474*n*1, 475–76
Fodor, Jerry 293–94
Frampton, Peter 77
Fredrickson, Barbara 235, 495
Freud, Sigmund 8–9, 8*f*, 19, 20, 46, 136
Frey, William 223
Friberg, Anders 143, 196
Frijda, Nico 224, 245–46
Frölich, Franz Joseph 342

Gabriel, Peter 116
Gabrielsson, Alf 40–41, 63–64, 71, 86, 144, 191, 215, 217, 223, 226, 234, 238–40, 266, 268, 288, 304*n*2, 320, 326–27, 331–32, 337–38, 387, 407, 434, 444, 447–48, 490, 492, 504
Gärdenfors, Peter 334–35
Gardner, Howard 88
Gaston, Thayer 275
Gaudí, Antoni 205
Gaut, Berys 430–32
Gaver, William 413–14
Gaye, Marvin - *What's Going On* 440
Gayford, Christopher 121
George-Warren, Holly 116–17, 118–19, 121, 207
Geringer, John 478
Getz, Russell 413
Gibson, James 148, 383–84
Glass, Philip 440
Goehr, Lydia 103–4
Gohm, Carol 214
Goldberg, Frances 333, 336
Goldinger, Stephen 510–11
Goldman, A. 75
Gomart, Emilie 507–8
Gopnik, Blake 428–29
Górecki - Symphony No. 3 267*n*2
Gould, Glenn 310
Goulding, P.G. 3, 213
Gracyk, Theodore 438, 439, 443, 455, 485
Grandjean, Didier 58, 279, 283
Greenberg, Leslie 487
Grewe, Oliver 4–5
Gridley, Mark 412–13
Grohl, Dave 389
Gross, James 226
Güell, Parc 223
Gutheil, Emil 9
Guy, Buddy 121, 199–201

Haidt, Jonathan 450–51
Hammond, K.R. 148, 152, 515
Handel - "Messiah, The" 117
Hanslick, Eduard 65*n*2, 103, 230, 444
Hargreaves, David 15, 413, 417, 418–19, 467–68
Harrer, Gerhart 282
Harris, Emmylou 6–7

Harrison, George 106, 339–40
Harris, Roy - *American Scene* 402
Harwood, Dane 14*n*3, 175, 205
Harwood, Richard 157
Hatfield, Elaine 287*n*1, 288
Hatten, Robert 81, 181
Hawk, Skyler 289
Haydn, Franz Joseph 449–50
  Symphony No. 94 in G major ("Surprise" symphony) 265–66, 269–71, 272
Hebb, Donald 53
Hedström, Peter 253
Hellström, Klas 311
Hendrix, Jimi 158, 175–77, 176*f*
Henley, Don 21, 116–17
Hennion, Antoine 507–8
Hevner, Kate 31–32, 63, 65, 66*f*, 71, 92, 106–7, 108*t*, 177
Heyduk, Ronald 415
Higgins, Kathleen 511–12
Hindemith, Paul 413
Hirschfield, L.A. 166
Hodges, Donald 216–17, 434–35
Höfel, Lea 475*n*2
Holiday, Billie 292
Honegger, Arthur - 'Pacfic 231' 66–67
Hooker, John Lee 116
Huron, David 4, 172–73, 217, 218, 242–43, 344, 348, 349, 351, 352*f*, 352, 353–54*n*5, 358, 359*n*7, 433*n*1, 437, 501, 502
Hursch, C.J. 152, 515
Hursch, J.L. 152, 515
Huygens, Christian 276, 277

Ice-T 116
Isaksson, S. 439
Istok, Eva 434
Iverson, J.R. 280–81*n*1
Ives, Charles 440

Jackendoff, Ray 350, 360, 488
Jacobsen, Thomas 464, 475*n*2
James, William 8, 44
Janata, Petr 322, 323, 330, 375
Janov, Dr Arthur 165*n*2
Jentschke, Sebastian 348
John, Elton 328–29
Johnson-Laird, Philip 100
Johnson, Robert 62–63
Joplin, Janis 292
Jørgensen, Harald 21–22
Joseph, Rhawn 270
Joyce, James 316

Kant, Immanuel 241, 434
Keil, Charles 278
Keith, Gillian 119–20
Key, Ivor 464
Kiedis, Anthony 116–17
Kiernan, Frederic 376
King, Albert 199–201
Kivy, Peter 9, 33–34*n*1, 103, 210, 222–23, 230, 255, 346, 463, 500, 501–2
Kleinginna, A.M. 44
Kleinginna, P.R. 44
Kneutgen, Johannes 283–84
Knopfler, Mark 426
Koelsch, Stefan 221, 325, 356
Konečni, Vladimir 116, 230
Kopiez, Reinhard 4–5
Kosslyn, Stephen 335–36*n*2
Kreutz, G. 81, 86–87
Kringelbach, Morten 362
Krugman, Herbert 413
Krumhansl, Carol 225–26, 318

Labbé Rodriguez, Carolina 279, 280, 283
Lahdelma, Imre 180–81
Laird, James 295
Lane, Richard 371
Langer, Susanne 79, 92, 94, 158
Lang, Peter 316
Larson, Reed 338–39, 386
Laszlo, Janos 460
Laukka, Petri 71, 132, 161–62, 186, 311
Lazarus, Richard 248

Leander, Zarah 504
Leder, Helmut 449–50, 454–55
Lee, Christopher 285
Leech-Wilkinson, Daniel 36, 111, 136, 188, 197
Lehmann, Andreas 444–45
Lennon, John 87, 165*n*2
Lerdahl, Fred 350, 488
Levenson, Robert 215
Levinson, Jerrold 86, 425–26, 491, 499–500
Levitin, D.J. 61, 87
Liljeström, S. 330
Lindström, E. 143, 144
Lindström Wik, Siv 41
Lipps, Theodor 288
Liszt, Franz 195–96, 497
  "Faust Symphony" 403
Lomax, Alan 278, 300
Lorand, Ruth 428, 434
Lundy, Duane 473–74

McCartney, Paul 87
MacDonald, R. 81
McIver Lopes, Dominic 432
MacLean, Paul 297
McPherson, Gary 439, 476
Mahler, Gustav 127–28
  Symphony No. 1 in D Major, IV: "Stürmich bewegt" 72
  Symphony No. 2 135
  Symphony No. 5 305, 403, 434
  Symphony No. 8 272
  Symphony No. 9 345*n*2
  Symphony No. 10 268
Mandler, George 413–14
Marcus, Greil 403*n*1
Margulis, Elisabeth Hellmuth 217, 218, 327–28, 349
Marks, David 338
Marr, David 148
Marsalis, Branford 116
Martindale, Colin 416, 417, 418, 420, 502
Marvin, Hank 116
Mascagni - Turridu's Farewell from "Cavalleria Rusticana" 91
Maslow, Abraham 505
Matravers, Derek 489
Melchionne, K. 404*n*2
Mendelssohn - "Wedding March" in C major 320
Menninghaus, Winfried 242
Menuhin, Yehudi 82, 115*b*, 206
Merriam, Alan 39–40
Metzler, Jacqueline 335
Meyer, Leonard B. 65, 67, 78, 82, 124, 161, 190, 212, 346–48, 351, 353–54, 356, 357–80, 382, 437
Miceli, Maria 354, 358, 359, 380
Miller, Glenn - "Moonlight Serenade" 312–13
Minassian, Caroline 121
Mitchell, Joni 116
  "A Case of You" 177
  Blue 117
Mitchell, L. 81
Moby - *Play* 300
Monk, Meredith 440
Moog, Robert 167*n*5
Moore, K. 417
Morey, R. 132
Morgan, Lee - "Moanin" 207
Morricone, Ennio 180–81*n*6
Morton, Eugene 297
Moser, Thomas 119–20
Mozart 69, 77, 136–37*n*6, 341, 438*n*5, 440, 444–45, 449–50, 485, 505
  Piano Sonata in A major 191, 191*f*
  "Requiem" 332
Mull, Helen 413
Mull, Martin 31
Myles, B. - "Have You Ever Loved a Woman?" 207*n*1

Narmour, Eugene 347
Nash, Graham 116, 207
Nesse, Randolph 304*n*1
Newman, Randy 116

Niccolini, Alberto 310
Nicks, Stevie 116
Niedenthal, P. 44
North, Adrian 417

Oakley, Kenneth 318*n*1
Oatley, Keith 54, 242
Obrecht, Jas 165–66*n*4
O'Connor, Sinéad 121
Offenbach - "Barcarolle" 492
Öhman, Arne 47
O'Neill, S.A. 316
Osborne, John 336–37
Oshinsky, James 143

Paganini, Niccolo 61–64, 62*f*, 71, 111, 444
Panksepp, J. 218
Pascal, Blaise 255
Patel, A.D. 280–81*n*1, 351
Pavarotti, Luciano 64, 167, 219–20, 219*f*
Pavlov, Ivan 174
Peirce, Charles 157
Peretz, Isabelle 9, 221
Persson, R.S. 331
Petty, Tom 108–9
Pilc, Jean-Michel 249
Pitts, Stephanie 247–48
Plato 8, 122, 401, 434, 443, 453, 488
Ploog, Detlev 296, 297
Plutchik, Robert 269
Pratt, Carol 158
Price, Harry 477
Prokofiev 135, 433*n*1
Proust, Marcel 160–61, 291
Puccini, Giacomo
  Madame Butterfly 91, 174–75
  "Nessun Dorma", *Turandot* 220
Pylyshyn, Zenon 335–36

Rachmaninoff, Sergei - "Vocalise", Opus 34, No. 14 301
Radford 34, 34*n*2
Randall, William 232
Ravel, Maurice - "Bolero" 272
Razran, Gregory 305–6
Redding, Otis - "Sitting on the Dock of the Bay" 177
Rembrandt 445
Repp, Bruno 196, 197
Reznor, Trent 379
Richards, Keith 63, 116, 206, 306–8, 307*f*
Rickard, Nikki 232
Riess Jones, Marie 278
Rigg, Melvin 67, 91, 104, 177–78
Risset, Jean-Claude 21, 32, 75, 127*n*2
  Mutations 9
Robertson, Enid 99–100
Robinson, Jenefer 250, 292, 443, 499
Robitaille, Brent 88
Rosch, Eleanor 416–17
Rossini, Gioachino 63
  "William Tell" 271
Rotten, Johnny 160*n*1
Rous, Samuel 271
Russell, J.A. 50, 106*n*6
Ruud, Even 324

Saint-Saëns, Camille 108–9, 136–37*n*6
Sakka, L.S. 6
Salieri, Antonio 440
Salimpoor, V.N. 252
Schellenberg, Glenn 137, 377
Schenker, Heinrich 170, 345
Scherer, Klaus 58, 119–20, 143, 227, 241, 491–92
Schoenberg, Arnold 102*n*1, 357–58, 413, 433*n*1, 440, 484
  'serial' compositions 66–67
  "Verklärte Nacht" 493*f*, 493
Scholes, Percy 401
Schubert, Emery 107, 108*t*, 206, 375, 438, 439, 476, 502*n*5, 503
Schubert, Franz 36, 111, 492
  Impromptus 174, 181, 493
  Piano Quintet in A Major, D.667 ("Trout Quintet") 125

Schulkind, M.D. 322*n*4, 326, 327
Schumann, Robert - "Träumerei" 151
Scruton, Roger 463
Seashore, Carl Emil 190
Seder, Patrick 450–51
Sessions, Roger 413
Shaffer, Henry 193
Shankar, Ravi 116, 129–30
Shaw, Woodie 207
Shepard, Roger 335
Shimp, Terrance 311
Shostakovich, Dmitri
  String Quartet No. 8 in C Minor, Opus 110 125
  Symphony No. 10 in E minor, Opus 93 125
Shove, Patrick 196
Silvia, Paul 418, 421, 470
Simner, Marvin 298
Simons, Ronald 266, 271, 273–74
Simonton, Dean Keith 118, 416, 441–42, 449–50
Sinatra, Frank 137
Sloboda, John 93, 120, 121, 157, 207, 218, 223–24, 234, 287–88, 316, 320, 348–49, 355–56, 444, 484, 500
Slonimsky, N. 401–2
Small, Christopher 39–40
Smith, Patti 116
Soares, Joaquim 47
Solomon, Robert 506–7
Spencer, Herbert 159
Sperber, D. 166
Spinoza, Baruch 252
Springsteen, Bruce - "Born to Run" 245
Starobinski, Jean 106
Steinbeis, Nikolaus 356
Stern, Daniel 93–94
Stockhausen, Karlheinz 440
Storms, Tim 292
Strauss, Richard 65*n*2
Stravinsky, Igor 65*n*2, 101–3, 101*f*, 117*n*10, 230, 433*n*1, 440, 484
  "Augures Printaniers, Les" 344
  "Firebird, The" 270–71
  "Rite of Spring" 343, 464
Sundararajan, Louise 245
Sundberg, Johan 196
Swanwick, Keith 240

Taruffi, Liila 325
Tchaikovsky, Pyotr 118
  Symphony No. 6 in B minor, Opus 74 ("Pathétique") 81–82, 117–18, 125
Thaut, Michael 278
Thayer, Robert 47
Thompson, Bill 131, 132, 159, 191–92, 339
Thompson, Robert 386
Thompson, Sam 468
Thompson, Virgil 514
Titchener, Edward B. 313
Todd, Neil 285
Tolstoy, L. 443
Tomaino, Concetta 326
Tomkins, Silvian 295
Trost, Wiebke 279
Tulving, Endel 317
Turino, Thomas 306, 311, 314

Van Zijl, Anemone 120
Varèse, Edgard 440
Västfjäll, Daniel 365
Verdi, Giuseppe
  "Aida" 271, 271*f*
  La Traviata 179
Vine, Carl - Piano Sonata No. 1 430
Vitz, Paul 412–3
Vivaldi, Antonio 485
  Concerto for Two Violins in A minor, Opus 3 No. 8 292–93, 301
  'Spring, The' 66–67
Von Helmholtz, Hermann 161
Vonnegut, Kurt 266
von Scheve, Christian 137
von Weber - "Oberon" 271
Vuilleumier, Patrik 279

Vuoskoski, Jonna 339, 503
Vuust, Peter 362

Wager, T.D. 57–58
Wagner, Richard 63, 65*n*2, 178–79, 309
  Siegfried's Funeral March from "Götterdämmerung" 91
  "Tristan and Isolde" 213, 272
Walter, Bruno 213
Warren, Jane 295–96
Waterman, Mitch 380*n*3
Waters, Roger 116, 117
Webern, Anton 440, 442
Webern, Anton, String Trio, Opus 20 39
Wedin, Lage 128
Weller, Paul 32
Whissel, Cynthia 87
Williams, Tony 116
Wilson, Nancy 158
Windsor, W.L. 121
Winwood, Steve 116
Wittgenstein, Ludwig 105, 359–61
Woody, Robert 15, 119

Xenakis, Iannis 440

Ylikoski, Petri 253
Yo-Yo-Ma 110

Zajonc, Robert 313
Zangwill, Nick 103, 109–10
Zentner, Marcel 58, 227, 241
Zeppelin, Led - "Kashmir" 411

SUBJECT INDEX

Tables and figures are indicated by an italic *t* and *f* following the page number.

ABBA 141
abductive reasoning 227
absolute music 65*n*2, 67–68, 483
absolutism/absolutists 65–67, 101–2, 103, 171, 199
  episodic memory 321, 327
  learning, prediction and expectancy 351
  utilitarian versus aesthetic uses 484
abstract labels - deep and sophisticated 90
abstract narrative 117
accelerando 93, 94, 284
achievement 151
acoustic conditions 22
acoustic cues 149, 162*t*, 331
acoustic features 161, 162, 259
acoustic parameters 139–40
action 28
action-perception links 296
action tendency 211, 224–26
activation 87
adaptive function 198
adaptive responses 52
additive combination 143
adjective scale 143
adjective checklist 70
adjective circle 106–7, 107*f*, 108*t*, 177
adjective ratings 70, 212
admiration 236–37, 463
adolescence/early adulthood 326–27, 338–39, 505, 507–8
advertising and music 311
aesthetic activities 261–62
aesthetic attitude 422–32
  aesthetic criteria 429–30
  aesthetic experience 425
  aesthetic judgment 423, 425, 426, 428, 429, 430–32
  aesthetic norms 428
  aesthetic response 422–23, 424–25, 429, 432
  aesthetic value 423, 425–26, 428, 430, 432
    individual and average ratings of criteria 431*f*
    objective 428
  definition 422–25
  emotional responses to fiction 498
  listeners thinking of music as art, grounds for 429–32
  new empirical aesthetics 430
  normative aesthetics 428
  philosophical aesthetics 425–26, 432
  properties distinguishing art 426–29
aesthetic criteria 433–51
  aesthetic judgment 433, 438, 441, 442, 443–44, 447–48, 449, 450
  aesthetic judgment, and other mechanisms, interactions between 495
  aesthetic norms 440
  aesthetic quality 450
  aesthetic value 433, 434, 437–38, 439, 441, 442–44, 446, 447, 449, 451
  arousal of emotions 442–44
  beauty 433–37

aesthetic criteria (*cont.*)
communication of idea or intention 446–48
contrarian aesthetic 433n1
expression 437–39
novelty 439–42
philosophical aesthetics 433
skill 444–46
style 448–50
sublime music 450–51
aesthetic distancing 498
aesthetic emotions
aesthetic judgment and other mechanisms, interactions between 495
functionalist analysis 53, 54*t*
investigation of specific mechanisms 397
unique and music-specific emotions 240–41
aesthetic goals 147
aesthetic judgment 12, 26–27, 26*f*, 34*n*2, 260, 452–68, 513
aesthetic attitude 454–56, 457, 463
aesthetic criteria 456, 459–61
aesthetic emotions versus everyday emotions 464–66
aesthetic experience 452, 456
aesthetic framing 455
aesthetic potential 455–56
aesthetic response 452–53
aesthetic threshold 462, 467
aesthetic value 452–53, 455–56, 459–60, 463
and affect 44
bias and content 473–77
brainstem reflex 273
cognitive inputs 457–58, 459
conceptualization of judgments: preliminary model 454–58
emotional inputs 457, 458, 459
evolution of brain functions 262
expectancy 344, 363
functionalist analysis 53
individual differences in reactions to music 383
induction mechanisms 376, 379
investigation of specific mechanisms 397
'live' music and intensity of emotions 390
negative emotions: 'pleasurable sadness' 503, 504
novel approach, necessity for 452–54
and other mechanisms, interaction between 493–97
'peak' experience 505–6
perceptual inputs 457, 458, 459
philosophical aesthetics 453
preference and emotion 461–64, 466–68
richness of music experience 489
see also BRECVEMA framework
aesthetic perspective on mixed emotions 492
aesthetic pleasure 241
aesthetic response 422–23
aesthetics
aesthetic attitude 410–11
aesthetic experience 407
aesthetic judgment 401, 404–5, 407–8, 420–21
aesthetic response: working definition 406–9
aesthetic value 420
aims and outline 404–6
classical aesthetics 410
complexity and familiarity 413–16
cultural context 392*f*
empirical aesthetics 410–13
evolutionary basis of emotions 256–57
experimental aesthetics 406
functionalist analysis 54*t*
interactionist view 406
neuroaesthetics 405
new empirical aesthetics 418–21
philosophical aesthetics 405, 410
prototype theory 416–18
taste 401–4

aesthetics and affect 469–87
aesthetic attitude 486
aesthetic criteria 470, 471, 485
aesthetic dimensions 470
aesthetic emotions 483–84, 485
aesthetic judgment 469–73, 472*t*, 480, 484, 485, 486
aesthetic judgment, bias and content 473–77
aesthetic value 470, 471–73, 474, 475
preference 477–83
preference and relation to emotion and choice 479–83
utilitarian versus aesthetic uses of music 483–87
aesthetics of feeling and sensation 11
aesthetic value 24, 382–83, 495, 497
musical feature-emotion link 127
aesthetics 15, 401–9, 410–21
affect 11, 23, 25*t*
aesthetics 404
associative coding 180
ideal 226–27
induced 366*t*, 370–71
as information 493–94*n*2
intrinsic coding 171
mild 313
negative 50*n*3, 242, 268–69, 312
phasic aspect 48
positive 50*n*3, 242, 312, 313, 333
programs for vocal expression, innate and universal 159
temporal focus 371
see also aesthetics and affect
affections, doctrine of 11
affective contrast, law of 490
affective response 322
affective states 47–48
affective trajectory 173
afferent physiological feedback 295
affordances 383–84, 449, 480
age factors 22
'chills' 219
episodic memory 326–27
iconic sources: formal resemblance 163
learning, prediction and expectancy 349
moderating variables 97–98
agency 324
agitation 107*f*, 108*t*
agreement 158
agreement criterion 83
aim and structure of book 11–27
definitive limits to human introspection (premise) 19–20
emotional responses to music are intrinsically social (premise) 20–21
emotions depend on evolved mechanisms (premise) 17–18
musical emotions depend on music-listener-situation interactions (premise) 21–23
music engages multiple emotion mechanisms (premise) 18–19
terminology and organization 23–27
working definitions 25*t*
Alzheimer's disease 326
ambiguity, emotional 110, 129
amino acid receptors (NMDA) 394*n*5
amplitude variation 143
amygdala 220–22, 270, 306, 373–74
anchor points 111–12
anger 84*t*, 84–85, 86–87, 108*t*
brainstem reflex 274
broad emotion categories 91
Brunswikian lens model 147, 149, 154
causal effects and music synthesis 143
collective, refined and meta-musical emotions 245
contagion 289
cross-modal patterns of acoustic cues for speech 162*t*
cultural context 392*f*
emotion terms vs. expression marks 111, 114, 114*t*
expression and passion 201, 439

anger (*cont.*)
 iconic sources: formal resemblance 160, 164
 individual differences in reactions to music 382
 induction mechanisms and context 386
 intrinsic coding 171–72
 logic of emotions 255
 multiple-layer model 187
 musical feature-emotion link 123, 125, 126, 128
 musical features used to express emotions by professional performers 194*t*
 musicians communicating emotions to listeners 88, 89–90
 negative emotions: 'pleasurable sadness' 500
 prevalence of emotional reactions 237*f*
 richness of music experience 490
 style and emotional expression 135
 two-dimensional emotion space 113*f*
 vitality affects 94
angry touch 199
animal studies 309–10
annoyance 260
antagonistic interactions 144
anticipation 245–46, 358, 359
anxiety 84*t*, 85, 237*f*
 brainstem reflex 274
 cultural context 392*f*
 emotion terms vs. expression marks 114*t*
 expectancy 344, 357–58, 359
 intrinsic coding 172, 173
 multiple-layer model 187
 musical expectancy 259
 pleasurable 504
 prevalence of emotional reactions 235
 temporal focus of affect 371
appraisal 248, 351, 352, 383, 392*f*
appreciation emotions 463, 464–65
Aqua - "Barbie Girl" 496
arbitrary association 157
arousal 24, 25*t*, 205–9, 210–30, 442–44
 action tendencies 224–26
 aesthetic attitude 430
 aesthetic judgment 452, 458, 459, 471
 aesthetic value 431
 aims and questions 208–9
 associative coding 177
 autonomic 216
 beauty 434*n*2
 brainstem reflex 267, 270–71, 274
 BRECVEMA framework 375
 categorical or dimensional emotions 50, 51
 'chills' (goosebumps) 217–20
 cognitivists 210–11, 228, 230
 contagion 287–88, 289
 emotional expression 222–24
 emotional regulation 226–27
 emotion as catalyst for embarking on musical career 206–8
 emotion terms vs. expression marks 111–12
 emotivists 210, 221, 226, 228, 230
 empirical aesthetics 410–12, 419, 420
 episodic memory 323
 expectancy 344
 expression 63–64, 84–85, 86, 438
 felt emotion 30, 53
 functionalist analysis 54*t*
 high 113*f*, 128
 'how' question 247–64
  'bad' category 250–52
  BRECVEMA model 258–60
  emotions have their own logic 255–56
  evolutionary basis of emotions 256–58
  'good' category 252–53
  mechanisms 253–54, 262–64
  mechanisms, evolution of 258–62
  previous accounts 249–53
  'ugly' category 249–50
 induced affect 371
 infant-directed speech 161

investigation of specific mechanisms 396–97
language factors 106*n*6
level 50–51
low 111–12, 113*f*, 128
mixed emotions 492
multiple-layer model 183
musical feature-emotion link 123, 128–29
negative emotions: 'pleasurable sadness' 500
neural activation 220–22
and perception distinction 229
physiological 43–44, 160, 282
positive 390
preferences 481
prevalence of emotional reactions 238–40
psychological approach 31, 35
psychophysiological measures 214–17
referential meaning 68
rhythmic entrainment 283
self-reported feelings 211–14
startle response 266
state goals 418
synchronization 227–30
undifferentiated 358
of unique and music-specific emotions 240–44
arousal-energy (alertness) 236–37, 237*f*
Art Blakey and the Jazz Messengers 207
articulation 22
causal effects and music synthesis 141–42, 143
combined effect of several features 143–45
communicative process quantification 151, 152
expression and passion 201
GERMS model 193
iconic sources: formal resemblance 160
musical feature-emotion link 123
musical features used to express emotions by professional performers 194*t*
see also legato articulation
artistic intention 431
artistic sensibility 261–62
artistic skill 431
associations 308–9
associative coding 168, 172, 173–81, 182*f*, 202
see also multiple-layer model: intrinsic, associative and iconic coding
associative learning 377
associative representations 365
associative sources of expression 157
assumption of realism 255
astonishment 237*f*
atonality 189, 442*n*7
attack 194*t*, 201–2
attention 68, 214, 260–61
attunement 94
audience support 476
audio platform 289
auditory imagery 333
auditory perception 333
auditory perception, and motor responses link 280
auditory regions 280–81*n*1
auditory stimulus 293
auditory style 505
authenticity project 75–76*n*3
autobiographical memories 375
autobiographical salience 322
autonomic responses 301–2
autonomous module of the brain 293
autonomous oscillators 277
availability to consciousness 366*t*, 372
awareness 213–14
expanded 333
primary 213
secondary 213
awe 107*f*, 236–37
brainstem reflex 273
categorical or dimensional emotions 40

awe (*cont.*)
'chills' 218
cultural context 392*f*
expectancy 358, 359
'live' music and intensity of emotions 390
preference 463
prevalence of emotional reactions 237*f*, 238–40
sublime 450–51
unique and music-specific emotions 243
universality/cross-cultural emotions 132–33

background music 314, 385
backward masking 47*n*1
balance 436
baroque music 122, 136, 180
basal ganglia 281
baselines 124, 130–31
basic emotions
Brunswikian lens model 154–55
causal effects and music synthesis 143
contagion 292–93, 297, 299
emotion terms vs. expression marks 111–12, 114
evaluative conditioning 312
expression and passion 84–85, 86, 202
functionalist analysis 52–53, 54*t*, 55
GERMS model 194
iconic sources: formal resemblance 160, 162–64
induced affect 370–71
modular view of information processing 294–95, 296
multiple-layer model 182–83, 186, 187
musical features used to express 126*t*, 194*t*
musicians communicating emotions to listeners 89–90
prevalence of emotional reactions 235–36, 238–40
super-expressive voice, music as 167–68
theories 49–50*n*2
unique and music-specific emotions 242
Beach Boys
"Caroline No" 177
Pet Sounds 135
Beastie Boys 443
beat induction 280–81
Beatles 87
Sgt Pepper album 440
"Yesterday" 177
beauty 433–37
aesthetic attitude 430
aesthetic emotions vs everyday emotions 465–66
aesthetic judgment 452, 455–56, 459, 460, 470, 471, 472*t*
aesthetic value 431
Brunswikian lens model 147
interactionist perspective 436
mate selection 436
musical feature-emotion link 127
negative emotions: 'pleasurable sadness' 503, 504
objective aspects 436
perceived 436, 459–60, 470
perceptual features 436
preference 463
referential meaning 69
subjective aspects 436
sublime 450
behavioral impact, degree of 44
behaviorism 14, 511*n*1
beliefs 69
belonging 324
'big five' personality traits - Openness to Experience and Extraversion 233
biographical stress 118
biological motion 196–97
blues music 116, 165, 199–202
Böhmish folk music (Czech Republic) 184
boredom 143, 237*f*, 358, 359, 392*f*
brain circuits 258
brain functions 222

brain levels and types of emotions, links between 371*f*
brain regions 365–70, 366*t*
brain size 20
brainstem 220–21, 373–74
brainstem reflex 251*n*3, 259, 265–74, 364, 366*t*, 376, 513
  aesthetic response 407
  cognitive goal appraisal 380, 381
  contagion 302
  cultural context 392*f*, 393
  cultural impact and learning 370
  empirical aesthetics 419
  episodic memory 323
  evolutionary order 260–61, 365
  expectancy 344–45, 353–54
  individual differences in reactions to music 382, 383
  induced affect 371
  induction mechanisms and context 385
  induction speed 371–72
  investigation of specific mechanisms 395
  'live' music and intensity of emotions 387–88
  mixed emotions 493
  ontogenetic development 370
  'peak' experience 505–6
  reason for 267–70
  richness of music experience 489
  role in music 270–74
  startle response 265–67
  temporal focus of affect 371
  visual imagery 342
  see also BRECVEMA framework
BRECVEMA framework 366*t*, 373–76, 377, 380, 383*n*1, 509
  aesthetic emotions vs everyday emotions 465–66
  aesthetic judgment *see* aesthetic judgment
  aesthetics 405, 408
  arousal: 'how question' 258–60
  brainstem reflex *see* brainstem reflex
  contagion *see* contagion
  empirical aesthetics 411–12*n*1
  episodic memory *see* episodic memory
  evaluative conditioning *see* evaluative conditioning
  investigation of specific mechanisms 396
  mixed emotions 491, 492
  musical expectancy *see* musical expectancy
  negative emotions: 'pleasurable sadness' 501, 503
  'peak' experience 506*n*8
  rhythmic entrainment *see* rhythmic entrainment
  utilitarian versus aesthetic uses 485
  visual imagery *see* visual imagery
brightness 107*f*, 108*t*
broad emotions 90–93, 154–55, 183
broaden and build theory 495
Broca's area of the brain 351, 374–75
Brunswikian lens model 147–55
  achievement 151
  communicative process quantification 151–52
  consistency 152
  cue weight 151
  definition 148–51
  expanded lens model (ELM) 152, 153*f*
  implications 153–55
  lens model equation (LME) 152
  matching 151–52

calm 84*t*, 84–85, 108*t*
  cultural context 392*f*
  episodic memory 323
  evaluative conditioning 310
  induction mechanisms and context 386
  mixed emotions 493
  prevalence of emotional reactions 236–37, 237*f*
  rhythmic entrainment 283–84
candidate cause 20
cantabile 114
Castrati opera singers 167, 292

catalytic interactions 144
categorical or dimensional emotions 49–52
category boundary 55
catharsis 11, 443
caudate nucleus 281
causal effects and music synthesis 140–43
causal factors approach 250–51
cause and effect 36
cello 259, 291, 292–93, 301
central nervous system 263–64, 266
cerebellum 220–21, 281, 306, 308, 373–74
certain emotions occur more frequently and consistently than others 236–40
certainty 173
checklists 212
cheerfulness 107*f*, 108*t*
children
  basic emotions decoding 164
  childhood amnesia 326
  childhood experiences, negative 320*n*2
  childhood memories 320
  development 405
  learning, prediction and expectancy 348–49
  ontogenetic development 370
  visual imagery 335
  see also adolescence/early adulthood; infants
children's songs 437
'chills' (goosebumps) 217–20, 242–43, 307–8, 355–56
chords
  expectancy 357
  I 170
  intrinsic coding 169, 170
  learning, prediction and expectancy 349
  major and minor 177
  major seventh 180–81
  minor seventh 180–81
  V7 170
cingulate cortex 220–21, 373–74
Circle of Fifths 356
circumplex model of emotions 50, 51*f*, 106*n*6, 128, 216
clarinet 291
clarity 214, 436
Clash, The 257
classical music 15
  action tendencies 224–25
  aesthetic attitude 424
  aesthetic judgment and other mechanisms, interactions between 495
  aesthetic judgment, preferences and emotions: independence 467–68
  aesthetics 401–3
  communication and emotion 121
  complexity preference and familiarity 416, 417
  composers: meaning 67
  composing: emotion and expression 117, 118
  emotion terms vs. expression marks 112–14
  evaluative conditioning 309
  expectancy 355
  expression: objections and obstacles 104
  GERMS model 199
  iconic sources: formal resemblance 158
  'live' music and intensity of emotions 387–88
  multiple-layer model 185–86
  preferences 481–82
  referential meaning 69, 70
  style 449–50
  universality/cross-cultural emotions 132
  utilitarian versus aesthetic uses 486
classic conditioning 173–74, 304
classicism 136–37
clichés, culture-specific in film music 180
climate 133
cluster analysis 201
co-activation of mechanisms 499
cognition 28, 41, 42*t*, 407, 408
  cold 304

embodied 302, 510–11
hot 304
cognitive empathy 287*n*1
cognitive goal appraisal 260, 344–45, 379–82, 464, 505–6
cognitive hedonics 502
cognitive inputs 457–58, 459
cognitive irony 241*n*2
cognitive judgment 459, 515
cognitive mastering 446–47, 463
cognitive revolution 14
cognitive security 359
cognitivists 210–11, 228, 230
coherence 448–49
collative variables 411–12
collective emotions 53, 54*t*, 244–46, 290
collectivist countries/cultures 323–25, 378, 391, 392*f*
color perception (hue, brightness, saturation) 184
comfort/comforting 107*f*, 181
communal associations 179
communal subsection 183
communication 25*t*, 121
accuracy 82, 110
of emotions by musicians to listeners 88–90
experience and affect 54, 55
expression 25*t*, 76*f*, 76, 77, 103–4, 105
external 54, 55
iconic sources: formal resemblance 162
of idea or intention 446–48
internal 54, 55
paradigm 91
performing: emotion and expression 119
symbolic 157
communicative process quantification 151–52
communicative sounds 21
completion 173
complex emotions
categorical or dimensional emotions 40
contagion 299
emotion terms vs. expression marks 111–12, 114
empirical studies 84–85
evaluative conditioning 312
expression 86
functionalist analysis 53, 54*t*
GERMS model 193–95
induced affect 371
moderating variables 97
multiple-layer model 182, 183, 186, 187
musical feature-emotion link 123
musical features used to express 126*t*, 194*t*
musicians communicating emotions to listeners 90
positive 53
prevalence of emotional reactions 235–36, 238–40
richness of music experience 490
super-expressive voice, music as 168
complexity 51
aesthetic attitude 430
aesthetic value 431
empirical aesthetics 420
and familiarity 413–16
objective 414, 415
physical 413–14
preference and familiarity 413
psychological 413–14, 415
component process theories 49–50*n*2, 491–92
composer cues 152
composer-related features 123
composing 28–29
emotion and expression in 116–18
composition 123–24
compositional style 87
composition rules 448
computational models 142
concept 39–40
conceptual layers 53
conceptual metaphors 331–32
conditioned response 354

conditioned stimulus (CS) 304, 306, 308, 309, 310, 311
conditioning 311, 317, 318*n*1, 375, 392*f*
confidence 236–37, 237*f*
confirmation emotions 359
conflicting emotions 193–94
conflicting outputs 263–64, 492
conflict theory 346
connectedness 284
conscious experience 68, 370
consciousness 15–16, 318*n*1
consistency 152
consonance 128, 171–72, 193, 267–68, 347
constant interpretation 30
constructed emotion 510, 511
consumer research 311
contagion 259, 287–302, 366*t*, 375, 509, 513
  aesthetic judgment and other mechanisms, interactions between 494, 495, 497
  in animals 296–97
  arousal 259
  cognitive goal appraisal 380, 381
  cultural context 392*f*
  emotional responses to fiction 498
  and entrainment distinction 300–2
  episodic memory 320*n*2, 328
  evaluative conditioning 303
  evolution of brain functions 261
  expression 438, 439
  group 298
  historical background 288–89
  individual differences in reactions to music 382, 383
  induced affect 370–71
  induction mechanisms 377, 385
  information focus 365
  investigation of specific mechanisms 395
  'live' music and intensity of emotions 389
  mixed emotions 491, 493
  modular account, support for 293–96, 372
  negative emotions: 'pleasurable sadness' 500, 502*n*5, 503*n*6
  occurrence in music 290–92
  'peak' experience 505–6
  perception versus arousal 56–57
  primitive 287*n*1
  psychological approach 34*n*2
  reasons for experiencing 296–98
  richness of music experience 489
  scepticism amongst scholars 292–93
  super-expressive voice, music as 167
  which emotions contagion arouses 299–300
  Wittgenstein's dilemma 361
  see also BRECVEMA framework
contempt 135, 237*f*
content analysis methods 41
contentment
  episodic memory 323
  expectancy 359
  induction mechanisms and context 386
  investigation of specific mechanisms 396–97
  musical features used to express emotions by professional performers 194*t*
  prevalence of emotional reactions 235, 236–37, 237*f*
contents of actual experiences 40
context
  and expression 73–74, 86
  and induction mechanisms 384–86
context-dependence 124
context effects 290
context-related variables 96*t*
contextual factors 338, 476, 477
contextual variables 95
continuous response method 70
contours 93, 161
contrast effects 97
contrasts 490
control 388, 480
conventions for expressing emotion 132–33

conveyance of emotions 72
core layer of musical expression 84–85, 123, 182–83, 202
cortex 220–21, 318*n*1
cost-benefit asymmetry 269–70
costly signal theory 436
country music 116
Cream 137
crescendo 93, 94, 272, 331
critical bandwidth 267–68
crooning singing style 137, 441
cruelty 86
crying *see* tears/crying
crying voice 290–91
cue-redundancy model (CRM) 131*f*, 131
cues
  acoustic 149, 162*t*, 331
  composer 152
  culture-specific 131
  former 152
  multiple 153–54
  probabilistic 149
  psychophysical 131, 132
  redundancy 149–51, 153–55
  secondary 474–75
  uncertain 216–17
  utilization for acoustic features 164
  weight 151
cultural factors 4, 22, 511–12
  aesthetic judgment 454
  arousal: self-reported feelings 213
  associative coding 178
  beauty 437
  brainstem reflex 273–74
  communicative process quantification 151–52
  contagion 288
  emotion regulation 226–27
  episodic memory 323–24
  evaluative conditioning 309, 314
  evolutionary basis of emotions 256–57
  expectancy 361
  expression 202, 439, 442
  functionalist analysis 53
  GERMS model 197–98
  iconic sources: formal resemblance 163, 164
  induction mechanisms 378
  intrinsic coding 170–71
  lullabies 283–84
  moderating variables 97–98
  multiple-layer model 182, 185, 186
  musical feature-emotion link 124
  nostalgia 324, 325
  predictions, implications and complications 389–93
  prevalence of emotional reactions 236–37
  rhythmic entrainment 278, 285–86
  super-expressive voice, music as 167–68
  utilitarian versus aesthetic uses 485, 486
  see also collectivist countries/cultures; individualist countries/cultures; language factors
cultural identity 68, 187
cultural impact and learning 370
culturally valued emotion 226–27
culture-specific cues 131
curiosity 194*t*

Daft Punk - "Around the World" 167
dancing 4, 225, 278, 284–85, 286*f*, 390
'dangerous music' 122
dark 107*f*
darkness (emotion) 108*t*
'Darling, they are playing our tune' phenomenon 316
dead-pan performances 88–89, 188, 292
death (portrayed as emotion) 91
decay 93
deceptive cadence 345
decoding accuracy 90, 153
decoding emotions 149, 294–95
definition of music 39–40
definitive limits to human introspection (premise) 19–20

delicate 107*f*, 108*t*
demand characteristics 212, 229
demographic variables 479
dependent variables 469
depressing 106, 107*f*, 108*t*
depth of emotion, multiple-layer model 184
Derek and the Dominos 340*f*
  Layla and Other Assorted Love Songs 207*n*1, 339–41
desire 84*t*, 114*t*, 120, 201
  sexual 180, 187
despair 84*t*, 165, 173, 183, 201
detachment 498
detection, context-dependent 189
deviations, expressive 190
devotion 86
diabolus in musica (augmented fourth or tritone) 171–72
diary studies 212
differential liking 477–78
differentiation 253
dignified 107*f*
dilution effect 359
diminuendo 93
direction 172
disagreement 158
disappointment 358, 359
discos 135, 285
discrete emotions 158–59, 172, 287–88, 294, 295, 301
discrimination 309
disgust 114*t*, 143, 194*t*, 237*f*, 289, 392*f*
dislike 466
display rules 226–27
displeasure center 412
displeasure inhibition 502–3
dissonance
  brainstem reflex 267–68, 273
  expectancy 347
  GERMS model 193
  intrinsic coding 171–72
  learning, prediction and expectancy 348–49
  multiple-layer model 183
  musical features and emotion dimensions 128
  sensory 344
  startle response 266
distinct feelings 49
distortion 199
Doctrine of Affections 180
dolce 114*t*
doleful 107*f*
dominant interval 172
Dorian mode 122*n*1
double aspect theory 252
dramatic 107*f*, 108*t*
dreamy 107*f*, 108*t*
drum machines 300
dual functionality 53–54, 55
dullness 88
duration 44, 161
durational contrasts 141–42
dynamic accent 193
dynamic form of emotional life 94, 158
dynamics 164–65, 189, 193, 293
dynamic social systems 245
dynamic systems theory 280

early auditory areas 281
early left anterior negativity 357*n*6
easygoing 107*f*
ecological variables 411–12
economic context of music 256–57
education 22
elation 111, 236–37, 237*f*, 386, 391
electric guitar 300
  string bending 165–66, 188, 201–2, 340–41
electromyography (EMG) 216, 223–24, 228
electronic dance music 283
electronic microphone 441
elicitation 253
elitist view 484
E major key 125–27
embodied cognition 302, 510–11

embodied emotions 124, 160
emotional granularity 105–6
emotional implications 56–57
emotional inputs 457, 458, 459
emotional intelligence 164
emotionality 357
emotional motor expression 365
emotional nuance 109
emotional overflow 492–93
emotional polyphony 185
emotional responses 30
  to music are intrinsically social (premise) 20–21
emotional speech 161–62, 186, 290–91
emotional surrender 492–93
emotional tone 172
emotion as catalyst for embarking on musical career 206–8
emotion causation theory 253
emotion episode 211
emotions depend on evolved mechanisms (premise) 17–18
emotions have their own logic 255–56
emotions or moods in responses to music 46–48
emotions in the music and emotions felt by performer, distinction between 120
emotion-specific acoustic patterns 160
emotion-specific patterns of musical features 147
emotion terms versus expression marks 111–21
emotivists 210, 221, 226, 228, 230
empathy 261, 288, 382, 503*n*6
emphasis 136
emphatic 107*f*
empirical studies 79–98
  broad emotion categories 90–93
  communication of emotions by musicians to listeners 88–90
  expression, conflicting views on 79–80
  moderating variables 95–98
  perceived expression, measurement of 80–83
  specific emotions 83–87
  vitality affects 93–95
encoding emotions 149
encoding habits, minor 449–50
energy arousal-tense arousal-valence 50*n*3
energy/energetic 107*f*, 323
enjoyment 236–37, 237*f*, 386
envy 463
episodic estimates 391
episodic memory 259, 316–29, 366*t*, 509, 513
  aesthetic judgment and other mechanisms, interactions between 496
  aesthetic response 408
  arousal 259, 260*f*, 261
  availability to consciousness 372
  beauty 435
  cognitive goal appraisal 380, 381
  complexity preference and familiarity 414–15
  cultural context 391
  definition and functions 316–19
  during development 326–27
  and evaluative conditioning distinction 303, 319–21
  evolutionary order 365
  individual differences in reactions to music 382, 383–84
  induction mechanisms 377, 379
  investigation of specific mechanisms 394–95
  'live' music and intensity of emotions 390
  mixed emotions 491, 493
  musical structure 372–73
  nostalgia 324–25
  'peak' experience 505–6
  preferences 480
  richness of music experience 489
  songs linked to 327–29
  temporal focus of affect 371

episodic memory (*cont.*)
visual imagery 330, 331, 342
within music 321–24
see also BRECVEMA framework
eroticism 86
espressivo 114*t*
euphoria 180
evaluation process 257–58
evaluative conditioning 303–15, 366*t*, 509, 513
aesthetic attitude 422
aesthetic emotions vs everyday emotions 466
aesthetic judgment and other mechanisms, interactions between 497
aesthetic judgment, preferences and emotions: independence 466–67
arousal 259
associative coding 175
characteristics 305–8
complexity preference and familiarity 414–15
definition 304–5
emotional responses to fiction 498
and episodic memory distinction 319–21
evolution of brain functions 261
individual differences in reactions to music 382, 383
induction mechanisms 377, 379
investigation of specific mechanisms 394*n*5, 394–95
investigation within music 308–12
mental representation 365
multi-component approach 304
musical structure 372–73
'peak' experience 505–6
preferences 480
richness of music experience 489
role of in everyday life 313–15
volitional influence 372
which emotions aroused by 312–13
see also BRECVEMA framework
event-related potentials (ERP) 357
events and objects 69
event-specific knowledge 319
everyday emotions 483, 495
evidence, introspective 32–33
evolutionary basis of emotions 17–18, 22*f*, 52, 256–58, 511–12
evolutionary order 371
exalting 107*f*
excerpts, short 70
excitement
contagion 290
episodic memory 323
expression 107*f*, 108*t*
intrinsic coding 172
musicians communicating emotions to listeners 88
rhythmic entrainment 259, 276, 282, 283–84
executive function 334–35
exhilaration 107*f*, 108*t*
existential and transcendental aspects 41, 42*t*, 187
expectancy 237*f*
schematic 360
veridical 360
experience sampling method (ESM) 232, 234–35, 323, 362, 381–82
induction mechanisms and context 385, 386
'live' music and intensity of emotions 386
experiences that cannot be described in words 69
experiential aspect of emotions 41, 211
experiments 35, 323, 362, 393–94
expression 24, 26*f*, 56, 61–78
aesthetic attitude 430, 431
aesthetic criteria 437–39
aesthetic judgment 459
investigation 470, 471, 472*t*
and other mechanisms, interactions between 494, 495
reliability: bias and context 475

aims and questions 63–64
appropriateness of emotional expression term 72–73
arousal 211, 214, 222–24
associative sources of 157
beauty 437
causal effects and music synthesis 143
as cognitive recognition 438
communication of emotions 76*f*
conflicting views on 79–80
different uses of the term 73–78
evaluative conditioning 15
functionalist analysis 53, 54*t*
historical context 135–38
iconic sources: formal resemblance 160
intra-musical aspects 94
intrinsic sources 128, 157
layers of 92, 156
meaning, different types of 65–68
objections and obstacles 99–121
  adjective circle 107*f*, 108*t*
  case against musical expression of emotions 99–105
  communication and emotion 121
  composing, emotion and expression in 116–18
  emotion terms versus expression marks 111–21
  language factors 105–10
  performing, emotion and expression in 118–20
  perspectives from musicians 115*b*
  two-dimensional emotion space 113*f*
and passion 201
perception versus arousal 56–57
performer's role 191–92
personal layer of 183
posed (acted) 299
preferences 481
referential views 67–72
role of the performer 193–95
spontaneous (genuine) 299
  and style 133–35
  theories 438
  without conscious thought 119
  see also iconic expression
expressionists/expressionism 67, 483
expression mark 123–24, 201
expressive acoustic patterns 291
expressive dialects of specific styles 133–34
expressive gestures 111
expressive intention 74
expressive modulations 164–65
expressive patterns 137–38
expressive qualia 94–95
expressive shape 183
expressivo expression mark 201
external movements - head bobbing, foot stamping 276
external world 67
extinction 306
extra-musical (designative) phenomenon 65, 67
extrinsic factors 482–83
eye-blink conditioning paradigm 308

face perception 166
facial expressions 298, 301–2
  and mimicry 289
facial feedback hypothesis 295
factorial experimental design 142*f*, 142, 143, 145
Fado music (Portuguese) 226–27, 324–25, 378
false alarms 269–70
'fame' and aesthetic value 477
familiarity
  aesthetic attitude 430
  beauty 437
  and complexity 413–16
  episodic memory 322
  modular view of information processing 294
  preferences 480, 481

familiarity principle *see* mere exposure effect
fanciful 107*f*
fantasy 11
fear
brainstem reflex 267, 274
causal effects and music synthesis 143
'chills' 218
combined effect of several features 144–45
contagion 297–98
cross-modal patterns of acoustic cues for speech 162*t*
emotion terms vs. expression marks 111, 114*t*
empirical studies 84*t*, 84–85, 86–87
evaluative conditioning 309
expression and passion 201
iconic sources: formal resemblance 164
logic of emotions 256
musical feature-emotion link 123, 125, 126*t*, 128
musical features used to express emotions by professional performers 194*t*
musicians communicating emotions to listeners 89–90
neural activation 222
prevalence of emotional reactions 237*f*
sublime 450–51
synchronization 228
two-dimensional emotion space 113*f*
unique and music-specific emotions 242–43
universality/cross-cultural emotions 132
visual imagery 337
feelings 25*t*, 41, 42*t*, 43, 45, 88, 211
knowledge of 88
negative 352
positive 352
see also subjective feelings
felt emotions 3–4
arousal 443–44
associative coding 175
BRECVEMA framework 375
and expression 74–75, 77, 438
iconic sources: formal resemblance 160
induction mechanisms and context 385
intrinsic coding 170–71
investigation of specific mechanisms 395
'live' music and intensity of emotions 390
perception distinction 215
singers avoidance of 119–20
super-expressive voice, music as 167
FEPNAR components 211, 227
festive songs 187
fiction, emotional responses to 497–99
field studies 393
film music 7, 177, 180–81, 279–80, 282, 496
filtration cut-off level 143
flageolet harmonics 340–41
flow 213*n*3, 245
flute 178*n*4
focus on music performance 119, 388
folk psychology/folk theories 49, 69, 111, 116, 213
forced-choice task 70, 90
forgetting 317–18
formalists 67, 483
formal resemblance 157, 158–65
fragments 85
frame of reference 448–49
free-labeling task 90
free phenomenological description 70, 212
frequency spectrum *see* timbre
fright 490
frontal gyrus 220–21, 373–74
frontal lobe 334–35
frustration 107*f*, 120
fun 107*f*
functional analysis of emotions 52–55
functional definition of art 427
functionalist framework 159

functionlessness 486
functions of music 135
funeral music 135
furioso 112, 114*t*

gaiety 91, 107*f*, 111
gaming industry 7
gender factors 22, 68, 97–98, 223, 233
general characteristics 41, 42*t*
general events 319
generalization 309
generative theory of tonal music 488
genre 22, 30–31, 95, 124, 236–37, 478–79, 481–82
gentle 86, 107*f*
geographical factors 178
GERMS model 192–99
  emotional expression (E) 193–95, 197–99, 200*t*
  generative rules (G) 193, 198, 199, 200*t*
  hypothesized characteristics 200*b*
  lessons learned from 198–99
  motion principles (M) 196–97, 198, 200*t*
  random fluctuations (R) 195–96, 198, 199, 200*t*
  stylistic unexpectedness (S) 197–98, 200*t*
gestalt theory 29, 170–71, 346, 347, 347*f*, 437, 442
gesture 197
gleeful 107*f*
glissando 9, 188
gloominess 106, 107*f*, 108*t*
good continuation, law of 347
gospel music 391
graceful 107*f*, 108*t*
grave 114*t*
gravitational forces between musical tones and chords 170
'groove' 94–95, 137–38, 309
group boundaries 197–98
group cohesion 298
group entrainment 389
guided imagery and music (GIM) 333, 336
guilt 237*f*
'guilty pleasures' 495–96, 497
guitar
  expression and passion 199–201
  fretboard 196–97
  gut-string 205
  rhythmic entrainment 277
  slide guitar 165
  see also electric guitar

habituation 267, 378, 441–42
habitus of listening 391
happiness
  broad emotion categories 90
  Brunswikian lens model 147, 149, 154
  causal effects and music synthesis 143
  combined effect of several features 144–45
  contagion 289, 299
  cross-modal patterns of acoustic cues for speech 162*t*
  cultural context 391, 392*f*
  emotional expression 222–23
  emotion terms vs. expression marks 111, 114*t*
  empirical studies 84*t*, 84–85, 86
  episodic memory 323
  evaluative conditioning 259, 304
  expression 107*f*, 108*t*, 201
  iconic expression 156
  induction mechanisms and context 386
  investigation of specific mechanisms 395, 396–97
  language factors 106
  mixed emotions 491, 492
  moderating variables 97
  multiple-layer model 187
  musical feature-emotion link 123, 125, 126*t*
  musical features used to express emotions by professional performers 194*t*

happiness (*cont.*)
musicians communicating emotions to listeners 89–90
negative emotions: 'pleasurable sadness' 500, 501
prevalence of emotional reactions 235–40, 237*f*
psychophysiological measures 216
richness of music experience 490
synchronization 228
two-dimensional emotion space 113*f*
unique and music-specific emotions 242, 243
vitality affects 94
hard rock 137, 386
harmony/harmonic 22
'chills' 218
complexity 128
expectancy 355–57
GERMS model 193–94
integration 348
learning, prediction and expectancy 349
musical feature-emotion link 123
progression 125
structure 193
universality/cross-cultural emotions 130–31, 132
visual imagery 337*n*3
hate 84*t*, 490
health benefits and well-being 7, 486, 510
see also music therapy
heart reactions 355–56
'heat' of the emotion 45
heavy 107*f*, 108*t*
heavy metal music 135, 382
hermeneutic analyses 81, 181
hierarchical levels of music 354–55
hierarchy of perceived relations, stabilities, attractions and directionality 169
high C's in opera tenors 167
hip-hop music 116, 391
hippocampus 220–22, 318*n*1, 373–75
historical factors 4, 37, 133, 439, 442, 511–12
homologies 52–53
'hooks' 309
hope 86–87, 97, 173, 354, 358, 359
hopelessness 183
horn section 344
horror 176–77
human character 68
human gesture 182–83
humor 84*t*, 85, 107*f*, 108*t*
hyperbole 213
hypothalamus 270

iceberg theory of the mind 33
iconic coding
associative coding 180, 181
Brunswikian lens 154*n*1
expression and passion 202
GERMS model 197–98
multiple-layer model 182–83, 182*f*
see also multiple-layer model: intrinsic, associative and iconic coding
iconic expression 156–68
acoustic cues: cross-modal patterns 162*t*
coding 156–57
icon 157
iconic sources: formal resemblance 158–65
index 157
sources 157, 331
super-expressive voice, music as 165–68
symbol 157
Iconic-Intrinsic-Associative layers (ICINAS framework) 202, 489, 509
ideal affect 226–27
ideal resolution 170
idée fixe 178–79, 179*f*
idiographic approach 470
idiosyncratic subsection 183
imagination 261, 351, 352
impetuous 107*f*
implicit dimensionality 106*n*6

implicit learning 437
importance of emotions 48–49
imposing 107*f*
independent variables 469
index 157
Indian music 129–30
indifference 237*f*
individual differences 47–48, 382–84, 430
individual features 22
individualist countries/cultures 323–24, 378, 391, 392*f*
individual listener 86
individual variables 95
induced affect 366*t*, 370–71
induction of emotion 25*t*, 26*f*
induction mechanisms 258–59, 324–25, 342, 376–79
  BRECVEMA framework 374–75
  cognitive goal appraisal 381
  and context 384–86
  individual differences in reactions to music 383
induction speed 371–72
infant-directed speech 161
infants
  attachment 297
  contagion 298
  parent-infant bonding 4, 278
  post-natal behavior effects of pre-natal exposure 313–14
  rhythmic entrainment 284
inferior colliculus 269
information
  empirical aesthetics 411–12
  focus 365
  selection principle 394
  theory 412
in-group advantage 132
inspiration 323
instructions 97
instrumental music 21, 22, 86, 164, 165
instrumental music *see also* classical music
instrument-related variables 96*t*
instruments
  cello 259, 291, 292–93, 301
  clarinet 291
  flute 178*n*4
  horn section 344
  oboe 291
  organ music 174
  piano 151, 196–97, 301, 415
  saxophone 180
  strings 344
  violin 259, 291, 292–93, 301
  see also guitar
insula 220–21, 373–74
in 'sync' 284
integrative framework 13
intended emotion felt whilst playing 119
intense affective reactions 48
intensity of emotions 44, 49, 51, 214
  categorical or dimensional emotions 50–51
  contagion 291
  evaluative conditioning 313
  intrinsic coding 171
  language factors 109
  multiple-layer model 183
  vitality affects 93
intentional objects 47
intentional sounds 21
intention to express a specific emotion 76
interaction between music, listener and situation 22*f*
interactions between features 22*f*, 143–46
intercorrelation between musical features 140
interest
  aesthetic judgment 465
  categorical or dimensional emotions 40
  cultural context 392*f*
  expectancy 236–37, 237*f*
  preference 463
  prevalence of emotional reactions 235–36
  unique and music-specific emotions 243

interference principle 394
inter-individual agreement 92
inter-judge reliability 473, 474*n*1, 475
internal representation 76
interoception 257–58
intervallic leaps 128
interviews, in-depth 212
intimacy, feelings of 284
intra-class correlation coefficient 474
intra-judge reliability 473, 475–76
intra-musical aspects of expression 94
intra-musical (embodied) phenomenon 65, 67
intra-musical patterns 171
intrinsic coding: 'will' of the tones 168, 169–73, 180, 181, 182*f*, 202, 345
  see also multiple-layer model: intrinsic, associative and iconic coding
intrinsic factors 482, 483
intrinsic sources of emotional expression 128, 157
introspection 255, 257
intuition and instinct 11, 19, 49, 111, 122–23
irrationality of emotions 257
irritation 237*f*, 386
isomorphism 158
ITPRA theory 351–53
  appraisal 351, 352
  imagination 351, 352
  post-outcome phase 351–52
  prediction 351, 352
  pre-outcome phase 351–52
  reaction 351, 352
  tension 351–52

Jaws (film) 282
jazz music 116, 121, 199, 413, 417, 481–82
jealousy 86, 91, 194*t*
jovial 107*f*
joy 84*t*, 107*f*, 108*t*
  associative coding 180
  broad emotion categories 91
  composing: emotion and expression 118
  contagion 290
  emotional expression 223
  emotion terms vs. expression marks 111
  episodic memory 323
  iconic sources: formal resemblance 164
  individual differences in reactions to music 382
  logic of emotions 255
  multiple-layer model 184
  musicians communicating emotions to listeners 88
  neural activation 222
  prevalence of emotional reactions 235
  vitality affects 94
judgment analysis 469, 470
judgment policies 474–75
judgment process: affective outcomes 461*f*

Katrina and the Waves - "Walking on Sunshine" 75
Kenya 391
key change 273
Kivy-Radford debate 34, 80*n*1, 210*n*1

language factors 4, 105–10, 260*f*, 261–62, 350–51
large-scale musical form 125–27
lateral amygdala 394*n*5
laughter 274
layers of emotional expression 92, 156
learned schemata 348
learning
  associations 261
  GERMS model 197–98
  intrinsic coding 170–71
  and prediction 348–49
  stylistic 357
left temporo-occipital regions 336
legato articulation 143, 144–45, 152, 183, 212, 501
leisurely 107*f*
leitmotif strategy 178–79
lens model equation (LME) 515–40

communication accuracy or achievement 515
linear component 515
listener consistency 515
matching 515
performer consistency 515
unmodeled component of communicative process 516
unmodeled matching 516
unsystematic and systematic variance 516
'licks' 309
life-time periods 319
light 107*f*, 108*t*
likeability scale 415
liking 466, 467–68
limbic system 261, 285, 297
linear combination 143
listener agreement 110
listener-related variables 96*t*
listening 28–29
listening experiments 212
listening strategies 507
listening tests 95, 124
operant 478
'live' concerts
brainstem reflex 272
contagion 290
expression 77
moderating variables 97
visual imagery 337–38
'live' concerts producing more intense emotions than recorded music 386–89
control over music 388
focus on music performance 388
multimodal experience 388
shared emotions 389
volume 387–88
locations 22, 385
locus of emotions 57
Loma villagers, Zealua, West Africa 132
loneliness 84*t*, 86–87, 120, 337
longing 84*t*, 84–85, 86–87, 107*f*
associative coding 177, 178, 180–81
cultural context 391
induction mechanisms and context 386
intrinsic coding 173
prevalence of emotional reactions 236–37, 237*f*
loss 324–25
loudness
associative coding 177
brainstem reflex 268, 272, 273
'chills' 218
contagion 291
expression and passion 199
GERMS model 193
historical context and emotional expression 137
infant-directed speech 161
musical feature-emotion link 127
rhythmic entrainment 285
universality/cross-cultural emotions 132
love 84*t*, 84–85, 86–87
collective, refined and meta-musical emotions 245
cultural context 392*f*
emotion terms vs. expression marks 111
episodic memory 323
expression and passion 201–2
iconic sources: formal resemblance 164
multiple-layer model 187
musical features used to express emotions by professional performers 194*t*
prevalence of emotional reactions 235, 236–37, 237*f*
richness of music experience 490
universality/cross-cultural emotions 132
Love - *Forever Changes* 312–13
love songs 187
lullabies 187, 283–84
Lydian mode 122
lyrical 107*f*, 108*t*

lyrics 21
cultural context 392*f*
expression 86–87
induction mechanisms 378–79
meaning 66–67
message 447–48
visual imagery 339

'mad artist' syndrome 341
maestoso-pride 114
majestic 107*f*, 108*t*
mannerism 445
marching music 278, 279–80
marketing music 7
Marshall stacks (amplifiers) 137
martial 107*f*
matching emotion 71, 151–52, 295
meaning 30–32, 65–68, 324
mechanisms 253–54, 262–64
evolution of 258–62
mechanisms, unique characteristics of 364–73
availability to consciousness 366*t*, 372
brain levels and types of emotions, links between 371*f*
cultural impact and learning 370
induced affect 366*t*, 370–71
induction speed 371–72
information focus 365
key brain regions 365–70, 366*t*
mental representation 365
modularity 372
musical structure, dependence on 372–73
ontogenetic development 370
order, evolutionary 365
specific mechanisms, investigation of 393–97
survival value of brain function 365, 366*t*
temporal focus of affect 371
volitional influence, degree of 372
see also BRECVEMA framework
medial pre-frontal cortex 370
mediant 172
mediation of musical emotions, single versus multiple 374*f*
mediator variables 253
melancholy 86, 106, 107*f*, 108*t*, 184, 504
cultural context 391
induction mechanisms and context 386
prevalence of emotional reactions 236–37, 237*f*
melody/melodic 22
appoggiaturas 183, 355–56
associative coding 173
contour 123
evaluative conditioning 309
expectancy 347, 355–56, 357
GERMS model 193–94
intervals 123, 125–27
originality 416, 441
originality quantitative index 118
progression 144
themes 118, 174–75
universality/cross-cultural emotions 130–31
visual imagery 331, 337*n*3
memory
autobiographical 322
cultural context 392*f*
declarative 317
evoked 318
negative 323–24
non-declarative 317
nostalgia 324–25
positive 323–24
procedural 260*f*, 317
recognition memory 502
semantic 260*f*, 317
spontaneous 318
working 459
see also episodic memory
mental imagery 318*n*1, 331
mental representations 263, 365, 417, 511
analogical 263
associative 263

complex 263
evaluative conditioning 303
intentional 263
sensori-motoric 263
mental rotation experiment 335
mental simulation 334
mere exposure effect 313, 377
mere recognition 502–3
merry 107*f*, 108*t*
message and aesthetics 430, 431, 459, 460, 472*t*
meta-musical emotions 244–46
meter 169–70*n*1
method triangulation 236
metric accents 197–98
microphones 96–97, 137, 441
microstructure 189
micro-timing 123
mighty 107*f*
military drills 278, 279–80
mimesis 11
mimicry 261*n*7, 288
minor triad 180–81
mirroring response 295
mirror neurons 295–96, 301, 498
MIR toolbox 139–40*n*1
misattributions 33
mixed emotions 491–93
aesthetic judgment and other mechanisms, interactions between 495–96
arousal 263–64
associative coding 176–77
emotional responses to fiction 498–99
functionalist analysis 54*t*
GERMS model 193–94
induced affect 371
ITPRA theory 352, 353
multiple-layer model 185
negative emotions: 'pleasurable sadness' 504
prevalence of emotional reactions 238
unique and music-specific emotions 242
mobility 173
mode
arousal: self-reported feelings 212
combined effect of several features 144
historical context and emotional expression 137
major 128, 348
minor 137
multiple-layer model 183
musical feature-emotion link 123
negative emotions: 'pleasurable sadness' 501
moderate universalism 390
moderating variables 95–98, 253
modularity 172, 293–96, 360*f*, 372
automaticity 294
autonomy 294
domain-specificity 294
hardwiring 294
information capsules 294
innate specification 294
special-purpose modules 293–94
speed 294
mood 25*t*, 43–44, 46
mood-induction technique 334
Moog synthesizer 143, 145–46, 178
moral emotions 53, 54*t*, 464–65
moral judgments 464
moral outrage 464
mother-infant interactions - emotion regulation and bonding 278
motifs 85
motion 68, 158
principles 196–97
tonal and harmonic 170
motives for listening to music 382–83
motor cortex 281, 295–96, 373–74
motor mimicry 261*n*7
motor regions 374–75
mournful/mourning 107*f*, 108*t*, 187
moved-touched 237*f*
multimodal experience 388

multiple attributes or clusters 430–32
multiple-layer model: intrinsic, associative and iconic coding 182–87
multiple regression analysis 144–45, 151, 469–70, 471
musical conventions 69
musical emotions depend on music-listener-situation interactions (premise) 21, 23
musical expectancy 161, 259, 343–63, 366*t*, 375, 376*n*2, 509, 513
  aesthetic judgment and other mechanisms, interactions between 494
  arousal 354–58
  brainstem reflex 273
  'chills' 218–19
  critical appraisal 361–63
  cultural context 370, 391, 392*f*, 393
  definition 343–46
  distinction from other mechanisms 353–54
  evolution of brain functions 261
  individual differences in reactions to music 382, 383
  induction mechanisms and context 371–72, 385
  information focus 365
  investigation of specific mechanisms 395
  language-music parallels 350–51
  learning and prediction 348–49
  mental representation 365
  musical structure 372–73
  ontogenetic development 370
  'peak' experience 505–6
  richness of music experience 489
  temporal focus of affect 371
  theoretical foundations (Meyer) 346–48
  which emotions are aroused by 358–59
  Wittgenstein's dilemma 359–61
  see also BRECVEMA framework; ITPRA theory
musical features 22, 122–38
  cue-redundancy model (CRM) 131*f*
  emotion dimensions link 127–29
  expression and historical context 135–38
  expression and style 133–35
  feature-emotion links 123–27
  and perceived emotions 122–23
  universality of expressed emotions 129–33
  used to express basic emotions and complex emotions 194*t*
musical form 125
musical nuance 92, 109, 172
musical score 139
musical setting 95
musical shape 109
musical structure 29, 30–31
  associative coding 174–75
  dependence on 372–73
  GERMS model 193, 197
  modular view of information processing 294
  musical features and emotion dimensions 128
  and non-verbal expression of emotions 158–59
  visual imagery 331
musical training 97–98, 233
music education 510
music engages multiple emotion mechanisms (premise) 18–19
music, experience and affect 39–58
  affect 43–44
  categorical or dimensional emotions 49–52
  definition of music 39–40
  emotions or moods in responses to music 46–48
  experience 40–43
  functional analysis of emotions 52–55
  importance of emotions 48–49
  perception versus arousal of emotion 56–58

psychology of emotions 44–46
SEM descriptive system 42*t*
subtypes of emotions 54*t*
musicking 39–40, 121
musicology 37
music therapy 7, 94, 333, 510

N5 brain response 348
narrative and narration 86, 117, 173, 261
nativist fallacy 250–51
negative emotions
aesthetic judgment and other mechanisms, interactions between 495
arousal 251
evaluative conditioning 309, 311
GERMS model 193
induction mechanisms and context 386
'pleasurable sadness' 499–504
preference 463–64, 481
prevalence of emotional reactions 234–35, 239*t*
visual imagery 333–34
negative feedback loop 276
neo-classicism 448
neocortex 19, 261
neural activation 211, 220–22
neural networks 417
neurochemical interference strategy 394*n*5
neurophysiology 29
neuroticism 325
new-age music 259
nightclub music 135, 285
noble 107*f*
non-emotional content 86
non-emotional ideas 90
non-verbal expressions of performers 290, 290*f*
normative analyses in musicology 37
norms
absolute 124
preference 464
stylistic 348
nostalgia 107*f*, 114
aesthetic judgment and other mechanisms, interactions between 496
associative coding 177–78, 179, 180–81
categorical or dimensional emotions 40
cultural context 391, 392*f*
emotion terms vs. expression marks 114
episodic memory 259, 323, 324–25
evaluative conditioning 312–13
induction mechanisms and context 378, 386
investigation of specific mechanisms 395, 396–97
'live' music and intensity of emotions 390
multiple-layer model 184, 187
negative emotions: 'pleasurable sadness' 500–1
prevalence of emotional reactions 235–37, 237*f*, 238–40
temporal focus of affect 371
unique and music-specific emotions 241, 243–44
visual imagery 342
note(s)
accents on 123
attacks 199, 273, 340–41
bass 273
expectancy 353
falling 180
intrinsic coding 169–70
lengthening 189
non-diatonic 169–70, 172
patterns 30
abstract 30
autonomous 67
pure 67–68
rhythmic entrainment 275
novelty 439–42
aesthetic emotions vs everyday emotions 465–66

novelty (*cont.*)
  aesthetic judgment 455–56, 460, 470, 471
  aesthetic judgment and other mechanisms, interactions between 494
  beauty 434*n*2
  Brunswikian lens model 147
  complete 440–41
  empirical aesthetics 420
  GERMS model 197–98
  long-term 440–41
  music as art 432
  preference 463
  short-term 440–41
  style 448, 450
  Wittgenstein's dilemma 361
nucleus accumbens 221–22, 252

oboe 291
occipital cortex 336
offense 463–64
one-dimensional models (arousal) 50*n*3
onion metaphor 293
onsets 166
ontogenetic development 335, 370
openness to experience 505
opera 167, 174, 179, 220, 271, 498
operant listening tests 478
operationalization 35
optimal music performance 121
orbitofrontal cortex 220–21, 270, 373–74
order 436, 459–60
  effects 124
  evolutionary 365
  x complexity 437
organ music 174
originality 430, 431, 450, 459, 471, 472*t*, 475
oscillators 277, 279, 280–81, 301
outrage 463–64
oxytocin 21

P3 component 357
P300 357

pain 84*t*, 86–87
pairs of emotions 49
Paradox 1 13
Paradox 2 80
Paradox 3 148
Paradox 4 208, 254–55
Paradox 5 500
paradox of fiction 497
parahippocampal gyrus 220–21
parahippocampus 221
parent-infant bonding 4
parietal cortex 280–81*n*1
passion/passionate 107*f*, 108*t*, 199–202
pathetic 107*f*
patriotism 176–77
pattern matching 149
pauses 141–42
peacefulness 88, 107*f*, 500–1
peak activations (in brain) 57–58
'peak' experience 40–41, 71, 505–8
  aesthetics 410
  beauty 434
  collective, refined and meta-musical emotions 245
  'live' music and intensity of emotions 387
  mixed emotions 492–93
  prevalence of emotional reactions 238–40
  skill 444
  utilitarian versus aesthetic uses 486
  visual imagery 337–38
  see also sublimity
peaks and valleys 184
pentatonic scales 199
perceived emotions 3–4, 31, 35
  BRECVEMA framework 375
  expression 79
  induction mechanisms 377
  intrinsic coding 171
  and musical features 122–23
  negative emotions: 'pleasurable sadness' 500
  referential meaning 68

perceived expression 86
perceived expression, measurement 80–83
perception of emotion 3–4, 24, 25*t*, 26*f*, 28, 41, 42*t*, 43
  aesthetic response 407
  brain regions 370
  BRECVEMA framework 375
  contagion 63–64, 302
  episodic memory 318*n*1
  evolution of brain functions 260*f*, 261
  expectancy 346
  and expression 73–75, 438
  functionalist analysis 53
  induction mechanisms 377
  intrinsic coding 171
  musical features and emotion dimensions 128
  neural activation 221–22
  rhythmic entrainment 279, 280
  subjective 470
  versus arousal of emotion 56–58
perceptual fluency theory 418, 436–37, 460
perceptual inputs 457, 458, 459
perceptual processes 14, 165, 347
perceptual qualia 106
perceptual system 266
performer-related variables 96*t*, 123
performer, role of 188–202
  expression and passion 191–92, 199–202
  GERMS model 192–99
  musical features used to express basic emotions and complex emotions 194*t*
  'unlimited resources for instrumental art' 189–90
performing, emotion and expression in 118–20
periaqueductal grey 370
personal aspects 41, 42*t*
personal associations 179, 181
personal experience 111, 122–23
personal expression 136–37
personality traits 22, 25*t*, 69, 325
personal layer of expression 183
personal meaning 185
personal significance 43
perspectives from musicians 115*b*
perturbations 277, 282
perturbations, phasic 46
phenomenological aspect of emotions 211
phonation 160
phrasing 22, 174–75, 193
Phrygian mode 122
physical aspects 69
physical coupling processes 260–61
physical proximity to sound source 30–31
physical reactions and behaviors 41, 42*t*
physical work efficiency and music 278
physiological arousal 43–44, 160, 282
physiological responses 45, 47–48, 175, 334, 501–2
piano 151, 196–97, 301, 415
piano forte 137
pictorial representation of events 335
piece-related moderating variables 95, 96*t*
piece-specific features 193–94
pious 107*f*
pitch
  arousal: self-reported feelings 212
  brainstem reflex 272
  combined effect of several features 144
  contagion 287, 291, 293
  contour 143, 164–65, 183, 292, 331, 501
  discrete 459
  empirical aesthetics 412
  factorial experimental design 142*f*
  iconic expression 156
  infant-directed speech 161
  intrinsic coding 169
  learning, prediction and expectancy 349
  level 143
  musical feature-emotion link 123, 127, 128
  musicians communicating emotions to listeners 88
  performer's role 189

pitch (*cont.*)
  portamento (pitch sliding) 9*n*1, 165–66
  range 166
  universality/cross-cultural emotions 130–31
  variation 143
  visual imagery 331
pity 86
plaintive 107*f*
planning 260*f*, 261
play behavior 297
playful 107*f*, 108*t*
playing with feeling 119
playlist positioning 97
play-offs 444–45
pleading 107*f*
pleasantness 87, 143, 267–68, 274
pleasurable anxiety 504
'pleasurable sadness' 499–504, 510
pleasure
  aesthetic emotions vs everyday emotions 465
  aesthetic judgment 260
  beauty 435
  categorical or dimensional emotions 50
  cultural context 392*f*
  expectancy 359*n*7, 363
  induction mechanisms and context 386
  language factors 106*n*6
  preference 463
  prevalence of emotional reactions 236–37, 237*f*
  unique and music-specific emotions 243
pleasure center 412
plurality of music types 40
politics of music 103–4, 175, 244, 256–57, 309–10
ponderous 107*f*
pop music
  aesthetic attitude 424
  aesthetic judgments, preferences and emotions: independence 467
  aesthetics 403*n*1
  associative coding 178
  beauty 437
  brainstem reflex 268–69
  communication and emotion 121
  complexity preference and familiarity 417
  composing: emotion and expression 116
  evaluative conditioning 309
  historical context and emotional expression 137
  'live' music and intensity of emotions 387–88
  musical feature-emotion link 127, 128*n*2
  nostalgia 325
  novelty 440
  preferences 481–82
  rhythmic entrainment 285–86
  synchronization 228
portamento (pitch sliding) 9*n*1, 165–66
portraying emotions 72
Portuguese Fado music 226–27, 324–25, 378
positive emotions
  aesthetic emotions vs everyday emotions 465–66
  aesthetic judgment and other mechanisms, interactions between 495–96
  aesthetic judgments, preferences and emotions: independence 468
  arousal 251
  beauty 435
  complexity preference and familiarity 414–15
  induction mechanisms and context 386
  and negative emotions: 'pleasurable sadness' 501
  preference 463–64, 479, 480
  prevalence of emotional reactions 234–35, 239*t*
  rhythmic entrainment 283
  visual imagery 333–34
positive valence 50–51, 113*f*, 128–29, 177
  episodic memory 321–22, 323

evaluative conditioning 313
psychophysiological measures 216
rhythmic entrainment 284
post-natal behavior effects of pre-natal exposure 313–14
potency 107*f*, 143
power of music 93, 173
PRAAT software package 139–40*n*1
practice-based emotions 120
precision 197
prediction 351, 352
effect 437
and learning 348–49
see also predictions, implications and complications
predictions, implications and complications 364–97
cognitive goal appraisal 379–82
cultural context 389–93
individual differences among listeners and non-arousal 382–84
induction mechanisms 376–79, 384–86
'live' concerts producing more intense emotions than recorded music 386–89
specific mechanisms, investigation of 393–97
see also mechanisms, unique characteristics of
preferences 25*t*, 26*f*, 461–64, 466–68, 477–83
aesthetic response 408
and affect 43–44
empirical aesthetics 420–21
individual differences in reactions to music 382–83
induction mechanisms 377
long-term 478
negative 461–62
positive 461–62
for prototypes theory 449
and relation to emotion and choice 479–83
pre-frontal cortex 220–21, 381
pre-genual cingulate cortex 221
pre-motor cortex 295–96
preparation techniques 507
prestige effects 404, 476–77
prevalence of emotional reactions 231–46
arousal of unique and music-specific emotions 240–44
basic and complex emotions 235–36
certain emotions occur more frequently and consistently than others 236–40
collective, refined and meta-musical emotions 244–46
individual prevalence 233
listeners, situations and pieces of music 237*f*
negative emotions 239*t*
positive bias 240
positive emotions 234–35, 239*t*
specific emotions 233–40
times of day/days of week 233
pride 114, 194*t*, 235–37, 237*f*, 238–40, 392*f*
primary auditory cortex 370
primary concepts, default relationships between 26*f*
primary emotions *see* basic emotions
procedural history principle 394–95
procedural memory 260*f*
program music 65*n*2
program notes for classical concerts 447
prolactin 501
proper emotions 93
properties distinguishing art 426–29
proportion 436
propositional representation of events 335
proprioceptive feedback 276, 279
prosocial behavior 284
protest and war songs 187
prototypes/prototypicality 52–53, 416–18, 450
aesthetic judgment 460, 471, 472*t*
beauty 437
multiple-layer model 187

proximal explanations for evolution 256
psychological approach 28–38
  aesthetic attitude 430
  aesthetic judgment 452–53, 454
  consciousness 32–34
  limitations 35–38
  meaning 30–32
  scientific analysis, levels of 29
  unique role of psychological inquiry 34–35
psychological experiment 231–32
psychological mechanisms 17–18, 256, 466
psychological processes 222, 459
psychological status 22
psychology of emotions 44–46
psychophysical principle 436
psychophysical processes 14
psychophysical relationships between musical features and perceptual impressions 82
psychophysical variables 411–12
psychophysiological measures 214–17
psychophysiological reactions 498
psychophysiology 211, 279, 501
psychotherapy 486
pulse 279–80, 285
punk music 135
pure and contentless form 11
pure sound 30
purpose 172

quaint 107*f*
qualia 172, 173, 284–85
qualified listener 130
quality of emotion 50–51, 467–68
questionnaire studies 362, 429
'quick and dirty' versus 'slow and accurate' processing 264, 269–70
quiet 107*f*, 108*t*

rage 132
random fluctuations 195–96
range 141
raves 283–84, 285
raw feeling 213
reaction 212–13, 351, 352
real emotion 334
recall of specific events 261
reciprocal feedback model 418
recognition of emotion 76
recognition memory 502
reconstructive analysis in history 37
recorded music 77, 96–97, 278–79
reductionism 36–37
redundancy 412, 413–14, 430
  cue 149–51, 153–55
  functional 18, 263–64
reference class problem 134
reference level 124, 130
referential information 74
referentialists 65–67, 199, 484
referential meaning 100–1
refined emotions 244–46, 485, 498
reflective awareness/consciousness 213, 257
register 292
regression models 152, 515, 516
  see also multiple regression analysis
regret 176–77
regulation of emotion 211, 226–27, 381
reinforcer
  primary 268–69
  secondary 268
relaxation 86, 108*t*, 128, 236–37, 237*f*, 259
release 93, 158, 172, 183, 184
relevant features, extraction of 139–40
relief 97, 173, 223, 358
religious context of music 68, 69, 91, 187, 256–57, 278
reminiscence bump 326
repetition 337*n*3, 414, 437
representations 56, 72, 103, 128, 431
  associative 365
  schematic 365
  sensori-motoric 280–81, 300, 315, 354, 511
representative design 141
resonance 160

response format 97
rest 158
restless 107*f*, 108*t*
restraint 498
reticular system 270
reticulospinal tract 270, 281
retrieval cue 174–75, 316, 331, 372–73
reverberations 273
reverence 132
rhythm 22, 282
  associative coding 174–75
  'chills' 218
  combined effect of several features 144
  complexity 128
  contagion 300
  expectancy 357
  musical feature-emotion link 123
  physiological 282
  regularity 128
  visual imagery 337*n*3
  see also rhythmic entrainment
rhythmic entrainment 259, 275–86, 303, 366*t*, 511, 513
  action tendencies 225
  asymmetrical 278–79
  characteristics 276–78
  cognitive goal appraisal 380
  and contagion distinction 300–2
  cultural context 392*f*
  episodic memory 323, 328
  evaluative conditioning 308
  evidence of in music 281–83
  evolution of brain functions 260–61
  expectancy 344
  external manifestation 281–82
  hierarchical relationships 280
  individual differences in reactions to music 383
  internal manifestation 281–82
  'live' music and intensity of emotions 390
  manifestation 279
  mechanism 279
  motor level 279
  in musical setting 278–80
  neural 279
  passive 281
  'peak' experience 505–6
  perceptual level 279
  period 277
  phase 277
  physiological level 279
  richness of music experience 489
  sensori-motoric representations 280–81
  social level 279
  subdivisions 280
  subjective 283
  symmetrical 278–79
  types of effect induced by 283–86
  see also BRECVEMA framework
richness of music experience 489–91
ritardando 93, 141–42, 196
robust 107*f*
rock music 116, 199, 259
  concerts 224–25, 272–73
Rococo 448
romance 205
romanticism 136–37, 201, 448
rostral anterior cingulate 370
rubato 189

sacred 107*f*, 108*t*
sad 107*f*
sadness 84*t*, 84–85, 86–87, 107*f*, 108*t*
  aesthetic judgments, preferences and emotions: independence 466–67
  arousal 212, 251
  associative coding 175, 176–77
  broad emotion categories 90, 91
  causal effects and music synthesis 143
  'chills' 217–18
  combined effect of several features 145
  communicative process quantification 151
  composing: emotion and expression 117–18

sadness (*cont.*)
contagion 259, 287–88, 289, 293, 299, 301–2
cross-modal patterns of acoustic cues for speech 162*t*
cultural context 391, 392*f*
emotional expression 222–23
emotion terms vs. expression marks 111, 114*t*
episodic memory 323
expression and passion 201
GERMS model 195
historical context and emotional expression 135–36, 137
iconic expression 156
induction mechanisms 378, 386
investigation of specific mechanisms 395, 396–97
language factors 106
logic of emotions 255
mixed emotions 491, 492
moderating variables 97
multiple-layer model 183, 185, 187
musical feature-emotion link 123, 125, 126*t*
musical features used to express emotions by professional performers 194*t*
musicians communicating emotions to listeners 88*f*, 89–90
nostalgia 324–25
performing: emotion and expression 120
prevalence of emotional reactions 235–37, 237*f*, 238–40
style and emotional expression 133
synchronization 228
two-dimensional emotion space 113*f*
unique and music-specific emotions 242
visual imagery 339
vitality affects 94
see also 'pleasurable sadness'
salsa music 284–85
sarcasm 135
satisfaction 107*f*, 359, 463
savoring 498
saxophone 180
scale 169
scherzando 114*t*
scientific analysis, levels of 29
screams 290–91
secondary emotions 283
secondary responses 274, 284, 285, 299, 301, 325
segmentation of events 461
sehr Langsam 112
self-awareness 318
self-chosen music 480–81
self-consciousness 260*f*, 261
self-identity 326–27
self-reflection 318*n*1, 498
self-reports
arousal 207–8, 211–14
brainstem reflex 273–74
cognitive goal appraisal 381–82
contagion 288, 289, 301–2
cultural context 391–93
emotional responses to fiction 498–99
expectancy 355, 362
and expression 75
induction mechanisms and context 385
investigation of specific mechanisms 393, 395
language factors 106, 107
negative emotions: 'pleasurable sadness' 501–2
preferences 478
prevalence of emotional reactions 231
psychophysiological measures 215, 216–17
referential meaning 68
rhythmic entrainment 283, 285–86
synchronization 228
visual imagery 338
self-selected music 217–18
semantic associations 377
semantic content 377

semantic estimates 391
semantic memory 260*f*, 317
semantic snowballing 314
SEM descriptive system 42*t*
semitones, falling 251*n*4
sending intention 74
sensational 107*f*, 108*t*
sensations 260–61, 260*f*, 318*n*1
sensitization 267
sensorimotor cortex 281
sensori-motoric representations 280–81, 300, 315, 354, 511
sensory dissonance 344
sensual seduction 187
sentimental 107*f*, 108*t*
separation call 218–19
sequence of thirds 180
serenity 106, 107*f*, 108*t*, 333
serious 91, 107*f*, 108*t*
serious music 128
Sex Pistols
  "Anarchy in the UK" 39
  "I'm a Lazy Sod" 135
  Never Mind the Bollocks 160*n*1
sexual courtship 4
sexual desire 180, 187
shame 194*t*, 195, 237*f*
shared emotions 389
shared meaning 185
shock 463–64
sighs 180, 290–91
significance 31
significant world events 87
signify emotions 72
signs 157
similarity judgments 106*n*5
simultaneous activities 22
sincerity 299, 437, 439
singing 4
  see also songs; voice
single-factor view 192
situational factors 22, 47–48, 491
skill 30–31, 444–46
  aesthetic attitude 430
  aesthetic judgment 455–56, 459, 471, 472*t*, 475
  beauty 434*n*2
  preference 463
  technical 432
slide guitar 165
soaring 107*f*, 108*t*
sober 107*f*
social aspects 41, 42*t*
social belonging 187
social benefits 298
social bonding 284
social ceremonies 20
social coherence 4
social companion, music as 302
social components 322, 328
social conditions 68, 69
social connectedness 284
social context 22, 30–31, 256–57
  aesthetics and affect 469
  arousal 253
  evaluative conditioning 314
  expression and passion 202
  induction mechanisms and context 384, 385
  moderating variables 95
  style 448–49
social conventions 17–18
social element 20
social functions 20
social identity 68, 187
social interaction 298
social intimacy and bonding 300
sociality 297
social organization 68, 133
social relationships/interactions 321
socio-cultural variables 37
sociology 29, 37
soft rock 386
solemnity 84*t*, 84–85, 107*f*, 108*t*, 128, 174, 187
somato-topic body maps 280–81

songs
  and episodic memory linkage 327–29
  sequencing 97
sonic 'finger-print 196–97
sonic play 361
soothing 107*f*, 108*t*
sorrow 88, 91, 164, 183, 490
soul music 116
sound effects 96–97
sound intensity 266, 267, 493
sound level 387–88
  brainstem reflex 259, 267, 272–73
  Brunswikian lens model 149
  causal effects and music synthesis 141–42, 143
  combined effect of several features 144
  contagion 287
  empirical aesthetics 412
  expression and passion 201
  GERMS model 195
  investigation of specific mechanisms 395
  musical feature-emotion link 123, 128
  musical features used to express emotions by professional performers 194*t*
  musicians communicating emotions to listeners 88
  relevant features, extraction of 139–40
sound patterns 69
sound pressure level 137
source of the sound 30–31
sparkling 106, 107*f*
spatial localization 96–97
special music events 320
specific emotions 83–87
specification of structure of feelings 158
specific emotions
  intrinsic coding 173
  language factors 109–10
  musical features 122–23, 127
  neural activation 222
  performing: emotion and expression 119
  prevalence of emotional reactions 233–40
specific object 47–48
speculation 122–23
speed 164–65, 166, 259, 291, 293, 411–12
Spencer's law 160
spiritoso 114*t*
spirituality 107*f*, 108*t*
  associative coding 174
  cultural context 391, 392*f*
  multiple-layer model 187
  prevalence of emotional reactions 236–37
  style and emotional expression 135
sprightly 107*f*
stability 173
staccato 128, 143, 144–45, 152, 331
standard content paradigm 89
standard deviations 192
standard paradigm 161–62
startle response 259, 265–67, 269–70, 271, 273–74, 396–97
statistical-ideographic approach 396
statistical learning 170–71
stereotyping 476
stimulus choice 97
stimulus order 97
stimulus-response relationship 346
stratified random sampling 471
striatum 220–22, 373–74
strings 344
strong experience *see* 'peak' experience
strong order effects 476
study of music and emotion links 139–46
  causal effects and music synthesis 140–43
  interactions between features 143–46
  relevant features, extraction of 139–40
style 448–50
  aesthetic judgment 460, 494
  expression 86, 439
  moderating variables 95
  music as art 432
  -specific conventions 181

stylistic evolution 197–98
stylistic learning 357
stylistic norms 348
stylistic unexpectedness 197–98
stylometric analysis 87
subconscious 19–20
subcortical brain areas 220–21, 281, 306, 318*n*1
subdominance 172
sub-genres 478–79
subjective feelings 11, 211–12, 216, 257, 284–85
subjective impression 92, 136–37
sublimity 107*f*, 431, 450–51, 498
subtle emotions 40
subtypes of emotions 54*t*
suggestive analyses in musicology 37
sunny 107*f*
super-expressive voice, music as 165–68, 188, 291, 292–93
super-natural quality of voice 167
supervenient relationship 426
supplementary motor area 281
surprise
  aesthetic response 407
  brainstem reflex 259, 270–71, 274
  causal effects and music synthesis 143
  'chills' 218
  cultural context 392*f*
  emotion terms vs. expression marks 114*t*
  expectancy 353–54, 358, 359, 363
  investigation of specific mechanisms 395
  ITPRA theory 352
  preference 463
  prevalence of emotional reactions 235–36, 237*f*
  startle response 266
  temporal focus of affect 371
  visual imagery 342
  Wittgenstein's dilemma 360, 361
surveys 212, 323
survival value of brain function 365
suspense 347
swan-song phenomenon 441–42
'swing' music 94–95
symmetry 436, 459–60
sympathy 299
synchronization 227–30
  period and phase 280
  rhythmic entrainment 277, 278, 279, 282, 285
  spontaneous 284
synchrony 277
  implicit 284
  interpersonal 284
  variation 277
syncopation 128, 169, 171–72, 183, 218, 355–56, 415
synonymous affect terms 111
syntactical relationships 157
syntactical violations 348
syntactic processing 261, 331, 351, 365
synthesized music 140
  combined effect of several features 144, 145–46
  contagion 300, 301
  GERMS model 199
  visual imagery 336–37
  see also Moog synthesizer
systematic design 141, 142
systematic experimentation 509
systematic listening tests 363

tacit aspect of emotional expression 119
taste 401–4, 431, 471–73, 477
tears/crying 223–24, 226–27, 355–56, 492–93
technological development 133, 137–38
techno music 259, 279–80
temoroso 114*t*
tempo 22
  arousal 212, 250–51
  associative coding 177
  brainstem reflex 267, 272
  Brunswikian lens model 147, 149, 151

tempo (*cont.*)
causal effects and music synthesis 141–42, 143
'chills' 218
combined effect of several features 143–45
communicative process quantification 151
contagion 287, 291
expression and passion 201
factorial experimental design 142*f*
GERMS model 193, 195, 196
historical context and emotional expression 137
investigation of specific mechanisms 395
mean 137
multiple-layer model 183
musical feature-emotion link 123–24, 127, 128
musical features used to express emotions by professional performers 194*t*
musicians communicating emotions to listeners 88
negative emotions: 'pleasurable sadness' 501
performer's role 188, 189
relevant features, extraction of 140
rhythmic entrainment 278, 280
startle response 266
universality/cross-cultural emotions 130, 132
visual imagery 331, 337*n*3
temporal patterns 291
temporal poles 221
temporal structure 344
tenderness 84*t*, 84–85, 107*f*, 108*t*
associative coding 177
causal effects and music synthesis 143
communicative process quantification 152
cross-modal patterns of acoustic cues for speech 162*t*
emotion terms vs. expression marks 114, 114*t*
expression and passion 201
GERMS model 195
iconic expression 156
intrinsic coding 173
multiple-layer model 184, 187
musical feature-emotion link 123, 125, 126*t*
musical features used to express emotions by professional performers 194*t*
musicians communicating emotions to listeners 89–90
prevalence of emotional reactions 236–37, 237*f*
style and emotional expression 135
two-dimensional emotion space 113*f*
unique and music-specific emotions 241
tension 50*n*3, 68, 84*t*, 85, 108*t*
expectancy 345, 356, 357
GERMS model 197
iconic sources: formal resemblance 158
intrinsic coding 169–70, 171, 172, 173
ITPRA theory 351–52
multiple-layer model 183, 184
musical feature-emotion link 123, 128–29
psychological 69
rhythmic entrainment 282
vitality affects 93
terminative interactions 144
terminology and organization 23–27
texture 22
thalamus - intralaminar nuclei 270
thinking 260*f*
thinking of music as art, grounds for 429–32
three-dimensional models (energy arousal-tense arousal-valence) 50*n*3
timbre 22, 85
arousal 207
associative coding 173, 174–75, 178
brainstem reflex 273

Brunswikian lens model 149
causal effects and music synthesis 141–42, 143
'chills' 218
combined effect of several features 144
contagion 287, 291, 292, 293
evaluative conditioning 312–13
expression and passion 201
frequency spectrum 139–40
GERMS model 193
iconic sources: formal resemblance 160, 164–65
infant-directed speech 161
investigation of specific mechanisms 395
musical feature-emotion link 123
musical features used to express emotions by professional performers 194*t*
performer's role 189
startle response 266
super-expressive voice, music as 166
universality/cross-cultural emotions 132
timing 22
causal effects and music synthesis 141–42
GERMS model 193
historical context and emotional expression 137–38
musical feature-emotion link 123
patterns 292
performer's role 189
relevant features, extraction of 139–40
time signature 284
tiredness 86–87
tonal closure 173
tonal hierarchies 349
tonality 123, 130–31, 169
tonal music 70, 348
tonal perception 170–71
tonal progression 144
tonal sequence 189
tone
attacks 123, 141–42, 143, 201
brainstem reflex 267–68
emotional 172
empirical aesthetics 412
evaluative conditioning 309
expectancy 344–45
leading 170, 172
multiple-layer model 184
quality 165
super-expressive voice, music as 165–66
of voice 158
see also atonality
tonic affective background 46
tonic notes 169–70, 172
topics 94–95
touching/touched 107*f*, 237*f*
tragic 107*f*, 108*t*
trait anxiety 382
trance 283–84
tranquil 107*f*, 108*t*
transcendence 236–37, 391
transient sync 277
transitions 277, 333
transmission model 77, 103–4, 121
triumphant 86, 107*f*, 108*t*, 135
triviality 128
trust 358
tumultuous 107*f*
'tuning in' 507
twelve-tone technique 357–58, 442*n*7
two-dimensional emotion space 52, 113*f*
two-dimensional models (positive affect-negative affect) 50*n*3
typicality 459

uncertainty 172, 173, 345, 347, 420
unconditioned stimulus (US) 304, 308, 313
unique impressions of individual 81
unit-weight models 132–33*n*5
universal character 156
universality of expressed emotions 129–33
unpleasantness 266, 267–68, 274
unrest 84*t*
U-shaped (Wundt) curve 411–13, 411*f*

utilitarian versus aesthetic uses of
music 483–87

valence 43–44, 50*n*3
categorical or dimensional emotions 51
emotion terms vs. expression
marks 111–12
empirical aesthetics 419
evaluative conditioning 305
expression 86
functionalist analysis 55
intrinsic coding 172, 173
language factors 109
musical feature-emotion link 123, 128
negative 50–51, 111–12, 113*f*, 128, 177, 337
preference 462
response, contrastive 218–19
see also positive valence
value of pieces of music 15–16
value of responses to music 15–16
variability in musical features 147–48,
190, 196–97
verbal fluency 213
veridical expectation 360
vestibular system 285, 301
vibration 285
contagion 290–91, 292–93
expression and passion 199, 201–2
extent and speed 123, 128, 141–42
musical features used to express
emotions by professional
performers 194*t*
performer's role 188
rate, musical features used to express
emotions by professional
performers 194*t*
super-expressive voice, music as 165–66
visual imagery 340–41
vicarious functioning 153
vigorous 106, 107*f*, 108*t*
violence 86
violin 259, 291, 292–93, 301
visual cortex 336, 338, 365–70, 373–75
visual imagery 259, 303, 330–42, 366*t*, 509, 513
aesthetic judgment and other
mechanisms, interactions
between 497
cognitive goal appraisal 381
cultural context 392*f*
emotional reaction to images 333–35
emotional responses to fiction 498
evidence for in music 336–38
extra-musical information influence
on 339–42
individual differences 338–39, 383
induced affect 370–71
induction mechanisms 379, 385
investigation of specific mechanisms 394
modularity 372
in music listening 331–33
'peak' experience 505–6
pictorial forms 335–36
richness of music experience 489
visual cortex 365–70
volitional influence 372
see also BRECVEMA framework
visual impressions 22, 95, 476
vitality affects 93–95, 324
iconic sources: formal resemblance 158
language factors 109
musical features and emotion
dimensions 128–29
visual imagery 331
vivacious 107*f*
Vividness of Visual Imagery Questionnaire
(VVIQ) 335
vocal emotion 164–65
vocal expression 163, 164, 182–83
vocal feedback 295
vocal learning 280–81*n*1
vocal signaling 297
vocoder 167
voice 158, 159, 160–62
hypothesis 165
-related cues iconic sources: formal
resemblance 164

super-expressive voice, music as 165–68, 188, 291, 292–93
super-natural quality of 167
volitional influence, degree of 372
volume *see* sound level

wellbeing 325
'will' of the tones 169–73, 345
wistful 107*f*
wittiness 431, 434*n*2, 446–47
wonder 241, 450–51, 463, 465–66, 500–1
work coordination 4
working definitions 25*t*
working memory 459

yearning 107*f*, 108*t*